Understanding Textiles

Understanding

PHYLLIS G. TORTORA

Professor
Department of Home Economics
Queens College

Textiles

3rd Edition

Macmillan Publishing Company
New York

Collier Macmillan Publishers
London

Macmillan Publishing Company
866 Third Avenue, New York, New York 10022

Collier Macmillan Canada, Inc.

Library of Congress Cataloging-in-Publication Data

Tortora, Phyllis G.
  Understanding textiles.

  Bibliography: p.
  Includes index.
  1. Textile industry.   2. Textile fibers.   3. Textile
fabrics.   I. Title.
TS1445.T63   1987   677   85-32043
ISBN 0-02-421140-0

Printing: 3 4 5 6 7 8   Year 8 9 0 1 2 3 4 5 6

ISBN 0-02-421140-0

The purpose of this book is to provide a common background for students who are making a study of textiles. Some students may be planning to enter one of the many career areas that require some knowledge about textiles. Others may be interested in becoming better informed consumers. Whatever may motivate students to enter an introductory course in textiles, certain basic concepts are essential to their understanding of the subject. It is my hope that these concepts are presented in a clear, logically developed format.

It has been my intention to emphasize the interrelationships of fibers, yarns, fabric constructions, and finishes and to apply what has been learned about each of these components to the understanding of textile behavior and performance. To this end, diagrams and photographs were selected with care to illustrate the concepts and processes described in the text. Where possible, pictures of machinery or steps in textile processing are included to provide a visual as well as a written description.

The recommended references at the end of each chapter have been selected to complement the subject matter of the chapters. I have made a conscious effort to include both relatively elementary and highly technical material so as to introduce students to the variety of resources in the field. I have also tried to include readings from the most widely used periodicals in the field. An extensive bibliography, broken down under special subject headings, is appended to the book.

A new Chapter 1 introduces the reader to the various elements from which textiles are made, their historical development, and the present-day organization of the textile industry. Chapters 2 and 3 establish the relationship of fiber properties to fiber behavior. Chapter 2 focuses on physical properties of fibers, and Chapter 3 deals with the chemistry of textile fibers. Chapter 3, which presents in an elementary way some of the basic concepts in textile chemistry, is written for the reader who has had no previous chemistry training. The student should be able to gain some understanding of these elementary concepts and to appreciate not only the integral role that chemistry plays in the manufacture and finishing textile products, but also the role of chemistry in the use and care of textiles by consumers. Often this kind of material is integrated into varying parts of a text. I have not done so here because a separate chapter on the subject offers a better opportunity to explain elementary chemical terminology and concepts and to relate these concepts to the science of textiles. Some teachers may prefer to emphasize this chapter a great deal, whereas others may wish to discuss it briefly. Either approach may be taken.

The chapters on textile fibers (Chapters 4 to 13) are each organized in much the same way with the same topic headings being used in each chapter. These topic headings are also used in the introductory chapter dealing with textile fiber properties—to facilitate comparisons between fibers. Each chapter ends with a table summarizing some of the more

Preface

important characteristics of the major fiber groups discussed in that chapter.

From fibers the text moves to yarns and their production (Chapter 14) and from yarns the text goes on to fabric structures. Fabric structures are divided into woven fabrics (Chapter 15), knitted fabrics (Chapter 16), and other methods of fabric construction (Chapter 17). These chapters deal with the newest processes for the manufacture of yarns and fabrics as well as the more traditional methods.

The various methods of adding color and giving special finishes to fabrics are discussed in Chapters 18 to 21. Much of the appeal of textile fabrics results from the color and decoration that are applied to them. A number of photographs selected for Chapter 18 and 19 are of historic textiles and are meant to provide a special emphasis on the aesthetic qualities of textiles.

Each of Chapters 22 to 25 fulfills a special purpose in the organization of the book. Chapter 22, "The Care of Textile Products," is included as a separate chapter, even though some material about the care of textiles is also included in preceding chapters, because of the importance of care in relation to consumer satisfaction with textiles.

Chapter 23 deals with textiles and the environment, a topic of concern to both the consumer and the textile industry. The chapter is addressed not only to ways in which textile production and use affect the environment but also raises questions about the complex "trade-offs" between environmental quality and increased costs of consumer goods.

Chapter 24 provides a brief introduction to the subject of textile testing. Many colleges and junior colleges have little or no textile testing equipment. Others may have extensive and elaborate textile laboratories. For the former, this chapter provides photographs of basic equipment and some brief discussion of types of equipment used in testing, as well as descriptions of some simple tests that can be performed in the classroom or at home. For the latter, this chapter provides a very general introduction to the subject of textile testing that may be expanded in other courses. This chapter does not serve as a substitute for technical or laboratory manuals.

The last chapter provides a summary for the text. It explores some of the ways in which fiber, yarn, fabric construction, and finishes contribute to the total structure of the fabric, and how the structure of the fabric is, in turn, related to its performance.

Each college or university organizes its course work in unique ways. While it is not possible for a single text to meet the needs of all programs, I believe that this book includes all the information essential to an introductory textiles course and offers the student and the teacher neither too much nor too little. It will be up to the faculty and students who use this book to tell me whether I have indeed reached that goal.

The contributions of individuals to the preparation of previous editions continue to be basic to the structure and form of the third edition, and those contributions are still very much appreciated. My husband

Vincent, my son Christopher, and my daughter Giulia continued to provide constant encouragement, assistance, and support throughout the process. A friend, Marianna Norris, helped with a great many small, detailed tasks.

A number of persons were especially helpful in suggesting revisions for this edition. They include the readers selected by the publisher. Of these, particular thanks are given to Dr. Robert Merkel of Florida International University whose meticulous reading and many excellent suggestions have certainly strengthened the quality of the text; Dr. Kitty Dickerson, Missouri State University; Professor Rinn M. Cloud, Louisiana State University; Professor Robert Merkel, Florida International University; Dr. Lorayne Roberds, Western Illinois University; Dr. Jeanette M. Cardamone, Virginia Polytechnic Institute and State University; Professor Ardis M. Rewerts, University of Texas at Austin; and Dr. Sue Bailey, formerly of James Madison University.

A number of friends and colleagues who have used the book were very generous in responding to my request for suggestions. These included Linda Snyder and Constance Sussman of Queens College and the students in the Department of Home Economics.

Typing of portions of the manuscript was ably done by Marguerite Fenick and Mary Coelo.

As before, I owe appreciation to the many segments of the textile industry who were so generous with information and photographs and other illustrative materials. Fisher Rhymes and the technical committee of the Man-made Fiber Producers Association were especially helpful in reviewing the chapters that dealt with man-made fibers. Picture sources are acknowledged with each reproduction, but it is impossible to identify all of the many firms and individuals who provided source materials and other forms of assistance.

P. T.

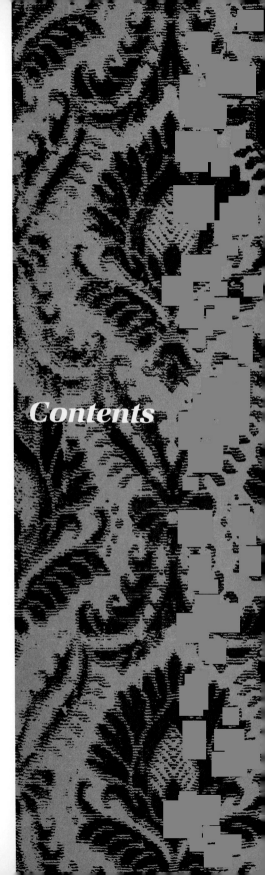

Contents

1 *Introduction*   1

2 *Textile Fibers and Their Properties*   21

3 *The Chemistry of Textiles*   41

4 *Natural Cellulosic Fibers*   61

5 *Man-made Cellulosic Fibers*   85

6 *Protein Fibers*   101

7 *Inorganic, Metallic, and Carbon Fibers*   133

8 *Nylon and Aramid Fibers*   141

9 *Polyester Fibers*   151

10 *Acrylic and Modacrylic Fibers*   161

11 *Olefin Fibers*   171

12 *Elastomeric Fibers*   177

13 *Other Man-made and Bicomponent Fibers*   183

14 *Making Fibers into Yarns*   193

15 *Woven Fabrics*   231

16 *Knitted Fabrics*   281

17 *Other Methods of Fabric Construction*   305

18 *Adding Color to Textiles*   327

19 *Textile Printing and Design*   343

20 *Routine and Mechanical Finishes*   369

21 *Chemical Finishes*   389

22 *The Care of Textile Products*   417

23 *Textiles and the Environment*   441

24 *Textile Testing and Standards*   453

25 *Fabric Structure: The Sum of Its Parts*   473

Appendixes

A *Bibliography*   487

B *Glossary*   497

C *Summary of Regulatory Legislation Applied to Textiles*   505

D *Man-made Fibers and Trademark Names*   509

Index   519

Introduction

Each day each of us makes decisions about textiles. From the simplest choice of what clothes to wear to the commitment of a major portion of the family budget to buy a new carpet, judgments about the performance, durability, attractiveness, and care of textiles are consciously or unconsciously made. The economic implications of decisions about fibers, yarns, and fabrics obviously increase if someone is involved professionally with textiles. But whether or not understanding textiles is required for personal or for professional purposes, the key to informed decision making is knowledge about fibers, yarns, fabrics, and finishes and the ways in which these are interrelated.

Textiles fulfill so many purposes in our lives that their study can be approached in a number of ways. Textiles may be seen as being purely utilitarian, in relationship to the numerous purposes they serve. On awaking in the morning, for example, we climb out from under sheets and blankets and step into slippers and a robe. We wash our faces with washcloths, dry them with towels, and put on clothing for the day. We even brush our teeth with toothbrushes, the bristles of which are made from textile fibers. If we get into a car or bus, we sit on upholstered seats and the machine moves on tires reinforced with strong textile cords. We stand on carpets, sit on upholstered furniture, and look out of curtained windows. Even the insulation of our houses is glass textile fiber. Not only are golf clubs, tennis rackets, and ski poles reinforced with textile fibers, but so are roads, bridges, and buildings. Strong, heat-resistant textile fibers in the nose cones of space ships travel to the moon with the astronauts. Physicians implant artificial arteries made of textiles or use fibers for surgery that gradually dissolve as wounds heal. Few of our manufactured products could be made without textile conveyor belts. Even our processed foods have been filtered through textile filter paper. There is truly no aspect of modern life that is untouched by some area of textiles. (See Figure 1.1.)

Even though we all personally experience textiles at home, at work, and at play, we usually encounter only the completed product; rarely do we deal with the individual components. But each finished product makes a long journey from its beginnings in the laboratory or on the farm to the place where it is acquired by the ultimate consumer. An

FIGURE 1.1. *Fibers are used in applications that range from fashion to high technology. (top, left) Designer dress made of Avetex polyester, (top, right) Fabric softener backing made with Avril® rayon, (bottom) Exhaust nozzles of Columbia space shuttle and Trident missile are made with carbonized rayon fiber. Courtesy of Avtex Fibers Inc.*

introductory course in textile study can be a sort of road map or itinerary of that journey; therefore, this text is organized to begin with the first steps in the long progress from fiber to completed fabric and goes on to examine subsequent steps in a generally chronological sequence.

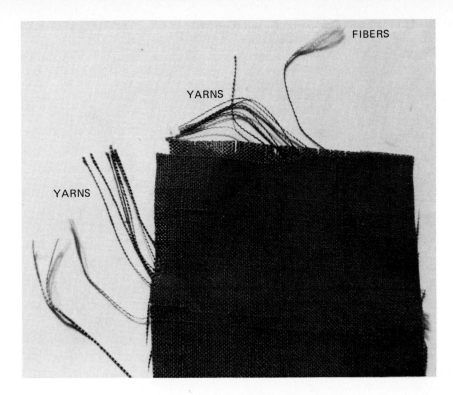

FIBERS

YARNS

YARNS

FIGURE 1.2. *Fabric unravels into separate yarns. Yarns untwist into individual fibers.*

If you were to take the shirt or sweater that you, the reader, are wearing at this moment and break it down into its intermediate components, you would have to work backward, taking apart the fabric structure. Most likely your garment is woven or knitted. Weaving and knitting are the two most common means of creating fabrics for apparel, although other methods do exist. Both weaving and knitting are subject to a great many possible variations, and these differences contribute to the enormous variability in appearance, drapability, texture, crease recovery, handle, and the many other qualities of fabrics.

To take a woven or knitted structure apart requires that the fabric be unraveled into the yarns from which it was constructed. The yarns (with some few exceptions) are likely to have been made from shorter or longer fibers that are twisted together. By untwisting the yarns, it should be possible to separate the yarn into a number of small, fine, hairlike fibers. These fibers are the basic units that make up the majority of textile products that are encountered in apparel and home furnishings. (See Figure 1.2.)

Fibers

Textile fibers exist in nature or are created through technology. Technical definitions of the term *textile fibers* tend to stress their dimensions. For example, a textile fiber may be defined as "a unit of measure of hairlike dimensions with a length at least one hundred times greater than the width."[1] Although this may explain how a fiber looks, some materials that do fit this definition are not suitable for use in textiles. The fibrous structure of an overcooked pot roast, for example, is obviously not suitable for use in a textile. Fibers appropriate for use in textiles must have not only fineness and flexibility, but also sufficient strength and durability to withstand conditions encountered in use.

Particular fibers may be suitable for use in some textile applications, but not in others. Glass fiber, excellent for use in curtains or lamp shades, is not useful in wearing apparel. Even among those fibers used in many apparel and home furnishing items, some are preferred for particular applications. Nylon has become synonymous with sheer women's hosiery—women may refer to their stockings as "nylons"—although in fact in the past fibers such as silk or rayon were used to make women's dress hosiery. On reflection, then, it is obvious that we tend to prefer some kinds of fibers for certain uses because those particular fibers offer some special advantages. For example, a particular fabric may seem to be more comfortable in warm or cool weather, may soil less easily, may dry more quickly, or may have an appearance that is best suited to a particular kind of occasion. The reasons for these differences among fibers reside in the specific properties of each fiber. If we are to have a clear understanding of the finished products and what qualities are to be expected of them, we need to know the fibers from which the product is made—and the characteristics of those fibers.

Yarns

Fibers alone cannot make a textile. Although it is possible to entangle groups of fibers or to bond them together in some way to create a textile (as is done with felt, for example), most of the cloth that is made into wearing apparel is formed from yarns. Yarns are assemblies of fibers twisted or otherwise held together in a continuous strand. An almost endless variety of yarns can be created by using different fibers, by twisting fibers more or less tightly, by combining two or more individual yarns to form a more complex yarn, or by giving yarns a wide range of other special treatments.

Just as different fibers will vary in their individual properties, different kinds of yarns have varying characteristics. (See Figure 1.3.) And to complicate matters still further, two yarns of the same structure will have different properties if they are made from markedly different kinds of fibers.

Fabric Structures

Yarns must be united in some way if they are to form a cohesive structure. The transformation of individual yarns into textile fabrics can be accomplished by an individual with a pair of knitting needles, a cro-

[1]A glossary of technical terms is provided in Appendix B.

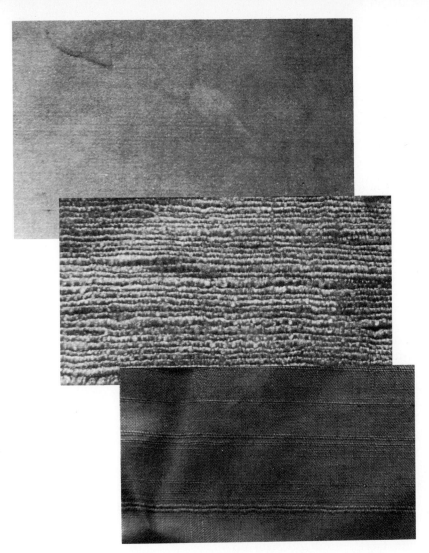

FIGURE 1.3. *Fabrics made from the same fiber and in the same (plain) weave look different because different kinds of yarns are used.*

chet hook, or a hand loom or through the use of powerful machines that combine yarns by weaving, knitting, or stitch-bonding to produce thousands of yards of completed fabrics. As with fibers and yarns, the potential for variations in the structure is enormous, and a walk through any department store will reveal to even the most casual observer the almost endless variety of textile structures produced and consumed by the public in the form of apparel or household textiles.

And, once again, if the construction being used is varied, the resulting properties will differ. Furthermore, even when the same weave or knit construction is used, the end product will be distinctive if the fiber or yarn type is varied. (See Figure 1.4.)

FIGURE 1.4. *Fabrics made from the same fiber and from similar types of yarns look different because different types of weaves were used in their construction.*

As the reader will learn, certain properties are inherent to each fiber, yarn, or fabric structure. Consumers find some of these properties desirable, while others are not valued. For example, fabrics of man-made fibers dry quickly after laundering. Most consumers value this quality. But the same fabrics may tend to build up static electric charges, producing small electrical shocks or "static cling." Consumers do not like this quality. When a fiber, yarn, or fabric has unacceptable properties, special treatments called "finishes" may be given to the fiber, yarn, or fabric to overcome undesirable properties. Finishes may be used to give to the fibers, yarns, or fabrics some properties that they do not normally possess but that will enhance performance. The aforementioned static cling of some man-made fibers can be decreased or overcome by giving fibers, yarns, or fabrics special finishing treatments. Most of you know about durable press finishes, for example, or you may have purchased upholstered furniture with soil-resistant finishes. Other examples will be discussed in the chapters dealing with finishes.

Appearance—color, pattern, or texture—is one of the major factors that leads consumers to purchase one product over another. Most textile fabrics intended for personal, household, or architectural use have been decorated in some way, by dyeing the fabric, printing designs on it, or weaving with varicolored yarns. Large segments of the textile industry are devoted to dyeing and/or printing fabrics, yarns, or fibers.

Finishing and Dyeing

The place of textiles in the world economy is enormously complex. How the production of textiles moved out of the home to become the business of huge multinational corporations is a part of the history of the evolution of modern society. The origin of textile production is lost in prehistory.

No one knows exactly when the spinning and weaving of textiles began, but archeologists tell us that woven plant fiber fabrics were made more than eighty-five hundred years ago in Catal Huyuk, a hunting village in what is today the country of Turkey, and that a number of Mex-

Textile History

ican textiles date between 7000 and 5000 B.C.[2] For most of the time that people have made fabrics, the only fibers available for use were found in nature, and the processes used to make these fibers into cloth were carried out by hand.

In spite of limited technology, people created a wide variety of fabrics for themselves and for use in their homes. Some of these fabrics, such as the simple, plain homespun cloth used for every day were strictly utilitarian. Others were elaborately patterned, printed, or dyed in order to satisfy the universal human need for beauty.

As the complex social and political organizations of people evolved, some of the small hunting villages were replaced by larger towns, and eventually by cities and urban centers. Along with the growth of cities, nations, and empires, there were improvements in technology and the development of international trade, both of which involved textiles. Changes in textile technology and trade had come about as early as the time of the Roman Empire. The Romans not only traded actively with nearby Egypt to import cotton, but they had developed trade in silk with faraway China by the year A.D. 1. Close to storehouses in Roman settlements excavated in India, archeologists have found facilities for dyeing and finishing cotton fabrics. In the remains of many Roman towns there is evidence of installations for finishing and dyeing fabrics.

During the Middle Ages the production and trading of the plant called *woad*, an important source of dye, was a highly developed industry. Returning Crusaders brought luxurious silk and cotton fabrics from the Middle East to their homes in Europe, and these "foreign novelties" became an important item in trade. During the fifteenth century, the trade fairs of southern France provided a place for the active exchange of wools from England and silks from the Middle East. The economic activities surrounding these events gave rise to the first international banking arrangements.

Even the discovery of America was a result of the desire of Europeans to find a faster route not only to the spices but also to the textiles of the Orient. Once the American colonies had been established, the colonists sold native dyes such as indigo and cochineal to Europe and bought cottons from India. At the time when textiles were assuming an increasingly important role in international trade, advances were being made in the technology of textile production. Even so, the manufacture of cloth was still essentially a hand process. By 1700 in Western Europe spinning was still being done on a spinning wheel, by hand. Fabrics were woven by hand on looms for which the power was provided by the weaver.

The production of textiles was the first area to undergo industrialization during the Industrial Revolution, which occurred during the latter half of the 1700s in Western Europe, especially in Great Britain,

---

[2]Mary Elizabeth King, "Archeological Textiles," in the *Proceedings of the Irene Emery Roundtable on Museum Textiles* (Washington, D.C.: The Textile Museum, 1974), p. 10.

France, and the Low Countries. The vast changes that took place during this period, not only technological but also sociological, economic, and cultural, included a major reorganization of manufacturing of a variety of goods. This came about during the seventeenth and eighteenth centuries when good-quality textile products, produced inexpensively in India and the Far East, were gradually replacing European goods in the international market. In England, this competition produced a severe economic crisis within the textile field, and it became imperative that some means be found to increase domestic production, to lower costs, and to improve quality of textiles. The solution was found in the substitution of machine or nonhuman power for hand processes and human power.

Many important inventions were made during this period that improved the output and quality of fabrics. The most important of these were spinning machines, automatic looms, and the cotton gin. These inventions provided the technological base for the industrialization of the textile industry. Each invention that improved one step of the manufacturing of the textiles also had an effect on the parts of the process. For example, an improvement that increased the speed of spinning meant that looms were needed that consumed yarn more rapidly. More rapid yarn production required greater quantities of fiber. The growth of the textile industry was further hastened by the use of machines that were driven first by water power, then by steam, and finally by electricity.

The full mechanization of the textile industry was accomplished by the early part of the nineteenth century. The next major developments in the field were to take place in the chemist's laboratory. Experimentation with the synthesis of dyestuffs in the laboratory rather than from natural plant materials led to the development and use of synthetic dyestuffs in the latter half of the nineteenth century. Other experiments proved that certain natural materials could be dissolved in chemical solvents and re-formed into fibrous form. This principle was used to produce "artificial silk" (now called rayon) from cellulosic materials such as mulberry leaves, wood chips, or cotton linters. By 1910, the first plant for manufacturing rayon had been established in the United States.

The manufacture of rayon marked the beginning of the man-made textile industry. Since that time, enormous advances have been made in the technology for making fibers, spinning them into yarns, constructing fabrics, and coloring and finishing them. Today the textile industry utilizes a complex technology based on scientific processes and a vast economic organization. With the application of advanced technology to the textile field, textile use has expanded from the traditional areas of clothing and home furnishings into the fields of construction, medicine, aerospace, sporting goods, and industry. These applications have been made possible by the ability of textile chemists to "engineer" textile fibers for specific uses. At the same time that textile technology is making strides in new directions, the fabrics that consumers buy for clothing and household use also benefit from the development of new fibers, new methods of yarn and fabric construction, and new finishes for existing fibers and fabrics.

Today a huge international industrial complex encompasses the production of fiber, spinning of yarns, fabrication of cloth, dyeing, finishing and printing, and manufacture of goods for purchase. Consumers purchase products made of textiles. The story of the journey that these products make as they progress from fiber to yarn to fabric to finished product is not just the story of spinning yarns, weaving or knitting fabric, or constructing the end product. It is also the story of a complex network of interrelated industries.

From the Fiber Producer to the Fabric Manufacturer

Natural Fibers

The producer of natural fibers and the producer of man-made fibers are engaged in two very different businesses. The farmer who raises cotton, the rancher who herds sheep, or the grower of silkworms is trying to produce a maximum quantity of fiber from animal or vegetable sources. The grower may attempt to improve the quality of the seeds or breeding stock, but is limited in production by natural factors. If the demand for the product increases or decreases, the grower cannot, like the man-made fiber producer, simply increase or decrease the short-term supply of fiber.

The natural fiber producer sells fibers to mills or to wholesalers for resale. Fibers may be sold to domestic buyers or exported. Much of the supply from natural fibers is produced abroad and imported into the United States. Natural fiber producers have little direct involvement in what happens to their products after they have been sold. The spinning, weaving, and finishing of the fabrics are undertaken by other segments of the textile industry.

There is, of course, economic self-interest on the part of the fiber producer in the promotion of the fiber. To stimulate interest in or demand for products made of wool, cotton, linen, or silk fibers, fiber producers and others involved in their manufacture, processing, and sale have formed trade associations. The purpose of such trade associations is to stimulate interest in fabrics made from natural fibers through advertising, educational materials, and other promotional campaigns.

Some trade organizations maintained by natural fibers groups include the Wool Bureau, the Cotton Council, the International Silk Association, the Mohair Council, and the International Linen Promotion Association. These organizations produce educational materials for use in schools and by consumer groups, provide publicity photographs and information to the press, and sponsor a variety of public relations campaigns designed to keep the name of the fiber constantly before the public. Such publicity emphasizes the name of the fiber, not the fiber producer.

Man-made Fibers

An industrywide Man-made Fiber Producers Association produces public relations materials for the industry in general, but publicity in many segments of the man-made field is also centered on brand or trademarked fibers. (See Figure 1.5.)

Production in the man-made fiber industry differs from the production of natural fibers in a number of ways. Man-made fibers are manufactured, and while the industry must depend on available supplies of the raw materials from which the fibers are made, this industry is not dependent on natural forces that regulate the supply of fiber. Instead, the manufacturer can regulate production according to supply and demand. Manufacturers can also help to create demand for increased quantities of fiber products through advertising and other publicity.

Many man-made fiber producers and firms are, or were originally, chemical companies. The fiber manufacturer generally sells the fibers produced to a firm that will make yarns and/or fabrics. These fibers may be sold as unbranded products or commodities. When sold in this way, the purchaser has no obligation to the fiber manufacturer to produce a product of any specific quality. Products must meet no minimum standards. In short, the buyers can do whatever they wish with the fibers they have purchased.

Other fibers may be sold as "trademarked fibers" or as "brand-name fibers." Here the fiber manufacturer's trademarked name is carried by the finished product. The fiber manufacturer has some control over the quality of the fabric, although it is still possible that a poorly made garment could be constructed from the fabric. One advantage to the fabric and garment manufacturers of buying a trademarked fiber is that they can capitalize on the publicity and promotional materials distributed by the fiber manufacturer.

"Licensed trademarked fibers" are sold only to those manufacturers whose fabrics meet the standards established by the fiber manufacturer. Standards may be set in regard to the construction of fabrics, the manufacture of garments, and, in blends or combinations of two or more fibers, the appropriate proportion of fibers to be combined. Not only do the fabric and garment manufacturers benefit from customer familiarity with the brand name of the fiber, but the fiber manufacturer often shares the costs of advertising or mounts intensive publicity campaigns to promote the fabric, the garment, and even retail outlets where the products are sold.

The interest of man-made fiber producers in their products does not end when the fiber is sold. Because techniques for spinning and fabri-

FIGURE 1.5. *Man-made Fiber Producers'*
Association prepares educational exhibits for
professional meetings and trade shows.
Courtesy of the Man-made Fiber Producers'
Association.

cating man-made fibers may not be uniform for all fibers, the fiber producer provides technical assistance to the fabric manufacturer. Technical bulletins are published that recommend the most effective ways of processing fibers. Consultants from the fiber companies provide information about new developments in textile machinery and finishing. Research and development in fiber-producing companies is often focused on more effective ways of handling man-made fibers during fabrication.

Fiber producers assist manufacturers of fabrics and of garments or other products to locate sources of yarns and fabrics. The marketing department of a fiber-producing company also maintains a library of fabrics that can be used by garment manufacturers and their designers.

A wide variety of other services are offered to the direct customers of the fiber companies and to the general public. Exhibits of current products are presented, often at trade and professional meetings. Educational materials for schools, retailers, and consumers are prepared and distributed. Retail stores may be assisted in promoting trademarked products through fashion shows, publicity materials, or cooperative advertising in which the fiber producer pays some part of the advertising costs. Fashion consultants may be available to assist the designers of fabrics and clothes.

Many of these activities are part of an organized advertising and public relations program. In addition to the services offered that result indirectly in publicity and goodwill for the company, other forms of direct advertising are also utilized. In addition to advertising cooperatively with manufacturers of retail products and retail stores, fiber companies also advertise in publications ranging from those for the trade to general women's magazines.

Research and development (often abbreviated as R & D) is an important function in most large textile fiber companies. Researchers are constantly looking for new fibers, fiber modifications, and improvements in processing at all steps of manufacture. The synthetic fiber industry might be said to have grown out of the research and development program at DuPont, for it was in this program that W. H. Carothers first synthesized nylon.

From the Fiber Manufacturer to the Fabric Producer

Fiber must be converted into yarn, except in some specialized "nonwoven" products where the fibers themselves are united into a cohesive structure. The production of yarns from short, staple fibers is done by *spinners*. When continuous filament yarns are given special treatments such as texturing, this is done by *throwsters*. *Yarn converters*, who may also be throwsters, dye yarns or add special protective finishes that facilitate knitting or weaving.

Textile mills produce knitted, woven, or nonwoven goods. Completed cloth that has not been given any special finishes or been dyed is known as *greige goods*.

The organization of the textile manufacturing industry differs from company to company and also exhibits some differences from one type of textile to another. Cotton fabrics, for example, may be made in a series of steps. One mill may take the raw fiber and turn it into yarn. Then the yarn may be sold to another mill that, in turn, weaves it into cloth. The cloth may be sold to yet another plant where it is dyed or finished.

The wool industry, by contrast, has traditionally processed the fiber from beginning to end. The same mill buys the fiber, spins the yarn, weaves or knits the goods, and finishes the cloth.

Since World War II there has been an increased tendency for all segments of the fabric manufacturing industry to follow the pattern of the wool mills. Although all the operations may not necessarily be carried out in the same location, one company performs all these operations as part of the overall production of the fabric. This form of business organization is known as *vertical integration.*

Vertically integrated companies produce their own yarn, make that yarn into fabric, and finish the fabrics. Some textile firms, especially those making knits, may also manufacture the final product. Burlington Industries, for example, manufactures hosiery as well as produces yarns and fabrics for a variety of other uses.

The mills sell their products to garment or home furnishings manufacturers. Some yard goods are sold to retail stores for resale to the home sewer. The mill may also sell unfinished fabric to jobbers and converters.

Since the number of vertically integrated companies has expanded, converters no longer play as important a role in the textile business as they once did. In these large integrated companies, the conversion of unfinished (greige) goods is done within the framework of the company. The traditional role of the converter has been to buy greige goods from mills, to arrange for dyeing and finishing companies to dye or finish the fabric, and then to resell the finished goods.

Converters serve a useful purpose in the textile industry: because they do not have a large commitment of money to machinery and buildings, they, therefore, have great flexibility. They can, for example, produce smaller runs of high-fashion dress fabric for a manufacturer without having to be concerned about keeping their machines working over the long term. Converters can be more responsive to fashion trends, as they enter only into the very last stages of production.

Mills and converters may have excess fabrics to dispose of. These are often sold to a jobber, who buys lots of fabrics for resale to garment manufacturers or retail stores. The jobber sells in smaller quantities, as a rule, than does the mill or the converter. Manufacturers of garments who want to buy small yardages or specialty fabrics may be able to obtain these more easily from a jobber than from a mill or a converter.

In addition to vertical integration of fabric-producing companies, some companies have moved as well into *horizontal integration* of functions. Here, a parent company joins with other companies that produce related kinds of goods. Burlington Industries, for example, has taken in such companies as Klopman fabrics, Lees Carpets, J. G. Furniture Systems, and Raeford Uniform Fabrics. Formerly separate companies, these groups are now divisions of Burlington Industries.

The advertising and publicity functions of fabric manufacturers are similar to those of the fiber producers. As noted before, the fiber producers and fabric manufacturers may cooperate in publicity campaigns. Fabric producers provide fashion consultants to work with apparel designers and manufacturers, participate in trade and professional shows, produce educational materials, and assist retailers in promoting retail items made from their fabrics.

From the Fabric Manufacturer to the Retailer

After the fabric manufacturer has sold his cloth to the garment manufacturer or to the manufacturer of household goods, the fabrics are converted into the products found on the racks and shelves of the retail store. The garment industry, and the household textile industry, must be involved in the identification of current fashion trends.

The garment industry works four to five months in advance of the time at which the garment will be sold. The textiles from which these garments are made must be made 12 to 18 months ahead of the time that the garments are to be sold. For this reason, textile fabric manufacturers keep up with current trends in design in general, and with fashion trends in particular. They must anticipate the direction in which fashion will move.

Designs for garments made by manufacturers are originated by a fashion designer. Some fashion designers have attained sufficient prominence that they own their own manufacturing companies. Others work for specific manufacturing houses; still others may work on a free-lance basis, selling individual designs to smaller fashion houses. The fashion designer often works closely with the textile company. The fabric company provides the fashion designer with swatches of fabrics from their new lines, or, in some instances, the company may make an "exclusive" fabric that will be sold only to this particular fashion house. It is rare for fabric manufacturers to grant exclusive rights to a fabric to one manufacturer. When this is done, the fashion house is generally a very good customer, and the exclusive rights to the fabric usually last for only a limited period of time before the fabric becomes available more widely.

Fiber companies sometimes plan and execute fashion promotion of new fibers with well-known fashion designers. A promotional campaign of this sort not only creates a high-fashion image for the fabric, but the designs made by top fashion designers are also featured widely in the fashion press.

After the designs for a particular season have been prepared, the garment manufacturer shows the line to retail buyers and to the press. Retail store buyers place orders for the items shown in the line. If sufficient orders are placed, the garment is manufactured, and the orders are delivered to the store for sale.

Because the garment manufacturer does not sell directly, but through retail outlets, advertising and promotional campaigns of manufacturers are most often tied directly or indirectly to retail store promotions. Some garments are selected by manufacturers for national or regional advertisements. Knowing that a particular garment is slated for advertisement in *Vogue*, *Bazaar*, or *Seventeen* magazine may encourage a buyer to place orders for the item. The additional press exposure may enhance the salability of the garment. Retail stores that are especially good customers may be singled out for cooperative advertising in which the names of several stores at which the item is available are specifically mentioned in the advertisement. Other cooperative promotional efforts between retail store and manufacturer include fashion shows, provision of counter cards and other display materials for the retailer, and training programs for sales personnel.

Industrial Textiles

Most consumers are not aware of the segment of the textile industry known as *industrial textiles.* According to J. Donald Keen of Celanese Fibers, "If you don't wear it, sit on it, or walk on it, it is an industrial textile."[3]

Industrial textiles may be woven, knitted, or nonwoven, often of manmade fibers. Fashion is not a factor in industrial textiles, but instead such functional characteristics as strength, stability, chemical resistance, and weight are likely to be important. Examples of industrial textiles range from small products such as filters and auto safety belts to enormous structures such as rooves, tents, and storage tanks. Consumers of industrial products include the construction, mining, sanitation, and transportation industries; medicine; and the military. Some of the more dramatic examples of progress in textile technology have come in the area of industrial textiles, particularly those for the aerospace industry and for "geotextiles." Geotextiles are those used in soil and soil-based structures such as road building, dam construction, and erosion control. (See Figure 1.6.)

FIGURE 1.6. *Earthen wall of a dam being reinforced by inclusion of Supac® geotextiles. Courtesy of Phillips Fibers Corporation.*

[3]J. Donald Keen, Celanese Fibers, in a presentation to the New York City Chapter of the American Association for Textile Technology, January 14, 1985.

No discussion of the textile industry can be complete without mention of the international nature of the production, distribution, and consumption of textiles. All the operations mentioned thus far—namely, fiber production, yarn manufacture, spinning and weaving products, the fabrication of garments, and other dyeing and finishing of textiles—can be and are carried out in many different parts of the world.

Many factors ranging from the wages paid to laborers to the exchange rate paid for American dollars make textiles and textile products manufactured abroad cheaper than those produced in the United States. As a result, retailers have tended to increase the quantity of imported apparel and household textiles. As imports have increased, the domestic textile production industry has suffered severe economic losses.

International agreements concerning trade in textiles have been negotiated both with individual countries *(bilateral agreements)* and with many countries *(multilateral agreements)*. The General Agreement on Tariffs and Trade (GATT) includes a special Multifiber Agreement (MFA) that deals with textile trade. Specific quotas and procedures have been established that were intended to provide some degree of protection to both the exporting and importing countries. Negotiations for renewal of these agreements are initiated at specified intervals. In spite of these agreements, the import problem continues to plague American manufacturers of textile products. (See Figure 1.7.)

International Textile Concerns

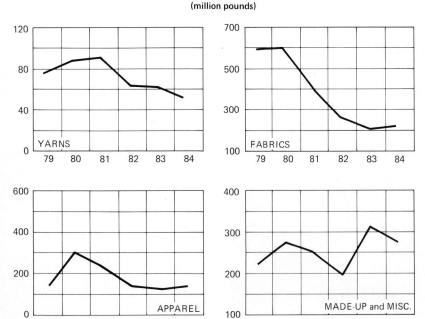

U.S. EXPORTS OF TEXTILE MANUFACTURES
(by calendar years)
(million pounds)

*Annual Rate

FIGURE 1.7. Graphs show clearly that trends in exports and imports of textile manufactures from 1979 to 1984. Source: Economic Information Division, American Textile Manufacturers Institute.

To combat the influx of competing textile products, American companies have taken a number of countermeasures. For example, the American apparel industry sometimes utilizes lower-cost foreign labor. Under Item 807 of the Tariff Schedules of the United States, (TSUS), cut garments can be sent to low-wage countries for assembling and finishing. This kind of production is known as *offshore production*. Finished garments shipped back to the United States under the 807 provision are charged duty not on the whole product, but only on the "value added" abroad. Although this benefits the apparel sales segment of American industry and may not affect the sale of fibers, yarns, and fabrics, textile and apparel unions understandably object to this practice as it decreases jobs for persons working in these segments of industry in the United States.

Organizations representing textile producers have lobbied in favor of laws to impose greater restrictions on imports. Counterarguments have been made by some elected and appointed officials that the imposition of restrictions on imports in textiles would lead to the imposition of restrictions on exports of other kinds of American products to the countries whose imports would be affected by American limits.

Recently, activities to counter imports have centered on increasing the awareness of consumers about imports and their effect on the American industry. Congress has acted in support of American textiles

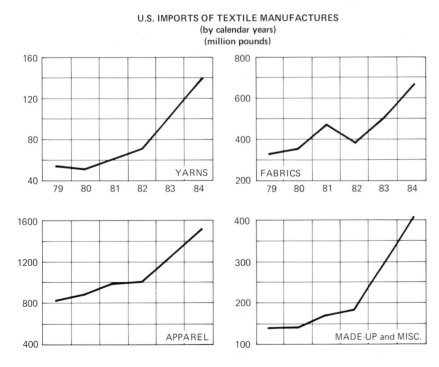

U.S. IMPORTS OF TEXTILE MANUFACTURES
(by calendar years)
(million pounds)

*Annual Rate

by passing legislation requiring that all textile products carry labels indicating the country of origin of the product, including a designation showing that the product was produced in the United States. A "Crafted with Pride in the U.S.A." campaign sponsored by a number of trade organizations and textile- and apparel-producing companies has been initiated with print and other media publicity designed to tell the consuming public about American products and the importance of purchasing "Made in America" textiles. (See Figure 1.8.)

Many experts in the textile field believe that the most important advantage the American textile industry has over foreign competition in the long run is its technological sophistication and, particularly, its potential for automation. These persons believe that increased automation can cut costs and make American products more competitive. They also point out the needs of the retail industry for a "fast turnaround." For example, if a particular item of fashionable apparel sells exceptionally well and fast, the retailer cannot reorder the item from Hong Kong and expect to have it for the same season. Moreover, the Hong Kong quota may already have been filled, and additional items cannot then be shipped. If American manufacturers can supply quickly and dependably, some retailers have indicated that they are willing to pay slightly more for products.

It is likely, then, that American textile firms and trade associations will continue to work on a number of fronts to counteract the negative import situation. Efforts will continue to support legislation that would protect American textiles, campaigns to educate the public about American-made products will be mounted, research will stress improvement of technology in regard to increased automation, and companies will seek to improve their ability to meet their customers' needs for merchandise that can be supplied quickly.

FIGURE 1.8. Publicity and educational materials distributed as part of the "Crafted with Pride in the U.S.A." campaign.

The Responsibility for Quality

All segments of the textile products industry—the fiber producer, the fabric manufacturer, the product manufacturer, and the retailer—are responsible to some extent for the maintenance of quality and for complying with legal requirements for labeling. The maintenance of a certain standard of performance is not required by law, but many segments of the textile industry accept this as a moral obligation. If the producer makes specific claims about performance, the manufacturer then has a more binding legal obligation to be sure that the product does meet the stated claims.

The point of contact for the consumer is usually the retail store where merchandise is returned and complaints are taken. If a retail store values its reputation in the community, justified complaints are handled promptly, merchandise is exchanged, or purchase price is refunded. The retailer then passes the item back to the manufacturer. If the fault is in the construction, the manufacturer must assume responsibility. If the fabric is at fault, the manufacturer may pass the complaint along to the fabric manufacturer.

Some labeling information, however, is required by law. Provisions of the Textile Fiber Products Identification Act mandate labeling of fabrics for fiber content and country of origin. Permanent-care labeling regulations require that permanent labels giving care instructions be affixed to clothing and that the manufacturer of the fabric must supply information about fiber content to the garment manufacturer. The garment firm then affixes to the garment sewn or hanging tags carrying this information as well as all other information required by the law. (See Appendix C for a summary of regulatory legislation applied to textiles.)

The garment manufacturer is also responsible for sewing care label instructions into the garment. Because care is dependent not only on the fashion fabric, but also on trimmings, interfacings, linings, and the like, the garment manufacturer must ascertain the appropriate care to be given the item before selecting the label. While the manufacturer provides the labels, the retail store is responsible for seeing that these labels are not removed before the item is sold to the customer.

Career Opportunities in the Textile Field

From the preceding survey of the organization of the textile industry, it is evident that a wide variety of employment opportunities exist in this field and its related areas. The following brief, and very general, list provides not only a view of the breadth of the field, but also an appropriate summary for this chapter.

Textile careers include the areas of
Business Management
    In textile fiber, fabric, finishing, garment, and retail segments of the industry.
Textile Chemistry
    In manufacturing fibers, research and development, and finishing.
Textile Technology
    In manufacturing fibers, yarns, and fabrics.
    In research and development of new techniques for manufacturing fibers, yarns, and fabrics.
    In developing new machinery for garment manufacture.
    In the application of dyes and finishes.
Marketing
    Of fibers, yarns, fabrics, textile auxiliaries, and finished products.
    Market research.
    Retail sales.
    Of textile machinery and equipment.
Advertising and Public Relations
    For fiber, fabric, garment, and retail segments of the industry.

Design

Of yarns, fabrics, garments, household and industrial textile products.

Buying

Of fibers, fabrics, or textile items for the fabric, garment, or retail industries.

Education

Through industry, trade organizations, technical schools, colleges, and universities.

Recommended References

American Fabrics and Fashions (issue devoted to international textile concerns), No. 131, 1984.

"Burlington CEO Updates Apparel Project," *Textile World*, p. 35 (February 1985), p. 35.

CLUNE, R. "Robotics Seen Aid to Textile Import Battle," *Daily News Record*, June 4, 1985, p. 12.

DICKERSON, K. G., and S. B. HESTER. "The Purchase of a Shirt: International Implications," *Journal of Home Economics*, 76 (Spring 1984), p. 20.

FORTRESS, F. "Responsibility in the Textile/Apparel Interface," *Textile Industries*, 147 (October 1983), p. 62.

FRINGS, G. S. *Fashion from Concept to Consumer*. Englewood Cliffs, N.J.: Prentice-Hall, Inc., 1982.

HASSELBRACK, S. A. "Textiles Is Ready When You Are," *Textile World*, 132 (May 1982), p. 96.

"How Geotextiles Work," *Textile Industries*, 147 (May 1983), p. 40.

Made in the U.S.A.: The Story of How Textiles Are Crafted with Pride in the U.S.A. Washington, D.C.: American Textile Manufacturers Institute, 1985.

PACKARD, S. *The Fashion Business*. New York: Holt, Rinehart, and Winston, Inc., 1983.

SHULMAN, L. "Fabric Quality: The Mill Perspective," *Americas Textiles*, 12 (September 1983), p. 88.

TOYNE, B., et al. *The Global Textile Industry*. Boston: George Allen and Unwin, 1984.

TOYNE, B., et al. *The U.S. Textile Mill Products Industry*. Columbia: University of South Carolina Press, 1983.

WOODRUFF, J. L., and J. M. McDonald, eds. *Handbook of Textile Marketing*. New York: Fairchild Publications, Inc., 1982.

YALE, J. P. "The Economic Structure of the Textile Industry," *Modern Textiles*, 58 (April 1977), p. 9.

Textile Fibers and Their Properties

Textile fibers may be found in nature or created through technology. Natural fibers are taken from animal, vegetable, or mineral sources. A few examples of widely used natural fibers include animal fibers such as wool and silk; vegetable fibers, especially cotton and flax; and asbestos, a mineral fiber.

Man-made fibers are those created through technology. Man-made fibers can be made from natural materials that cannot be used for textiles in their original form but that can be *regenerated* (re-formed) into usable fibers by chemical treatment and processing. These *regenerated fibers* can be made from such diverse substances as wood, corn protein, milk protein, small cotton bits (called *linters*), and seaweed. The first commercially successful man-made fiber was a forerunner of modern rayon, a regenerated cellulose fiber, production of which began around the beginning of the twentieth century. The second, also regenerated, was cellulose acetate, first used after World War I. Synthetic fibers, those synthesized from chemical substances, represent another type of man-made fiber, the first of which was developed by W. H. Carothers for DuPont.

Nylon, the generic name given to this fiber by DuPont, was first marketed in 1938, and its commercial distribution was beginning when the outbreak of World War II required the diversion of nylon and its constituent materials into wartime use. It was not until after the war that commercial nylon production for the civilian market was initiated on a large scale.

The invention of nylon, and its successful marketing after the war, stimulated the synthesis of additional fibers. Gradually, a wide variety of man-made fibers were introduced: vinyon, 1939; saran, 1941; olefin and modacrylic, 1949; acrylic, 1950; polyester, 1953; triacetate, 1954; spandex, 1959; aramid, 1961;[1] olefin, 1961; anidex, 1970; and novoloid, 1972.[2] (The last two of these fibers are no longer produced.)

---

[1]Although the generic category of aramid fibers was established in 1974, these fibers have been produced since 1961 under the generic classification of nylon.

[2]*Man-made Fiber Fact Book* (Washington, D.C.: Man-made Fiber Producers Association, Inc., 1978), pp. 14ff.

Groups of fibers that are related in their chemical structure may be compared with large, extended families. Each fiber family group is made up of smaller family units. These smaller family units are, in turn, composed of a number of individual units. For example, some fibers have a structure made of protein (the large extended family). Subunits of the "protein" family include silk, which has no other close relatives; animal hair fibers, including wool, mohair, cashmere, camel's hair, and the like; and regenerated protein fibers that can be made from corn, soybean, peanut, or milk protein.

Within the family are certain "family resemblances," or ways in which the members of each group are alike. Most protein fibers, for example, show these similarities: they are harmed by the same chemicals, are fairly resilient, are harmed by dry heat, and are weaker wet than dry. Like human family members, however, each fiber has its own talents or eccentricities: silk has high luster, wool does not; vicuña and cashmere are exceptionally soft and luxurious to the touch; and the color of camel's hair cannot be removed easily.

As a result of legislation known as the Textile Fiber Products Identification Act, the Federal Trade Commission has established names and definitions for each of the families of man-made fibers. The "family" name is called the *generic* name or generic classification of the fiber. Manufacturers of man-made fibers also give each of their fibers a name that is known as the *trademark*. Mary Smith, John Smith, and George Smith may be members of the same human family, each with the same family name, but each with a different given name. In the same way, Orlon® acrylic, Zefran® acrylic, and Acrilan® acrylic are all members of the generic group of acrylics, but each has a different trademark. The symbol ® indicates that the name is a registered trademark.

By law, all manufactured items must (at the point of purchase) carry the generic name of the fiber on the label. Most manufacturers of man-made fibers use the generic term along with their own trademark, so that the consumer will find such terms as Dacron® (trademark of E. I. du Pont de Nemours & Company) polyester (generic name) or Kodel® (trademark of Eastman Kodak company) polyester on labels of textile products. (See Appendix D for a listing of generic and trademark names of man-made fibers.)

Generic Fiber Classification

Fiber manufacturers introduced ever-increasing varieties of new fibers to the public after World War II. No regulation was made of the use of man-made fiber names, so that each manufacturer that made its own version of a fiber gave it its own trademark. The consumer was confronted with a variety of fiber names and had no ability to distinguish one from the other. Furthermore, two or more fibers might be blended together without the consumer's knowledge. The purchaser of a man's shirt had no way of knowing whether it was made of cotton, rayon, or a cotton and polyester blend.

Textile Fiber Products Identification Act

The consumer confusion resulting from this situation led to the Textile Fiber Products Identification Act (often abbreviated TFPIA), which provided for fiber content labeling of all textile products. The law, which became effective March 3, 1960, has been amended several times since that date. The legislation assigned responsibility for the enforcement and drafting of rules and regulations under the act to the Federal Trade Commission.

Under the provisions of the TFPIA, all fibers, either natural or man-made, all yarns, fabrics, household textile articles and wearing apparel are subject to this law. One of the first tasks assigned to the Federal Trade Commission was the establishment of generic names or classifications for man-made fibers. (See Figure 2.1.)

Natural fibers, which are each to be called by their own name, are defined in the act as "any fiber that exists as such in the natural state." The terms for natural fibers, such as *cotton, linen, silk,* and *wool* appear on labels. Man-made or, as the act defines them, manufactured fibers are defined as "any fiber derived by a process of manufacture from any substance which, at any point in the manufacturing process, is not a fiber." The law charged the Federal Trade Commission with the responsibility of classifying the many different manufactured fibers that had been introduced. These categories or generic classifications were based on similarities in chemical composition. Along with similarities in chemical composition, fibers in these groupings had many common physical properties, care requirements, and performance characteristics. New generic classes may be added when manufacturers are able to demonstrate that fibers are sufficiently unique to warrant a separate classification from those already in existence, so that it is possible that further generic classes may be established in the future as new fibers are synthesized.

In May 1985, for example, the Federal Trade Commission issued a call for public comment on the request of two companies for the establishment of new generic names for fibers that they believe meet the com-

FIGURE 2.1. *Major classifications of textile fibers.*

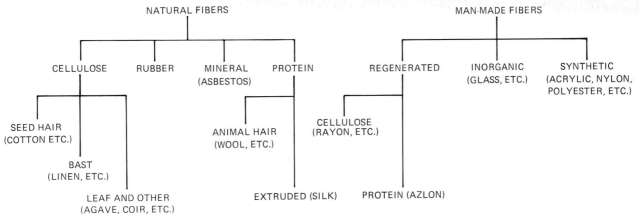

mission's criteria for granting new generic names. These criteria are "that the fiber must have a chemical composition 'radically different' from other fibers and that chemical composition must give it significantly different physical properties; the fiber must currently be, or soon be, in active commercial use; and the granting of the generic name must be of importance to the consuming public 'at large,' rather than to a small group of knowledgeable professionals.' "[3] If the evidence collected by the FTC leads to the conclusion that these criteria have been satisfied, then one or two new generic names may be established within the next few years.

The TFPIA requires that all textile products have a label attached that lists the names of the fibers, either natural or generic, from which they are made.[4] Fiber listing must be done in order of the percentage of fiber by weight that is present in the product. The largest amount must be listed first, the next largest second, and so on. Thus, for example, a fabric might be labeled

60% polyester
30% cotton
10% acetate

The manufacturer must list the generic name of the fiber but may also list the trademark. So, for example, the same label could also read as follows:

60% Dacron® polyester
30% cotton
10% Avetex® acetate

Note that the trademark is capitalized but that the generic term is not.

Fiber quantities of less than 5 per cent must be labeled as "other fiber," unless they serve a specific purpose in the product. If they are listed, the function of these minor components must be stated. For example, a manufacturer could say, "96 per cent nylon, 4 per cent spandex for elasticity," because spandex is an elastic fiber and does perform a specific function. The intent of this provision is to prevent manufacturers from implying that 5 per cent or less of a fiber will produce some positive benefit. Quantities of less than 5 per cent of most fibers normally have little or no effect on fabric performance. Examples of exceptions are in the use of elastomeric fibers such as spandex or metallic fibers that control static.

---

[3]Federal Trade Commission information sheet requesting public comment, May 28, 1985.

[4]With these exceptions: upholstery stuffing; outer coverings of furniture, mattresses, and box springs; linings, interlinings, stiffenings, or paddings incorporated for structural purposes and not for warmth; sewing and handicraft threads; and bandages and surgical dressings.

Where products are made from fibers that have not been identified, for instance, from mixed reused fiber, the label may indicate that such a product is "composed of miscellaneous scraps, rags, odd lots, textile by-products, secondhand materials, or waste materials." Such a label might read, for example,

45% rayon
35% acetate
20% miscellaneous scraps of undetermined fiber content

No trademarks or other terms may be used that imply the presence of a fiber that is not actually a part of the product. For example, it would be illegal to use the following labels:

SILK-SHEEN Blouses   or   Wooly Warm Blankets
  100% nylon   100% acrylic

The law also requires that either the name of the manufacturer, a registered trademark, or a registered identification number appear on the label. All the mandated information must appear on the same side of the label, and all fiber content information must appear in type or lettering of equal size or conspicuousness, except for the manufacturer's name or identification number. This information may be placed on the reverse side of the label or on a separate label close to the fiber content label.

The TFPIA was further amended in 1984, the purposes of the amendment being to clarify and improve country-of-origin labeling requirements and to increase consumer awareness of origin. (A parallel amendment was added to another law, the Wool Products Labeling Act, at the same time. See Chapter 6.)

The specific requirements under the amendment are as follows. The country of origin, whether foreign or domestic, must be disclosed in a label placed in the neck of any garment having a neck; for those without necks, it must be placed on a conspicuous spot on the inside or outside of the product. All products are to be separately labeled except when several pairs of hosiery are enclosed in one retail package that will not be opened prior to sale. Not only the product itself but also packages must be labeled unless the individual product label can be seen clearly through the package. Mail-order catalogs and mail promotional materials such as department store advertising flyers must disclose whether a product advertised was made in the United States or imported or both.

Once the law had been passed, major questions surfaced as to how to identify the point of origin of an item that, for example, was made from fiber produced in one country, spun and woven into cloth in another, and constructed into apparel in yet another. The rules promulgated following the law were hotly debated by individuals in the textile industry during a period when comments were invited. The report in the *Federal Register*, April 17, 1985 (pp. 15101–15107), makes fascinating reading, as the debate over the implementation of the provisions of the law is summarized. After considering the comments offered, the following rules went into effect in May 1985. Products made entirely in the United States must carry a label that says "Made in the U.S.A." or some other "clear and equivalent" term. (Acceptable examples include "Crafted with Pride in the U.S.A." or "Made in New York, U.S.A.")

Products made in the United States using foreign materials are required to carry a label such as "Made in the U.S.A. of imported fabric" or equivalent terms. The Federal Trade Commission requires only that the manufacturer go back one manufacturing step to determine origin. For example, the manufacturer of knitting yarn sold at retail needs to identify the origins of the fiber; the manufacturer of retail piece goods needs to identify origins of yarn, but need not identify origin of the fiber; and the apparel manufacturer would identify the origin of the cloth. The specific country of origin need not be identified, although it may be given. Therefore, for example, a knitting yarn spun in the United States of Australian wool would need to be labeled as "Made in U.S.A. of imported wool fibers." However, if the manufacturer wished, it could say "Made in U.S.A. of Australian wool fiber."

Properties of Textile Fibers

Fibers, which are primary materials from which most textile products are made, can be defined as units of matter of hairlike dimensions, with a length at least one hundred times greater than the width. Many substances found in nature can be classified as fibers according to this definition; however, only a limited number of these materials are useful in the production of yarns or fabrics.

Whether a fiber can be utilized in the creation of a yarn or fabric depends upon the physical, mechanical, and chemical properties of the fiber. Many fibrous substances lack one or more essential qualities required of textile fibers. They may not, for example, be sufficiently long to be spun into a yarn. Or they may be too weak to use, too inflexible, too thick in diameter, or too easily damaged in spinning and weaving.

Comparison of fiber qualities and characteristics requires the use of certain basic terms and a technical vocabulary. Definition of these terms and of their meanings as they relate to textile performance and/or behavior is important for communication and understanding.

Physical Properties

Some qualities of textile fibers are related to their physical characteristics. Since most single fibers are so small that they cannot be examined adequately with the naked eye, the physical appearance of these fibers is best observed under a microscope. With a microscope, it is possible to observe such properties as length, diameter, surface contour, and color. The physical characteristics of each individual fiber affect the appearance and behavior of the yarns and fabrics into which they are manufactured.

Color

The color of natural fibers varies. Some, like cotton, have just enough pigment to make them yellow or off-white; others, like wool, may range from white to black. If their color interferes with dyeing or printing, the color may be removed by bleaching. Man-made fibers are usually white or "bright."

Luster

Luster is the amount of light reflected by the fiber. Luster may be desirable in some products and undesirable in others. Current fashion trends may increase or decrease consumer acceptance of bright or dull fabrics. Man-made fibers may have bright luster. If it is desirable to decrease the luster, the chemical titanium oxide is added to the material from which the fiber is made. The small particles of the chemical break up the reflected light, giving the fiber a lower luster. They are said to "deluster" the fiber. Untreated fibers may be known as "bright" fibers; delustered fibers may be called "dull" or "semidull" fibers.

Shape

The shape of a fiber can be examined both in *cross section* and in its *longitudinal* form. Since cross section is a practical way in which to view the three-dimensional form of a fiber, cross sections are often used as a means of comparisons. Cross sections vary from fiber to fiber, ranging from circular to oval, triangular, dog-bone shaped, U shaped, and hollow. (See Figure 2.2.)

The cross-sectional shapes of man-made fibers are uniform. Some irregularities in shape will occur in natural fibers, but the range of these differences is slight enough that fabric appearance is not much affected.

Differences in cross section are responsible for differences in fiber characteristics such as appearance, hand or feel, surface texture, and body. Luster and covering power are also affected by cross-sectional shapes.

Fabrics are often used to cover that which is placed beneath them. The ability of a fabric to cover an object is known as its *covering power.* The covering power of fibers and fabrics has two aspects: the visual and the geometric. Visual covering power is related to the ability of the fiber to hide what is placed beneath it. The more transparent the fiber, the less covering power it has. The second aspect, that of geometric covering power, might be described as the quantity of fiber required to make a yarn that will cover a specific area.

Geometric covering power is measured by filling a standard sized container with yarn, then weighing the amount of yarn required to fill the container. When a small quantity of yarn is required to fill the container, the fiber is said to have good covering power. When a large quan-

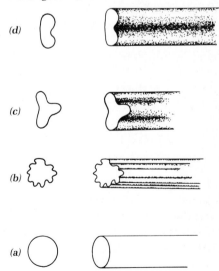

FIGURE 2.2. *Typical variations in fiber cross-sectional shape together with the resulting longitudinal appearance: (a) round, (b) serrated, (c) trilobal, (d) dog bone. Notice how the shape of the cross section forms visual lines and/or shadows in the appearance of the longitudinal view.*

(d)

(c)

(b)

(a)

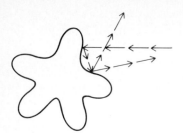 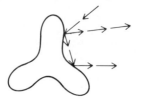 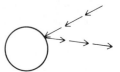

FIGURE 2.3. *Diagrams showing differences in reflection of light in round, trilobal, and pentalobal fibers.*

tity of yarn is required to fill the container, the fiber is said to have poor covering power. The better the covering power, the less expensive it will be to manufacture a yarn or fabric, because a smaller quantity of fiber will be required.

Round, cross-sectional–shaped fibers have a soft, smooth, sometimes slippery feel. Unless a special treatment has been given to the fiber to decrease its luster, the luster of round fibers is high. Covering power is, however, poor. This is because the surface area of round fibers is less than that of any other shape. Also being both round and smooth, the fiber will pack closely together into a yarn.

Dog-bone–shaped and flat cross-section fibers have a harsher, less smooth handle. The covering power of these fibers is excellent. Completely flat cross sections have a high luster, and some manufacturers have produced flat fibers with a glittering luster, but those with less regular surface, such as cotton, which has a somewhat flat but irregular cross section, do not have high luster.

Fibers with three- and five-lobed shapes have been manufactured. Three-lobed fibers are known as trilobal fibers; those with five lobes are known as pentalobal. The term *multilobal* is used to refer to all fibers with a number of lobes in the cross section. Trilobal fibers with triangular-shaped cross sections have increased covering power, a more silk-like feel, and an increased luster. The luster results from the reflection of light not only from the surface of the fiber but also from the light being reflected from one lobe to another. (See Figure 2.3.) Pentalobal fibers also have this tendency to reflect light from one lobe to another, but because there are more lobes among which the light can be reflected, the fibers have a soft, subdued sheen.

When the lobes of the fiber are increased still further, light rays are broken up and the luster decreases. Octolobal fibers have been made to decrease luster or glitter.

Hollow fibers (Figure 2.4) are made of a sheath of fiber material and a hollow space at the center. This hollow may be formed in a number of different ways. The fiber may be made with a core of one material and a sheath of another, and then the central material is dissolved out. Or an inert gas may be added to the solution from which the fiber is formed, with the gas bubbles creating a hollow area in the fiber. Other specialized techniques also appear to be utilized to make hollow fibers,

FIGURE 2.4. *Photograph of the cross-section of a hollow rayon fiber mounted in wax and photographed through a scanning electron microscope. Courtesy of Courtaulds North America, Inc.*

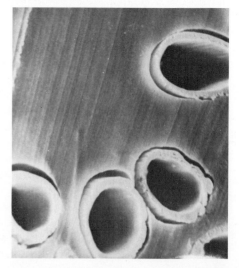

but details of the processes are not released to the public. Hollow fibers provide greater bulk with less weight. They are, therefore, often used to make insulated clothing. For absorbent fibers such as rayon, hollow fibers provide increased absorbency. Some have been put to such specialized uses as filters or as carriers for carbon particles in safety clothing for persons who come into contact with toxic fumes. The carbon serves to absorb the fumes.

Surface Contour

Some fibers have smooth, even contours when examined longitudinally; others are rough and uneven. Wool, for example, is covered with many small scales that cause wool fibers to cling closely together. Cotton is twisted, making it reflect light unevenly and giving it a dull appearance. Horizontal lines or other markings may appear in the length of some man-made fibers as a result of irregularities in the cross-sectional shape of the fiber. The valleys between the lobes of multilobal fibers cause shadows, which (under the microscope) appear as dark lines and are known as *striations*. (See Figure 2.5.)

Crimp

Some fibers possess a wavy, undulating physical structure. This characteristic is called *crimp*. Wool has a natural three-dimensional crimp. A number of "texturing" processes can be used to add crimp to man-made fibers or yarns. Fabrics made from crimped fibers and/or yarns tend to be more resilient and have increased bulk, cohesiveness, and warmth. *Cohesiveness* is the ability of fibers to cling together.

Length

By microscopic examination of textile fibers, one can readily observe the ratio (or comparison) of the length of the fiber in relation to its width. Although fibers are, by definition, always long and narrow, the length of the fiber is one basis for division or classification. Fibers of relatively short length, measured in centimeters or inches, are called *staple* fibers. Long fibers, those measured in yards or meters, are known as *filament* fibers.

All natural fibers except silk are staple fibers. Man-made fibers are manufactured in filament form, but the filaments can be cut into shorter, staple lengths. Therefore, man-made fibers may be found in either staple or filament form.

The length of the fiber will have an effect on the appearance of the yarn into which it is made. Filament fibers can be made into yarns with little or no twisting. These will look smooth and lustrous. Staple fibers, being short, must be twisted together or spun to make them into a long, continuous yarn. Shorter fibers will produce more fiber ends on the surface of a yarn, thus creating a duller appearance.

The *hand* or *texture* of the fabric is affected by the use of either filament or staple fibers. If an untextured filament form is selected, there

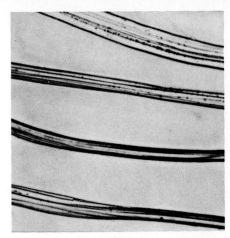

FIGURE 2.5. *A longitudinal view of rayon showing striations. Courtesy of E. I. du Pont de Nemours & Company.*

are fewer fiber ends on the surface of a fabric, creating a smooth, even surface. If staple fibers are used, the short fiber ends on the surface of a fabric can create a fabric that feels soft and fluffy to the touch. Judicious selection of short staple, longer staple, textured, or untextured filament yarns enables the manufacturer to vary the appearance, the texture, or other properties of fabrics.

Diameter or Fineness

The diameter of the fiber is the distance across its cross section. In natural fibers the diameter usually varies from one part of the fiber to another because of irregularities in fiber size. Unless manufactured to have an uneven diameter, man-made fibers usually have a uniform diameter throughout.

Fiber diameter is measured in millimeters or in microns. One micron is 1/1000th of a millimeter or 0.000039th of an inch. Cotton fiber diameter is usually from 12 to 20 microns in width, for example.

Fiber diameter is an aspect of *fineness*. Fineness is not a direct but a relative measure of size, diameter, linear density, or weight per unit length. Instead of measuring the distance across the fiber, a calculation is made of the weight in grams of 1,000 meters of fiber. The term used to express this measurement is *tex*. In reading technical reports on fibers, you may see one fiber identified as having a measurement of 0.33 tex, (or 0.33 grams per 1,000 meters), another of 0.17 tex, and yet another of 5.5 tex. The fibers with the lower tex numbers would be finer; those with higher numbers would be less fine.

A new system of measurement is being adopted worldwide. Called the International System of Units, abbreviated SI, its details are controlled by the International Bureau of Weights and Measures. The system of measurement used for fibers and yarns before the adoption of the SI system utilized the term *denier*, which is the weight of 9,000 meters of fiber or yarn. The use of denier measurements has not been entirely replaced by tex measures and will be found in many readings. To convert from denier to tex measurements, multiply by 1.111×10^{-7}. As in the case of tex measures, a lower denier measure means a finer fiber or yarn and a higher denier measure means a coarser fiber or yarn.

Man-made fibers can have any diameter that the manufacturer chooses, and the selection of diameter is generally related to the projected end use of the fiber. Clothing fibers are made in relatively small diameters, whereas heavy-duty fibers for household items or industrial uses are made with larger diameters. Fineness of fibers is related to softness, pliability, and handle, characteristics that consumers often take into account when choosing products. Fine man-made fibers are more costly to produce than are coarser sizes, and finer natural fibers generally command higher prices as well.

Extrafine fibers, called *microdenier fibers* or *microfibers*, are manufactured for specialized uses. These fibers are at least half the diameter of conventional fibers. Most man-made fibers have diameters ranging from 10 to 50 microns, whereas microfibers have diameters of about 5 microns or less. The fineness of these fibers makes them particularly useful in forming fabrics with very fine pores and a dense surface. Applications include surgical masks, filtration materials, ski jacket insulation, and surgical wrapping materials.

Mechanical Properties

Determination of Textile Properties and Performance

A number of specific textile properties are defined and discussed in the following pages. The determination of the properties of specific fibers is made through one or more of a variety of different fiber-, yarn-, or fabric-testing methods. Test methods are standardized by organizations such as the American Society for Testing Materials (ASTM), the American Association of Textile Chemists and Colorists (AATCC), the American National Standards Institute (ANSI), or by the government through federal test method standards.

When textile materials are tested, not only must standardized procedures be utilized but testing must be done under controlled conditions. Even the temperature or the quantity of moisture present in a room may affect the results of tests. For this reason, testing is done only under conditions of controlled humidity and temperature, and samples are "conditioned" for a specific period of time prior to testing at a temperature of 70°F and 65 per cent relative humidity. The conditioning time is usually at least 24 hours, temperature may be plus or minus 2°F, and humidity may be plus or minus 2 per cent. (See Chapter 24 for fuller discussion of textile testing.)

Strength or Tenacity

The strength of textile fibers is referred to as their *tenacity*. According to the American Society for Testing and Materials, tenacity is determined by measuring the force required to rupture or break the fiber.[5] Tenacity of fibers is measured either in grams per tex or grams per denier. *Grams per tex* (abbreviated *g/t*) is the number of grams of weight required to break a fiber of 1 tex. *Grams per denier* (abbreviated *g/d*) is the number of grams of weight required to break a fiber of 1 denier.

Tensile strength measures textile strength in terms of pounds of weight required per square inch to break a yarn or fabric. The word *tensile* means "tearing apart." This measure is applied more frequently to woven fabrics than to fibers.

Although measuring the tenacity of a fiber will provide some guide to potential strength in a woven fabric, many other factors will also affect the durability of the fabric into which the yarn is made. The strength of

[5]*Compilation of ASTM Standard Definitions* (Philadelphia: American Society for Testing Materials, 1982), p. 733.

filament fibers is more comparable to the strength of yarns and fabrics than is the strength of staple length fibers. Such factors as the twist of a yarn will also be important in determining the ultimate durability and strength of a woven fabric.

Specific Gravity

Density and *specific gravity* are terms that are used in relation to the weight of fibers. Both terms show a relationship, but each has a somewhat different technical definition.

Density is the ratio of a mass of a substance to a unit of volume. In the case of a fiber, density is expressed as grams of fiber per cubic centimeter of fiber. The concept of linear density has already been discussed under the heading of diameter and fineness and is measured as grams per tex or grams per denier.

The concept of specific gravity is an alternative means of expressing density and is defined as the density of the fiber in relation to the density of an equal volume of water at a temperature of 4°C. The specific gravity of water is 1. If a fiber has a specific gravity of more than 1, it is heavier than water; if it has a specific gravity that is less than 1, it is lighter than water. Only a few textile fibers have a specific gravity that is less than that of water, so that the specific gravity of most fibers will fall in a range of from 1.0 to 2.0 or slightly above. (See Table 2.1.)

Density has significance for the consumer in a number of ways. Olefins, with a specific gravity of less than that of water, will float on the top of water during laundering. The low density of olefin fibers makes possible the manufacture of fibers from smaller amounts of raw materials. This results in lower costs for the fiber. Glass fiber has a high specific gravity. Therefore, if a cotton fabric and a glass fabric are made of yarns of comparable size and of similar weave, the glass fabric will be much heavier than the cotton.

Flexibility

Flexibility of fibers refers to their ability to be bent or folded and is an essential quality of textile fibers. The consumer perceives fiber flexibility in terms of stiffness. Not only is it difficult to spin inflexible fibers into yarns, but fabrics made from such fibers feel stiff, do not drape well, and are not comfortable to wear; therefore, except for special-use fabrics for household or industry, fabrics that lack flexibility have poor consumer acceptance. Furthermore, the fiber must bend or flex often without breaking or splitting; as in many end products the textiles are subject to manipulation that causes fibers to bend or fold. Wood, for example, is composed of fibers, but these fibers lack flexibility and cannot be spun into textiles.

Elongation and Elastic Recovery

Elongation is the stretching or lengthening of a fiber. Elongation does not imply that the fiber will return to its original form, but merely that

TABLE 2.1. Some Properties of Man-made Fibers (standard laboratory conditions for fiber tests: 70°F and 65% relative humidity)

Fiber	Breaking Tenacity[1] (grams per denier)		Specific Gravity[2]	Standard Moisture Regain (%)[3]	Effects of Heat
	Standard	Wet			
Acetate (filament and staple)	1.2–1.5	0.8–1.2	1.32	6.0	Sticks at 350°F (177°C) to 375°F (191°C). Softens at 400°F (205°C) to 445°F (230°C). Melts at 500°F (260°C). Burns relatively slowly.
Acrylic (filament and staple)	2.0–3.5	1.8–3.3	1.14–1.19	1.3–2.5	Sticks at 450°F (232°C) to 497°F (258°C), depending on type.
Aramid					
Regular-tenacity filament	4.8	4.8	1.38	5.0	Decomposes above 800°F (427°C).
High-tenacity filament	22.0	22.0	1.44	2.7–7.0	Decomposes above 900°F (482°C).
Staple	3.0–4.5	3.0–4.5	1.38	5.0	Decomposes above 800°F (427°C).
Modacrylic (filament and staple)	2.0–3.5	2.0–3.5	1.30–1.37	0.4–4.0	Will not support combustion. Shrinks at 250°F (121°C). Stiffens at temperatures over 300°F (149°C).
Nylon					
Nylon 66 (regular-tenacity filament)	3.0–6.0	2.6–5.4	1.14	4.0–4.5	Sticks at 445°F (229°C). Melts at about 500°F (260°C).
Nylon 66 (high-tenacity filament)	6.0–9.5	5.0–8.0	1.14	4.0–4.5	Same as above.
Nylon 66 (staple)	3.5–7.2	3.2–6.5	1.14	4.0–4.5	Same as above.
Nylon 6 (filament)	6.0–9.5	5.0–8.0	1.14	4.5	Melts at 414°F (212°C) to 428°F (220°C).
Nylon 6 (staple)	2.5	2.0	1.14	4.5	Melts at 414°F (212°C) to 428°F (220°C).
Olefin (polypropylene; filament and staple)	4.8–7.0	4.8–7.0	0.91	—	Melts at 325°F (163°C) to 335°F (168°C).
Polyester					
Regular-tenacity filament	4.0–5.0	4.0–5.0	1.22, 1.38[a]	0.4, 0.8[a]	Melts at 480°F (249°C) to 550°F (288°C).
High-tenacity filament	6.3–9.5	6.2–9.4	1.22, 1.38[a]	0.4, 0.8[a]	Melts at 480°F (249°C) to 550°F (288°C).
Regular-tenacity staple	2.5–5.0	2.5–5.0	1.22, 1.38[a]	0.4, 0.8[a]	Melts at 480°F (249°C) to 550°F (288°C).
High-tenacity staple	5.0–6.5	5.0–6.4	1.22, 1.38[a]	0.4, 0.8[a]	Melts at 480°F (249°C) to 550°F (288°C).
Rayon (filament and staple)					
Regular-tenacity	0.73–2.6	0.7–1.8	1.50–1.53	13.0	Does not melt. Decomposes at 350°F (177°C) to 464°F (240°C).
Medium tenacity	2.4–3.2	1.2–1.9	1.50–1.53	13.0	Burns readily.
High tenacity	3.0–6.0	1.9–4.6	1.50–1.53	13.0	
High wet modulus	2.5–5.5	1.8–4.0	1.50–1.53	13.0	
Spandex (filament)	0.6–0.9	0.6–0.9	1.20–1.21	0.75–1.3	Degrades slowly at temperatures over 300°F (149°C). Melts at 446°F (230°C) to 518°F (270°C).
Saran (filament)	≤1.5	≤1.5	1.7	—	Softens at 240°F (116°C) to 280°F (138°C). Self-extinguishing.
Triacetate (filament and staple)	1.2–1.4	0.8–1.0	1.3	3.2	Before heat treatment, sticks at 350°F (177°C) to 375°F (191°C). After treatment, above 464°F (240°C). Melts at 575°F (302°C).
Vinyon (staple)	0.7–1.0	0.7–1.0	1.33–1.35	≤0.5	Becomes tacky and shrinks at 150°F (66°C). Softens at 170°F (77°C). Melts at 260°F (127°C). Will not support combustion.

Note: Data given in ranges may fluctuate according to introduction of fiber modifications or additions and deletions of fiber types.
Source: Table reproduced courtesy of Man-made Fiber Producers Association, Inc.

[1]Breaking tenacity: the stress at which a fiber breaks, expressed in terms of grams per denier.
[2]Specific gravity: the ratio of the weight of a given volume of fiber to an equal volume of water.
[3]Standard moisture regain: the moisture regain of a fiber (expressed as a percentage of the moisture-free weight) at 70°F and 65 per cent relative humidity.
[a]Depending on type.

the fiber length can be elongated or extended. Measurement of elongation is commonly made as "elongation to break," the amount of stretch the fiber can withstand before it will break. A fiber that will stretch or elongate more before breaking will therefore show greater strength or tenacity, as it will require more force to both stretch and then break the fiber.

Elastic recovery is the ability of fibers to return to their original length after being stretched. Elastic recovery can be quantified or measured and is calculated in numerical terms as the percentage of elastic recovery. A measured fiber (or fabric) is elongated or stretched to a specific degree, for a specified period of time. The stress is then removed, and the fiber is allowed to recover for a short period of time. After recovery, the fiber is remeasured, and the percentage of recovery is calculated. A fiber with 100 per cent recovery has returned to its original length. A fiber with 80 per cent recovery is 20 per cent longer after stretching.

Elongation and elastic recovery are separate qualities. One fiber (fiber A) may stretch (elongate) but not return to its original length, while another (fiber B) may stretch to the same extent and return to (recover) its original size. Both fibers show similar qualities of elongation, but differ in their elastic recovery. For the manufacturer who wishes to produce a serviceable product that has some "give" but will not stretch out of shape, use of fiber B will produce the better product.

Dimensional Stability

Fibers that neither stretch nor shrink are dimensionally stable. Recovery from stretching is related to elastic recovery, as fibers with good elastic recovery retain their shape. Shrinkage is a decrease in the length of fibers and may be accompanied by an increase in the width of the fiber.

Many fibers are described as being inherently dimensionally stable, yet the fabrics into which they are made may shrink. This fabric shrinkage results from the stretching of fabrics during their construction and/or finishing. Fabrics that are distorted during processing tend to relax to their natural dimensions after the first few launderings. This type of fabric shrinkage is called *relaxation shrinkage*. If fabrics continue to shrink each time they are washed, even after many launderings, then they are displaying *progressive shrinkage*.

Man-made fibers that are thermoplastic or heat sensitive may shrink when subjected to heat. Special treatment with heat called *heat setting* can, however, be used to set the fiber and make it dimensionally stable. The man-made fibers or fabrics that have been heat-set do not shrink unless the heat-setting temperature is exceeded.

Resiliency

Resiliency refers to the ability of a fiber to spring back to its natural position after folding, creasing, or deformation. Fibers differ in their natural resiliency, and those that are resilient are likely to recover from creasing or wrinkling more quickly. Although resiliency and elasticity are not the same, high elastic recovery is necessary for good resilience.

The term *loft* is related to resiliency. Sometimes known as *compressional resiliency*, loft is the ability of fibers to return to their original thickness after being flattened or compressed. A fabric with "loft" is one that is springy and resists flattening.

Abrasion Resistance

One of the most important physical properties of a fiber in relation to durability is its ability to withstand abrasion. *Abrasion* is the rubbing or friction of fiber against fiber or fiber against other materials. Fibers with poor abrasion resistance break and splinter, which produces worn or broken areas in fabrics.

Abrasion of fabrics may take place when they are flat, folded, or curved, so that fibers can be subjected to three types of abrasion: flat, flexed, and edge abrasion. For example, flat abrasion may be seen on carpets as the feet of passers-by constantly rub against the surface; flexed abrasion takes place at the back of the knee in trousers or with the folding and unfolding of linens as they are stored; and edge abrasion occurs at the permanently folded edges of collars and cuffs. Prediction of performance in relation to abrasion is considered to be difficult (see Chapter 24 for a discussion of the methods of evaluating abrasion) as many factors influence abrasion.

Pizzuto lists five variables that must be considered in evaluating abrasion resistance. They are

1. *Type of abradant.*
2. *Amount of pressure between fabric and abradant.*
3. *Position of the fabric while being abraded.*
4. *Frequency and time duration of the abrading sequence.*
5. *Tension exerted on the fabric while it is being abraded.*[6]

Morton and Hearle, who note that abrasion depends largely on construction of yarn and fabric, state that no way has been found to eliminate the influences of these factors and calculate a basic fiber property.[7] For this reason, fiber abrasion properties are not discussed in the following chapters as a separate category. Table 2.2 does, however, present a summary of general evaluations of abrasion resistance for a number of widely used fibers.

Pilling takes place when a fabric has been subject to abrasion that causes fiber ends to break, migrate to the surface, and form into a small ball that clings to the surface of the fabric. Pilling is a more serious problem in strong fibers, as weaker fibers tend to break and fall off the surface of the fabric when pills are formed, whereas the stronger fibers do not break away and the pills stay on the surface of the cloth.

[6]J. Pizzuto, *Fabric Science* (New York: Fairchild Publications, Inc., 1974), p. 367.
[7]W. E. Morton and J. W. S. Hearle, *Physical Properties of Textile Fibers* (New York: John Wiley & Sons, Inc., 1975), p. 435.

TABLE 2.2 A Comparison of Abrasion Resistance in Selected Fibers as Evaluated by Several Sources

Fiber	Abrasion Resistance Evaluated as[1,2,3]	
Nylon	"Outstandingly durable fiber"	"Good to excellent abrasion resistance"
Polyester	"Very durable in comparison with natural fibers"	Ratings range from "good" to "excellent" depending on variety
Acrylics	"Quite sufficiently durable"	"Good resistance to abrasion"
Viscose	"Tested in the laboratory, does not have good resistance to abrasion, but in use blends have been found to be as durable as cotton"	"Fair resistance to abrasion"
Acetate and triacetate	"Low abrasion resistance"	"Fair resistance to abrasion"
Cotton	"More resistant to abrasion than other natural fibers"	Sometimes rated higher than wool, sometimes rated lower
Wool	"More resistant to abrasion than other natural fibers"	Sometimes rated higher than cotton, sometimes rated lower
Linen	"Good resistance to abrasion, but durability is less than hoped for because is damaged by repeated flexing"	Not rated
Silk	"Poor abrasion resistance"	Consistently rated lower than cotton and wool

[1]Fiber evaluations in second column summarized from H. M. Taylor, "Abrasion in Fabrics," *Textiles*, 7 (June 1978), pp. 36 ff.
[2]Evaluations of man-made fibers in third column from *Textile World Man-made Fiber Chart*, 13 (August 1980).
[3]Evaluations of natural fibers in third column from W. E. Morton and J. W. S. Hearle, *Physical Properties of Textile Fibers* (New York: John Wiley & Sons, Inc., 1975), p. 437.

Chemical Properties

Absorbency

The ability of a fiber to absorb or take water into itself affects many aspects of its use. The ability of a bone-dry fiber to absorb moisture is called *moisture regain.* In calculating the properties of textile fibers, textile technologists will take a sample of fibers or fabric, dry it thoroughly, and return the sample to a controlled atmosphere in which temperature and humidity are accurately maintained at a temperature of 70°F and 65 per cent relative humidity. The amount of moisture that is taken up by the sample is then measured. *Saturation regain* is measured at 95 to 100 per cent relative humidity.

A fiber that permits some moisture absorption is comfortable to wear, especially in hot weather. Absorbent fibers accept water-borne dyes and special finishes readily and are easy to launder. On the other hand, fibers that absorb moisture readily dry slowly and may be stained by water-borne soil.

Some fibers *adsorb* moisture rather than absorb it. When water is adsorbed, it is held on the surface of the fiber rather than being taken into the fiber itself. If such fibers have a low moisture regain, they dry more quickly than do absorbent fibers and stain less readily. *Wicking* takes place when moisture travels along the surface of the fiber but is not absorbed into the fiber. Some fibers both absorb moisture and also have wicking ability. Most synthetics have low absorbency, but some also have wicking properties that make them more comfortable to wear, since perspiration can travel to the surface of the fiber where it can evaporate.

The strength of some fibers is affected by the moisture that they contain. Cotton, for example, is stronger when wet than when dry, whereas rayon is weaker wet than dry. For the consumer this means that handling some fabrics during laundering may require greater care. For the manufacturer, it means that processing of fibers during dyeing or finishing must be modified.

Electrical Conductivity

Electrical conductivity is the ability of a fiber to carry or transfer electrical charges. Fabrics with low or poor conductivity build up electrical charges with the result that these fabrics cling or produce electrical shocks. The mechanical action of automatic dryers also serves to build up static electricity on fabrics of low conductivity, thereby producing "static cling." Many synthetic fibers have low conductivity, and when several layers of clothing of low electrical conductivity are worn, the problem of charge buildup is aggravated.

Poor conductivity is related to low moisture regain. Water is an excellent conductor of electricity, and fibers with good absorbency are not as likely to build up static electricity as are those that are nonabsorbent. Furthermore, some fibers with fairly good moisture absorbency but poor conductivity display static buildup, and fabrics "cling" only when weather conditions are dry. Treatments given to fabrics to decrease static accumulation involve finishes that enable fibers to hold moisture on the surface or to absorb more moisture. Some man-made fibers are modified in chemical structure during manufacture so as to increase electrical conductivity.

Effect of Heat

Textile products may be subjected to heat not only during manufacture and processing but also in use. In home care, for example, fabrics may be pressed or dried in a hot drier. The way in which various fibers respond to the application of heat depends upon their chemical composition. Many synthetic fibers soften or melt at various temperatures. Cellulosic and protein fibers scorch or turn brown. The specific behavior exhibited by each fiber will, of course, determine the way in which the fiber must be handled during manufacture and use.

Some man-made fibers are said to be thermoplastic because they soften or melt on exposure to heat. This characteristic is used to advantage in the manufacturing of some textile products because the application of the right amount of heat will permanently set pleats or shape into the fabric. Careful control of heat causes physical changes to take place within the fiber that alters its form, thereby establishing a permanent shape. In fabrics made from thermoplastic fibers, heat may be used to fuse seams and make buttonholes.

Flammability

Some fibers ignite and burn, some smoulder, and others are noncombustible. Fibers that burn when they are held in a direct flame and stop burning when the flame is removed are designated "self-extinguishing."

Burning of small quantities of textile fibers may be used as a means of differentiating one fiber group from another. Although precise identification of individual fibers cannot be made by burning, burning can help to establish the general fiber group to which the fiber belongs. Cellulosic fibers, for example, exhibit flammability characteristics much like that of paper, protein fibers burn in a manner similar to hair, and some synthetics melt when they burn. The odor produced when a fiber burns and the kind of ash that remains after burning may also aid in the identification of the fiber.

The flammability of textile fibers may be related to their selection for use in particular products. Certain fibers are inherently noncombustible, whereas others exhibit flame-retardant or flame-resistant properties. Glass fiber draperies are often used in public places because they are noncombustible, thereby decreasing the hazards of fires. Special finishes are applied to fabrics to retard flammability. Children's sleepwear and certain household products, such as carpets and mattresses, must, by law, be tested to determine whether they pass established test standards relating to flammability.

Chemical Reactivity and Resistance

The chemical reactivity and resistance of textile fibers are discussed at length in the next chapter. Many of the substances used in the manufacture of fibers, in their finishing, and in the care of fabrics in the home are chemical. Therefore, the behavior of textiles when they are exposed to these chemical substances is important to the consumer as well as to the textile technologist.

Environmental Properties

Sensitivity to Microorganisms and Insects

Some fibers support the growth of microorganisms (such as molds or mildew) that will deteriorate the fibers. Others may permit such bacterial growth without damage to the fabric. Still other fibers do not support bacterial growth at all. Fiber characteristics in this respect will affect the choice of fibers for certain uses. Boat sails made of cotton are subject to the conditions favorable to the development of mildew when they become wet. Synthetics, which resist mildew, thus compete favorably with cotton in making sails for boats. Mildew will develop on some fabrics if they are stored in warm, dark, damp areas.

Carpet beetles, clothes moths, and silverfish are the most common insect pests that attack certain textile fibers. Special finishes may be given vulnerable fabrics to make them resistant to insects. Proper care and storage of susceptible fabrics can prevent insect damage.

Sensitivity to Environmental Conditions

A number of general environmental conditions may have an adverse effect on textile fibers. These include exposure to sunlight and air pollution. For example, many fabrics lose strength after long exposure to sunlight, whereas others may be discolored. Acetate fibers may be discolored by air pollution, and some fabrics lose strength or degrade as they age.

Interrelatedness of Fiber Characteristics

The particular qualities that distinguish one textile fiber from another result from the combination of the characteristics that have been discussed. No one single fiber characteristic stands alone, but each property contributes to, and modifies, fiber behavior. (Fabric properties are further changed or modified by yarn and fiber.) For example, a fiber might have good tensile strength, but poor abrasion resistance. This fiber would, therefore, be less serviceable than a fiber of moderate strength with better abrasion resistance. Another fiber might possess excellent abrasion resistance but have poor resiliency or poor elastic recovery. *In short, it is the sum of its qualities or characteristics that determines the usefulness of a fiber.*

Some of the negative qualities of fibers can be overcome through special finishes or processing. A finish is a treatment given to a fiber, yarn, or fabric to enhance or alter some of its qualities. It is possible to treat wool fabrics so that they become mothproof, or to treat cotton so that it gains in luster and in strength. Some finishes increase absorbency and/or resilience, whereas others decrease flammability. Special texturing processes for man-made yarns can increase the stretch, bulk, and covering power of the yarn or decrease pilling.

Relation of Care Procedures to Properties

Care procedures that are appropriate for fabrics are determined by an evaluation of the behavior of the fiber in relation to many of the factors discussed earlier in this chapter. Laundering or dry cleaning, ironing, and storage procedures must be determined by taking into account the reaction of the fiber to the chemical substances used in home and professional cleaning, sensitivity to heat, and resistance to microorganisms, insects, and environmental conditions. The last consideration affects the type of care that is necessary in the storage of textiles.

Care procedures are not determined by fiber content alone. In ready-to-wear garments, the care requirements for all components from trimmings to interfacings must be taken into account.

Recommended References

"Amendment to Rules and Regulations Under the Wool Products Labeling Act of 1939 and Textile Fiber Products Identification Act," *Federal Register*, 50, (April 17, 1985), p. 15100.

CHAPMAN, C. B. *Fibres*. Plainfield, N.J.: Textile Book Service, 1974.

COOK, J. G. *Handbook of Textile Fibers*, Vols. 1 and 2. Watford, England: Merrow Textile Books, 1975.

CORBMAN, B. P. *Textiles, Fiber to Fabric,* 6th ed. New York: McGraw-Hill Book Company, 1983.

Encyclopedia of Textiles, American Fabrics, 3rd ed. Englewood Cliffs, N.J.: Prentice-Hall, Inc., 1980.

FORD, J. E. "Textile Units for Fibers and Yarns," *Textiles,* 14 (Spring 1985), p. 17.

GOHL, E. P. H., and L. D. Vilensky. *Textile Science: An Explanation of Fibre Properties.* London: Longman Group Ltd., 1981.

HEARLE, J. W. S., and R. H. PETERS. *Fiber Structures.* London: Butterworth & Co., 1970.

HOLLEN, N., and J. SADDLER. *Textiles,* 6th ed. New York: Macmillan Publishing Company, 1986.

JOSEPH, M. *Introductory Textile Science,* 5th ed. New York: Holt, Rinehart and Winston, Inc., 1986.

LINTON, G. E. *Applied Textiles: The Modern Textile and Apparel Dictionary,* 4th ed. Plainfield, N.J.: Textile Book Service, 1973.

LYLE, D. S. *Modern Textiles.* New York: John Wiley & Sons, Inc., 1982.

MONCRIEFF, R. W. *Man-Made Fibres,* 7th ed. London: Butterworth and Company Ltd.,) 1987.

The Chemistry of Textiles

Those who undertake an intensive study of textile science will need to develop a solid background in organic chemistry. Many introductory courses in textiles, however, do not have chemistry prerequisites. It is, therefore, the purpose of this chapter to explore certain quite elementary concepts that relate to the chemistry of textiles and that are basic to a more complete understanding of the behavior of textiles and textile products.

In Chapter 1, a number of physical properties of textiles were outlined. It is the chemical structure of each fiber that determines what its physical characteristics will be. All matter is made up of combinations of one or more of some one hundred elements. An *element* is a substance that cannot be broken down any further by chemical means. An element is the simplest form of matter. Some elements exist free in nature; others are found only in combination.

All textile fibers except glass, metal fibers, and asbestos are organic. An organic material—by chemical definition—is one that contains the chemical element carbon. In natural fibers the chemical construction of the fiber has been determined by nature, whereas the structures of synthetic and regenerated fibers have been "engineered" by textile chemists.

The basic building block of an element is the *atom*, which is the smallest amount of an element that can exist. Atoms, however, do not generally exist in isolation, but can combine into larger units called *molecules*. In turn, matter, even small bits of simple substances, is composed of many millions of molecules. Each atom of an element can combine with only a limited number of atoms of other elements. Chemists, who call this combining capacity *valence*, have established the combining capacity of each element, which is expressed as an integer (1, 2, 3, 4, . . .). Oxygen, for example, has a valence of 2; that is, it can combine with up to two other elements; hydrogen, which has a valence of 1, can combine with only one other element; and carbon has a valence of 4 can combine with as many as four other elements. One molecule of water, for example, is made up of one atom of oxygen, which has two bonding points available, in combination with two atoms of hydrogen, each of which has one bonding point. Factors beyond valence alone enter into determination of which elements can combine, but for this simplified discussion, these concepts will not be explored.

As mentioned previously, almost all fibers are organic and all organic compounds contain carbon together with a few other elements such as hydrogen, oxygen, nitrogen, the halogens (fluorine, chlorine, bromine, and iodine), and sulfur. Carbon with four valence points offers opportunity for combinations with many other elements. "The carbon atom can be imagined as a small ball with four arms sticking out of it . . . these arms represent carbon's valence bonds. Each one is a point of attachment, it can (and readily does) grasp the valence arm of another atom."[1]

A carbon atom can combine with another carbon atom by using one, two, or three of its valence points. When each carbon atom uses one valence, the bond that forms is called a single bond. When each carbon atom uses two of its valence points, a double bond is formed, and when three valence points are used from each carbon atom, a triple bond obtains. These second and third bonds between carbon atoms are very reactive. This property of carbon compounds can be used in forming new compounds by breaking some double or triple bonds between carbons so as to add on new elements. The single bond between the carbon atoms remains after this alteration takes place.

There are many thousands of different organic compounds, and all are made from a relatively small number of elements. Dr. Bruce Hartsuch used the following analogy to describe organic compounds: "we realize that we can take a very few types of building materials and construct an almost unlimited number of houses. All these houses differ from each other in only a very few things—the kind of structural elements, the number of them, and their arrangement with respect to each other . . . [likewise] organic compounds differ from each other not only in the number of the elements in the molecule, but also in the arrangement of the elements."[2]

The arrangement of atoms within the molecule may take a variety of forms. The most common form of molecules with which the textile chemist deals is a linear, chainlike arrangement as in the following:

Carbon to carbon to carbon to carbon
$\longrightarrow$ $\longrightarrow$ $\longrightarrow$ $\longrightarrow$

Not only the elements that make up the molecule but also the way in which the elements are arranged determine the behavior of a specific compound. The structure of the molecule, its elements and their arrangements, is so important to the organic chemist that chemists make

[1]H. Mark, *Giant Molecules* (New York: Time, Inc., 1966), p. 52.
[2]B. Hartsuch, *Introduction to Textile Chemistry* (New York: John Wiley & Sons, Inc., 1950), p. 19.

diagrammatic representations or formulas of the molecules. These formulas, a kind of chemical shorthand, show the positions occupied by all the elements.

Signs and symbols represent elements and the ways in which they connect. Each of the elements has an abbreviation or symbol, usually the first letter or a combination of several letters found in the name of the element. The symbol for carbon is abbreviated C; oxygen, O; hydrogen, H; chlorine, Cl; and so on. The connections between elements may be shown by drawing a line between the elements:

C—C—C—C— and so on

If a double bond is formed between two elements, a double line may be drawn: C=C.

A six-carbon ring formation may sometimes be shown by a simple diagram, without showing all of the carbons, as follows:

The double lines represent double bonds between carbon atoms. This compound is part of so many organic compounds that the shortened form of the formula is generally utilized by the textile chemist; it is a convention that the corners of these geometric figures represent carbon atoms.

To simplify the formulas somewhat more, other combinations of elements that are readily recognizable to the chemist may be written without the lines showing chemical bonding. For example, a combination of oxygen with hydrogen to form a common group, the hydroxyl group, is written as —OH. When more than one atom of an element is required for a compound in which the bonds and specific position of the element is not shown, a small number is written to the right and slightly below the symbol of the element. The formula for water, for example, is written H_2O, showing two atoms of hydrogen and one of oxygen. H_2SO_4 (sulfuric acid) contains two atoms of hydrogen, one of sulfur, and four of oxygen.

So far the formulas used to illustrate the "shorthand" of chemistry have been simple. Formulas of organic compounds, however, are rarely simple. The formula for cellulose, the basic material of which cotton is composed, is shown as the chemist would write it:

The generic definitions of textile fibers (see Appendix D) identify the major units that make up the fiber, and in most of these definitions, the unit is named and its formula shown. For example, acrylic fibers are defined as "a manufacturered fiber in which the fiber-forming substance is any long-chain synthetic polymer composed of at least 85 per cent by weight of acrylonitrile units ($-CH_2-CH-$)."

$$\begin{array}{c} | \\ CN \end{array}$$

Textile Molecular Structure

The chemistry of textile fibers is but one branch of the field of organic chemistry. Much of organic chemistry is concerned with fairly small, complex molecules, few of which are composed of as many as one hundred atoms, whereas textile materials are composed of giant molecules known as *macromolecules*. Analysis of these large molecules shows that they are composed of molecular subunits containing perhaps two to twenty atoms and that the large molecules were built up from many of these smaller units joined together. In textile fibers the individual molecules join together in a very special way, into long chains. The individual, subunit compounds are called *monomers*, and the long-chain macromolecules made from the monomers are called *polymers*. In cellulose, for instance, the subunits are derived from glucose. Interestingly, the subunits of the constituents of another well-known macromolecule, starch, are also derived from glucose. Starch and cellulose have completely different properties, however, because the subunits are bonded to each other differently; starch is not fibrous but can be digested by humans, whereas the opposite is true for cellulose.

Polymerization

The formation of polymers, or *polymerization*, is accomplished through the joining of monomers, one to the other. In the formation of polymers, several intermediate steps take place. Two monomers (small, nonpolymerized compounds) may join to form a *dimer* (two-monomer molecule), a dimer and a monomer join to form a *trimer* (three-monomer molecule), two dimers join to form a *tetramer* (four-molecule structure), and so on.

The combining monomers may be similar or dissimilar and can be arranged in a number of different formats. *Homopolymers* are polymers composed of identical units of the same substance. *Copolymers* contain two or more unidentical units. Copolymerization is likely to be utilized in creating textile fibers when one polymer exhibits a negative quality in homopolymer form that can be overcome by combining it with another substance.

The arrangement of repeating units (which may be homopolymers or copolymers) can vary. A homopolymer might be represented as AAAAAAAAAAA, with A representing the linked polymer units. A normal copolymer structure (A representing one part of the copolymer and B representing the other) might be arranged in sequence ABABABABAB. Block copolymers have different structures, for example, AAABBB-AAABBB, with each of the copolymers blocked together before being repeated. Yet another structure can also be formed, that of graft polymers that are made by attaching monomers onto long-chain polymers. The long chain forms the base structure, rather like the trunk of a tree, with the side chains branching off. Grafting makes possible the addition of qualities not present in the "mother" fiber. Grafting of monomers, for example, can reduce static electricity buildup, improve dyeability, improve soil resistance, increase strength, or decrease shrinkage. Grafting is a relatively new technique and, though not yet widely used, will undoubtedly be further developed for a variety of applications. A graft polymer, in general, would have a structure something like this:

```
AAAAAAAAAAAA
  B      B
  B      B
  B      B
```

Linear polymers are formed either by *addition polymerization* or by *condensation polymerization*. In condensation polymerization, as a small molecule (usually water, ammonia, or hydrogen chloride) is eliminated, monomers join other molecules:

$$\text{monomer} + \text{monomer} \longrightarrow \text{dimer} + \text{water (eliminated)}$$
$$\text{dimer} + \text{dimer} \longrightarrow \text{tetramer} + \text{water (eliminated)}$$

Monomers may link up with monomers, monomers with polymers, polymers with polymers, and so on to form a growing chain, with the elimination of water or another compound during the process. Examples of this process are, among the natural fibers, cellulose from glucose and, among the man-made fibers, nylon from its components.

Addition polymerization differs from condensation polymerization in that no compound is split off. Monomers with the capacity to react (unsaturated monomers) can add to each other in a chemically effected chain reaction to join into a long-chain molecule. This is generally accomplished under conditions of high pressure and high temperature and in the presence of a *catalyst* (a substance that does not take part in the reaction but facilitates the reaction):

$$\begin{array}{c}\text{monomer}\\+\\\text{activator}\end{array} = \begin{array}{c}\text{reactive}\\\text{monomer}\\+\\\text{monomer}\end{array} = \begin{array}{c}\text{reactive}\\\text{dimer}\\+\\\text{monomer}\end{array} \rightarrow \textit{polymer}$$

FIGURE 3.1. *Amorphous arrangement of polymers within fiber.*

An example of this process is the polymerization of acrylonitrile to create acrylic fibers. Acrylonitrile is a nitrogen-containing three-carbon molecule.

This, in highly simplified terms, is part of the chemical process that takes place in the manufacture of synthetic fibers. Most of the specific processes utilized by companies to make their trademarked textile fibers are carefully guarded secrets. Such confidential processes are known as *proprietary processes.* Textile chemists, however, can make reasonably accurate estimates of the processes used by each company by reading research reports and by analyses of the properties and physical structure of the fibers.

Polymers and Their Arrangement

The molecules within each polymer are held together by chemical bonds formed as monomer joins monomer. But each individual fiber is made of many chemically alike polymer molecules that may occupy different positions within the fiber. The arrangement of polymers within the fiber may be either random or parallel. A random or unorganized arrangement of long-chain molecules creates an *amorphous* area within the fiber. (See Figure 3.1.) Orderly, parallel arrangement of polymers is known as *crystallinity.* Crystalline arrangements of molecules may lie in a variety of positions relative to the fiber shape. However, if the crystalline polymers are parallel to the length of the fiber, they are said to be *oriented.* (See Figure 3.2.)

Most fibers possess largely crystalline structures, but they also have some amorphous areas. Textile chemists believe that amorphous areas are weaker than are crystalline areas and that those fibers with the highest levels of crystallinity are the strongest fibers. A high degree of orientation of crystalline areas (that is, the crystalline areas lie parallel to the length of the fiber) is said to produce still greater strength.

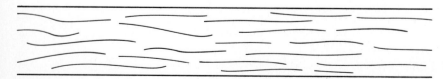

FIGURE 3.2. *Crystalline arrangement of molecules in fiber, with molecules oriented to fiber length.*

Moncrieff illustrates this concept by contrasting the structures of cotton and flax:

Molecules of cellulose which constitute both cotton and flax are similar . . . the reason for the difference in the physical properties of cotton and flax lies in the arrangement of the molecules. In flax, they are highly oriented, they are very well parallelised, and they lie side by side along the length of the fibre; in cotton some of the fibres lie parallel to the fibre axis, but quite a large proportion of them lie at an appreciable angle to the fibre axis. [See Figure 3.3.] When tension is applied to the fibre nearly all of the molecules in flax take their fair share of the load, and a high breaking load is the result; but in the case of cotton, the strain has to be taken by those molecules that are facing in the right direction, i.e., roughly parallel to the fibre axis—those molecules lying approximately at right angles to the fibre axis take little or none of the load. Consequently the tenacity of cotton is lower than that of flax.[3]

The structures of some man-made fibers are quite amorphous when they are formed. By stretching or "drawing" the fiber, these amorphous areas can be made more parallel and crystalline. Stretching the fiber causes the polymers within the fiber to arrange themselves along the direction of stretch.

This principle can be seen by taking a strip of polyurethane plastic cut from a storage bag and slowly stretching it. As the strip narrows, the plastic becomes clearer, finer, and much stronger. (See Figure 3.4.)

Internal Bonds or Forces

In addition to the internal bonding that holds the individual molecules together to form the long-chain molecule, there are attractive forces that hold the polymers together within the fiber. These forces are of two primary types: *Van der Waals* forces and *hydrogen bonding*.

Van der Waals forces are relatively weak attractions based on proximity of the molecules. Chapman points out that, although the forces of attraction of this type may be small individually, the cumulative effect of a large number of groups of polymers is significant. When molecules are crystalline and highly oriented, the strength of these forces is enhanced, because there is a greater area over which the polymer molecules may be in close contact.[4]

COTTON FLAX

FIGURE 3.3. Orientation of molecules in cotton and flax. Note that although many of the cotton molecules are shown to be parallel, they are not oriented. Reprinted from R. W. Moncrieff, Man-Made Fibres *6th ed. Butterworth & Co. (Publishers) Ltd., 1975, pp. 74, 75. Courtesy of R. W. Moncrieff.*

FIGURE 3.4. Effect of drawing of fibers on polymer orientation.

[3]R. W. Moncrieff, *Man-Made Fibres* (London: Butterworth & Co., Ltd, 1975), pp. 74, 75.
[4]C. B. Chapman, *Fibres* (Plainfield, N.J.: Textile Book Service, 1974), p. 19.

Hydrogen bonding in well-oriented fibers is a powerful force for binding molecules together. Hydrogen bonding occurs in situations in which one atom of hydrogen links together two other atoms. For hydrogen bonds to be formed, molecules must be packed closely together, as occurs in textile fibers with closely packed, highly oriented molecules. Furthermore, the appropriate reactive elements must be present in the molecules. Reactive atoms are nitrogen, oxygen, and fluorine, which are small electronegative elements. Hydrogen bonds are present in natural cellulose and protein fibers, as well as in manufactured fibers that contain hydrogen and appropriate reactive atoms.

When long polymers are attracted to parallel long polymers by Van der Waals forces, hydrogen bonding, or both, fibers are stronger than if short polymers are attracted to short polymers. In longer molecules, the area over which these forces bond is greater. When the area of attraction between molecules is greater, then more force is required to break the cohesive forces. This generalization is true only up to a certain point, however. Chain length will eventually reach the point where any further increase in the length of the chains will not result in an increase in strength. At the same time, no decrease in strength takes place either.

Cross-linkages

A third means by which molecules are held together is by *cross-linking*. (See Figure 3.5.) Cross-linking is the attachment of one long-chain molecule to another by covalent chemical bonds; these are bonds of a strength equivalent to that along the polymer chain. A small amount of cross-linking in fibers will produce such desirable properties as ability to resist creasing and increased crease recovery. In some instances, cross-linkages seem to increase chemical stability and improve resistance to attack by insects and bacteria. Wool and animal hair fibers have naturally cross-linked structures. It is thought that the cross-links in wool are one of the factors responsible for the excellent resiliency of wool.

Special chemical finishes can be used to create cross-linkages in some fibers that do not possess them naturally. Such finishes when applied to cotton, for example, improve crease resistance and wrinkle recovery but decrease strength and abrasion resistance. It may be helpful to imagine that the cross-links serve to return the molecules to their original position within the fiber after it has been bent or folded, thus providing wrinkle recovery.

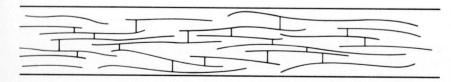

FIGURE 3.5.   *Cross-linking of molecules within fiber.*

Fringed Fibril Theory

With continuous research and investigation into the chemical structure of fibers, new theories and knowledge concerning the arrangement of molecules continue to evolve. One such theory, the "fringed fibril theory," put forth by Hearle and Peters suggests that within the fiber are both highly oriented and amorphous regions. "Polymer molecules may pass from a crystalline to a noncrystalline region and may also pass through a second (and more) crystalline region. Thus we develop a picture of small, ordered crystalline zones which are separated by less well-ordered amorphous regions, but which are all connected together by a random network of polymer molecules."[5] (See Figure 3.6.)

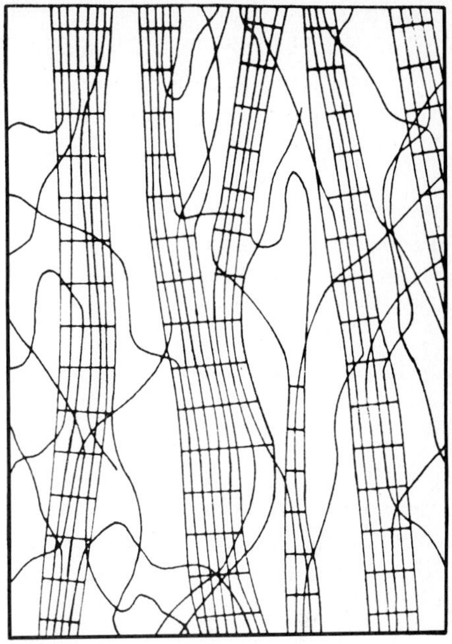

Effect of Side Chains

Although most polymers are of straight-line formation, some polymeric substances react to form side chains as well. These side chains cause the molecules to function differently than either the long, straight molecules or cross-linked molecules. Such polymers do not crystallize as readily as do regular unbranched polymers, because the side chains prevent the polymer chains from coming in close enough contact for Van der Waals attractive forces to operate. (See Figure 3.7.)

Such side-chain polymers are sometimes formed purposely in the synthesis of elastic fibers or to introduce or alter other properties not inherent to a polymer.

FIGURE 3.6. *Fringed fibril structure. Reprinted from* Fiber Structures *by J. W. S. Hearle and R. H. Peters, Courtesy of Newnes-Butterworth Publishers, London, England.*

Relationship of Fiber Structure to Properties

To examine in depth the variations of fiber structure as they relate to the various properties of fibers is beyond the scope of this book. The following summary of properties common to fibers with a high or low degree of orientation may, however, be useful.

These characteristics are those associated with the extremes of molecule orientation and crystallization. Polymeric fibers possess both amorphous and crystalline regions and show characteristics that fall somewhere between these extremes.

Views differ concerning fiber structure. Morton and Hearle point out that it is now recognized that different polymers produced in different

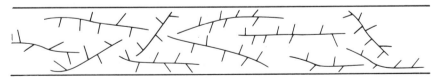

FIGURE 3.7. *Polymers with side chains within fiber.*

[5]W. E. Morton and J. W. S. Hearle, *Physical Properties of Textile Fibers* (New York: John Wiley & Sons, Inc., 1975), p. 32.

Table 3.1

Properties Common to Fibers with a High Degree of Orientation and High Crystallinity	Properties Common to Fibers with Low Degree of Orientation and Low Crystallinity
High tenacity	Low tenacity
Low elongation	High elongation
Brittle	Extremely pliable
Increased luster	Subdued luster
Low moisture absorption	High moisture absorption
High chemical stability	Low chemical stability
Low dyeing affinity	High dyeing affinity
May have less pleasant handle	Warm, soft handle

SOURCE: R. W. Moncrieff, *Man-Made Fibres* 6th ed. (New York: John Wiley & Sons, Inc., 1975), pp. 107ff.

ways may have major structural differences. "In particular," they state, "there will be differences between natural fibers, which grow very slowly as living cells, and man-made fibres, formed by high-speed extrusion and drawing."[6]

Summary

In summary, then, requirements for the formation of a substance that can be utilized as a textile fiber would be

1. Long-chain molecules, molecules that are too short will have inadequate strength.
2. More or less parallel arrangements of molecules.
3. Forces acting laterally between molecules to hold the molecules together and give cohesion to the structure.
4. Enough freedom of molecular movement to allow fiber extensibility and flexibility.
5. Enough openness to allow room for moisture and dye absorption.[7]

The chemical principles outlined heretofore apply to both natural and man-made fibers. In man-made fibers chemists have succeeded in creating through chemical means substances that have the qualities necessary to make them useful in textiles. Man-made fibers may be either regenerated or modified natural substances, or synthetic.

All the early procedures (in the man-made fiber industry) started with materials similar in structure to natural fibers. These materials were dissolved chemically and were then re-formed into long, filament fibers. It was not until chemists came to understand the chemical structure of fiber molecules that they realized that it might be possible to create fibers entirely from simple chemical substances.

Man-made Fibers: Chemical Creations

[6]Ibid.
[7]Ibid., p. 22.

An analytical process called X-ray diffraction revealed that fibrous qualities depended on the presence of long-chain polymers. This understanding led to attempts to put together long-chain polymers in the laboratory from chemical materials. Chemists had synthesized a type of large molecule known as a *polypeptide*. A polypeptide is any polymer containing an abundance of amide linkages, that is, linkages made up of carbon, oxygen, nitrogen, and hydrogen (CONH). Silk and wool are, chemically speaking, polypeptides. Scientists believed that synthesis in the laboratory of polypeptides might lead to the invention of a totally synthetic fiber that was not derived from any natural substance.

E. I. du Pont de Nemours & Company, a chemical-manufacturing firm, had established an extensive basic research program, and those doing research in this program were given wide latitude as to the areas in which they might work. In particular, W. H. Carothers, a chemist at DuPont, chose to work in the synthesis of long-chain molecules; he was not searching for textile fibers, but the work he initiated in the formation of long-chain polymers was applied widely to the creation of a number of fibers and to their subsequent manufacture. The direction in which Carothers was working might be described as follows: "Take molecules that can react at both ends, react them, and long molecules will result. If these molecules are very long in relation to their dimensions, they will exhibit fiber-forming properties."[8]

The basic research done by Carothers resulted in the invention of nylon, the first truly synthetic fiber to be marketed. Nylon, like silk and wool, is a polypeptide.

Fiber Formation

Most synthetic polymers must be converted into liquid form to be spun. This is done either by dissolving the polymer in a suitable solvent or by melting the polymer and then extruding the liquid polymer through a spinneret. Each spinneret has a number of holes, and each hole produces one filament. Filament yarns are described by denier (i.e., size) and number of filaments; for example, filaments described as 70/34 represent 70 denier/34 filaments. When fibers being extruded are intended for conversion into staple lengths, spinnerets with larger numbers of holes are used to produce more filaments.

Melt Spinning

Melt spinning or extrusion utilizes the thermoplastic characteristics of fibers. Chips of solid polymer about the size of rice grains are dropped from a hopper into a melter where heat converts the solid polymer into a viscous liquid. The liquid forms a "melt pool" that is pumped through filters to remove any impurities that would clog the spinneret and is delivered to the spinneret at a carefully controlled rate of flow. Melt

[8]R. W. Moncrieff, op. cit., p. 319.

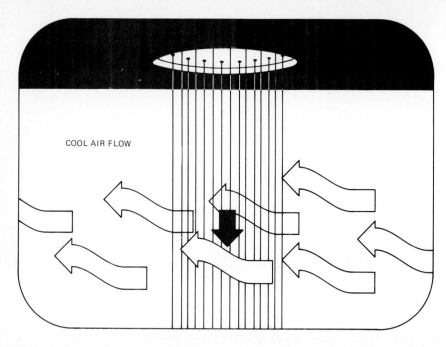

COOL AIR FLOW

FIGURE 3.8. *Melt spinning. Courtesy of the Man-made Fiber Producers Association, Inc.*

spinning is simpler and cheaper than other processes; therefore, it is utilized except when polymers cannot be melt spun.

The spinneret holes are usually round, but noncircular holes are also used to make filaments of various cross-sectional shapes. Melt-spun fibers may be made through Y-shaped holes that yield a three-lobed fiber or C-shaped holes to produce a hollow filament, for example.

The diameter of the fiber is determined by the rate at which the polymer is supplied to the hole in the spinneret and the windup speed, not by the diameter of the hole. When the molten polymer emerges from the spinneret hole, a cool air current is passed over the fiber, causing it to harden. (See Figure 3.8.) Failure to maintain constant feeding speed of molten polymer or changes in the temperature of cooling will cause irregularities in the diameter of the fiber.[9] Nylon is a melt-spun fiber.

Dry Spinning

Many polymers are adversely affected by heat at or close to their melting temperatures, so that they cannot be melt spun; other methods of spinning, such as dry spinning, are thus employed. Dry spinning requires the dissolving of the polymer in a solvent to convert it into liquid form. Substances used as solvents are chosen not only because they will

[9]Chapman, *Fibres*, p. 37.

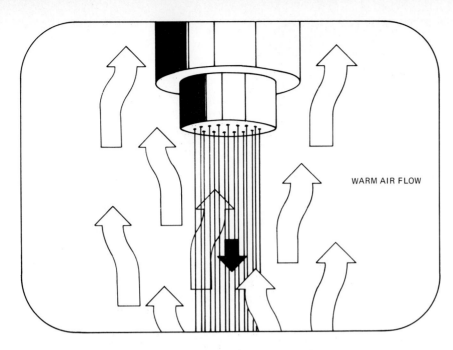

WARM AIR FLOW

FIGURE 3.9.   Dry spinning. Courtesy of the
Man-made Fiber Producers Association, Inc.

dissolve the polymer but also because they can be reclaimed and reused.

The polymer and solvent are extruded through a spinneret into a circulating current of hot gas that evaporates the solvent from the polymer and causes the filament to harden. (See Figure 3.9.) The solvent is removed and recycled to be used again.

Dry-spun filaments generally have an irregular cross section. Because the solvent evaporates first from the outside of the fiber, a hard surface skin of solid polymer forms. As the solvent evaporates from the inner part of the fiber, this skin "collapses" or folds to produce an irregular shape. If the rate of evaporation is slowed, the cross section of the filament will be more nearly round. Acetate fibers are dry spun.

Wet Spinning

Wet-spun polymers are, like dry-spun polymers, converted into liquid form by dissolving them in a suitable solvent. The polymer is extruded through a jet into a liquid bath. The bath causes coagulation of the fiber. (See Figure 3.10.) Solvents are recovered from the liquid bath and are recycled. Viscose rayon is wet spun.

It is possible to add special chemical reagents to the liquid bath that produce selected changes in the fiber. This is done in the manufacture of some high-strength rayons, for example.

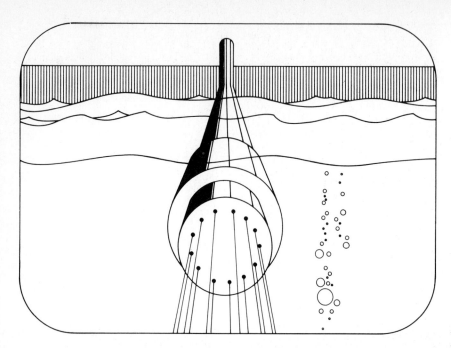

FIGURE 3.10. Wet spinning. Courtesy of the
Man-made Fiber Producers Association, Inc.

Drawing or Stretching

Both crystalline and amorphous arrangements of molecules exist within
newly formed fibers. It is possible to orient these molecules to make
them more parallel to the walls of the fiber, and therefore more crystalline and stronger, by stretching the fiber before it is completely hardened.

Newly formed fibers, whether formed by melt, wet, or dry spinning,
are, therefore, subjected to drawing or stretching. Depending on the
fiber, this may be done under cold or hot temperature conditions and
has the additional effect of making the fiber both narrower and longer.

Heat Setting

Some man-made fibers are thermoplastic, so that when exposed to heat,
they may shrink. To prevent this shrinkage, fibers are treated with heat
after spinning to "set" them into permanent shape. Not only can fibers
be heat-set to make their dimensions permanent, but many man-made
fabrics can also be heat-set into pleats, creases, or other permanent
shaping.

The molecular structure of the fiber is involved in heat setting. Heat-
sensitive fibers have not only a melting temperature but also a temperature at which the amorphous regions of the fiber become rubbery or
soft. This temperature is called the *glass transition temperature* and is

abbreviated T_g. The glass transition temperature may be reached without causing the fiber to melt.

For heat setting to take place, the fabric is put into its new shape. The fiber or fabric is then heated enough for the crystalline structure of the fiber molecules to "lock" into the new shape. The fiber after cooling will remain in this position until the heat-setting temperature is again reached or exceeded. If the T_g is low, the fiber cannot be successfully heat-set for ordinary uses as hot water in washing or heat from a dryer will negate the effect of heat setting.

If, in use and care, heat-set fabrics are subject to temperatures above their respective heat-setting temperatures, heat setting will be lost. Likewise, thermoplastic fabrics lying in a wrinkled state in a very hot dryer may have wrinkles "heat-set" after the temperature in the dryer goes above the heat-setting temperature.

Chemical Substances Commonly Used with Textiles

Fibers are composed of long-chain molecules or polymers that are arranged in positions roughly parallel to the lengthwise direction of the fiber. If we were to diagram each of the smaller molecules from which the polymers are formed, we would see precisely the elements of which they are made. When chemists see a molecular diagram or formula, they recognize that there are "functional chemical groups" within the polymers, that is, places at which chemical reactions are likely to take place. Some of these reactions take place when textiles come into contact with substances used in processing or in everyday use.

Materials with which textile fibers come into contact might be divided, roughly, into two basic groups: (1) materials used in processing fibers or fabrics, such as bleaches, dyestuffs, and special finishing materials used to alter fabric characteristics such as crease resistance, soil resistance, and flame retardancy, and (2) materials used in home or professional care or cleaning of fabrics, such as soaps, detergents, cleaning solvents, and moth repellants. Some of these substances are organic (having carbon in the compounds), and some are inorganic. Some are acid, some are alkaline, and some are neutral. Many processes in manufacturing, finishing, and care of textiles utilize the reaction of fibers to acids or alkalis.

The term "pH" is often encountered in discussions of acidic or basic substances. The pH of a substance is expressed as a number. A solution with a pH of 7 is neutral (i.e., neither acid nor basic), one with less than 7 is acidic, and one with more than 7 is basic.

Acids

Acids are both strong and weak, and organic and mineral. Acids are characterized by the ability to neutralize bases or alkalis and the ability to turn a special indicator paper, called litmus paper, from blue to red. Among the better known strong inorganic acids are sulfuric acid and hydrochloric acid. Acetic acid is a weak organic acid (vinegar is a dilute solution of acetic acid.) Other organic acids include lactic acid, present in sour milk, and ascorbic acid or vitamin C. These few examples may serve to illustrate the diversity of types of acids.

Action of Acids. The action of acids when they come into contact with various textile fibers varies not only with the type of textile fiber but also with the strength and type of the acid. It is important for the textile manufacturer to be acquainted with the effect of acids on textile fibers to avoid damaging fibers or fabrics during finishing. Also, some specialized textile processes rely on the action of acids on various textile fibers.

Acid hydrolysis is a chemical reaction that is important for textile fibers. Hydrolysis results in the breaking of long-chain molecules into shorter chains. In these cases, the bonds connecting the subunits are unstable to acid, and the result is a loss of tensile strength. If the reaction goes on for a sufficiently long time, susceptible fibers will actually be dissolved. Cellulosic fibers are damaged by strong mineral acids and are harmed even by quite diluted concentrations of these substances. This quality is not especially important to the consumer, but it is utilized in the manufacture of some man-made cellulosic fibers. For example, acid hydrolysis is used to convert short cotton fibers into a substance called oxycellulose as the first step in the manufacture of rayon.

The same reaction, in a highly controlled process, is used to make permanently stiffened sheer cotton fabrics. The acid is applied so that it breaks down the outermost layer of fabric. The outer layer softens, the reaction is stopped, and the fabric is given a hard press that forms the outer fabric layer into a smooth, clear, permanently stiffened finish.

Because dilute acids do not readily harm protein fibers (the bonds connecting the subunits are relatively stable to acid), especially wool, acid treatments can be utilized in cleaning wool of vegetable matter prior to spinning. The controlled acid solution destroys the bits of wood and burrs caught in the wool, the acid is neutralized, and the wool is left unharmed. Such processes are carried out under rigidly controlled conditions to avoid any harm to the fibers. Strong mineral acids will destroy wool fiber.

Fibers that are sensitive to the action of acids cannot be dyed in dyestuffs that require the presence of strong acids.

Alkalis

Alkalis are members of a class of substances called bases and are opposite in nature to acids. Bases react with acids to form salts or neutral compounds. Alkalis when dissolved in water are slippery to the touch, have an acrid taste, and change litmus paper from red to blue. The most important strong alkali is caustic soda or lye, known chemically as sodium hydroxide or NaOH. Sodium hydroxide is used extensively in textile and related industries in making soap, in special treatments given cotton, and in manufacturing rayon fiber. Borax, baking soda, household ammonia, and washing soda are also bases.

Action of Alkalis. Alkalis, even strong caustic alkalis at high temperature, do not harm natural cellulosic fibers. Alkalis do, however, cause radical physical changes to take place within these fibers, and, as a result, a special treatment with the alkali sodium hydroxide is sometimes given to cellulosic fibers to take advantage of these changes that improve the strength and appearance of cellulosic fibers.

Sensitivity to alkalis is important in the care of protein fibers (silk, wool, and animal hair fibers) in which the bonds between the subunits are broken by alkali. Some synthetic fibers are negatively affected by alkalis. Many strong soaps and detergents have alkali material added to increase their cleaning power. These soaps and detergents should be avoided for use with fibers that are sensitive to the action of alkaline substances.

Oxidation and Oxidizing Agents

Many fibers are not white enough in their natural state or after manufacture to permit dyes to be fully effective. These colors and/or stains accumulated during spinning and weaving are removed by the action of bleaches that causes oxygen to be added to the coloring matter by a process called oxidation. This leads to the removal of the colors and the stains.

During bleaching, coloring matter from some stains is converted into a colorless substance. However, the oxidizing agent (bleach) may also react with the fiber itself. If the fiber is sensitive to the action of the oxidizing agent, the fiber may be damaged.

Chlorine bleach is an oxidizing agent that may damage protein fibers and spandex. Chlorine bleach must be carefully controlled in bleaching cellulose fabrics, but it does no appreciable harm to other fibers such as polyester or nylon. Other bleaching agents made from substances such as sodium perborate will oxidize stains without damage to fibers.

Both the consumer and the manufacturer benefit from understanding the action of oxidizing agents on different fibers.

Chemical Reactions and Their Importance to the Textile Industry

The textile industry is the greatest consumer of industrial chemicals of all industries known today. Some sixty-five hundred special chemicals are now manufactured for the textile industry.[10] In addition to the chemical reactions utilized in the manufacture of fibers, of which more

---

[10]"Textile Chemistry," in *Encyclopedia of Science and Technology*, Vol. 13 (New York: McGraw-Hill Book Company, 1977), p. 551.

is said in later chapters, textile manufacturers are concerned with the chemical reactions between textile chemical specialties (known as textile auxiliaries) and textile fibers. These auxiliaries are used as cleaning agents, as chemical finishing agents, and as dyestuffs.

Cleaning agents are selected for use both on the basis of their ability to remove foreign matter from the fiber and their compatibility with the fiber. As has been mentioned earlier, strongly alkaline cleaning agents cannot be used on protein fibers because of the likelihood that these substances will degrade the fibers.

Chemical finishing agents vary widely in type and purpose. In some instances the chemicals used alter the physical appearance of the fiber without changing the chemical nature of the fiber. Mercerization is an example of such a reaction. In mercerization, cotton or linen fibers are treated with a strong alkali. The action of the alkali on the cotton causes the fibers to become stronger, more lustrous, and more chemically reactive.

In other cases, the chemicals utilized react in such a way that some parts of the chemical substance become a permanent part of the fiber structure. This is true in the case of mothproofing wool. Within the wool molecule are a number of cross-links of different chemical composition. Apparently the moth larvae attack a particular cross-link called a dilsufide cross-linkage. Wool is treated with a process that first breaks the dilsufide linkage and then rejoins the broken ends of the links by a short hydrocarbon residue supplied by further treatment with other chemicals. The resulting linkage is different chemically from the natural linkage and will not be attractive to moths.

Modern dyestuffs are synthesized chemically. In dyeing, three substances of a chemical nature are utilized: the fiber, the dyestuff, and the solvent. The solvent is the material in which the dyestuff is carried and must penetrate the fiber to carry the dye within the fiber. Water may be used as a solvent, or other organic substances may be used.

Dyes enter fibers most easily in the amorphous regions; then, as the fiber swells from the entrance of the solvent and dye, the dyestuff spreads throughout both crystalline and amorphous regions. Fibers with highly oriented, crystalline structures are, therefore, more difficult to dye, and special dyestuffs and dyeing techniques must be utilized to color these fibers.

The retention of the dyestuff within the fiber relies on reactions between the fiber molecules and the dyestuff molecules. Positively or negatively charged ions—one on the dye, the other on the fiber—may be attracted to each other. Hydrogen bonding, that is, the sharing of electrons between dye and fiber molecules, or the attraction of molecules of dye and fiber by Van der Waals forces may account for the retention of dye materials. The dyestuff may form a covalent bond with the fibers. Other dyes form insoluble particles within fibers. Selection of the appropriate dyestuff depends upon the chemist's understanding of the properties of fibers and dyestuffs and the reactions they will undergo.

Colorfastness, or the ability of a fiber to retain the color to which it has been dyed, may require further chemical treatments. If the fiber has been penetrated easily to carry the dye into the fiber, then when the fiber is laundered, water may enter as easily to carry the dye back out again. During dyeing, additional treatments are sometimes given the dyed fibers to transform the soluble dyestuffs into insoluble compounds within the fiber.

As with other chemical finishes, the application of dyestuffs must also take into account the effect of acids, alkalis, organic solvents, and the like on textile fibers. Protein fibers, which are always sensitive to alkali, cannot be dyed in a highly alkaline medium, and cellulosic fibers cannot be dyed by highly acid dyes.

The importance of the chemical aspects of textile science cannot be underrated. Man-made fibers, both synthetic and regenerated, dominate the modern textile industry in the United States. In 1910 only 40 per cent of the fibers utilized by American mills were man-made. In 1984, man-made fibers supplied about 75 per cent of the U.S. mill consumption of fibers.[11] And the manufacture of fibers is only the beginning. Subsequent cleaning, finishing, dyeing, and even home care aspects all relate in some way to chemically induced reactions.

Recommended References

BILLMEYER, F. W., JR. *Textbook of Polymer Science.* New York: John Wiley & Sons, Inc., 1984.

COWIE, J. M. G. *Polymers: Chemistry and Physics of Modern Materials.* New York: Intext Educational Publishers, 1973.

CHAPMAN, C. B. *Fibres.* Plainfield, N.J.: Textile Book Service, 1974.

GOHL, E. P. G., and L. D. Vilensky. *Investigations in Textile Science.* Glasgow: Blackie and Sons, 1980.

GRAYSON, M., ed. *Encyclopedia of Textiles, Fibers, and Nonwoven Fabrics.* New York: Wiley-Interscience, 1984.

HEARLE, J. W. S. *Polymers and Their Properties.* Vol. 1: *Fundamentals of Structure and Mechanics.* Chichester, England: Ellis Horwood Ltd., 1982.

HEARLE, J. W. S., and R. H. PETERS. *Fiber Structures.* London: Newnes-Butterworth Publishers, 1963.

HIEMENZ, P. C. *Polymer Chemistry: The Basic Concepts.* Brookfield Center, Conn.: Society of Plastics Engineers, 1984.

KAUFMAN, H. S., and J. J. Falcetta, eds. *Introduction to Polymer Science and Technology.* Brookfield Center, Conn.: Society of Plastics Engineers, 1977.

MARK, H., ed. *Giant Molecules.* New York: Time, Inc., 1966.

MONCRIEFF, R. W. *Man-Made Fibres.* 7th ed. London: Butterworth and Company, Ltd., 1987.

MORTON, W. E., and J. W. S. HEARLE. *Physical Properties of Textile Fibers.* New York: John Wiley & Sons, Inc., 1975, Chap. 1.

NEEDLES, H. L. *Handbook of Textile Fibers, Dyes, and Finishes.* New York: Garland STPM Press, 1981.

[11]Data provided by the Man-made Fiber Producers Association.

PETERS, R. H. *Textile Chemistry*, Vol. 1. New York: American Elsevier Publishing Co., 1967.

ROBINSON, J. S., ed. *Fiber-Forming Polymers: Recent Advances*. Park Ridge, N.J.: Noyes Publications, 1980.

"Textile Chemistry," *Encyclopedia of Science and Technology*, Vol. 13. New York: McGraw-Hill Book Company, 1977, pp. 551 ff.

TROTMAN, E. R. *Dyeing and Chemical Technology of Textiles and Fibres*. New York: Wiley-Interscience, 1984.

Natural Cellulosic Fibers

Cellulosic fibers are composed of natural and regenerated cellulose, or of regenerated chemical variants of cellulose. Natural cellulosic fibers are derived from a wide variety of plant sources, which are classified as follows:

1. Seed hair fibers, or those fibers that grow in a seed pod on plants.
2. Bast fibers, or those fibers that are removed from the stems of plants.
3. Leaf fibers, or those fibers that are found on the leaves of plants.
4. Miscellaneous fiber from mosses, roots, and the like.

Man-made cellulosic fibers include rayon, a regenerated cellulosic fiber and acetate and triacetate, which are modified cellulosic fibers.

Cellulose Family

Table 4.1 lists fibers of the cellulose family. Included in this list are not only those fibers that have extensive commercial production and distribution but also fibers that have little or no importance to the consumer.

Each of these cellulosic fibers possesses distinctive qualities or properties that distinguish it from others and make it especially suitable for certain end uses. Most cellulosic fibers also share a "family resemblance" in their physical and chemical properties.

In all subsequent discussions of the properties of different fibers, statements about fiber characteristics are made in relation to the characteristics of other fibers. For example, when flax is said to be a relatively strong fiber, what is meant is that, in comparison with other fibers, flax is fairly strong. If the strength of flax were measured against that of a strand of steel or aluminum wire, for example, it would seem relatively weak.

Table 4.1

Natural Fibers	Man-made Fibers
A. *Seed hair fibers*	A. *Rayon*
1. *Major fibers*	1. Viscose rayon
Cotton	high-wet-modulus
2. *Minor fibers*	rayon
Kapok	2. Cuprammonium rayon
B. *Bast fibers*	B. *Modified cellulose fibers*
1. Flax	1. Acetate
2. Jute	Saponified rayon[1]
3. Ramie	2. Triacetate
4. Hemp	
C. *Leaf fibers*[1]	
1. Abaca[1]	
2. Sisal[1]	
3. Henequin[1]	
4. Pina[1]	
D. *Fruit*	
Coir	
E. *Miscellaneous*[1]	
1. Spanish moss[1]	
2. Sacaton (root fiber)[1]	

[1]Of limited use or discontinued.

General Characteristics of Cellulosic Fibers

The following discussion summarizes the general characteristics of natural cellulosic fibers and rayon as a class or group. Cellulose acetate and cellulose triacetate are chemical variants of cellulose and, as such, do not share in many of the "family characteristics." Their specific fiber characteristics are discussed at length later, in Chapter 5.

The density of cellulosic fibers tends to be relatively high, making fabrics woven from yarns of these fibers feel comparatively heavy. Cellulosic fibers have relatively low elasticity and resilience. As a result, they wrinkle easily and do not recover from wrinkling readily. Absorbency and moisture regain are generally good. Most cellulosic fibers are, therefore, slow to dry after wetting, comfortable to wear, and easy to dye.

Cellulosic fibers are good conductors of heat and electricity. As good conductors of heat, they carry warmth away from the body and are favored for use in hot weather and warm climates. Since they conduct electricity, cellulosic fibers do not build up static electricity, which produces shocks when garments are worn.

Cellulosic fibers tend to burn easily, with a quick, yellow flame, much as paper (which is also cellulose). Most cellulosic fibers can, however, withstand fairly high dry heat or ironing temperatures before they scorch. On an electric iron, cotton and linen settings are the highest settings on the dial.

Chemical properties of cellulosic fibers include good resistance to alkalis. Excessive bleaching will harm cellulosic fibers, although carefully controlled bleaching is less detrimental. Strong mineral acids are quite damaging, and most natural cellulosic fibers will withstand high water temperatures. Such properties permit laundering of cellulosic fibers with strong detergents, controlled bleaching, and hot water temperatures. Regenerated cellulosic fibers are more sensitive to chemicals and require more careful handling and gentle agitation with lower water temperatures.

Most insects do not attack cellulosic fibers. However, silverfish are likely to attack heavily starched cellulosic fabrics. Most cellulosic fabrics are susceptible to attack by fungi, especially mildew. Extended exposure to sunlight tends to damage the fibers.

Seed Hair Fibers

Seed hair fibers belong to a class in which the fibers grow from the seeds that are formed in pods on certain plants. The most widely used seed hair fiber is cotton. Other seed hair fibers include kapok, milkweed, and cattail.

Cotton

History

The cotton plant appears to have been native to the area known today as India and Pakistan, and the cultivation and use of cotton is thought to have begun there. Eventually the use of cotton spread into other areas in which the climate was compatible with its cultivation. Some archeologists and anthropologists believe that cotton was imported into South America from Asia during prehistoric times. Others, who point out that cotton plants of South America differ genetically from the Asian varieties, believe that cotton cultivation and spinning developed independently in the Western Hemisphere.

The earliest evidence of actual woven cotton fabrics was found in India during the excavation of the city called Mohenjo-Daro. The date assigned to these fabrics was 3000 B.C., so that we know that the use of cotton for fabrics was well established by this date. Fabrics of comparable age have been unearthed in excavations of Peruvian grave sites.[1]

Historians note that among the fabrics made in India were cottons so fine that they were called by names such as "flowing water" or "evening dew." One pound of cotton could be made into yarn 250 miles in length.[2] The species of cotton fiber from which these fabrics were made is now extinct, and their fineness has never been equaled.

From India, cotton cultivation spread west to Egypt and east into China and the South Pacific. Roman writers speak of importing cotton fabrics from Egypt and the East. Since cotton cannot be cultivated in the cooler European climates, cotton fiber and fabrics used in the Mid-

[1]M. D. C. Crawford, *The Heritage of Cotton* (New York: G. P. Putnam's Sons, 1924).
[2]W. Born, "Spindle and Distaff as Forerunners of the Spinning Wheel," *CIBA Review* (December 1939), p. 982.

dle Ages had to be imported. Because Europeans had never seen cotton plants, the belief was widespread that cotton came from the fleece of a beast that was half-plant and half-animal.[3]

One of the purposes of Columbus's voyage was to find a shorter trade route to India to import the fine Indian cotton fabrics. When Columbus found the Indians of Santo Domingo wearing cotton garments, he was convinced that he had, indeed, discovered a new route to India.

Large-scale cotton cultivation in the American colonies is thought to have begun as early as 1556 when cotton seeds were planted in Florida. By 1616, colonists in Virginia were growing cotton along the James River.

Cotton provides an interesting illustration of the ways in which the value of a textile fiber can vary. In the eighteenth century and before the invention of the cotton gin, cotton was a costly luxury fabric used chiefly by the wealthy. After its processing became less labor intensive through mechanization, the price decreased, and for many decades cotton was a utilitarian fabric available at relatively low cost.

Since the development of man-mades, cotton production and manufacture has had its ups and downs. Fluctuations in supply affect the price of cotton. But supply is not the only factor involved in establishing the price of cotton. Fashion trends towards or away from natural fibers will also serve to increase or decrease demand and, thus, prices.

The southern states of the United States proved especially hospitable to the cultivation of cotton, and the production of cotton soon became a major factor in the economy of the South. As Americans migrated westward, the cultivation of cotton also moved west in those areas where the climate was suitable. Texas now produces the largest quantity of cotton of any state (4,028,000 bales in 1984), and Arizona, California, Louisiana, and Mississippi each produce upward of 1,000,000 bales. Alabama, Arkansas, Georgia, Missouri, New Mexico, North Carolina, Oklahoma, South Carolina, and Tennessee also produce substantial quantities (at least 109,000 bales or more in 1984).[4]

FIGURE 4.1. Cotton flower (below); closed boll (opposite, top); mature, open boll (opposite, bottom). Courtesy of the United States Department of Agriculture.

Economic Importance of Cotton Production

Worldwide, more cotton is used than any other single fiber. In 1984, cotton accounted for about 47 per cent of total world fiber consumption. Outside the United States, cotton made up about 55 per cent of all fibers consumed. In the United States, about 23 per cent of total fiber utilized by textile mills in 1984 was cotton, while at the retail level, cotton was about 29 per cent of total consumption. Among staple fibers

[3]Frank Anderson, "Medieval Beasties," *Natural History*, 82 (January 1973), p. 61.
[4]Statistics provided by the National Cotton Council of America, January 1985. (Each bale weighs 480 pounds.)

cotton accounts for about 41 per cent of the U.S. total use, polyester staple being second, with about 26 per cent of the total. However, consumption of polyester filament plus staple was about 19 per cent greater than total U.S. cotton consumption.

U.S. cotton growers produce about 15 per cent of total world production, which amounted to about 18.5 million metric tons in the 1984–85 crop year. This ranks second behind the People's Republic of China, which produced approximately a third of the global crop. Russia ranked third with about 14 per cent of the word total, and the remaining 38 per cent of global cotton production was divided among about 70 other countries, with most of the remainder accounted for by only 7 countries (India, Pakistan, Brazil, Egypt, Mexico, and Australia).

Cotton is grown primarily for fiber in the United States. However, 10 to 15 per cent of the value of a cotton crop is due to cottonseed, which yields a high-quality oil and makes good livestock feed.

Cotton fiber is one of the major U.S. agricultural exports, with slightly over half of total sales being for export during the last five years. The United States accounts for about a third of the total world trade in raw cotton.

The cotton industry estimates that approximately 3 million Americans live wholly or in substantial part on incomes earned from cotton, including those who farm, gin, store, process, and market the fiber and seed.[5]

Botanical Information

Cotton fiber is removed from the boll or seed pod that grows on a plant of the botanical genus, *gossypium*. (See Figure 4.1.) Cotton is a member of the mallow family, related to the common garden hollyhock, hibiscus, and okra. Each fiber is a single plant cell that develops as an elongation of a cell in the outer layer or epidermis of the cotton seed. These seed hairs are called *lint*. A secondary growth of much shorter fibers accompanies the growth of cotton lint. These fibers, which are too short to be spun into yarn, are called *linters*.

Types of Cotton

Many different species are included within the genus *gossypium*, and each species of cotton includes many varieties that will produce different results under various field and weather conditions. Robert Merkel has likened these differences to those that can be seen among wine grapes grown in different climates and soils.[6]

[5]Ibid.

[6]Comment to author by Dr. Robert Merkel, Florida International University, in review of manuscript, Spring 1985.

Cotton fibers are sometimes classified according to the length to which they grow. Longer fibers command higher prices. These are as follows:

1. *Short-staple fiber:* ⅜ to ¾ inches in length. Short fibers come from Asiatic species of cotton that are both short and coarse. (Botanically, these are either *G. arboreum* or *G. herbacium*.)
2. *Intermediate-staple fiber:* ¹³⁄₁₆ to 1¼ inches in length. The variety known as American Upland is of intermediate length and coarseness. This variety of cotton makes up by far the largest quantity of cotton fiber grown in the United States. (Botanically, *G. hirsutum*.)
3. *Long-staple fiber:* 1½ to 2½ inches. This includes varieties known as Sea Island, Egyptian, and pima (or American-Egyptian), all of which are used for good-quality cotton fabric. Peruvian and Brazilian fibers also fall into this classification. However, the Peruvian variety, known as *tanguis*, has a slight crimp and rougher feel, somewhat like that of wool with which it is sometimes blended. (Botanically, *G. barbadense*.)

Cultivation

For optimum growth the cotton plant requires a warm climate, with adequate rain or other water supply. A favorable distribution of rain is more important than is the quantity of rain because the plant needs plenty of moisture during the growing season and warm, dry weather during havesting. For this reason, cotton is also grown successfully in warm, dry climates with adequate water for irrigation.

Blooms appear on the plant from 80 to 110 days after planting. The blooms are creamy white or yellow in color when they first appear. From 12 hours to 3 days after the blooms have appeared, they have changed in color to pink, lavender, or red and have fallen off the plant, leaving the developing boll on the stem. Fifty to 80 days later the pod has matured, the pressure of the full-grown fiber has caused the pod to burst, and the cotton is ready to be picked. Failure to pick the ripened bolls promptly detracts from the quality of the fiber.

To facilitate harvesting, plants may be treated with defoliants that cause a shedding of the leaves and prevent further development of the plant or with desiccants that kill the plant by causing a loss of water from the tissue. When desiccants are used, the leaves remain on the plant and contribute to the trash content of harvested cotton, whereas defoliants remove and thereby decrease this material.

Picking of the cotton is done either by hand or machine. In the United States a great deal of cotton production and harvesting has been mechanized (Figure 4.2), but in underdeveloped parts of the world much of the cotton planting, cultivation and harvesting is done by hand.

FIGURE 4.2. *Cotton harvesting machines.*
Photograph courtesy of The Mississippi
Cooperative Extension Service.

Production of the Fiber

Once the cotton fiber has been picked, it must be separated from the cotton seeds. This is accomplished by ginning. The cotton gin removes the fibers from the seeds. (See Figure 4.3.) Cotton linters, too short for spinning, are utilized in making rayons and acetates; as stuffing materials for mattresses, upholstery, and pillows; and in nontextile materials such as paper. Seeds are used in making cotton seed oil and fertilizer.

The quality of cotton fiber varies not only as to the length and variety of fiber but also as to physical condition from ginning; the amount of vegetable matter, dirt, and sand present; and color.

To provide an objective means of evaluating cotton quality, the Department of Agriculture establishes a classification system that provides information to the sellers and buyers of unprocessed cotton so that they can evaluate its value and the requirements for further processing.

FIGURE 4.3. Cotton gin in which cotton fibers are separated from cotton seeds. Courtesy of Mississippi Cooperative Extension Service and Crossroads Gin, Schlater, Mississippi, owner Jack Colquett.

Different grades are established for different kinds of cotton, with the trash content, color, ginning preparation, and brightness being the factors taken into account. Standards for length of staple fiber have also been established.

Measures for fineness and maturity are made by an indirect method, known as *micronaire fineness.* Micronaire is determined by using a standard-weight cotton specimen that is compressed to a standard volume and subjected to standard air pressure. The resultant air flow is the *micronaire reading.* Optimum micronaire measurements fall somewhere around the middle of the scale. Lower readings indicate immaturity, and higher readings may be produced by fibers that lack the fineness required for some high-quality products.

Individuals who work in the cotton industry in jobs where they come into contact with a great deal of cotton dust often develop a serious lung disease called "brown lung." This condition, known medically as *byssinosis,* appears to be related to inhaling cotton fiber or contaminants present in cotton fiber. Research is underway to try to find the precise cause and methods of production that will eliminate this illness.

Recent developments of machinery for processing cotton have focused on closed systems that protect workers from cotton dust exposure. Air quality is monitored and legislative requirements for safe levels of exposure have been established under the Occupational Safety and Health Act (OSHA). (See Chapter 23 for further discussion.)

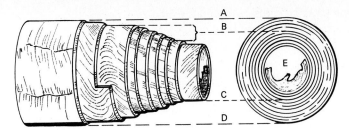

FIGURE 4.4. *The structure of cotton fiber. As the cotton fiber matures, the cell formed by the primary wall (A) is filled by successive daily deposits of cellulose in layers. (D) is the first layer deposited within the original cell. (B) shows the central layers. (C) is the innermost layer. (E) is the lumen. Courtesy of the National Cotton Council of America.*

Properties of Cotton

Physical Appearance

Color of Fiber. Cotton fiber is generally white or yellowish in color.

Shape. The length of an individual cotton fiber is usually from 1,000 to 3,000 times its diameter. The diameter may range from 16 to 20 microns. in cross section, the shape of the fiber varies from a U shape to a nearly circular form. Seen in microscopic cross section, the fiber displays a hollow, central canal known as the *lumen*. During growth this channel carries nutrients to the developing fiber.

After the fiber has reached its full length, layers of cellulose are deposited on the inside of the thin, exterior wall. The fiber grows much as a tree does, with concentric rings of growth. (See Figure 4.4.) Each layer is made up of small fibrils, or minute fibrous segments. As these fibril layers are deposited, they form a complex series of spirals that reverse direction at some points. The reverse spiral, fibril structure of cotton gives it some small degree of elasticity and is responsible for its twisted shape. The mature cotton fiber has a natural twist, called *convolutions*, which can be seen clearly when the lengthwise direction of the fiber is examined with a microscope. (See Figure 4.5.) This twist gives the magnified cotton fiber the appearance of a twisted ribbon, and it makes cotton easier to spin. Long, staple cotton has about 300 twists per inch; short cotton has less than 200. In spite of the twisted shape of the cotton fiber, it is relatively uniform in its size.

Luster. The luster of cotton is low, unless it has been given special treatments or finishes. This is, in part, a consequence of the natural twist of cotton and its resultant uneven surface that breaks up and scatters light rays reflected from the fiber surface.

Other Properties

Strength. Strength of cotton on a scale of high, medium, and low would rank as medium. (Tenacity is 3.0 to 4.9 g/d.) In comparison with other cellulosic fibers, cotton is weaker than flax and stronger than rayon.

FIGURE 4.5. *Photomicrograph of cotton in a cross section and a longitudinal view. Courtesy of E. I. du Pont de Nemours & Company.*

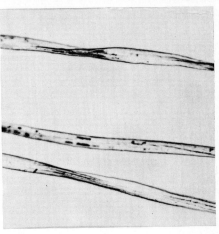

Cotton is 10 to 20 per cent stronger when wet than when dry. Its strength can be increased by a process called *mercerization* in which yarns or fabrics held under tension are treated with controlled solutions of sodium hydroxide. The alkali causes the fiber to swell and straighten out and to become more lustrous and stronger.

Density and Specific Gravity. Cotton has a specific gravity of 1.54. (Compare this with that of polyester at 1.38 or nylon at 1.14.) This means that cotton fabrics will feel heavier in weight than will comparable fabrics made from polyester or nylon.

Elasticity and Resilience. Like most other cellulosic fibers, the elasticity and elastic recovery of cotton are low. Not only does cotton stretch relatively little, but it also does not recover well from stretching. Its resilience is low. Through the application of durable press resin finishes, however, resilience can be improved.

Cotton fabrics wrinkle easily and do not recover well from wrinkling, although they drape well. Unfinished cotton fabrics generally must be ironed after laundering.

Absorbency and Moisture Regain. Cotton is an absorbent fiber. Its good absorbency makes cotton comfortable in hot weather, suitable for materials where absorbency is important (such as diapers and towels), but it is relatively slow to dry, because the absorbed moisture must be evaporated from the fiber. For the same reason, cotton fibers take waterborne dyes readily. The percentage moisture regain of cotton is 7 to 8 per cent at standard temperature and humidity.

Dimensional Stability. Cotton fibers exhibit neither shrinkage nor stretching in their natural state. Woven or knitted cotton fabrics may shrink in the first few launderings because the laundering releases tensions created during weaving or finishing. The relaxation of these tensions may cause changes in the fabric dimensions. Cotton fabrics can be given special finishes to prevent this *relaxation shrinkage.*

Heat and Electrical Conductivity. Cotton conducts electricity and thus does not build up static electrical charges. It has moderately high heat conductivity, which makes the fabric comfortable in hot weather.

Effect of Heat; Combustibility. Cotton is not thermoplastic and will not melt. Exposure to dry heat at temperatures above 300°F, however, does cause gradual decomposition and deterioration of the fiber. Excessively high ironing temperatures cause cotton to scorch or turn yellow.

Cotton is combustible. It burns upon exposure to a flame and will continue to burn when the flame has been removed. Burning cotton fabric smells like burning paper, and a fluffy, gray ash residue remains.

It is not possible to distinguish cotton from other cellulosic fibers by burning.

The Behavior of Cotton Fibers in Relation to Selected Conditions

Chemical Reactivity. Cotton that has been cleaned and bleached is about 99 per cent cellulose. Its chemical reactions are typical of cellulosic materials. Table 4.2 shows the reaction of cotton to treatment with certain chemical substances in the laboratory.

Implications for Manufacture. Some of the chemicals listed are utilized in the finishing of cotton. For example, acids may be employed to stiffen permanently the cotton fabric called organdy. The reaction of cotton to strong alkalis, in which the fiber swells and becomes stronger with (when the process is carried out under tension) an increase in luster as well, is used for mercerization. The same process done without tension and under slightly different conditions is used to make stretch fabrics. Dyestuffs that are too acidic in reaction cannot be applied to cotton fabrics.

Implication for Care. Chemical reactivity of the fiber also has implications for care. Cotton can be cleaned successfully using either synthetic-built detergents, which are generally quite alkaline, or natural soaps. The alkalinity of the detergents has no effect on the fiber. Dry-cleaning solvents do not harm cotton, so, where construction details or trim would make wet laundering undesirable, dry cleaning could be used.

Stains can be removed from cotton by using the stronger oxidizing bleaches as long as water temperature, concentration of bleaching

Table 4.2

Substance	Effect on Cotton Fiber
Acids	
Mineral acids such as sulfuric, hydrochloric, nitric, etc.	Concentrated acids destroy. Cold, diluted acids, if not neutralized and washed out, degrade and destroy the fiber.
Volatile organic acids: formic, acetic	No harmful effect.
Nonvolatile organic acids: oxalic, citric, etc.	Degrade fiber slightly if not removed.
Alkalis	
Strong alkalis: sodium hydroxide, etc.	No harmful effect. Causes fiber to swell and become stronger.
Weak alkalis: borax, soap, etc.	No harmful effect.
Oxidizing agents	
Chlorine bleaches	Destroy if uncontrolled.
Organic solvents (used in spot and stain removal)	No harmful effect.
Perchloroethylene	
Naptha	

SOURCE: J. LaBarthe, *Elements of Textiles* (New York: Macmillan Publishing Company, 1975), pp. 22–23.

agent, and time of exposure are controlled. Strong chlorine bleaches should not be poured directly on cotton since pinholes can be formed in the fabric from direct contact with the chlorine bleach.

Resistance to Microorganisms and Insects. Mildew grows on cotton fibers, especially if they are stored under conditions of dampness, warmth, and darkness. This fungus stains the fiber and eventually rots and degrades it. Other bacteria and fungi that grow in soiled, moist areas will also deteriorate or rot cotton fabrics.

Moths and carpet beetles do not attack cotton, but silverfish may eat the fiber. Heavily starched fabrics are liable to be damaged by silverfish.

Environmental Conditions. Although cotton shows better resistance to sunlight than do many fibers, extended exposure to sunlight will cause weakening and deterioration of cotton fabrics. Cotton draperies will last longer if lined with another layer of fabric.

Age does not seriously affect cotton fabrics; however, it is important that the fabrics be stored in clean condition and in dry areas to prevent mildew.

Special acid-free tissue paper can be used to store antique cotton garments, and cotton quilts and spreads. Ordinary tissue paper should not be used for wrapping fabrics for long-term storage, as the paper contains an acid residue that may damage the cloth.

Use

The range of items for which cotton fabrics are used is enormous. In wearing apparel the qualities of comfort, dyeability and launderability have caused cotton to be used widely in articles of apparel ranging from underwear to evening gowns. In the home, bed linens, table linens, draperies, upholstery and slipcover fabrics, and towels are frequently made from cotton.

Cotton has been increasingly blended with other fibers, especially with man-made fibers. This blending may be done to create cottonlike fabrics with better resiliency or those that require less ironing.

Along with its many positive qualities, cotton has some disadvantages such as combustibility and low wrinkle recovery. Various finishes developed for cotton can compensate for some of these less desirable qualities. Special finishes are discussed in Chapters 20 and 21.

Minor Seed and Fruit Hair Fibers

Kapok

Kapok, like cotton, grows in a seed pod. The kapok tree, sometimes called the silk cotton tree, is native to the tropics. Seed pods are gathered when they fall or are cut from the tree. The dried fiber is easily separated from the seeds.

The fiber has exceptional resiliency and buoyancy, but it is too brittle to be spun readily into yarns. As a result, the uses of kapok have been limited chiefly to stuffings and insulation materials. Because of its buoyancy and resistance to wetting, kapok has been used as a filling for life preservers. Having a hollow, air-filled structure, kapok could remain in the water for hours without an appreciable absorption of water, while holding up considerable weight.

Some kapok stuffings are used in household furnishings. The fibers have a tendency to deteriorate and to break down after a time. In general, kapok is little used, having been replaced by foam.

Coir

Coir is a fiber obtained from the outer hull or shell of the coconut and is therefore classified as a fruit hair fiber. Most of the coir produced is utilized in the geographic areas where the fiber is grown.

The production of the fiber is carried out by hand using rather primitive methods. The coconut is picked, the nut is removed, and the husks are collected.

The fibrous material of the husk is held tightly in place, so the husks must be soaked in water for a long period of time to facilitate fiber removal. This step of soaking is called *retting*. Husks are cut into two or three sections and remain in the water from five to six months. Salt water and tidal action seem to produce the best conditions for retting coir.

After retting, the husks are dried in the sun. Next they are placed on a plank and are either beaten with a club to separate out the fiber or placed in a breaker drum. The breaker drum contains rollers with nails set into them that pull the fiber from the husk.

The brown coir fibers, which are from 5 to 10 inches long, are used for brushes, ropes, and mats. Among the useful qualities of coir are resistance to rot, lightness coupled with elasticity, and resistance to abrasion. Face yarns of coir on a polypropylene backing are being used in broadloom carpet, carpet tiles, and floor mats.[7]

Bast Fibers

Bast fibers are those that grow in the stems of plants. Located in the inner bark of the stalk, these fibers are often several feet in length. The best known of the bast fibers is linen, which comes from the flax plant. Other important bast fibers include jute, ramie, and hemp. Minor fibers of historical interest but of little or no commercial importance are kenaf, urena, and nettle.

[7]Vera Montgomery, "Coir Yarn Specialists," *Modern Textiles*, vol. 58 (February 1977), p. 18.

Certain plants are native to a particular geographic area. During prehistoric times, flax had the widest distribution of any of the fiber-bearing plants. The oldest archeological evidence of the use of flax shows that the flax plant stem was used in basket making long before flax fiber came into use. Techniques for removing the long fibers from flax stems were developed at a later period. At first, wild flax was gathered, but subsequent cultivation of the plant spread it rapidly throughout the Middle East, Northern Africa, and Europe.

Actual samples of woven linen fabrics have been recovered from Egyptian tombs dating from 4000 B.C. The hot, dry climate of Egypt has preserved samples of both coarse and fine linen materials. Additional samples of linen fabrics have been excavated from the dried-out lake mud of prehistoric villages in Switzerland where the mineral salts of the lakes preserved the textiles. These samples are thought to be as much as seven thousand years old.[8]

In Europe, before world trade routes were developed, linen fabrics were widely utilized for most of the items in which cotton is used today. Cooler northern climates were not suited to the cultivation of cotton, but they did permit the growth of flax. The widespread use of linen

FIGURE 4.6   *Photgraph of flax plants in bloom. Courtesy of the United States Department of Agriculture.*

[8]G. Schaefer, "On the History of Flax Cultivation," *CIBA Review*, 9 (April 1945), pp. 1763 ff.

for many purposes is reflected in terminology still employed, such as *bed linens* or *table linens*. In modern products, bed linens and table linens are often made from fibers other than flax.

The United States does not produce linen for textiles (although flax seed is produced here) but imports the fibers, yarns, or fabrics. The largest part of these imports are of finished fabrics and manufactured goods such as yarns and fabrics. Countries that produce substantial quantities of linen are the Soviet Union, France, Belgium, Ireland, Egypt, Poland, and China.[9]

Botanical Information

The botanical name of the flax plant is *linum usitatissimum*. Some varieties of the plant are grown for fiber, whereas others are grown for seeds. The plant grows to a height of 2 to 4 feet. The varieties grown for fiber have long stems, with few branches and seeds. (See Figures 4.6 and 4.7.)

FIGURE 4.7 *Mature flax stalks after pulling. The stalks have been bundled. Threshing machines will remove the seeds which are used for linseed oil. Courtesy of the United States Department of Agriculture.*

[9]Information provided by the International Linen Promotion Commission.

Cultivation

In most countries the flax crop is sown in the early spring. The plant thrives best in temperate climates with adequate rainfall. Harvesting is done about 80 to 100 days after sowing when about one half of the seeds are ripe and leaves have fallen from the lower two thirds of the stem. In those countries where inexpensive labor is readily available, flax is still harvested by hand, but in developed countries, much of the labor of flax pulling is now done by machine. Whether done by hand or machine, the flax plant is pulled completely from the ground. Removing plants from the ground retains as long a stem as possible and prevents discoloration of fibers through wicking.

Stalks are dried sufficiently so that they can be threshed, combed, or beaten to remove the flax seeds, which are used for sowing future crops or for making linseed oil or livestock feed.

Preparation of the Fiber

Bast fibers require extensive processing to remove the fibers from the woody stem in which they are held. The procedure is similar for all bast fibers. The deseeded flax straw has to be partially rotted to dissolve the substances that hold the fiber in the stem. This first step in preparing the fiber is called *retting*.

Retting processes are of three types:

1. *Dew retting*. Dew retting takes place in the fields. The flax is laid out in swaths in the fields where the action of rain and dew together with soil-borne microorganisms causes the bark of the stems to become loosened. This may take from 7 to 21 days, depending on weather conditions. After retting, the bark is removed and retted straw bundles are set up in the fields to dry.
2. *Water retting* takes place when flax is submerged in water from 6 to 20 days. When water temperature is cooler, the process takes the longer amount of time. Water retting may be done in ponds, in vats, (Figure 4.8), or in sluggish streams. As in dew retting, the bacterial action causes the bark to be loosened.
3. *Chemical retting* is done by using chemicals to perform the retting function. Only limited use is made of chemical retting, and often it follows a short period of "half retting" during which bacterial action on the bark is begun.

Retting only loosens the bark from the stem. Following retting, *breaking* and *scutching* finish the job of separating the fiber from the stem. In breaking, the flax straw is passed over fluted rollers or crushed between slatted frames. This breaks up the brittle, woody parts of the stem, but does not harm the fiber. In scutching, the broken straw is

FIGURE 4.8 *The men are loading bundles of flax into retting tanks filled with heated water. The soaking action loosens the outside flax fibers from the woody center stalk. Courtesy of the International Linen Promotion Commission.*

passed through beaters that knock off the broken pieces of stem. The fibers are baled and shipped to spinning mills.

At the mill the fibers go through yet another process before they are ready for spinning. The fibers are *hackled* or combed to separate shorter fibers (called *tow*) from longer fibers (called *line fibers*) and to align fibers parallel preparatory to spinning. Even with all this processing, individual fibers do not separate out, and bundles of fibers continue to cling together.

Linen fibers are quite long; therefore, they must be processed on specialized machinery. (See Chapter 14 for discussion of spinning linen fibers.)

Properties of Linen

Physical Appearance

Color. Unbleached flax varies in color from a light cream to a dark tan. Different types of retting may produce differences in fiber color.

Shape. Fiber length may be anywhere from 5 to 20 inches, but most line (longer) fiber averages from 15 to 20 inches, whereas tow (shorter fiber) is less than 15 inches. Fiber diameter averages 15 to 18 microns.

In microscopic cross section, flax has a somewhat irregular, many-sided shape. Like cotton, it has a central canal, but this lumen is smaller and less distinguishable than is that of cotton. Looking at the length-wise direction of fiber under the microscope is rather like looking at a stalk of bamboo. Flax has crosswise markings spaced along its length that are called *nodes* or *joints.* (See Figure 4.9.)

Luster. Because it is a straight, smooth fiber, flax is more lustrous than is cotton. Many linen fabrics are designed to take advantage of this natural luster.

Other Properties

Strength. Flax is stronger than is cotton, being one of the strongest of the natural fibers. It is as much as 20 per cent stronger wet than dry.

Density and Specific Gravity. The specific gravity of flax is the same as that of cotton (1.54). Linen fabrics are, therefore, comparable in weight to cotton fabrics, but feel heavier than silk, polyester, or nylon, even in cloth of similar weave.

Elasticity and Resilience. Elongation, elasticity, and resilience of flax are still lower than are those of cotton because linen lacks the fibril structure that gives some resilience to cotton. Linens crease and wrinkle badly unless given special finishes.

Absorbency and Moisture Regain. Moisture regain of linens is in the same range as cotton (about 8 to 12 per cent). Unlike cotton, linen has very good wicking ability; that is, moisture travels readily along the fiber as well as being absorbed into the fiber. The fiber gives up its moisture readily, making it quick drying. Both absorbency and good wicking ability make linen useful for towels and for warm-weather garments.

Dimensional Stability. Like cotton, flax has good natural dimensional stability, neither shrinking nor stretching. However, it is also like cotton in that tension from manufacturing may result in relaxation shrinkage of fabrics. Preshrinkage treatments can be applied to linen fabrics to prevent relaxation shrinkage.

Heat and Electrical Conductivity. Linen conducts heat more readily than does cotton and is even more comfortable for summer wear. Conductivity of electricity prevents static electricity buildup.

Effect of Heat; Combustibility. Higher temperatures are required to scorch linen than to scorch cotton. Linen is slightly more resistant to

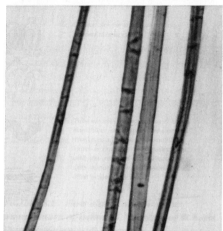

FIGURE 4.9 *Photomicrograph of flax in a cross section and a longitudinal view. Courtesy of E. I. du Pont de Nemours & Company.*

damage from heat than is cotton. The burning characteristics of linen are similar to those of cotton; it is combustible, continues to burn when the flame is removed, and burns with an odor like that of burning paper.

Behavior of Linen in Relation to Selected Conditions

Chemical Reactivity. The chemical reactions of linen closely parallel those of cotton. Like cotton, linen is destroyed by concentrated mineral acids, not harmed by alkalis or decomposed by oxidizing agents and not harmed by organic solvents used in dry cleaning. Linen could be mercerized, but because the flax is naturally strong and lustrous, there is little to be gained by the mercerization of flax.

Resistance to Microorganisms and Insects. If linen is stored damp and in a warm place, mildew will attack and harm the fabric. Dry linen is not susceptible to attack. It generally resists rot and bacterial deterioration unless it is stored in wet, dirty areas. Moths, carpet beetles, and silverfish do not usually harm unstarched linen fabrics.

Environmental Conditions. Linen has better resistance to sunlight than does cotton. There is a loss of strength over a period of time, but it is gradual and not severe. Linen drapery and curtain fabrics are quite serviceable.

The resistance of linen to deterioration from age is good, especially if fabrics are stored properly. Linen, however, has poor flex abrasion resistance and should not always be folded at the same place in order to avoid abrasion at folded edges.

Care Procedures. Linen can be dry cleaned or laundered at home with heavy-duty detergents. Being stronger wet than dry, the fabric requires no special handling during laundering. Excessive chlorine bleaching will damage linen, but linen fabrics can be whitened by the periodic, controlled use of chlorine or other bleaches.

Ironing temperatures for linen are at the highest end of the dial of electric irons. Linen fabrics can be ironed safely at a temperature of 450°F. Dryer drying at the highest setting is satisfactory.

Uses

Linen fabrics are utilized in wearing apparel and in household textiles. Yarns spun from flax range from very fine for weaving into sheer, soft "handkerchief" linens to coarse, large-diameter yarns for "crash," a fabric that is frequently used for making dish towels.

In wearing apparel, linen fabrics are popular for summer clothing. The major disadvantage of linen clothing, its wrinkling, may be overcome by giving the fabrics special crease-resistant finishes. Blending of fabrics with synthetics may also help to improve wrinkle recovery.

Table 4.3 Comparison of the Characteristics of Cotton and Linen Fibers

	Cotton	Linen
Specific gravity	1.54	1.54
Tenacity (g/d)		
Dry	3.0–5.0	5.5–6.5
Wet	3.3–6.4	6.0–7.2
Moisture regain[1]	7–11%	8–12%
Resiliency[2]	poor	poor
Burning	burns, does not melt	burns, does not melt
Conductivity of		
Heat	high	high
Electricity	high	high
Resistance to damage from		
Fungi	damaged	damaged
Insects	silverfish damage	silverfish may eat sizing
Prolonged exposure to sunlight	causes loss of strength	loss of strength
Strong acids	poor resistance	poor resistance
Strong alkalis	excellent resistance	excellent resistance

[1]At 70°F, 65% relative humidity.
[2]Characteristics such as resiliency, conductivity, and resistance are compared on the following scale: poor, fair, moderate, good, and excellent. Conductivity is characterized as being low or high.

SOURCE: Data on this and subsequent fiber characteristics charts obtained from *Man-made Fiber Fact Book* (Washington, D.C.: Man-made Fiber Producers Association, Inc., 1978); "Man-made Fiber Desk Book," *Modern Textiles*, 62 (March 1981); "Identification of Fibers in Textile Materials," *Bulletin X-156* (Wilmington, Dela.: E. I. du Pont de Nemours & Company, December 1961); *Textile Handbook* (Washington, D.C.: American Home Economics Association, 1974); R. W. Moncrieff, *Man-Made Fibres* (New York: John Wiley & Sons, Inc., 1975); and *Textile World Man-made Fiber Chart*, 130 (August 1980).

For household textiles, linen fabrics are often used in table linens. The launderability of linen combined with its good luster and attractive appearance make it quite popular for use in tablecloths and place mats. Other important uses for linen fabrics in the home include tea towels, especially those used for drying glasses. Linen produces less lint (small bits of fiber that break off from the yarn) than does cotton and is, therefore, preferred for drying glassware as it does not leave a lint deposit on the dried glass. Linen is used alone or in blends for household products such as curtains and in slipcover and upholstery fabric.

The fabric is in relatively short supply and tends to be rather expensive. Both the cost factor and desirability in increasing wrinkle resistance have led to blending flax with other fibers. In those periods when a "wrinkled look" has been fashionable, garments of linen have been popular, although expensive.

Other Bast Fibers

Ramie

Ramie or China grass is obtained from a plant in the nettle family. It is a perennial shrub. The fibers are taken from the stalk. Ramie plants are grown in semitropical regions. (See Figure 4.10.) At the present time, ramie growth and processing are concentrated in the Philippines, Bra-

FIGURE 4.10   Ramie plants growing in Florida. Courtesy of R. V. Allison, Ph.D.

zil, and the Peoples Republic of China. Hong Kong, Taiwan, Korea, and Japan process but do not grow ramie.

Ramie stalks are planted and the fiber is harvested the third year after planting. Three crops may be cut each year. After cutting the stems, the leaves of the plant are beaten off, the stems are split lengthwise, and the bark is stripped from it. This yields "ribbons" of bast that are soaked in water until the green outer layer can be scraped off. After drying, this substance, sometimes called China grass, is bundled and shipped.

Before spinning, the fiber must be retted out of the ribbons. Both dew and wet retting, similar to that used with flax, can be done. A chemical retting process that uses caustic soda and an acid rinse has been patented and is used in the industrially developed countries.

Ramie has a fine diameter, very good strength, and high luster. It is white in color, its absorbency is excellent, it dyes rapidly, and it has good resistance to attack by microorganisms.

The commercial use of ramie had been limited by difficulties of processing that made it expensive to produce. Until the chemical retting process was developed, only hand methods could be employed to remove the fiber from the stem. The control of quality of fibers was also difficult. Researchers have developed controls for growth and processing that have made possible the production of uniform quality fibers. Advances in the processing of ramie fibers are proprietary; that is, they are not made available to the public by the manufacturers.

In recent years, ramie imports into the United States have increased. This greater availability is attributed to a number of factors. Production has increased abroad. The Peoples Republic of China is a major ramie producer, and the opening of trade relations between China and the

United States has served to increase supplies. Fabrics made chiefly from ramie are not subject to U.S. import quotas. Recent fashion trends have increased demand for natural fibers in general, and ramie has the advantage of having many linenlike qualities but a lower price than linen.[10]

Ramie is used alone or in blends. Blends are most frequently made with polyester, cotton, linen, and acrylics. One hundred per cent ramie fabrics do not require any special care. They are machine washable and require ironing. If blended with adequate quantities of polyester or acrylics, these fabrics will have easy-care characteristics. The major uses for ramie fabrics or blends are in table linens, home furnishing materials, and wearing apparel.

Jute

Jute fiber is taken from the stem of the jute plant. Successful cultivation of the plant requires fertile soil and a hot, moist climate. Jute plants grow from 6 to 16 feet high.

The stalks are cut just after the flowers begin to fade. Like other bast fibers, separation of the fiber requires retting. After retting, the stems are broken and the fiber is removed.

Jute is shorter than most other bast fibers. Its length is only about 150 times its breadth, which makes it difficult to spin. It ranges in color from light to dark brown, and it is soft, fine, and lustrous, but not very pliable. On exposure to air, jute becomes somewhat brittle. It absorbs moisture readily, resists deterioration by microorganisms, and is weakened by exposure to sunlight.

Jute is in demand as a cheap, useful packaging material, although polypropylene is a major competitor. In 1979 the United States imported more than 665 million pounds of jute. Burlap is one of the major jute bagging fabrics. Jute is also used for making carpet backings and cordage.

Hemp

Hemp is a member of the mulberry family and a type of marijuana plant. The fiber bundles come from the bast layer of the stem. Mature plants are cut off and spread on the ground where they are left to dry for 5 or 6 days. Leaves and seeds are beaten off, and bundles or sheaves of hemp are formed after additional drying. Retting, breaking, and scutching complete the fiber extraction process.

Hemp has tensile strength comparable to that of linen; it is one of the strongest of the natural fibers. It has good absorbency and poor elasticity. In its chemical properties, hemp is similar to cotton and flax.

The major uses of hemp are in the production of industrial fabrics, twine, and ropes of great tensile strength. If it finds some limited use in clothing and household textiles in some countries such as Italy.

[10]Correspondance with Lorenzo P. Lesaca, senior vice-president, Ramie Textiles, Inc., Manila, Philippines, June 10, 1985.

Leaf Fibers

Leaf fibers are of limited usefulness and, for the most part, are made into cordage. They are taken from a variety of plants, most of which are perennials that produce fiber for from 5 to 20 years. The leaves are harvested, and through mechanical methods, the extraneous matter is scraped and broken away from the fiber.

The most widely used leaf fibers are those from cactuslike plants, such as those that have long, fleshy leaves with spiny edges (agave, henequen, sisal), yuccas, the banana family (abaca or Manila hemp), and the bromeliad family (pina or pineapple). Pina cloth is used in the Philippine Islands to make a sheer, lustrous fabric that is often used in Philippine national costumes.

Miscellaneous Fibers

A few fibers are obtained from roots and mosses. Sacaton, a coarse, stiff, root fiber from Mexico has been used as bristle for brushes. Spanish moss, an air plant, has been used for inexpensive upholstered furniture and mattress filler. In recent years, synthetic fibers have, to a large extent, replaced these materials.

Recommended References

"Coir," *CIBA Review*, No. 116 (August–September 1956).

"Cotton," *CIBA Review*, No. 95 (December 1952).

"Cotton" *Textiles*, 11 (Autumn 1982), p. 58.

"Fibres Under the Microscope. No. 2—Flax," *Textiles*, 11 (Spring 1982), p. 16.

"Flax," *CIBA Review*, No. 2 (1965).

FORD, J. E. "Jute and Other Vegetable Fibers," *Textiles*, 4 (October 1975), p. 58.

GUHA ROY, T. K., A. K. MUKHOPADHYAY, and A. K. MUKHERSEE. "Surface Features of Jute Fibers Using Scanning Electron Microscopy," *Textile Research Journal*, 54 (December 1984), p. 874.

"Hemp," *CIBA Review*, No. 5. (1962).

"Jute," *CIBA Review*, No. 108 (February 1955).

KAMAL, M. M., S. H. ZERONIAN, and M. S. ELLISON. "Selected Single Fiber Mechanical Properties of Different *Gossypium barbadense* Cotton Varieties," *Textile Research Journal*, 54 (May 1984), p. 343.

"Natural Fibers: Cotton," *American Fabrics and Fashions*, Nos. 124/125 (Fall/Winter 1982–83), p. 43.

"Natural Fibers: Flax, Jute," *American Fabrics and Fashions*, Nos. 124/125 (Fall/Winter 1982–83), p. 50.

PAL, B. K., S. K. SHARMA, and P. SEN GUPTA. "A Study of the Properties of Polyester-Ramie Blended Yarns," *Textile Research Journal*, 52 (June 1982), p. 415.

PETKAR, B. M., P. GOKA, and V. SUNDARAM, "Cross-sectional Shape of Cotton Fibers Belonging to Different Species," *Textile Research Journal*, 53 (December 1983), p. 778.

ROLLINS, M. L. *Cotton Fiber Structure.* Watford, England: Merrow Publishing Company Ltd., 1975.

"Ramie," *CIBA Review,* No. 123 (November 1957).

SCHAEFER, G. "On the History of Flax Cultivation," *CIBA Review,* No. 49 (April 1945), pp. 1963 ff.

SLATER, K., "The Superiority of Egyptian Cotton over Pima Cotton," *Canadian Textile Journal,* 102 (May 1985), p. 37.

U.S. Department of Agriculture. *The Classification of Cotton, Agricultural Handbook,* No. 566. Washington, D.C.: USDA, 1980.

VARMA, D. S., M. VARMA, and I. K. VARMA, "Coir Fibers. Part I: Effect of Physical and Chemical Treatments on Properties," *Textile Research Journal,* 54 (December 1984), p. 827.

Man-made Cellulosic Fibers

For thousands of years the only fibers used for textiles were those found in nature, even though, as early as 1664, Robert Hooke, an English writer, suggested that people ought to be able to create fibrous materials that had the same qualities as natural fibers. However neither Hooke nor any of his contemporaries were equal to the task. In the nineteenth century, a number of scientists had begun to look seriously for techniques for creating fibers. Their search was successful. Nitrocellulose, the first rayon fiber, was obtained as early as 1832. Further experimentation and development followed, and by the end of the century, Count Hilaire de Chardonnet, a Frenchman, had set up a factory for the production of "artificial silk" (rayon), the first "man-made" fiber.[1]

Rayon

The earliest processes for making rayon utilized natural materials that were fibrous, such as short cotton linters that could not be spun into yarns or fibrous wood pulp. Chardonnet used the pulp of mulberry trees because silkworms ate the leaves. The pulp was dissolved in chemicals that broke down the molecular structure of the fiber somewhat, while still retaining a substantial quantity of long-chain molecules. The solution was forced through a metal plate that had small holes in it, exposed either to heated air or to a chemical solution, and then formed into a long, hairlike filament. This substance was called artificial silk.

This fiber was given the name *rayon* in 1924. It is a regenerated cellulose. The specific process that was used is now obsolete in the United States and has been replaced by other methods of manufacture, but the basic principle of taking a natural material that is not usable in its original form and regenerating it into usable textile form remains the same. The manufacture of "artificial silk" by Chardonnet in 1891 marked the beginning of the man-made fiber industry.

[1]R. W. Moncrieff, *Man-Made Fibers* (New York: John Wiley & Sons, Inc., 1975), p. 147.

Federal Trade Commission definitions of generic fiber names always are written to specify the chemical makeup of the fiber. The FTC definition of rayon identifies rayon as "a manufactured fiber composed of regenerated cellulose, as well as manufactured fibers composed of regenerated cellulose in which substituents have replaced not more than 15 per cent of the hydrogen of the hydroxyl groups." The major fiber groups that fall within this definition are viscose rayon, cuprammonium rayon, high-tenacity rayon, and high-wet-modulus rayon. Viscose rayon accounts for by far the largest amount of rayon manufactured.

Viscose Rayon
Manufacture

The following steps are employed in the process for manufacturing viscose rayon (See Figure 5.1):

Purified cellulose, the base material from which viscose rayon is made, is provided, usually in the form of wood pulp, although cotton fibers, especially the short cotton linters, are also used. This material is supplied in the form of blotterlike sheets about 2 feet square.

The quantity of cellulose is measured carefully by weight, then placed in a "soaking press" where it remains immersed in a solution of caustic soda (sodium hydroxide) for about an hour. The excess solution is pressed out and the pulp material has been changed into a substance called alkali cellulose.

Alkali cellulose is shredded into small, fluffy particles called "white crumbs." These are aged under carefully controlled conditions for several days.

Carbon disulfide is then added to the white crumbs, which produces sodium cellulose xanthate and changes the color to bright orange-yellow. The orange-yellow "crumbs" are placed in dissolving tanks of dilute caustic soda. The resulting solution is thick and viscous and is known as viscose. In color, it is gold with a consistency similar to that of honey.

The viscose is filtered to remove any insoluble particles. This is important because the particles would interfere with the spinning process. Now, the viscose must be aged or ripened a second time.

The final step in the formation of the fiber is the spinning. Man-made fibers are created by forcing the solution or viscous liquid through a spinneret, a metal plate with small holes arranged in a precise pattern. These holes are spaced to allow the filaments to be extruded without touching each other. The holes must be exactly the same size to produce uniform fibers. The metal used in the plate must be capable of withstanding high pressures. For spinning viscose, the spinneret is made of gold, platinum, or rhodium.

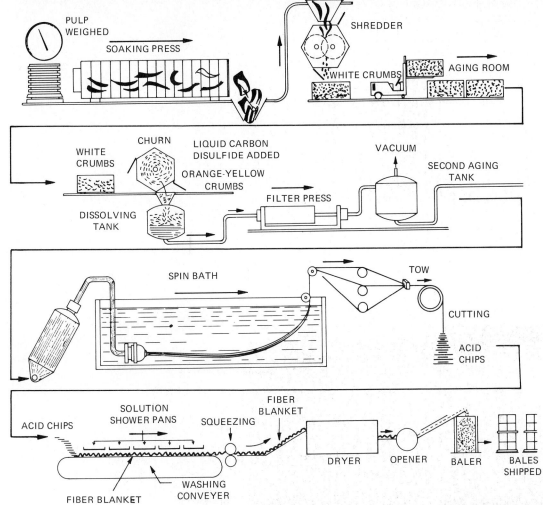

PULP
WEIGHED
SOAKING PRESS
SHREDDER
WHITE CRUMBS
AGING ROOM

WHITE
CRUMBS
CHURN
LIQUID CARBON
DISULFIDE ADDED
ORANGE-YELLOW
CRUMBS
VACUUM
SECOND AGING
TANK
DISSOLVING
TANK
FILTER PRESS

SPIN BATH
TOW
CUTTING
ACID
CHIPS

ACID CHIPS
SOLUTION
SHOWER PANS
SQUEEZING
FIBER
BLANKET
DRYER
OPENER
BALER
BALES
SHIPPED
FIBER BLANKET
WASHING
CONVEYER

FIGURE 5.1. *Flow chart for the manufacture of viscose staple fibers. Courtesy of American Enka Company.*

When man-made fibers are extruded into a liquid bath that causes the fibers to solidify or coagulate, the process is known as *wet spinning*. Wet spinning is a crucial step in the formation of viscose. The solution is wet spun into a dilute sulfuric acid bath. The acid hydrolyzes the xanthate, thereby reversing the xanthate formation and regenerating the cellulose in the form of long, continuous fibers or filaments.

These newly formed filaments are handled differently depending on the type of fiber and yarn that is to be formed. If the fiber is to be used in filament form, the yarn is formed immediately by drawing out the coagulated viscose and winding it onto spools or making it into other types of yarn packages. If the manufacturer wishes to make staple fiber lengths, the filaments are drawn and then cut into short staple lengths.

Whether the fiber is formed into filament or staple fiber, it must be washed to remove chemicals or other impurities.

Properties of Viscose Rayon

In the manufacture of man-made fibers, many qualities can be built into the fiber. For this reason it is difficult to generalize about all rayon fibers, since each manufacturer may produce viscose rayons that differ somewhat. The following discussion refers to the properties of viscose rayon that has not had any special modifications.

Rayons have generally been used in many of the same kind of products for which cotton is used. When compared with cotton, rayons have displayed certain disadvantages. They are not equal in firmness and crispness; they have poorer dimensional stability, stretching and shrinking more than cotton; and they lose strength when wet so that rayons must be handled carefully both in industrial processing and in home laundering.

Physical Appearance

Color and Luster. Rayon fibers are normally white in color. The luster of rayon can be modified by the addition of titanium dioxide, a delustering agent, to the solution before the fibers are extruded. Delustering agents break up light rays and decrease shine. Man-made fibers that have not been delustered are called *bright* fibers; those that have been delustered are called *dull* or *semidull* fibers. Figure 5.5 shows a bright fiber; Figure 5.6 shows a delustered fiber.

Shape. Man-made fibers can be manufactured in any length and diameter. In cross section the rayon fiber is an irregular circle with serrated edges. When lengthwise fibers are examined microscopically, longitudinal lines called *striations* are seen. (See Figure 5.2.)

In 1976 the Courtaulds Company marketed Viloft, now called Courcel® in the United States. Courcel® is a viscose fiber with a hollow space at the center, which is intended to simulate the hollow space or lumen within the cotton fiber. (See Figure 2.3.)

The hollow space is created by dissolving sodium carbonate in the viscose solution. When the carbonated viscose comes into contact with the acid in the spinning bath, carbon dioxide gas is formed and the bubbles of gas inflate the fiber. Careful control of the spinning allows the hollow shape to be set and the carbon dioxide gas dissipated.

The manufacturer says of Courcel® that it provides more bulk for a given weight, that it has high moisture absorption properties, and that, in comparison with other viscose fabrics, it has lower air permeability and light transmission. Courtaulds suggests that the fiber be used in blends with polyester and also with cotton. It is used for diapers, terry towels, active wear, and thermal underwear and in nonwovens where its absorbency is an advantage.

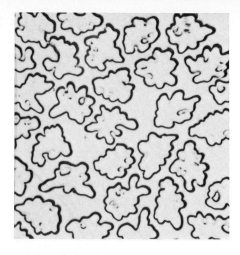

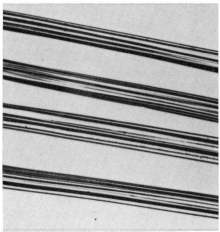

FIGURE 5.2 *Photomicrograph of regular viscose rayon in a cross section and a longitudinal view. Courtesy of E. I. du Pont de Nemours & Company.*

Other Physical Properties

Strength. The strength of viscose rayon is low. The lower polymer-chain length of viscose when compared with polymer length of cotton and linen is responsible for this lower strength of viscose. Furthermore, rayon is weaker than cotton because its physical structure is different. During the growing process, cotton develops a fibril structure, the layers or rings of which protect the fiber and provide greater strength. Ordinary rayon has no fibril layers in which the crystallinity of the physical structure is increased. Instead, rayon has a more amorphous inner structure. There is a considerable decrease in strength when the fiber is wet. Rayon fabrics must be handled carefully during laundering. Tenacity of regular viscose when dry is 0.73 to 3.2 g/d; when wet, it is 0.7 to 1.8 g/d.

Exceptionally high-tenacity rayons are also manufactured. These are generally utilized in specialized and industrial applications. Tenacities for such viscose fibers range from 3.0 to 5.7 g/d, dry, and 1.9 to 4.3 g/d, wet.

Density and Specific Gravity. The specific gravity of rayon is 1.51. Rayon fibers are comparable in density and specific gravity with cotton (1.54)and linen (1.54). Viscose, cotton, and linen fabrics of similar weave, and construction will be of comparable weight.

Elasticity and Resilience. The elastic recovery of rayon is low, as is its resiliency. Untreated rayons tend to stretch and wrinkle badly. However, wrinkle-resistant finishes can be given to viscose to overcome these disadvantages. Tebilized®, is the trademark of one wrinkle-resistant finish applied to rayon and other cellulosic fibers.

Absorbency and Moisture Regain. The molecular structure of viscose is more amorphous than is that of cotton or linen, making the viscose fibers more absorbent than the natural cellulosic fibers. Moisture regain is 1 per cent. Viscose accepts dyes readily, because of its increased absorbency. Also, fibers with larger surface areas dye more readily, and the serrated edge of the rayon fiber provides greater surface area. The absorbency of the fiber makes clothing of viscose comfortable to wear.

Dimensional Stability. Viscose rayons stretch and, having low elastic recovery, tend to remain stretched. For some time after stretching, the distorted fabric tends to "creep" toward, but not completely to, its original length.

Fabrics may be stretched during processing and exhibit relaxation shrinkage upon a first laundering. Fibers may continue to shrink in subsequent launderings, as the "creep" effect continues. Tightly woven fabrics made of viscose rayon tend to shrink less than loose weaves. Special finishes can be given to viscose to overcome some of the problems of shrinkage. Treating fabrics with resin finishes has been the most commonly used means of stabilizing viscose rayon fabrics.

Heat and Electrical Conductivity. The conductivity of both heat and electricity of viscose rayon is satisfactory, so that the fiber is reasonably comfortable in hot weather and does not build up static electricity.

Effect of Heat; Combustibility. Viscose fabrics must be ironed at lower temperatures than cotton. Too high ironing temperatures will produce scorching. The recommended ironing temperature of viscose rayon is 250°F. Long exposure to high temperatures deteriorates the fiber.

The fibers burn with characteristics similar to those of cotton. Viscose rayon fabrics continue to burn after the source of the flame has been removed, and burning fabrics have the odor of burning paper. A soft, gray ash remains after burning.

Behavior of Viscose Rayon in Relation to Selected Conditions

Chemical Reactivity. The amorphous molecular structure of viscose makes viscose more susceptible to action of alkalis and acids. Acids attack viscose more readily than cotton or other cellulosic fibers. Viscose is more susceptible to damage from alkalis as well.

Resistance to Microorganisms and Insects. Viscose is subject to damage from mildew and rot-producing bacteria. Silverfish will attack the fiber. Care in storage is necessary to prevent exposure of the fabric to conditions that encourage mildew and silverfish.

Environmental Conditions. Exposure to sunlight will deteriorate viscose rayons more rapidly than cotton. Although it is often used in these products, viscose rayon is not especially satisfactory for curtains or draperies unless they are lined to protect against sunlight. Age has no deleterious effect on viscose rayons if care is taken to be sure fabrics are stored in a clean, dry condition.

Care Procedures. Viscose rayons can be dry cleaned successfully. Laundering requires care because the fiber is weaker when wet and can be damaged more easily by rough handling. Unless given special finishes, viscose rayons tend to shrink as they dry. Drying in an automatic dryer may accentuate this tendency. When pressing rayon fabrics, lower ironing temperatures should be utilized. Chlorine bleaches can be used with rayon; however, if they are not controlled carefully, bleaching with chlorine may cause fabric deterioration. Oxygen (or perborate) bleaches are safer for rayon fabrics, if bleaching must be done.

Uses

Viscose rayon fabrics are used in wearing apparel and in household textiles. Fabrics made from rayon have a broad range of quality and price. For optimum serviceability, rayons should have been given special finishes to control shrinkage and wrinkling.

There is such a great variation in the quality of these fabrics that consumers should be sure to follow care-labeling instructions closely. Some rayon fabrics require dry cleaning for best results, whereas others can be laundered quite successfully.

For apparel, viscose rayons are made into a wide variety of garments and accessories, ranging from millinery to lingerie, suits, dresses, and sportswear. Viscose rayon is often blended with other fibers. In the home, rayon fabrics or blends of rayon and other fibers may be utilized for tablecloths, slipcovers, upholstery, bedspreads, blankets, curtains, and draperies. Rayon fibers are now being used to manufacture a wide variety of nonwoven fabrics, both disposable and durable.

Cuprammonium Rayon

The manufacture of cuprammonium rayon was discontinued in the United States in 1975. It is still being manufactured abroad in Italy, Japan, and East Germany. Water waste from the cuprammonium process is contaminated with chemicals that must be removed to meet clean water standards in the United States. The cost of removing chemical pollutants from the water is significant, and it is this factor that has resulted in discontinuance of its manufacture in the United States.

Properties of Cuprammonium Rayon

Properties of this type of rayon are quite similar to those of viscose rayon. The fiber has a somewhat more silklike appearance and feel and is often manufactured in finer diameters.

Under the microscope cuprammonium rayon appears to have a round cross section and a smooth longitudinal appearance. No striations, or very faint striations, appear on the surface.

The fiber can be made into very lightweight fabrics. A good conductor of heat and fairly absorbent, it is especially suitable for use in warm-weather clothing. Films and hollow fibers of cuprammonium rayon are used in making artificial kidneys as they exhibit superior performance in removing impurities and cause less blood clotting than do other man-made fibers.

High-Wet-Modulus Rayon

Attempts have been made to produce rayon fibers that possess some of the advantages of cotton. These experiments have centered on the development of rayon fibers with fibril structures similar to that of the natural cellulose fibers.

A Japanese researcher, S. Tachikawa, discovered a process for manufacturing rayon that develops a physical structure more like that of cotton. In this process, the severity of the chemical processing was decreased, the manufacturing time was decreased, and careful control was maintained over the chemical materials used. More specifically, Tachikawa's process eliminated the aging of alkali cellulose, dissolved the cellulose xanthate in water rather than in caustic soda, and eliminated the ripening of cellulose xanthate. A lower concentration of acid was used in the spinning bath with little or no salts.

These rayons are known as *high-wet-modulus rayons*, which means rayons that have greater resistance to deformation when wet. Trade names currently in use for high-wet-modulus rayons include Avril® from Avtex fibers and both Zantrel® and Fiber 700®, manufactured by American Enka Company.

Properties

The microscopic appearance of high-wet-modulus rayon is similar to that of cuprammonium rayon; its cross section is round but may show grainy-looking texture in the lengthwise direction. However, the granular features are not clearly pronounced dark spots like those in delustered fibers. (See Figure 5.3.) Fibers are made in both staple and filament form. Table 5.1 lists those properties of high-wet-modulus rayons that differ from regular viscose rayon.

Uses

Producers of high-wet-modulus rayons say that they are suitable for use in the same kind of products as cotton. These rayons have a crisp, lofty feel. High-wet-modulus rayons, which offer better dimensional sta-

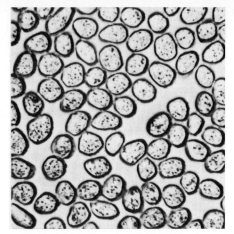

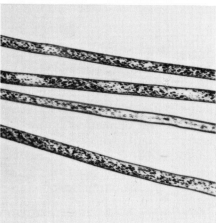

FIGURE 5.3 *Photomicrograph of high-wet-modulus fiber in cross section and a longitudinal view. Courtesy of E. I. du Pont de Nemours & Company.*

Table 5.1

Property	Differences from Regular Viscose Rayon
Strength	
Dry	Increased strength.
Wet	Weaker wet than dry, but has much better wet strength than viscose or cuprammonium rayon.
Elasticity and resilience	Improved resilience, better elastic recovery.
Absorbency and moisture regain	Decreased absorbency, making fabrics somewhat harder to dye than viscose rayons, but still easy compared with many synthetics.
Dimensional stability	Does not stretch or shrink excessively.
Effect of heat	Can tolerate higher ironing temperatures (slightly above those suitable for cotton).
Chemical reactivity	Can be mercerized.
Resistance to sunlight	Although deteriorated by sunlight, resistance is better than regular viscose rayon.

bility and strength during laundering than do conventional rayons, are often made into wind jackets, sportswear, and sweaters as well as shirts, dresses, and a variety of household fabrics. High-wet-modulus rayons are frequently blended with cotton. Typical blends include those with polyester in durable press fabrics and blends with cotton.

In the 1920s experimentation with regeneration of cellulosic materials led to the discovery of a by-product called cellulose acetate. (See Figure 5.4.) This substance, a chemical derivative of cellulose, was used as a coating for the fabric wings of World War I airplanes. It caused the fabric to tighten up and become impervious to air. After the war, the demand for this material decreased, and the manufacturers of cellulose acetate sought another market for their product. Intensive research yielded a process for converting cellulose acetate into a fiber with high luster and excellent draping qualities. Like rayon, acetate was known as "artificial silk."

The resulting confusion between real silk and "artificial silk" led the Federal Trade Commission to establish a separate name for the man-made fibers. In 1924 the term *rayon* was established to include both regenerated cellulose and cellulose acetate. In 1953 an FTC ruling established separate categories for rayon and acetate and for triacetate, another modified cellulose fiber.

Cellulose acetate and cellulose triacetate are classified as modified cellulose fibers. These fibers should be distinguished from the rayons, which are regenerated cellulose fibers. The production of both fibers begins with cellulose, but unlike rayon, the chemical composition of acetate and triacetate fibers is not cellulose but chemical variations of cellulose known as esters of cellulose. For this reason, the behavior of cellulose acetate and cellulose triacetate differs somewhat from the other cellulosic fibers.

The diagram of the cellulose molecule subunit shows that it possesses three —OH groups, known in chemical terminology as *hydroxyl groups.* In the chemical reactions that take place during the manufacture of cellulose acetate (and cellulose triacetate), acetyl groups ($CH_3 CO_2$) are substituted for —OH groups on the cellulose molecule. This process is known as *acetylation.*

cellulose subunit

Cellulose Derivative Fibers

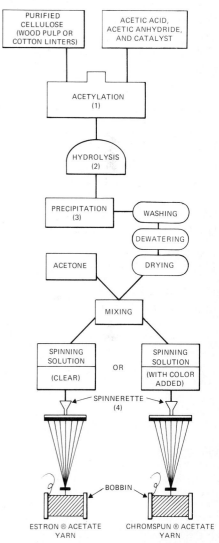

FIGURE 5.4 *Flow chart for the manufacture of cellulose acetate. Courtesy of Eastman Kodak Company.*

All three hydroxyl groups in the cellulose molecule can be acetylated. When a substance is formed from cellulose in which all three hydroxyl groups have been acetylated, the material is called cellulose triacetate. If a smaller number of hydroxyls are acetylated, the substance is called cellulose acetate. Cellulose acetate is, technically, a diacetate. Both are used in forming textile fibers.

cellulose triacetate

The initial stages of formation of both cellulose acetate and cellulose triacetate are the same. Cotton linters or wood pulp are treated to remove any impurities. In making acetate, the purified cellulose is steeped in acetic acid for a time to make the material more reactive. After further treatment with still more acetic acid, acetic anhydride is added. This mixture is stirred until it is thoroughly blended, but no reaction takes place until sulfuric acid is added to the mixture. The sulfuric acid begins the acetylation reaction. The temperature is kept low, and the mixture stands for 7 or 8 hours until it takes on a thick, gelatinlike consistency. The material formed is triacetate, also known as the primary acetate. From this point, the procedure differs, depending on whether cellulose diacetate or triacetate is being made.

Cellulose Triacetate

Cellulose triacetate having been formed, water is added to the viscous solution. The triacetate can no longer be held in this weak solution and precipitates out in the form of small, white flakes. These flakes are collected, dried, and then dissolved in a solution of methylene chloride and a small quantity of alcohol. The fibers are dry spun through a spinneret into warm air, solidify, and are formed into yarns. See dry-spun illustration and discussion on pages 52 and 53.

Cellulose Diacetate (Regular Acetate)

To follow the steps in the spinning of regular acetate, we must return to the formation of triacetate, or the base acetate. The next step is the conversion of the base acetate into a diacetate. The primary acetate (triacetate), excess acetic acid, and acetic anhydride from the first reaction are combined with sufficient water to produce a 95 per cent solution of acetic acid. This mixture stands for 20 hours, during which time acid hydrolysis takes place and some of the acetylated hydroxyl groups are reconverted to their original form. This mixture is tested constantly so that the reaction is stopped at the appropriate point. The mixture is poured into water, and the cellulose acetate precipitates into chalky white flakes that are collected, washed, and dried. This is the secondary acetate or cellulose acetate.

Flakes from different batches of cellulose acetate are mixed together to maintain a uniform quality of acetate. The flakes are soluble in acetone. Before spinning, the flakes are dissolved in acetone to form the solution or dope. This takes about 24 hours. The dope is filtered and then extruded through spinnerets into warm air that evaporates the acetone. In winding the fiber into yarns, fibers are given a slight stretch that orients or parallels the molecules, making the fiber somewhat stronger.

Appearance of Cellulose Acetate and Cellulose Triacetate

Shape. In microscopic appearance cellulose diacetate and cellulose triacetate are very similar. Normally both fibers are clear and have an irregular, multilobed shape in cross section rather like popcorn. Acetate may be manufactured in other cross sections as well; however, most commercially available acetate fibers with unusual cross-sectional shapes have been withdrawn from manufacture.

The longitudinal appearance of regular acetate and triacetate fibers shows broad striations. It is not possible to distinguish normal acetate fibers from triacetate fibers by microscopic examination. (See Figures 5.5 and 5.6.)

FIGURE 5.5. *Photomicrograph of cellulose acetate fiber in a cross secton and a longitudinal view. Courtesy of E. I. du Pont de Nemours & Company.*

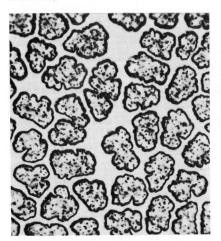 

FIGURE 5.6. *Photomicrograph of delustered cellulose triacetate fiber in a cross section and a longitudinal view. Courtesy of E. I. du Pont de Nemours & Company.*

Luster and Color. If acetate and triacetate have not been treated to decrease luster, both fibers will have a bright appearance and good luster. Fibers that have been delustered show small, black spots of pigment in the microscopic longitudinal view and cross section. Fibers are white unless they have been solution dyed.

Other Properties

Strength. Both acetate and triacetate have very low strength. Both are weaker wet than dry. The abrasion resistance is poor. Nylon hosiery wearing against acetate satin linings in coats provides sufficient abrasion to cut these fibers.

Density and Specific Gravity. Acetate and triacetate are both lower in specific gravity, at 1.32 and 1.3, respectively, than is rayon or cotton. Comparable fabrics, therefore, feel lighter when made of acetates or triacetates than if they are woven of cotton, linen, or rayon.

Elasticity and Resilience. Acetate and triacetate differ markedly in their elastic recovery and resilience. Acetate has poor elastic recovery and poor wrinkle recovery. By contrast, triacetate has increased elastic recovery, is resilient, and has good wrinkle recovery.

Absorbency and Moisture Regain. Acetate is more absorbent than is triacetate. (Acetate has a moisture regain of 6.3 to 6.5 per cent, whereas triacetate regains only 3.5 per cent of moisture.)

Dimensional Stability. Triacetate fibers have good resistance to stretch or shrinkage. Acetate fabrics may exhibit relaxation shrinkage on laundering unless they are pretreated. Knit fabrics are especially prone to relaxation shrinkage with as much as 10 per cent shrinkage during laundering. Exposure to high temperatures may also cause acetates to shrink.

Heat and Electrical Conductivity. Neither heat nor electrical conductivity of acetate and triacetate is as good as the conductivity of other cellulosic fibers. Both fibers tend to build up static electricity charges, and neither acetate nor triacetate is as cool to wear as cotton, linen, or rayon.

Effect of Heat; Combustibility. Both acetate and triacetate are thermoplastic fibers; they will soften and melt with the application of heat. Triacetate is normally given a special heat treatment that makes it much less sensitive to heat than acetate. Surface designs such as moiré can be heat-set in acetate. Heat treatments given to triacetates increase the crystallinity of the molecule. Along with the increase in crystalline structure, the moisture regain decreases. Heat-treated triacetates can be permanently set into pleats or other shapes. Table 5.2 contrasts the effect of heat on each fiber.

If ignited, acetate and triacetate burn with melting. When the flame has been put out, a small, hard, beadlike residue remains at the edge of the burned area.

Behavior in Relation to Selected Conditions

Chemical Reactivity. Table 5.3 compares the chemical reactivity of acetate and triacetate.

Resistance to Microorganisms and Insects. Mildew will grow on acetate or triacetate if the fabrics are incorrectly stored. The growth causes discoloration of the fabric but no serious loss of strength. Triacetate is more resistant to mildew than is acetate.

Moths or carpet beetles do not attack either fiber. However, heavily starched or sized acetates are prone to attack from silverfish.

Environmental Conditions. Extended exposure to sunlight will cause a loss of strength and deterioration of acetate fabrics. Draperies should be lined to protect them from the sun. Triacetate has moderate resistance to sunlight. The resistance of acetate to ultraviolet light is decreased if the fiber has been delustered.

Acid fumes in the atmosphere may adversely affect some dyes used for acetates. The low absorbency of acetates requires that they be dyed with a type of dye known as "disperse" dye. Certain of these dyes are subject to atmospheric fading or "fume" fading. Blue and gray shades,

Table 5.2 Effect of Heat on Acetate and Triacetate

Acetate	Triacetate
Sticks at 350°F to 375°F	464°F (after heat treatment)
Melts at 500°F	575°F

Table 5.3

	Acetate	Triacetate
Effect of acids	Resistant to cold, dilute acids. Decomposed by strong acids; dissolves in acetic acid.	Resistant to cold, dilute acids. Damaged by strong acids; slightly better acid resistance than acetate.
Effect of alkalis	Good resistance to weak alkalis. Saponified by strong alkalis.	Like acetate.
Effect of bleach	Hydrogen peroxide or sodium perborate bleach recommended at temperatures below 90°F.	Like acetate.
Effect of organic solvents	Petroleum products safe for use; dissolved by acetone, an ingredient in some fingernail polish remover, and in cresol, phenol, and some lacquer solvents.	Like acetate—partially disolved by acetone with heat.

after exposure to atmospheric gases produced by heating homes with gas, turn pink or reddish. Greens may turn brown.

To overcome this problem, acetate fibers may be colored in the solution before the fiber is extruded from the spinneret. Pigment that is added to the acetate solution is locked into the fiber permanently and cannot change in color.

In addition to solution dyeing, special finishing agents called diethanolamine or melamine can be applied to acetate and triacetate fabrics to stabilize colors and prevent fume fading. Also some blue dyes that are not reddened by gas fumes have been developed.

Acetate does lose some strength through aging. Triacetates resist deterioration with age.

Care Procedures

Acetate. If handled with care, acetates can be laundered successfully. However, acetates that have not had special shrink-resistant finishes should be dry cleaned. Woven acetate goods may shrink as much as 5 per cent and knits as much as 10 per cent in laundering.

During laundering, acetate fabrics should not be subjected to undue stress through wringing or twisting. Fibers are weaker wet than dry, and acetates will wrinkle badly if creased or folded when wet.

Hydrogen perioxide or sodium perborate bleaches can be used if necessary for whitening of fabrics. Bleaching should be carefully controlled. Ironing temperatures for acetates must be kept low. The fabric will stick and melt if ironed at temperatures above 275°F.

Acetone, a component of some fingernail polishes and polish removers, will dissolve acetate. Care should be taken to avoid spilling acetone-containing substances on the fabric.

Triacetate. Triacetate fabrics can be hand or machine washed. Hydrogen peroxide and sodium perborate bleaches can be used. Triacetates have better wrinkle recovery and crease resistance than acetates. If the fabrics require touch-up ironing after laundering, triacetates can be ironed at the rayon setting on the iron dial.

Dry-cleaning solvents will not harm triacetates. These fabrics can be successfully dry cleaned.

Acetone will also damage triacetate fabrics. Spills from nail polish or remover that contains acetone will dissolve the fabric.

Uses

Acetate is used for many household and apparel textiles because it has an attractive appearance and pleasant hand or texture. Decorative fabrics are woven to take advantage of the high luster and wide color range available in acetate fabrics.

Table 5.4 Comparison of Characteristics of Regenerated Cellulosic Fibers and Cellulose Derivative Fibers

	Regular-Tenacity Rayon	High-Wet-Modulus Rayon	Acetate	Triacetate
Specific gravity	1.51	1.51	1.32	1.25[a]
Tenacity (g/d)				
Dry	0.73–3.2	2.5–5.5	1.2–1.4	1.1–1.3
Wet	0.7–1.8	1.8–4.0	0.8–1.0	0.8–1.0
Moisture regain	11–14%	11–14%	6%	4%
Resiliency	poor	fair	poor	fair
Burning	burns, does not melt	burns, does not melt	burns, melts at 500°F	burns, melts at 575°F
Conductivity of				
Heat	high	high	moderate	moderate
Electricity	high	high	moderate	moderate to high
Resistance to damage from				
Fungi	damaged	damaged	fair resistance	resistant
Insects	attacked by silverfish	attacked by silverfish	silverfish may eat sizing	silverfish may eat sizing
Prolonged exposure to sunlight	loss of strength	some loss of strength	some loss of strength over time[b]	moderate resistance
Strong acids	poor resistance	poor resistance	poor resistance	poor resistance
Strong alkalis	poor resistance	excellent resistance	causes saponification and eventual loss of strength	causes saponification and eventual loss of strength

[a]Average of major commercial brands.
[b]Sunlight-resistant acetate is available for draperies.

Acetates are used for items of clothing such as blouses, dresses, and lingerie. Handsome drapery and upholstery fabrics are often made of acetate brocade, taffeta, or satin. Acetate yarns are used in some fabrics together with yarns of other fibers to provide a contrast between the luster of acetate and a dull appearance of, for example, cotton or rayon. Cigarette filters are a major and growing use of acetate tow.

Triacetate fabrics have the advantage of being able to be heat-set. Apparel in which pleat or shape retention is important is often made from triacetate. The major use of this fabric is in wearing apparel; however, the manufacturer recommends its use for comforters, bedspreads, draperies, and throw pillows, as well. Arnel®, the only triacetate produced at present, is manufactured by the Celanese Corporation.

Recommended References

"Artificial Silk," *CIBA Review*, Vol. 2 (1967).

"Cellulose: Rayon and Acetate," *American Fabrics*, No. 84 (Fall 1969), p. 51.

CHEEK, L. "Dyeing High Wet Modulus Rayon Yarns with Fiber Reactive Dyes," *Clothing and Textiles Research Journal*, 1 (1982), p. 9.

"Courtaulds' Courcel Hollow Cross-section Rayon Introduced," *Knitting Times*, 53 (June 1984), p. 62.

CUMBERBIRCH, R. J. E. "High Absorbency Viscose Fibres," *Textiles*, 13 (Autumn 1984), p. 58.

"Fibres Under the Microscope. No. 4—Viscose," *Textiles*, 11 (Autumn 1982), p. 72.

FORD, J. E. "Viscose Fibres," *Textiles*, 9 (February 1980), p. 2.

"High Performance Cellulosics Explored," *High Performance Textiles*, 5, (1984), p. 9.

MONCRIEFF, R. W. *Man-Made Fibres*, 7th ed. London: Butterworth and Company Ltd, 1987.

MCNEIRNEY, F. "Acetate," *Modern Textiles*, 58 (March 1977), p. 6.

"Solvent Spinning Reduces Rayon Processing Time at Avtex," *Knitting Times*, 53 (October 1984), p. 73.

"Special Report on Rayon and Acetate Fibers and Fabrics," *American Fabrics and Fashions*, No. 83 (Summer 1979), p. 99.

Protein Fibers

Protein fibers are those fibers in which the basic chemical structure is composed of amino acids joined in polypeptide chains. They may be separated into three basic groups:

1. *Those fibers that are animal hair.* The major fiber in this group is sheep's wool. Other fibers of commercial importance are those obtained from animals such as the alpaca, camel, cashmere goat, llama, vicuña, and guanaco and the fleece of the angora goat, called mohair. Also used are qiviut or hair from the musk ox; angora rabbit hair; fur fiber from animals such as beaver, mink, and rabbit; and cow and horse hair.
2. *Those fibers formed from extruded filaments.* Silk, produced by the silkworm caterpillars, is the only important fiber in this group. In the past such unusual materials as spider silk and byssus from mussels were said to have been made into fabrics.
3. *Those fibers that are regenerated from vegetable or animal protein.* Corn, soybeans, and milk are some of the base materials from which regenerated protein fibers have been made.

All protein fibers contain the elements carbon, hydrogen, oxygen, and nitrogen. Wool contains sulfur as well. In each protein fiber these elements are combined in different arrangements. As a result, properties of the various protein fibers may show some striking differences.

Even so, these fibers share a number of common properties. Protein fibers, except silk, tend to be weaker than cellulosic fibers, and they are weaker wet than dry. Fabrics made from protein fibers must be handled with care during laundering or wet processing.

Density and specific gravity of protein fibers tend to be lower than that of cellulose. Fabrics made from these fibers feel lighter in weight than do comparable fabrics made from cellulosic fibers.

Protein fibers have greater resilience than cellulosic fibers. They are more resistant to wrinkling and hold their shape well. Moreover, fibers from the protein family do not burn readily. When set aflame, they may extinguish themselves. Burned fibers smell like burning hair, flesh, or feathers. Protein fibers tend to be damaged by dry heat and should be

Table 6.1 *Protein Fiber Family*

Natural Fibers	Man-made Fibers
Animal hair fibers	*Regenerated protein or azlon fibers*
Major fibers	Minor fibers
Wool (from sheep)	Animal protein
	Milk protein[1]
Specialty hair fibers	Vegetable protein
Camel family	Peanut protein[1]
Alpaca	Corn protein[1]
Huarizo	Soybean protein fiber[1]
Guanaco	Chinon
Misti	
Vicuña	
Llama	
Goat family	
Cashmere	
Mohair (from the angora goat)	
Qiviut (from the musk ox)	
Fur fiber	
Beaver	
Fox	
Mink	
Chinchilla	
Rabbit (especially angora rabbit)	
Other	
Horsehair	
Cow hair	
Extruded fibers	
Major fibers	
Silk (from the silkworm)	

[1]No longer in production.

ironed with a press cloth or steam. Wool and silk require lower ironing temperatures than do cotton and linen, with recommended temperatures around 300°F.

Chemical properties common to most protein fibers include susceptibility to damage by alkali and by oxidizing agents, especially chlorine bleach. Care in laundering is required to avoid damaging fibers through the use of strongly alkaline soaps and detergents and chlorine bleach. Fabrics can be bleached safely with hydrogen peroxide. Acids are less damaging to protein fibers than to the cellulose fibers.

Sunlight discolors white fabrics made from protein fibers, turning them yellow after extended exposure to the sun. Although wool has better resistance to sunlight than does cotton, it will degrade on prolonged exposure. Silk degrades quite readily on exposure to sunlight.

The hair of a number of different kinds of animals has been used for textile fibers for many centuries. If one looks briefly at the early history of textile fibers, it appears that the widespread use of animal hair fibers for construction of yarns may have developed later than the use of plant fiber since the prehistory of northern Europe shows no evidence of the use of wool until considerably after flax and other cellulosics. The belief that wool use for fabrics was developed later in Europe and South America is supported by the fact that the herding of sheep and goats was not widespread in Europe until the Bronze Age, or about 2000 to 3000 B.C., whereas in South America, herding is dated at about 1000 B.C.[1]

Early hunting peoples undoubtedly made some use of wool fibers from the fleeces that hunters took from animals. After people recognized that these fibers were useful in constructing cloth, sheep, goats, and other animals such as camels, llamas, alpacas, and the like were domesticated in different parts of the world, and their hair was removed for spinning and weaving.

Of the many varieties of animal hair from which textile fibers are derived today, the fleece of the sheep is most widely used. In Central Asia, the camel is an important source of textile fiber, and South America is the home of a number of camellike animals that produce fibers used for spinning and weaving. The alpaca and llama are native to the Andes Mountains regions and have been domesticated. Vicuña and guanaco are wild or semiwild animals from the same geographic region. Other animal hair fiber comes from domesticated goats such as the angora goat and the cashmere goat.

Hair from other wild or domesticated animals such as rabbits, musk oxen, horses, and cows have some minimal use in textile products.

Under the Wool Products Labeling Act, wool is defined as "the fiber from the fleece of the sheep or lamb or hair of the angora or cashmere goat (and may include the so-called specialty fibers from the hair of the camel, alpaca, llama, and vicuña)."[2] Fiber taken from the domesticated sheep makes up by far the largest quantity of fiber sold under the name of wool.

Approximately two hundred different breeds and crossbreeds of sheep produce wool fiber. The fiber produced by these animals varies widely in quality not only because of the conditions under which the sheep may graze and the quality of the pasture land, but also because some breeds of sheep produce finer quality wool than do others.

The sheep that produces the most valuable and finest wool is the Merino variety. (See Figure 6.1.) This type of wool accounts for about 30

Animal Hair Fibers

Sheep's Wool

[1]J. G. Clark, *Prehistoric Europe* (New York: Philosophical Library, Inc., 1952).
[2]*Rules and Regulations Under the Wool Products Labeling Act of 1939* (Washington, D.C.: Federal Trade Commission, 1980), p. 25.

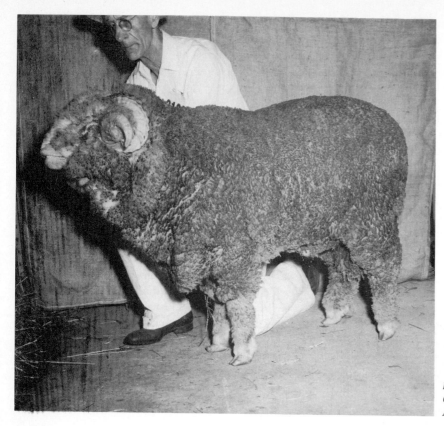

FIGURE 6.1 Champion Merino sheep. Courtesy of the United States Department of Agriculture.

per cent of wool production. Merino sheep originated in Spain, but are now prevalent all over the world, the largest proportion of Merino fleeces today coming from Australia. Merino wool is fine, strong, and elastic, though relatively short—from 1 to 5 inches. French Rambouillet sheep, descendants of the Merino blood line, were imported to the United States in 1840 and make up 27 per cent of all the sheep in the United States. These, too, produce fine, high-quality wool.

A second group of sheep that originated in the British Isles produces fibers that are not quite so fine as Merino and Rambouillet but are also of quite good quality. Fibers range from 2 to 8 inches in length. Some of the breeds of sheep from this group are Devonshire, Dorset, Hampshire, Oxford, Southdown, and Wiltshire. Like Merino sheep, these breeds are raised worldwide.

Coarser, longer fiber is produced by a group of sheep known as Long British or Long Crossbreeds. The fiber length is 4 to 16 inches, and the better known breeds include Leicester, Lincoln, Cotswold, Romney Marsh, and Cheviot. Much of this fiber is made into outerwear in tweed, cheviot, homespun, and shetland fabrics.

A fourth group of sheep is made up of a variety of crossbred sheep that produce fibers of from 1 to 16 inches in length, fibers that are coarse and have lower elasticity and strength. These wools are used largely for carpets and inexpensive, low-grade cloth.

Climatic conditions can have an adverse effect on the quality of the wool, as can the condition of the grazing area. Australian flocks are enclosed in large fenced areas where underbrush and burrs are kept to a minimum, whereas American sheep are permitted to graze on open ranges. This free grazing results in fleece in which sticks, leaves, burrs, and other vegetable matter may be caught.

Wool Consumption

Mills in the United States utilized 340.2 million pounds of raw wool in 1984, 276.2 million pounds for apparel and 64.0 million pounds for carpets. A little more than a third of this quantity was produced in the United States. Of the 210.2 million pounds of wool product imported in 1984, about half was from Australia. This wool was used largely for apparel. Other major shippers of wool to the United States include New Zealand, which produces wool used mostly for carpet and nonapparel products, and South Africa, which produces apparel fiber. Of the wool produced in the United States, Texas, California, and Wyoming supply the largest quantities with 30 per cent, 10 per cent, and 10 per cent, respectively, of the domestic totals.[3]

Fleece Removal

Sheep are sheared to remove the fleece in the spring season. (See Figure 6.2.) Expert shearers move from place to place removing fleece or clip wool. In Australia, fleece is removed in sections with the underbelly section kept separate from the sides. This is done because the fleece from the undersection and legs tends to be inferior in quality to that of the sides, as it contains more vegetable matter and is more tangled, matted, and torn than is fleece from the upper part of the body. In the United States, it is customary to remove the fleece in one piece.

Fleece that is sheared from sheep at eight months of age or younger is called *lamb's wool*. Because this is the first growth of hair, it tends to be softer and finer. Products made from this soft, fine wool are generally labeled "lamb's wool."

Wool removed from animals that have been slaughtered is referred to as *pulled wool*. Wool is taken from hides by one of several methods. A chemical depilatory, a substance that loosens the wool from the hides, may be used. This material does not seriously damage the hide and is the preferred method as it allows full utilization of both hides and fleece. Another method is to allow bacterial action to loosen the fiber so that it can be pulled from the hide.

---

[3]Data provided by the Wool Bureau, Inc.

FIGURE 6.2. *A line of sheep shearers remove fleece from sheep. Courtesy of the United States Department of Agriculture.*

Pulled wool is taken from the hide after the animal has been slaughtered for meat and is inferior in quality to fleece or clip wool as it is less lustrous and elastic. Pulled wool is generally blended with other types of wool. The chemical treatment given to the pulled wool in its removal from the skin degrades the fiber and allows the fiber to swell more readily in the dyebath. For this reason, pulled wool dyes more unevenly than does sheared wool.

From time to time stories will appear in the media about experimentation with feeding chemicals to sheep that cause their hair to fall out by itself, without shearing. Michael Koch of the Wool Bureau, Inc., points out that although this process exists, it causes the hair to fall out from deep within the skin so that it then becomes necessary to provide each sheep with a jacket for the sheep to avoid hypothermia and possibly death from exposure. Said Mr. Koch, "As you can imagine, there is currently little enthusiasm for this process—but research continues."[4]

Grading

Grading of wool is done at the time the fleece is sheared. In grading, the fleece is judged for its overall fiber fineness and length. An alterna-

[4]Letter to the author, June 14, 1985.

tive to grading is found in *sorting*, in which the fleece is divided into sections of differing quality. The best fiber comes from the sides and shoulders; the poorest comes from the lower legs.

Preparation for Spinning

The first step taken to prepare the fleece for use is *scouring*, which removes oil, grease, perspiration, and some of the dirt and impurities from the fleece. The fleece is washed a number of times in a warm, soapy, alkaline solution. A fleece of about 8 pounds in weight will be reduced by scouring to about 3 to 4 pounds. Much of the weight loss results from the removal of lanolin, a natural oil secreted by the sheep, which keeps the fleece soft and waterproof. This lanolin is recovered for use in cosmetics and other oil-based preparations. Even though lanolin can be recovered, the refuse produced by scouring of wool may be a cause of water pollution in areas where wool is processed.

If wool retains significant quantities of vegetable matter after scouring, it must be carbonized to remove this substance. *Carbonization* is the treatment of the fleece with sulfuric acid that destroys burrs, sticks, or other woody material. Careful control is maintained to assure that fibers are not damaged by the process. An alternative method is to lower the temperature of the fleece below freezing so that dirt, burrs, or vegetable matter become brittle and can be knocked or brushed from the fleece.

As a result of these processes, the wool may become overly dry and brittle. To avoid this, a small amount of oil is added to the fiber to keep it flexible, and the wool is kept somewhat moist during handling.

All wool fibers are carded. Fine wire teeth, mounted on a cylinder, separate the fibers and make them somewhat, although not completely, parallel. This procedure also helps to remove remaining vegetable matter from the fiber.

Combing is an additional processing procedure that further aligns longer fibers in a parallel manner so that the resulting yarns are smoother and stronger. Combed yarns may have a tighter twist, but it is not necessary that they do because of the longer fiber length used. The term *woolen* is applied to yarns spun from shorter fibers that have been processed on the *woolen system. Worsted* yarns are made from longer combed yarns that have been processed by the *worsted system.* (See Chapter 14 for a full discussion of these spinning systems.) Worsted yarns are more lustrous, less fuzzy, and often smaller in diameter than are woolen yarns.

Wool Products Labeling Act of 1939

Wool fabrics can be made from new or from used wool, but you cannot tell by looking at the fabric whether the wool it contains is new or reused. To assure that products made from used fibers are clearly labeled as such, the Wool Products Labeling Act of 1939 was enacted. This legislation regulated the labeling of sheep's wool and other animal hair fibers. The provisions of this act are as follows:

All wool products must be labeled.

The fibers contained in the product, except for ornamentation, must be identified.

The following terms used in identifying wool products are defined by the statute.

The term *wool* "means the fiber from the fleece of the sheep or lamb or hair of the Angora or Cashmere goat (and may include the so-called specialty fibers from the hair of the camel, alpaca, llama, and vicuña) which has never been reclaimed from any woven or felted wool product."

The term *recycled wool* means (1) "the resulting fiber when wool has been woven or felted into a wool product which, without ever having been utilized in any way by the ultimate consumer, subsequently has been made into a fibrous state," or (2) "the resulting fiber when wool or reprocessed wool has been spun, woven, knitted, or felted into a wool product which, after having been used in any way by the ultimate consumer, subsequently is made into a fibrous state."[5]

The terms *new wool* or *virgin wool* may be used "only when the product or part (of a product) referred to is composed wholly of new or virgin fibers which has [sic] never been reclaimed from any spun, woven, knitted, felted, bonded or similarly manufactured product."[6]

Recycled wools are often made from the cutting scraps left from the manufacture of wool items. The fibers are pulled apart and returned to the fibrous state through a process known as *garnetting*. In the garnetting procedure, fibers may be damaged and can, therefore, be lower in quality than some new wool. Less frequently, wool is recycled from fabrics used by the ultimate consumer. These fabrics are also returned to the fibrous state by garnetting. Because these fibers have been subject to wear not only from the garnetting process but also by the normal wear and tear of a garment or product in use, these are the lowest-quality wool fibers. Recycled wools are often made into interlining materials for coats and jackets. or other inexpensive wool products. They are sometimes referred to as *shoddy*.

[5]Text of the Wool Products Labeling Act of 1939 as amended effective July 4, 1980. Reported in *Rules and Regulations Under the Wool Products Labeling Act of 1939* (Washington, D.C.: Federal Trade Commission,), p. 25.

[6]"Questions and Answers Relating to Textile Fiber Products Identification Act and Regulations" (Washington, D.C.: Federal Trade Commission, October 17, 1974), p. 14.

Although the terms *virgin* or *new* wool guarantee that fabrics are made from wool that has not been previously fabricated, the terms carry no guarantee of quality. It is possible that a poor quality of virgin wool may be inferior to a fabric made from excellent quality recycled wool.

In pile fabrics the face and the backing may be made of different fibers. The contents of the face and the backing may be listed separately, such as "100% wool face, 100% cotton back." If listed separately, the proportion of these fibers must also be indicated in percentage, so that in addition to the designation of "100% wool face, 100% cotton back," the label must also say "Back constitutes 60% of the fabric and pile 40%."

The contents of paddings, linings, or stuffings are designated separately from the face fabric, but must be listed.

The 1984 amendments to the Wool Products Labeling Act requiring country of origin labeling are the same as those required by the TFPIA and are described on pages 25 and 26.

Molecular Structure

Wool is made of a protein substance known as *keratin*. The fiber is composed of nineteen amino acids, but the relative amounts of amino acids vary from one type of wool to another. In addition to its long-chain, polyamide structure, wool has covalent cross-linkages called *cystine* or *sulfur linkages* and ion-to-ion bonds called *salt bridges*. Like other fibers, wool also possesses hydrogen bonds. (See Figure 6.3.)

Chemists are still trying to determine the exact effect the chemical structure of wool has on the behavior of the fibers. Some of the findings can be summarized as follows:

1. Diagrammatic representation of the fiber is usually made in the form of a ladder, showing the cross-links. Although this format is visually clearer, the wool structure is actually more in a helical form rather like a coil or spiral, like that of DNA. It is supposed that this coiled form of the molecule permits the marked elongation that is characteristic of wool fibers.[7] (See Figure 6.3G.)
2. Wool can be pressed into pleats or creases by the application of heat, moisture, and pressure. Hydrogen bonds are thought to permit this shaping of wool. Because hydrogen bonding takes place when molecules are close together, and because these bonds can be broken and re-formed in other areas, it is thought that shape can be set in this way: heat and moisture break the hydrogen bonds in one area, the fabric is shaped, heat is applied, and new hydrogen bonds are formed that hold fabric in the new shape. This

[7]J. W. S. Hearle and R. H. Peters, *Fiber Structure* (London: Newnes-Butterworth Publishers, 1963), p. 58.

A.

A. Here is a simplified outline of a single wool fiber: This is the invisible, filmy epicuticle or outer skin of the fiber.

B.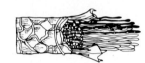

B. The epicuticle encases the imbricated (overlapping) outer layer.

C.

C. The outer layer encloses masses of cortical cells.

D.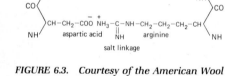

−CH⟨CO / NH⟩CH−CH₂−S−S−CH₂−CH⟨CO / NH⟩CH−
cystine linkage

CH−CH₂−CH₂−COO⁻ ⁺NH₃−CH₂−CH₂−CH₂−CH₂−CH−
glutamic acid   lysine

CH−CH₂−COO⁻ ⁺NH₃−C−NH−CH₂−CH₂−CH₂−CH−
aspartic acid   ‖   arginine
              NH
salt linkage

D. Each cell is made up of carbon, oxygen, nitrogen, hydrogen and sulfur, constituents of 19 different amino acids.

E.
Alanine	Lysine
Arginine	Methionine
Aspartic acid	Phenylalanine
Cystine	Proline
Glutamic	Serine
Glycine	Thereonine
Histidine	Tryptophan
Hydroxylysine	Tyrosine
Isoleucine	Valine
Leucine	

E. 19 Amino Acids (the "building blocks" of wool)

F-1.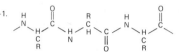

F. These are linked up in polypeptide chains.

F-2.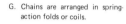

G.

G. Chains are arranged in spring-action folds or coils.

H-1.

H-2.

H. Here we see a cross section of the wool fiber, so skillfully "engineered" that it is more reactive on the outer or convex side of each crimp, and less reactive on the concave side—nature's way of ensuring the fiber's crimp retention.

FIGURE 6.3. Courtesy of the American Wool Council.

shape will remain only until the fabric is dampened again, at which point the molecular structure reverts to its former shape.[8]

3. The cross-linkages in wool are thought to provide the resiliency of the fiber by pulling the fiber back to its original shape after it has been distorted through stretching or folding.

4. The cystine linkages in wool are chemically reactive to such substances as alkalis, bleaches, heat, sunlight, and certain finishing agents such as those used in mothproofing and shrink-resistant finishes. They are thought to be involved in permanent setting.

5. The salt bridges of wool are reactive to acids and dyestuffs. They are thought to be involved in temporary setting.

[8]"What Happens When Setting Wool," *Textile Industries*, 1 (October 1966), p. 344.

Properties of Wool Fibers

Physical Appearance

Color. Wool fibers vary in natural color from white to creamy white to light beige, yellow, brown, and black. Wool may be dyed easily; however, it is difficult to keep white wool snow-white. The fiber tends to yellow from exposure to sunlight and with age. Bleaching is not a satisfactory means of keeping wool white, as chlorine bleaches are harmful to the fiber and bleaching itself tends to cause some yellowing.

Shape. The length of the fiber depends on the breed of sheep from which it comes and on the length of time during which it has been permitted to grow. In general, the range of fiber length is from 1 to 14 or more inches, with finer fibers usually being shorter and coarser fibers usually being longer.

The diameter of the fiber ranges from 8 to 70 microns (1 micron equals 0.00004 inch). Merino fleece fibers are usually about 15 to 17 microns in width. In cross section the fiber is oval or elliptical. The cross section may show three parts: the innermost part is called the *medulla*. Not all wool fibers possess a medulla, which is the section in which the pigment or color is carried and which provides air space. Most finer wools do not have a medulla. The next segment is the *cortex*. Research has shown that the cortex is made up of microscopic fibrils that pack this area. The outer layer is made up of a fine network of small overlapping scales. The scale structure is responsible for the behavior of wool in felting and in shrinkage and for its insulating qualities. (See Figure 6.4.)

The scales on the surface of the fiber overlap "like the tiles on a roof, with the protruding end of the scales pointing toward the fiber tip."[9] Because of the way the scales are arranged, the fiber can move in only one direction. As fibers are placed close together in a mass of fiber, or in yarns, or in fabrics, they entangle with one another. During washing the cloth is compressed and manipulated and the individual fibers are bent. The fiber, being highly elastic, slides through the entanglement but can move only in one direction. As all the fibers exhibit this unidirectional movement, the fibers are drawn closer together, causing the whole structure to become smaller or *shrink*.

Wool fiber possesses one further quality that is important in its physical appearance and behavior: it has a natural crimp, or curly, wavy shape. This crimp increases the bulk and springiness of wool and makes it quite resilient. It also makes wool fiber relatively easy to spin into yarns.

Mixed into wool fleece are a number of *kemp* hairs. Kemp hairs are coarse, straight hairs that are often white and shiny and do not absorb

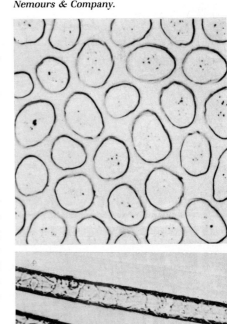
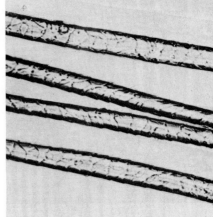

FIGURE 6.4. *Photomicrograph of Merino wool fiber in a cross section and a longitudinal view. Courtesy of E. I. du Pont de Nemours & Company.*

---

[9]W. S. Boston, "Wool," *Encyclopedia of Textiles, Fibers, and Nonwoven Fabrics* (New York: John Wiley & Sons, Inc., 1984), p. 523.

dye easily. A large proportion of kemp hairs lowers the quality of the fleece.

Other Properties

Luster. The luster of wool varies, although sheep's wool does not have a great deal of luster. Luster varies among different breeds of sheep, different sections of the fleece, and the conditions under which the animal has been raised. In general, the luster of poor-quality wool is greater than the luster of better grades of wool.

Density or Specific Gravity. The specific gravity of wool is 1.32. This relatively low density makes wool fabrics feel light in relation to their bulk. The ability of wool fibers to trap air also gives them an ability to provide warmth without excessive weight. This is fortunate since wool is so weak that a large amount of fiber is usually necessary to make fabrics of adequate strength.

Elasticity and Resilience. The elasticity and resilience of wool are excellent. These qualities contribute to the appearance of wool products by giving them very good resistance to, and recovery from, wrinkling. Wrinkles will hang out of wool garments, especially if they are hung in a damp atmosphere, as will creases, pleats, or other shape provided by pressing.

Absorbency and Moisture Regain. Wool is a very absorbent fiber. Wool also gives up its moisture slowly. Paradoxically, wool is also water repellent. Spilled liquids run off wool, because the scale structure of wool inhibits wicking of moisture along the fiber surface. Surface moisture is absorbed slowly. The behavior of wool in relation to moisture can be summarized by saying that wool is naturally water repellent, but upon prolonged exposure to moisture, the fiber does absorb substantial quantities of water. The moisture is held inside the fiber, not on the surface. Furthermore, wool retains its resilience even when wet, so that wool can become wet yet retain the ability to insulate the wearer from cold.

Dimensional Stability. Wool has poor dimensional stability. As mentioned previously, the tendency of wool to shrink and felt can cause fabrics and garments to decrease in size. The shrinkage of wool is progressive. In the first laundering, fabrics stretched in the weaving process tend to relax. But wool will continue to shrink with subsequent launderings if it is not washed in cool water with a minimum of handling.

Consumers should preshrink wool fabrics before sewing unless the fabric is labeled as having been treated to prevent shrinkage. Purchasers of wool ready-to-wear should look for labels indicating shrinkage control. Finishes can be given to wool to render the fabric washable. Such finishes are discussed at length in Chapter 21.

Conductivity of Heat and Electricity. The conductivity of wool of both heat and electricity are low. Both the poor heat conductivity of wool fiber and its ability to trap air between the fibers contribute to its excellent qualities for cold-weather clothing. Even though the electrical conductivity of wool is rated as poor, wool fibers do not build up static electrical charges unless the atmosphere is very dry. The ability of the fiber to absorb moisture improves its conductivity when humidity is present in the atmosphere. For this reason, wool garments sometimes generate static electrical charges indoors in winter when central heating of homes makes them warm and dry.

Combustibility; Effect of Heat. Wool will burn if a flame is held to the fabric, but it burns slowly, and when the flame is removed, the fabric may self-extinguish. The danger of flammability exists, but this factor is not so great as with many other fabrics. Wool can be treated for fire retardancy. Dry heat damages the fiber, producing a negative effect on both appearance and strength.

Wool Fabrics and Their Behavior in Relation to Selected Conditions

Chemical Reactivity. Wool fibers are damaged quickly by strong alkali solutions, even relatively weak alkalis have a deleterious effect on wool. Strong laundry detergents and soaps have "free" alkali added to increase their cleaning power, and extended exposure to this additional alkali may be harmful to wool. Wool fabrics should be washed with special mild detergents.

Acids do not harm wool except in very strong concentrations. This makes it possible to carbonize wool fleece to remove vegetable matter without harming the wool fiber.

Chlorine compounds used for bleaching damage wool. Hydrogen peroxide or sodium perborate bleaches can be used safely. Organic dry-cleaning solvents will not harm the fiber.

Insects. One of the major problems in the care of wool is its susceptibility to damage from insect pests. Moths and carpet beetles are particularly destructive because the chemical structure of the cross-linkages in wool is especially attractive to these insects. Care in the storage of wool is required to minimize attack by insects. Soiled clothing is damaged more readily than are clean fabrics, as the insects may attack the spilled food as well as the wool. Fabrics of wool that have special finishes that prevent moth attack are referred to as being "moth-proofed." Some of these finishes can be applied at the time of dry cleaning. Other moth-repellent substances can be placed in storage containers in closets or sprayed on fabrics. Paradichlorobenzene crystals or napthalene flakes may be used in an airtight container with garments.

Chemicals should be placed above the garments since their vapors are heavier than air.[10]

Microorganisms. Mildew will not form on wool unless the fabric has been stored in a damp condition for an extended period of time. Fabrics should be put away only after they are completely dry.

Environmental Conditions. Exposure to sunlight will cause deterioration of wool, although it is less severely affected than cotton. Sunlight also yellows white wool fabrics.

Age will not affect wool adversely. However, because of their susceptibility to attack by moths, wool fabrics require careful storage.

Care Procedures

Wool fabrics can be either laundered or dry cleaned, although dry cleaning is preferable for wool fabrics that have not been specially finished to make them "washable." Dry cleaning minimizes shrinkage problems. Also, dry-cleaning solvents may include mothproof finishes that will protect wool garments from moth attack during storage.

Fabrics that have been given special finishes to render them "washable" should be laundered according to care directions attached to the fabric. Fabrics without special finishes must be handled gently as a result of the fact that the fabric is weaker wet than dry and also to prevent felting of fibers because of friction. Water temperatures used in washing wool products should be lukewarm, and synthetic detergents may be used. Washing can be done by hand or machine, provided that the wool fabrics are not agitated for more than 3 minutes. Agitation and friction produced in handling wool is more detrimental to the fabric than are high washing temperatures, so that care must be taken to avoid placing undue stress on wool fabrics during laundering. Knitted garments, such as sweaters, should be measured before laundering, and while the garments are drying they can be gently reshaped into their original size.

Wool fabrics should not be dried in an automatic dryer. The pounding action caused by tumbling damp fabrics in the dryer may cause excessive felting shrinkage of the fabrics. The dryer provides all the conditions conducive to felting: heat, moisture, and friction. Drying fabrics flat will prevent strain on any one part of the garment.

Chlorine bleaches must not be applied to wool because this type of bleach will damage the fabric. Hydrogen peroxide may be used for bleaching.

Solvents used for spot and stain removal do not harm wool fabrics. However, care should be taken in the application of spot remover. Ex-

---

[10]"Protecting Woolens Against Clothes Moths and Carpet Beetles," *Bulletin No. 113* (Washington, D.C.: U.S. Department of Agriculture, 1970).

cessive friction or rubbing on the surface of the fabric may cause matting and felting of fibers in the treated spot. Pat the fabric gently rather than rubbing hard.

Because of the detrimental effect of heat on wool fibers, ironing temperatures should not exceed 200°F, and fabrics should always be pressed with a press cloth or steam.

Wool Use

The excellent insulating qualities of wool leads to its use for cold-weather clothing. Winter coats, warm sweaters, and men's and women's suits are frequently made of worsted or woolen fabrics or blends of wool and other fabrics.

Tailored garments utilize the qualities of wool that make it possible to shape the garment through pressing techniques that depend on wool's capacity for shrinkage. By using different kinds of wool yarns and variations in weave, a wide variety of attractive garments and accessories are manufactured from wool.

In the home, wool fabrics are made into carpets, blankets, upholstery fabrics, and sometimes draperies. Special coarse, resilient, durable wool fibers are produced for manufacture into carpets. Blankets of wool are warm without excessive weight and have the advantage of inherent flame retardancy. The durability of upholstery fabrics will depend upon the construction of the yarn and fabric, and those fabrics made from tightly twisted yarns with close, even weaves are most serviceable.

The disadvantages of wool used for apparel and in the home center on the tendency of fabrics to shrink and the susceptibility of wool to moth damage. Fabrics that have been finished to overcome both these problems are available, and appropriate handling during use and care will minimize these disadvantages. A disadvantage of wool for some individuals is that they may have allergic reactions from contact with the fiber. Some wool fabrics may have a rough or "scratchy" feel.

Specialty Hair Fibers

Many hair fibers possess qualities similar to those of wool. These fibers are produced in comparatively small quantities, but they do have an important place in the textile industry, particularly among high-status, prestige clothing items.

Cashmere

Cashmere fiber is obtained from the fleece of the cashmere (or kashmir) goat, an animal that is native to the Himalaya Mountains region of India, China, and Tibet. (See Figure 6.5.) Iran and Iraq also produce cashmere fiber.

The animals are domesticated, and fiber is gathered by combing hairs from the fleece during the shedding season. Only the fine underhair is

FIGURE 6.5. Cashmere goat.

useful for cashmere fabrics, and one goat produces about 4 ounces of usable fiber each year.

The softest fibers are 1½ to 3½ inches in length. Coarser and stiffer fibers range from 2 to 5 inches. The natural color of cashmere is gray, brown, or, less often, white.

Microscopically, cashmere displays a scale structure like that of wool, but the scales are spaced more widely apart. Fibers are finer than are those in wool, about 15 microns in diameter. The cross section of cashmere fibers is round.

The chemical and physical behavior of cashmere is much like that of wool, although cashmere is more quickly damaged by alkalis.

The softness and luster of cashmere combined with its scarcity put this fiber in the category of luxury fibers that are quite expensive. The fiber abrades easily, because of its softness, and since many of these fabrics are constructed with napped or fleecy surfaces, they require careful handling. Sweaters, coatings, and soft luxurious fabrics and yarns account for the largest proportion of the items made from cashmere.

Camel's Hair

The two-humped Bactrian camel of Central Asia is the source of the camel's hair fiber. (See Figure 6.6.) In the spring when the weather begins to warm, the camel begins to shed. (Although some hair is collected at other times of the year, the largest quantity is taken in the spring.) A trailer follows the camel caravans as they move from place to place. As the hair drops, the trailer collects it, placing it in a basket that is carried by the last camel in the caravan. It has been estimated that one camel produces from 5 to 8 pounds of hair each year. When sufficient quantities have been collected, the hair is baled and prepared for shipping.

Within the collected hair are found both fine, soft down or *noils*, and coarse, bristly hairs. The soft noils are used for making cloth. Coarser hairs are separated out before processing.

Under the microscope, camel's hair shows a scale structure similar to that of wool, but the scales are less visible and less distinctly seen. The cortex is distinct; the medulla is discontinuous. Both the cortex and medulla are pigmented. This pigment produces the light brown or tan color associated with camel cloth, and because it is not discolored by oxidation, it cannot be removed by bleaching. Therefore, camel fabrics are usually left in their natural color or are dyed to darker shades.

Camel's hair provides excellent warmth without weight. It is said to have better insulating qualities than any of the other hair fibers. It is a relatively weak fiber and is subject to damage from abrasion because of its softness. Other physical and chemical properties of camel's hair are like those of wool.

FIGURE 6.6. Bactrian camel.

Most fine camel's hair fiber is used for clothing, especially coating fabrics. Like other hair fibers there is great variety in quality of camel's hair fibers, and the consumer must evaluate these products carefully. Because it is easy to dye wool camel color and to blend it with camel's hair, there may be misrepresentation of the final product as "camel's hair" when, in fact, the quantity of camel's hair is relatively low. Camel's hair fabric is expensive and should not be selected for its durability, as it tends to wear readily. Coarse camel's hair is used for industrial fiber, ropes, and paintbrushes.

Mohair

Mohair fiber is taken from the angora goat. (See Figure 6.7.) The United States produces the largest quantity of mohair, much of it in Texas. Other important sources of the fiber are South Africa and Turkey where the angora goat originates.

Goats are sheared in the same way as sheep. Fleece is removed twice a year. Each animal yields from 3 to 5 pounds a year of 4- to 6-inch fiber. To obtain a supply of slightly longer fiber, some goats are sheared only once a year, in which case the fibers are 9 to 12 inches in length.

The natural color or unscoured fleece is yellow to grayish white. In cleaning, 15 to 25 per cent of the weight is removed. The clean fibers are white in color, silky, and fine in feel and appearance. Fibers are graded, with kids' or young goats' fleeces especially valued for their fine-

FIGURE 6.7.   *Angora goat. Courtesy of the United States Department of Agriculture.*

ness. The cross section of the fiber is round, with the medulla being only rarely visible. Small air ducts are present between the cells of the fiber, which give it a light, fluffy feeling. The microscopic appearance of mohair is similar to that of wool.

Most of the physical and chemical properties of mohair are very similar to those of wool. The major differences between wool and mohair are the very high luster of mohair and its slippery, smooth surface. Mohair is especially resistant to abrasion. When viewed under the microscope, mohair shows fewer scales than does wool. As a result, the fiber sheds dust and soil and neither shrinks nor felts as readily as wool. Mohair is easier to launder, as well.

The current uses of mohair stress products, where its luster can be used to good advantage, and these include men's and women's suitings, upholstery fabrics, carpets, and draperies. Novelty yarns, such as looped or bouclé yarns, are often made of mohair, and it is blended with other fiber. (See Figure 6.8.)

The cost of mohair fabrics tends to be higher than that of wool. The quality of mohair can vary a good deal, so the consumer must evaluate mohair products carefully.

Qiviut

Qiviut is the underwool of the domesticated musk ox. (See Figure 6.9.) Herds of musk oxen are cultivated in Alaska where Eskimo women have been taught to spin and knit qiviut into articles for sale. The fiber is similar to cashmere in texture and softness. One-half pound of qiviut will make a large, warm sweater. An equivalent garment in sheep's wool would require 6 pounds of fiber.

FIGURE 6.8. Sweater knitted from mohair yarn. Courtesy of Elite Specialty Yarns, Inc., Lowell, MA.

FIGURE 6.9. Musk ox.

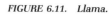

FIGURE 6.10.   *Alpaca.*

FIGURE 6.11.   *Llama.*

Alpaca

Native to Peru, Bolivia, Ecuador, and Argentina, the domesticated alpaca, (Figure 6.10), produces a fleece of fine, strong fibers that have a glossy luster. The alpaca is sheared once every two years in the spring (November and December in the Southern Hemisphere). Hairs average 8 to 12 inches in length and range in color from white to brown to black.

Alpaca fiber is used in suits, dresses, and upholstery fabrics. It may be made into blends with other fibers.

Llama

Another domesticated Andean animal, the llama, (Figure 6.11), produces a fine, lustrous fleece, similar to alpaca. Its colors are predominantly black and brown, but some lighter colors are found. Slightly weaker than alpaca or camel's hair, llama fleece is used by many Indian artisans to produce decorative shawls, ponchos, and other products.

The fibers which are often blended, are used for coatings, suitings, and dress fabrics.

Huarizo and Misti

Llamas and alpacas have been crossbred, and the resulting animals have fleece with many of the same qualities and characteristics as those of the parents. The huarizo has a llama sire and an alpaca dam. The misti has a llama dam and an alpaca sire.

Vicuña

A wild animal, the vicuña lives at very high altitudes in the Andes Mountains. (See Figure 6.12.) Although attempts are being made to domesticate this animal, most of the fiber must be obtained by hunting and killing the vicuña. One vicuña yields 4 ounces of very fine fiber and 10 to 12 ounces of less fine fiber. The Peruvian government sets a limit on the number of vicuña that can be taken in any year, so that the fiber is in very short supply.

One of the softest fibers known, vicuña is also the costliest. A vicuña coat will be comparable in cost to a good fur coat. Its use is limited to luxury items. The natural color—a light tan or chestnut brown—is usually retained, as the fiber is hard to dye.

Guanaco

Another wild animal, the guanaco, has been domesticated successfully. Although supplies of the fiber are more readily available than vicuña, it remains a relatively expensive fiber.

FIGURE 6.12. Vicuña herd. Photograph by W. L. Franklin.

It has a soft, fine fleece of reddish-brown color. Often blended, guanaco is similar to alpaca in its qualities.

Fur Fiber

Fiber from the pelts of the fur-bearing animals is sometimes blended with other wool fibers. It provides interest, and softness, in texture. Fur fibers from animals such as the beaver, fox, mink, chinchilla, rabbit, and the like are used.

Angora rabbits have long, fine, silky, white hair. These rabbits are raised in France, Italy, Japan, and the United States. The fiber is obtained by combing or clipping the rabbits. Angora rabbit fiber is exceptionally fine (13 microns) and is very slippery and hard to spin. Angora is used chiefly in novelty items and is often knitted. The fibers tend to slip out of the yarns and increase in length on the surface of fabrics so that some persons have the mistaken notion that angora hair "grows."

Fur Products Labeling Act of 1951

Relatively small quantities of fur fibers are used in the production of textiles. If fur fiber has been removed from the skin and incorporated in a textile product, it is designated as "fur fiber" and is subject to regulation under the Textile Fiber Products Information Act and the Wool Products Labeling Act. Fur that is attached to the animal skin is regulated by the Fur Products Labeling Act of 1951. This legislation requires that all fur products carry the true English name of the fur-bearing animal from which the fur comes. It also requires that furs be labeled with the country of their origin.

No fur may be given a trademark name of a fictitious or nonexistent animal. If furs have been worn or used by the ultimate consumer, they must be designated as "used fur." When fur is damaged from natural causes or from processing, it must be labeled as containing damaged fur. Any dyeing or bleaching or other treatments given to artificially color the fur must be disclosed.

Cow Hair and Horsehair

Cow hair is sometimes blended with wool in low-grade fabrics used for carpeting and blankets and in felts. Horsehair is utilized as a filling or stuffing material for mattresses and upholstered pieces. In the past, it was woven into a stiff braid for use in millinery or dressmaking, but this use has been replaced, for the most part, by synthetic fibers. Rubberized horsehair has been used to make carpet underlays.

History of Silk Culture   Silk

Silk originates in China, the first habitat of the silkworm, which grew wild and lived on the leaves of a species of mulberry tree. Although some animal hair and flax fibers can grow to considerable length, silk is the only natural fiber that is hundreds of meters long.

Silk is made by the silkworm as it builds its cocoon. The substance is *extruded* from its body in one continuous thread from beginning to end. It is possible to unwind the cocoons and obtain long, silk filaments. The Chinese discovered this process and, recognizing the potential value of the fiber it produced, guarded the method closely for hundreds of years. Silk has a natural beauty, and its history has been surrounded by legends. Chinese folklore credits the discovery of silk to Princess Si Ling Chi, who reigned about 2650 B.C. According to legend, after watching a silkworm spin its cocoon in her garden, she attempted to unwind the long filaments. After much experimentation she succeeded. She instructed her serving women in the art of weaving rich and beautiful fabrics from the long, silk threads. So grateful for her discovery were the Chinese that they transformed Princess Si Ling Chi into a goddess and made her the patron deity of weaving.[11]

History agrees with legend at least insofar as the approximate dates for the first use of silk by the Chinese. In spite of the close guarding of the secret of *sericulture* or the controlled production of silk, other countries managed, often by somewhat devious means, to obtain silkworms. The Japanese supposedly abducted four Chinese maidens who were experts in sericulture and forced them to disclose the process. Another princess carried silkworm eggs and the seeds of the mulberry tree in her headdress when she left China to marry a prince of another kingdom. Even as late as the sixth century A.D., the secrets of silk manufacture were sought by the Byzantine emperor Justinian who sent two monks to the East to discover how to produce and weave these handsome fabrics. The monks returned from a lengthy trip bringing back silkworm eggs and mulberry seeds in their hollow bamboo walking sticks. From these seeds a flourishing silk industry developed in Byzantium. The cultivation of the silkworm spread to Italy and later to France.[12]

Silk Production

Cultivation of the Silkworm

Silk is the only natural filament fiber that has significant commercial value. Produced by a caterpillar known as a "silkworm," silk can be obtained either from cultivated silkworms *(Bombyx mori)* or wild species.

Silk from wild species is limited in quantity and produces a coarser, stronger, short fiber known as *tussah silk*. Tussah silk has short fibers because the cocoons from which it is taken have been broken or pierced. When wild silk is spun by caterpillars that feed on oak leaves, the silk is light brown or tan in color and cannot be bleached.

By far the largest quantity of silk is obtained through sericulture, or the controlled growth of domesticated silkworms to produce the silk fiber. Whether the silkworms be domesticated or wild, they go through four basic stages of development.

1. Laying of the eggs by the silk moth.
2. Hatching of the eggs into caterpillars.
3. Spinning of a cocoon by the caterpillar.
4. Emerging of the silk moth from the cocoon.

The science of sericulture has been perfected over many thousands of years. Today all stages of development are carefully controlled and

[11]Ethel Lewis, *The Romance of Textiles* (New York: Macmillan Publishing Company, 1937), pp. 31 ff.
[12]Ibid.

only the healthiest eggs, worms, and moths are used for the production of silk. (See Figure 6.13.)

Selected moths of superior size lay from four hundred to six hundred eggs or seeds on prepared cards or strips of cloth. Each seed is about the size of a pinhead. These eggs can be stored in cool, dry places until the manufacturer wishes to begin their incubation.

Incubation is done in a mildly warm atmosphere and requires about 30 days. At the end of this time the silkworms hatch. They are about one eighth of an inch in length. The young silkworms require constant care and carefully controlled diets. Shredded or chopped young mulberry leaves are fed to the worms five times each day. Worms that appear to be weak or deformed are discarded, and the areas in which they are grown are kept scrupulously clean. For about a month the worm grows, shedding its skin four times. When fully grown, worms are about 3½ inches in length.

FIGURE 6.13. (Upper left) *silk moth laying eggs;* (upper right) *silkworms on a bed of mulberry leaves;* (lower left) *silkworm beginning to spin cocoon;* (lower right) *completed cocoon. Photographs courtesy of the Japan Silk Association.*

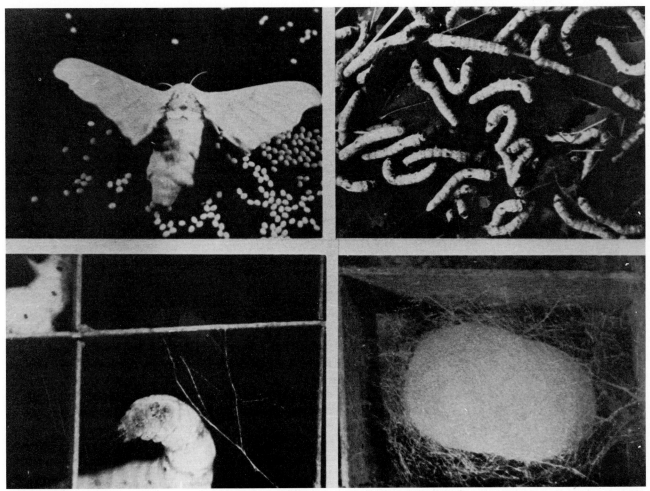

When its size and activity show that the worm is about ready to begin to spin a cocoon, the silkworm is transferred to a surface of twigs or straw. From two sacs located in the lower jaw, the worm extrudes a substance made up of two strands of silk (fibroin) and a gummy material (sericin) that holds them together. Moving its head in the shape of a figure eight, the worm surrounds itself with a cocoon of perhaps 1,000 meters of fiber. The completed cocoon is about the size of a peanut shell and takes 2 to 3 days to spin. If the worm is permitted to live, it will change into a pupa or chrysalis and then to a moth. After 2 weeks the moth breaks through the cocoon and emerges, mates, lays eggs, and begins the cycle again.

Only those moths selected as breeding stock are permitted to complete the cycle. These are selected from the largest and heaviest cocoons. The remainder of the cocoons is subjected to dry heat that kills the pupa.

Occasionally two silkworms will spin a cocoon together. This produces a cocoon made of a double strand of silk and is known as *doupion* silk.[13]

Reeling of Silk

The whole, unbroken cocoons are sorted according to color, texture, size, shape, and other factors that will affect the quality of the fiber. Reeling of silk is, to a large extent, a hand operation done in a factory called a *filature*. Several cocoons are placed in a container of water of about 140°F. This warm water serves to soften the gum or sericin that holds the filaments of silk together. Very little gum is actually removed in reeling. The outer fibers are coarse and short and not useful in filament silk. They are separated and are used for spun silk, which is made from short fiber lengths.

The filaments from four or more cocoons are held together to form a strand of yarn. As the reeling continues, a skilled operator adds or lets off fibers as needed to make a smoother strand of uniform size. A number of skeins of silk weighing 50 to 100 grams each are combined into bundles. Each bundle is called a *book* and weighs from 5 to 10 pounds. These are packaged into bales for shipping.

Locale of Production

Because the culture of silkworms requires so much hand labor, sericulture has been most successful in countries where labor is less expensive. Major silk-producing areas include China, India, Southeast Asia, and Japan. European countries such as France and Italy that once had thriving silk industries no longer produce a great deal of silk fiber. These countries may still weave silk fabrics, but most of the silk fiber is produced elsewhere. No silk is produced in the United States.

Silk imports are in the form of raw silk in bales, spun silk and thrown

---

[13]*Doupioni,* in Italian.

silk yarns, woven or knitted fabrics, and completed garments or household textiles. In 1984 more than 6,000 bales (weighing 132 pounds each) of raw silk were utilized in the United States. Almost 266,000 pounds of spun and 160,000 pounds of thrown silk yarns were imported along with upwards of 2.5 million square yards of pure silk fabrics. No reliable statistics are kept that record the total quantities of imported ready-to-wear and other manufactured articles made of silk.[14]

Silk Yarns

The making of silk filament yarns is called *throwing*. Reeled silk filaments can be made into yarns immediately. Short, staple-length silk fibers must be spun. Short outside fibers of the silkworm's cocoon, the inner fibers from the cocoon, and the fiber from pierced cocoons are known as *frisons* and are made into spun silk yarns. Fibers are cut into fairly uniform lengths, combed, and twisted into yarns in the same way that other staple fibers are spun.

Gum Removal

The sericin or gum that holds the silk filaments in place in the cocoon is softened but not removed in reeling. This material makes up about 25 per cent of the weight of raw silk. It is removed before throwing, after throwing, or after the fabric has been woven. A soap solution is used to wash the gum from the silk. In some silk fabrics, called "raw silk," the sericin has not been removed.

Regulation of Silk Weighting

During the latter part of the nineteenth century, the technique of weighting was employed extensively to add body and weight to silk fabrics after removal of the gum. In passing silk through a solution of metallic salts, the salts are absorbed by the fiber, with a corresponding increase in the weight of the fabric. Silk can absorb more than its own weight in metallic salts, so that this excess weight on the fiber will, eventually, cause the fabric to break.

This practice had become so widespread that a good deal of poor-quality fabric was being sold. Because the buyer could not tell from its appearance or hand that the silk had been weighted, the Federal Trade Commission, in 1938, began overseeing silk weighting by passing its pure silk regulation.

These FTC regulations are still in effect even though little or no weighting is done at present. The regulations require that fabrics labeled "silk" or "pure dye silk" contain from 0 to 10 per cent of weighting. All silk fabrics that have more than 10 per cent weighting must be labeled as weighted silk, unless they are black in color. Black silks are able to hold a greater quantity of weighting than are other colors without degradation, and, so, black silks can be weighted up to 15 per cent.

---

[14]Data supplied by the International Silk Association, U.S.A.

Properties of Silk Fibers

Physical Appearance

Color. The natural color of cultivated silk is off-white to cream. Wild silk is brown.

Shape. In microscopic cross section silk is triangular in shape. (See Figure 6.14.) The double silk filaments lie with the flat sides of the triangles together.

The fiber has a smooth, transparent rodlike shape with occasional swelling or irregularities along its length. It is fine, having a diameter of 9 to 11 microns, and filaments may be as short as 300 meters or as long as 1,000 meters. Individual filaments as long as 3,000 meters have been measured.

Luster. The luster of degummed silk is high, but not so "bright" as man-made fibers with round cross sections.

Other Properties

Strength or Tenacity. Silk is one of the strongest of the natural fibers. (Its tenacity is 2.8 to 5.2 g/d.) Its wet strength is slightly less than its dry strength.

Density or Specific Gravity. The specific gravity of silk of 1.25 is less than that of cellulose fibers and is similar to that of wool.[15] Lightweight fabrics can be made of silk because of the fine diameter of the fiber and its high tenacity.

Elasticity; Resilience. The elasticity of silk is good and its resilience is medium. Creases will hang out of silk, but its wrinkle recovery is slower and not as good as that of wool.

Absorbency; Moisture Regain. The absorbency of silk is good (the moisture regain is 11 per cent), making it a comfortable fiber to wear. Although silk is more difficult to dye than is wool, it can be printed and dyed easily to bright, clear colors if appropriate dyes are used.

Dimensional Stability. The dimensional stability of silk is good. Silk does not tend to stretch or shrink to any significant extent.

Heat and Electrical Conductivity. The heat conductivity of silk is low so that densely woven fabrics can be relatively warm. However, because very sheer, lightweight fabrics can be woven from silk, it can be used for lightweight, summer clothing.

---

[15]"Identification of Fibers in Textile Materials," *Bulletin X-156*. Wilmington, Del.: E. I. du Pont de Nemours, 1961. Varying sources list specific gravity of silk that ranges from 1.25 to 1.34.

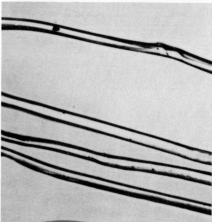

FIGURE 6.14 *Photomicrograph of degummed silk fiber in a cross section and a longitudinal view. Courtesy of E. I. du Pont de Nemours & Company.*

The electrical conductivity of silk is poor and silk tends to build up static electricity charges, especially in dry atmospheres.

Combustibility; Effect of Heat. When placed in a direct flame, silk will burn, but when the flame is removed, it will not continue to support combustion. Therefore, silk is not considered to be an especially combustible fabric. Like wool, silk is damaged by dry heat and should be ironed damp, at low temperatures and using a press cloth.

Effect of Selected Conditions on Silk

Chemical Properties. Like other protein fibers, silk is sensitive to the action of alkalis but is damaged more slowly than is wool. Acids will harm silk more quickly than they harm wool. Chlorine bleach deteriorates the fiber, but hydrogen peroxide or other peroxygen bleaches can be used. Organic chemical solvents used in dry cleaning will not affect silk. Perspiration will cause deterioration of the fabric. Perspiration can have a negative effect on dyestuffs, causing discoloration after repeated exposure; therefore, silk fabrics should always be cleaned before they are stored.

Insects and Microorganisms. Mildew is not a problem with silk. Moths do not harm clean silk, but carpet beetles will attack the fabric.

Environmental Conditions. Sunlight deteriorates silk even more rapidly than wool, causing white fabrics to yellow. Age will lead to eventual deterioration of fabric strength. Silk fabrics should be stored away from light. Antique fabrics should be sealed off from the air.

Weighting of silk causes it to crack, split, and deteriorate much more quickly than would otherwise be true. (See Figure 6.15.) Historic costumes made of silk before silk weighting was introduced are still in good condition. Weighted silk garments, made in later times, break apart into shreds.

FIGURE 6.15. Silk fabric from the skirt of an historic costume of the 1890s that has deteriorated as a result of silk weighting.

Care Procedures

Most silk garments should be dry cleaned for best results. Some of the dyestuffs used on silk are susceptible to bleeding or loss of the dyestuff into the washing water so that dry cleaning is preferable to laundering. Small items such as silk scarves or other accessories made of silk can be laundered if mild detergents and lukewarm water are used and if the fabrics are handled carefully. Chlorine bleaches should never be used on silk fabrics. If silk fabrics must be bleached, hydrogen peroxide can be used.

Silk fabrics should be stored away from direct sunlight, both to avoid yellowing of white fabrics and to prevent loss of strength. Long-term storage of silk wedding gowns or other items is best done in containers that are sealed against air and carpet beetles.

When ironing silk, protect the fabric with a dry press cloth. Keep ironing temperatures low, at 300°F, or lower. Test silk fabrics to be sure they will not watermark before using steam or a damp press cloth. Although badly wrinkled silk fabrics will require pressing, many creases will hang out of silk fabrics without ironing.

Uses

The beauty of silk fabrics is legendary. For many centuries, silk was synonymous with luxury and was used for garments worn on feast days, festivals, and other occasions of great importance. Wall hangings of silk were used to decorate the homes of the wealthy, and carpets woven of silk were used in the homes of the rich in Persia and China.

At present, the relatively smaller supplies of silk, as compared with synthetics, have tended to maintain the position of silk as a "luxury" fiber. Silk is relatively expensive and is used chiefly for dresses, blouses, and other garments and accessories that sell at fairly high prices.

Silk may also be found in some high-priced drapery and upholstery fabrics. The performance of silk fabrics in these uses is rather poor. Upholstery fabrics of silk are often made in weaves that show up the luster of the fabric but abrade rather easily. Sunlight will deteriorate drapery fabrics of silk. Draperies made of silk should be lined with some other fabric to protect the silk from constant exposure to the sun.

Table 6.2 offers a comparison of the two major protein fibers, silk and wool.

Regenerated Protein or Azlon Fibers

With the commercially successful regeneration of cellulosic fibers, research was initiated to find suitable protein materials for regeneration in the hope of creating fibers with the highly desirable qualities of wool. As a base material, a protein was required that was readily available, as well as one that had a chemical structure similar to that of wool. Milk was selected, and in 1904 the first method for making filaments from the protein of milk (casein) was disclosed, but the filaments were too

Table 6.2 Comparison of the Characteristics of the Protein Fibers, Wool and Silk

	Wool	Silk
Specific gravity	1.32	1.25 (boiled off)
Tenacity (g/d)		
Dry	1.0–1.7	2.4–5.1
Wet	0.8–1.6	1.8–4.2
Moisture regain	about 15%	10–11%
Resiliency	excellent	good
Burning	burns slowly, sometimes self-extinguishing when flame is removed	burns slowly, sometimes self-extinguishing when flame is removed
Conductivity of		
Heat	good insulator, low conductivity	moderate
Electricity	rather low, builds up static electricity	rather low, builds up static electricity
Resistance to damage from		
Fungi	good	good
Insects	poor, attacked by moths, carpet beetles	fair, not attacked by moths, but attacked by carpet beetles
Prolonged exposure to sunlight	yellows, loses strength eventually	yellows and degrades
Acids	resists action of mild or dilute acids, damaged by strong acids	more readily damaged by acids than wool, more resistant than cotton
Alkalis	damaged by even mildly alkaline substances	damaged by even mildly alkaline substances

brittle to be used. In the 1930s, a usable fiber known as Lanital® was developed in Italy and one called Aralac® was made in the United States. Since that time other regenerated protein fibers have been made from corn, peanuts, and soybeans.

Regenerated protein fibers had a pleasant, soft handle, but their strength was poor and their lack of durability presented a problem. Some of the milk-based proteins also developed an unpleasant odor when wet.

These fibers are only of historic significance as they are not now being produced, the one exception being Chinon®, a graft fiber of milk protein and polyacrylonitrile. Chinon® is shown in the *Textile Organon* list of man-made fibers for 1985 as being manufactured in Ireland by a Japanese company. It does not appear to be distributed in the United States.

Table 6.3 depicts the period of production of those fibers and the country in which each was produced. The generic name for the regenerated protein groups is *azlon*. Worldwide shortages of foodstuffs, especially protein foods, make it unlikely that new regenerated protein fibers will be developed.

Table 6.3 Regenerated Protein Fibers

Substance	Trade Name	Country	Dates
Milk protein	Aralac®	United States	1939–1948
	Fibrolane®	Britain	discontinued in 1965
	Lanital®	Italy	1937 into 1940s
	Merinova®	Italy	discontinued in late 1960s
Milk protein grafted with acrylic	Chinon®	Japan	early 1970s to present
Peanut protein	Ardil®	Britain	1938–1957
Corn protein	Vicara®	United States	1948–1957
Soybean protein	Ford Motor Company experimented with for car seats		never in major production

BERGEN, W. B. *Wool Handbook.* Plainfield, N.J.: Textile Book Service, 1963.

CHADWICK, A. "Silk," *Textiles,* 6 (October 1977), p. 58.

"Fibers Under the Microscope. No. 1—Silk," *Textiles,* 10 (Autumn 1981), 74.

"Flame Resistance of Wool Fabrics," *Textile Topics,* 13 (November 1984), p. 1.

FRANKLIN, W. L. "Biology, Ecology and Relationship to Man of the South American Camelids," in M. Mares and H. H. Genoways, eds., *Mammalian Biology in South America,* p. 457. Pittsburgh: University of Pittsburgh Press, 1981.

FRANKLIN, W. L. "Living with Guanacos—Camel of South America," *National Geographic,* 160 (1981), p. 63.

FRANKLIN, W. L. "Turnabout in the Andes," *International Wildlife,* 13 (May–June 1975), p. 42.

Homespun to Factory Made: Woolen Textiles in America, 1776–1876. North Andover, Mass.: Merrimack Valley Textile Museum, 1977.

HYDE, N. "The Queen of Textiles," *National Geographic,* 165 (January 1984), p. 2.

LEWIS, ETHEL. *The Romance of Textiles.* New York: Macmillan Publishing Company, 1937.

"The Musk Ox Project," *American Fabrics and Fashions,* No. 95 (Fall 1972), p. 40.

"Natural Fibers: Silk," *American Fabrics and Fashions,* No. 124/125 (Fall/Winter 1982–83), p. 48.

"Natural Fibers: Wool, Camel, Cashmere, Angora, Mohair," *American Fabrics and Fashions,* No. 124/125 (Fall/Winter 1982–83), p. 45.

RUSSELL, K. P. "The Specialty Animal Fibres," *Textiles,* 6 (February 1977), p. 8.

"Spun Silk," *CIBA Review,* 2 (1967).

STINCHECUM, A. M. "Harris Tweed: An Island Legend," *American Fabrics and Fashions,* No. 129 (Fall 1983), p. 20.

STOCKWELL, J. "American Woolen Mills and Wool from American Sheep," *American Fabrics and Fashions,* No. 129 (Fall 1983), p. 32.

VARRON, A. "The Origins and Use of Silk," *CIBA Review,* No. 11 (July 1938), p. 350.

WEIBEL, A. C. *Two Thousand Years of Textiles.* New York: Pantheon Books, 1952.

"Wool," *CIBA Review,* 6 (1962).

Recommended References

Inorganic, Metallic, and Carbon Fibers

The small number of fibers that can be classified as mineral fibers might also be called inorganic fibers, because these fibers lack carbon, the essential element in the chemical composition of organic fibers. Of these fibers, only asbestos is found in the fibrous state. Glass and metallic fibers are considered to be man-made fibers because they are subjected to a reformation to make them into fibrous form.

Asbestos

Asbestos fiber is obtained from mineral deposits. As it is naturally fireproof, it has been used alone or in blends to make textile products in which fire resistance was important, for example, in fire curtains for theaters, insulating materials, and household products such as ironing board covers or pot holders.

Continued inhalation of asbestos fiber can cause serious lung disease, and asbestos fiber is considered to be carcinogenic. For this reason the use of asbestos fiber is being limited to products in which persons are not exposed to the fiber. The consumer, therefore, is unlikely to encounter new products made from asbestos.

Glass Fiber

During World War I, the Germans found that they were running short of asbestos fiber. In an effort to find a substitute fiber that was noncombustible, they attempted to make fibers from glass, with only a limited success.

Following World War I, researchers continued to look into ways of using glass to produce fibers. This technology had been sufficiently advanced by the late 1930s, when the Owens-Corning Glass Company initiated the mass production of glass fiber.

Glass fiber is made from glass that has been melted and extruded into long, fine filaments. Glass is made from silica sand and limestone, plus small amounts of other constituents such as soda ash, borax, and aluminum hydroxide. The quantities of these ingredients are varied depending on the qualities desired in the glass fiber.

Production of Glass Fiber

Glass fiber is produced in both continuous filament form and in staple lengths. Selected ingredients are mixed together, and that mixture is melted in a high-temperature furnace. Molten glass is then drawn from the furnace in the form of filaments, the diameter of which is controlled by the viscosity of the glass melt and the rate of extrusion. (See Figure 7.1.)

If staple fiber lengths are required, an air jet "cuts" the filaments and pulls the glass onto a revolving drum from which they are gathered into a strand. Filament fibers are wound onto a spool by high-speed winders. Bare glass fibers have poor abrasion resistance, so a sizing or lubricating material is applied to fibers to provide some degree of protection. Fibers made of glass are subject to the usual textile processes for making yarns and for weaving.

Properties of Glass Fiber

Physical Appearance of Glass Fiber

Under the microscope, glass fibers look like small glass rods (which is just what glass fibers are). The fiber diameter is determined by the size of the orifice through which it is extruded. Size is selected accord-

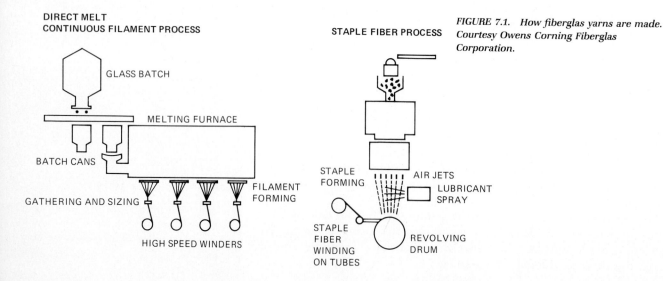

FIGURE 7.1. How fiberglas yarns are made. Courtesy Owens Corning Fiberglas Corporation.

ing to the end use of the fiber. Finer fibers are more flexible and have certain other advantages that are discussed later.

The longitudinal view of the fiber has a very smooth, round surface that produces a high luster. The fiber is colorless, unless a ceramic pigment has been added to the glass melt before it is formed into fibers.

Properties

Strength or Tenacity. Glass fiber has exceptionally high breaking strength and has been called the strongest fiber. Nevertheless, one of the major problems encountered in glass fabrics is their lack of flex abrasion resistance. They tend to break where creased and to wear at points where the fabric rubs against other objects.

Density or Specific Gravity. Glass fibers have a specific gravity of from 2.5 to 2.7, which causes fabrics made from glass fibers to feel heavy. When made into draperies, glass fabrics must be supported with curtain rods that will withstand this increased weight.

Dimensional Stability and Resiliency. Glass has excellent dimensional stability but lacks resilience and stretch. At the same time, its ability to recover from strain is excellent, and, therefore, glass fiber has excellent wrinkle resistance.

Absorbency. Glass fiber is completely nonabsorbent and, therefore, has no affinity for dyes. For best colorfastness, color can be added to the molten glass before it is spun by incorporating ceramic pigment into the glass melt. Manufacturers, however, prefer to add color later, so as to retain flexibility in producing fabrics in colors and patterns that are fashionable. A process called *coronizing* has been developed that enables glass fiber to be colored and improves the hand, softness, and dimensional stability of glass fibers.

Coronizing is done in three stages. First, a silica dispersion is impregnated onto the fabric. The silica material helps to hold the weave firm and decreases yarn slippage. In the second step, the fabric is heat-set with a slight crimp, which improves the hand. The heat treatment also causes the silica to adhere more closely. From this stage the fabric passes into a water bath that holds pigment for color and a resin that will bind the pigment to the fabric. A final treatment is given to fasten the binding resin, and the fabric is dried.

Heat and Electrical Conductivity. Glass fiber conducts neither heat nor electricity. For this reason it is used in staple form in a variety of insulation materials.

Effect of Heat, Combustibility. The fiber is completely noncombustible. When held in a flame, the finish of the fabric will darken as the pigments and resins used in finishing are destroyed, but the fibers, yarns, and woven structure of the fabric will remain intact. Glass fiber softens at 700°C or 1350°F or above.

Behavior of Glass Fiber in Relation to Selected Conditions

Chemical Reactivity. Acids do not generally affect glass fiber; however, alkalis can have a deleterious effect. Organic solvents do not affect the fiber, but some dry-cleaning solvents will adversely affect resin finishes used on glass fibers. Chlorine bleach does not harm glass fiber, but bleaching is not required because the fibers do not discolor or stain.

Resistance to Insects, Microorganisms, Sunlight, and Aging. Glass fiber is attacked by neither mildew nor insect pests. Sunlight does not damage the fabric, nor is it harmed by aging.

Care Procedures. Glass fiber fabrics should not be dry cleaned, as the tumbling that fabrics undergo in a dry-cleaning machine may damage glass fiber fabrics. Broken fibers will contaminate other fabrics cleaned with glass fabric. As has been mentioned before, some dry-cleaning solvents will damage resin finishes given to some glass fabrics. Hand laundering is the recommended method of cleaning. As a general rule, items made from glass fiber should not be laundered in a washing machine as the action of the washer may cause some fiber breakage. These broken fibers remain in the washer and may be picked up by other clothing during subsequent launderings. When clothing in which the fibers are embedded is worn, the small bits of glass can cause severe skin irritations. For the same reasons, glass fabric should not be tumble dried.

Instead, glass fiber fabrics can be hand washed in soapy water or detergent and rinsed. In summer, drapery fabrics can be hung on a clothesline outside and rinsed off with a garden hose. Soil will be removed easily, as the fiber is totally nonabsorbent and all soil is held on the surface of the fabric. When glass fiber fabrics are hung to dry, they should be supported at several points to avoid putting too much pressure on the fabric at one place. Glass fiber fabrics do not require ironing. Characteristics of glass fiber are summarized in Table 7.1.

Uses

Glass fiber is not used for wearing apparel primarily because, as the ends of the fibers break, they scratch or irritate the skin and also because of its poor resistance to abrasion, lack of absorbency, and lack of stretch. For the most part, glass fiber is utilized in draperies, curtains, lamp shades, window shades, and table linens. Industrial uses are more varied, with glass fiber being utilized for products in aerospace, construction, electrical industries, transportation, recreation, packaging, and filtration and for insulation purposes.

Table 7.1 Chart of Selected Characteristics of Glass Fiber

Specific gravity	2.54
Tenacity (g/d)	
Dry	6.3 to 9.6
Wet	5.4 to 6.0
Moisture regain	none
Resiliency	very good
Burning	will not burn; softens at 1350°F
Conductivity	
Heat	low
Electricity	low
Resistance to damage from	
Fungi	excellent
Insects	excellent
Prolonged exposure to sunlight	excellent
Acids	attacked only by hot phosphoric acid and by hydrofluoric acid
Alkalis	attacked by strong alkalis and by hot solutions of weak alkalis

Manufacturers of glass fiber are continuing to experiment with modifications of glass fiber that would make it useful for additional products. *Beta glass fiber*, manufactured by Owens-Corning, has an exceptionally fine diameter—as little as 3 microns. This low-diameter fiber is more flexible and has better abrasion resistance. The manufacturer suggests that it may eventually prove useful in new products.

Other Inorganic Fibers

Several other types of fibers have been developed for use in the aerospace and aircraft industries. These fibers are not used for commercial textile products for the home or in garments. They include the following:

1. *Aluminum silicate fibers.* Used in high-temperature insulation, filters. Spinning is similar to that of glass fiber.
2. *Ceramic fibers.* Used in the aerospace program or in aircraft. A modification of the viscose process is used to spin a fiber with a proportion of cellulose and of metal oxides. The cellulose is burned off to yield ceramic fiber.
3. *High-purity silica fibers.* Produced by purifying glass of specified composition through an acid leaching treatment, the resulting fibers are composed of 99 per cent silica. These fibers will withstand very high temperatures.
4. *Silicon carbide fibers.* These fibers are used as reinforcement materials in resins, some ceramics, and metals.
5. *Boron fibers.* Made by depositing boron vapor onto fine tungsten wire, these fibers have uses in reinforcement, especially of aluminum. Cloth made in part from boron fibers was used in the drill stems for collecting lunar rock samples during NASA's moon mission.

Metallic Fibers

Metallic fibers were the first man-made fibers. Gold and silver "threads" have long been used to decorate costly garments, tapestries, carpets, and the like. These threads were made either by cutting thin sheets of metal into narrow strips and weaving these strips into decorative patterns or by winding a thin filament of metal around a central core of another material.

Examination of historic costumes and fabrics reveals the disadvantage of using metals in this way. Except for gold, the metals tended to tarnish and become discolored. Threads were relatively weak and broke readily. Durability was limited, and, of course, the cost of precious metals was very high.

Fashion fabrics today make use of a wide variety of metallic fibers that are both inexpensive and decorative. Other metallic fibers are used for purely practical purposes. Many decorative metallic fibers are made in the form of large monofilaments. These are discussed later under the heading of "Monofilament Yarns" in Chapter 14.

Forming fibers from metal is difficult; therefore, metal fibers are largely limited to those made from steel (carbon, stainless, and low-alloy types); iron, nickel, and cobalt-based superalloys. These particular metals lend themselves more readily to fiber formation. The manufacture of fibers from metal is usually done by one of three methods. A rod of metal may be used as the starting material, and from this rod fine-dimension metal wire is drawn to form fibers. Another method begins with the formation of metal foil that is sheared or slit into fibers. Metal as a substance does not lend itself well to the traditional method of forming man-made fibers from a liquid melt; however, research has resulted in the development of some specialized techniques by which this can be done.

Most applications of metal fibers are for industry and the aerospace industry where such products as filters, seals, abrasives, and insulation are used. The automotive industry uses metal fibers in products such as tires or brake linings. Some limited applications of metal fibers are made in consumer products, particularly in certain household textile products. Superfine filaments of stainless steel and aluminum are made and are added to fabrics in any one of a number of ways. Sometimes metal fibers are used as the core of yarns, sometimes they are wrapped around other core yarns, and sometimes they are used alone. Steel and copper and aluminum fibers are being blended into some industrial carpets where they cut down on static electricity buildup and have the side effect of decreasing flammability. As the heat of a fire increases, the metallic fibers conduct some of the heat away from the fire, thereby decreasing the heat of the flame. This tends to slow the rate of burning or to lower temperatures below the kindling point. Other projected end uses for metal fibers include upholstery, blankets, and work clothing and in blends with polyester for hospital gowns. Trademark names of some metal fibers include Brunsmet® (stainless steel), Hudstat®, Metlon F® and Fairtex®.

Carbon Fibers

Carbon fibers are also known as graphite fibers. Like other fibers discussed in this chapter, carbon fibers find their major application in industrial use.

Manufacture

Graphite fibers are made from rayon or polyacrylonitrile fibers that are treated with heat in four separate stages under carefully controlled conditions. The final product is a fiber from which all of the elements but carbon have been driven off.

The Japanese firm Mitsubishi recently announced that it is producing industrial-grade carbon fibers from coal tar pitch. Because the starting material is readily available and relatively inexpensive, it is expected that these fibers can be produced much more cheaply than can those made from rayon or polyacrylonitrile.[1]

[1]*Daily News Record,* December 20, 1984, p. 12.

Characteristics

Carbon fibers are black in color, with a silky appearance. They have a stiff hand, possess high strength, and are light in weight.

Uses

Graphite fibers are used in many of the same ways that glass and high-strength polyamide fibers are used. Graphite fibers have been used in light-weight structures for aircraft and spacecraft and as brake discs for jet airplanes. Graphite fibers see use in such diverse areas as sporting goods (Figure 7.2), the construction industry, the automotive industry, and medicine. For example, the spinnaker pole of the yacht *Intrepid* contained 23 miles of graphite yarn. Golf club handles have been made with graphite fibers, and tennis racquets and fishing poles are made of graphite. Graphite fibers are used for the reinforcement of bridges and buildings, and graphite materials have been used for implantation to replace bone.

Because inorganic and carbon fibers have less use in ready-to-wear and household textiles, they are generally assigned a position of less

Summary

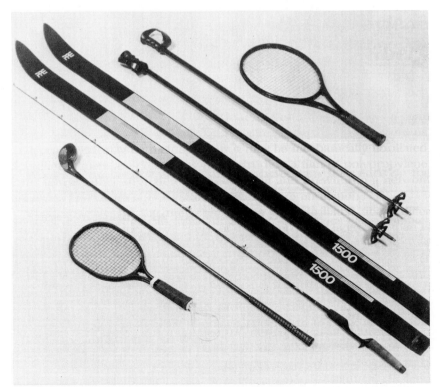

FIGURE 7.2. *A variety of sports equipment that is made using graphite fibers. Courtesy of Hercules Aerospace Products Group.*

importance in the study of textiles. Except for glass fiber, they are not of major interest to the average consumer. These fibers, however, do demonstrate clearly the enormous range of textile fiber uses in a technological society.

Recommended References

ANSELL. M. P., C. A. S. HILL, and C. ALLGOOD. "Architectural PTFE-Coated Glass Fabrics—Their Structure and Limitations," *Textile Research Journal*, 53 (November 1983), p. 692.

BARRY, G. F. "Static Control Metal Yarns in Carpets," *Modern Textiles*, 54 (January 1973), p. 46.

BROWNELL, J. E., JR. "Fiber Glass: Looking to 1980," *Modern Textiles*, 58 (January 1977), p. 35.

"Carbon Fibres," *Textiles*, vol. 4 (January 1975), p. 2.

"Chemical Warfare Fabrics: New Textile Market?" *Textile World*, 131 (September 1981), p. 115.

DENHAM, M. "Textile Glass," *Modern Textiles*, 61 (November 1980), p. 8.

GRAHAM, C. O., and G. F. RUPPENICKER. "Cotton Outdoor Fabrics Reinforced with Glass Fiber," *Textile Research Journal*, 53 (February 1983), p. 120.

HAWORTH, W. "Glass Fibre in Modern Industry," *Textiles*, 7 (October 1978), p. 79.

"High-Performance Carbon Fibres," *Textiles*, 4 (January 1975), p. 2.

MILLER, W. C "Refractory Fibers," in *Encyclopedia of Textiles, Fibers, and Nonwoven Fabrics*. New York: John Wiley & Sons, Inc. 1984, p. 438.

"Produce Asbestos Yarn, Safely," *Textile World*, 131 (March 1981), p. 69.

SEIDEL, L. E. "Industrial Fabrics: Candidates for Composites," *Textile Industries*, 147 (September 1983), p. 102.

SEIDEL, L. E. "Manmade Fiber Variant Update: Two Celanese High-performance Fibers," *Textile Industries*, 147 (January 1983), p. 60.

TOWNE, M. K., and M. B. DERVELL. "Properties and Uses of Carbon Fiber Cloth," *Modern Textiles*, 57 (May 1976), p. 51.

Nylon and Aramid Fibers

Nylon

The generic term for polyamide fibers is *nylon*. Under the most recent Federal Trade Commission definition, nylon is "a manufactured fiber in which the fiber-forming substance is a long-chain synthetic polyamide in which less than 85 per cent of the amide ($-\overset{\parallel}{\underset{O}{C}}-NH-$) linkages are attached directly to two aromatic rings." This definition covers a variety of structures, two main classifications of which are used in the United States: nylon 6 and nylon 66.

Nylon 66

Although the processes for making both nylon 66 and nylon 6 have been known since the earliest experimentation on nylon, DuPont, which pioneered the development of nylon in the United States, chose to utilize the nylon 66 process. Nylon 66 predominates in the United States, whereas nylon 6 predominates in Europe, although a number of U.S. textile companies produce nylon 6.

Manufacture of Nylon 66

The chemicals from which nylon 66 is synthesized are adipic acid and hexamethylene diamine:

Adipic acid	Hexamethylene diamine
$COOH(CH_2)_4COOH$	$NH_2(CH_2)_6NH_2$
1 + 4 + 1 = 6	(6)

Note that there are six carbon atoms in each molecule of adipic acid and six carbon atoms in each molecule of hexamethylene diamine. For this reason this nylon was designated as nylon 6.6 (six carbons in each molecule of reacting chemical). In time it came to be known as nylon 66. These materials are synthesized from benzene.

Polymerization. The first step in the manufacturing process is to cause the reacting materials to form long-chain molecules or polymers. Nylon is formed by condensation polymerization. The reaction of adipic acid and hexamethylene diamine takes place in an air-free atmosphere. Water, which is split off during polymerization, is allowed to escape from the reacting tank. If the manufacturer wishes to produce a delustered nylon, titanium dioxide can be added to the material during this step.

The molten polymer that forms is extruded from the tank as a ribbon, several inches in width. The material is quenched in cold water, which reduces the size of the crystals formed.

Spinning. The ribbon is broken into smaller nylon "chips." Nylon is melt spun. The chips fall onto an electrically heated grid that is too small to allow the chips to pass through until they have been melted. The melted polymer is delivered from an extruder, from a metal grid melter, or directly from a polymerizer and then passes through a filter that removes any impurities on to a meter pump. The pump delivers measured polymer to the *pack*, which consists of a small filter and spinneret.

As they exit from the spinneret, the molten filaments enter a chimney where they are air cooled and simultaneously stretched. Spinning finish, a complex mixture of oil lubricants emulsified in water together with additional materials such as wetting agents, antistatic agents, and adhesives is coated onto the fiber. The finish lubricates fibers for subsequent processing and disperses static electrical charges that would interfere with yarn formation. The finish is eventually washed from the fabric.

FIGURE 8.1 Flow charts showing the manufacture of nylon 66. Courtesy of E. I. du Pont de Nemours & Company.

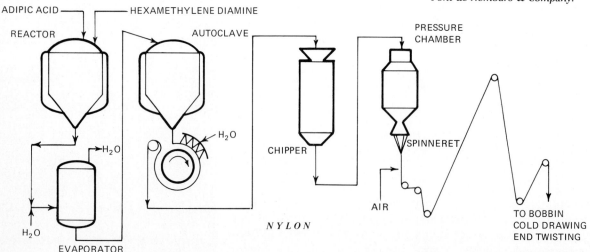

Drawing. After addition of the finish, the fiber is wound onto a bobbin. In this state nylon is not especially strong or lustrous, so fibers are heated and stretched to 400 to 600 per cent of their original length. The stretching orients the molecules, making the fiber more crystalline, increasing luster, and improving tensile strength.

Students can observe the effect of the drawing process by taking a strip cut from a polyethylene plastic bag and gently but firmly stretching it. As the strip is stretched, a sort of neck forms at some point in the strip, and beyond the neck, the strip both narrows and stretches. A comparison of the unstretched and stretched strips shows clearly the improvement in strength that follows drawing.

Not all yarns are drawn to their maximum extensibility, because when a fiber reaches its maximum length, the extensibility of the yarn and fiber are lowered. As is true of many other textile processes, precise control of the process must be maintained so that the manufacturer can achieve the qualities needed in the final product.

Other steps may be added, such as texturing the fiber (in which crimp is added to the filaments) or heat relaxation treatments to assure very low shrinkage as is required in fiber for auto tires. Sometimes two or more steps may be combined into consecutive operations to reduce manufacturing costs, so that the fibers may go from spinning directly to drawing, or from spinning to drawing to texturing. Figure 8.1 presents a diagrammatic summary of the manufacture of nylon 66.

Appearance of Nylon Fibers

Normal nylon in microscopic appearance looks like a long smooth cylinder. Its cross section is circular, and it is naturally lustrous, unless it is delustered. (See Figure 8.2.)

Properties

Strength or Tenacity. The tenacity or strength of nylon is excellent. It is produced in a variety of tenacities. Regular-tenacity nylon is rated at 3.0 to 6.0 g/d; high-tenacity nylon is rated 6.0 to 9.5 g/d. The exceptional strength of nylon has led to its use not only for tire cords but also for a variety of industrial items. Its abrasion resistance is good, being four to five times that of wool. The strength and abrasion resistance plus the elasticity of nylon have led to its predominance in the field of women's hosiery.

Density or Specific Gravity. A relatively low-density fiber, the specific gravity of nylon is 1.14, which is lower than most other fibers. (Rayon, for example, has a specific gravity of about 1.5, polyester of 1.22 or 1.38). Nylon can be made into very light, sheer fabrics, of good strength.

FIGURE 8.2 *Photomicrograph of delustered, regular nylon 66 in a cross section and a longitudinal view. Courtesy of E. I. du Pont de Nemours & Company.*

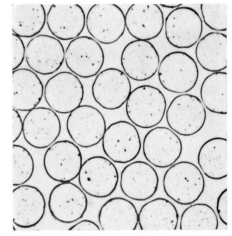

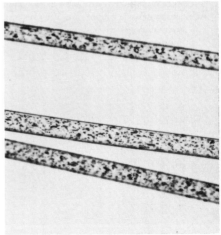

Elasticity and Resilience. The elasticity of nylon is very high. Its resilience is good.

Absorbency. Nylon is moderately hydrophilic, having better moisture regain than many man-made fibers. Nylon fabrics dry quickly after laundering.

Dimensional Stability. Nylon has good dimensional stability at low to moderate temperatures, neither shrinking nor stretching out of shape. At high temperatures, nylon fabrics may shrink. Washing and drying temperatures should be kept low.

Electrical Conductivity. Nylon is a poor conductor of electricity, and it builds up static electricity, especially when humidity is low. Nylon serves as a good insulator in electrical materials because of its nonconducting qualities. Some special nylons have been manufactured to improve conductivity and decrease static electricity.

Combustibility; Effect of Heat. The melting point of nylon 66 is about 500°F. It will soften and may start to stick at 445°F. If a hot iron is used on nylons, the fibers may glaze, soften, or stick. The fiber burns in a flame, but usually self-extinguishes when the flame is removed. However, nylon fibers do melt, and as with any fiber that melts, if the molten fiber drips onto the skin, it may cause serious burns. The thermoplasticity of nylon allows it to be heat-set.

Behavior of Nylon Fibers in Relation to Selected Factors

Chemical Resistance. Like most synthetics, nylon is chemically stable. Dry-cleaning solvents will not harm the fiber. It is not seriously affected by dilute acids, but is soluble in strong acids. Treatment with concentrated hydrochloric acid at high temperatures will break nylon 66 down into adipic acid and hexamethylene diamine, the substances from which it is made. This reaction could be used to reclaim these basic materials and permit this fiber to be recycled after use. Prolonged exposure to acidic fumes from pollution will decrease the dyeability of nylon.

Resistance to Microorganisms, Insects, Sunlight, and Aging. Moths, mildew, and bacteria will not attack nylon. The fiber is degraded by long exposure to sunlight, but age has no appreciable effect if fabrics are stored away from sunlight. Sheer nylon fabrics are unsuitable for use in curtains.

Variations of Nylon 66

Varying the cross-sectional shape of man-made fibers is one means of producing fibers that may have some particularly desirable appearance or performance quality. Nylon 66 is sometimes made in trilobal or multilobal forms. The trilobal shape reflects more light, thereby increasing luster. Antron® is the trademark name of one of the multilobal nylon 66 fibers made by DuPont.

Nylon 6

Nylon 6 is made from *caprolactam*, which has the following chemical structure:

$$
\begin{array}{c}
\quad\quad CH_2 \\
CH_2 \quad\quad C{=}O \\
| \quad\quad\quad\quad NH \\
CH_2 \quad\quad CH_2 \\
\quad\quad CH_2
\end{array}
$$

Since there are six carbons in caprolactam, the fiber is known as nylon 6.

After DuPont chose to develop nylon 66 rather than nylon 6, the development of nylon 6 was left to researchers in Europe, where it is the most common type of nylon manufactured. Nylon 6 has some cost advantages over nylon 66.

Manufacture

Polymerization. Caprolactam is polymerized by one of two methods. In one, caprolactam is melted, heated, and filtered under high pressure, during which process condensation polymerization takes place. In the second method, water in the amount of 10 per cent of the weight of the caprolactam is added, after which the water and caprolactam are heated to a high temperature, steam escapes, and polymerization takes place.

In both these methods a certain amount of monomer material remains. The polymerized material is given a water bath in an extractor to remove the monomer, which, if it remained, would weaken the final fiber. The polymer is dried and made into nylon chips.

Spinning. Nylon 6 is melt spun. It has a lower melting point than does nylon 66. It melts at a temperature of 414° to 428°F. The fiber is spun into air, cooled and liquified, and finish is applied.

Drawing. The fibers are stretched to orient the molecules and to improve strength and luster. They are then wound onto a cone.

Characteristics of Nylon 6

The characteristics of nylon 6 are essentially the same as those of nylon 66 with these particular exceptions:

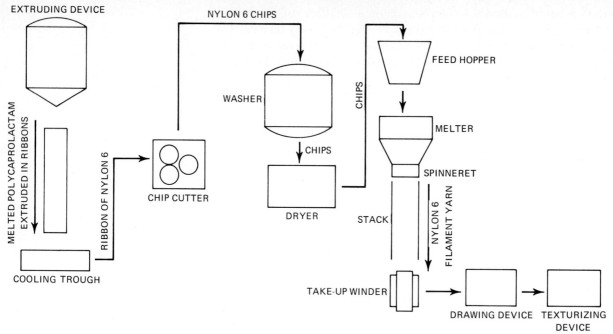

FIGURE 8.3. *Flow chart for the manufacture of nylon 6. Courtesy of Badische Corporation.*

1. The tenacity of regular tenacity nylon 6 is 4 to 7 g/d; that of regular nylon 66 is 3 to 6 g/d.
2. The affinity of nylon 6 for acid dyes is greater than that of nylon 66, because there are more acid sites (places where the fiber combines with the dyestuff) in nylon 6 than in nylon 66.
3. Elastic recovery is claimed to be slightly better in nylon 6, as is fatigue resistance.
4. Nylon 6 has a lower melting point than nylon 66, which imposes some limitations on handling nylon 6.

Multilobal varieties of nylon 6 are also made. Enkaloft® and Enkalure® are multilobal nylon 6 fibers made by the American Enka Company. See Figure 8.3 for a diagram summarizing the manufacture of Nylon 6.

Consumer Considerations Concerning Nylon

The availability of a wide variety of types of nylon (from fine to coarse, from soft to crisp, from sheer to opaque) has resulted in the use of nylon in an enormous range of products for apparel, the home, and industry.

Nylon has long been of major importance in the manufacture of women's hosiery because it can be heat-set and it is strong and elastic. Sheer fabrics of nylon have been popular because of their inherent strength and abrasion resistance. Special-purpose nylons have been manufactured for upholstery and carpets.

Nylon is also considered to be an "easy-care" fabric. Most nylon items are machine washable and can be tumble dried at normal drying temperatures.

However, some aspects of the care of nylon require special attention. Like many synthetics, nylon has an affinity for oil-borne stains. These should be removed with a grease solvent before laundering.

Nylon has a tendency to "scavenge" colors, picking up surface color easily from other fabrics. This is why many white nylons gradually become gray or yellowed; therefore, it is advisable to wash white nylons alone, never with other items of color.

Nylon's resilience usually precludes its ironing, but the heat sensitivity of nylon requires that it be pressed with a warm, not hot, iron if pressing seems necessary. Also, nylon items should be removed from the dryer as soon as the cycle is ended. Nylons that remain in a hot dryer in a wrinkled condition may retain these wrinkles until the item is pressed.

Spun yarns may tend to pill, as the fabric wears. Pilling on synthetics including nylon is a particular problem because the strength of the fibers causes tangled fiber ends to cling tightly. These fiber ends do not fall off, which makes wearing apparel unsightly.

Other Types of Nylon

Nylon 612, a low-moisture variant, and nylon 11 or Rilsan®, a French product made from castor oil and having a relatively low melting point, are commercially available in the United States but are not used in apparel or household textiles. Other nylon variations cited in the literature but not available to the public at this time include nylon 7, which is being developed in Russia. It is claimed to be more stable to heat and light than is nylon 6.

Nylon 4 was developed by the General Aniline and Film Corporation. The advantage of nylon 4 is said to be an increased moisture regain, which decreases static buildup. Nylon 4 is supposedly closer to cotton in its physical characteristics than are other nylons.

Qiana

Qiana® is the trademark of a nylon formerly produced by DuPont. Its manufacture was discontinued in the winter of 1981–82. Given the time required for using up existing stocks, consumers may still find some products made from Qiana® nylon. Care of Qiana® is much the same as for other nylon products.

In a 1974 revision of generic fiber categories, the Federal Trade Commission established a separate category of fibers that is designated "aramids." Like nylon, aramid fibers are polyamides. However, in its redefinition, the FTC separated polyamides into those in which *less* than 85 per cent of the amide linkages are attached directly to the aromatic rings (nylon) and those in which 85 per cent or *more* of the amide linkages are attached to two aromatic rings (aramid). Nomex® and Kevlar® are DuPont trademarks of fibers that belong to the aramid classification.

Characteristics of aramids include high strength and good dimensional stability. Standard moisture regain is 5 per cent; absorbency is relatively low. Figure 8.4 shows cross-section view of Nomex® aramid fiber.

The color range of aramid fibers is limited. Some dyes will increase its flammability. Since aramid fibers are used primarily in industrial applications, the demand for a wide range of colors is not very great.

The outstanding property of aramid fibers is their flame resistance.

Aramid

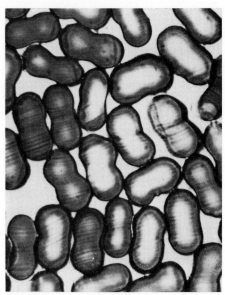

FIGURE 8.4 Photomicrograph of a cross section of Nomex® aramid fiber. Courtesy of E. I. du Pont de Nemours & Company.

Table 8.1   Selected Characteristics of Nylon and Aramid Fibers

	Nylon (regular tenacity)	Aramid (Nomex® filament)
Spectific gravity	1.14	1.38
Tenacity (g/d)		
Dry	3.0–6.0	4.8–5.8
Wet	2.6–5.4	3.8–4.8
Moisture regain	4.0–4.5%	5%
Resiliency	excellent	excellent
Burning characteristics	burns slowly with melting in flame, usually self-extinguishing after flame is removed	low flammability
Melting point	415°F (nylon 6) 482°F (nylon 66)	decomposes above 700°F; does not melt
Conductivity of		
Heat	low	low
electricity	low	low
Resistance to damage from		
Fungi	excellent	excellent
Insects	excellent	excellent
Prolonged exposure to sunlight	degrades	degrades
Acids	degraded by concentrated acids	degraded by hot, concentrated acids
Alkalis	degraded by hot, concentrated alkalis.	degraded by hot, concentrated alkalis

Aramid fibers have no melting point (they do not melt), and they have extremely low combustibility. The fiber decomposes at a temperature above 700°F. Selected aramid and nylon characteristics are compared in Table 8.1.

Aramids degrade and lose strength on exposure to ultraviolet rays. Their resistance to radiation from gamma, beta, and X rays is, however, excellent, and this resistance is utilized for some industrial applications. Their resistance to most chemicals and organic solvents is generally good.

Aramid fibers are used in industrial and military protective clothing, (Figure 8.5), industrial hot-air filtration fabrics, ropes, cables, sailcloth, and marine and sporting goods. Nomex® aramid is used in applications that take advantage of its flame resistance. For example, highly temperature-resistant papers are made from Nomex® aramid fibers.

Kevlar® aramid is being used in products that take advantage of its strength. In industry it may reinforce of plastics with strong but lightweight fiber material. It is substituted for glass fiber in the aircraft industry because it is lighter in weight than glass. Sports equipment, such as sailboats, hockey sticks, tennis rackets, fishing rods, and golf clubs, also make use of Kevlar® fibers. Kevlar® is gaining popularity for canoes in that it is both light and strong. Whereas aluminum canoes weigh 70 to 80 pounds and fiberglass 50 to 70 pounds, a Kevlar® canoe of the same size will weigh only 40 to 50 pounds. It will, however, cost almost twice as much as the heavier canoes. Alone or with other fibers, Kevlar® may be made into bullet-resistant garments and coated fabrics, and it is used in automobile tires.

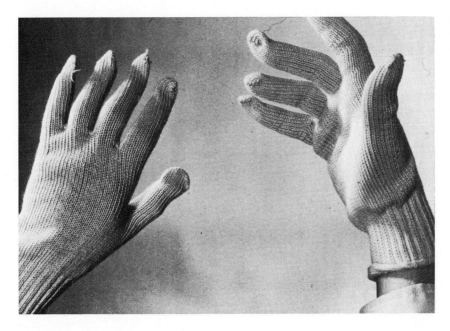

FIGURE 8.5 *Aramid fibers have been spun and knitted into cut-resistant gloves. Courtesy of E. I. du Pont de Nemours & Company.*

Recommended References

GRAYSON, M., ed. "Polyamide Fibers," in *Encyclopedia of Textiles, Fibers, and Nonwoven Fabrics.* New York: John Wiley-Interscience, 1984.

HILLERMEIER, K. "Prospects of Aramid as a Substitute for Asbestos," *Textile Research Journal,* 54 (September 1984), p. 575.

HILLERMEIER, K. "Aramid's Asbestos Replacement Potential," *Textile Industries,* 147 (July 1983), p. 55.

HORSFALL, G. A. "Factors Influencing the Daylight Photodegradation of Nylon 66, Nylon 6 and Polyester in Commercial Fabrics," *Textile Research Journal,* 52 (March 1982), p. 197.

"Kevlar: A New Concept in Fiber Strength," *American Fabrics and Fashion,* No. 105 (Fall 1975), p. 67.

MONCRIEFF, R. W. *Man-Made Fibres. 7th ed.* London: Butterworth and Company, Ltd., 1987.

NEEDLES, H. L. *Handbook of Textile Fibres, Dyes and Finishes.* New York: Garland SFM Press, 1981, Chap. 8.

"Polyamides and Polyester," *CIBA Review,* No. 127 (July 1958).

"Properties of Nomex," *Technical Bulletin N-236.* Wilmington, Del.: E. I. du Pont de Nemours & Company.

SITTIG, M. *Polyamide Fiber Manufacture.* Plainfield, N.J.: Textile Book Service, 1972.

WILFONG, R. E., and W. G MIKELL. "Kevlar Aramid," *Modern Textiles* (November 1976), p. 26.

Polyester Fibers

In his first experiments with the synthesis of polymers, W. H. Carothers concentrated his attention on compounds called polyesters. Encountering some difficulties in this research, he turned his attention to polyamides, from which he synthesized nylon.

After the discovery of nylon, a group of English researchers at Imperial Chemical Industries concentrated on the polyester group. Their experimentation led to the development and subsequent manufacture of polyester fibers. DuPont bought the English patent, and the first DuPont plant for the production of Dacron® polyester in the United States opened in March 1953.

Polyester fibers are defined as "a manufactured fiber in which the fiber-forming substance is any long-chain synthetic polymer composed of at least 85 per cent by weight of an ester of a substituted aromatic carboxylic acid, including but not restricted to substituted terephthalate units $p(-R-O-C-C_6H_4-C-O-)$ and parasubstituted hydroxybenzoate units $p(-R-O-C_6H_4-C-O-)'$ (as amended September 12, 1973). British publications may refer to polyester as terylene.

Manufacture

The raw material from which most polyesters are made is petroleum from which the constituent acids and alcohols are derived. The most commonly used acid is terephthalic acid or its dimethyl ester. The processes that are used for manufacturing different types of polyesters vary. Many of the details of these processes are not known because the companies that hold the patents on the manufacturing processes have not released full information on precisely how these processes are carried out. A generalized description of the process for synthesizing polyesters follows.

Polymerization

Condensation polymerization takes place during the reaction of the acid and alcohol, in a vacuum, at high temperatures. Polymerized material is extruded in the form of a ribbon onto a casting wheel or cooling trough. The ribbon hardens, and small polyester chips are cut from the ribbon.

Spinning and Drawing

The chips are dried to remove any residual moisture and are then put into hopper reservoirs ready for melting. The melted polymer (polyester is "melt spun," like nylon) is extruded through the spinnerets, solidifies on hitting the air, and is wound loosely onto cylinders. How the solidified filaments are processed next depends upon the projected end use of the fiber.

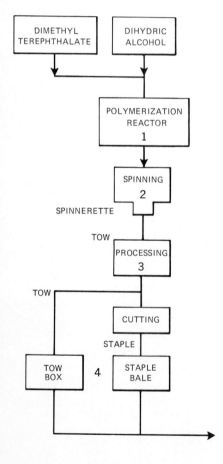

FIGURE 9.1   Flow chart showing the manufacture of polyester. Courtesy of the Eastman Kodak Company.

STARTING CHEMICALS: The production of KODEL polyester fiber begins with dimethyl terephthalate and a special suitable dihydric alcohol.

1 POLYMERIZATION: The dihydric alcohol and dimethyl terephthalate are placed in a polymerization reactor where, under the proper conditions, they combine to form long chain-like molecules called **polymer.**

2 SPINNING:
The liquid polymer is forced through microscopic holes in a device similar to a miniature shower head, called a **spinnerette.**
The thin strands formed by the spinnerette are cooled and gathered into bundles of continuous fiber called **tow,** which looks like untwisted rope.

3 PROCESSING:
The tow is drawn and heat-treated to make it resistant to shrinking or to stretching.
Lubricants are added to aid in spinning yarns.
The tow may also be crimped like a "permanent wave" to add bulk and texture to the fiber.
The tow may be cut into short lengths called **staple** fiber or it may be left uncut, in continuous tow form . . . depending upon the customer's (mill's) requirements.

4 PACKING:
Staple fiber is compressed into bales.
Continuous-form tow is packed into boxes.

SHIPPING: These forms of KODEL polyester fiber are then shipped to textile mills where the fibers are spun into yarns and woven into fabrics.

Tennessee Eastman Company produces the KODEL polyester fiber. It does not weave fabrics or make garments or home furnishings.

If filaments are to be made into staple fiber, several sets of filaments, each containing 250 to 3,000 filaments, are brought together and coiled in a large can in preparation for drawing. The yarns are heated, drawn to several times their original length to orient the molecular structure, and then allowed to relax to release stresses and strains and reduce shrinkage of drawn fibers. Drawn tow is crimped, dried, and heat-set for stability. At this point, tow may be cut into required staple lengths, usually 38 to 152 millimeters in length, and baled, ready for sale.

Fiber intended for continuous filament yarn is either drawn directly and packaged for sale—a process requiring more complex machinery—or wound on bobbins preparatory for draw twisting or draw texturing. Yarn for weaving or knitting or yarn intended for texturing is often processed on a draw twister that heats, draws the fibers, and imparts a small amount of base twist. Additional heating and drawing is given to high-strength industrial yarns in a second stage of processing.

Although draw-twisted yarns can also be textured, recent developments in spinning polyester have led to the use of an alternative process. High-speed spinning processes yield partially oriented yarn (POY), which is preferred for draw texturing because it eliminates the expensive draw-twisting operation and allows the POY to be both drawn and textured in the same operation, one in which the drawing, texturing, and heat-setting operations are carried out in an integrated manner. See Chapter 14 for a fuller discussion of texturing. For a diagram summarizing the manufacture of polyester, see Figure 9.1.

Appearance

Polyester fibers are manufactured in a variety of cross sections, including round, trilobal, pentalobal, and hollow shapes. Under the microscope, round fibers appear as long, smooth rods with spots of pigment. This pigmented appearance decreases the luster or brightness of polyesters. Longitudinally, multilobal fibers appear striated. (See Figure 9.2.)

Characteristics of Polyesters

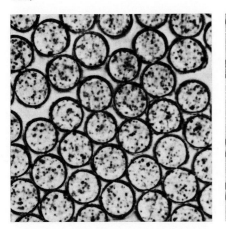 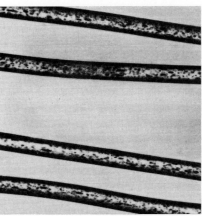

FIGURE 9.2. *Photomicrograph of regular Dacron® polyester in a cross section and a longitudinal view. Courtesy of E. I. du Pont de Nemours & Company.*

Properties

Strength or Tenacity. The strength or tenacity of polyester varies with the type of fiber; however, as a general category, polyester would be considered a relatively strong fiber. Regular filaments have a breaking tenacity of 4 to 7 g/d; high-tenacity filaments are rated at 6.3 to 9.5 g/d.

Specific Gravity or Density. The density or specific gravity (1.38 or 1.22 depending on type) is moderate. Polyesters have a density greater than nylon (1.14) and lower than rayon (1.50). Fabrics made from polyesters are medium in weight.

Elasticity and Resilience. The elasticity of polyester is generally good. Polyester recovers well from stretching but is inferior to nylon in its elasticity. Resilience is excellent. For this reason, polyesters are often blended with less wrinkle-resistant fibers to make easy-care fabrics.

Absorbency and Moisture Regain. The moisture regain of polyester is low, only 0.2 to 0.8 per cent. Although polyesters are nonabsorbent, they do have wicking ability. In wicking, moisture can be carried on the surface of the fiber without absorption. This quality makes polyester relatively comfortable to wear in warm weather, as perspiration is carried to the surface of the fiber and evaporated. Multilobal fiber cross sections improve the wicking qualities of polyesters. Special finishes can be applied to polyester to make it more hydrophilic.

Dimensional Stability. Polyesters that have been given heat-setting treatments have excellent dimensional stability, so long as the heat-setting temperature is not exceeded. If polyester fabrics have not been heat-set, they may shrink at high temperatures.

Effect of Heat; Combustibility. The melting point of polyester is close to that of nylon, ranging from 480° to 550°F. Polyesters usually need no pressing because of their excellent wrinkle recovery. If they must be pressed, it should be with a warm, not hot, iron. Polyesters can be heat-set into pleats with especially good results. Not only will heat setting stabilize size and shape, but wrinkle resistance of polyesters is enhanced by heat setting.

Polyester shrinks from flame and will melt, leaving a hard black residue. The fabric will burn with a strong, pungent odor. Some polyesters are self-extinguishing. Melted polyester fiber can produce severe burns.

Polyester Fiber Behavior in Relation to Selected Conditions

Chemical Resistance. Polyesters are not harmed by solvents used in professional dry cleaning, nor are they susceptible to damage from bleaching. Although polyesters are not harmed by acids, they may be adversely affected by strong alkalis. Alkalinity encountered in detergents is not harmful.

Resistance to Microorganisms, Insects, Sunlight, and Aging. Bacteria, mildew, and moth larvae will not attack polyesters.

Although polyesters will degrade after long exposure to sunlight, they have better sun resistance than do most fibers. This resistance is enhanced when the fibers are placed behind glass that screens out some of the harmful ultraviolet rays. Polyesters are, therefore, quite suitable for use in curtains and draperies.

Age has no appreciable effect on polyesters.

Varieties and Modifications of Polyesters

Polyester fiber accounted for about 40 per cent of all fiber used in textile mills in the United States in 1983. Among man-made fibers, it dominates the market, accounting for about 43 per cent of all the man-made fiber consumed. *Textile Organon* for June 1984 listed twenty-one American manufacturers of polyester fiber.[1]

The major polyester in manufacture and use is polyethylene terephthalate, abbreviated PET. Eastman Kodak Company manufactures a polyester variant, poly-1,4-cyclohexylenedimethylene terephthalate, which it calls Kodel II® or identifies in its product list as items carrying numbers from 200 to 299. This polyester has properties that are similar to PET (see Table 9.1) but is said to have better recovery from stretch, better resistance to pilling, and superior resilience. For these reasons, it is recommended for blending with cellulosics and wool, for carpet fiber, and in fiberfill.

Table 9.1 Comparison of selected properties of Kodel® 200 series fibers (poly-1,4-cyclohexylenedimethylene terephthalate) and Kodel 400 (PET) fibers

Property	200-series fiber round cross section	400-series fiber round cross section
Break tenacity, grams per denier	2.0–2.5	4.7
Elongation at break	35%	42%
Melting point	554°F	482°F
Specific gravity	1.23	1.38
Compression recovery from 5,000 pound force per square inch	44%	31%
Fiber shrinkage		
In dry air at 190°C	<1%	<6%
In boiling water	<1%	<1%

SOURCE: Eastman Kodak Company, *Eastman Textile Fibers Publication No. K-230*, Rochester, N.Y., June 1981.

[1]*Textile Organon*, June 1984, p. 110.

The quantity of polyester in use is a reflection of its versatility. A number of different companies produce specialized varieties of the fiber for different end uses. Cross-sectional shapes may be varied to alter handle and appearance. Some varieties of polyester are solution dyed. The fiber is produced as staple, filament, tow, and fiberfill, which may be made either in filament or crimped staple form.

Filament yarns of polyester may be textured to create stretch yarns or to produce a filament yarn with aesthetic qualities of a staple spun yarn. Such yarns decrease pilling, which may occur in spun staple polyester yarns.

Researchers have concentrated on modifications of polyesters to improve aesthetics and comfort. Alkaline hydrolysis is used to improve hydrophilic properties and also to produce silklike qualities. Considerable attention has been addressed to these experimental techniques in the research and technical literature, and some commercial applications are being made.

A wide range of filament sizes and yarn counts, modified cross-sectional shapes, bicomponent fibers, texturing, and blending with other fibers has made possible the production of a tremendous range of polyester and polyester-containing fabrics. The enormous variety of polyester materials available is dramatically illustrated by the fact that the DuPont Company alone produces more than seventy polyester variants. See Table 9.2 for a summary of polyester characteristics.

Care

Polyester is blended with so many other fibers that consumers should consult care labels for specific instructions on care. Those procedures that are appropriate for 100 per cent polyester fabrics may not be suitable for the fibers with which polyester is blended.

Polyester fabrics are generally machine washable. Water temperatures should be warm, not excessively hot. Ordinary laundry detergents can be used. Household bleaches will not harm white fabrics. Oily stains should be removed before laundering by treatment with a grease solvent.

Polyesters should be dried at moderate temperatures, and items should be removed from the dryer as soon as the cycle is complete to avoid creases that must be removed by ironing. As a general rule, polyesters should not require pressing after drying, although polyester fabrics may be ironed on the wrong side with a moderately warm iron. Some blends of polyesters and cottons can be difficult to iron because the suitable ironing temperature for polyester fibers may not be high enough to press wrinkles from cotton, whereas the cotton temperature is too high for the polyester.

Most fabrics made from polyesters can be dry cleaned safely. Some polyester double knits printed with pigment colors cannot be dry cleaned. Care labels should be checked to determine whether dry cleaning should be avoided.

Table 9.2 Selected Characteristics of Polyester Fiber

	Polyester (regular tenacity)	
Specific gravity	1.22 or 1.38[a]	
Tenacity (g/d), filament		high tenacity
Dry	4.0–7.0	6.3–9.5
Wet	4.0–7.0	6.3–9.5
Moisture regain	0.4–0.8[a]	
Resiliency	excellent	
Burning and melting point	In flame, burns slowly with melting; usually self-extinguishing after flame is removed; melts at 482–550°F[a]	
Conductivity of		
Heat	low	
Electricity	low	
Resistance to damage from		
Fungi	excellent	
Insects	excellent	
Prolonged exposure to sunlight	good if behind glass	
Acids	good	
Alkalis	good to weak alkali	
	fair to strong alkali	

[a]Depending on type.

Uses

Polyester is used in a wide range of wearing apparel, home furnishings, and industrial products, either alone or in blends. The exceptional resilience of polyester makes it especially suitable for use in easy-care fabrics.

Blends of polyester with other fibers are made to take advantage of durability and easy maintenance. Durable press fabrics are frequently made from blends of cotton and polyester. Wool and polyester blends have a woollike feel and appearance and some of the easy-care aspects of polyester. Furthermore, creases and pleats can be heat-set through the thermoplastic properties of polyester. Other blends with rayon and with acetate as well as blends with other synthetics such as acrylics and with natural fibers such as silk, flax, and ramie are produced.

Polyesters and their blends are used for carpets, curtains, draperies, sheets, and pillowcases for the home-furnishings market. Sleeping bags, insulated outdoor clothing, and pillow and comforter fillings of polyester are being promoted by manufacturers as easy-care, nonallergenic substitutes for goose down. Hollow polyester fibers are said to offer advantages in this use over traditional polyester fiber forms.

Industrial uses of polyesters include fire hoses, power belting, ropes, and nets. Tire cord for automotive uses and sails for sports are also made from polyester fibers. Nonwoven polyester fiber webs may be used in construction projects for reinforcement.

The relatively low cost of polyester fiber makes it the fiber of choice for many of the foregoing applications.

"Polyester gets no respect!" This was the lead sentence in an article discussing manufacturers' efforts to enhance the image of polyester. After more than two decades of constant growth in demand for and use of polyester by consumers, apparel manufacturers in the 1970s flooded the market with polyester double knits. The public came to associate polyester with these garments, many of which had questionable design quality, aesthetics, and comfort. These negative experiences have continued to haunt polyester producers in spite of major improvements in polyester fabrics. As a result, six fiber producers—Celanese, DuPont, American Enka, Eastman Chemical Products, Hoechst, and Avtex—formed the Polyester Council, which has attempted to fight the "image" problem through a concerted public relations campaign directed not only at consumers but also at retailers. (See Figure 9.3.)

Polyester Marketing Problems

FIGURE 9.3   *Polyester high fashion. Both outfits in Trevira® by Shamask. Courtesy of Hoechst Fibers Industries.*

American Fabrics & Fashions, No. 132 (1985). Entire issue devoted to polyester.

"Fiberfill," *American Fabrics and Fashions*, No. 115 (Spring 1979), p. 64.

GRAYSON, M., ed. *Encyclopedia of Textiles, Fibers, and Nonwoven Fabrics.* New York: Wiley-Interscience, 1984, pp. 381 ff.

HOUSER, K. "Some Observations: Caustic Reduction of Polyester Fabrics," *Textile Chemist and Colorist*, 5 (April 1983), p. 37.

JANECEK, C. and H. LUNDE. "Hydrophilic Finishes: Effect on Selected Properties of Polyester Fabric," *Clothing and Textiles Research Journal*, 2 (Fall/Winter 1983–84), p. 31.

MITTAL, F. M., and V. R. BHATT. "Process for Improving Comfort and Aesthetic Properties of Polyesters," *American Dyestuff Reporter*, 74 (June 1985), p. 26.

NEEDLES, H. L. *Handbook of Textile Fibers, Dyes and Finishes.* New York: Garland STPM Press, 1981, Chap. 9.

"New Luster for Polyester," *Apparel Merchandising* (September 1983), p. 13.

OLSON, L. M., and M. WENTZ. "Moisture Related Properties of Hydrolized Polyester Fabrics," *Textile Chemist and Colorist*, 16 (February 1984), p. 48.

"Polyester Producers Launch All-out Market Drive," *Textile World* (August 1983), p. 59.

YOON, H. N., A. BUCKLEY, et al. "Improved Comfort Polyester Series," *Textile Research Journal.*

Part I: "Transport Properties and Thermal Comfort of Polyester/Cotton Blend Fabrics," 54 (May 1984), p. 289.

Part II: "Mechanical and Surface Properties," 54 (June 1984), p. 357.

Part III: "Wearer Trials," 54 (July 1984), p. 447.

Part IV: "Analysis of the Four Wearer Trials," 54 (August 1984), p. 544.

Part V: "Results from Two Subjective Wearer Trials and Their Correlation with Laboratory Tests," 54 (September 1984), p. 602.

Recommended References

Acrylic and Modacrylic Fibers

Acrylic fibers are "manufactured fibers in which the fiber-forming substance is any long-chain synthetic polymer composed of at least 85 per cent by weight of acrylonitrile units ($-CH_2-CH$)."

$$\begin{array}{c} | \\ CN \end{array}$$

Acrylics

The second synthetic fiber to be produced commercially by DuPont, Orlon® acrylic fiber, entered production in 1950. Acrilan® acrylic was produced commercially in 1952 by Monsanto.

Early acrylic fibers were somewhat yellowish in color, and a clear white fiber was difficult to obtain. In time this problem was overcome, and the fiber is now available in a clear white as well as in a variety of other colors.

Manufacture of Acrylics

Acrylic fibers are produced from acrylonitrile usually in combination with one or more comonomers. The reaction that takes place during polymerization is an addition reaction. Some acrylics are dry spun, others are wet spun. Most acrylics are used in staple form, and the fiber is crimped before cutting.

A number of variations in the processes used to manufacture acrylic fibers are possible. Many of these processes are proprietary, and their details are not available. The general characteristics common to most acrylic fibers are as follows.

General Properties of Acrylics

Appearance

The microscopic cross section of acrylic fibers may be round, bean shaped, dog-bone shaped, or multilobal. Likewise, the longitudinal appearance of acrylics is either smooth or twisted and may have wide striations (lengthwise markings). (See Figure 10.1.)

Elasticity and Resilience. The elasticity of acrylic fibers varies from one trademarked fiber to another. In general, however, elastic recovery is lower than that for most other synthetic fibers. Resilience ranges from good to excellent.

Absorbency and Moisture Regain. The moisture absorption of acrylics is low, and moisture regain is 1.0 to 2.5 per cent.

Dimensional Stability. Heat setting will produce good dimensional stability in fabrics made from acrylics. However, there are many varieties of acrylics with somewhat different performance in regard to their dimensional stability. For this reason, instructions on care labels should be followed carefully in laundering acrylics. For example, some fabrics are manufactured from specially crimped fibers that require dryer drying after laundering to restore the crimp. If hung wet on a line, some of these fabrics may stretch out of shape.

Electrical Conductivity. The poor electrical conductivity of acrylics is related to their low moisture absorption. Static electricity charges are built up unless special finishes have been given to the fabrics.

Effect of Heat; Combustibility. Untreated acrylic fibers ignite and burn readily. As fabrics of acrylic burn, flaming melt drips away and burns sufficiently to ignite flammable surfaces on which the melt may fall. The residue is a hard, black bead at the edge of the fabric. Flame-retardant finishes can be given to the fibers. The melting point of the fiber is 450° to 497°F, depending on the type of fiber. Fibers shrink in steam. Exposure to high dry heat may cause yellowing. Fibers can be heat-set.

Acrylic Fibers and Their Behavior in Relation to Selected Factors

Chemical Resistance. The resistance of acrylics to acids is very good, except to nitric acid in which it dissolves. Resistance to alkalis is moderate and degradation by sodium hydroxide at high concentrations and/or temperatures, is cited by Moncrieff for Orlon®, Acrilan®, Creslan®, and Zefran®. Solvents used in commercial dry cleaning do not affect the fiber adversely. Most acrylics are not harmed by household bleaches.

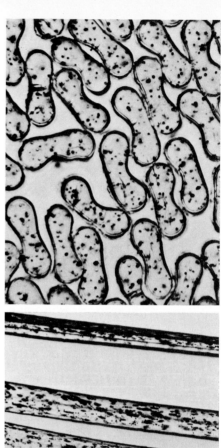

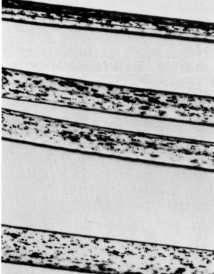

FIGURE 10.1 Photomicrograph of regular Orlon® acrylic fiber in a cross section and a longitudinal view. Courtesy of E. I. du Pont de Nemours & Company.

Resistance to Microorganisms, Mildew, Sunlight, and Aging.
Mildew, microorganisms, and moths will not harm acrylic fibers. Resistance to sunlight ranges from very good to excellent. Age has no detrimental effect on fabric strength.

Some Acrylic Trademarks

Acrylic fibers differ more from one manufacturer to another than do most man-made fibers. This is a result of differences in synthesis and the specific techniques used to produce the polymer. Differences are also attributed to variations in the means of spinning the fiber, which may be either wet or dry spun. The reaction that takes place during polymerization is an addition reaction. In general, one can say that acrylics have a woollike hand and good bulking qualities, so that they give warmth and good cover without excessive weight. In addition, acrylics are easily laundered, can be machine dried, and are considered "easy-care" fabrics. For these reasons, acrylic is made into many of the same products for which wool is used, such as sweaters, knits, socks, sportswear, pile fabrics, blankets, and carpets.

Orlon®

DuPont's acrylic, Orlon®, is manufactured by a series of complex processes in which the basic material is acrylonitrile. In simplified terms, a catalyst and an activator are dissolved in water. Over a period of several hours, acrylonitrile and 10 to 15 per cent of an undisclosed monomer are added and polymerization takes place.

The polymer precipitates out of the solution and is collected, filtered, washed, and dried. The polymer is dissolved in a suitable spinning solution, heated, and extruded into a heated spinning cell. The solvent evaporates and is collected and recycled for reuse. The filaments are hot stretched.

Orlon® acrylic is made in staple or tow lengths.

Fiber manufacturers may produce a number of specialized types of their trademarked fibers. Orlon® acrylic is an excellent example of this practice. The fiber is produced in a wide variety of types for special purposes, each carrying a different number or name. Some Orlon® fibers are designed for rug or carpet use; some are delustered; and some are suitable for apparel, hosiery, or other items.

Bicomponent Orlon®

DuPont introduced a bicomponent acrylic fiber with a permanent crimp in 1959. To form the fiber, two different types of acrylic material are extruded together as one fiber from the spinneret. Each has somewhat different shrinkage properties, and when the fiber is subjected to heat and moisture during the processing, one polymer shrinks more than the other, producing a spiral crimp that is permanent. This provides increased bulk and resilience. Bicomponent acrylics are used extensively in knitted goods such as sweaters and socks, and this type of fiber is produced by several different firms.

Certification marks are names established by a fiber manufacturer for use with products made from that manufacturer's fiber. For example, a company such as DuPont that makes only fibers sells its fiber to a yarn manufacturer. If the yarn manufacturer uses the fiber in the ways that DuPont specifies, that yarn may carry DuPont's established certification mark. Wintuk® is the certification mark given to yarns of Orlon® acrylic based on bicomponent fibers. Sayelle® is DuPont's certification mark for yarns made from 100 per cent bicomponent. Civona® is DuPont's certification mark for yarns containing a specified amount of bicomponent Orlon®.

Acrilan®

Acrilan®, a product of the Monsanto Company, is manufactured in a process that utilizes slightly different materials than does Orlon®. Whereas Orlon® is dry spun, Acrilan® is wet spun and then dried, stretched, and crimped. The fiber is made in both staple and tow lengths, and in bright and delustered versions. (See Figure 10.2.) Monsanto also supplies a range of bicomponent products.

FIGURE 10.2. Flow chart for the manufacture of Acrilan® acrylic fiber. Courtesy of Monsanto Company.

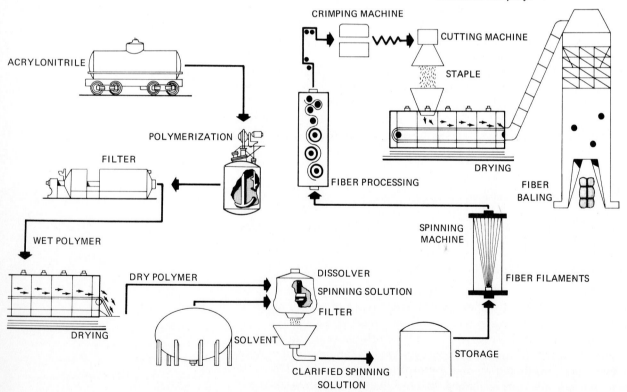

The qualities of Acrilan® are like those described for acrylics in general. Monsanto also manufactures variations of Acrilan® under the trademarks Bi-loft® and Paquel®.

Monsanto also produces a line of precolored Acrilan® products for use in apparel, home furnishings, and craft and carpet end uses. The range of colors offered is wide, and this product eliminates the need for dyeing at the mill level. Producer-dyed fabric of Acrilan® is sold under the trademark of So-Lara®.

Creslan®

Creslan® is the trademark given to the acrylic fiber produced by American Cyanamid Company.

Like Orlon® and Acrilan®, Creslan® is polymerized from acrylonitrile and other monomers. It is considered to be a copolymer and has a somewhat different composition from the acrylics already discussed. It is wet spun, washed, stretched, and made into staple and tow.

Its resilience is rated slightly better than Orlon® and Acrilan®, but otherwise its characteristics are comparable to the other acrylics.

Zefran® Acrylic

Zefran® acrylic fiber is manufactured by Badische. The manufacturer identifies Zefran® acrylic as a "second-generation acrylic textile fiber." Zefran® is rated as slightly stronger than other acrylics. The rest of its characteristics are typical of the acrylics as a class, and it is used in the same types of products. (It should be noted that the trademark Zefran® is applied by Badische to all its synthetic fibers. Fibers are distinguished by their generic class in accordance with TFPIA, for example, Zefran® acrylic, Zefran® nylon, and so forth.) Badiche also supplies producer-dyed fibers for a variety of end uses.

Uses

Acrylic fibers as a class are utilized in a wide variety of different apparel and home-furnishings products. Their woollike handle and bulk combined with easy-care characteristics make them popular for use in sweaters, fleece fabrics, hand-knitting yarns, blankets, and carpets. Resistance to degradation by sunlight leads to use of acrylics in drapery fabrics. Acrylic fibers are fabricated into woven and knitted cloth constructions in a variety of textures and weights that are used for clothing, draperies, and upholstery. Acrylic fibers can be used alone or in blends.

Care

Different acrylic fibers may vary in their care requirements. For this reason it is especially important to follow care labels of these fabrics. In general, acrylic fabrics can be laundered and dry cleaned. Acrylics may be sensitive to heat, so that when dryer drying is recommended for acrylic products, low heat settings should be used, and fabrics should be removed from the dryer immediately after tumbling. Pressing temperatures should not exceed 250°F.

Modacrylics

Modacrylic fibers were first manufactured commercially by Union Carbide Company in 1949 before the production of acrylics. Because the composition of modacrylics is very similar to the acrylics, both fibers were at first included in the acrylic classification, but in 1960, the Federal Trade Commission ruled that a separate category should be established for them.

Modacrylics are defined as a"a manufactured fiber in which the fiber-forming substance is any synthetic polymer composed of less than 85 per cent but at least 35 per cent by weight of acrylonitrile units (—CH—CH$_2$—) except fibers under category (2)[1] of paragraph (j) of Rule

|
CN

7 of the Textile Fiber Products Identification Act."

Manufacture of Modacrylics

Modacrylic fibers are made from chemicals derived from natural gas, coal, air, salt, and water. Combinations of acrylonitrile and other materials, such as vinyl chloride, vinylidene chloride, or vinylidene dicyanide, are made in a polymerization reactor. The polymer formed in the reaction is dissolved in an appropriate solvent, and the fiber is spun, drawn, and cut into staple lengths. Varying degrees of crimp may be added to the fiber depending on its projected end uses. Modacrylics can be produced by dry- or wet-spun processes but are only sold as staple products.

Modacrylics were produced in the United States by Union Carbide (Dynel®), Eastman Kodak (Verel®), and Monsanto (SEF®). Union Carbide and Eastman have terminated production, leaving Monsanto as the only domestic producer. See Figure 10.3 for diagram of modacrylic manufacture.

General Characteristics of Modacrylics

Appearance

The microscopic appearance of various types of modacrylics differs. Cross sections range from an irregular flat shape, through a U shape, to a peanut shape. The longitudinal appearance usually shows some striations, or it may have a grainy effect. (See Figure 10.4.)

---

[1]This category excepts certain synthetic rubber products that have a substantial quantity of acrylonitrile in their composition.

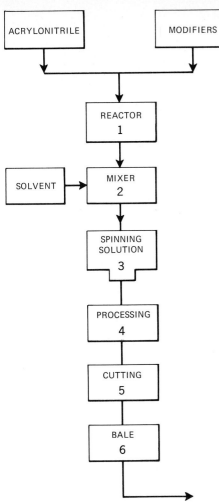

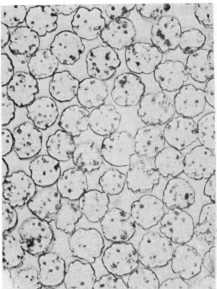

FIGURE 10.3 (left) *Flow chart for the manufacture of modacrylic fiber. Provided by the Technical Committee of the Man-made Fiber Producers' Assn.*

1 **POLYMERIZATION IN REACTOR:** The production of modacrylic fiber begins in a polymerization reactor where acrylonitrile and certain modifiers are combined into long chain-like molecules called polymer.

2 **MIXING:** A suitable solvent and the polymer are placed in a tank where they are stirred together until the polymer has dissolved and the mixture has a consistency similar to molasses.

3 **SPINNING:**
■ This mixture, called **spinning solution**, is forced through the microscopic holes of the **spinnerette** . . . a device similar to a miniature shower head . . . forming thin, continuous strands of solution.
■ The solvent is removed leaving the **polymer.**
■ The strands are gathered into bundles of continuous fibers called **tow,** which looks like untwisted rope.

4 **PROCESSING THE TOW:**
■ The tow is moved to the processing area where it is treated to make it resist shrinking or stretching.
■ Lubricating oils are added to aid in spinning yarns.
■ A crimp (like a permanent wave) is added to give texture and bulk.

5 **CUTTING:** The tow now moves to a cutting machine where the continuous strands are cut into short lengths called **staple fiber.**

6 **BALING:** The staple fibers, looking very much like wool, are compressed into bales and wrapped for shipment.

SHIPPING: The fiber is shipped to textile mills where it will be spun into yarn and woven into fabric.

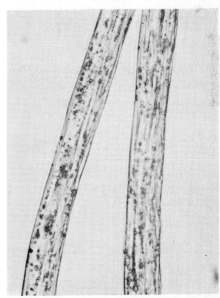

FIGURE 10.4 *Photomicrograph of modacrylic fiber in a cross-section and a longitudinal view. Courtesy of Monsanto Fibers and Intermediates Company.*

Properties

Strength. The strength of SEF® modacrylic is **1.7**, weaker than acrylics. Abrasion resistance is moderate.

Density and Specific Gravity. The specific gravity of modacrylics is 1.3, which is comparable to wool, so that the fibers feel light but also have good insulating qualities.

Elasticity and Resilience. The resilience is high, and the combination of high resilience with abrasion resistance makes modacrylic fibers especially suitable for use in high-pile fabrics. Elastic recovery is good.

Absorbency and Moisture Regain. The absorbency of the fibers is low, and the moisture regain is 0.4 to 4 per cent. As a result, the stain resistance to water-borne soil is good.

Dimensional Stability. Modacrylics have good dimensional stability. However, their sensitivity to heat may result in some shrinkage if they are dried in a dryer at high temperatures.

Effect of Heat; Combustibility. Modacrylics are inherently fire retardant. Although they will burn when placed in a direct flame, they are self-extinguishing as soon as the flame is removed. Furthermore, the melted polymer does not drip off the fabric, so that there is no danger of burns from melted polymer. For these reasons, modacrylics are being widely used in the manufacture of children's sleepwear for which the law mandates the use of flame-retardant fabrics. (See Chapter 22.)

The melting point of modacrylics is low (about 370° to 410°F). Only the olefins and saran are more sensitive to heat. If modacrylic fabrics are ironed, very low temperature settings must be used. If a dryer is used, temperatures should be set for "no heat."

Behavior of Modacrylic Fibers in Relation to Selected Factors

Chemical Resistance. Dry-cleaning solvents will not affect modacrylics adversely. These fibers are soluble in acetone, and some modacrylics may be discolored by strong alkalis. Their resistance to acids is good to excellent.

Resistance to Selected Environmental Factors. The resistance to deterioration from light is fairly good. Neither moths nor mildew attack modacrylics. Age has no apparent effect.

Uses of Modacrylic Fibers

The major areas of use for modacrylic fibers include carpets, wallcoverings, pile and fleece fabrics for apparel, blankets, flame-resistant draperies and curtains, paint roller covers, filters, wigs, and hairpieces. As a result of the fact that modacrylics have a low softening temperature and a high shrinkage potential, a variety of texturizing treatments can be given to the fibers that allow them to simulate the textures and characteristics of fur fibers. Most simulated fur fabrics are made from modacrylic or acrylic fibers. The same characteristic of modacrylics makes it possible to create hairlike fibers, which leads to their use in wigs and hairpieces.

As mentioned previously, modacrylics are naturally flame retardant, so that they are used in sleepwear, especially garments with fleecy or pile fabric constructions, carpets, curtains, and draperies, blankets, and in some industrial fabrics where their flame resistance and good chemical resistance are both utilized.

Considerations in Care of Modacrylics

Deep-pile garments must be cleaned professionally to avoid crushing or altering the appearance of the pile. Other modacrylic fabrics are machine washable, but special care should be taken to avoid exposing them to very high temperatures because of their heat sensitivity. Low dryer temperatures must be used, and ironing should only be done with a warm, not hot, iron. Some modacrylic fibers are discolored by the use of chlorine bleaches.

Trademarked Modacrylic Fibers

For many years three modacrylic fibers were made commercially: Dynel® by Union Carbide Company and Verel® by Eastman Kodak Company. During 1974–1975, Dynel® was phased out of production by Union Carbide Company. Verel® was phased out in 1984.

Monsanto manufactures modacrylics under the trademark SEF®. SEF® has been especially recommended by Monsanto for use in flame-resistant sleepwear. (See Figure 10.5.)

FIGURE 10.5 Flame resistant sleepwear made of SEF® modacrylic fiber. Courtesy of Monsanto Fibers and Intermediates Company.

Table 10.1 Selected Properties of Acrylic and Modacrylic Fibers

	Acrylic	Modacrylic
Specific gravity	1.14–1.19	1.30–1.37
Tenacity (g/d)		
Dry	2.0–3.5	2.0–3.5
Wet	1.8–3.3	2.0–3.5
Moisture regain	1.0–2.5	0.4–4.0
Resilience	good	good
Burning and melting point	in flame, burns with melting, continues after flame removed; softens at 450° to 497°F; indeterminate melting point	in flame, burns very slowly with melting; self-extinguishing after flame removed; melting point 371° (approximate) to 410°F
Conductivity of		
Heat	low	low
Electricity	low	low
Resistance to damage from		
Fungi	excellent	excellent
Insects	excellent	excellent
Prolonged exposure to sunlight	excellent	excellent
Acids	good, except nitric	good
Alkalis	good to weak alkali	good

Recommended References

HOBSON, P. H., and A. L. McPETERS. "Acrylic and Modacrylic Fibers," in Martin Grayson, ed., *Encyclopedia of Textiles, Fibers and Non-woven Fabrics*, p. 1. New York: Wiley-Interscience, 1984.

MONCRIEFF, R. W. *Man-Made Fibres*, 7th ed. London: Butterworth and Company, Ltd., 1987.

NEEDLES, HOWARD L. *Handbook of Textile Fibers, Dyes and Finishes*. New York: Garland STPM Press, 1981, Chap. 10.

SITTIG, M. *Acrylic and Vinal Fibers*. Plainfield, N.J.: Textile Book Service, 1972.

Olefin Fibers

Although olefin monofilaments have been manufactured for specialized applications since 1949, the widespread use of olefin fibers for a variety of textile products has been a relatively recent development. (British publications may refer to these fibers as polyalkenes.)

The FTC definition of olefin fiber is "a manufactured fiber in which the fiber-forming substance is any long-chain synthetic polymer composed of at least 85 per cent weight of ethylene, propylene, or other olefin units, except[1] amorphous polyolefins qualifying under category (1) of paragraph (j) of rule 7."

Two major categories of olefin fibers exist. One is polypropylene; the other is polyethylene. Of the two, polypropylene is used more extensively for textiles and constitutes the larger quantity of olefin fibers in use today.

Polypropylene Fibers

Manufacture

Polymer flakes and chips are manufactured from propylene gas, a component of natural gas. The fiber is then formed by one of two means: polypropylene may be melt spun, or it may be mechanically fibrillated. Fibrillated fibers are created by first extruding a film of polypropylene. This film is either stretched and split or slit and drawn into a network of fibers. (See Chapter 14 for a discussion of film fibrillation.)

The properties of the melt-spun fibers and fibrillated fibers differ somewhat. The denier (size) range of melt-spun fibers is greater than is that of fibrillated fibers. Fibrillated fibers have branchlike structure that may eliminate the need to add texture to the fiber. Also, fiber-to-fiber interlocking is better in fibrillated fibers, but fiber length is not so uniform, and fibrillated fibers are less regular in shape than are those from melt-spun fibers. Spun fibrillated yarns are smoother and softer. Less pigment is required to color fibrillated fibers than to color comparable spun yarns from melt-spun fibers.

---

[1]This exception refers to a type of synthetic rubber with a substantial proportion of polyolefin material.

Properties of Polypropylene Fibers

Appearance

In microscopic appearance, the polypropylene fiber may have any of several cross-sectional configurations depending on the shape of the holes of the spinneret used in extruding the fibers. The surface of the fiber is smooth. (See Figure 11.1.)

Strength. Polypropylene olefins are strong. The breaking strength is from 4.8 to 7.0 g/d (regular-tenacity nylon 66 is 3.0 to 3.6 g/d), and the abrasion resistance is good.

Density and Specific Gravity. The density of polypropylene is especially low. Its specific gravity is 0.92, or less than that of water. As a result, olefin fabrics float on water when they are washed. The low density of polypropylene also is related to the relatively low cost of olefin fiber, as a small quantity of raw materials can be used to produce a large quantity of fiber.

Elasticity and Resilience. The elastic recovery of polypropylene olefin fibers is excellent. The resilience of the fiber is fair to good.

Absorbency. Almost completely nonabsorbent, polypropylene is difficult to dye. Best results in coloring fibers are attained when the pigment is combined with the polymer before the fibers are formed. Low absorbency also makes the fiber exceptionally resistant to water-borne soil and stains. Grease and oil do stain polypropylene fabrics, and since they are oleophilic (or oil attracting), stains may be difficult to remove. Olefin fabrics have good wickability.

Dimensional Stability. The dimensional stability of heat-set polypropylene is good, as long as it is not subjected to temperatures above 250°F. Elevated temperatures will result in fabric shrinkage.

Electrical Conductivity. The electrical conductivity of polypropylene is poor. Its low absorbency contributes to problems of static electricity buildup, although finishes used in the spinning and processing of the fiber can overcome this problem in the finished product.

Effect of Heat; Combustibility. The melting point of polypropylene is quite low: 338°F. Hot bacon fat dropped on olefin carpets will melt fibers. Olefins are combustible and melt as they burn. They produce a sooty smoke.

Behavior of Olefin Fibers in Relation to Selected Factors

Chemical Resistance. In general, polypropylene's resistance to alkalis and to acids is good. Some organic solvents used in dry cleaning

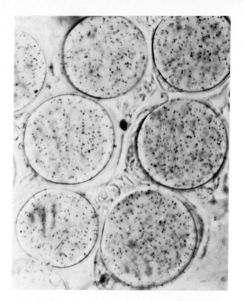

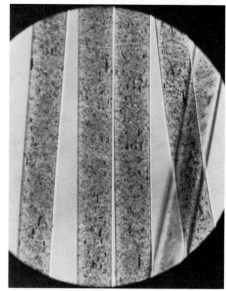

FIGURE 11.1 *Photomicrograph of Marvess®* *olefin fiber in a cross section and a* *longitudinal view. Courtesy of Phillips Fibers* *Corporation.*

may affect the fabrics adversely. Perchloroethylene should not be used. However, Stoddard solvent will not deteriorate the fibers. Home laundering is preferable to dry cleaning in the care of polypropylene fabrics.

Resistance to Environmental Factors. Mold, mildew, and insects to not attack olefins. Sunlight does gradually deteriorate the fabric, and age has no appreciable effect. Hindered amine light stabilizers, a newly introduced product, can be added to the fiber to control light degradation.

See summary of characteristics in Table 11.1.

Uses of Polypropylene

Propropylene fibers are used in the manufacture of carpets, especially indoor/outdoor carpeting. Being nonabsorbent and having good weather resistance, polypropylene can be made into carpets that will withstand exposure to outdoor conditions in areas where sunlight is not intense or prolonged. However, unless they are given a sunlight-resistant finish, such carpets will deteriorate in climates like those of the American Southwest. When polypropylene is used for traditional indoor carpets, soil- and water-borne stain resistance are exceptional. Other characteristics such as good abrasion resistance, good lightfastness if solution dyed, and resistance to moths have contributed to the successful use of polypropylene for carpetings. (See Figure 11.2.)

Table 11.1 Selected Properties of Polypropylene Fibers

Specific gravity	0.92
Tenacity (g/d)	
Dry	4.8–7.0[a]
Wet	4.8–7.0
Moisture regain	none
Resiliency	good
Burning and melting point	in flame, burns with melting; continues to burn after flame is removed; melts at 325° to 335°F
Conductivity of	
Heat	low
Electricity	low
Resistance to damage from	
Fungi	excellent
Insects	excellent
Prolonged exposure to sunlight	slowly loses strength, but can be ultraviolet stabilized effectively
Acids	excellent
Alkalis	excellent

[a]*Man-made Fiber Fact Book* (Washington, D.C.: Man-made Fiber Producers Association, Inc., 1974).

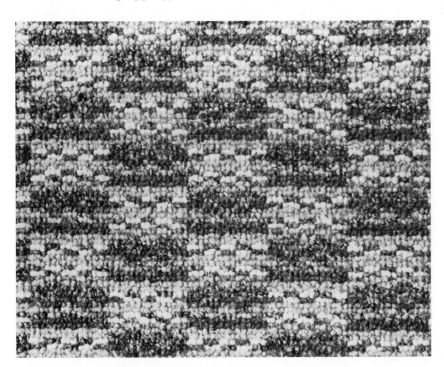

FIGURE 11.2 Nouvelle® olefin carpet fabric. This carpet is of tufted construction and has uncut loops on the surface. Courtesy Hercules Incorporated.

Upholstery fabric manufacturers have made extensive use of polypropylene in a variety of fabrics including velvets. Again, stain resistance and resistance to abrasion are important in this application. Marvess® olefin fibers (Phillips Petroleum Company) are being formed into DUON®, the trademark for nonwoven fiber webs designed for use in upholstered furniture for spring covers and cushion backing, as lining for skirts, and in other structural elements of the furniture. It is recommended by the manufacturer to replace woven fabrics in these uses. One of the advantages cited is that it is a "quiet fabric" and does not make noise or rustle when subjected to stress or movement.

Other products made from polypropylene include blankets and wall coverings, and polypropylene serves as replacement for jute and other bast fibers in twine, rope, carpet backings, and the like. It is also utilized in a variety of nonwovens, including industrial filters and diaper stock, where thermobondability is an essential property. Good wicking qualities also contribute to its use in diaper liners.

Industrial applications of olefins are numerous and include ropes, cordage, filter paper, netting, and bagging. Nonwoven olefin materials are used in road construction and in other engineering projects. Stabilizing soil to prevent erosion is one such application. (See Figure 11.3.)

Although industrial and home furnishings areas are the major outlet for polypropylene fiber, activewear apparel manufacturers are beginning to use polypropylene in garments such as knit shirts, sweaters, thermal underwear, glove liners, and sweatsuits. Hand-knitting yarns of polypropylene are also available.

Characteristics that encourage these applications are its excellent wicking qualities by which moisture is transmitted to the outer surface, thereby reducing the cold, clammy feeling next to the skin, good thermal insulating qualities, and excellent abrasion resistance.

Polypropylene is being seen in a variety of apparel applications, most often from spun yarns. It may be blended with wool, particularly for men's hosiery. Wool and polypropylene blends are being evaluated for possible use in blankets. The low specific gravity of polypropylene together with its low thermal conductivity would offer the advantage of a lighter blanket that retains the desirable properties of a heavier all-wool blanket.

Olefin fibers are also being used for insulation materials for gloves, footwear, and apparel. Very fine olefin and polyester fibers are made into a nonwoven batting that the manufacturer, 3M, calls Thinsulate®. The batting provides, according to the manufacturer, approximately two times the thermal insulation of competitive materials including 100 per cent polyester fiberfill, down, and wool. One advantage, therefore, is that warmth without excessive bulk is possible.

One of the major advantages of the fiber is the low cost of production. The *Textile Organon* for June 1985 lists seventy-five manufacturers of olefin fiber or nonwovens in the United States alone.

FIGURE 11.3 Supac® olefin engineering fabric being rolled over river sand and covered with granite and sandstone shale in order to stabilize marshy riverfront soil. Courtesy of Phillips Fibers Corporation.

Care of Polypropylene

Polypropylene carpet and upholstery fabrics are relatively care free. Stains can be wiped off with a damp cloth. Routine vacuuming and periodic shampooing will help to maintain and preserve both appearance and durability.

Garments and other items such as blankets can usually be laundered. Polypropylene is injured by some dry-cleaning fluids. Care labels should be checked carefully, as blends of polypropylene with other fibers may require special care.

All polypropylene fabrics can be laundered at moderate temperatures. This fiber is heat sensitive at about 250°F. Most dryers do not exceed temperatures of 180° to 190°F so that drying at low temperatures is permissible; however, line drying may be preferable as it generally eliminates any need for pressing. Hot irons will damage these fabrics, so only cool iron temperatures should be used if any pressing is done.

Polyethylene

Polyethylene fibers are made by the polymerization of ethylene gas. Fibers are melt spun and then drawn to orient the molecules.

Polyethylene shares many qualities in common with polypropylene and exhibits some differences, including a lower melting point for polyethylene and some tendency to be deformed if stretched more than 10 per cent. Polyethylene, not a textile fiber of major importance, is widely used for plastic films and packaging materials.

Recommended References

ANDERSON, D. F. "Polypropylene Fibers," *Textiles*, 5 (February 1976), p. 8.

BADRIAN, W. H. "Polypropylene," *Modern Textiles*, 55 (July 1974), p. 58.

COOK, J. G. *Handbook of Polyolefin Fibers.* Watford, England: Merrow Publishing Company Ltd., 1967.

"The Latest on Polypropylene," *Textile Month* (December 1975), p. 40; (January 1976), p. 38; (February 1976), p. 47

MANSFIELD, R. G. "Polypropylene in Nonwovens: Products and Participants," *Nonwovens Industry*, 16 (February 1985), p. 26.

MONCRIEFF, R. W. *Man-Made Fibres*, 7th ed. London: Butterworth and Company, Ltd., 1987.

"Polypropylene Fiber: 4000% Growth in Two Decades," *Textile World*, 134 (November 1984), p. 48.

RIDGEWAY, B. "Enter Practical, Dyeable Polypropylene," *Textile Industries*, 147 (February 1983), p. 63.

SZLOSBERG, E. "Polypropylene in Home Furnishings," *American Textiles*, 14 (March 1985), p. 84.

"Twenty Years of Polypropylene," *Modern Textiles*, 58 (October 1977), p. 7.

WISHMAN, M. "Polypropylene Fibers: Developments and Markets," *Fiber Producer International* (October 1984).

Elastomeric Fibers

Elastomeric fiber is defined as fiber made of "a natural or synthetic polymer which at room temperature can be stretched repeatedly to at least twice its original length and which after removal of the tensile load will immediately and forcibly return to approximately its original length."[1]

Natural rubber has been made into fiber for many years. Natural rubber has certain disadvantages in fiber use, however. It is difficult to dye, has poor abrasion resistance, is deteriorated by sunlight, and has relatively poor chemical resistance. Textile chemists have synthesized several new fibers that compare favorably in elasticity with rubber without some of its disadvantages.

Three generic fiber classifications have been established for elastomeric fibers: spandex, rubber, and anidex. Other elastomeric fibers have been made by modifying cellulose fibers, and still other elastomers are in experimental stages of development. Of these generic fiber groups only rubber and spandex are currently being manufactured.

Rubber Fibers

Rubber

The Federal Trade Commission has established a category that is designated as rubber fibers. The definition established is divided into three parts and includes both natural and synthetic rubber.

Natural rubber is obtained from rubber plants. From a liquid form, the rubber can be extruded into fibrous form. For many years, natural rubber was used as the core for fiber-covered elastic materials. Its advantages include elasticity, flexibility, good strength, and nonabsorbency. Its disadvantages include deterioration by temperatures above 200°F and by sunlight, oils, petroleum, and aging.

Globe Manufacturing Company, the largest domestic producer of natural latex rubber–based thread, indicates that these products are used

---

[1] *Compilation of ASTM Standard Definitions*, 3rd ed. (Philadelphia: American Society for Testing and Materials, 1982), p. 205.

in such areas as hosiery, elastic waistbands for underwear, foundation garments, surgical support stockings and stretch bandages, and industrial stretch items.

A variety of synthetic rubber products was marketed after World War II. These products are made from hydrocarbons such as polyisoprene, polybutadiene, and noncrystalline polyolefins. Copolymers of dienes and hydrocarbons are also used in the manufacture of some synthetic rubber.

The FTC also identifies synthetic rubber made from "polychloroprene or a copolymer of chloroprene in which at least 35 per cent by weight of the fiber-forming substance is composed of chloroprene units." Synthetic rubbers exhibit similar characteristics to natural rubber in their behavior but in general show better resistance to deterioration than does rubber.

Spandex

Manufactured in the United States since 1959, spandex fibers have attained extensive use in stretch fabrics for foundation garments, sports apparel, and other products where elasticity is important.

The FTC defines spandex fibers as "a manufactured fiber in which the fiber-forming substance is a long-chain synthetic polymer comprised of at least 85 per cent of a segmented polyurethane." The polyurethane components are structured into linear polymers in combinations with other substances such as polyesters, polyamides, polyglycols, or copolymers of these compounds. The methodologies and compounds used by manufacturers are not released to the public.

Appearance

The microscopic appearance of spandex fibers differs from one trademarked fiber to another. In cross section, some are round, some are shaped like peanut shells, and others are shaped like dog bones. Longitudinal views display even, smooth, though dark, surfaces. (See Figure 12.1.)

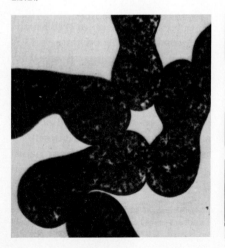 

FIGURE 12.1   Photomicrograph of Lycra® spandex fiber in a cross-section and a longitudinal view. Courtesy of E. I. du Pont de Nemours & Company.

Properties

Because spandex is selected for use in many products in which rubber might be used, it may be helpful to compare the properties of spandex to rubber as well as to other fibers.

Strength or Tenacity. Spandex is relatively weak when compared with nonelastomeric fibers. It is about twice as strong as rubber. Breaking strength ranges from 0.7 to 1.0 g/d depending on type.

Density or Specific Gravity. Spandex has a moderate density. Specific gravity is 1.2.

Elasticity and Elastic Recovery. The most important property of spandex is its ability to stretch and recover. It will stretch 500 to 600 per cent without breaking. This amount of stretching is comparable to that of rubber. Recovery from stretching is slightly better for rubber than for spandex. The improved strength of spandex combined with its excellent strength give it an advantage over rubber. Other properties of spandex that are described in the following paragraphs also make spandex more practical to use than rubber.

Absorbency and Moisture Regain. Although the absorbency and moisture regain of spandex fibers are low, water will penetrate the fiber.

Effect of Heat; Combustibility. Spandex fibers will burn. The melting point varies from trademarked fiber to trademarked fiber, and the specific melting point is difficult to ascertain. Apparently most spandex fibers melt at temperatures of about 430° to 450°F. These fibers stick at temperatures around 340°F.

Spandex can be heat-set. Spandex fibers can be dried safely in an automatic dryer. Hot water tends to yellow white spandex.

Spandex Fiber and Its Behavior in Relation to Selected Conditions

Chemical Resistance. The resistance to chemicals is generally good. Chlorine compounds in strong concentrations will cause the fiber to be degraded and yellowed, but spandex will withstand chlorine concentrations such as those used in swimming pools. Chlorine bleaches should be avoided.

Sea water has no deleterious effect on spandex fibers. Perspiration and suntan oils do not seriously affect spandex, although some suntan oils may cause yellowing of white fibers. (Suntan oils *do* deteriorate rubber.)

Resistance to Microorganisms and Light. Spandex has satisfactory resistance to microorganisms. Exposure to light does cause yellowing of

Table 12.1 Selected Properties of Spandex Fibers

Specific gravity	1.21
Tenacity (g/d)	
Dry	0.7–1.0
Wet	0.7–1.0
Moisture regain	1.3%
Breaking extension	500–600%
Elasticity and resilience	excellent
Burning and melting point	in flame, burns with melting; continues to burn after flame is removed; melts at 446° to 518°F
Conductivity of	
Heat	difficult to assess because fiber is used in combination with other fibers
Electricity	difficult to assess because fiber is used in combination with other fibers
Resistance to damage from	
Fungi	excellent
Insects	excellent
Prolonged exposure to sunlight	resists degradation, yellows
Acids	good—acid fumes may cause yellowing.
Alkalis	fair

white spandex but does not deteriorate the fiber seriously. See summary of spandex characteristics in Table 12.1.

Use of Spandex Fibers

Spandex fibers are always used in conjunction with other fibers. This combination may be made in one of several ways. The spandex fiber may be made as bare yarn, single-covered yarn, double-covered yarn, or core-spun yarn.

Bare core spandex yarns are uncovered filaments. They may be woven into fabrics in combination with other yarns. This provides additional strength to the spandex and stretch to the fabric. More often, the spandex is covered with another fiber and the spandex serves as the core. Single-covered yarns are wrapped inside the filament yarn of another fiber.

Double-covered yarns are wrapped in companion filament fibers in which one layer is twisted around the core in one direction, and the second layer is twisted around the core in the opposite direction. These can be made into very sheer yarns and are often used for support hose. Where it is desirable, two different types of fibers can be used, one in each layer. Core-spun yarns are made by holding spandex filaments at tension while a staple fiber is spun around the core. (See Figure 12-2.)

Spandex yarns are woven or knitted into a variety of garments in

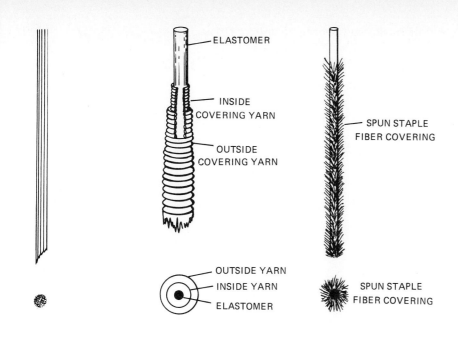

Bare Filament   Covered Yarn   Core-spun Yarn

FIGURE 12.2 *Types of elastomeric yarns (length and cross section).*

which stretch is desirable. These may include power nets for foundation garments, underwear, lingerie, and active sportwear used in sports such as swimming, skiing, golf, and tennis. Attractive stretch laces and other decorative fabrics may be made with spandex.

Cost of spandex fibers is relatively high. As a result, the use of spandex is made chiefly in those applications where alternative forms of providing stretch, such as stretch-texturing nylon or polyester, are inadequate.

Care of Spandex Fibers

Spandex fibers are used in combination with other fibers, so that care must take into account not only the characteristics of spandex but also of the other fiber. Spandex should not be subject to excessive heat in ironing. It is recommended that ironing temperatures not exceed 300°F or the "synthetic" setting on a hand iron. Dryer temperatures should be moderate. Chlorine bleaches should not be used in laundering spandex.

Trademarks of Spandex

Trade names for spandex fiber include Lycra®, a DuPont trademark, and Glospan® and Cheerspan® by Globe Manufacturing Company.

Cook, J. G. *Handbook of Textile Fibers*, Vol. 2. Watford, England: Merrow Publishing Company Ltd., 1967.

"Lycra: A World of Difference," *American Fabrics and Fashions*, no. 126 (1982), p. 31.

Meredith, R. *Elastomeric Fibres*. Watford, England: Merrow Publishing Company Ltd., 1971.

Moncrieff, R. W. *Man-Made Fibres*, 7th ed. London: Butterworth and Company, Ltd., 1987.

Recommended References

Other Man-made and Bicomponent Fibers

13

In addition to the man-made fibers discussed in earlier chapters, there are a number of fibers that have somewhat limited use or represent relatively recent developments in the technology of man-made fiber production. These include a number of synthetic fiber types that are manufactured either in the United States or abroad.

Saran

Saran is a textile fiber of limited use. It is defined as "a manufactured fiber in which the fiber-forming substance is any long-chain synthetic polymer composed of at least 80 per cent by weight of vinylidene chloride units ($-CH_2-CCl_2-$)."

Introduced by Dow Chemical Company in 1941, saran is now made in the United States by Ametek. It is a stiff, nondrapable fiber with specialized uses in agricultural and industrial fabrics. Upholstery fabrics for deck chairs and garden furniture have been made from saran.

Production and Processing

The molten vinylidene chloride/vinyl chloride copolymer is forced through the spinneret, air spun into cold air, quenched in water, and stretched. Saran fibers can be delustered and/or solution dyed.

Appearance

In microscopic view, filaments of saran have a round cross section. The longitudinal view shows a smooth surface. Saran can also be produced in flat and oval shapes.

Properties

Strength. Saran is generally made with a large diameter, so that its strength is very good. It also has excellent tear and abrasion resistance.

Density and Specific Gravity. A high-density fiber (specific gravity is higher than that is of most other synthetics at 1.70), the weight and inflexibility of the fiber eliminate it from use in apparel fabrics.

Elasticity and Resilience. Fibers made of saran have excellent elastic recovery and are quite resilient.

Absorbency. Saran is nonabsorbent. The moisture regain is less than 0.1 per cent.

Dimensional Stability. If saran is not exposed to excessive temperatures, its dimensional stability is good.

Conductivity of Heat and Electricity. Because of the low heat and electrical conductivity of saran, it may be used for insulation purposes.

Combustibility; Effect of Heat. Saran burns very slowly if placed in a direct flame. The fiber is self-extinguishing after removal of the flame. The melting point of the fiber is relatively low: 335°F.

Effect of Selected Conditions on Saran Fibers

Chemical Resistance. Neither acids nor alkalis affect the fiber adversely to any extent.

Resistance to Insects, Microorganisms, and Sun. Saran is not attacked by moths, mildew, or bacteria. Sunlight resistance is very good, although some discoloration may take place after long exposure to the sun.

Uses of Saran

Upholstery fabrics made from saran have been used for public conveyances, deck chairs, garden furniture, and the like. Its low absorbency, good sunlight and weather resistance, and strength and abrasion resistance make saran appropriate for this use.

Agricultural fabrics take advantage of the weather and flame-resistant characteristics of saran. Such fabrics are used to provide shade for growing plants. The chemical resistance of the fiber results in a variety of industrial uses. Saran grille fabrics are used in sound systems because they distort sound less than other materials do. Some saran drapery fabrics made of saran in combination with other fibers, such as modacrylics, are used for making drapery fabrics that are flame resistant.

Furniture with saran webbing can be cleaned easily with soap and water. Because the fiber is nonabsorbent, these items will dry quickly. They do not stain readily.

Vinyon fibers are used most frequently in industrial applications where their high resistance to chemicals is useful. Vinyon has a low melting point and is, therefore, useful as a bonding agent in nonwoven fabric construction.

FTC defines vinyon as "a manufactured fiber in which the fiber-forming substance is any long-chain synthetic polymer composed of at least 85 per cent by weight of vinyl chloride units ($—CH_2——CHCl—$)."

The low melting point of vinyon has prevented its use to any extent in apparel. (The fiber is combined with vinal, however, in making a bi-constituent fiber Cordelan®; see page 190.) Vinyon has high resistance to chemicals. Major uses are as a bonding agent in industrial nonwoven applications and for tea bags and other speciality uses.

Fibers Not Currently in Production in the United States

The production of novoloid, vinal, and nytril fibers has been discontinued in the United States. Imported items made from vinal can sometimes be purchased; however, nytril is no longer being manufactured.

Novoloid

Novoloid fibers are manufactured fibers "containing at least 85 per cent by weight of a cross-linked novolac." Novoloid fibers are no longer produced domestically, nor is the fiber used extensively in the domestic market. Characteristics included low tenacity and fair abrasion resistance; it is noncombustible and nonmelting. Chemical resistance is good. Major uses were in industrial products, and some protective garments were woven from blends of novoloid and Nomex® aramid.

Nytril

"A manufactured fiber containing at least 85 per cent of a long-chain polymer of vinylidene dinitrile ($—CH_2—C(CN)_2—$) where the vinylidene dinitrile content is no less than every other unit in the polymer chain," nytril fibers are soft and resilient. They have a low melting point, softening at temperatures similar to those of modacrylic fibers. Nytril fibers are most suitable for items that do not require pressing.

Major uses of nytril fibers were in garments where the softness was desirable, in pile fabrics, and in blends with wool. Like most synthetics, nytrils had low absorbency, washed and dried quickly, and had good wrinkle recovery.

Vinal

The FTC calls vinal "a manufactured fiber in which the fiber-forming substance is any long-chain synthetic polymer composed of at least 50 per cent by weight of vinyl alcohol units ($—CH_2—CHOH—$) and in which the total of the vinyl alcohol units and any one or more of the various acetal units is at least 85 per cent by weight of the fiber."

Most of the development of vinal has taken place in Japan. The fiber has a melting point close to that of nylon 6 (around 425°F) and very good chemical resistance and is especially resistant to rot-producing micro-organisms.

The use of vinal fibers is largely in industrial applications, although some blends of vinal fiber with cotton, rayon, or silk have been used abroad. Vinal scarves imported from Japan are available in the United States both in 100 per cent vinal or in blends.

In some countries vinal fibers are called polyvinyl alcohol fibers.

Fluorocarbons and Fluoropolymers

Used for industrial purposes, fluorocarbon and fluoropolymer material may be formed into fibers, extruded as a molded form, or formed into sheets. It can also be applied as a coating to other substances.

Consumers may know Teflon®, a fluorocarbon manufactured by DuPont as a coating for cooking utensils. Teflon® fluorocarbon polymer is also made into a thin, microporous membrane that is used in making GORE-TEX® fabrics, which have wide use in outdoor apparel. (See Chapter 21 for a discussion of GORE-TEX® fabrics.)

Fluoropolymer fibers differ somewhat in chemical composition from fluorocarbons but have generally similar properties and can be used in comparable applications. All have excellent chemical resistance, are usable over a wide temperature range, resist abrasion, and are nonabsorbent. Trademark names for fluoropolymers are Kynar®, Halar®, and Tefzel®. Industrial uses include pump and valve packing, gaskets, filtration materials, bearings, and office copy equipment.

Uses of Teflon® TFE fibers include protective clothing, chemical and heat-resistant sewing thread, conveyer belts, and other industrial fabrics.

Polyphenylene Sulfide Fiber

Rhyton® polyphenylene sulfide fiber is manufactured by Phillips Petroleum Company. The company has petitioned the Federal Trade Commission to establish a new generic category for this fiber. It has suggested any of these names: "arofide, sulfar, or arosul." A decision is pending.

Rhyton® is described by Phillips as having tenacity, elongation, modulus, elastic recovery, boiling water shrinkage, and moisture regain that are satisfactory for textile applications. Its melting point is very high (545°F, 285°C); chemical resistance is described as excellent.

Suitable applications for the fiber include filter bags for filtration of

Fibers for Industrial or Specialty Uses

high-temperature materials, woven and nonwoven filter fabrics for gas and liquids, papermaker felts, and protective clothing.

The manufacturer suggests that Rhyton® has advantages over competing high-temperature-resisting, chemically resistant fibers in that it is less expensive and easy to process.

Polybenzimidazole Fiber

Celanese Corporation has asked the Federal Trade Commission to establish a new generic name for polybenzimidazole or PBI fiber. It has suggested the generic name of "arasole."

PBI entered commercial production in May 1983. The largest present end use of PBI is in civilian and military protective apparel. It is being used as a successful alternative to asbestos in protective gloves, gaskets, and packing materials in industrial applications and to construct fire-blocking material in places such as aircraft.

The fiber is nonflammable in air, emits little or no toxic gases or smoke up to temperatures of 1040°F, and has excellent resistance to acids, organic solvents, and fuels. The fiber is currently produced in staple form.

Soluble Fibers

Fibers that will dissolve are useful for rather specialized applications in the textile industry. Alginates, regenerated fibers made from seaweed, are soluble. In a preliminary step during the manufacture of vinal, a soluble form of this fiber is created. (Nonsoluble vinals or polyvinyl alcohols—PVA Fibers are given additional treatments to render them insoluble.)

Production of alginates is reported to have ceased in the United Kingdom, where their manufacture had been concentrated. PVA fibers, manufactured in Japan, seem to have superseded the alginates in most uses.

Soluble yarns may be used as "support" yarns in fabric construction where open, sheer, or lacelike effects are desired but are not attainable through normal weaving processes. The fabric is woven then laundered, causing the yarns to dissolve, leaving only the insoluble yarns in a lacy open pattern.

Soluble yarns may also be used when wool socks are manufactured in a continuous "string" with a few rows of stitches between the toe of one sock and the top of the next. The socks are cut apart, and when subjected to finishing processes, the remaining soluble threads dissolve out, leaving a smoothly finished edge. Only hot water is required to dissolve polyvinyl alcohol fibers, whereas alginates must be laundered in water with dilute sodium carbonate or sodium phosphate added.

As the technology for the manufacture of man-made fibers has become more highly developed, increasingly sophisticated techniques for creating new fibers have been utilized. Not only are new generic fibers being created, but different polymers or variants of the same polymer can be combined into a single fiber in order to take advantage of the special characteristics of each polymer. Such fibers are known as bicomponent and biconstituent fibers.

Different sources define these terms in different ways. Definitions of the American Society for Testing Materials (ASTM) are as follows.

Bicomponent fiber is defined as "a fiber composed of two physically and chemically distinct polymeric components in continuous, longitudinal contact within the fiber."

Bicomponent fibers can be made from two variants of the same generic fiber (for example, two types of nylon, two types of acrylic) or from two generically different fibers (for example, nylon and polyester or nylon and spandex).

Bicomponent fibers may be of two types: side-by-side bicomponent fibers or sheath-core fibers. In making a side-by-side bicomponent fiber, the process requires that the different polymers be fed to the spinneret orifice together so that they exit from the spinneret opening, side by side.

Sheath-core fibers require that one component be completely surrounded by the other, so that the polymer is generally fed into the spinneret as shown in the diagram. (See Figure 13.1.) Variation in the shape

Bicomponent and Biconstituent Fibers

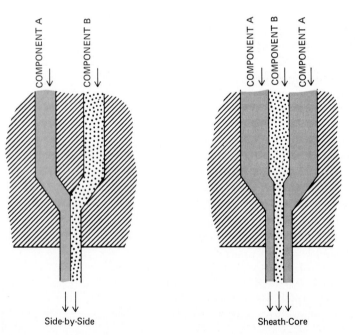

FIGURE 13.1   Formation of bicomponent fibers.

FIGURE 13.2 *Photomicrograph of cross section of Monvelle® biconstituent fiber. The spandex portion of the fiber shows as black; the nylon is transparent. This fiber is no longer manufactured. The photograph shows clearly how different constituents can be combined. Courtesy of the Monsanto Fibers and Intermediates Company.*

of the orifice that contains the inner core can produce fibers with different behavioral characteristics. (See Figure 13-2.)

Most bicomponent fibers are made to provide stretch or crimp to the fiber. Each of the polymers used in the bicomponent fiber has slightly different characteristics. Often one polymer is made to shrink in heat or chemical treatment more than the other, which pulls the fiber into a permanent crimp. If sufficient crimp is provided or if the fiber is elastic, the bicomponent fiber may also have increased stretchability. Cantrece® nylon is a bicomponent fiber with good stretch that is used in hosiery. Other uses for bicomponent fibers have been suggested. For example, components with different melting points could be used to bond fibers together in the construction of nonwoven fabrics. When heat is applied, one fiber softens, serving as a glue to hold the other fiber in place. A less absorbent core fiber could be sheathed in a more absorbent fiber, in order to increase comfort or increase dyeability.

Biconstituent fibers are defined as fibers "consisting of a continuous matrix of one polymer in which a different fiber-forming polymer is dispersed as a second, distinct, discontinuous phase." This type of fiber is also referred to as a "matrix" fiber. A matrix fiber is one in which the fiber-forming components are dispersed one within the other before they are extruded. Figure 13.3 illustrates the structure of a matrix fiber. Few commercial matrix or biconstituent fibers have been manufactured.

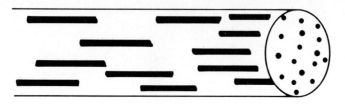

FIGURE 13.3. *Longitude and cross section of matrix fiber structure. The black areas represent fibrils of one generic fiber; the second fiber is represented by the white.*

One, Cordelan®, a Japanese fire-retardant fabric recommended for children's sleepwear, was distributed in the United States for a time, but is no longer available.

Under the Textile Fiber Products Information Act, those products made from bicomponent or biconstituent fibers that are composed of different generic fibers must have listed on their labels the generic fibers present. Constituents are to be listed in the order of "predominance by weight" and must state the "respective percentages of such components by weight." The ruling goes on to state, "If the components of such fibers are of a matrix-fibril configuration, the term 'matrix-fibril' or 'matrix fiber' may be used."

The label of a Cordelan® fiber might, therefore, have read as follows:

100% matrix fiber
(50% vinal, 50% vinyon)

Bicomponent fibers made from the same generic fiber are not covered by this regulation. They are composed of the same generic fiber type throughout, even though the different types of the same polymer may each exhibit somewhat different characteristics. Orlon Sayelle®, for example, is 100 per cent acrylic and would be labeled as such.

Future Directions of Man-made Fiber Technology

Bicomponent fibers represent one of the newer techniques for producing man-made fibers. Some authorities refer to these fibers as "third-generation man-made fibers."

The American Fabrics *Encyclopedia of Textiles* identifies the three phases or generations of man-made fiber development as being invention, diversification, and sophistication.[1]

In the first or invention phase, the basic polymer technology for man-made fibers was developed. During the diversification phase, scientists modified the various generic types of man-made fibers so that their performance would be improved and they would be more widely accepted by consumers. Now in the present phase of sophistication, fibers are being modified to make them appropriate for specialized end uses.

[1]*Encyclopedia of Textiles. American Fabrics* (Englewood Cliffs, N.J.: Prentice-Hall, Inc. 1980), p. 63.

The bicomponent fibers represent one aspect of this phase. The other aspect is seen in the manufacture of specialized varieties of the same generic fiber in high, medium, and low tenacities; more or less absorbent types; and those for special end uses such as carpets and knits or for nonwovens.

Representatives of the textile industry who predict the future of man-made fiber development say that they expect to see few new generic fibers based on radically different polymers from those known today. Exceptions to this projection will probably occur in areas in which a specific need for new fibers has been demonstrated, such as noncombustible generic fiber types suitable for clothing and household goods and fibers for high-technology applications.

Predicted, instead, is the continued development or refinement of special properties of existing fibers. Alteration of properties may be accomplished by varying spinning techniques, changing the cross-section shapes, grafting side-chain molecules onto polymers, and expanding the variety of matrix and bicomponent fibers.

Recommended References

DE MARTINO, R. N. "Comfort Properties of Polybenzimidazole Fiber," *Textile Research Journal*, 54, (August 1984), p. 516.

NETHERBY, S. "Beat The Rain," *Field and Stream*, 89, (September 1984), p. 102.

Properties, Processes and Applications of Teflon TFE Fluorocarbon Fiber," *Bulletin TF-2* Wilmington, Del.: E. I. du Pont de Nemours & Company, May 1978.

"Report on U.S. Fiber Companies," *American Fashions and Fabrics*, No. 119 (Spring 1980), p. 4.

Making Fibers into Yarns

For the production of cloth woven or knitted from either natural or synthetic fibers, fibers must be made into yarns. The type of yarn chosen for a fabric affects the appearance of the fabric, its durability, and its hand and draping characteristics. Yarn construction can serve either to enhance or to detract from the inherent qualities of the fiber from which the yarn is spun.

Fiber for yarns is supplied either in the form of long, continuous filaments or short, staple lengths. Being long, continuous strands themselves, filaments may require little more than some additional twisting to make them into yarns. Sometimes they are put through an additional process called *texturing*. Being short, staple fibers must be held together by some means in order to be formed into a long, continuous yarn. Although the multiple processes required to make a staple yarn add significantly to the cost of the yarn, the aesthetic qualities such as comfort, warmth, softness, and appearance make these yarns highly desirable in many products.

Short, staple yarns require fairly complex spinning processes. Moreover, the physical characteristics of different fibers require that machinery utilized in the construction of yarns be adapted to the requirements of spinning that fiber. For example, the machinery for spinning wool is different from the machinery for spinning cotton. Even so, the spinning of a staple yarn, whether by hand or machine and whether cotton, wool, or man-made, utilizes certain fundamental processes. These are

1. Preparing the fibers.
2. Making the fibers more or less parallel.
3. Forming a long strand of aligned fibers.
4. Drawing the strand to reduce its size.
5. Inserting twist or by some other means holding the fibers together to form a yarn.
6. Winding the completed yarn onto a bobbin or some other package.

Hand Spinning

Before the invention of man-made fibers, all yarns except those made from silk had to be spun from short, staple fibers. At first these staple fibers were twisted together by hand. A simple experiment will easily demonstrate how this can be done. Take a small bunch of cotton from a roll of absorbent cotton. Pull off a long strand and begin to twist the fibers in one direction. You will soon find that you have a rather short, coarse, but recognizable, cotton yarn. Rolling the fiber between the hand and the leg is another primitive method of spinning. Hand twisting by an experienced spinner can produce an acceptable yarn. Ancient textiles have been found in Peruvian graves that were woven from hand-twisted cotton yarns of excellent quality.

Before fibers could be twisted into yarns, some attempt had to be made to bring them into a more parallel alignment. This could be done by hand by running fingers through a bundle of fibers in order to straighten the fibers somewhat. Tools were designed to do the job more efficiently, and hand spinners still use an ancient device called a *carder*, a pair of wooden paddles on which is mounted a leather piece set with bent wire hooks. The process of straightening fibers prior to spinning, be it done by hand or by machine, is called *carding*. (See Figure 14.1.)

A small quantity of fiber was placed on one carder. The second carder was laid against the first, and each was pulled in the opposite direction. This process was repeated several times until the fibers were roughly parallel and any extraneous material had fallen out. The carded fibers were put aside for spinning.

Fibers were made more completely parallel by a further step called *combing*. Combing was generally reserved for fibers of longer lengths, and the process, using a device shaped like a comb, pulled the fibers into alignment.

After the fiber had been carded or carded and combed, the actual twisting together of the fibers was begun. The spinner who twisted fibers together by hand needed a place to put the completed yarns. The solution was to wind them onto a stick. In time, the stick itself became a tool for spinning. By notching the stick to hold the thread and by adding a weight (called the *whorl*) to the end of the stick, a spindle was made. With the whorl to provide momentum, the spinner could use the stick to help in twisting the yarn. The spinner stood erect and held the mass of fiber under the left arm, leaving both hands free to work. A long, untwisted strand of fiber was fed to the spindle by the left hand. With the right hand, the spinner gave the stick a twist and let it fall, whirling, toward the ground. The momentum and weight of the falling spindle twisted the fibers into a continuous yarn. The right hand was used to control the quantity of fiber feeding onto the spindle. When the spindle reached the ground, the spinner bent over, picked up the spindle, and wrapped the newly made yarn around the stick. Pulling out a new

Steps in the Historical Development of Spinning

FIGURE 14.1 Woman uses hand carders to card wool prior to spinning. The uncarded fiber is placed in a basket to the right of the picture, and rolls of carded fiber are seen on top of a basket to the left.

bunch of fiber, the spinner twisted the end of the unspun fiber to the end of the completed yarn, and began the process again.

For better control of spinning, bundles of fiber were mounted on a long staff. The staff also prevented the fibers from becoming entangled. The Old English word for a bundle of flax was *dis*, and so the staff on which the fiber was placed came to be known as the *distaff*. (See Figure 14.2.)

So closely were women associated with the tasks of spinning that many of these terms have taken on interesting connotations in modern language usage. The spinning was often done by the unmarried girls and adult women, and so the terms spinster has become a synonym for an unmarried woman. The distaff was used almost exclusively by women, and in time the term has come to connote women's activities or interests.

For many thousands of years this hand method of spinning was the only way in which yarn could be made. A major improvement in this technique originated in India when the action of a wheel was added to the spinning of the yarn. The Indian *charka* or spinning wheel seems to have been invented sometime between A.B. 500 and A.D. 1000.[1] Since the production of cotton was paramount in India, this wheel was devised to spin cotton. The spinning wheel did not come into wide use in Europe until the fourteenth century, and it is thought to have been carried to Spain by way of the Arab countries that occupied Spain until the late 1400s. The original Indian wheel that had been used for cotton was small and close to the ground. A modification of this wheel that allowed the spinner to stand was made in Europe, but the same basic wheel, with minor modifications, was used for spinning flax, cotton, or silk. Wool, however, required a bigger wheel, and the wool spinning wheel was always made with a much enlarged wheel. (See Figure 14.3.)

With the earliest European wheels, the spinner had to move back and forth in front of the wheel, turning it first in one direction to spin, then in the opposite direction to wind the yarn. Modifications of design produced a treadle mechanism for turning the wheel, and this made it possible for the spinner to sit at the wheel to spin. Another advance came in the sixteenth century with the invention of a "flyer and detachable bobbin" mechanism. This device allowed the simultaneous spinning and winding of yarn onto the bobbin, thus eliminating the interruptions occasioned by the older operation in which (1) the yarn was spun, (2) the spinning was interrupted to wind the thread, and then (3) the spinning was begun anew.

Throughout the development of all these processes, power was always supplied by the spinner, either through hand- or foot-and-hand motions.

FIGURE 14.2 *Hand spinning with spindle and distaff. The woman holds the distaff under her left arm, draws fibers from the bundle tied to the distaff, and spins fibers into a yarn by lowering the spindle with a spinning motion. Spun yarn is wrapped around the spindle as it is formed.*

[1]W. Born, "The Indian Hand-Spinning Wheel," *CIBA Review*, No. 28 (December 1939), pp. 988 ff.

WHEEL, CARD, AND REEL.   WOOL WHEEL.

FIGURE 14.3   Spinning wheels. The wheel on the left is a flax wheel. On the ground under the wheel stands a device for winding skeins of yarn and one for hackling (carding) flax fibers. The wheel on the right is a wool wheel.

Mechanization of Spinning

The invention of the spinning wheel may be thought of as the first mechanization of spinning. In 1741, John Wyatt and Lewis Paul built the first of a series of machines for spinning cotton yarn. Wyatt and Paul used a roller-drafting principle; that is, they fed a long strand of carded or combed fibers through a series of rollers. Each set of rollers moved at a different speed, thereby drawing out or elongating the strand of fibers. This strand of fibers was called the *roving*. From the roller the strand of fibers was stretched to a bobbin-and-flyer twisting mechanism, like that of a spinning wheel. Arkwright utilized this same principle in 1769 when he constructed a spinning machine called the "water frame," which was given this name because it was operated by water power.

A second spinning machine was invented by James Hargreaves sometime in the 1760s. Utilizing the basic principles of the spinning wheel, Hargreaves's "spinning jenny" made eight yarns at the same time. A later patent shows that the number of yarns that could be made was increased to sixteen, and eventually the jenny was modified to make as many as one hundred yarns.

Both the spinning jenny and the Arkwright machine had certain limitations. Yarns made on these machines were not as strong as hand-spun yarns and were, therefore, not as suitable for use in the warp where greater tension was placed on the threads.

Samuel Crompton combined both the Arkwright machine and the

spinning jenny into one basic machine that utilized both rotating rollers in drawing out the yarn and a moving carriage that provided the twist needed to make strong, fine yarns. This machine, known as the spinning mule, was the basic machine for producing cotton yarn in England until well into the twentieth century.

Although each of these methods made it possible for the quantity of yarn produced by one spinner to be enormously increased, they still required supervisory personnel to keep the machines operating. In about 1830, a device was developed that could be added to the spinning mule to make its operation completely automatic. These first machines were made for spinning cotton yarns, but the spinning jenny and subsequent modifications of this machine allowed the mechanization of wool spinning as well.

At about the same time that the automatic spinning mule was developed, an American inventor named John Thorpe devised a ring spinning machine. This machine has been used in the United States since about 1830 and is a basic machine used for spinning cotton and other staple fibers today.

The most recent development in the spinning of yarns from staple fibers is a process known as "open-end spinning." In this method of spinning, air suction takes the fibers through a spinning tube in which twist is imparted to the fiber.

Modern Spinning

Natural fibers, except for silk, are all staple in length. Silk and all man-made filament fibers can be cut or broken into staple length, so that it is possible to spin any natural or man-made fiber into a yarn.

Preparation of the Staple Fiber for Spinning

From the time staple fibers are supplied to the manufacturer until they have been made into yarns, they go through a series of steps, some of which are required for all yarns and fibers and some of which are optional.

Blending of Staple Fibers

It is sometimes desirable to blend two or more different fibers into one yarn. Frequently, man-made fibers are blended with natural fibers to take advantage of the best qualities of each fiber. In other blends the combination may be made to reduce the cost of the fabric by blending a less expensive fiber with a more expensive one, or blending may be done to achieve decorative effects.

Blending may be done at one of several steps in the preparation of yarns from staple fibers: during formation of the lap, during carding, or during drawing out. No matter when blending is done, quantities of each fiber to be used are measured carefully, and the proportions of one fiber to another are consistently maintained.

Breaking and Opening Bundles and Cleaning Fibers

Bales of fiber may be opened either by hand or by machine. (See Figure 14.4.) Many modern textile mills have completely mechanized this process. The trend toward mechanization of opening cotton bales has been accelerated by the requirements of the Occupational Safety and Health Act that workers' exposure to cotton dust be limited. As noted earlier, high levels of cotton dust appear to be associated with a lung disease called byssinosis.

Cotton contains impurities such as sand or grit and particles of leaf, stalk, and seeds. New wool that has not previously been cleaned contains vegetable matter, sand, dirt, and grease. Both may require special cleaning after the bales have been opened.

FIGURE 14.4 *Bales are opened and cotton from several different bales is blended together in the opening room. Photograph courtesy of the National Cotton Council of America.*

Man-made fibers do not require cleaning, but if they have been compressed for packing and shipping, they need to be opened and the fibers separated so that bunches of fibers do not cling together and form thick areas or *slubs* in the yarn.

Spinning Systems

Processing of fibers in preparation for spinning may be done on one of three major spinning systems: the cotton, the worsted or long-staple, or the wool system. These systems developed at the time when only natural fibers were in use; therefore, the different characteristics of the fibers, including their length, helped to shape the processes used. Man-made staple fibers can be handled on any of these systems. More yarn is produced on the cotton system than on the worsted or wool systems.

Yarn Formation by the Cotton System

Once the bales of fiber are opened, the lumps of fiber are loosened and separated by the *picker*, which also cleans off heavier impurities. The resulting *lap*, a flattened, fairly uniform layer of fibers, is fed directly into a *carder*. Blending of fibers may be done by combining two or more types of fibers in the lap if subsequent handling of the different fibers is compatible.

Carding. The carding machine is set with hundreds of fine wires that separate the fibers and pull them into somewhat parallel form. A thin web of fiber is formed in this machine, and as the web is moved along it passes through a funnel-shaped device that forms it into a rope-like strand of roughly parallel fibers. (See Figure 14.5.)

Blending can take place at the point of carding by joining laps of different fibers. Carding mixes the blend fibers together, distributing them evenly throughout the mass of fiber.

Carding is done to all fibers. In processing linen fiber, carding is done but is called *hackling*.

Combing. Whereas carding is a step in the production of all fibers, combing is an optional step in the preparation of some yarns. When a smoother, finer yarn is wanted, fibers are subjected to a further paralleling called *combing*. A comblike device arranges fibers into parallel form. At the same time, the short fibers fall out of the strand. (See Figure 14.6.)

Combed yarns have smooth surfaces and finer diameters than do carded yarns. Fewer short ends show on the surface of the fabric and the luster is increased. Combed yarns are more expensive to produce, and fabrics made from combed yarns are, therefore, higher in price. Far more of the yarn produced on the cotton system is carded than that which is both carded and combed.

FIGURE 14.5 Cleaning and separation of individual fibers takes place in the carding machine. A web of fibers is formed into a thin ropelike strand or sliver. Photograph courtesy of the National Cotton Council of America.

Drawing Out. After carding or combing, the fiber mass is referred to as the *sliver*. Several slivers are combined before the drawing out process. Blending of fibers can be done by combining slivers of different fibers. During the drawing out, a series of rollers rotating at different rates of speed elongate or draw out the sliver into a single more uniform strand that is given a small amount of twist and fed into large cans. (See Figure 14.7.)

Within the card sliver are a substantial proportion of fibers with hooked ends. These hooks are formed as the fibers are moved along by the machinery. Their presence reduces the effective length of the fiber, and if these hooks are not removed, the yarns produced will be weaker. Subsequent drawing steps help to eliminate some hooks.

Carded slivers are drawn twice following carding. Combed slivers are drawn once before combing and twice more after combing.

FIGURE 14.6   A lap composed of slivers is passed through a comb that combs out short fibers. The output of the comb is formed again into a sliver. (Not all fibers are combed.) Photograph courtesy of the National Cotton Council of America.

FIGURE 14.7   In drawing, several slivers are combined into a strand and reduced to about the same diameter as the original sliver. Drawing blends fibers and arranges them in parallel order. Photograph courtesy of the National Cotton Council of America.

Twisting. The sliver is fed to a machine called the *roving frame*. Here the strands of fiber are elongated still more and are given additional twist. The product of the roving frame, an elongated, slightly twisted strand of fibers, is called the *roving*. (See Figures 14.8, 14.9, and 14.10.)

Yarn Formation by the Woolen System

A wide range of wool types, but generally the shorter fiber varieties, can be spun on the wool system. Man-made staple fibers can be blended with the wool fibers and spun on the wool system as well.

After cleaning, the fibers to be used in the yarn are blended, a small amount of oil is added to the fiber to facilitate processing, and the fibers are carded. The carded web is divided into strips by a "condenser," following which a very slight amount of twist is introduced by subjecting the strips to a rubbing motion to form rovings. Final twist and yarn formation is subsequently imparted, usually on a ring spinner.

FIGURE 14.8   Slivers are fed into a roving frame where the fibers are twisted slightly and are drawn into a smaller strand. Photograph courtesy of the National Cotton Council of America.

FIGURE 14.10 *Roving is fed to ring spinning frame where it is drawn out to final size, twisted into yarn, and wound on bobbins. Photograph courtesy of the National Cotton Council of America.*

Woolen yarns are soft and bulky. They have many fiber ends on the surface of the yarn, giving them a fuzzy appearance and handle.

Yarn Formation by the Worsted System

The worsted system is used for longer varieties of wool and can also be used for man-made staple fibers in appropriate lengths. If wool fiber is being processed, it is cleaned and then processed either dry or with oil added to lubricate the fibers. Carding is followed by preparation of fibers for combing. Prior to combing, the fibers are subjected to *gilling*, or passage of fibers through gill boxes in which pins control the movement of short fibers and minimize the development of unevenness in slivers while also assisting in straightening of fibers. Slivers are subjected to three gillings, after which they are combed, gilled again, then drawn, and, finally, spun.

Worsted yarns are smooth, sleek, and compact in appearance, with few fiber ends on the surface of the yarn. Their strength is better than that of woolen yarns and their handle is crisper.

The Semiworsted System

A variation of worsted spinning is particularly popular for spinning man-made fibers. Called semiworsted spinning, this process omits combing but is otherwise very much like the worsted process. Yarns produced are not so smooth, lean, or lustrous as are worsted yarns.

Processing of Linen Yarns

The length of linen fibers requires that they be processed somewhat differently from either wool or cotton. The final cleaning of flax is accomplished by a hackling machine, a device that has a revolving belt set with pins that remove short fibers, entangled fibers, and vegetable matter. The pins bring the linen fibers into alignment.

Linen fibers that are comparable to carded fiber after hackling are referred to as tow or hackled fibers; those comparable to combed fibers are referred to as line or well-hackled fibers. The same terms are applied to the yarns made from these fibers. Table 14.1 summarizes the terms used in referring to combed and carded yarns from different fibers.

The processes used in preparing linen fiber for spinning are intended to take advantage of the strength and luster of these long fibers. Precise steps vary, depending on whether tow or linen fibers are being handled. Also, either a wet or dry processing can be utilized. Wet processing produces the finest, strongest, and smoothest yarns.

Figure 14.11 compares steps in the major yarn preparation processes.

Making Filaments into Staple Lengths

Cut Staple

One of the advantages of utilizing cut tow for spinning is that, unlike cotton, wool, and other natural fibers, the tow fibers are aligned and parallel and need not be combed or carded to make them ready for spinning. The fibers can be said to go from tow to sliver (or as the industry terms the process, "tow-to-top") in one operation. Specialized machines make this conversion.

The Pacific converter cuts the staple into the desired length. Fibers may be cut into uniform lengths or into variable lengths. The steps performed in this machine include

1. Heat stretching man-made fibers, if needed.
2. Forming a flat web of tow.
3. Cutting the web by a blade cutter.

Table 14.1

Fiber	Yarns from Carded Fiber	Yarns from Combed Fiber
Linen	Tow or hackled yarns	Line or well-hackled yarns
Wool	Wollen yarns	Worsted yarns
Cotton and other staple fibers	Carded yarns	Combed yarns

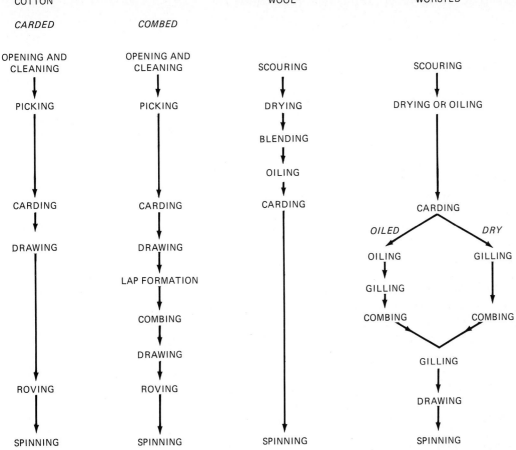

COTTON		WOOL	WORSTED
CARDED	COMBED		

OPENING AND CLEANING
↓
PICKING
↓
CARDING
↓
DRAWING
↓
ROVING
↓
SPINNING

OPENING AND CLEANING
↓
PICKING
↓
CARDING
↓
DRAWING
↓
LAP FORMATION
↓
COMBING
↓
DRAWING
↓
ROVING
↓
SPINNING

SCOURING
↓
DRYING
↓
BLENDING
↓
OILING
↓
CARDING
↓
SPINNING

SCOURING
↓
DRYING OR OILING
↓
CARDING
OILED ↙   ↘ DRY
OILING   GILLING
↓   ↓
GILLING   COMBING
↓   ↙
COMBING ↘ ↙
GILLING
↓
DRAWING
↓
SPINNING

FIGURE 14.11 *Comparison of the steps in the major yarn preparation systems*

4. Moving the cut fibers in such a way that not all cut ends fall at the same place in the web.
5. Rolling the web diagonally into a continuous sliver of staple fibers.

A second method of converting tow to top is to break the fibers into staple lengths. The Perlock system performs this operation.

The Perlock system applies tension to the tow and pulls the stretched tow across a tow breaker wheel, a cog wheel with sharp, protruding edges. The filaments then break on the sharp edges of the tow breaker wheel. Stretch breaking is most effective with synthetic fibers, less useful in cutting regenerated cellulose.

A variation of this process called the Turbo-stapler process is used for producing high-bulk fibers, especially acrylics. During stretch breaking, the fibers are extended and must be treated to relax the fiber or else yarns will show a good deal of relaxation shrinkage. In the Perlock process, breaking is followed by adding crimp to the fiber, heat setting the crimp, and relaxing the fiber by a steam heat treatment. If a sliver of stretch-broken, crimped, relaxed staple is blended with a sliver of stretch-broken, crimped, but not relaxed staple, the bulking properties of acrylic fibers are much improved.

The yarns made in this way are woven or knitted into a garment, the garment is subjected to treatment with hot water and the unset fibers shrink, causing the preshrunk fibers to stand up in bulky, fuzzy surface texture.

Spinning

The aforementioned systems for preparations of fibers for spinning are preliminary to the final yarn formation. A variety of different means can be used to join fibers together to form a yarn. Some of these yarn-forming methods are well established, others are beginning to be used commercially, while others are in various stages of noncommercial research and development.

The predominant commercial systems of yarn formation are ring spinning and open-end spinning. On the following pages the methods of spinning that are now used or that are likely to be commercialized in the near future are summarized. The major focus of discussion will be ring and open-end spinning because of their dominant position in the industry.

Ring Spinning

The ring spinner is made up of the following parts:

1. Spools on which the strand of carded fiber or roving is wound.
2. A series of rollers through which the roving passes.
3. A guiding ring or eyelet.
4. A traveler or small U-shaped clip.
5. A stationary ring around the spindle.
6. A spindle.
7. A bobbin.

The strand of fibers or roving is fed from the spool through the rollers. The rollers elongate the roving, which passes through the eyelet, moving down and through the traveler. The traveler moves freely around the stationary ring. The spindle turns the bobbin at a constant speed. This turning of the bobbin and the movement of the traveler impart the twist to the yarn. The traveler moves around the ring at from 4,000 to 12,000 revolutions per minute. The yarn is twisted and wound onto a bobbin in one operation. (See Figures 14.12 and 14.13.)

FIGURE 14.12   Ring spinner.

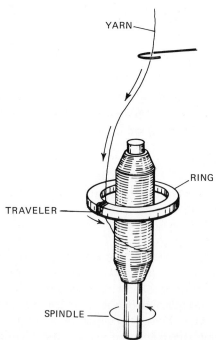

FIGURE 14.13 *Ring spinning machine in operation. Note the cones of roving at the top of the machine. The filled bobbins of spun yarn are being removed automatically at the center of the picture, ready to be moved into position for spinning. Courtesy of Zinser Textilmaschinen GmbH.*

Open-End Spinning

In ring spinning, insertion of twist requires that the entire bobbin rotates. As a result there is a limit to the speed with which the machine can operate. Researchers, therefore, concentrated on developing techniques for inserting twist into yarns that would permit more rapid production. A result of this search was the introduction, in the 1960s, of the *open-end spinning machine*, which operated at higher speeds but which produced a yarn with slightly different characteristics that conventional ring-spun yarns.

Open-end spinning omits the step of forming the roving. Instead, a sliver of fibers is fed into the spinner by a stream of air. Figure 14.14 shows an open-end spinner of the rotor type and describes its operation. The sliver is delivered to a rotary beater that separates the fibers into a thin stream that is carried into the rotor by a current of air through a tube or duct and is deposited in a V-shaped groove along the sides of the rotor. Twist is provided by the turning of the rotor.

Fibers from the side of the rotor are "peeled off" to join the "open end" of a previously formed yarn that extends out of the delivery tube;

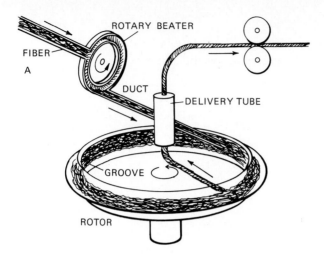

FIGURE 14.14   *Open-end spinner. The fibers are separated into a thin stream by the rotary beater. The fibers moved by an air stream enter the rotor and through centrifugal force are carried in a V-shaped groove. The fibers are drawn off from the groove to become attached to the open end of an already formed yarn. The rotor produces the twist. From "Yarn" by Stanley Backer. Copyright December 1972 by* Scientific American.

hence the name "open-end spinning." As the fibers join the yarn, which is constantly being pulled out of the delivery tube, twist from the movement of the rotor is conveyed to the fibers. A constant stream of new fibers enters the rotor, is distributed in the groove, and is removed at the end of the formed yarn, becoming part of the yarn itself.

The fineness of the yarn is determined by the rate at which it is drawn out of the rotor relative to the rate at which fibers are being fed in. In other words, if fewer fibers are being fed in while fibers are being withdrawn rapidly, a thinner yarn will result, and vice versa. The twist is determined by the ratio of the speed of turning of the rotor to the linear or withdrawal speed of the yarn (i.e., the higher the speed of the rotor, the greater the twist).

Theoretically, a variety of different means may be used to form the yarn and insert twist. These have been divided into the following categories: mechanical spinning (of which rotor spinning is an example), electrostatic spinning, fluid spinning, air spinning, and friction spinning. Fluid spinning has had no significant commercial application, although it has been utilized experimentally.

The electrostatic spinning process utilizes an electrostatic field for the movement and orientation of fibers during spinning. An electrostatic field is formed by giving the rollers that feed the sliver to the machine a negative charge and giving the twisting device a positive charge. The movement of the electrostatic field is from the negative toward the positive pole, so that the fibers are arranged and moved in the same direction. Fibers are separated, made parallel, stretched, oriented, and transferred to the twisting device under the influence of the electrostatic field. Twist is, however, imparted by a specific twisting device.[2] This process has not attained commercial feasibility in the United

[2]I. Doga, "The Fundamentals of Electrostatic Spinning," *Textile Research Journal*, 45 (July 1975), p. 521.

States. Most open-end spinning machines now in use are of the mechanical rotor spinning type; however, air jet and friction open-end spinning equipment are available. Figures 14.15 and 14.16 show an air jet-type spinner and a friction-type spinner and describe their operation.

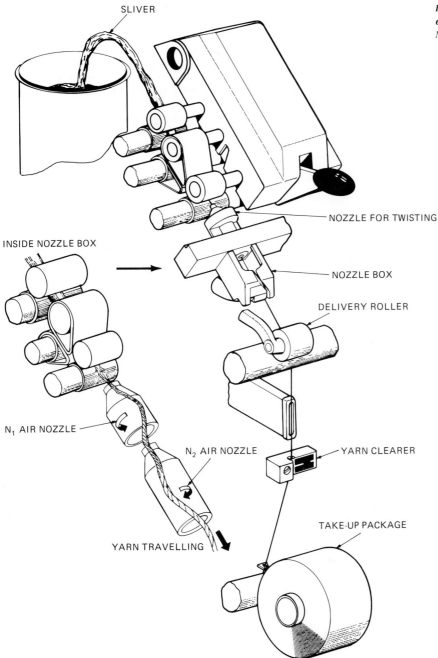

SLIVER

NOZZLE FOR TWISTING

INSIDE NOZZLE BOX

NOZZLE BOX

DELIVERY ROLLER

N_1 AIR NOZZLE

N_2 AIR NOZZLE

YARN CLEARER

YARN TRAVELLING

TAKE-UP PACKAGE

FIGURE 14.15 *Murata jet spinner, and enlarged view inside nozzle box. Courtesy of Murata of America, Inc.*

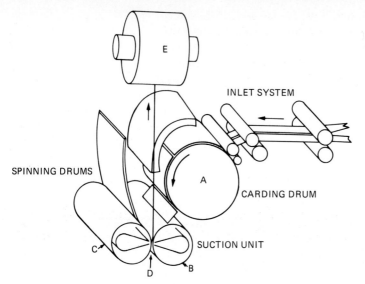

E

INLET SYSTEM

SPINNING DRUMS

A

CARDING DRUM

SUCTION UNIT

C

D

B

FIGURE 14.16   DREF-2 spinning system. The DREF-2 system utilizes friction as the means of inserting twist. A mixture of air and fibers is fed to a moving, perforated surface. (A) Suction holds the fibers against the drum. (B) A second perforated drum rotates in the opposite direction. (C) Twist is inserted as the fibers pass between the two drums. (D) The newly forming yarn is added to the open end of an already-formed yarn, and the yarn is continuously drawn away and wound as it is formed. (E) Courtesy of Fehrer AG.

The advantages of open-end spinning are that it increases the speed of production, eliminating the step of drawing out the roving prior to spinning, it permits finished yarns to be wound on any sized bobbin or spool, and it produces yarns of more even diameter than does ring spinning. Yarns are more uniform in diameter, bulkier, more absorbent, and less variable in strength than are ring-spun yarns.

Properties of fabrics made from open-end spun yarns compared with ring-spun yarns are said to be more uniform and more opaque in appearance, lower in strength, less likely to pill, and inferior in crease recovery. A number of sources indicated that they are more subject to abrasion. At least one wear test study indicated that, when woven into boy's denim jeans, fabrics from open-end spun yarns were less durable. The evaluation included abrasion resistance. However, the researchers reported, "the differences were small, and durability of both fabrics was acceptable to consumers."[3]

The quantity of yarns being produced by this method is increasing; however, in spite of predictions that open-end–spun yarns would gain a substantial share of world spinning capacity, ring spinning is still the predominant method. What seems to have happened is that ring-spun yarns and open-end spun yarns are each used for the kinds of applications to which they are best suited.

Although air jet-spun yarns can be made in diameters finer than those made by rotor spinning, neither method will produce yarns as fine and strong as ring-spun yarns. Open-end–spun yarns have a handle that has been characterized as "harsh." Some of the kinds of products

[3]M. A. Morris and H. H. Prato, "End-Use Performance and Consumer Acceptance of Denim Fabrics Woven from Open-End and Ring-Spun Yarns," *Textile Research Journal*, 48 (March 1978), p. 177.

that seem to be especially well suited to the use of open-end spun yarns are in warp and filling yarns for denims, toweling pile yarns, and heavier weights of bed sheeting. Their smooth, even surface makes them desirable as base fabrics for plastic-coated materials. On the other hand, the more acceptable feel of ring-spun yarns has led knitwear manufacturers to prefer them, and they are better for fine polyester/cotton blends.

Other Methods of Manufacturing Yarns

In addition to ring and open-end spinning, techniques that insert true twist into yarn, three other types of yarn construction have been utilized. These are false twist, yarn wrapping, and glueing or welding fibers together. Assessment of the viability of these processes for commercial purposes varies. Josef Derichs, analyzing textile spinning, predicted that thread wrapping is likely to gain in importance, but that it is too early to evaluate some of the other systems.[4]

False or Self-twist Spinning

Self-twist spinning is used to make ply yarns, yarns made from two or more yarns twisted together. The process follows these steps:

Two rovings are utilized. Each one is passed through a pair of rollers that are both rotating and oscillating. Each set of rollers twists its roving in a direction opposite to the other. The uneven motion of the rollers forms a yarn that has both twisted and untwisted areas. Adjacent ends of the two yarns are allowed to untwist around each other. Care must be taken to space the untwisted areas of each yarn in such a way that a loosely twisted section of one yarn never coincides with a loosely twisted section of the other yarn, or a weak spot would result. (See Figure 14.17.)

Repco® is the trademark of one commercially available self-twist spinner. Officials of the manufacturer cite the following benefits from the use of self-twist yarns: less space required for producing the same weight of yarn, reductions in annual maintenance costs and time, less waste in spinning, lower power utilization, and lower labor costs. This

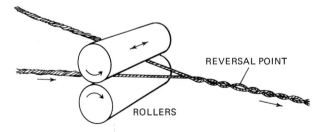

FIGURE 14.17   *Self-twist spinning. Two separate rovings are fed between a pair of rollers that move both forward and side to side. The twisted rovings, each with opposite directional twist, when placed side by side, twist around each other to form a ply yarn. From "Yarn" by Stanley Backer. Copyright December 1972 by* Scientific American.

[4]"Sorting Out the Spinning Systems," *Textile World*, 134, No. 9 (September 1984), p. 69.

system is currently being used in Europe as a substitute for worsted manufacture.[5]

Self-twist yarns can, of course, only be used in those fabrics that require two-ply yarns. The process also requires that fiber lengths not be too short. Wool and long man-made staple fibers are especially suitable.

Wrapped Yarns

Yarns can be made from a bundle of parallel fibers held in place by surface wrapping of other staple or filament fibers. The first of these wrapped yarns were made by DuPont and were called *fasciated yarns*. (See Figure 14.18.) The term derives from the Latin word *fasces* meaning "a bundle of rods wrapped with ribbons."

Untwisted, relatively long parallel fibers (averaging 5 to 6 inches in length) predominate in these yarns. The fiber ends and wrappings also appear on the surface. As a result, these yarns have something of the qualities of both filament and staple yarns. Fasciated yarns are less fuzzy, more lustrous, and cleaner in appearance than are conventionally spun yarns.

Such yarns are no longer made by DuPont; however, wrapped or core-spun yarns, similar in concept, but produced by a special hollow core spindle, are exciting interest in the manufacture of fancy yarns for woven and knitted goods. The specific techniques utilized vary from one machine to another. Three different processes now in or approaching commercialization are shown in Figures 14.19, 14.20, and 14.21.

An interesting application of the technique has been made in the manufacture of towels, in which the wrapped yarns are used in the pile. In this instance, the wrapping yarn is made from polyvinyl alcohol fibers (see page 187), which are soluble. After the fabric has been put through the finishing processes, these yarns dissolve, leaving a soft, all-cotton twistless and absorbent yarn in the pile.

Yarns Held Together by Adhesives

Twistless Spinning. Reiter Machine Works Ltd. has developed a yarn manufacturing process that is said to produce colored yarns of high breaking strength and increased bulk. Fibers are handled in such a way as to eliminate several steps in the conventional spinning process. One system is referred to as the Pavena-Pavil system, the other the Pavena-Paset system. The former produces a twisted colored yarn, the

FIGURE 14.18   Diagram of the structure of a fasciated yarn.

[5]C. G. Tewksbury, "New Spinning Systems," *American Fashions and Fabrics*, No. 123 (1981), p. 17.

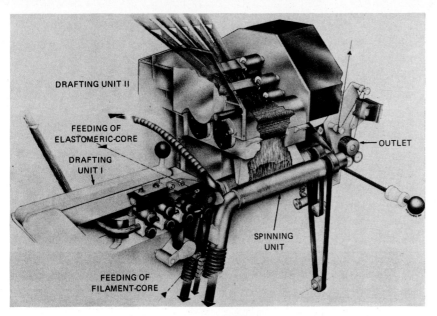

DRAFTING UNIT II

FEEDING OF
ELASTOMERIC-CORE

DRAFTING
UNIT I

OUTLET

SPINNING
UNIT

FEEDING OF
FILAMENT-CORE

FIGURE 14.19 *The basic construction of a DREF-3 spindle. Drafting Unit I is positioned before the central element of the spinning unit and it feeds the drafted core fibers on the inlet side to the spinning unit. It is possible to feed different kinds of filament core in addition to, or in place of the core fibers, in order to achieve specified yarn properties. For example, elastomeric core filaments can be fed. Drafting Unit II, which is positioned above the spinning nip, separates sheath fibers from several drawn slivers. These are then fed via the funnel to the spinning unit. After passing the take-up rollers, the yarn can be wound. Courtesy of Dr. Ernst Fehrer, Textilmaschinenfabrik.*

FIGURE 14.20 *Saurer-Allma GmbH ESP-X Hollow Spindle Spin Twister. Yarn to be wrapped is fed in at point A. A tube (B) containing the wrapping yarn is placed over a hollow spindle. The wrapping yarn is threaded through the hollow spindle together with the yarn to be wrapped and at the twist former (C) is wrapped around the central yarn. Courtesy of Saurer-Allma GmbH.*

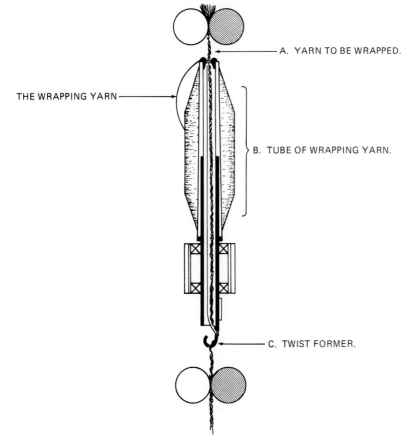

A. YARN TO BE WRAPPED.

THE WRAPPING YARN

B. TUBE OF WRAPPING YARN.

C. TWIST FORMER.

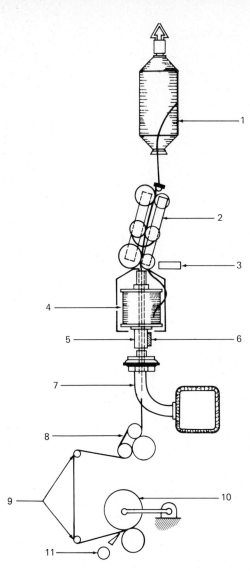

FIGURE 14.21 *Wrap spinner. Roving (1) feeds through 3-roll, durable-apron drafting (2), past broken-end collector (3). Spool (4) contains wrapper filament. It rotates around hollow spindle (5), driven by belt (6). Drafted staple yarn passes through hollow spindle. Rotating spool causes filament to wrap around spun yarn with predetermined frequency. Yarn passes through suction tube (7) to feed roll (8) and through yarn guides (9) to cylindrical takeup (10). Threadup aspirator (11) aids package startup. Courtesy of* Textile World Magazine, *copyright McGraw-Hill, Inc.*

latter an untwisted colored yarn. Table 14.2 compares the steps followed in the Pavena systems with conventional spinning of carded cotton, synthetics, or blends.

Similar techniques, for the production of no-twist cotton yarns are reported periodically in the research literature. Progress is apparently being made toward the combining of fibers from a narrow strip of card web that are aligned and condensed by a special combing and drafting device. The strand is impregnated with a water-soluble binder, is dried, and is wound on a package. The yarn is knitted or woven into cloth and

Table 14.2 Comparison of Conventional and Bonded Silver Spinning

Conventional System	Pavena-Pavil System	Pavena-Paset System
1. Opening and cleaning	1. Opening and cleaning	1. Opening and cleaning
2. Carding	2. Carding	2. Carding
3. Breaker drawing	3. Bonding together and coloring of fibers in a silver	3. Bonding together and coloring of fibers in a silver
4. Finisher drawing		
5. Roving		
6. Ring spinning of uncolored fibers	4. Ring spinning of colored fibers	4. Doubling, drafting, and rebonding colored fiber
7. Rewinding of dyeing tubes		
8. Dyeing		
9. Dyeing		

the binder is removed; the fabric construction serves to hold the fibers together.

Yarn strength is reported as low; however, when the yarns are used in the widthwise direction of fabric, strength of the materials is said to be comparable to fabrics woven with open-end or ring-spun yarns.

Integrated Composite Spinning. A relatively new machine called the Bobtex® integrated composite spinning machine is being used to form yarns from a composite of synthetic polymer monofilament and staple fibers. The yarn is made of three separate components. A continuous filament feeder yarn is passed through a spinneret that contains a molten synthetic polymer resin. The filament yarn and the polymer resin may be of the same or different synthetic polymers. Staple fiber slivers are fed on both sides of the feeder yarn that has been coated with polymer resin. Twist is inserted by a friction false twister. The molten resin solidifies, holding the staple fibers in place. (See Figure 14.22.)

Variation in yarn properties can be achieved by varying the three components used. These yarns possess the properties of both filament and spun yarns and have great potential for the creation of a wide variety of interesting yarns.

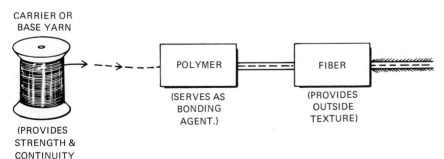

CARRIER OR BASE YARN

POLYMER

(SERVES AS BONDING AGENT.)

FIBER

(PROVIDES OUTSIDE TEXTURE)

(PROVIDES STRENGTH & CONTINUITY

FIGURE 14.22 Bobtex® integrated composite spinning system.

Making Fibers into Yarns   **215**

Filament Yarns

Yarns made from continuous filaments are divided into two groups: monofilament yarns, or yarns made from one filament, and multifilament yarns made from more than one filament. Filament yarns are generally multifilament. Monofilament yarns find limited use in nylon hosiery where an exceptionally sheer fabric is wanted and in saran fabric webbing used in some lightweight beach or casual furniture as well as in a variety of industrial uses.

Monofilament yarns can be made by the conventional extrusion of large single filaments from spinnerets. The slit film technique in which a film of synthetic polymer is cut into strips will also make single filaments, each of which can be used as a monofilament yarn.

Multifilament yarns can be given either tight or loose twist. The characteristics of each fiber—its luster, handle, and cross-sectional shape—will determine the appearance and feel of the yarn into which it is made. In general, most smooth filament yarns are characterized by greater luster, have less tendency to pill, and require more yarn to cover the same area than do spun yarns.

Textured Filament Yarns

Man-made filament yarns can be treated with processes that utilize heat setting or mechanical entangling of fibers to alter their texture. Yarns made from filament fibers are smooth and slippery to the touch. They lack the warmth, bulk, and comfort of yarns spun from staple fibers. Texturing of man-made filament fibers can produce softer, bulkier yarns, with increased warmth, comfort, and absorbency; can decrease pilling of the fibers; or can impart stretch.

The American Society for Testing and Materials (ASTM) assigns textured yarns to the general category of bulk yarns. In the ASTM compilation of standard definitions, *bulk yarns* are described as yarns prepared so as to have greater covering power or apparent volume than similar conventional yarns with normal twist. The category of bulk yarns is further subdivided into *bulky yarns*, *textured yarns*, and *crimped yarns*.[6]

Bulky Yarns. Bulky yarns are formed from fibers that are inherently bulky and cannot be closely packed because of such characteristics as cross-sectional shape, fiber resilience, natural crimp, or some other quality. No special treatments need to be given to bulky yarns to make them bulky, although the fibers may have been engineered to obtain some of the aforementioned qualities. Bulked yarns are used in those applications in which bulk is more important than stretch, although

---

[6]*Compilation of ASTM Standard Definitions* (Philadelphia: American Society for Testing and Materials, 1982), pp. 89–90.

many bulked yarns do have moderate stretch. Products in which bulked yarns are most often found are sweaters, warm hosiery, carpets, wool-like knits, and upholstery.

Textured Yarns. Textured yarns may be filament or spun yarns that have been given "noticeably greater volume" through physical, chemical, or heat treatments or a combination of these. In the ASTM standard definitions compilation, textured yarns are separated into the categories of *loopy yarn*, *high-bulk yarn*, and *stretch yarn*.

Loopy yarns have a relatively large number of randomly spaced and sized loops along the filaments or fibers. Loopy yarns may be produced through air jet texturing in which texture is not produced by heat, but by feeding yarns into a system in which slack yarns are formed into loops by jets of air. (See Figure 14.23.)

Loopy yarns can also be made by core-spun processes. These yarns are relatively free from stretch unless they are made with a core of elastomeric fiber. (See Figure 12.2.)

High-bulk yarns have a random crimp produced by the combination of fibers that shrink markedly with those that do not tend to shrink. The fibers or parts of fibers that shrink pull the other fibers or fiber sections into permanently crimped position. High-bulk yarns do not usually exhibit a great deal of stretch. Bicomponent Orlon Sayelle® is produced by this technique.

Crimped Yarns. Crimped yarns are often made from thermoplastic fibers. These yarns are deformed from a straight configuration to a saw-toothed or curled shape. Heat setting of the fibers in the deformed position makes these shapes permanent.

At the present time the dominant process used for texturing crimped yarns is the *false-twist* process. The means of inserting twist varies, depending on the process, with some machines using a series of disks over which the yarn passes, others using a friction belt device, and others a spindle, but no matter how the twist is developed, the yarn is heat-set in the twisted position and then untwisted, whereupon it kinks. Unless a yarn with stretch is required, this textured shape is treated to stabilize it. (See Figures 14.24, 14.25, and 14.26.)

Other processes that introduce crimp include the *stuffer box* process, in which fibers are fed into a small chamber in which the crimped shape is heat set (Figure 14.27); gear crimp, imparting crimp by passing filaments between the teeth of two heated gears (Figure 14.28); and edge crimp (Figure 14.29) in which heated thermoplastic yarns are drawn over a sharp knife edge causing some areas of the fiber to fuse slightly and imparting a spirallike curl to the yarn. Agilon® is a trademarked nylon yarn made by the edge-crimp process and is used in women's hosiery, socks, sweaters, and household textiles.

Earlier processes such as three-stage twist and knit-deknit have been

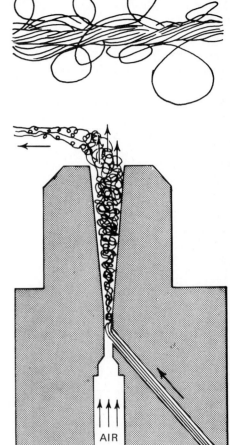

FIGURE 14.23 *Texturing of yarns by the air-jet method.* From "Yarn" by Stanley Backer. Copyright December 1972 by Scientific American.

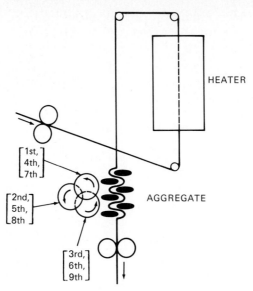

HEATER

1st,
4th,
7th

2nd,
5th,
8th

AGGREGATE

3rd,
6th,
9th

FRICTION FALSE TWISTING

FIGURE 14.24 (left)   Friction false twisting.
Courtesy of Celanese Corporation.

FIGURE 14.25 (left)   Disk system for insertion
of false twist.

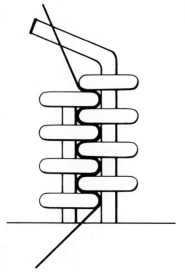

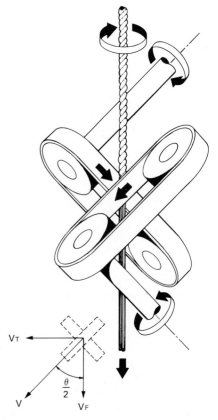

V_T
V
$\frac{\theta}{2}$
V_F

VECTOR V : FORCE APPLIED TO YARN
V_T : TWIST COMPONENT
V_F : FEED COMPONENT
θ : TWISTER ANGLE

FIGURE 14.26 (above)   Belt friction false
twisting on the murata VIP twister. The yarn
is nipped securely and twisted by Twister
Belts. Slippage is almost zero.
In this diagram, the force applied to the yarn,
V, is divided into V_T and V_F. V_T is twist force.
V_F is yard feed force. Values of V_T and V_F are
decided according to V and angle θ. That is,
in the NIP SYSTEM, the twist level, twist
tension (T_1) and untwist tension (T_2) can be
set by adjusting V and θ. Courtesy of Murata
of America, Inc.

superseded by processes that are more economical. It should be noted
that texturing filament yarn is much less expensive than spinning staple
yarns. Customers seem to show a preference for spun yarns in many
applications; thus, texturing filament yarns, especially those of polyester, has become an important manufacturing step. With the widespread
use of partially oriented yarn (POY, see Chapter 9 for fuller discussion),
the texturer, who may also be the fiber producer, simultaneously draws
and textures the yarn.

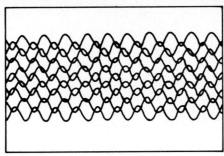

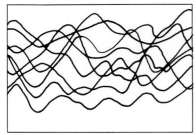

FIGURE 14.27 (below) Texturing of yarns by the stuffer box method. From "Yarn" by Stanley Backer. Copyright December 1972 by Scientific American.

FIGURE 14.29 (below) Texturing of yarns through the edge crimp process. From "Yarn" by Stanley Backer. Copyright December 1972 by Scientific American.

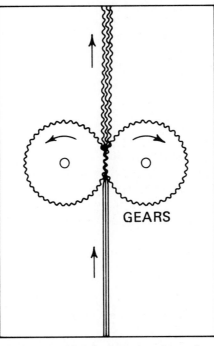

GEARS

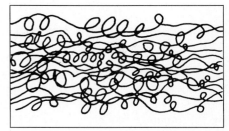

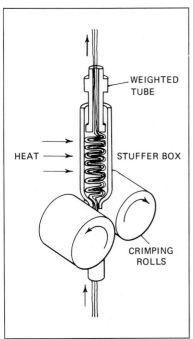

WEIGHTED
TUBE

HEAT

STUFFER BOX

CRIMPING
ROLLS

FIGURE 14.28 (above) Texturing of yarns by the gear crimp method. From "Yarn" by Stanley Backer. Copyright December 1972 by Scientific American.

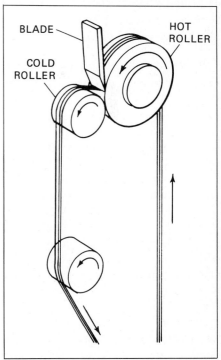

BLADE

HOT
ROLLER

COLD
ROLLER

Making Fibers into Yarns 219

Stretch Yarns

ASTM defines stretch yarns as yarns with a high degree of potential elastic stretch and rapid recovery. They are said to have a high degree of yarn curl achieved by deforming the yarn and heat-setting the yarn in this position. When the yarn is placed under stress, it will stretch, flattening the curls; but when stress is removed, it returns to the permanent heat-set shape. False-twist and edge-crimp processes can produce stretch yarns.

Consumers as well as those in the textile industry use the term "stretch" more broadly, applying it to any yarn or fabric that exhibits stretch and recovery. Most of these alternative routes to provision of stretch have been discussed elsewhere, and they include the use of elastomeric fibers (Chapter 12), bicomponent or biconstituent fibers with differential shrinkage (Chapter 13), and treatment of fabrics to provide moderate amounts of stretch. (See Chapter 20, p. 375.)

Network and Film Yarns

Recently, various new techniques have emerged that allow the formation of yarns directly from synthetic polymers without the formation of fibers or the twisting of fibers into yarns. These processes include the formation of yarns by the split film process, or the slit film process, or by the creation of network yarns from foam. Slit film yarns could be classified as monofilaments. Yarns made by the split film process or the network yarns made from foam do not fit neatly into the categories of staple or filament yarns.

Split Films

In the creation of yarns by the split film technique, a sheet of polymer is formed. The formed sheet is drawn in the lengthwise direction. Through drawing, the molecules in the polymer are oriented in the direction of the draw, causing the film to be strengthened in the lengthwise direction and weakened in the crosswise direction. This causes a breakdown of the film into a mass of interconnected fibers, most of which are aligned in the direction of the drawing, but some of which also connect in the crosswise direction.

The process is known as *fibrillation*. These materials can be twisted into strings or twines or other coarse, yarnlike materials. The usefulness of split film yarns is limited because the yarns created are coarse. Olefins are made into split film yarns for use in making bags, sacks, ropes, and other industrial products. (See Figure 14.30.)

Slit Films

Slit films are made by cutting film into narrow, ribbonlike sections. Depending upon the process used for cutting and drawing the film, the tapes may display some degree of fibrillation, like that described for

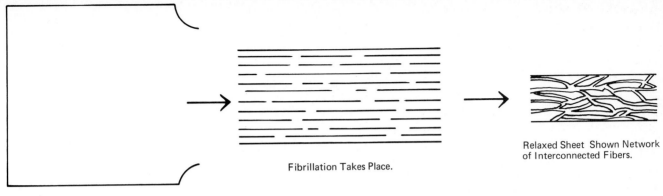

Sheet of Polymer Is Drawn.

Fibrillation Takes Place.

Relaxed Sheet Shown Network of Interconnected Fibers.

FIGURE 14.30   Film fibrillation.

split films. When tapes are made that do not fibrillate, they are flatter and are more suitable for certain uses. Flat tapes are used as warp yarns in weaving and can be made into carpet backings that will be more stable, remaining flat and even. All types of tape yarns are used in making wall coverings, packaging materials, and carpet backing and as a replacement for jute in bags and sacks.

Lurex®, a flat, ribbonlike yarn with a metallic appearance, is a slit film yarn that is often used to add decorative touches to apparel or household textiles. Lurex® is made from single or multiple layers of polyester film. Multilayered types are made by placing a layer of aluminum foil between two layers of polyester film. Mono-ply types are cut from metallized polyester film, protected by a clear or colored resin coating. The natural color of Lurex® is silver. Other colors are produced by adding pigments to the lacquer coating or to the bonding adhesive. The width of these yarns ranges from 0.069 to 0.010 inches. The manufacturer claims that the use of polyester film increases the strength and flexibility of the yarn but notes that these yarns are decorative rather than functional.

Network Yarns

A third type of yarn is created from foamed polymers in a three-stage process. A polymer is formed in which air is added to create a foam structure. The foamed polymer is fed into a buffer zone or area where the quantity of material can be regulated. Material from the buffer zone is fed into a draw chamber in which the foamed polymer is stretched.

The foaming of the polymer has created small cells or bubbles of polymer. As the material is drawn, the cell walls crack, forming individual fibers that are interconnected. The resultant yarn is made up of a network of small, interconnected fibers.

Network yarns resemble staple yarns but lack the hairiness of staple yarns because there are no free ends. They have bulk. Experimental yarns formed in this way display a range of tenacities that can be increased by the addition of some twist. However, the tenacity of network yarns is lower than is that of yarns made from corresponding filament fibers. Fabrics woven on an experimental basis showed good drape and handle, but poor crease recovery. Researchers believe that network yarns offer potential for a variety of uses, especially in coarse yarns, but that further research and development is required before they will be commercially viable.[7]

Effects of Twist

The degree of twist given to a yarn affects a number of aspects of its appearance, behavior, and durability. The fineness of yarns is related to twist. As a general rule, increasing twist decreases yarn size. This can be demonstrated easily by taking a strand of loose fiber, such as absorbent cotton, and twisting it. The more one twists, the smaller in diameter the "yarn" will become.

Strength increases in staple yarns as twist increases up to a certain point. Beyond this point, the strength of the yarn begins to decrease, and yarns with exceptionally high, tight twist may become brittle and weak. Filament yarns are stronger untwisted.

Elasticity is increased if yarns are twisted very tightly. Very tightly twisted yarns are known as *crepe* yarns, which are generally very fine. The twist of crepe yarns is so high that they curl up unless they are held under tension, as they would be on a loom during weaving. A simple and easy test to identify crepe yarns is to unravel a yarn from the fabric and run it between the fingernails, thus removing the tension produced by sizing material. If the yarn curls up into corkscrewlike curls, it has been creped. This tendency of crepe yarn to twist makes fabrics constructed from these yarns less dimensionally stable than other fabrics, as they are more elastic (see page 257).

More tightly twisted yarns shed soil more easily. Because their surface is smoother, there are fewer fiber ends to attract and hold soil. In yarns made from absorbent fibers, absorbency is lower in more tightly twisted yarns.

Abrasion resistance is increased by tighter twist. This is a logical result because in a more tightly twisted yarn many fibers are held in such a way that they appear on the surface, then into the center of the yarn, and then back to the surface again. As a result, more fibers are subject to a relatively even distribution of abrasion. Loose surface fibers in low-twist yarns also snag and pull up, creating points of wear.

The appearance of a fabric is determined to a large extent by the twist of the yarn. For example, if filament yarns of higher luster are given very low twist, they will reflect greater quantities of light and, therefore, appear brighter than the same yarns when they are more tightly twisted.

[7]P. R. Lord, *Spinning in the 70's* (Watford, England: Merrow Publishing Company Ltd., 1970), pp. 73 ff.

Crepe fabrics achieve a nubby, somewhat crinkled, effect by using creped yarns that have a less even surface texture. Loosely twisted worsted yarns produce a smooth, more even surface. The fabric designer takes advantage of these effects to create a wide variety of surface textures and designs.

Keeping these points in mind is helpful when evaluating products in relation to performance. For example, abrasion resistance is an important factor to consider in selecting an upholstery fabric, as abrasion is related to the durability of a product on which people will sit. Not only can the consumer look for a fiber that has reasonably good abrasion resistance but also for a yarn that has reasonably high twist. Low-twist yarns abrade and snag more easily than do those with higher twist. Also, tighter-twist yarns shed soil more readily.

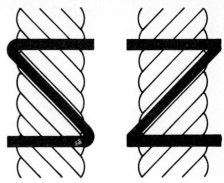

FIGURE 14.31   S and Z twist.

Direction of Twist

In twisting fibers together to form yarns, the fibers can be twisted either to the right or to the left. In textile industry terminology, this twist is called *S* or *Z twist*. (See Figure 14.31.) Z twisted yarns are twisted so that the direction of the twist follows the center bar of the letter "Z." Z twist is also known as "right" twist. In S twist yarn, the twist direction follows the center bar of the letter "S." S twist is also known as "left" twist. This concept will be more easily understood if the reader takes a small bunch of absorbent cotton and makes a vertical line on the fibers with a pen. Then, suspending the fibers from the thumb and forefinger of the left hand to that of the right, rotate the fibers to the right with the upper left-hand fingers. The line you have made will take a diagonal direction similar to that of the bar in a Z. If the upper fingers are twisted to the left, the line will follow the bar of the S.

Most yarns are made with a Z twist. However, in certain fabric constructions special effects can be achieved by combining yarns in which the fibers have been twisted in either the same or opposite directions.

Size of Yarns

Since the textile industry requires some means for distinguishing between yarns of different sizes, standards of measurement have been established. There are different systems of measurement for cotton and wool, and different systems for staple and filament yarns.

This variety of measurement systems may seem unnecessarily complicated. They had their origins in measurements that were appropriate for particular uses in isolated textile manufacturing localities and may go back for hundreds of years. The present trend is toward establishing metric measurements, but one will still encounter the use of traditional terminology.

The basic principles underlying these systems that should be borne in mind are these: the system is different for each type of fiber, is different for staple and filament yarns, and may be either a direct measure of size or an indirect measure.

Direct methods of measurement rely on the measurement of fixed lengths of yarn. A specified length of yarn is measured, and this length is weighed. The measures used are *tex, decitex,* or *denier*. As explained earlier, tex is defined as the weight in grams of 1 kilometer length of staple yarn; decitex is the weight in grams of 10,000 meters of filament yarn; and denier is the weight in grams of 9,000 meters of yarn. In all these measures, the higher the number, the coarser the yarn.

Indirect methods of measurement rely on the measurement of fixed weights of yarn. The numbering system establishes a number of hanks of yarn that make up either a pound or a kilogram of yarn weight. Pounds are used for measurements in the English system and kilograms for measurements in the metric system. The size of the hanks used is different for each kind of fiber, with the measures being as follows: cotton count equals the number of hanks of 840 yards in 1 pound; linen count (also called *linen lea*) equals the number of hanks of 300 yards in 1 pound; woolen count equals the number of hanks of 256 yards per pound; worsted count equals the number of hanks of 560 yards per pound. All these yarn numbers are reported in technical or research literature followed by the abbreviation "Ne," which stands for "number in the English system." Metric yarn numbers in the indirect measurement system equal the number of 1,000-meter hanks in each kilogram, and this measurement is designated followed by the abbreviation "Nm," which stands for "number in the metric system."

Table 14.3

Denier (weight in grams of 9,000 meters of yarn)	Worsted (no. of 560-yard hanks per pound)	Woolen (no. of 1,600-yard hanks per pound)	Cotton (no. of 840-yard hanks per pound)	Linen (no. of 300-yard hanks per pound)	Tex (weight in grams of 1,000 meters of yarn)
thinnest					thinnest
50	160	56	106	298	5.6
75	106	37	71	198	8.3
100	80	28	53	149	11.1
150	53	19	35	99	16.6
200	40	14	27	74	22.2
300	27	9.3	18	50	33.4
400	20	7	13	37	44.4
500	16	5.6	11	30	55.5
700	11.4	4.0	7.6	21	77.7
1000	8.0	2.8	5.3	15	111
1500	5.3	1.9	3.5	10	166
2000	4.0	1.4	2.7	7	222
coarsest					coarsest

SOURCE: Adapted from J. Pizzuto, *Fabric Science* (New York: Fairchild Publications, Inc., 1974), p. 88.

In the indirect system, the higher the count, the finer the yarn. For example, if 2 hanks of yarn of the same fiber weigh 1 pound, and 10 hanks of another yarn of the same fiber weigh 1 pound, obviously the higher number (10) would be finer than the lower number (2).

The amount of twist in a given yarn can also be measured. The ASTM standard definition of twist is "the number of turns about its axis per unit length observed in a yarn or other textile strand." Twist may be expressed as turns per meter (tpm), turns per centimeter (tpcm), or turns per inch (tpi).

Blends

Blending is the process of mixing fibers together. As noted earlier, it can take place at any of several points during the preparation of a yarn. The American Society for Testing Materials (ASTM) differentiates between *blended yarn*, which it defines as "a single yarn spun from a blend or mixture of different fiber species," and *self-blended yarn*, which is defined as "a single yarn spun from a blend or mixture of the same fiber species."[8]

The purposes of blending are (1) the thorough intermixing of fibers and/or (2) combining fibers with different properties to produce yarns with characteristics that cannot be obtained by using one type of fiber alone. Self-blending of bales of the same fiber is done routinely in processing natural fibers because from bale to bale, the fibers may vary. In this type of blending, the mixing of as many bales as possible is done early in the processes preparatory to spinning so that the subsequent steps can help to mix the fiber still more completely.

For the same reasons even when two or more different fiber types are combined, blending is done as early as possible. Carding helps to break up fiber clusters and intermix fibers more thoroughly. However, if the fibers being blended require different techniques for opening, cleaning, and carding, then slivers can be blended.

Blending is not limited to staple-length fibers. Filament fibers of different generic types can be combined into a single yarn. This can be done by extruding these fibers side by side during drawing or during texturing.

Sometimes a blended yarn is core spun with one fiber at the center and a different fiber as the covering or is wrapped with one fiber making up the central section and another the wrapping yarn. As yarn spinning and texturing technologies grow more sophisticated, the possibilities of combining several different fibers into one yarn expand. DuPont, for example, has introduced a yarn called Monece® that it calls a "cospun" yarn and describes its production as "filaments of both Dacron® polyester and Antron III® nylon are extruded together side by side and then air entangled into a single bundle."[9] Lanese® produced by the Celanese

[8]*Compilation of ASTM Standard Definitions* (Philadelphia: American Society for Testing and Materials, 1982), p. 833.

[9]DuPont news release, New York, February 21, 1984.

Company is described as an "acetate-bulked, polyester-core yarn with a voluminous wooly-like texture . . . created when the acetate-covered polyester-core filaments are fed down through air jets."[10]

It should be noted that fabrics woven from two or more yarns each made of different fibers are not considered blends. These fabrics are, instead, called *combination fabrics*. They do not behave in the same way as those fabrics in which the fibers are more intimately blended and may require special care procedures. Regrettably, the TFPIA labeling requirements do not distinguish between blended fabrics and combination fabrics when fiber percentage contents of fabrics are given.

The properties affected by blending may be aesthetic or functional or both. Among the aesthetic qualities that may be affected by blending are luster, texture, hand or draping qualities, and color. Blending for color may be done to combine already colored fibers or those that will show different affinities for dyestuffs when they are dyed subsequently.

Functional qualities that may be affected by blending include strength, resilience, abrasion resistance, absorbency, or, in fact, any desirable quality that any fiber used in the blend will confer. Blending less expensive fibers with more costly fibers may be done to lower the cost of fabrics.

Even through considerable study and evaluation has been made of optimum proportions of fiber required to achieve desired results in blends, no certain conclusions have been reached. It is clear that very small proportions of fibers have no appreciable influence on performance, although they may have some effect on appearance.

Classification of yarns can be made on a variety of bases, and authorities often differ when they define yarn types. The following classifications are based on those included in the *Textile Handbook* of the American Home Economics Association.

Types of Yarns

Yarns Classified by Number of Parts

Yarns that have been classified by the number of parts they possess are divided into *single*, *ply*, and *cord yarns*. A single yarn is made from a group of filament or staple fibers twisted together. If a single yarn is untwisted, it will separate into fibers.

Ply yarns are made by twisting together two or more single yarns. If ply yarns are untwisted, they will divide into two or more single yarns, which, in turn, can be untwisted into fibers. Each single yarn twisted into a ply yarn is called a *ply*.

Cord yarns are made by twisting together two or more ply yarns. Cord yarns can be identified by untwisting the yarn to form two or more ply yarns. Cord yarns are used in making ropes, sewing thread, and cordage and are woven as decorative yarns into some heavyweight novelty fabrics. (See Figure 14.32.)

[10]Celanese Corporation informational bulletin.

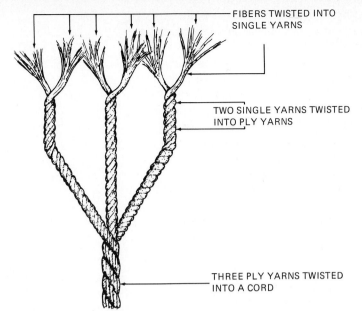

FIBERS TWISTED INTO
SINGLE YARNS

TWO SINGLE YARNS TWISTED
INTO PLY YARNS

THREE PLY YARNS TWISTED
INTO A CORD

FIGURE 14.32 *Single, ply, and cord yarns.*

Yarns Classified by Similarity of Parts

Simple yarns are those yarns with uniform size and regular surface. They have varying degrees of twist, ranging from loose to moderate, tight or hard twist. Single, ply, and cord yarns can all be simple yarns if their components are uniform in size and have a regular surface. When one strand of fibers is twisted together evenly, it is classified as a simple, single yarn. Two simple, single yarns twisted together create a simple ply yarn. (See Figure 14.33.)

Yarns made to create interesting decorative effects in the fabrics into which they are woven are known as *novelty* yarns. Some authors also call these yarns *complex* yarns. Novelty yarns can be single, ply, or cord, staple or filament.

In the industry, novelty yarns tend to be referred to as *fancy* yarns. Terminology identifying these yarns is confusing. A Saurer Corporation (manufacturers of spinning equipment) spokesperson commented on the difficulties in a 1982 presentation, saying "it is most difficult to find the correct terminology, due to the fact that, say, five twisting specialists may have about seven terms for the same yarn alone." The following list of terms and their definitions represent an attempt to define these terms as they appear to be accepted by most authorities.

1. *Bouclé* yarns are ply yarns. An effect yarn forms irregular loops around a base yarn or yarns. Another yarn binds or ties the effect yarn to the base. Some sources use the terms *loop* or *curl* yarns

FIGURE 14.33 *Yarns depicted are (A) monofilament—solid single strand of unlimited length, (B) multifilament—many continuous filaments, (C) staple—many short fibers twisted together, (D) two-ply—two single yarns twisted together. Drawings reproduced courtesy of John Wiley & Sons, Inc., from* Textile Yarns: Technology, Structure, and Applications, *by B. C. Goswami, J. G. Martindale, and F. L. Scardino, p. 2.*

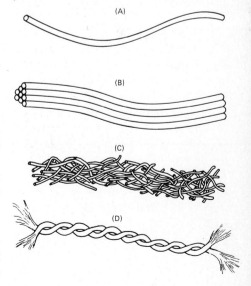

(A)

(B)

(C)

(D)

interchangeably with bouclé.[11] Ratiné yarns are similar to bouclé in construction. The loops in ratiné yarns yarns are spaced evenly along the base yarn.

2. *Flake, flock,* or *seed yarns* are made of loosely twisted yarns that are held in place either by a base yarn as it twists or by a third or binder yarn. These yarns are relatively weak and are used in the filling to achieve decorative surface effects.

3. *Nub yarns* are ply yarns in which an effect yarn is twisted around a base yarn a number of times in a small area to cause an enlarged bump or "nub." Sometimes a binder yarn is used to hold the nubs in place. The spacing of the nubs may be at regular or irregular intervals. Nubs are often of different colors than the base yarn. The terms *knot, spot,* or *knop* are also applied to this type of yarn.

4. *Slub yarns* may be either ply or single yarns of staple fibers. The slub effect is created by varying the twist in the yarn, allowing areas of looser twist to be created. This produces a long, thick, soft area in the fabric called a slub. Slub yarns are irregular in diameter. The surface of fabrics woven with slub yarns shows these irregularities. Yarns made in this way have areas of varying twist, causing weaker areas in the yarn. In many fabrics, slub yarns are placed in the filling direction where fabrics receive less strain. Slubs are the same color as the rest of the yarn and cannot be pulled out of the fabric without damaging the structure of the fabric. Filament yarns can be spun with varying degrees of twist. These yarns also create a slubbed appearance in fabrics. Such filament yarns are known as *thick-and-thin yarns.*

5. *Snarl yarns* are ply yarns in which two or more yarns held at different tension are twisted together. The varying tension allows the effect yarn to form alternating unclosed loops on either side of the bsae yarn.

6. *Spiral* or *corkscrew yarns* are made of two plies, one soft and heavy, the other fine. The heavy yarn winds around the fine yarn.

7. *Chenille yarns* are made by a totally different process and require several steps in their preparation. First, leno-weave fabric is woven (See pages 265 and 266). This fabric is cut into strips, and these strips, which have a soft pile on all sides, are used as yarns. These are not yarns in the traditional sense of twisted fiber, but have been taken through a series of preliminary stages before being readied for use.

8. *Core-spun yarns* are made with a central core of one fiber around which is wrapped or twisted an exterior layer of another fiber. Core-spun yarns may be made with an elastomer core, such as spandex, covered by another fiber to produce a stretch yarn. Other

[11]M. D. Potter and P. B. Corbman, *Textiles, Fiber to Fabric* (New York: McGraw-Hill Book Company, 1967).

1. BOUCLÉ YARN

2. FLAKE, FLOCK, OR SEED YARN

3. NUB, SPOT, OR KNOP YARN

4. SLUBYARN

6. SPIRAL OR CORKSCREW YARN

7. CHENILLE YARNS

core-spun yarns include sewing thread made with polyester cores and cotton cover. Lanese® is a core-spun and textured yarn with a polyester core and an acetate wrapping. (See Figure 12.2.)

Thread

The terms *yarn* and *thread* are sometimes used interchangeably. A distinction should, however, be made between yarns, which are fiber assemblies intended for weaving, knitting, or otherwise combining into a textile fabric, and sewing threads, which are used for sewing together sections of garments or other products.

Sewing threads may be made from one kind of fiber or from more than one kind of fiber. The most important threads have been those made from cotton or from a multifilament core of polyester covered with a cotton, rayon, or spun polyester. Except for yarns made from nylon or polyester, single yarns are not suitable for sewing threads; therefore, two or more plys are used.

To perform well, sewing threads must have high stability to bending, good strength, limited elongation, minimal shrinkage, and good abrasion resistance. Consider the stresses to which sewing thread is exposed. On the sewing machine, it must slide through various thread guides, it is hit back and forth under tension by the sewing machine needle, and it is permanently held in a bent position as it interlocks with the thread from the bobbin. Seams in tarpaulins, shoes, pants, and safety belts are subject to considerable tension and abrasion. If threads used shrink more or less than the fabrics in garments, puckering and wrinkling will appear at seam lines.

Home sewers purchase thread for their personal use, but 95 per cent of the sewing thread produced goes to industry. The development of high-speed industrial sewing machines requires manufacturers of sewing thread to improve constantly the quality and performance of these products.

Recommended References

"Air Jet Spinning Goes into Production," *America's Textiles*, 148 (June 1984), p. 24.

BARELLA, A. and A. MANICH. "Relation Between Twist and Abrasion Resistance of Rotor Yarns," *Textile Research Journal.*
  Part I: "Cotton Yarns, Viscose and Acrylics," 54 (February 1984), p. 453.
  Part II: "Polyester and Blend Yarns," 54, (May 1984), p. 314.

BECKWITH, N. R. "Hand Knitting Yarns," *Textiles*, 13 (Summer 1984), p. 30.

BORN, W. "Spindle and Distaff as Forerunners of the Spinning Wheel," *CIBA Review*, No. 28 (December 1939), pp. 982 ff.

BRUNET, I. "ITMA Perspective: Spinning Systems," *Textile Industries*, 148 (January 1984), 44.

BURNIP, M. X., and J. CASTLE-MALLORY. "Yarn as a Design Tool: How It Applies to Knitting," *Knitting Times*, 53 (December 1984), p. 67.

CATLING, H. "A History of Spinning and Weaving," *Textiles*, 12 (Spring 1983), p. 20.

Fannin, A. *Hand-Spinning Art and Technique*. New York: Van Nostrand Reinhold Co., 1970.

"Fine Count Friction Spinning: How It Works," *Textile World*, 134 (January 1984), p. 57.

Ford, J. E. "Spun Yarns—Ring or Rotor?" *Textiles*, 13 (Summer 1984), p. 36.

Ford, J. E. *Fibrillated Yarns*. Watford, England: Merrow Publishing Company Ltd., 1975.

"The Future of Yarn Manufacturing," *America's Textiles*, 148, (June 1984), p. 20.

Goodman, P. L. "Developments in Sewing Thread," *Textile Industries*, 147 (September 1983), p. 84.

Gross, D. "Spunfibers' Repco Spinning Operation Based on Service to the Customer," *Knitting Times*, 53 (February 20, 1984), p. 35.

Haldon, R. A. "The New Yarn Spinning Processes: Their Role and Requirements," *Canadian Textile Journal*, 101 (October 1984), p. 28.

"Increase Sophistication for O-E Spinning," *America's Textiles*, 148 (January 1984), p. 26.

Kullman, R., C. O. Graham, Jr., and G. Ruppenicher. "Air Permeability of Fabrics Made from Unique and Conventional Yarns," *Textile Research Journal*, 51 (December 1981), p. 781.

Linnert, A. "Open-End Spinning," *Textiles*, 5 (October 1976), p. 64.

Morris, M. A., and H. H. Prato. "End-Use Performance and Consumer Acceptance of Denim Fabrics Woven from Open-End and Ring-Spun Yarns," *Textile Research Journal*, 48 (March 1978), p. 177.

"New Developments in Fiber Cleaning," *America's Textiles* 13 (May 1984), p. 26.

"Rotor Spinning: Maturing in End Use," *Textile World*, 129 (March 1979), p. 51.

Salun, H. L., and L. Garn. "An Improved SRRC No-Twist Yarn System," *Textile Research Journal*, 53 (February 1983), p. 103.

"Stowe Adds Twistless to Its Yarn Repertoire," *Textile World*, 134 (September 1984), p. 61.

"Sorting Out the Spinning Systems," *Textile World*, 134 (September 1984), p. 69.

"Spin Fine Counts at Higher Speeds with Lower Costs," *Textile World*, 132 (February 1982), p. 64.

"Technology Update: Core Spinning," *Textile Industries*, 147 (April 1983), p. 45.

"The Ultimate Sewing Thread?" *America's Textiles*, 147 (November 1983), p. 30.

Walton, W. "Ways of Joining Yarns," *Textiles*, 13 (Spring 1984), p. 14.

Ward, D. "Tomorrow's Yarns—Does Ring Spinning Still Have a Place in Yarn Production?" *Textile Industries*, 148 (November 1984), p. 55.

"Yarn and Thread," *CIBA Review*, 3(1965).

Woven Fabrics

Fabrics can be constructed in a variety of ways, ranging from the matting together of fibrous materials to the intricate interlacing of complex yarn systems. The following discussion outlines and defines the major classifications of fabric constructions. The specific techniques and processes by which these different fabrics are made are discussed in the chapters that follow.

Woven Fabrics. Weaving of fabrics consists of interlacing systems of yarn. By varying the interlacings, a wide variety of different fabric constructions can be made.

Looped Fabrics. Fabrics can be constructed from one continuous yarn by the formation of a series of interconnected loops. Knitting, though a complex form, is one type of looping construction. Crochet is another.

Knotted Fabrics. Some fabrics are created by knotting yarns together. Lace, nets, macramé, and tatting are created by knotting.

Braided Fabrics. Fabrics may be created by plaiting together yarns or strips of fabrics. The components are interlaced in a diagonal pattern over and under one another to form a flat or tubular fabric of relatively narrow width.

Films. Since films are not made from fibers, they are not considered to be true textiles. They are sometimes laminated to textiles and therefore may be part of the structure of some textile products. They are synthetic polymers extruded in the form of sheets rather than as fibers. In some cases, these films are eventually made into fibrous form by a process called *fibrillation* or by cutting the sheet into fibers.

Fiber Webs. Masses of fibers can be held together into a fabric by interlocking of fibers by mechanical action or by fusing fibers together with heat, adhesives, or chemicals. Examples of a few fabrics constructed by these means include felt, bark cloth, spun lace, spun-bonded and needle-punched fabrics, and bonded webs. In the textile literature, these structures are most commonly referred to as "nonwovens."

Stitch-through Fabrics. Stitch through or stitch bonding is a relatively new technique for constructing fabrics in which two sets of yarns or a mass of fibers are sewn together into a fabric structure by another set of yarns.

Fabrics can be woven from yarns on a simple hand loom or on a highly complex, totally automated power loom. In either case, the fabric that is produced will be made by interlacing one yarn with another. The lengthwise-direction yarns in a woven fabric are called the *warp yarns* or *ends*. Crosswise yarns are called *filling* or *weft* yarns or *picks*. Warp and weft yarns interlace with each other at right angles.

The Creation of Woven Fabrics

The Hand Loom

Weaving requires that the warp yarns be held under tension. Having stretched out one set of yarns, the weaver then takes a second yarn and interlaces it with the warps. The simplest interlacing is made by moving the filling over the first warp, under the second, over the third, and under the fourth, and so on. In the second row, the filling moves under the first warp, over the second, under the third, and so on. The third row repeats the pattern of the first, and the fourth row repeats the pattern of the second row. Known as a *plain weave*, this is the simplest form of weaving.

An ancient craft, hand weaving was well known in North America, South America, and the Middle East at least eight thousand years ago. Two separate types of looms developed in different geographic areas. These looms differ in their means of providing tension to the warps. Northern Europeans utilized warp-weight looms, a vertical type of loom on which the warps were suspended from an upper bar and weighted at the bottom by small stone or clay loom weights. The force that gravity exerted on the weights provided the tension.

The second type of loom was the *two-bar loom* in which the warps stretched from one bar to another. This loom could be made either vertically or horizontally, as a frame of stakes in the ground held the two bars taut. Looms from Asia, the southern shores of the Mediterranean, and South America were of this type. South American looms often added a waist strap to the lower bars. The weaver suspended one bar from a tree or wall, and by placing the strap around the waist, the weaver could increase or decrease tension on the yarns by moving backward or forward.

The filling yarns, those running at right angles to the warps, could have been introduced by hand, but it was easier to use a needle or to wrap the yarns around a stick. This latter method had the advantage of allowing the yarn to be unwound as the stock was moved across the warps. Ultimately, yarn was wound onto a bobbin, and the bobbin was placed into a boatlike *shuttle*. The pointed end of the shuttle allowed the thread carrier to move smoothly while the bobbin allowed the yarn to unwind as it was needed.

Filling yarns tended to be somewhat loose in placement and had to be pushed into place more firmly. The earliest weavers painstakingly pushed each yarn into place with a small stick. A later, more efficient method utilized a wooden stick, shaped like a sword, that was slipped behind the filling yarns and pushed them tightly against the fabric that had already been woven. This weaver's sword or *batten* became a permanent part of the loom, although its shape was transformed gradually into a comblike device called a *reed* that was mounted on a frame. The frame retained the name batten, and a pull of the hand on the batten frame moved the reed forward, swinging the reed against the filling yarn and pushing it firmly into place.

The finished cloth on both horizontal and vertical looms was at first most probably the same dimensions as the loom. At some point, this changed and horizontal looms were adapted to making lengths of fabric longer than the loom. Egyptian fabrics of quite long dimensions have been found, and it is possible that they may have used a roller beam system. A beam with warp yarns wrapped around it allowed yarns to be fed continuously to the weaver and as the fabric was woven, it was wrapped around a roller at the other end of the loom. In this way continuous lengths of fabric, longer than the loom, could be constructed.

As long as each warp yarn had to be raised by hand before the filling was interlaced with it, the process of weaving remained slow and tedious. Inventive weavers improvided a means of speeding up the procedure of raising and lowering warp yarns. Alternate rows of warps were placed over a "shed rod" or a stick that lifted them above the level of their neighboring yarns. This formation of raised and lowered yarns is called the *shed*. The bobbin could be thrust across the entire width of the cloth through the shed without stopping to raise each individual warp yarn. The alternate set of warp yarns was threaded through a series of string loops that were tied to another rod. This rod could raise the second set of yarns past those on the shed rod, and now by thrusting the bobbin under this second set of yarns that had been raised by an upward pull on the rod, the filling interlaced with an alternate set of yarns. Alternate raising and lowering of the rod made it possible to interlace warp and filling yarns quickly and efficiently. The rod that held the second set of warps was called a *harness;* the loops were called *heddles*. Heddles were used in Egypt before 2000 B.C. and in Peru at a comparable period.[1] Variety in weave could be achieved through the use of multiple harnesses, each raising a different set of warps.

[1]Anni Albers, *On Weaving* (Middletown, Conn.: Wesleyan University Press, 1957), p. 20.

The widespread use of silk probably brought about certain improvements in loom structure. Since silk filament fibers spin into fine yarns, these small, somewhat slippery threads made weaving more difficult. In silk weaving, the shed rod was replaced by a second heddle, as the smooth, fine yarns tended to slide against the shed rod, while the heddle held them securely.

The change from hand manipulation of harnesses to operation by foot treadle was another improvement. The loom was constructed so that pressure on a foot treadle raised and lowered the harness frame. This released the hand to operate the shuttle and the batten and increased the speed with which the weaver could work.

Probably the single most important invention that preceded automation of the loom was the flying shuttle. The *flying shuttle*, designed by John Kay, who patented it in 1733, was a device wth a spring mechanism that threw the shuttle across the loom from one side to the other. In hand weaving, Kay's device was activated by a cord on either side of the loom that was pulled by the weaver. When the machine was mechanized, the flying shuttle was incorporated into the loom and operated mechanically.

Figure 15.1 depicts the basic hand loom that had developed by the time of the Industrial Revolution. Hand looms used by weavers today have the same basic structure.

Automation of Weaving

To transform weaving from a hand to a mechanical operation, several conditions had to be satisfied. The various motions made in hand weaving had to be automated. "The power loom of today is essentially the hand loom adapted to rotary driving."[2] The motions made in hand weaving included (1) the alternate raising and lowering of warp yarns to allow the shuttle to pass between them, (2) passing of the shuttle from one side of the loom to the other, (3) pressing filling yarns into place, and (4) winding up the completed cloth as it is woven.

A further requirement of power looms was that a power-operated loom had to stop automatically when a warp or filling yarn had broken. If the loom continued to function, the cloth would be flawed.

The first automatic loom was devised by Edmund Cartwright in 1784. Although it had a number of defects, this loom did work well enough to demonstrate that automatic loom weaving was feasible. Gradually, inventions by different individuals each contributed to the development of an economically viable automatic loom.

Eventually upper limits on production speed of shuttle looms were reached. Also, shuttle looms are extremely noisy. To overcome these deficiencies, looms were invented that transported filling yarns without

[2]*Encyclopedia of Textiles, American Fabrics* (Englewood Cliffs, N.J.: Prentice-Hall. Inc., 1980), p. 330.

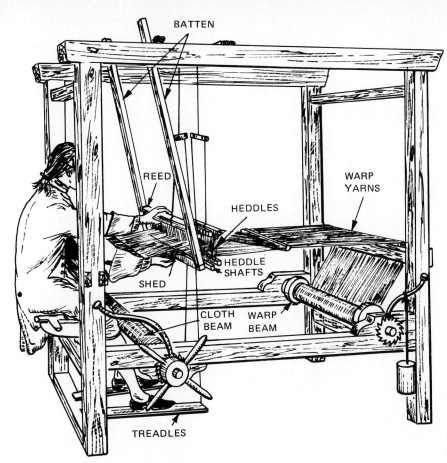

BATTEN

REED

HEDDLES

WARP
YARNS

HEDDLE
SHAFTS

SHED

CLOTH
BEAM

WARP
BEAM

TREADLES

FIGURE 15.1. Hand loom with the parts labeled.

a shuttle. These shuttleless weaving machines are faster and less noisy than are shuttle looms, and their operations are monitored by computer.

Modern Weaving Processes

Present-day looms can be divided between two major classifications: those that produce cloth in flat form and those that produce cloth in tubular form. Looms that produce flat woven cloth predominate. Flat looms can be further subdivided into two categories: those that use a shuttle to transport filling yarns and shuttleless looms, those that use some other means for carrying the filling from side to side.

Preparing the Yarns for Weaving

Prior to their use on the loom, warp and filling yarns must be prepared for weaving. (See Figure 15.2.) The essential characteristics of suitable warp and filling yarns differ. Warp yarns undergo greater stress and

FIGURE 15.2. *Warp beam being prepared from several hundred "cheeses" of yarn. Courtesy of the National Cotton Council of America.*

abrasion during weaving than do filling yarns; therefore, warp yarns must be strong enough to withstand these pressures. Warp yarns must be clean, free from knots, and uniform in size. A single warp yarn is called an "end."

To strengthen and lubricate warp yarns, *sizing* or *slashing* is added. Size is made up of starches, resins, or gums that act as lubricants. The yarns are passed from one warp beam through a solution of sizing material. The sized yarns are dried immediately after treatment and are wound onto another warp beam.

The warp beam containing the sized yarns is placed on the loom. In preparation for weaving, each warp end (yarn) must be threaded through its own drop wire, heddle eye, and reed dent. The *drop wire* is a device that will stop the loom if an end should break, the *heddle eye* is the opening in the heddles that carries the yarn, and the *reed dent* is the opening in the reed, a comblike device that will push each filling yarn close against the completed fabric.

To draw each end in by hand would be enormously time consuming; therefore, a variety of machines have been developed for drawing in. A separate machine can be used for each step (i.e., drawing through the drop wire, the heddle eye, and the reed dent), or one machine can perform all three steps.

Heddle wires are held in frames called *harnesses.* The number of harnesses required for the loom is determined by the weave.

Inserting the Filling Yarn

Once the warp yarns have been set into place, the loom goes through a series of motions: shedding, picking, beating up, and letting off. The shed is formed by raising the harnesses to form an open area between sets of warps. The formation of the shed is known as *shedding.*

While the shed is open, the yarn is transported across the opening, laying a filling yarn across the width of the loom. The insertion of the filling is known as *picking.* A single filling yarn is known as a *pick.* Speed of weaving machines is generally expressed as the number of picks per inch that the loom can insert.

The carrier used for transporting the filling yarn may differ from one kind of loom to another. The different devices used form the basis for organizing the following discussion of types of looms.

Shuttle Looms

In shuttle looms, the device that carries the yarn across the shed is called a shuttle and is made up of a wooden carrier into which a *quill* or *pirn* is placed. (See Figure 15.3.) As the shuttle traverses the cloth, the filling yarn unwinds from the quill. Quills or pirns in the shuttle must be replaced when the yarn supply is exhausted. The frequency with which a quill has to be replaced depends upon the fineness of the filling yarn. Coarse yarns require more frequent replacement; finer yarns need to be replaced less often.

In the mechanical changer, full quills are kept ready in a revolving case. The machine rams them into the shuttle when the shuttle comes to rest briefly after crossing the yarn. The pressure of the full quill crowds the empty quill out of the shuttle. It falls through a slot into a container under the loom. The new quill is pushed mechanically into place in the shuttle, which has a self-threading device that automatically picks up the yarn when the new quill is inserted. This allows the weaving to continue without a stop.

A specialized process has been developed that allows winding of quills to take place at the loom. In the *Unifil* system, empty quills are

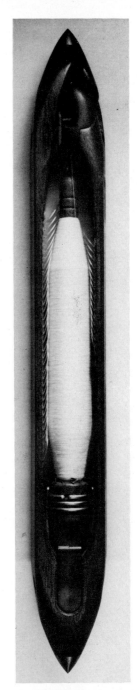

FIGURE 15.3. *The wooden shuttle (into which is fitted a quill or pirn on which yarns are wound) carries yarn across the loom. Courtesy of Steel Heddle.*

carried on a conveyer belt to a point where yarn from a large package is wound onto an empty quill that is then returned to a position where it can be placed in the shuttle. This system requires that fewer wound quills be supplied, but it has several limitations. It is useful only for single color picks, and because the cost of the system is high, it is most economical for coarse yarns that would require especially frequent quill replacement. (See Figure 15.4.)

The rapid crossing of the shed by the shuttle leaves a layer of filling yarn. When the shed is changed, the yarn is locked into place by the change in warp positioning. However, to make the yarn lie flat and in its proper position, it must be beaten into place. *Beating up* is done by the *reed,* a comblike device that pushes the filling yarn close against the woven fabric.

As the woven fabric is formed, it must be moved or *let off* the loom to make room for the formation of more fabric. All these functions are synchronized so that they occur in the appropriate sequence and do not interfere with one another.

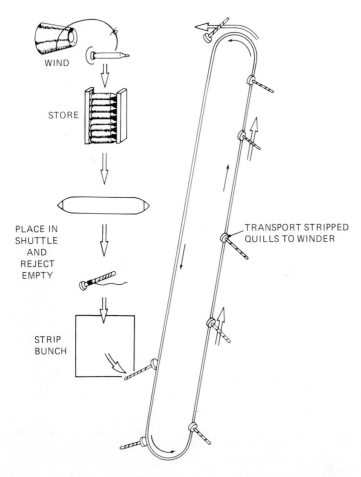

FIGURE 15.4   Flow cycle for Unifil. From P. R. Lord and M. H. Mohamed: Weaving: Conversion of Yarn to Fabric. *Copyright Merrow Publishing Co. Ltd. Reproduced by permission.*

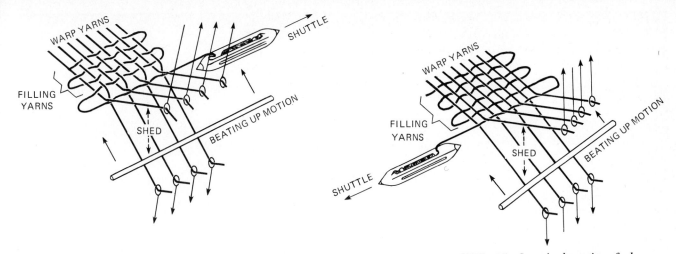

There is always the danger that a warp or filling yarn may break during weaving, causing a flaw in the cloth. Modern looms use electronic scanners that signal when a yarn is broken. A break in the electronic contact shuts off the loom, allowing the broken yarn to be repaired.

Except for the means of transporting the yarn across the shed, the steps in the weaving process are similar for shuttle and shuttleless looms. (See Figure 15.5.) The primary source of energy for automatic looms is an electric motor that transmits the motions of the various parts of the loom through a series of mechanical devices called *cams*. Several other looms have been developed that use different devices for regulating loom motions. These are the *Jacquard* and the *dobby* looms. Jacquard and dobby looms can use either shuttle or shuttleless transportation of yarns across the shed.

FIGURE 15.5. Steps in the action of a loom when a filling yarn is inserted in a plain weave fabric. Step 1, shed is formed by separating warp yarns to create space through which the shuttle can travel. Step 2, shuttle is projected through the shed. Step 3, beating up of yarn takes place to push new filling firmly against the others already in place. Step 4, positions of warp yarns are reversed to reform shed, and the process is repeated with the shuttle traveling in the opposite direction.

Jacquard Loom

The *Jacquard loom* (Figure 15.6.) is the descendant of an oriental loom, the draw loom, which was used to weave complex patterned fabrics. Operation of the draw loom required two workers: the weaver who threw the shuttle and operated the batten and a "drawboy" who raised and lowered a series of cords that controlled the pattern. The drawboy had to work from a platform above the loom while the weaver sat below.

Since the drawboy could make mistakes in the selection of cords, later modifications of the loom structure introduced a mechanical device for raising and lowering the cords. In 1805, Joseph Jacquard, a Frenchman, perfected the principle of the mechanical draw loom. To this day this same type of loom used in weaving complex patterns is known as the Jacquard loom and the weave is known as the *Jacquard weave*.

The ability of the Jacquard loom to weave a variety of complex fabrics is a result of the ability of this machine to control each warp yarn sep-

STEP 15.6. Two Jacquard weaving machines of the shuttleless type. Courtesy of Sulzer Ruti Inc.

arately. Each warp yarn is threaded through a loop in the end of a leash or cord.

Before the loom is set up, a design is worked out on graph paper and the position of each of the yarns in the design is analyzed. A punched card is prepared that corresponds to each of the filling yarns. The card contains a "code," a set of punched holes that will determine which warp yarns must be lifted for each passage of the filling. The punched cards are laced together in the correct order for the design. As the cards rotate, needles rest against the card. The needles are held under the pressure of a spring. When a needle position coincides with a hole in the card, the needle moves through the hole. The movement of the needle engages a hook, which in turn lifts the cords attached to the hook. The cords raise the yarns they hold to form the shed. When the filling has been inserted, the needles retract, the cards rotate to the next position, and different sets of needles engage holes in the next cards. This, in turn, causes other warp yarns to be lifted to form a different shed.

The Jacquard loom installation requires a large area, and particularly a very high ceiling. The loom operates more slowly than do simpler looms, so that the fabrics produced on this loom are more expensive.

Dobby Loom

The *dobby loom* (Figure 15.7.) might be considered a simplified version of the Jacquard. It can be used under normal mill conditions, as it requires only the installation of a somewhat enlarged dobby "head" on a conventional loom. The dobby mechanism uses a pattern chain (comparable to the pattern punched onto the cards in a Jacquard loom) on which there are pegs. Needles or feelers contact the pegs in the pattern chain and are positioned by the pegs. The feelers cause hooks within the dobby head to be connected or disconnected, and the motion of the hooks is translated to the harnesses that move from up to down or to in-between positions as dictated by the pattern.

From twenty-four to thirty shedding combinations are controlled in this way, so that the repeats are limited to about thirty rows in size. A machine called the double-cylinder dobby loom has been developed that approximately doubles the size of the repeat that can be made. The fabrics woven on this loom are less complex than are Jacquard patterns and usually consist of small fancy or geometrical figures or designs. Plain terry towels are also woven on dobby looms.

FIGURE 15.7. *Shuttleless rapier weaving machine with dobby head. Rapier-holding cases can be seen extending on either side of the machine. Courtesy of American Dornier Machinery Corp.*

Shuttleless Weaving Machines

Shuttleless weaving machines were invented to increase the speed of weaving. The modern loom with a shuttle, although much faster in operation than the earliest automatic looms, is not susceptible to further increases in speed because of the variety of operations that the machine must perform. For this reason, future loom developments are likely to be in the area of shuttleless weaving.

Shuttleless looms may be classified as to the method used in inserting the filling yarns. Four basic types have been developed:

1. Looms with grippers (Figure 15.8a).
2. Looms with mechanically operated gripper arms or rapiers (Figure 15.8b).
3. Looms employing water or air jets to carry the filling (Figure 15.8c).
4. Looms that mechanically propel the unsupported filling into the shed.

Only types 1, 2, and 3 have substantial commercial applications. In hand weaving and automatic shuttle weaving, the filling yarn is continuous and runs back and forth across the fabric, but in most shuttleless weaving, the filling yarn extends only from selvage to selvage, as it is cut off before it passes across the shed. In all shuttleless weaving, the yarn

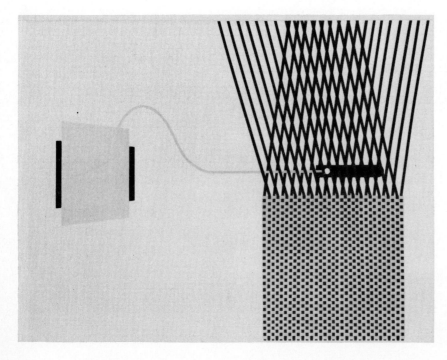

FIGURE 15.8 (a) Weaving with projectiles. A gripper projectile carries the weft thread into the shed. Its small size enables the moving parts of the machine to be kept small and the motions short, resulting in high picking rates even with large working widths.

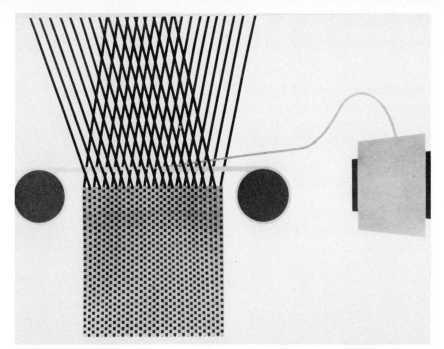

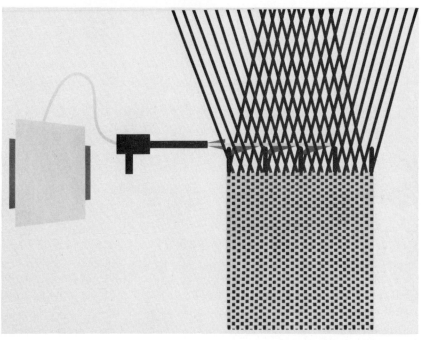

for the filling is unwound from large, stationary packages of yarn that are sometimes set on one side and at other times are set on both sides of the loom.

Gripper Loom

In the gripper type of loom, a small hooklike device grips the end of the filling yarn. As the gripper is projected across the warp shed, it tows the filling behind it. The gripper can move more quickly than can a conventional shuttle because of its decreased size; it can travel farther more easily, thereby making possible the weaving of wider fabrics, and it does not require the step of filling the shuttle; it pulls the yarn directly from a prepared yarn package.

Two types of gripper looms are used. In one, the gripper travels only in one direction. It is returned to the starting point by a conveyor belt. To maintain the speed of weaving, each loom must have several grippers, although only one is in use at any one time.

In the other, a single gripper inserts one filling yarn alternately from the right- and left-hand side of the loom. This gripper serves the same function as s conventional shuttle, but instead of holding a quill, it carries the yarn behind it. Packages of yarn must, therefore, be placed on both sides of the loom.

The gripper loom not only weaves fabric more quickly than does the shuttle loom, but it runs with less noise, making it possible for manufacturers to comply more easily with government regulations that restrict noise levels.

There is also a saving in power costs for wide-width fabrics. Narrow fabrics are not economically woven on this loom since too much time is spent in periods of acceleration of the gripper. Wide fabric widths are quite productive, as the power consumed is less than that for a conventional shuttle loom of the same size. Sheets are woven side by side on some of these looms to take advantage of these savings. According to data from producers of these machines, operation is at speeds of up to 330 picks per minute, or 1,260 yards of fabric per minute.

Rapier Loom

As in the gripper loom, a stationary package of yarn is used to supply the filling yarns to the rapier loom. One end of a *rapier*, a rod or steel tape, carries the filling. The other end of the rapier is connected to the control system. The rapier moves across the width of the fabric, carrying the filling across through the shed to the opposite side. The rapier is then retracted, leaving the new filling in place.

In some versions of the loom, two rapiers are used, each half the width of the fabric in size. One rapier carries the yarn to the center of the shed, whereas the opposing rapier picks up the yarn and carries it the remainder of the way across the shed. A disadvantage of both these techniques is the space required for the machine if a rigid rapier is used. The housing for the rapiers must take up as much space as the width of the machine. To overcome this problem, machines with flexible rapiers have been devised. The flexible rapier can be coiled as it is withdrawn and will therefore require less space. However, if the rapier

FIGURE 15.9. Figure 15.9 (left) In the two-rapier type of shuttleless machine, one rapier carries the yarn to the center of the shed where a second rapier grasps the yarn (right) and carries it across the rest of the width of the fabric. American Dornier Machinery Corp.

is too stiff, it will not coil; if it is too flexible, it will buckle. The double rapier is used more frequently than is the single rapier. (See Figure 15.9.)

Rapier looms operate at speeds of up to 325 picks per minute, or 732 yards per minute.

Water Jet Loom

Water-soluble warp sizings are used on most staple warp yarns. Therefore, the use of water jet looms is restricted to filament yarns, yarns that are nonabsorbent, and those that do not lose strength when wet. Furthermore, these fabrics come off the loom wet and must be dried. In this technique, a water jet is shot under force and, with it, a filling yarn. The force of the water as it is propelled across the shed carries the yarn to the opposite side. This loom is quite economical in its operation. A water jet of only 0.1 centimeter is sufficient to carry a yarn across a 48-inch shed. The amount of water required for each filling yarn is less than 2.0 cubic centimeters. Water jet looms are exceptionally fast: 600 to 800 picks per minute, (or 1,227 to 1,610 yards per minute.)

Air Jet Loom

Air jet looms operate in a manner similar to water jet looms. Instead of projecting a stream of water across the shed, a jet of air is projected. The initial propulsive force is provided by a main nozzle. (See Figure 15.10.) Electronically controlled relay nozzles provide additional booster jets to carry the yarn across the shed. Data from manufacturers indicate that air jet looms operate at speeds of up to 630 picks per minute, or a production rate of up to 1,420 yards per minute. They can weave multicolored yarns and are available in both dobby and Jacquard patterning mechanisms.

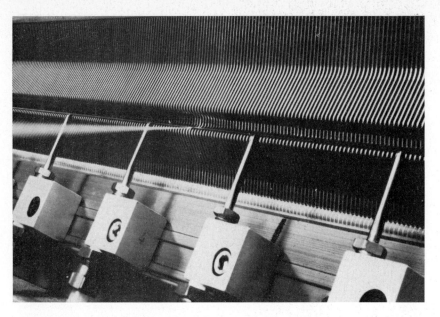

FIGURE 15.10 *Air jet nozzles spaced across the weaving machine transport filling yarns. Courtesy of Sulzer Ruti Inc.*

Multiphase Loom

All the weaving techniques discussed thus far require that the shed be open all the way across the loom for the device carrying the filling yarns to pass through the shed. This imposes a limit on loom speed.

The multiphase loom overcomes this limitation by forming many different sheds at different places across the loom and forming these only as the filling yarn is inserted. In this way, a number of filling yarns can be inserted, one behind the other. As a section of the shed opens, the filling passes, and the shed closes, opening again in the new pattern as the next filling yarn arrives. (See Figure 15.11.) Speed is increased because of the number of yarns that can be inserted one right after the other, but the actual speed of movement of the filling yarns is lower than in other types of looms. For this reason, filling yarns that are

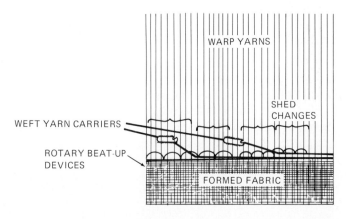

FIGURE 15.11. *Multiphase loom continually inserts weft yarns from yarn carriers. Rotary beat-up devices press inserted yarn firmly against previously formed cloth. If the pattern requires frequent shed position changes, small groups of yarns are changed into a new shedding position after each new yarn carrier has passed.*

weaker can be used. Nuovo Pignone, the manufacturer of a multiphase loom, states that its loom will insert up to 2,000 meters (2,176 yards) of picks per minute.

Selvages

Many shuttleless weaving techniques insert filling yarns from one side. In the shuttle type of loom, the carrying of the shuttle back and forth across the fabric creates a normal woven selvage, with no loose yarns to fray or ravel. In shuttleless looms, however, one or both of the selvages is fringed. It is necessary to reinforce this edge if the fabric is not to fray at the edges. The methods of reinforcement that are used include providing for tucking in the yarns at the open edge or use of a *leno* self-selvage, in which two warp yarns at the edges of the fabric twist around each filling. The tucked-in finish is the more durable. For heavy industrial fabrics made from heat-sensitive or thermoplastic fibers, hot melting devices cause the yarns to fuse together to form a selvage. (See Figure 15.12.)

Advantages and Disadvantages of Shuttleless Looms

When patterned fabrics are woven on shuttleless looms, colors can be changed more easily. Unlike shuttle looms in which a different shuttle must be provided for each different color, the shuttleless looms can be provided with a variety of colors directly from the yarn package. Other advantages include lower power requirements, lower sound levels, smaller space requirements, and higher speeds of fabric production. On the other hand, the higher production rates of shuttleless looms require that yarn quality be high to assure trouble-free operation.

Some Basic Concepts and Terminology

Woven fabrics, with a few exceptions (see triaxial fabrics, pages 278 and 279) are constructed by interlacing warp (lengthwise) yarns and filling (crosswise) yarns at right angles. In theory, warp and filling yarns should intersect at right angles. When this relationship is perfect, the fabric is said to be "on true *grain*." As a result of the stresses and strains imposed during weaving or finishing, these yarns may not lie in the proper position, and when this occurs, the fabric is said to be *"off grain."*

The off-grain relationship of warp and filling yarns is described by different terms, depending on how the distortion lies. Warp yarns are usually straight, as they are subject to lengthwise tension throughout the processing of fabrics. Filling yarns are usually responsible for the distortion, but they may be distorted in a straight line or in a *bowed* or *skewed* configuration. (See Figure 15.13.)

Within the textile and apparel industries, comparative measurement systems are necessary. The concept of yarn size expressed as yarn num-

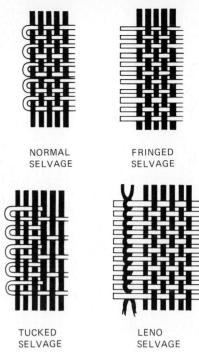

NORMAL SELVAGE

FRINGED SELVAGE

TUCKED SELVAGE

LENO SELVAGE

FIGURE 15.12. *Alternative selvage finishes*

The Weaves

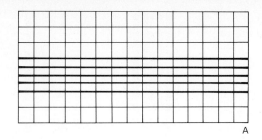

A. Warp and filling interlace at 90° angle. Fabric is on "true grain."

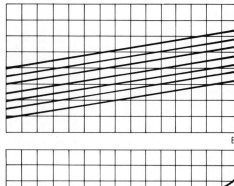

B. Filling is off the square; though straight, the filling is not at 90° to the warp.

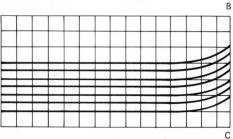

C. Filling is "skewed," i.e. straight for part of the way, then curved toward one selvage.

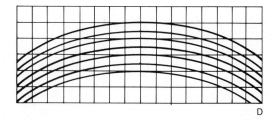

D. Filling is "bowed," or curved from selvage to selvage.

FIGURE 15.13   Grain positions.

ber has been discussed in Chapter 14. When dealing with fabrics, comparisons of size are made in terms of the number of yarns per inch or fabric count, the width of the fabric, or the weight of the cloth.

The closeness of the weave is expressed as the *fabric count*. With a small magnifying glass calibrated to measure an inch or fractions of an inch, it is possible to count the number of yarns in 1 inch of warp and in 1 inch of the filling. When the number of yarns in the warp is the same as the number of yarns in the filling, the weave is said to be a balanced weave. The fabric count is often expressed in numerical form as 80 × 64, indicating that there are 80 warp yarns per inch by 64 fillings. When warp and filling are balanced or equal, the count may be stated as 80 square, meaning there are 80 yarns per inch in the warp and 80 yarns per inch in the filling, or, alternatively, the number may be doubled, in which case a count of 180 would indicate a count of 90 yarns per inch in each direction. Balanced-weave fabrics with the same type of yarns in warp and filling are more durable because the fabric wears evenly in both warp and filling directions.

In those fabrics where yarn counts are not balanced, the larger number of yarns will usually be found in the warp direction. Costs increase more rapidly as the number of picks (filling yarns) increases; therefore, fabrics with balanced weaves or those with more yarns in the filling than in the warp are more costly to manufacture.

Counts are taken in the greige (i.e., unfinished) goods, and since fabrics may shrink during finishing, the count provided may not be exactly accurate. If one number only appears, it can generally be assumed that the fabric has a balanced weave.

Fabric widths will vary with the size of the loom on which they were woven. Since the introduction of automated looms and with improvements in the technology for transporting the filling yarns, fabric widths have increased dramatically. A survey of the specifications of air jet shuttleless looms, for example, notes width possibilities of as much as 157 inches, while narrow looms are available for weaving specialty items such as tapes.

Fabric weight is expressed as ounces per yard, yards per pound, or ounces per square yard. Woolens, worsteds, and fabrics of similar weight made from blends or man-made fibers are often measured in ounces per yard. For example, one may see designations such as a 14-ounce tweed or an 8-ounce tropical worsted. In this system of measurement, the higher the number, the heavier the fabric.

Yards per pound is a measure of the number of yards of cloth in 1 pound. In this measure, higher numbers indicate lighterweight fabrics. This system of measurement is used mostly for cottons, cotton blends, or lightweight man-made fabrics.

When measuring ounces per yard or yards per pound, the width of the fabric is not taken into account. These measures are, therefore, less precise than is the measure of ounces per square yard, which is the weight of a piece of fabric measuring 36 inches by 36 inches.

Fabric weights may range widely. Fabrics weighing less than 1 ounce per square yard would be very lightweight, as for example in some sheer curtain fabrics, gauzes, or even mosquito netting. Fabrics weighing from 2 to 3 ounces per square yard are also relatively lightweight. These are often referred to in the industry as "top-weight" fabrics and are typically used for shirts or blouses. Medium-weight fabrics, 5 to 7 ounces per square yard, are referred to as "bottom-weight" fabrics and are used for items such as skirts or slacks. Heavyweight fabrics range from from 9 to 11 ounces, and weights over 14 ounces are classified as "very heavyweight." As measurements tend to move to the metric systems, these weights may be expressed in grams per square meter rather than in ounces.

The appearance of a fabric will be affected by the number and placement of the yarns, as will the handle and draping qualities. As warp yarns are placed on the warp beam, they must be spaced so as to allow room for the filling yarns to interlace. In a "jammed" weave with minimum possible space for interlacing, a stiff, less flexible structure will be created. In general, it is true that those fabrics with fewer interlacings and more space between the yarns will be softer and more supple and will drape better. Fabrics with closer, denser weaves are likely to be more durable than are loosely woven, open weaves.

If warp yarns are set close together, they may obscure filling yarns. This is most evident when yarns of different colors or types are used. Such fabrics are often called "warp-faced" fabrics. If, as is relatively uncommon, fewer warp and many more weft or filling yarns are used, the weft may obscure the warp to produce a "weft-faced" fabric. Although the production of warp or weft-faced fabrics is possible in any of the basic weaves, it is more often twill or satin weave fabrics that utilize this effect.

Three types of weave structure form the basis of even the most complex weaves. Known as basic weaves, these are the plain weave, the twill weave, and the satin weave.

Visual representation of weaves is often made on graph paper. Each square of the paper represents the thread that appears on the upper side or surface of the fabric. Darkened squares represent the warp yarns crossing over filling yarns.

Diagramming of weaves or graph paper is a useful exercise, but students will probably find that the concepts relating to weaves are made clearer if they use colored yarns or strips of colored paper to create small samples of each of the basic weaves. A small hand loom, or a child's loom, can be used for this purpose.

FIGURE 15.14.   The plain weave.

Basic Weaves

The Plain Weave

The plain weave is the simplest of the weaves. It consists of interlacing warp and filling yarns in a pattern of over one and under one. Imagine a small hand loom with the warp yarns held firmly in place. The filling yarn moves over the first warp yarn, under the second, over the third, under the fourth, and so on. In the next row, the filling yarn goes under the first warp yarn, over the second, under the third, and so on. In the third row, the filling moves over the first warp, under the second, and so on, just as it did in the first row. (See Figure 15.14.)

The weave can be made in any type of yarn. Made with tightly twisted, single yarns that are placed close together both in the warp and filling, and with the same number of yarns in both directions, the resulting fabric will be a very durable, simple, serviceable fabric. If, however, the warp were to be made from a single yarn and the filling from a colorful bouclé yarn, a quite different, much more decorative fabric would result. Both are the product of the same, basic, plain weave.

Plain-weave fabrics are constructed from many fibers and in weights ranging from light to heavy. Weaves may be balanced or unbalanced. Decorative effects can be achieved by using novelty yarns or yarns of different colors. Together with many of these novelty fabrics, there are a number of standard fabric types made in the plain weave. In the past, these standard fabrics were always constructed from specific fibers. At present, suitable man-made fibers are also woven into many of the standard fabric constructions.

Among the best known of the plain-weave, standard fabrics are the following:

Open-weave, low-thread-count fabrics include *crinoline, cheesecloth, buckram*, and *gauze*. The openness of the weave and the wide spacing of the yarns in these fabrics make them limp. The durability of these fabrics is poor, and most of them have somewhat specialized uses. Cheesecloth, as the name implies, is used in producing cheese, serving as a wrapper or strainer for the curds. Cheesecloth, buckram, and crinoline can be heavily sized to serve as backing or stiffening fabrics. Gauze is often used for theatrical costumes, and medical dressings, as well as for blouses and dresses.

Sheer, soft, crisp finish plain-weave fabrics of close weave are generally made with high twist yarns. Often the yarns are combed. *Organdy*, a sheer cotton with a crisp finish, and *organza*, a similar fabric made with filament yarns, are examples of this type of construction. Organdy may be given either a temporary or permanently stiffened finish. Thread counts for organdies generally range from 72 × 64 up to 84 × 80. Other sheer, softer fabrics include *batiste*, made of mercerized cotton, linen, or cotton blended with man-made fibers. Batiste has acount of about 88 × 80. *Nainsook, longcloth*, and *voile* are other fabrics of slightly heavier weight than is batiste, which was, traditionally, made of cotton. Like batiste, they are now made of man-mades and/or blends, as well. Voile has a distinctive two-ply warp and good drapability.

Chiffon is made from fine, highly twisted yarns. Sheer evening dresses, blouses, lingerie, and other dressy garments are constructed from the fabric. Although delicate in feel and appearance, chiffon is relatively durable.

Medium-weight, plain-weave fabrics include such basics as *calico*, a low-count, coarse fabric, which is often printed with small designs, and *challis*, formerly made of worsted wool in a soft construction, but now made in a number of other fibers that attempt to simulate the original wool fabric. *Percale* is a closely woven, plain weave of cotton or blended fibers, made from yarns of moderate twist. Percale yard goods are generally carded, but percale sheets are finer and more luxurious in feel and are combed. Percale sheets have a count of 180 to 200 threads (warp plus filling) per inch. *Muslin* is generally woven from cotton or cotton blends. It is made in both heavily sized, bleached qualities and in better grades for sheets and pillow cases. Muslin sheets are not combed and have a lower count (128 to 140 total threads per inch) than do percale sheets.

Heavy or coarse plain-weave fabrics include *butcher linen, crash, osnaburg, and homespun.* All these fabrics have coarse, uneven yarns and an uneven texture.

Patterned effects are created by varying the color of the yarns. If the warp yarns are made up of alternating colors, a two-colored lengthwise stripe can be made. If warp yarns are of one color and filling yarns are of another color, the resulting fabric (usually made of cotton or a cotton blend) is called *chambray. Checks* can be made by alternating colors not only in the warp but also in the filling direction. *Plaids* are made in the same way, but with greater variety in the color. *Gingham* is a standard fabric of medium weight, usually made of cotton or a cotton blend, that has a woven check or plaid.

When these filling color variations are made on a shuttle loom, a special loom called a *box loom* is required in which there are as many shuttles as there are colors in the pattern. The shuttle release of each color is timed carefully so that the pattern repeat is always the same. On shuttleless looms, yarns of varying colors are drawn from yarn packages of different colors.

Plain-Weave Variations

Basket Weave. Using the principle of the plain weave, variations are made. The basket weave utilizes two or more warp and/or two or more filling yarns side by side as one yarn. (See Figure 15.15.) The resultant cloth is fairly loose in weave.

Among the more common basket-weave fabrics are

1. *Monk's cloth* is a coarse cloth of large yarns. Monk's cloth uses four or more yarns as one in the weave. Its major uses are in household textiles such as curtains, spreads, and the like. (See Figure 15.16.)
2. *Hopsacking* is made of many different fibers. This fabric simulates the fabrics used in bags for gathering hops. It has a 2-2 or 3-3 basket weave.
3. *Modified basket weaves* may utilize double yarns in one direction but not in the other. *Oxford cloth*, which is made in this way, is a soft fabric, often made of cotton or cotton blends, which is used for shirts. Frequently, it is made with narrow colored stripes in the warp.

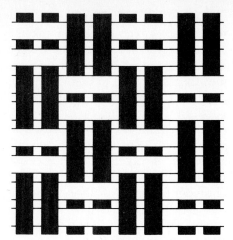

FIGURE 15.15. *The basket-weave variation of the plain weave.*

FIGURE 15.16. *Monks' cloth, a basket-weave fabric with four warp and four filling yarns.*

Rib Variation. Ribbed or corded fabrics are created by grouping a number of yarns together in one direction before they are crossed by the yarns from the opposite direction or by using larger yarns in one direction than in the other. If the resultant fabric shows an enlarged crosswise yarn, a crosswise *rib* is formed. (See Figure 15.17.) If the enlarged yarn is in the lengthwise direction, a lengthwise *cord* is formed. (See Figure 15.18.) Ribs and cords can be either relatively small or quite pronounced.

Some standard fabrics with small ribs include *broadcloth, poplin,* and *taffeta.* Broadcloth and poplin are most often woven from cotton or cotton blends, and sometimes from wool, whereas taffeta is made of filament yarns such as acetate and silk. *Faille, grosgrain,* and some *reps* have a larger rib. *Bengaline, ottoman,* and *large reps* have still larger, very pronounced ribs.

Shantung has a nubby, irregular rib in the filling. Formerly made almost exclusively of silk, shantung is now made from a variety of manmade fibers as well.

Dimity is a sheer cotton fabric that is often made with a lengthwise cord effect. Some dimity fabrics use larger yarns in both the warp and filling direction to achieve a checked or "barred" effect. *Bedford cord* is another example of a sturdy fabric constructed with a pronounced lengthwise cord.

Ribbed and corded fabrics may wear unevenly, as crossing the larger yarns exposes a greater surface area of the covering yarn to abrasion. The problem is aggravated if the crossing yarns are not closely spaced, if the rib is especially pronounced, or if the crossing yarns are loosely twisted or made from a weak fiber.

Seersucker. Another plain-weave variant, seersucker is created by holding some warp yarns at tight tension, some at slack tension. Those at slack tension puff up to form a sort of "blister effect." Seersucker surface effects are permanent. Often the slack and tight yarns are each made from a different color yarn, to provide a decorative striped effect. Seersucker should not be confused with fabrics having puffed effects created by chemical finishes, such as *plissé,* which are much less durable.

Twill Weave

Twill fabrics are readily identified by the diagonal lines that the weave creates on the surface of the fabric. The yarns in twill fabrics are usually spaced closely together, packed tightly, and held firmly in place. Therefore, twill fabrics are usually quite strong and durable, while at the same time they are supple and drape well. The compact structure of twill fabrics enables them to shed soil more readily, although when soiled they may be more difficult to get clean. Depending on their construction, twill fabrics generally show good resistance to abrasion. Twill fab-

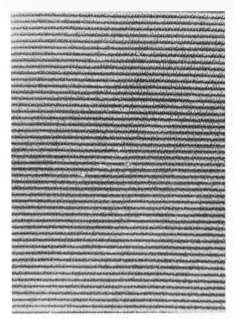

FIGURE 15.17. *Faille fabric with pronounced crosswise rib.*

FIGURE 15.18. *Dimity fabric with pronounced lengthwise cord.*

rics are often used for tailored garments, particularly when made of worsted wool yarns.

The simplest twill weave is created by the filling's crossing over two warp yarns, then under one, over two, under one, and so on. In the next row, the sequence begins one yarn farther on. (See Figure 15.19.) The area in which one yarn crosses over several yarns in the opposite direction is called a *float*.

The lines created by this pattern are called *wales*. When the cloth is held in the position in which it was woven, the wales or diagonal lines will be seen to run either from the lower left corner to the upper right corner or from the lower right to the upper left. If the diagonal runs from the lower left to the upper right, the twill is known as a right-hand twill. About 85 per cent of all twill-woven fabrics are right-hand twills.[3] When the twill runs from the lower right to the upper left, the twill is known as a left-hand twill. (See Figure 15.20.)

There are a number of types of twill weaves. All use the same principle of crossing more than one yarn at a regular, even progression. Descriptions of twills may be made in terms of the pattern of warp yarns crossing filling yarns. The description of twill weaves is notated as 2/1, 2/2, 3/2, and so on. The first digit refers to the number of filling yarns crossed by the warp and the second digit to the number of filling yarns the warp passes under before returning to cross the filling again. When the crossing is over and under the same number of yarns, the fabric is called an even twill. When warps pass over a larger or smaller number of filling yarns than they pass under, the fabric is an uneven twill.

Even-Sided Twill. The even-sided twill has the same number of warp and filling yarns showing on the face of the fabric. Figure 15.21 shows how such a weave is achieved in a 2/2 twill. Even-sided twills can also be made in 3/3 patterns.

Even-sided twill fabrics include *serge*, a popular, basic twill fabric made from any of a number of different fibers. When serge is made from wool, it is often woven from worsted yarns. Serge will take a crease well, but wool serge tends to become shiny with wear. It tailors well. *Surah* is an even-sided twill that is made of silk or other filament fibers. Often printed, or woven into plaids, surah is used for neckties, scarves, blouses, dress goods. Some twilled *flannels* are made from even-sided twill constructions.

Warp-Faced Twill. Warp-faced twills have a predominance of warp yarns on the surface of the fabric with patterns of 2/1, 3/1, 3/2, and so on.

Warp-faced twills include very popular basic twill fabrics such as *denim, jean,* and *drill,* which are durable fabrics often made from cotton or cotton blends. The major uses of these fabrics include work clothes, sportswear, and mattress and pillow ticking. *Gabardine* is a warp-faced twill fabric that is durable and closely woven. It is made into a variety

[3]*Ibid.,* p. 325.

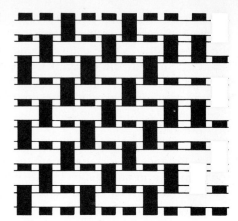

FIGURE 15.19.   *Right-handed twill weave.*

FIGURE 15.20.   *Left-handed twill weave.*

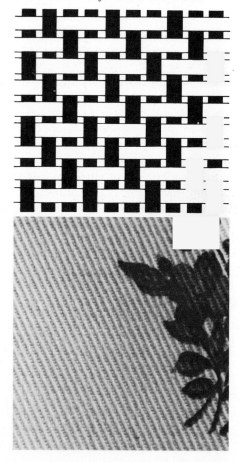

of weights from many different fibers such as wool, rayon, cotton, and man-made fibers. (See Figure 15.22.)

Filling-Faced Twill. Filling-faced twills have a predominance of filling yarns on the surface of the fabric. Filling yarns are generally weaker than are warp yarns, so that relatively few filling-faced twills are made.

Herringbone Twill. In a herringbone twill, the direction of the twill reverses itself to form a broken diagonal that appears like a series of V's: herringbone patterns create a decorative effect. (See Figure 15.23.)

Twill Angles. When the face of a twill fabric is examined, the diagonal of the wales will be seen to move at a more or less steep angle. The steepness of the angle is dependent upon two factors in the construction of the fabric: the number of warp yarns in the fabric and the number of steps between movement of yarns when they interlace. (See Figure 15.24.)

The more warp yarns in the construction, the steeper the angle of the wales will be provided that the number of filling yarns per inch remains the same. This is because the point of interlacing of the yarns will be closer together, thereby making a steep climb upward. When the steepness of the angle is the result of close spacing of warp yarns, these steeper angles are an indication of good strength.

Generally the interlacing of yarns in a twill changes with each filling yarn. There are, however, fabrics in which the interlacing of yarns changes only every two filling yarns or every three filling yarns. As can be seen in the diagram, the less often the interlacing changes, the steeper the angle of the twill will be.

FIGURE 15.21. *Right-handed, even-sided twill (2/2).*

FIGURE 15.22. *Right-handed, warp-faced twill weave (2/1).*

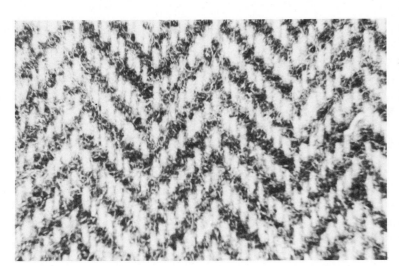

FIGURE 15.23. *Herringbone twill fabric*

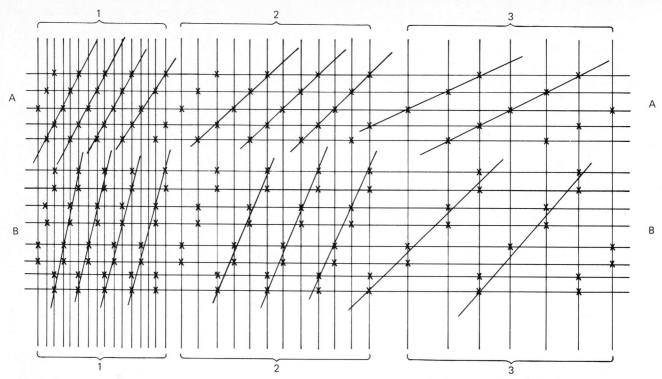

FIGURE 15.24. A and B. Twill angles decrease as yarns in the warp are spaced more widely apart. Compare sections A-1 with A-2 and A-3, and B-1 with B-2 and B-3. Twill angles become steeper as the frequency with which yarns change their pattern of interlacing decreases. In Figure A yarns change their pattern of interlacing with every weft yarn. In Figure B, yarns change their pattern of interlacing every two weft yarns. Compare the steepness of the angles in A-1 to that of B-1, A-2 with B-2, and A-3 with B-3.

Satin Weave

Satin-weave fabrics are made by allowing yarns to float over a number of yarns from the opposite direction. Interlacings are made at intervals such as over four, under one, over seven, under one, or over eleven, under one. Floats in satin fabrics may cross from four to twelve yarns before interlacing with another yarn. No pronounced diagonal line is formed on the surface of the fabric because the points of intersection are spaced in such a way that no regular progression is formed from one yarn to that lying next to it.

When warp yarns form the floats, the fabric is referred to as *satin*. (See Figure 15.25.) When filling yarns float, the fabric is called *sateen*. (See Figure 15.26.) Much of the beauty of satin-weave fabrics comes from the use of more loosely twisted yarns that reflect light to create a soft luster. Filament yarns do not require a tight twist to serve as warp yarns, whereas cotton, being a staple fiber, must be given a fairly high degree of twist if it is to serve as a strong warp yarn. Therefore *sateen* fabrics, in which the filling yarns float, are most often made from cotton or staple fibers, whereas low-twist filament yarns are often made to float in the lengthwise direction in constructing *satin*. Exceptions do exist in which cotton floats are formed in the warp, and filament floats are formed in the filling.

In *crepe-backed satin*, loosely twisted, lustrous warp yarns are combined with tightly twisted, creped filling yarns. The floats on the surface are created by the warp, so that the face of the fabric is chiefly made up of warp yarns with a satin appearance, whereas the back of the fabric is made up largely of the tightly twisted filling yarns that produce a crepe or rougher surface texture with a flat, less shiny appearance.

Satin-weave fabrics are quite decorative. They are usually made from filament yarns with high luster to produce a shiny, lustrous surface and tend to have high fabric counts. They are smooth and slippery in texture and tend to shed dirt easily. The long floats on the surface are, of course, subject to abrasion and to snagging. The longer the float, the greater the likelihood of snags and pulls. Satins are often used as lining fabrics for coats and suits because they slide easily over other fabrics. The durability of satin-weave fabrics is realted to the density of the weave, with closely woven, high-count fabrics having good durability. Satins made from stronger fibers will, of course, be more durable than those made from weaker fibers.

Some names given to satin fabrics include

1. *Antique satin*, a satin made to imitate silk satin of an earlier period, often using slubbed filling yarns for decorative effect.
2. *Double-faced satin*, a satin woven from two warps and one filling to obtain satin effects on both the face and the back of the fabric.
3. *Duchesse satin*, a satin with a plain back and a crisp texture. The fabric is smooth and lustrous.
4. *Peau de soie*, soft, closely woven satin with a flat, mellow luster.
5. *Slipper satin*, strong, compact satin, heavy in weight. It is often used for evening shoes.

Novelty Fabrics from Basic Weaves

Novelty effects in fabrics are in large part a result of selection of novelty yarns for incorporation into fabrics made in one of the basic weaves. Crepe fabrics are a good illustration. *Crepe fabrics* may be defined as fabrics characterized by a crinkled, pebbly surface.

Originally, crepe fabrics were made from crepe yarns, that is, yarns with an exceptionally high degree of twist, up to sixty-five turns per inch. Most standard crepe fabrics were made in the plain weave, some with rib effects, and some in satin weave, as in crepe-backed satin. With the advent of synthetic fibers, however, many *crepe effects* are achieved through the use of textured yarns, bicomponent yarns in which uneven shrinkage creates a crepelike surface, embossing or stamping a crepe-like texture on the surface of the fabric, or use of a crepe weave that breaks up the surface of the cloth into a random sequence of interlacings. Most fabrics made from these more recent processes will be durable only if they are made from heat-treated thermoplastic fibers. Careful examination of fabrics having a crepelike appearance will reveal that relatively few of them are actually woven with crepe yarns.

FIGURE 15.25.   *Satin weave. Warp yarns form floats, crossing over seven filling yarns between every interlacing.*

FIGURE 15.26.   *Sateen weave. Filling yarns form floats, crossing over four warp yarns between every interlacing.*

Variations of the Basic Weaves

Jacquard Weave

The operation of the Jacquard loom has been described earlier in this chapter. Jacquard patterns, when carefully analyzed, may be seen to contain combinations of plain, twill, and satin weaves, even in the same crosswise yarn. Many decorative fabric are made by the Jacquard technique. Jacquard woven fabrics should not be confused with true tapestries even though some fashion promotions may refer to Jacquard fabrics as being "tapestry fabrics."

The following are some of the best known Jacquard patterns:

1. *Brocade*, an embossed appearance is created in brocade fabrics. Elaborate patterns, often of flowers and figures, stand out from the background. Brocades are made from a wide range of fibers and with a wide range of price and quality. Fabrics are used for upholstery, draperies, and evening and formal clothing.
2. *Brocatelle*, a fabric that is similar to brocade, but with figures or patterns standing in high relief. Brocatelle is used mostly for upholstery fabrics and draperies.
3. *Damask*, a flatter fabric than brocade, many damasks have a fine weave. Damask figures often use a satin weave to reflect light from the pattern, whereas the background is made in a plain or twill construction. Linen damasks have long been used for luxurious tablecloths. Damasks are reversible. Cotton and linen damasks are made either with five-yarn float or a seven-yarn float in the satin weave. The longer floats are more lustrous, but the shorter floats are more durable, as they are less likely to snag or be subject to abrasion.

Dobby Weave

The dobby weave is rather like a Jacquard weave in miniature. The patterns created by the dobby weave are small, repeated patterns, usually geometric in form. (See Figure 15.27.)

Some of the fabrics made on the dobby loom include

1. *Bird's eye*, a cloth made with small diamond-shaped figures, the weave is said to resemble the eye of a bird. Bird's eye is allso called diaper cloth.
2. *Madras cotton shirting*, sometimes woven with a dobby pattern in the stripe. The figure woven may be in either contrasting or in the same color as the background fabric.
3. *Piqué*, medium- to heavyweight fabric, often of cotton, with a pronounced lengthwise cord, often combined with other small figures or patterns such as honeycomb or waffle effects.

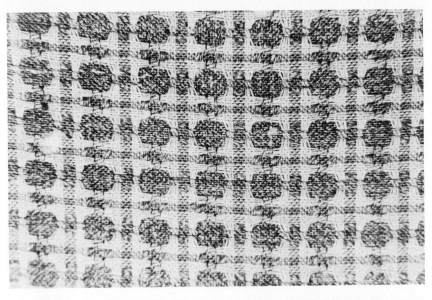

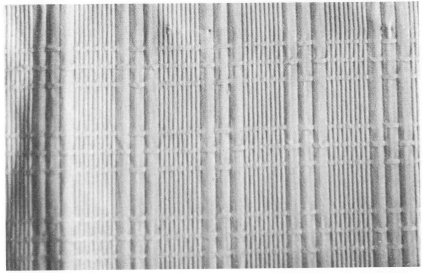

Figure 15.27. Dobby-weave fabrics with small geometric patterns.

4. *White-on-white,* a white dobby figure woven on a white background, often used for men's shirting.

Tapestry Weaving

Tapestry weaving differs from Jacquard weaving in that the former is essentially a hand technique. Whereas Jacquard weaving utilizes repeated patterns of finite size, tapestry weaving is used to produce enormous fabrics that can be one, large picture. Tapestry weaving may be compared with painting with yarn.

FIGURE 15.28. *Peruvian tapestry fabric from the ninth to the eleventh century. Courtesy of the Metropolitan Museum of Art, Fletcher Fund, 1959.*

Although tapestry weaving has been practiced in most cultures, the finest examples of this art are to be found in ancient Peru (Figure 15.28.), in Coptic Egypt in the fifth and sixth centuries A.D. (Figure 15.29), and in northern Europe from the fourteenth to the seventeenth centuries (Figure 15.30). Since it is basically a hand technique, tapestry is made on a very elementary loom. Even after the Europeans had built large factories in which tapestries were woven, particularly in Flanders and France, the operation remained a handcraft that had been moved into a factory setting.

In the weaving of European tapestries, the loom followed the basic form of the two-bar loom. The loom was set up either vertically or horizontally, and warp yarns were measured and affixed to the loom. Filling yarns were prepared in the appropriate colors. The design of the tapestry was first worked out in a drawing or *cartoon*, as it was called. The artist who created the drawing may have been one of great stature, and painters such as Raphael and Rubens served as designers of sixteenth- and seventeenth-century tapestries. The cartoon was sometimes traced onto the warp yarns. In other instances it was mounted behind the loom and the tapestry weaver looked through the warp yarns to the design, following the plan of the drawing. The tapestry was woven with the wrong side facing the weaver. Sometimes a mirror was set up beneath the tapestry so that the weaver could check the progress on the right side.

The various colors of yarns were wound onto sharp, pointed bobbins that were introduced into the warp, and the weaver proceeded to fill in the area of that particular color. When the weaver reached the end of one color, a new bobbin was used for the next section. This created a problem, because as the weaver worked back and forth in a particular segment of the design, the yarns of one color did not join with the yarns of the adjacent color. This produced slits in the fabric at the place where each new color began. In some forms of tapestry weaving these holes were purposely left open, and when the tapestry was hung, the

Figure 15.29. Egyptian (Coptic) tapestry woven in colored wools and undyed linen during the sixth or seventh centuries A.D. Courtesy of the Metropolitan Museum of Art, Rogers Fund.

Figure 15.30. French or Flemish tapestry of the late fifteenth century woven from wool and silk with metal threads. Courtesy of the Metropolitan Museum of Art, the Cloisters Collection. Gift of John D. Rockefeller, Jr., 1937.

light shining through the slits added to the decorative effect of the tapestry. This practice prevailed in ancient Peruvian tapestry design.

In many tapestries, however, these openings were not pleasing and a number of different techniques were used to avoid open spaces. Sections of the tapestry could be sewn shut, but this caused the fabric to be weaker at the spots where the fabric was seamed together. Two other methods were also utilized to prevent the formation of slits. Where the color of one section ended and another began, both the old and the new color could be twisted around the same warp yarns. This system worked well except that it created a slightly indistinct or shadowy line. Where clear, well-defined lines were required, the yarns of adjacent colors were fastened together by looping one yarn around the other.

In tapestry weaving all the warp yarns are completely covered by filling yarns, so it is the filling yarns that carry the design. The warp yarns serve only as the base.

Leno Weave

The leno weave is the modern descendant of a technique called "twining" that was used thousands of years ago for making fabrics. In leno-weave fabrics, the warp yarns are paired. A special attachment, the *doup* or *leno* attachment crosses or laps the paired warp yarns over each other, while the filling passes through the opening between the two warp yarns. (See Figure 15.31.)

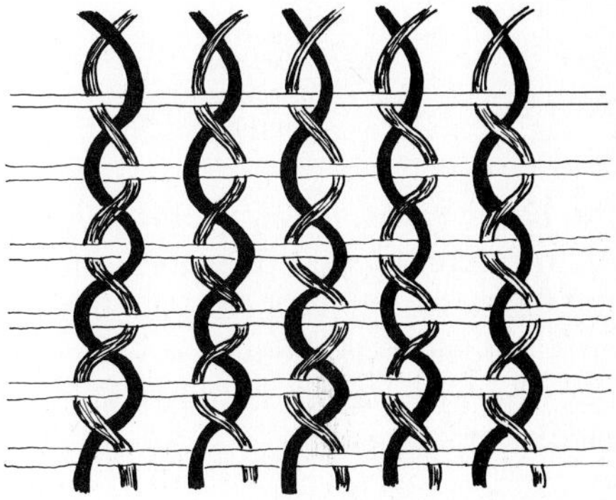

Leno-weave fabrics can be made in open, gauzelike constructions. The twined (not twisted) warp yarns prevent the filling yarns of these open fabrics from slipping. Curtain fabrics are often made with leno weave. Two of the more popular leno-weave fabrics are *marquisette* and *grenadine*.

Figure 15.31. Structure of a leno-weave fabric.

Woven Pile Fabrics

Pile fabrics have been defined as "fabrics(s) with cut or uncut loops which stand up densely on the surface."[4] Pile fabrics may be created by weaving or through other construction techniques, such as tufting, knitting, or stitch through. To create the loops that appear on the surface of *woven* pile fabrics, the weaving process incorporates an extra set of yarns that form the pile. Construction of woven pile fabrics, therefore, represents a complex form of weaving in which there are at least three sets of yarns.

Pile fabrics are woven by one of several methods: the wire method, the filling pile method, the double-weave method, or the terry method.

Wire Method. The wire method utilizes two sets of warp yarns and one set of filling yarns. One set of warp yarns and the filling yarn interlace in the usual manner and form the "ground" fabric. These two yarns may interlace in either a plain or a twill weave. The extra set of warp yarns forms the pile. When the pile yarns are raised by the heddles, the machine inserts a wire across the loom in the filling direction. When the warps are lowered, they loop over the wire to make a raised area. The next several filling yarns are inserted in the usual manner. The wire is then withdrawn, leaving the loop, which is held firmly in place by

[4]M. Klapper, *Fabric Almanac* (New York: Fairchild Publications, Inc., 1967), p. 64.

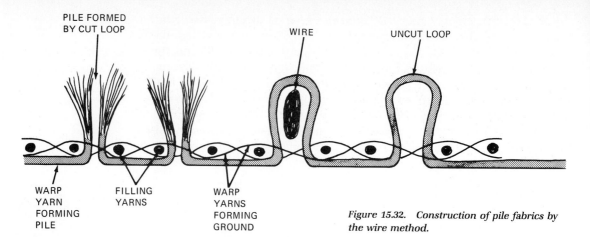

PILE FORMED
BY CUT LOOP

WIRE

UNCUT LOOP

WARP
YARN
FORMING
PILE

FILLING
YARNS

WARP
YARNS
FORMING
GROUND

Figure 15.32.   Construction of pile fabrics by the wire method.

the other yarns. *Frisé*, a fabric often used for upholstery, is an example of an uncut, looped pile fabric that can be made by the wire method. If the fabric is to have a cut pile, the wire has a knife blade at the end that cuts the yarns as the wire is withdrawn. If the fabric is to have an uncut pile, the wire has no cutting edge. *Velvets* may be made in this way. (See Figure 15.32)

Filling Pile Method. In the filling pile method there are two sets of filling yarns and one set of warp yarns. In this technique, the extra set of filling yarns forms floats that are from four to six yarns in length. The floating yarns are cut at the center of the float and these ends are brushed up the surface of the fabric. (See Figure 15.33.)

In some filling pile constructions, the filling yarn that makes the pile is interlaced with the ground one time before it is cut; in others, the filling pile interlaces twice. Those fabrics in which there are two interlacings are more durable than when only one interlacing has taken place. It is possible to distinguish fabrics by raveling pile loops from the fabric. Those that have been interlaced once will have the form of a small V, whereas those that were interlaced twice will look like a small W. The points of the V and W represent the places at which the yarns interlaced, and the W form is of better quality.

Corduroy floats are placed in lengthwise rows and *velveteen* floats are randomly spaced. The even spacing of corduroy floats produces the characteristic strip or wale of many corduroys, whereas velveteens are characterized by a uniform, overall pile. Other decorative effects can be achieved by cutting floats selectively to vary pattern and texture.

Both wire and filling pile grounds can be made in either plain or twill weaves. Twill-weave grounds will usually provide better wear.

Double-Cloth Method. The double-cloth method, like the filling pile method, is used for cut pile fabrics. Here two sets of warps and two sets of fillings are woven simultaneously into a layer of fabric. A third set of

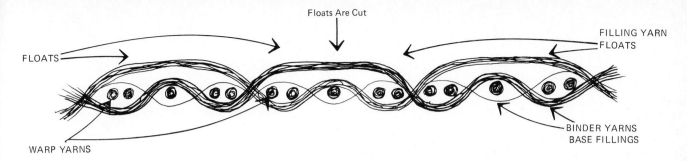

Floats Are Cut

FLOATS

WARP YARNS

Cut Floats Form Pile

FILLING YARN
FLOATS

BINDER YARNS
BASE FILLINGS

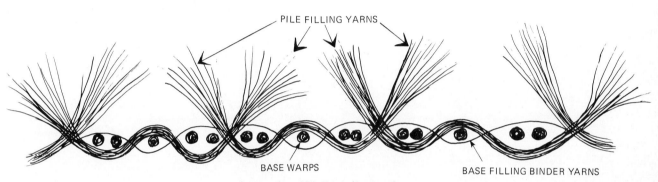

PILE FILLING YARNS

BASE WARPS

BASE FILLING BINDER YARNS

Cross-section of Pile Fabric (Corduroy)

Figure 15.33. Construction of corduroy by the filling pile method.

warp yarns moves back and forth between the two layers of fabric, holding them together and being held by each fabric. The resultant fabric is cut apart by a sharp knife, thereby creating two lengths of fabric, each with a cut pile. (See Figure 15.34.)

Velvets and *plushes* can be made in this way. Other nonpile fabrics can be made by the double-cloth method. These are discussed separately.

Terry Weave. *Terry cloth* is made by the slack tension method. Terry cloth is made with uncut loops. Two sets of warps and one of filling yarns are used. The ground of the fabric is made from one set of warp and one set of filling yarns, the warp yarns being held under tension. The warp yarns that make up the pile are allowed to relax, their tension being released. As the filling yarns are pushed firmly into place, the looser warp yarns loop up on the surface, forming the terry pile. Terry pile may appear on one or both sides of the fabric.

Chenille

Chenille fabrics have a pile that is created by the use of chenille yarns. (See Chapter 14.) The loose fiber ends that fluff up on the surface

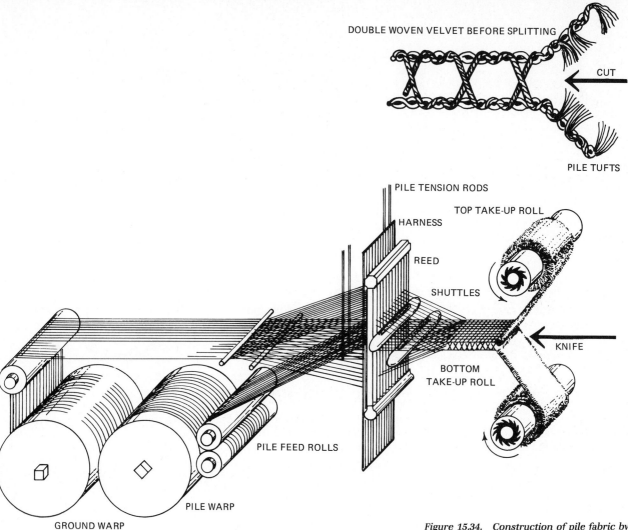

DOUBLE WOVEN VELVET BEFORE SPLITTING

CUT

PILE TUFTS

PILE TENSION RODS

TOP TAKE-UP ROLL

HARNESS

REED

SHUTTLES

KNIFE

BOTTOM TAKE-UP ROLL

PILE FEED ROLLS

PILE WARP

GROUND WARP

Figure 15.34. Construction of pile fabric by the double-cloth method. Courtesy of Crompton Company, Inc.

of the chenille yarn to form "caterpillars" create a soft, cut pile when woven into fabrics. The pile in this case is created not by the fabric structure, but by the characteristics of the yarn. Chenille fabrics may be woven or knitted.

Woven Effects

Hand embroidery has been used for many centuries to add decoration to fabrics. With the invention of the automatic loom came the invention of looms that would create ornamental effects similar to that of embroidery.

Decorative Surface Effects

Figure 15.35. Clipped spot design.

Clipped or Unclipped Spot Weave

Embroiderylike designs may be achieved through the use of extra warp and extra filling yarns. In the clip spot weave, either an extra shuttle or an extra set of warp yarns interlace to create a simple woven design. The extra yarns are carried along as a float on the wrong side of the fabric when they do not appear in the design. After the cloth is completed, the long floats are generally cut away. The clipped yarns form a characteristic "eyelash" effect. Sometimes these fabrics are used inside out for design interest. (See Figure 15.35.)

The durability of the design depends upon the closeness of the weave of the fabric into which they are woven. Some domestic dotted swiss fabric is constructed by the clip spot weave. This sheer cotton fabric uses small clip spot yarns in contrasting color to create a dotted surface design. (See Figure 15.36.) Dotted swiss may also be made with flocking (see pages 383–384).

Swivel Weave

Similar fabrics can be made in the swivel weave, which is now relatively rare. The design is made by supplying an extra filling yarn on a

Figure 15.36. Closeup of dotted swiss made by the clipped spot method.

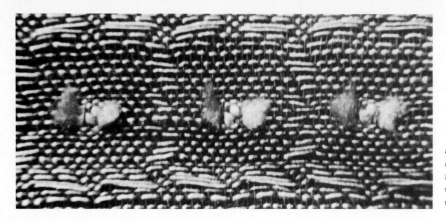

Figure 15.37. Closeup of dotted swiss made by the swivel weave. Note that in Figure 15.36 the fibers only interlace under one warp yarn, whereas in this figure the yarns appear to warp around the warp yarns.

small shuttle or swivel. The filling design yarns are carried several times around a group of warps by the motion of the swivel to prevent the yarn from pulling out of the background fabric. The long floats between designs are knotted and clipped off. Occasionally some imported dotted swiss fabrics are found that use a swivel weave rather than a clipped spot weave. The swivel weave is more durable than is the clip spot weave because the design yarns are woven in and cannot pull out of the fabric as easily as in the latter method. (See Figure 15.37.)

Lappet Weave

Lappet weave utilizes an extra warp yarn that may interlace in both the warp and filling direction with the ground fabric. The extra set of warps is threaded through needles set in front of the reed. The yarns are carried in a zigzag direction, back and forth to form an embroidery-like design. The design is created on the right side of the fabric, the excess yarn being carried along on the wrong side. Extra yarn is not clipped away from the back of the fabric, but can be seen as it is carried from one design area to another. Imported Swiss braids often utilize the lappet weave, but it is seldom found on merchandise sold in the United States.

Embroidery

Embroidery is not a method of constructing fabrics but, rather, a method of decorating them. It is mentioned at this point because the effects it produces are similar to those achieved by the surface weaves discussed in the preceding section. Embroidery is often used in conjunction with appliqué.

Appliqué is the cutting of small pieces of cloth or other materials that are then attached to the surface of a larger textile. The decoration of fabrics by appliqué is an old technique. Archeologists have identified appliqués from as early as the fifth century B.C. These very early forms were wall hangings or carpets in which the base material was felt and the designs were achieved by cutting other, smaller pieces of multicolored felt into designs that were sewn onto the larger piece of fabric.

Since appliqués are most often attached to the base fabric by hand stitches, they are often combined with embroidery. Embroidery is the use of yarns applied with a needle in a variety of stitches to form a decorative pattern. Embroidery is a skill that has been practiced for many centuries. The translation of writings from classical Greece includes many references to fine embroideries. The ancient Greeks considered weaving and embroidery to be fitting occupations for goddesses and noblewomen. One interesting Greek textile showing evidence of embroidery has been dated at 500 B.C. and provides some of the earliest evidence of the embroidery skills. It is believed, however, that embroidery was practiced long before this date.[5]

A wide variety of different types of embroidery and embroidery stitches have been developed in all parts of the world. Each area originated a style with a distinctive repertory of stitches and decorative motifs.

One of the most famous decorated textiles ever made was created by embroidery. Called the Bayeux tapestry, this representation of the conquest of Britain by the Normans is actually a large embroidery, not a tapestry. On its 231-foot length and 20-inch width, seventy-two embroidered pictures show the sequence of events that led to the Battle of Hastings and the conquest of England by William the Conqueror in 1066. The embroidery, made almost nine hundred years ago and now discolored with age, is still displayed in the Cathedral at Bayeux, France.[6]

American embroidery forms originated in Europe, especially in England. From the general category of embroidery, a number of specialized forms have broken off to become separate art crafts. These include crewel embroidery, cross-stitch embroidery, and needlepoint.

In embroidery, a wide variety of stitches are used to outline and fill in the design. The choice of stitch is usually related to the effect the sewer wants to achieve. The yarns may be made of any fiber.

Crewel embroidery is done with crewel wool, a loosely twisted fine yarn that probably was named after the English town of Crewel. Traditional crewel embroidery uses stylized forms and a repertory of specific basic stitches.

Made of two stitches that crossed in the center to form an X, the cross-stitch is one of the simplest of the embroidery forms. In Colonial American times it was the first embroidery technique taught to little girls. Combinations of the X-shaped stitches were used to make samplers or to decorate all kinds of household articles.

---

[5]A. T. B. Wace, "Weaving or Embroidery? Homeric References to Textiles," *American Journal of Archeology*, 52, No. 1 (January 1948), p. 51.
[6]R. W. Lane, *Book of American Needlework* (New York: Simon & Schuster, Inc., 1963), p. 19.

Figure 15.38. Machine-made Schiffli embroidery.

Needlepoint embroidery covers a canvas base with thousands of tiny stitches. Queen Elizabeth I of England was said to have preferred it to all other embroideries, and in the 1920s, Alice B. Toklas, companion to the writer Gertrude Stein, made a number of needlepoint chair covers after designs created for her by Picasso. Needlepoint has its own repertory of specialized stitches that are selected according to the pattern they will make in the often-complex needlepoint design.

Schiffli Embroidery

Schiffli embroidery machines mechanically apply embroidery to woven fabric. (See Figure 15.38.) The embroidery is not accomplished as an integral part of the weaving process but utilizes hundreds of needles to embroider patterns onto cloth after it is woven. Schiffli designs are often used by manufacturers in the United States and are successfully applied to a variety of fabrics of various fiber content and weave construction. By contrast with hand embroidery, machine-made embroideries utilize a limited variety of stitch types and pattern variations.

Only the process used to make interwoven fabrics actually involves weaving. Quilted and laminated fabrics are constructed by combining several layers of fabric into one united structure. Tufted fabrics utilize a base of completed fabric into which pile yarns are inserted.

Multicomponent Fabrics

Interwoven Fabrics

Interwoven fabrics are also called double-cloth fabrics. They are made with three, four, or five sets of yarns.

Double-faced fabrics are made with *three sets of yarns*. Woven either from two sets of warp yarns and one filling yarn or from two sets of filling yarns and one warp yarn, the effect of the weave is to produce the same appearance on both sides of the fabric. Some blankets and double-faced satins are examples of fabrics that are woven in this way.

Fabrics made with *four sets of yarns* use two sets of warp yarns and two sets of filling yarns. Yarns from both layers move back and forth from one layer to another, as required by the design. In some areas, the two fabrics are totally separated; in others, all four sets of yarns are interwoven. *Matelasse* is one fabric made by this process. The two layers of these fabrics cannot be separated without destroying the fabric. The cut edge of the fabric will show small "pockets" where fabric layers are separate. The pocket boundaries are the point at which yarn sets interchange from one side of the fabric to the other.

Fabrics with *five sets of yarns* are produced in the same way as double-woven pile fabrics. Two separate fabric layers are constructed. Extra yarns travel back and forth between the two layers to hold them together. These fabrics are often reversible, with one side being of one color and one side of another color. If the connecting yarn is cut, the two segments of the fabric can be separated into two individual pieces of cloth.

Quilted Fabrics

Quilted fabrics have been made for centuries. A filling material (usually cotton batting, wool, or down) is sandwiched between two layers of decorative outer fabric. These layers are sewn together with strong thread in selected areas to keep the filling material from shifting about. The location of the stitches forms a padded design that might take geometric, floral, or other shapes. (See Figure 15.39.)

Many quilted fabrics are produced commercially for apparel or household use. Synthetic fiberfill has, to a large extent, replaced the natural fillers because of its easy-care aspects.

The performance of quilted fabrics is related to the closeness of the quilting stitches, the size of the stitches, the type of thread used for stitching, and the durability of the outer fabric. If stitches are spaced too far apart, the filling will shift about and become uneven. If quilting stitches are too large, stretching of the cloth will tend to break the thread. The outer fabric layer should have a firm, close, well-balanced weave. Well-balanced fabrics will have better abrasion resistance and durability. A close weave is also important if the filling is not to work its way out through the covering fabric. Down-filled comforters or quilts

Figure 15.39.   Appliquéd and pieced quilt made in the United States in the midnineteenth century. The Metropolitan Museum of Art. Posthumous gift of Miss Eliza Polhemus Cobb (through Mrs. Arthur Bunker), 1952.

require the use of an inner layer of downproof ticking, a dense, closely woven ticking fabric that prevents the escape of small bits of down.

New Techniques of Quilting

Furthermore, changes have taken place in the methods by which some quilted fabrics are produced. Instead of sewing quilted fabrics with thread, sewing may be done with heat or adhesives. Thermal or heat stitching requires that all components be thermoplastic. The heat application causes the components to fuse together in the heat-stitched areas. One of these techniques uses high-frequency, ultrasonic vibrations to generate the heat in the stitching device. This "sonic sewing" can be used to construct apparel and household textiles made from synthetic fibers.

Another technique used to produce raised surface patterns with layered fabrics places a layer of fabric that is not thermoplastic over fabric, foam, or fiberfill that is heat sensitive. A design is printed on the fabric with a special chemical, which holds the layers together in the printed area. The fabric is subjected to heat that causes the backing fabric to shrink, thereby producing a raised pattern on the face fabric.

Laminated or Bonded Fabrics

The terms *laminated* and *bonded* have been defined by the American Society for Testing Materials as follows:

> *bonded fabric—a layered fabric structure wherein a face or shell fabric is joined to a backing fabric, such as tricot (a knit fabric), with an adhesive that does not significantly add to the thickness of the combined fabrics.*
> *laminated fabric—a layered fabric structure wherein a face or outer fabric is joined to a continuous sheet material, such as polyurethane foam, in such a way that the identity of the continuous sheet material is retained, either by the flame method or by an adhesive, and this in turn normally, but not always, is joined on the back with a backing fabric such as tricot.*

Several different methods can be used to join fabric to fabric, fabric to foam, or fabric to foam to fabric.

Fabric-to-Fabric Bonding

When two layers of fabric are joined, the purpose is to provide greater stability and body to the face fabric or to create a self-lined fabric. The underlayer in laminated fabrics is often knitted tricot or jersey, used because they have good flexibility, are relatively inexpensive, and slide readily, making them easy to wear over other garments. For the most part, fabrics used in laminating are less expensive and lower-quality fabrics that can be upgraded by this process.

Two methods can be used for laminating fabric to fabric. The *wet-adhesive* method places an adhesive material on the back of the face fabric and together they are passed between heated rollers that activate and set the adhesive.

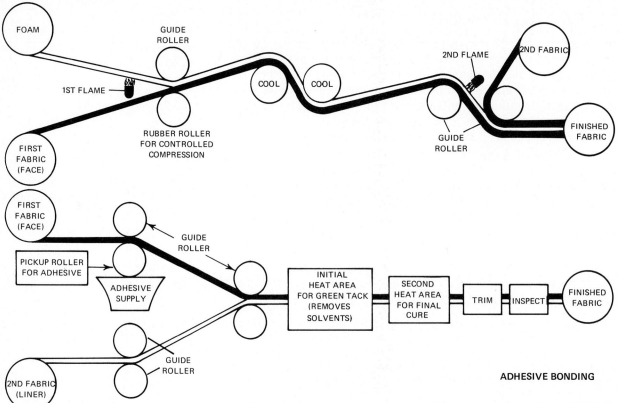

ADHESIVE BONDING

Figure 15.40. Flame-foam and adhesive bonding. Courtesy Celanese Corporation.

The second method is known as the *flame-foam* process. A thin layer of polyurethane foam is melted slightly by passing it over a flame. The two layers of fabric are sandwiched around the foam, which then dries, forming the bond between the two layers of fabric. Ideally, the layer of foam that is used should be so thin that it virtually disappears. (The foam in the finished fabric is about 0.010 inches thick.) The foam does, however, add body to the fabric and produces a somewhat stiffer fabric than does the wet-adhesive method. It is preferable that the foam method not be used with open-weave fabrics because of the possibility that some of the foam may appear on the surface of the fabric. (See Figure 15.40.)

Fabric-to-Foam Lamination

Fabrics are laminated to polyurethane foam when it is desirable to provide some degree of insulation. Winter coats and sportswear, for example, are made from these fabrics. The flame-foam process can be used to manufacture such fabrics. A thick layer of foam is utilized. Only one side of the foam, that to which the fabric attaches, must be heated. Still another foam process flows the sticky foam onto the fabric, cures the fabric, and causes the foam to solidify and adhere to the fabric at the same time.

When laminates first entered the retail market, customers found wide variation in the permanence of the bonding. Some fabrics separated during laundering, others separated during dry cleaning, and still others separated during use. Often the backing and face fabrics shrunk unevenly, causing wrinkling and puckering. Today many of these problems have been overcome. Although laminated fabrics of varying quality are still sold, many of these fabrics are labeled with guarantees of serviceability. The label term Certifab guarantees bonding and dimensional stability in dry cleaning or laundering for one year. Celabond is the same guarantee, but is applied to fabrics laminated with certain acetates.

Tufted Fabrics

Tufted fabrics are created by punching loops of yarn through a woven or nonwoven backing material. Handtufting is often used in "hooking" or tufting rugs. A hook is passed through the backing material, a loop is formed on the outside of the backing, and the needle is pulled back to the wrong side, leaving the loop to form the pile on the surface of the fabric. Loops can be left uncut or be cut to create a fluffy surface.

Machine-made tufted fabrics are created in much the same way as hand-tufted fabrics except that many needles punch through the fabric at the same time. A hook holds the loop in place when the needle is withdrawn. If a cut pile is being made, this hook has a small blade that cuts the loop. Tufted fabrics can be identified easily by looking at the wrong side of the fabric where parallel rows of stitches can be seen. (See Figure 15.41.)

Figure 15.41. Tufting. Needle carrying tufting yarn (1) carries yarn through the backing fabric (2). A hook catches the loop, holding it in place while the needle is withdrawn (3). If a cut pile is to be made, the hook carries a blade that cuts the pile yarn.

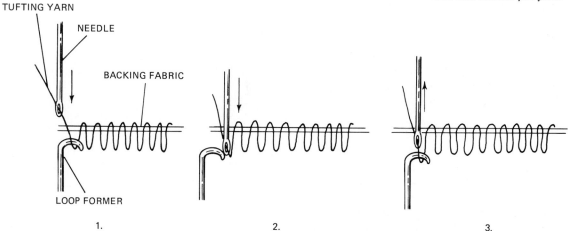

TUFTING YARN

NEEDLE

BACKING FABRIC

LOOP FORMER

1.   2.   3.

Carpet Manufacture

More than 90 per cent of the carpet produced in the United States is constructed by *tufting*. Tufts of pile yarn are punched through a woven backing of jute, heavy cotton, polypropylene, or other synthetic. The back of the carpet is given a coating of latex for greater stability and strength.

Tufting offers the advantages of being faster than more traditional methods of pile carpet construction and does not require such highly skilled craftsmen and -women, and the equipment used in its manufacture is less expensive. Although lower in cost than most other constructions, tufted carpet is not necessarily inferior in quality. The quality of carpets is more dependent upon the fibers, yarns, and backing materials used and the closeness of the pile than on the construction.

The major limitations in tufting are in the area of design. Woven designs cannot be made, although design variations can utilize cut and uncut pile or higher and lower levels of loops or cut pile. Designs can also be printed on the surface of the carpet.

Carpets are often made in *pile constructions*. In addition to tufting, several other major types of pile carpet construction are available to consumers. The names of the processes used for weaving carpets have become standard terminology in the carpet industry.

Velvet-weave carpets should not be confused with velvet-surface carpets. The term *velvet weave* refers to the construction of the carpet, the pile of which may be either cut or uncut. Simple in construction, the weave is similar to the construction of pile fabrics made by the wire method. (See Figure 15.32.) The pile is formed by wires inserted between the pile and warp yarns. The loops that are formed are held in place by the interlocking of warp yarns with the pile. The warps are, in turn, interlocked with the filling. Velvet-weave carpets are usually made in solid colors, but tweed effects are created by using multicolored tweed yarns. The cost of these carpets is moderate to low. (See Figure 15.42.)

Wilton carpets are made on a special Wilton loom. This loom is essentially a velvet loom with a a Jacquard attachment and can utilize up to six different colors. Patterns in Wilton carpets are woven, not printed. When yarns are not utilized in the surface design, they are carried along in the back of the carpet. This makes for a dense, strong construction. Wilton carpets of good quality are among the longest-wearing machine-made domestic rugs. Piles may be cut or uncut, loops may be high or low. (See Figure 15.43.)

Axminster carpets have the greatest versatility in machine-produced carpets in utilizing color. The loom draws pile yarns from small spools wound with yarns of various colors as they are needed for the design. The pile is a one-level, cut pile although textured effects may be attained by varying the twist or type of yarn used. Carpets made on an Axminster loom are readily identifiable because the construction produces a heavy ridge across the back of the carpet, and the carpet can

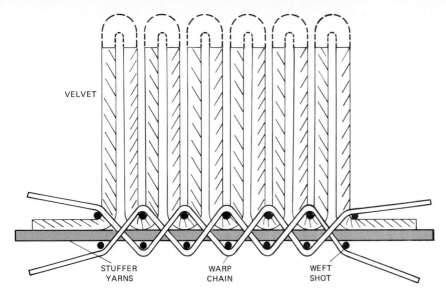

VELVET

STUFFER YARNS   WARP CHAIN   WEFT SHOT

Figure 15.42. Velvet carpet construction. Courtesy of Bigelow-Sanford, Inc.

Figure 15.43. Wilton carpet construction. Courtesy of Bigelow-Sanford, Inc.

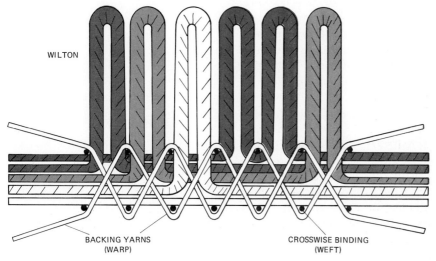

WILTON

BACKING YARNS (WARP)   CROSSWISE BINDING (WEFT)

be rolled only in the lengthwise direction. The quality of carpets made on the Axminster loom is medium. (See Figure 15.44.)

Chenille carpets are the most expensive and the most luxurious of all machine-made carpets and are rarely found. They are constructed on two looms. On one loom a fabric called a chenille blanket is woven. This blanket is cut into long strips called "caterpillars," which have a fuzzy surface. A second loom weaves the strips into the carpet. These strips are used in the filling direction, and are actually sewn into place. Chenille carpet pile is cut, carpets are made in solid colors, and the pile is dense, close, and velvety in texture.

Woven Fabrics **277**

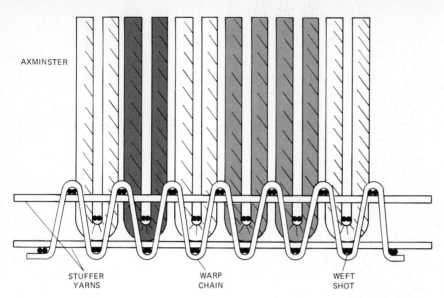

AXMINSTER

STUFFER
YARNS

WARP
CHAIN

WEFT
SHOT

*Figure 15.44. Axminster carpet construction.
Courtesy of Bigelow-Sanford, Inc.*

Carpets can also be made by knitting, needle punching, and flocking. These types of fabric construction are discussed in subsequent chapters. Designs can be added to carpets by printing as well as by weaving.

In addition to mass-produced, machine-made carpets, there are a number of one-of-a-kind, hand-woven carpets. The bibliography for this chapter includes some references for further reading about hand-woven and specialty carpets.

Many hand-woven carpets are made in the Near or Far East, using traditional designs, and are known as *oriental carpets.* Both antique and contemporary versions of these traditional design rugs can be purchased. Oriental designs can be printed or woven into machine-made carpets, but true orientals are made by hand-knotting a pile of wool or silk to a woven base of cotton or wool. The quality of these carpets depends upon the density rather than the length of the pile. There is a lively trade in new and antique oriental carpets, and prices are high. Purchasers should deal only with reputable merchants who can be depended upon not to sell counterfeit merchandise.

Rya rugs, another hand-made area rug type, are imported from the Scandinavian countries. These rugs have a long "shag" pile and are generally woven in contemporary designs.

Some traditional early-American–style rugs are made not by weaving but from strips of cloth braided or sewn together. Still others are made by "hooking," a hand process similar to tufting in which yarn or fabric strips are punched or pulled through a woven backing with a special hook.

Triaxally-Woven Fabrics

Although most of the fabrics used for clothing, for the home, and for industry are made by traditional weaving, tufting, or knitting methods, research into, and development of, new methods for constructing fabrics is constantly in progress. Several recent methods of fabric construction that are related to knitting are discussed in Chapter 16. There is, however, another method of constructing fabrics that is closely related to traditional weaving, and it is known as *triaxial weaving*. The term is derived from *tri-* meaning "three" and *axial*, meaning "of or pertaining to the axis or center line." In other words, triaxial fabrics have three axes or center lines. Traditionally, woven fabrics have a biaxial form or two axes, the lengthwise and crosswise axes. (See Figure 15.45.)

Triaxial fabrics can be woven by modifying the standard weaving procedure in one of two ways: one set of lengthwise yarns can be interlaced with two sets of crosswise yarns, or two sets of lengthwise yarns interlace with one set of crosswise yarns. The latter method, two warp yarns with one filling yarn, is most often used.

Special cams in the loom manipulate the yarns so that the double set of yarns (either warp or filling) is carried in a diagonal direction. All three sets of yarns interlace.

Triaxial weaves are not entirely new. The construction of snowshoes and some forms of basket work sometimes utilize a triaxial construction. Mass-produced fabrics have not, however, been made in a triaxial weave. The trademark Doweave® has been registered to refer to such constructions. The major advantage of triaxial weaving is in its stability not only in the length and crosswise directions but also in the bias; moreover, triaxial weaves do not stretch. Even those biaxial fabrics with good stability in the warp and filling will stretch in the bias direction. Triaxially woven fabrics have high burst resistance and strong resistance to tearing and raveling. Strength is uniform in all directions.

The research and development of triaxial fabrics was initiated in an attempt to produce fabrics of increased stability for use in the aerospace industry. Other suggested uses include apparel such as athletic and foundation garments, which take advantage of the form fit and strength of the fabrics, and household textiles for upholstery where it can be formed into neat corners and where its resistance to tearing is desirable. Industrial applications include such products as sail cloth, tarpaulins, and filter fabrics.

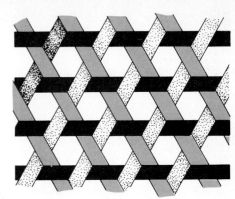

Figure 15.45. Triaxial fabric structure.

Recommended References

ADAMS, R. S., B. M. CALLAWAY, and D. M. HALL. "Shuttleless Weaving Needs Tailored Sizes," *Textile World*, 134 (May 1984), p. 77.

"Air Jet Weaving 1984: What Are the Options?" *Textile Industries*, 148 (September 1984), p. 26.

ALBERS, A. *On Weaving*. Middletown, Conn.: Wesleyan University Press, 1965.

BUHLER, K. "Basic Textile Technique," *CIBA Review*, No. 63 (January 1948), pp. 2297 ff.

CATLING, H. "The Development of Modern Weaving Machines," *Textiles*, 13 (Spring 1984), p. 5.

CATLING, H. "A History of Spinning and Weaving," *Textiles*, 12 (Spring 1983), p. 20.

"Corduroy," *Textiles*, 11 (Autumn 1982), p. 83.

FORD, J. E. "Carpets in Use," *Textiles*, 11 (Autumn 1982), p. 74.

D'HARCOURT, R. *Textiles of Ancient Peru and Their Techniques*. Seattle: University of Washington Press, 1962.

EMERY, I. *The Primary Structure of Fabrics*. Washington, D.C.: The Textile Museum, 1966.

"Evolution of Mills and Factories," *CIBA Review*, 1 (1968).

Handbook on Bonded and Laminated Fabrics. Research Triangle Park, N.C.: American Association of Textile Chemists and Colorists, 1974.

HEUSSER, A. "The Shape of Weaving Machines to Come," *Textile Industries*, 147 (September 1983), p. 109.

ISAACS, M. "Industrial Fabric Looms Promote Productivity," *Textile World*, 134 (March 1984), p. 79.

LENNOX-KERR, P. "Air Jet Machines Weave Toward Wider Horizons," *Textile World*, 133 (February 1983), p. 73.

LENNOX-KERR, P. "New Italian Loom: Wave of the Future," *Textile World*, 133 (January 1983), p. 76.

LORD, P. R., and M. H. MOHAMED. *Weaving: Conversion of Yarn to Fabric*, 2nd ed. Watford, England: Merrow Publishing Company Ltd., 1982.

NUTTAL, A. E. "Decorative Surface Effects in Woven Fabrics," *Textiles*, 7 (October 1978), and 8 (February 1979).

NUTTAL, A. E. "The Manufacture of Terry Towels," *Textiles*, 7 (February 1978), p. 17.

ORMEROD, A. "Air Jet Weaving," *Textile Horizons* (January 1984), p. 25.

"Poplin," *Textiles*, 12 (Spring 1983), p. 18.

"Rapier Looms: From ITMA to the Mills," *Americas Textiles*, 13 (July 1984), p. 64.

REED, S. *Oriental Carpets and Rugs*. London: Octopus Books, 1972.

REGENSTEINER, E. *The Art of Weaving*. New York: Van Nostrand Reinhold Co., 1970.

SCHWARTZ, P. "Complex Triaxial Fabrics: Cover, Flexural Rigidity, Tear Strength," *Textile Research Journal*, 54 (September 1984), p. 581.

SCHWARTZ, P. "Bending Properties of Triaxially Woven Fabrics," *Textile Research Journal*, 52 (September 1982), p. 604.

THOMAS, D. G. B. "Pile Fabrics," *Textiles*, 8 (October 1979), p. 59.

"Velvet Weaver Gets High Efficiency at High Speeds," *Textile World*, 134 (January 1984), p. 59.

Von Rosenstiel, H. *American Rugs and Carpets*. New York: William Morrow and Company, Inc., 1978.

WARD, D. T. "The Development of Tufting," *Textiles*, 9 (February 1980), p. 22.

"Which Fabrics for Air Jets?" *Americas Textiles*, 13 (July 1984), p. 64.

WHITON, S. *Interior Design and Decorating*, 4th ed. New York: J. B. Lippincott Company, Chap. 13, 1974.

WINGATE, I., K. GILLESPIE, and H. ADDISON. *Know Your Merchandise* 5th ed., New York: McGraw-Hill Book Company, 1984. Chap. 15.

WORTHINGTON, A. P., and J. FINDLOW. "Machine Embroidery," *Textiles*, 6 (June 1977), p. 41.

ZELLER, R. W. "Weaving Machine Manufacturing—Safeguarding the Future," *Canadian Textile Journal*, 101 (August 1984), p. 43.

Knitted Fabrics

Few segments of the textile industry have grown so rapidly in recent years as has the knitting industry. Advances in knitting production techniques along with the use of synthetic fabrics, such as acrylics and polyesters, for knit goods have led to the manufacture of knitted items, including such diverse products as men's tailored suits, table linens, blankets and bedspreads, carpeting, wall coverings, upholstery, shipping sacks, paint rollers, and vacuum cleaner bags.

The apparel knitting industry may be divided into four branches: knitted outerwear, knitted yard goods, knitted hosiery, and knitted underwear. Knitted yard goods mills produce a wide variety of fabrics in either flat or circular form that can be cut and sewn into apparel and other items. Those mills that produce outerwear, hosiery, or underwear may knit the item directly or may knit sections of a garment (such as sleeves, body sections, and the like) that are sewn, or cut and sewn, together. These mills complete the garment from knitting right through to construction in the same mill.

Historical Development of Knits

Although the earliest known fragment of knitted cloth dates from the fourth century A.D., hand knitting seems to have come to Europe from the Middle East during the medieval period. Apparently the Arab conquerors of Spain imported the technique of knitting from their homeland sometime after A.D. 1000. Knitting spread gradually to the rest of Europe. Because knits were more elastic than woven goods, they gained popularity, especially for making stockings and gloves.

Today one thinks of hand knitting as a process that uses two or more knitting needles, but the earliest hand knitting was done not on needles but on a frame into which a series of pegs had been set. Yarn was looped around each peg. To make the stitches, the knitter pulled a new loop of yarn through the old loop encircling the peg and placed the new loop around the peg while slipping the old loop off the peg with a hooked needle. The gradually increasing rows of loops formed the fab-

Figure 16.1. Knitted cap made in Italy in the seventeenth century. Courtesy of the Metropolitan Museum of Art, Rogers Fund, 1927.

ric. Eventually, a long, pointed knitting needle, such as those used today, replaced the pegs for holding the loops and a second needle replaced the hook for adding and subtracting loops.

The use of two needles or of the knitting frame made a flat fabric. A round tube of fabric could be made by using a circular needle, a round frame, or a set of four needles.

Since the knitting process was relatively simple, it lent itself to mechanization somewhat more easily than did weaving. By the late 1500s a knitting frame machine had been invented by William Lee. This machine made mechanically all of the kinds of knits that had previously been made by hand. Lee's machine continued in use until further refinements of machine knitting were made during the Industrial Revolution.

Machines for Knitting

"Knitting is the process of making cloth with a single yarn or set of yarns moving in only one direction. Instead of two sets of yarns crossing each other as in weaving, the single knitting yarn is looped through itself to make a chain of stitches. These chains or rows are connected side by side to produce the knit cloth."[1] The interlocking of these loops in knitting can be done by either vertical or horizontal movement. When

[1]*Encyclopedia of Textiles, American Fabrics* (Englewood Cliffs, N.J.: Prentice-Hall, Inc., 1980), p. 370.

the yarns are introduced in a crosswise direction, at right angles to the direction of growth of the fabric and run or interlock across the fabric, the knit is known as a *weft* knit. When the yarns run lengthwise or up and down, the knit is known as a *warp* knit.

Both warp and weft knits are made by machine. Knitting machines may be either flat or circular. The flat-type knitting machine has needles arranged in a straight line and held on a flat needlebed. The cloth is made by forming stitches on these needles. The resulting fabric is flat. Machines with flatbeds are used to make both warp and weft knits.

The circular knitting machine has needles arranged in a circle on a rotating cylinder. The resulting fabric is formed into a tube. Circular knitting machines produce weft knits almost exclusively. (See Figure 16.2.)

For nearly two hundred years after its invention in 1589, Lee's machine was used without further improvement. Using a *spring beard needle*, Lee's machine produced flat knitted fabrics by mechanically passing one loop of yarn through another.

Figure 16.2. Electronically-controlled circular Morat weft knitting machine. The yarn is held on the spools on frames on either side of the machine. The completed fabric will emerge in tubular form at the bottom of the machine. Courtesy of Sulzer Morat GmbH.

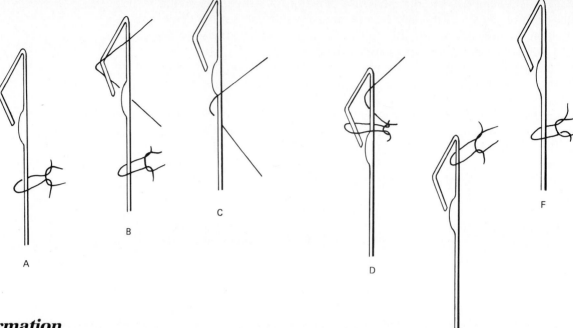

A

B

C

D

E

F

Loop Formation

The spring beard needle is formed from one piece of thin wire. (See Figure 16.3.) One end of the needle is drawn into thinner dimensions and is curved to form a hook. The flexible outer side of the hook can be pressed against the stem of the needle to close the hook. The loops are formed as follows:

1. The old loop is held on the stem of the needle below the hook. (A)
2. A new loop is formed around the outside of the hooked section of the needle. (B)
3. The needle rises, dropping the new loop to the stem. (C)
4. The needle falls again to bring the new loop into the hook. (D)
5. At the same time a presser comes in, closing the hook so that the old loop is held outside the hook. (D)
6. The needle falls further, sliding the old loop off the needle. The new loop is now held inside the hook. (E)
7. The needle is now ready to repeat the cycle. (F)

In 1847, Matthew Townshend invented a different type of hook known as the *latch needle*, which has come to be the most widely used type of needle. Its operation is similar to that of the spring beard needle, except that instead of having mechanically to press the flexible wire of the needle closed so that the new yarn loop will not slide off, a latch closes to hold the yarn in place. The steps in the cycle of the latch needle are

Figure 16.3. Formation of a loop by a spring beard needle.

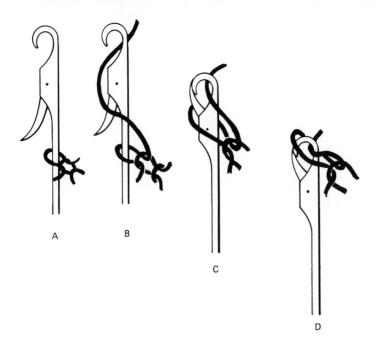

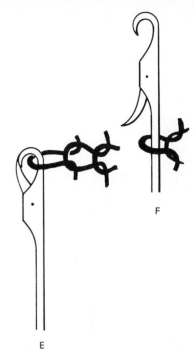

A B C D E F

Figure 16.4.   Formation of a loop by a latch needle.

Figure 16.5.   Tongue (A) of compound needle moves into position against the hook (B) in order to close the needle.

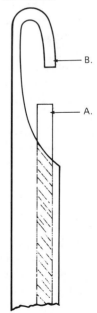

B.

A.

1. The old loop is held on the stem of the needle. The latch is open. (A)
2. A new loop is formed around the hook of the needle. (B)
3. The needle falls, the old loop rises, closing the latch of the needle. (C)
4. The old loop is cast off (D and E), the new loop pushes the latch open, the needle rises, and the new loop slides down to the stem of the needle. (F)

The needle is now ready to repeat the cycle. (See Figure 16.4.)

Yet a third type of needle, the compound needle (Figure 16.5.), is used almost exclusively for warp knitting. The compound needle has two components, a tongue and a hook. Its motion is as follows:

1. The old loop encircles the hook; the tongue is in such a position as to leave the hook open.
2. Both tongue and hook rise; a new yarn is fed to the hook.
3. Both tongue and hook descend, but the tongue descends more slowly, thereby closing the hook.
4. As the needle descends, the held loop slides off, forming a new loop.
5. The needle returns to its initial position, the hook ascending more rapidly, thereby opening the hook again.

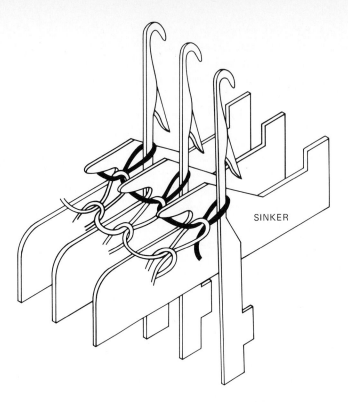

SINKER

FIGURE 16.6 *Sinkers used for weft knits, with latch needles in position ready for formation of new loop.*

The engaging by the needle of a new piece of yarn is called "feeding." Devices called feeders are located to introduce the yarn to the needles. The number of feeders can vary, but obviously the more feeders a machine has, the higher will be the speed of fabric forming of the machine, since each needle produces a loop each time it is activated and if many needles are activated more frequently, many courses can be formed at the same time.

Another important element of some knitting machines is the sinker. The already formed fabric may need to be controlled as the subsequent knitting action takes place. A thin steel device called a sinker may be used to hold the fabric as the needle rises, support the fabric as the needle descends, and push the fabric away from the needle after the new loop has been formed. Sinkers are generally mounted between each pair of needles. (See Figure 16.6.) Some machines, however, do not use sinkers but instead utilize the tensions placed on the completed fabrics for control.

In knitting terminology the rows of stitches that run in columns along the lengthwise direction of the fabric are known as *wales*. This corresponds to the warp direction of woven fabrics. Crosswise rows of stitches or loops are called *courses*. The direction of the courses corresponds to the filling of woven goods. (See Figure 16.7.)

The size of the needle and the spacing of the needles on knitting machines determine the number and size of the knit stitches and their

Figure 16.7. *Rows of stitches that run in a vertical column along the lengthwise direction of the fabric are called wales; crosswise rows of stitches or loops are called courses.*

WALES

COURSES

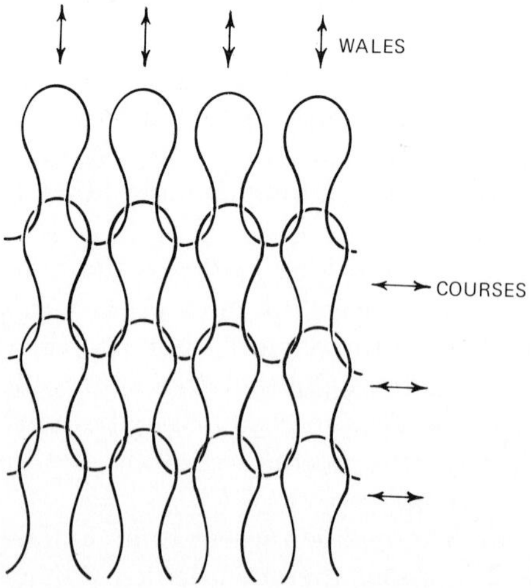

closeness. Each wale is formed on one needle. The number of needles is equal to the number of wales. The closeness of the stitches determines whether a knit fabric will be lightweight and open or heavier and more dense. The term *gauge* is used to describe the closeness of knit stitches. Gauge is the number of needles in a measured space on the knitting machine. Higher-gauge fabrics (those with more stitches) are made with finer needles; lower-gauge fabrics are made with coarser or larger needles.

The term *cut* is also used to designate the number of needles per inch in the needle bed of a circular filling knitting machine. To describe the stitch density of a single or double knit fabric, the fabric may be designated as an 18-, 20-, 22-, or 24-cut fabric. The higher the cut, the closer are the stitches; the lower the cut, the coarser is the fabric.

Varying types of knitting machines measure gauge over different distances on the machine. For example, circular knit hosiery measures the number of needles in 1.0 inch, full-fashioned knitting in 1.5 inches, and Raschel knits in 2.0 inches. Because of these differences, it is best to keep in mind the generalized principle that the higher the gauge, the closer the stitches.

The quality of needles used in manufacturing knit goods is related directly to the quality of the fabric produced. Needles of uneven size and quality will produce knit fabrics with uneven-sized stitches and imperfect surface appearance.

In *warp knits*, those knits in which the yarns interlace in the long direction, one or more yarns are allotted to each needle on the machine, and those yarns follow the long direction of the fabric. For *weft knits*, those in which the yarns interlace crosswise horizontally), one or more yarns are utilized for each course and these yarns move across the fabric. In weft knits, one yarn may have from twenty to several hundred needles associated with it. To summarize, weft knits can be made with one yarn, but warp knits must have a whole set of warp yarns, that is, one or more for each needle.

Once the basic distinction between warp and weft knits has been made, further subdivisions of knit classifications are usually based on the types of machines used in their production. The majority of knit fabrics are named after the machines on which they are constructed. For this reason, the discussion of knitted fabrics that follows is organized around the types of machines used in manufacturing knit fabrics and the types of knit fabrics made on these machines.

Weft Knits

The most important difference among weft knitting machines is in the number of needlebeds and the number of sets of needles used. On these bases, weft knits are divided among those made on each of these basic machines:

1. Flat or circular jersey or single knit machine: one needlebed and one set of needles.

2. Flat or circular rib machine: two needlebeds and two sets of needles.
3. Flat or circular purl or links-links machine: two needlebeds and one set of needles.

Jersey or Single Knits

Jersey or single knit machines have one needlebed and one set of needles. With one set of needles and one needlebed, all needles face the same direction; all stitches are pulled to the same side of the fabric. As a result jersey or single knit fabrics have a smooth face with a vertical grain on the right side of the fabric and a widthwise grain on the wrong side. The loops formed by the jersey machine are formed in one direction only (see Figure 16.8), which gives a different appearance to each side of the fabric. The basic fabric produced by this machine is known as a *plain*, *single knit*, or *jersey.*.

Plain, single knit, or jersey stretches equally in both the lengthwise and crosswise directions. If one stitch breaks, the fabric may ladder or "run." A great many items of hosiery, sweaters, and other wearing apparel are made in the plain knit. Jersey fabrics tend to curl at the edges and are less stable than are some other types of knits. This is the result of the pressures exerted during knitting. Special finishing techniques are used to overcome these tendencies and maintain fabric stability; the principal ones use starches, gum mixtures, polyvinyl acetate emulsions, and resins.

Plain knit fabrics can be made into two or more color designs by use of a patterning mechanism that controls the selection and feeding of yarns and types of stitches to create Jacquard knits. (See Figure 16.9.) Jersey machines can also produce terry and velour, fleece, and sliver knit fabrics.

High-Pile Fabric

High-pile fabrics, such as imitation furs and plushes, are usually knitted, utilizing a jersey machine. While the knitting is taking place, a sliver of staple fiber is fed into the machine. These fibers are caught in the tight knit and are held firmly in place. Although any staple fiber can be used for the pile, the greatest quantity of these fabrics are made with acrylic and modacrylic fibers in the pile. (See Figure 16.10.)

By using staple fibers of varying lengths, adding color through fiber dyeing or printing on the surface of the pile, and by shearing or brushing the pile, an enormous variety of effects can be achieved. The use of knitted pile fabric ranges from excellent imitations of furs, such as leopard, tiger, mink or mouton, to colorful pile outerwear, coat linings, or pile carpet fabrics.

FIGURE 16.8   Plain or jersey knit stitch.
Courtesy of the National Knitwear
Manufacturers Association.

TECHNICAL FACE

TECHNICAL BACK

A

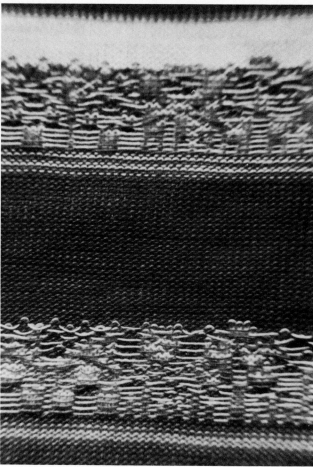

B

FIGURE 16.9. A and B. Face (A) and reverse (B) sides of a jacquard patterned plain knit fabric.

Knitted Terry and Velour

Jersey knits can also be made in the form of knitted terry fabrics and knitted velours. Two yarns are fed into the machine simultaneously, picked up by the same needle, and knitted in such a way that one of the yarns appears on the face of the fabric, the other on the back. The yarn that forms the pile is pulled up to the surface of the fabric. If the pile remains uncut, the resulting cloth is like a one-sided terry cloth. If the pile is cut, the fabric is called *velour*. (See Figure 16.11.)

Terry fabrics made by this process are not as durable as are woven terry cloth, nor do they hold their shape as well. On the other hand, they have softer draping qualities. The knitted velours are softer and more flexible than are woven pile fabrics, such as velveteen. Major uses for both fabrics are for sports and loungewear, for infants' and children's clothing, and for household items such as towels and slipcovers.

A

B

FIGURE 16.10   A and B. Back (A) and face (B) of a jersey knit, high pile fabric.

Fleece Fabrics

The soft texture or fleecy effect produced on the inside of sweatshirts is achieved by much the same techniques as in making velours. The fleece is created by cutting and brushing the loops that are formed on the underside of the fabric.

Plated Fabrics

In creating plated fabrics, the knitting machine feeds two separate yarns at the same time. By varying the color, texture, or type of yarn, interesting decorative effects can be achieved. It is also possible to utilize one yarn as the face yarn, and another as a backing yarn. Using an expensive face yarn with an inexpensive backing yarn can help to keep the cost of the fabric lower. Plating varies from relatively simple construction to very intricate pattern designs.

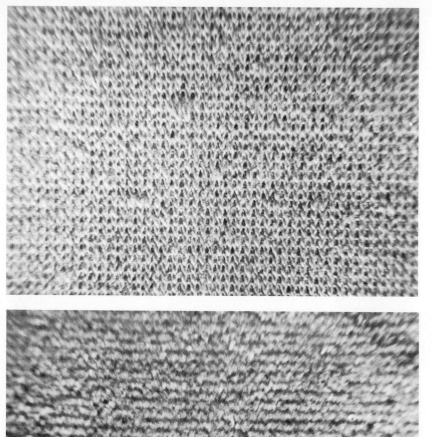

A

B

FIGURE 16.11   A and B. Back (A) and face (B) of a jersey knit velour fabric.

Rib Knits

Within the broad category of rib knitted fabrics are included rib knit fabrics, double knits, and interlock knits. The machine used to produce rib knits is different from the machine used for plain knits in that the former has two needle-holding beds and two sets of needles located opposite each other. The fabric is actually created between the two sets of needles. Rib knit machines may create flat or circular fabrics. Flat rib machines are also known as *V-bed flat machines* because the placement of the two rows of needles forms an inverted V.

"A rib knit fabric is characterized by lengthwise ribs formed by wales alternating on the face and back of the cloth. If every other stitch alternates from front to back, it is called a 1 × 1 rib. If every two stitches alternate, it is called a 2 × 2 rib."[2] The larger the number of stitches that alternate, the more pronounced the rib. A 1 × 1 rib made in a fine gauge may hardly be visible to the eye. Fabrics may appear to be a jersey on both sides.

Rib knits have greater elasticity in the width than in the length. They are stable and do not curl or stretch out of shape as do the jersey knits. For this reason they are often used to make cuffs and necklines on weft knitted garments. (See Figures 16.12 and 16.13.)

Double Knits

Double knits are made on a rib knitting machine. Twice as much yarn is incorporated into the double knit fabric as into comparable single knits. Double knit fabrics have the same appearance on both sides of the fabric, that is, exhibiting the appearance of the face or outer side of a single knit on both sides. (See Figure 16.14.) Double knit fabrics are more stable than are plain knits. When made from synthetic yarns, double knits should be heat-set for better dimensional stability. They do not run, have excellent draping qualities, and are easier for the home sewer to handle. Large quantities of double knits have been made in textured synthetic yarns, and double knits are widely used for easy-care clothing

1 X 1 RIB FABRIC

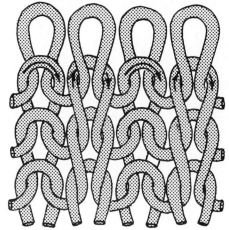

FIGURE 16.12. *1 × 1 rib fabric structure. Courtesy of National Knitwear Manufacturers Association.*

FIGURE 16.13. *2 × 2 rib fabric.*

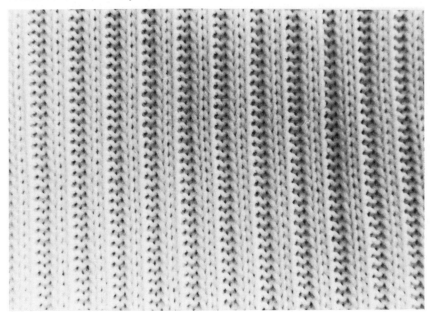

FIGURE 16.14. *Diagramatic representation of a double knit.*

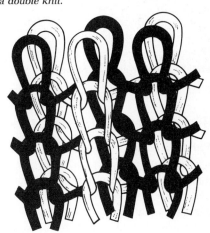

for men, women, and children. The home furnishings industry is beginning to utilize substantial amounts of double knit fabrics for upholstery, as well.

Interlock Knits

Interlock knits are produced on a special machine that has alternating long and short needles on both beds. The fabric created is an interlocking of two 1 × 1 rib structures. The resulting fabric, like double knit fabrics, is thicker than single knit fabric, and more stable in the widthwise direction. Interlock fabrics have been traditionally used for underwear. They are produced more slowly than are other rib knits and are generally made in plain colors or very simple patterns as the adding of pattern slows down the manufacture even further.

Purl or Links-links Machine

Purl or *links-links* machines have two needlebeds and one set of needles. Each latch-type needle has a hook at each end that allows the needle to pull stitches to either the back or the face of the fabric. The name *links-links* is given to the machine because the machine moves only to the left. *Links* is the German word for "left."

The links-links machine operates somewhat more slowly than do other knitting machines, causing the price of purl fabrics to be higher than those of other knits. The machine has a latch-type knitting needle with a hook on either end. This makes possible the construction of stitches on alternate sides of the fabric. The double needle arrangement makes this the most versatile of the weft knitting machines, as it can make plain, purl, or rib knits.

The simplest purl fabric is made by alternating courses so that every other course is drawn to the opposite side of the fabric, thereby producing a fabric with the same appearance on both sides. The raised courses produce a somewhat uneven texture. (See Figure 16.15.)

Purl knit fabrics are often made into a wide variety of decorative sweaters. Interesting textures can be achieved by the use of fluffy, soft yarns. The versatility of the machine makes possible the creation of a variety of patterns in these knits; however, relatively small quantities of fabrics are made in the purl stitch. (See Figure 16.16.)

Weft Knit Stitch Variation

The basic loop formed in the plain knit serves as the starting point for a wide range of weft knit stitches that can be used to vary the surface texture of weft knits. These include miss or float stitches, tuck stitches, and open stitches variously known as transfer or spread stitches. (See Figure 16.17.)

In miss or float stitches, some needles are immobilized, and instead

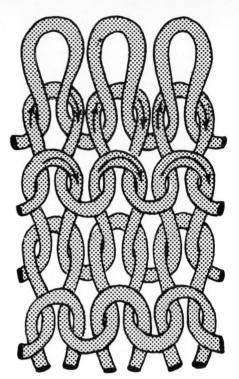

FIGURE 16.15   Purl knit structure. Courtesy of the National Knitwear Manufacturers Association.

FIGURE 16.16.   Close-up view of stitches in a purl knit fabric.

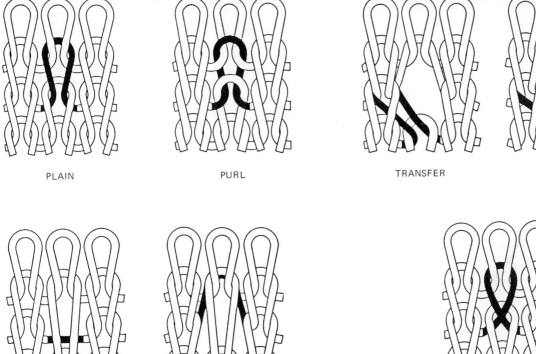

PLAIN   PURL   TRANSFER   SPREAD

MISS OR FLOAT   TUCK

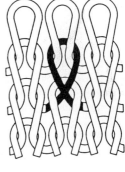

CROSS

FIGURE 16.17. *Basic weft-knitted stitches viewed from the front of the fabric. From J. A. Smirfitt,* An Introduction to Warp Knitting. *Copyright Merrow Publishing Company Ltd. Reproduced by permission.*

of catching the stitch, they allow the yarn to be carried across the back of the fabric. The float stitch can be used to hide colored yarns at the back of the fabric when they do not appear on the design in the face. When long, straight floats are used, the elasticity of the fabric is reduced, and long floats are likely to be caught or snagged in use.

The tuck stitch is made by programming certain needles to hold both an old loop and a new yarn without looping off the old stitch. This creates an elongated stitch that appears in the fabric as a variation in the surface pattern.

Loops can be transferred sideways to create decorative effects or open spaces. Transfer of loops can also be used in shaping of knits, as in "full-fashioning," which is accomplished on specialized machines. Combinations of the tuck, miss, and other stitches with basic rib, plain, or purl knit stitches can create such varied effects as raised cables, open work alternating with plain knit, and a wide range of other decorative fabrics. An almost infinite variety of patterns can be created by combining different colored or textured yarns and various stitches.

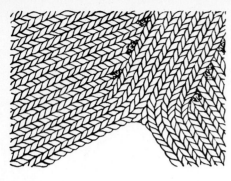

FASHION MARKS

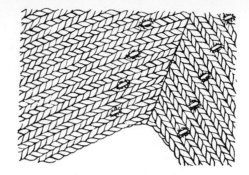

MOCK FASHION MARKS

FIGURE 16.18.   Fashion marks contrasted with mock fashion marks. Courtesy of E. I. du Pont de Nemours & Company.

Full-Fashioned Knits

Weft knits are usually circular unless they are made on full-fashioning machines. In hosiery and sweaters, the item itself or sections of the item are made on the specialized knitting machines. When sweaters or stockings are knitted, the shape may be incorporated by increasing or decreasing the number of stitches.

Where stitches have been dropped or added, *fashion marks* appear. Fashion marks—small alterations in the surface caused by the shifting of the needles and the change in position of the yarns—are an indication of better quality in that the consumer can be sure that the shaping of the garment is permanent. Items made in this way are referred to as "full-fashioned." Some manufacturers will create mock fashion marks to give the appearance of better quality. A careful examination of the area will show that in a true full-fashioned item, the number and direction of stitches change. In mock fashion marks, this does not occur. Mock fashion marks are usually produced by embroidery and have a long yarn float on the wrong side between "marks." (See Figure 16.18.)

Warp Knits

In warp knitting each yarn is looped around one needle at a time. The guide bar that carries the yarns moves sideways as well as forward and back so that the yarns are carried both lengthwise and, to a limited extent, diagonally. This diagonal motion is needed to assure that the yarns interlace not only with the loop directly below in the same wale, but also with loops to the side in adjacent wales. If the yarn interlaced only vertically, there would be no point at which each individual chain of stitches was attached to its neighboring chain.

This construction provides resistance to laddering or running, since each stitch is most directly connected not only with the stitch beneath but also with a stitch placed diagonally and lower. In forming the stitch, diagonal underlay moves the yarn from loop to loop.

Several types of warp knits are made on a number of different warp knitting machines.

Tricot

Tricot machines account for the largest quantity of warp knits. Tricot fabric is knit flat. On the right side the wales create the appearance of a fine, lengthwise line. On the wrong side, crosswise ribs appear in a horizontal position.

In the manufacture of tricot, a guide bar moves the yarns from side to side. The tricot machines may have from one to four guide bars. The greater the number of bars, the greater is the distance the yarn moves between stitches. In moving from one placement to the next, underlay yarns are carried across the back of the fabric. This extra yarn creates heavier weight fabrics. (See Figure 16.19.)

Tricot fabrics are identified as one-bar, two-bar, three-bar, or four-bar, depending on the number of guide bars used in their manufacture. One-bar or single-bar tricot is relatively unstable and is seldom used for garments. It is, however, used as backing for some bonded fabrics. It will run, because the loops interlace close together. Two-bar tricot is stable and fairly light in weight and is used extensively in lingerie, blouses, and the like. Three- and four-bar tricots are used for dresses and men's wear and are heavier than two-bar tricot. (See Figures 16.20 and 16.21.)

In addition to the basic tricot fabric, a number of variations can be made. A tricot satin is produced by allowing yarns to float further across

FIGURE 16.19   A to G. Tricot knitting cycle. In Figure 19.A the needle is in the up position, old loops are on the needle stems, and guides (bars) are ready to swing through the needles to the back. Figure 19.B shows the guides at the back and sideways one space. In Figure 19.C the yarns are laid across the needles; in 19.D the needle has risen to get the yarns around the stem; in 19.E the needle falls, moving the yarn into the hook of the needle while the presser bar presses the needle closed so that the new loops are held inside the hook. In 19.F a backward motion of the sinker moves the old loops over the closed needle. In 19.G the old loops have been cast off, and the needle is ready to rise into position as in 19.A. (Figure from D. G. B. Thomas; An Introduction to Warp Knitting. Copyright Merrow Publishing Co. Ltd. Reproduced by permission.)

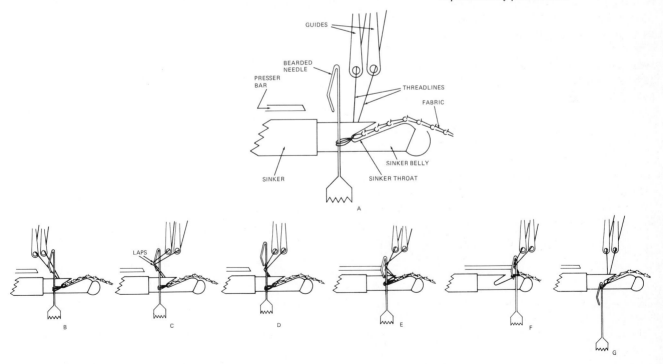

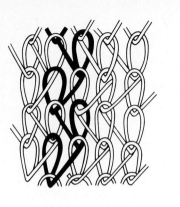

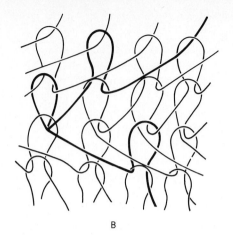

A   B

Figure 16.20. A and B. Figure A represents the simplest single guide bar tricot construction. Figure B represents a two guide bar construction. Darker areas show how one yarn is carried throughout the fabric.

the surface of the fabric before they interlace. Other textured tricots known as "brushed tricots" are made with raised, napped surfaces or with small loops. The fabric as knitted is smooth on both sides. The surface effects are achieved during finishing when the fabric is passed through a special machine equipped with wire rollers that either pull loops to the surface of the fabric or break some of the filaments to give a "brushed" or soft, napped surface. Brushed or looped tricot fabrics are made with long underlaps that form the pile or loops.

Three- and four-bar tricot constructions permit the carrying of hidden yarns through the fabric. Monofilaments that stabilize the fabric or spandex filaments for stretch may be concealed in the complex structure of the tricot fabric.

Tricot fabrics can be made with a variety of open-weave effects to create interesting lacelike patterns, as well. Figure 16.22 depicts a tricot knitting machine.

GUIDE BARS

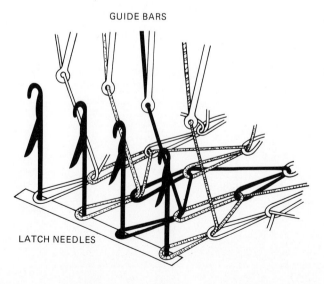

LATCH NEEDLES

FIGURE 16.21. Guide bars on warp knitting machine move from side to side while needles move up and down. Follow the path of each yarn as it changes its position in the fabric structure.

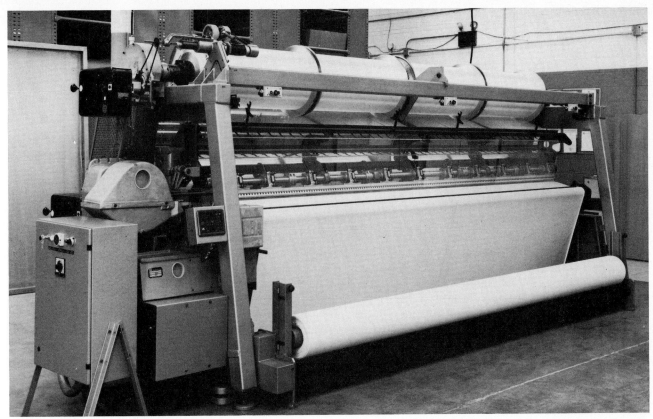

FIGURE 16.22. Tricot machine. Courtesy of American Liba Incorporated.

Raschel Knits

Raschel knitting machines are capable of enormous variation in construction. Raschel machines may have from two to forty-eight guide bars. The knits made on this machine range from fine knitted laces to heavy-duty fabrics. Elaborately patterned surface effects can also be achieved with the Raschel loom. Raschel fabrics may be knitted flat or tubular, although most are knitted flat. The versatility of this knitting machine makes it possible to knit fabrics that, to the eye, have the appearance of woven goods or lace. (See Figure 16.23.)

Among the most popular types of Raschel fabrics are power net of elastomeric yarns for foundation garments and swimsuits; thermal cloth for cold-weather underwear; lace; netting; carpet; and tailored men's wear fabrics. One of the parts of the Raschel machine that makes these variations possible is a special mechanism called a *fall plate*. In the normal knit stitch formation, the needle moves up and down, looping yarns on and off the needle to form a continuous chain. In the Raschel fall plate mechanism, a plate is lowered between two guide bars. This plate prevents the yarn that is held behind it from forming a normal loop. Instead, the yarn is carried along in the fabric in a horizontal or diagonal direction. In some fabrics, this technique is used to simulate the effect of embroidery; in others, it gives a woven appearance to the fabrics.

Simplex Knits

Simplex knitting machines create warp knits similar to tricot, but with a more dense, thicker texture—a sort of double knit tricot. Simplex knits are used in products requiring heavier fabrics, such as women's gloves, handbags, and simulated suede-textured apparel fabrics.

Milanese Knits

Milanese knitting machines knit fabrics that are used for many of the same items as tricots, but at higher price ranges. Milanese fabrics have a fine, riblike structure on the face and a diagonal rib on the back. They are similar in weight to a two-bar tricot and are runproof. Milanese knits are knit flat, but tubular variations of this construction can be made on a special machine, the *Marriati* knitting machine. In the period after World War II, rapid development of tricot machines made the Milanese process virtually obsolete, although the fabrics have certain advantages over tricot.[3]

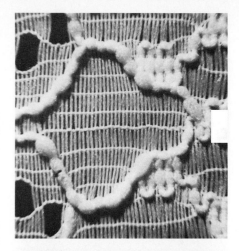

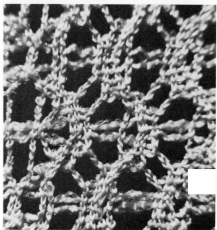

Cidega Knits

Cidega knitting machines produce fabrics in open-work patterns for apparel, curtains, upholstery, and trimming fabrics. A versatile machine, the Cidega is said by its manufacturer to permit knitting of several different fabrics simultaneously on different sections of the needlebed—for instance an entire series of different trimming fabrics or a "body" cloth and several matching trims.

Cidega knits may simulate crochet fabrics. Pile loop fabrics and tassellike fringes can also be made on the machine.

FIGURE 16.23. A and B. Close-up views of two open-structured raschel knit fabrics.

Creating Pattern and Design in Knitted Goods

Finished knit goods can be dyed. Patterns can be created by printing on the fabric or through the manipulation of multicolored yarns.

Weft knits are easily knitted into stripes. These stripes always run across the fabric, since the pattern is achieved through varying the colors of the yarns in the different courses. Since the yarns interlace horizontally, it is not possible to knit a vertical stripe in weft single knits.

A Jacquard attachment for weft knit machines makes possible the knitting of a wide variety of patterned fabrics. Like woven Jacquard patterns, Jacquard knit designs are plotted on paper and then are trans-

[3]A. Reisfeld, "Warp Knit Fabric Design," *Knitting Times*, (October 15, 1979), p. 40.

ferred to the Jacquard mechanisms where the machine automatically activates the appropriate needles and colored yarns.

The structure of patterns in warp knitting is determined by a system known as the *link-chain* system. Chains with links of variable heights control the movement of the guide bars. The height of the link transfers a motion to the guide bars. The guide bars set the yarn in position over a group of needles to form the pattern.

Performance and Care of Knitted Fabrics

Although there is a great variety in the quality of knitted goods sold, and the performance of any individual knit may differ markedly from that of other knits, some general guidelines for the care of knitted goods can be observed. The problems that consumers seem to encounter most often in the performance of knitted fabrics are in the areas of dimensional stability, pilling, and snagging.

Dimensional Stability

One reason for the popularity of knits for wearing apparel is their comfort. The looped construction of knit fabrics permits the fabric to give with the body as it moves. But the stretchiness of knits also results in lessened dimensional stability. Consumers have complained about shrinkage, stretching, and distortion of knits, although some interlock and doubleknit fabrics display little or no shrinkage.

Shrinkage control treatments, heat setting of synthetics, and special resin finishes can provide good dimensional stability for knits. Unfortunately not all manufacturers provide such treatment for their products. Consumers should check labels for percentage of shrinkage or for other special treatments to judge potential dimensional stability. (About 3 per cent shrinkage is a garment size.) If products fail to live up to specified performance standards, items should be returned to the retailer or the manufacturer.

Knits are considered to be easy-care fabrics, and many care labels recommend machine washing. Some labels will also specify that the fabric can be dried in an automatic dryer. In general, however, knits will shrink more in the dryer than if air dried. Knits maintain their shape best if they are dried flat. The weight of a wet knit, hung on a line, may cause the fabric to stretch out of shape.

The dimensions of knits usually will be retained best by professional dry cleaning. Coin-operated dry cleaning appears to offer no particular advantage over home laundering for double knit items that could be either washed or dry cleaned, as one research study has shown that double knits cleaned in a coin-operated dry-cleaning machine also shrink more than 3 per cent with repeated cleaning. Depending on fiber content, both methods produced substantial shrinkage.[4] Shrinkage in

[4]*Today's Knitwear*, Technical Bulletin, Vol. 27 (Columbus: Textile Research Laboratory, Ohio State University, August 1972).

coin-operated dry cleaning is a result of the tumbling action of the machine.

Hand knits, sweaters of wool or animal hair fiber, and other knits with a very open construction may require special hand laundering and blocking (stretching back into shape). Such items should be laid on a sheet of wrapping paper prior to washing, and the outlines traced. After washing, the garment should be stretched out on the paper to dry. While still damp, the garment should be gently stretched to fit the outline of the original dimensions.

In general, knits made of synthetics will have better resistance to stretching out of shape than will cotton, acetates, and rayons. Blending of synthetics with cottons, acetates, and rayons will improve the resiliency and dimensional stability of knitted fabrics made from these fibers. Price is a good guide—especially for children's knits.

Mechanical Damage

The loop structure of knitted fabrics makes them especially susceptible to snagging. If a loop catches on another object, it may be pulled up from the fabric surface and a long snag or pull of yarn may be formed. If the yarn that has been snagged is not broken, it can be pulled to the back of the fabric. It may be possible to gently stretch the fabric and work the pulled yarn back into place. This is difficult to do with very tightly knitted fabric structures.

If the yarn has been broken, the snag may produce a hole in the fabric. A few hand stitches with needle and matching thread should be made to secure the yarns so that the hole does not become enlarged during wearing or laundering.

Synthetic double knits or knits made from loosely twisted yarns may be subject to pilling. As the fabric is subjected to abrasion during wear, the short fiber ends that work their way to the fabric surface are rubbed into a small ball that hangs onto the fabric surface. When fibers are weak, as in cotton, rayon, acetates, wools, and the like, these fibers generally break off the fabric. But the stronger synthetic fibers cling to the fabric, making an unsightly area on the fabric surface. The use of textured yarns for knitting synthetics decreases the likelihood of pilling.

Knits may be damaged by sharp objects puncturing the fabric. If yarns are cut, a hole will result, and further pressure and strain on the fabric may enlarge the open area.

Combination Knit and Weave Constructions

A number of attempts have been made to combine the processes of knitting and weaving to create a fabric with some of the advantages of both processes. Some of these variations of knitting have been purely experimental; others have been commercialized for a time. For the most part, they have been based on the idea of integrating warp or filling yarns part or all of the way into the lengthwise or crosswise direction of a knitted structure. The knitting construction holds them in place.

At the present time only weft insertion systems have any substantial commercial distribution. A separate magazine feeds weft yarns to a tricot or Raschel warp knitting machine. The weft yarn crosses the entire width of the fabric. When the fabric is viewed from the back side, it can be seen that the weft always passes under the underlap of the knit stitch and over the loops. (See Figure 16.24.)

Manufacturers of magazine weft insertion machines recommend the fabrics for a wide variety of apparel, household textile, and industrial applications. The textile literature describes their potential for use in processing high-tenacity yarns that are difficult to handle in ordinary weaving. High-tenacity yarns will lose some strength as a result of stresses imposed by the interlacing of yarns required in weaving. In weft insertion, the knitting yarns serve to hold the weft yarn in place, and full advantage can be taken of the strength of the inserted yarn.[5]

Warp insertion techniques have also been developed, but their use is minimal at this time. One that is very similar in principle to weft insertion process is done on a VEEV system, but is used domestically on quite a limited scale. (See Figure 16.25.) Another warp insertion technique is a method for incorporating yarns walewise (lengthwise) rather than crosswise. This is done essentially for design flexibility rather than for stability. In this so-called "wrap-around" system the yarns are introduced by a device that pulls "warp" yarn from a cone and holds it in such a way as to allow it to be incorporated into the fabric in a mostly warpwise direction. A wide variety of patterned effects can be achieved, but unlike weft insertion or the VEEV process in which yarns are held

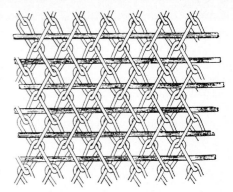

FIGURE 16.24. *Structure of weft insertion warp knit fabric. Reprinted by permission National Knitwear and Sportswear Association.*

[5]"Weft-Insertion Warp-Knits for Industrial Fabrics," *Textile Industries* (March 1983), p. 56.

FIGURE 16.25. *A. VEEV-type warp insertion. B., C. Two possible patterns of warp insertion using wrap-around method.*

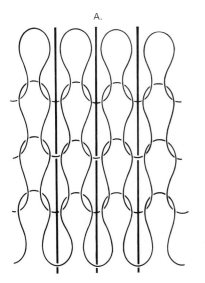

A.

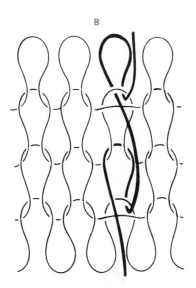

B

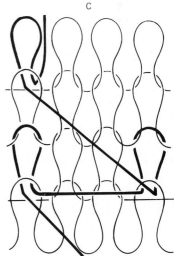

C

in place by the knit stitches, these yarns are formed into knit stitches as they are incorporated.[6] (See Figure 16.25.)

Recommended References

ESSIG, H. "Short Course in Knitting: Basic Fabric and Machine Types," *Knitting Times*, 48 (September 24, 1979), p. 18.

FRICK, J. G., JR. "Crimp and Resilience of Yarns in Knit Cotton," *Textile Research Journal*, 55 (February 1985), p. 132.

GETGOOD, J. "Built-in Computers in Knitting Machines: Advantages and Disadvantages," *Knitting Times*, 53 (July 1984), p. 54.

GAUCHER, M. L., and M. W. KING, "Predicting the Drape Coefficient of Knitted Fabrics," *Textile Research Journal*, 53, (May 1983), p. 297.

GROSS, D. "Cidega: Experienced Firm with New Image," *Knitting Times*, 50 (August 3, 1981), p. 6.

INNES, R. "Full-Fashioning Machine Developments," *Knitting Times*, 50:
  Part I: September 7, 1981, p. 8.
  Part II: September 21, 1981, p. 8.
  Part III: October 5, 1981, p. 10.
  Part IV: October 26, 1981, p. 10.
  Part V: November 2, 1981, p. 10.

KNAPTON, J. J. F. "Single Knit Technolgy: An Industry Overview," *Knitting Times*, (June 9, 1980), p. 52.

"Knitwear Dictionary for Ready Reference," *Knitting Times*, 48 (January 14, 1980), insert.

LENNOX-KERR, P. "No Needle Machine Uses Air to Knit," *Textile World*, 134 (July 1984), p. 35.

LEVENTHAL, L. "Plush Fabrics Replace Fake Furs as Mainstay for Sliver Knitters," *Knitting Times*, 52 (December 19, 1983), p. 67.

LOMBARDI, V. J. "Warp Insertion on Circular Knitting Machines: New Designing Tool," *Knitting Times*, 54 (May 1985), p. 59.

MUTARELLI, E. "The Missoni's Capture a World Audience with Knits as Art in Pattern, Color," *Knitting Times*, 54 (January 1985), p. 70.

NORWICK, B., "Quality Control in Knits: Production Techniques, Salability, Part 1," *Knitting Times*, 53 (June 1984), p. 90.

REISFELD, A. "History of Warp Knitting: An Outline," *Knitting Times Yearbook*, 52 (November 28, 1983), p. 79.

SHARMA, I. C., S. GHOSH, and N. K. GUPTA, "Dimensional and Physical Characteristics of Single Jersey Fabrics," *Textile Research Journal*, 55 (March 1985), p. 149.

SMITH, G. W., and C. SEASTRUNK. "Weft Knit Primer for Dyers and Finishers," *American Dyestuff Reporter*, 73 and 74 (December 1982–April 1984).

SPENCER, D. J. "Electronics in Knitting: A Primer," *Knitting Times*, 53 (January 23, 1984), p. 20.

TAYLOR, H. M. "Woven and Knitted Fabrics," *Textiles*, 8 (October 1979), p. 64.

"Technology Challenged by Shift in Legwear Market," *Textile Industries*, 148 (August 1984), p. 46.

THOMAS, D. G. B. *An Introduction to Warp Knitting*, Watford, England: Merrow Publishing Company Ltd., 1971.

"Weft-Insertion Warp-Knits for Industrial Fabrics," *Textile Industries*, 147 (March 1983), p. 56.

[6] V. J. Lombardi, "Warp Insertion on Circular Knitting Machines: New Designing Tool," *Knitting Times*, 54 (May 1985), p. 59.

Other Methods of Fabric Construction

Although woven and knitted goods make up the largest quantity of fabrics produced, various other construction methods are also used for the fabrication of textiles. Many of these techniques derive from processes utilized since prehistoric times, other have been developed more recently, and still others are the result of new technology within the textile industry.

The fabrication methods discussed in this chapter may be divided into several broad classifications: fabrics made by knotting, by looping, by stitching yarns or fibers together, and by bonding together a web of fibers. Netting, macramé, and lace are created by knotting, either by hand or by machine. Crochet, essentially a hand technique, is made from a series of loops in a process that is similar to knitting. A new fabric construction technique, known either as stitch bonding or stitch knitting, combines yarns and/or fibers by sewing them together. Ancient techniques such as felt making or bark cloth construction are similar in principle to the manufacture of modern nonwovens, fibers held together in a flexible web.

Fabric Webs

Felt

Although the evidence is scanty, it is believed that the first means of making fibers into cloth was through felting. Prehistoric remains of felt materials have been found in such diverse parts of the world as Anatolia, Siberia, Europe, Southeast Asia, and South America. To understand the process by which felt is formed, it is necessary to review the structure of the wool fiber from which it is made.

The surface of the wool fiber is covered with a fine network of small scales. This scaly structure causes wool fibers to cling closely together, as the scales from one fiber interlock with the scales of another. Furthermore, the natural crimp of wool assists in felting. When masses of wool fiber are placed together, the crimped fibers become entangled.

Friction increases this tangling. If the wool is subjected to conditions of heat and moisture, the scales open wider, interlocking with still more scales from neighboring fibers. Wool scales are so constructed that they shrink toward the fiber root, causing the mass to hold together more tightly. When pressure is added, the mass is flattened, producing a web of tightly joined fibers or felt. The factors essential for producing natural felt from wool are pressure, which increases the tangling, heat, and moisture.

It is not too difficult to imagine a situation in which felt might have been produced accidentally. Suppose a horserider placed a sheep fleece on the back of a horse as cushioning material. The body of the horse is both warm and moist; the rider provides the pressure and the friction. Over time, the fleece becomes matted, producing a primitive form of felt. Frequent repetition of the procedure could lead to the recognition that this material had potential for some of the same uses as the fleece from which it was made.

Eventually the natural process was reduced to a series of steps that included applying heat and moisture to a mass of wool fiber, placing the batt (or mass) of fibers on flat stones, and pounding the fibers with hammers or beaters. To vary the texture and quality of the material, fur fibers might be added, but it was the wool that served to hold the substance together.

In the commercial production of felt, a batt of cleaned wool fiber is fed into a carding machine that lays down a web of fairly even thickness. To improve strength and dimensional stability, two webs of carded fiber are laid across each other with the fibers of one web at right angles to the fibers of the other web.

Steam is forced through the mass of fiber, after which a heavy, heated plate or rollers are lowered onto the fibers. The plate or rollers are moved about to produce friction. The moisture, heat, and friction effectively interlock the fibers.

Following this operation, the fabric is passed through a solution of soap or acid that causes the fabric to shrink still further. From this stage the fabric goes to a "fulling mill" in which the fabric is subjected to further agitation, pounding, and shrinkage. After felting is complete, the fabric can be dyed or given any of the traditional finishes used on wool.

To decrease costs, manufacturers may blend other fibers with wool. A woven scrim (a plain, open, woven fabric) may sometimes be added as a framework to support felt to increase its strength.

Felt has the advantage of being easily cut, and because it has no yarns, it will not fray at the edges. Felt can be molded into shape and, so, has wide use in making hats. Because of its densely packed fibers, felt provides a good deal of warmth, and it is not easily penetrated by water. On the other hand, felt is a relatively weak fabric, may tear under pressure, and is subject to pilling. Being rather stiff, felt does not fall into graceful folds. Its use, therefore, is somewhat limited. Modern manufacturers of wool felt supply material not only for hats and fashion accessories but also for a wide range of industrial uses.

Bark Cloth

A process similar to that used for felt produces bark cloth or, as it is called in the Polynesian Islands, *tapa*. This nonwoven fabric was also known during prehistoric times in areas as widespread as Asia, Africa, Europe, South and Central America, and the South Pacific.

Made from certain trees, among them the paper mulberry, breadfruit, fig, or related species, bark cloth is produced by first removing strips of the inner layer of bark from the tree. This substance is softened by soaking it in water. The softened bark is placed on an anvil or flat surface, and special beaters are then used to pound the bark strips to interlace the fibers. When the mass is sufficiently integrated, the material is dried, producing a sheet of fabric. Special texture or surface markings are achieved by pounding the material with incised hammers or embossing the flat surface on which the fibrous materials are spread to be beaten and to dry.

The process is similar to that used in making paper, and the resulting fabric is somewhat like a soft, supple paper. Printed designs are added to the surface. Although woven cotton goods replaced native bark cloth in the South Pacific in the nineteenth century, small quantities are still made for native religious garb, and as an example of native handicrafts.

Like felt, *tapa* has limited usefulness. In medium to heavy weights, it does not drape or sew particularly well, and so is used chiefly for simple unsewn garments such as ponchos, sarongs, loincloths, or turbans. On the other hand, because pieces of tapa can be joined without sewing, simply by wetting the edge of two pieces and pounding them together, large pieces of fabric can be made without seams.

Other Fiber Webs

Techniques by which fabrics are made directly from fibers, bypassing both spinning and weaving, have been utilized for centuries in the production of felt and bark cloth. With the development of man-made fibers, and, in particular, the synthesis of thermoplastic fibers, technologies have evolved that have made possible the large-scale production of nonwoven fabrics. Marketed extensively for both durable and disposable items, nonwoven fiber webs range from throwaway diapers to blankets, from industrial filters to tea-bag covers.

The American Society for Testing Materials defines nonwoven textile fabrics as textile structures "produced by bonding or interlocking, or both, of fiber accomplished by mechanical, chemicals or solvent means and combinations thereof."[1] Excluded from this class are paper; fabrics that have been woven, knitted, or tufted; or those made by wool or other felting processes.

American Fabrics magazine recommends that nonwoven fabrics be classified as durable products or disposable products. They define a durable product as "one which is multi-use. It is not manufactured to be thrown away after a single application."[2] Examples of this type of product are blankets, carpetbackings, and furniture padding.

Disposable products were defined as "made to be disposed of after a single or limited number of uses." These are exemplified in disposable diapers, towels, or tea-bag covers. Some items, *American Fabrics* points out, are disposable not because of their durability but because of their purpose. Medical gowns, for example, or airplane and train headrests, might withstand multiple use, but for sanitary reasons they have limited use periods.

Nonwoven fabrics are made from both staple and filament fibers. Filament fibers are made into fabrics by spun bonding, which is discussed later. Staple fibers may be made into fabrics by several different processes.

Staple Fiber Web Formation

Both durable and disposable staple fiber nonwovens are manufactured in several stages. The first step, the forming of the web of fibers, is done by either *dry forming* or *wet forming*. Either of two different dry-forming processes may be used. Fiber-forming processes are explained in the following pages through the use of diagrams and captions reproduced courtesy of INDA (Association of the Nonwoven Fabrics Industry). This material appeared originally in INDA's publication *Guide to Nonwoven Fabrics*, New York, 1978. (See Figures 17.1, 17.2, 17.3.)

Paper is formed by a process very much like that described under the headings of "Wet Forming," and it is difficult to make a clear division between some paper and some nonwoven textile products.

Binding the Fibers Together

Once a web has been formed, some treatment must be given to bind the fibers together. This can be done by using a bonding or adhesive material or by entangling fibers.

Bonding. Bonding may be achieved by *applying an adhesive material* to the web and then setting the adhesive. This, in essence, "glues" the fibers together. When adhesive is applied to the surface of the fiber web, it tends to make the fabric stiff and more rigid. Also, fabrics exhibit the

---

[1] *Compilation of ASTM Standard Definitions* (Philadelphia: American Society for Testing Materials, 1982), p. 268.

[2] AAF Appraises the Non-Wovens," *American Fabrics* No. 101 (Summer 1974), p. 40.

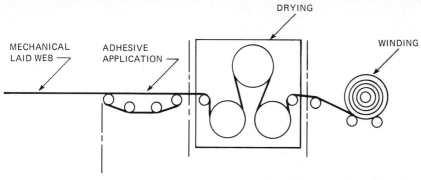

FIGURE 17.1 Dry process. Dry forming (carding or garnetting). Courtesy of INDA.

Process: *Individual natural or man-made fibers are metered and distributed uniformly by mechanical means to form a moving web. Fiber-to-fiber bonding is then achieved by the addition of binders or by heat fusion. Following drying of the binder chemicals, the resulting web is wound into a roll, ready for post-treatment or conversion into a finished product.*

Fabric characteristics: *Dry-formed fabrics generally exhibit a soft hand, have excellent drape, and have fabric strength highly oriented in the direction of web travel through the forming process (i.e., unidirectional). Fabric weights usually range from 0.3 to 6 ounces per square yard. Thicknesses generally range from 3 to 15 mils.*

Typical end uses: *Interlinings, coated fabric backings, carpet components, diaper cover stock, wipes, sanitary napkins.*

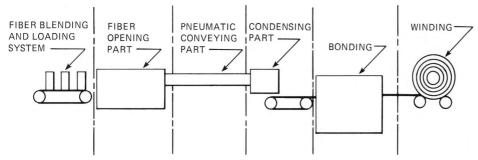

FIGURE 17.2 Dry process. Dry forming (airlaid). Courtesy of INDA.

Process: *Like carding or garnetting, the air-forming process meters individual natural or man-made fibers into a finished web. Distribution, however, is accomplished by suspending the fibers in an air stream and then forming them into a continuously moving web. By controlling the characteristics of the air stream, fiber direction can be more randomly oriented than in the previous process. The fibers in the web are then chemically or heat-bonded and the web is wound into a finished roll.*

Fabric characteristics: *Fabric properties are similar to those of a carded web, except that machine-direction strength and cross-machine-direction strength tend to be more nearly equal (i.e., isotropic) because of the random orientation of the fibers. Fabric weights usually range from 0.5 to 6 ounces per square yard. Thicknesses generally range from 5 to 70 mils.*

Typical end uses: *Battery separators, filter media, diaper cover stock, interlinings, carpet components, wipes, cushioning, insulation.*

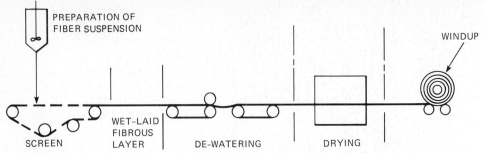

PREPARATION OF
FIBER SUSPENSION

WINDUP

SCREEN

WET–LAID
FIBROUS
LAYER

DE-WATERING

DRYING

FIGURE 17.3.   Wet Process. Courtesy of INDA.

Process: *In wet forming of nonwoven fabrics, individual natural or man-made fibers are suspended in water to obtain a uniform dispersion. As the fiber-and-water suspension flows onto a moving screen, the water passes through, leaving the fibers laid uniformly in the form of a web. Additional water is then squeezed out of the web and the remaining water is removed by drying. Bonding may be done completely during the drying step, or further bonding may be achieved through the use of rolls. Following bonding, the fabric is wound up into a finished roll ready for subsequent operations.*

Fabric characteristics: *Water suspension of fibers results in generally random orientation of fibers. The wet-lay process also permits chemicals, and sometimes the binder, to be added to the fibers as they are formed into a web. Since chemicals can be added before and after web formation, the manufacturer can be highly flexible in designing wet-formed fabric properties. Fabric weights usually range from 0.3 to 16 ounces. Thicknesses generally range from 2.3 to 190 mils.*

Typical end uses: *Wipes, towels, surgical gowns, diaper cover stock, shoe components, interlinings, filtration.*

characteristics of the adhesive material on the surface rather than the characteristics of the original fiber. To overcome this disadvantage, adhesives may be imprinted onto the surface in selected areas. The printing patterns are developed carefully to assure that adequate bonding takes place among fibers to maintain fabric strength. Such fabrics are less rigid and have better drapability and a more pleasant surface texture than do those that have been completely coated by an adhesive.

Instead of adhesive bonding, fibers may be bonded by spraying a mixture of chemicals and water onto the surface of the fibers. When subjected to heat, the water evaporates and the chemical vaporizes, dissolving a small amount of fiber, usually where one fiber crosses another. When the dissolved fibers resolidify, bonds are formed that hold the fibers together.

Thermoplastic fibers may be bonded by heat. The application of heat causes the fusing together of heat-sensitive fibers, which effectively fastens them together. As in bonding with adhesives, heat may be applied in a pattern to provide sufficient bonding for durability and to allow greater flexibility and softness in the end product.

Entangling the Fibers. Fiber webs produced by the dry-web methods may be joined by entangling the fibers in some way. One of these

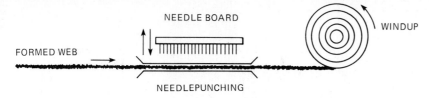

FIGURE 17.4. Needle-punched process.
Courtesy of INDA.

Process: *A needle punched fabric is produced by introducing a fibrous web—already formed by cards, garnetts, or air laying— into a machine equipped with groups of specially designed needles. While the web is trapped between a bed plate and a stripper plate, the needles punch through it and reorient the fibers so that mechanical bonding is achieved among the individual fibers. Often, the batt of fibers is carried into the needle punching section of the machine on a lightweight support material or substrate. This is done to improve finished fabric strength and integrity.*

Fabric characteristics: *The needle punching process is generally used to produce fabrics that have high density yet retain some bulk. Fabric weights usually range from 1.7 to 10 ounces per square yard. Thicknesses generally range from 15 to 160 mils.*

Typical end uses: *Blankets, filter media, coated fabric backings, carpeting and carpet backings, automobile landau top substrates, apparel interlinings, road underlay, auto trunk liners.*

methods will be discussed later under the heading of stitch-bonded fabrics. It is the technique (made by the Maliwatt and the Arachne machines) of *chain stitching* or knitting through a batt of fibers.

Another method, known as *needle punching*, has wide use in the home furnishings industry. (See Figure 17.4.)

Spun-laced goods are sheets of fibers made by fluid entanglement. No adhesive or binder is used. (See Figure 17.5.)

Sontara® is a class of spun-laced fabrics manufactured by DuPont.

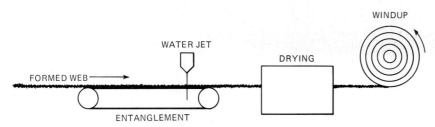

FIGURE 17.5. Spun-laced process. Courtesy of INDA.

Process: *In this system, a fibrous web is subjected to high-velocity water jets that entangle the fibers and achieve mechanical bonding. The fabric then travels through conventional drying and wind up operations.*

Fabric characteristics: *The substitution of mechanical bonding of fibers instead of chemical bonding results in very soft and drapable fabrics. Fabric weights usually range from 0.7 to 2.2 ounces per square yard. Thicknesses generally range from 3.5 to 25 mils.*

Typical end uses: *Quilt backings, mattress pad tickings, coated fabric substrates, interlinings, curtains, table cloths, apparel.*

Spun Bonding

Spun-bonded fabrics are manufactured from synthetic filament fibers in a process that has the economic advantage of taking the fiber directly from the spinning stage to the fabric-forming stage without costly intermediate processing. (See Figure 17.6.)

DuPont uses the process to produce Reemay®, Typar®, and Tyvek®. Reemay® is a polyester fabric used for apparel interlinings, backing layers for carpets, and furniture and bedding. Typar®, a spun-bonded poly-

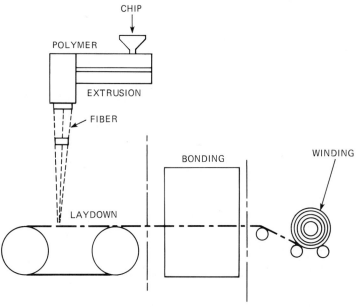

FIGURE 17.6. Spun-bonded process. Courtesy of INDA.

Process: *Spunbonding is a continuous process producing a finished fabric from polymer. A polymer, or several polymers, such as polyester, polyamide, polypropylene, polyethylene or others, is fed into an extruder. As it flows from the extruder it is forced through a spinneret, a device with tiny holes, like a shower nozzle. After cooling, the resulting continuous filaments are then laid down on a moving conveyor belt to form a continuous web. In the lay-down process, the desired orientation of the fibers is achieved by various means, such as rotation of the spinneret, electrical charges, introduction of controlled airstreams or varying the speed of the conveyor belt. The fabric is then bonded by thermal or chemical treatment before being wound up into finished roll form.*

Fabric characteristics: *A wide range of fabric characteristics can be achieved by controlling the various elements in this process. High performance-low weight fabrics are characteristic of this process because of the continuous nature of the fibers. Fabric weights usually range from 0.3 to 6 ounces per square yard. Thicknesses generally range from 3 to 25 mils.*

Typical end uses: *Coated and laminated fabrics, carpet underlay, packaging material, durable papers, sanitary napkin and diaper covers, road underlay, filtration, interlinings, disposable apparel, wallcoverings, battery separators, building materials.*

propylene, is used in bagging, packaging, furniture construction, filtration, and carpet backing. Tyvek® is an olefin sheet that is tough and durable. A kind of cross between paper, fabric, and film, Tyvek® is extensively used for wall coverings, tags, packaging materials, charts, maps, and the like.

Cerex® is a nylon spun-bonded fabric produced by Monsanto and used as carpet backing, in furniture manufacture, and for industrial fabrics. Mirafi 140S®, a porous heat-bonded fabric made from biconstituent fibers by Celanese, is used by engineers for road building, in combating soil erosion, and in other forms of construction. (See Figure 1.6.) Many companies now make spun-bonded fiber webs from a number of different fibers. Bidim® is a polyester manufactured by Monsanto; Celestra® and Evolution® are olefin products made by Crown-Zellerbach and Kimberly-Clark, respectively. Enkamat® is a spun-bonded nylon matting by Enka.

Stitch Bonding

A process known variously as *stitch bonding*, *stitch through*, *stitch knitting*, or *mali* (from one machine used in its manufacture) produces fabrics for apparel, household, and industrial uses. First developed in East Germany, stitch-through machines work at faster speeds than do knitting or weaving machines. Such fabrics have the advantage of being less expensive to produce, not only because of the increased volume of cloth produced by each machine but also because less yarn is required for stitch-through fabrics than for woven fabrics. Some stitch-through fabrics may also have greater bursting strength and tear strength than do conventionally woven fabrics of comparable yarn size and fiber type. Some stitch-through fabrics will run and are subject to fraying.

Three basic types of stitch-through fabrics are produced: a flat fabric of stitched yarns that is most similar to conventional fabrics, a pile fabric, and batting.

Heinrich Mauersberger, an East German inventor, developed the stitch-bonding concept after having observed his wife mending a fabric in which the filling threads had been worn away. Mauersberger called his process and the fabric it produced Malimo®.

Malimo® fabrics are made with two or three sets of yarns: weft yarns, stitching yarns, and for some fabrics, warp yarns. Figure 17.7 shows the possible structural variations. The stitch-bonding machine has been described as looking like a modified warp knitting machine. (See Figure 17.8.)

Design variations in Malimo® can be produced by varying the color, placement, and size of warp and filling yarns. Fabrics can be printed; sculptured or relief designs can be made, as can filetlike open work and striped or checked patterns. (See Figure 17.9.)

End uses for Malimo® stitch-bonded fabrics include products for the home such as draperies, vertical blinds, upholstery, textile wall coverings, bed sheets, table linens, towels and dishcloths, and industrial and

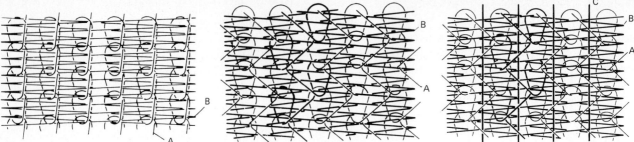

Figure 17.7. Malimo structural variations. (A) Weft yarn system and stitching yarn system intermeshed by plain chain stitch. (B) Weft yarn system and stitching yarn system intermeshed by locking chain stitch. (C) Weft yarn system and warp yarn system and stitching yarn system intermeshed by interlocking chain stitch. Courtesy of Chima Inc.

KEY: A = STITCHING YARN
B = WEFT YARN
C = STITCHING YARN

Figure 17.8. Construction of malimo-type stitch-bonded fabric. Courtesy of Chima Inc.

1 Stitching needles
2 Closing wires
3 Stitching yarn guide needles
4 Knocking-over sinkers
5 Retaining pins
6 Backing rail
7 Stitches of the preceding course
8 Newly laid stitching threads
9 Weft threads
10 New stitches

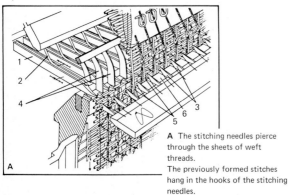

A The stitching needles pierce through the sheets of weft threads.
The previously formed stitches hang in the hooks of the stitching needles.

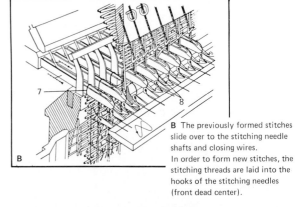

B The previously formed stitches slide over to the stitching needle shafts and closing wires.
In order to form new stitches, the stitching threads are laid into the hooks of the stitching needles (front dead center).

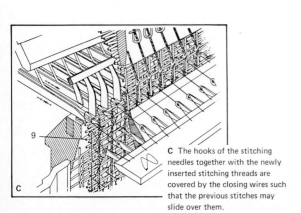

C The hooks of the stitching needles together with the newly inserted stitching threads are covered by the closing wires such that the previous stitches may slide over them.

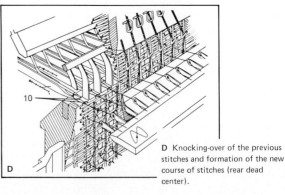

D Knocking-over of the previous stitches and formation of the new course of stitches (rear dead center).

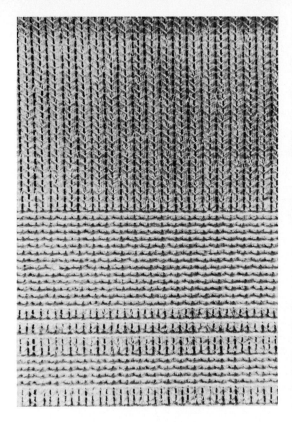

Figure 17.9.a & b Fabrics constructed by the stitch-through technique.

high-technology fabrics. Apparel applications are possible, but have been somewhat limited.

Pile fabrics are made by the Malipol and Schusspol (East German processes), and Araloop (Czechoslovakian) machines. Liropol machines make a two-sided pile, whereas the Malipol, Araloop, and Schusspol machines create pile on one side of the fabric. These processes may attach the pile loops to a basic fabric such as conventionally woven cloth, knits, or nonwovens. The Schusspol machine stitches warp, weft, and pile yarns together at the same time and does not require a preformed base fabric. Major applications of these fabrics are in carpeting, upholstery and other decorative fabrics, and terry fabrics.

The Maliwatt and Arachne machines stitch together a batt of fiber rather than yarns. (See Figure 17.10.) The process offers the advantage of low production costs, since fabrics can be made directly from fibers and the step of spinning fibers into yarns is omitted. Manufacturers find that the insulation qualities of fabrics made in this way are excellent.

In the Arabeva and Malivlies processes, a web of fibers is stitched together by using fibers from the web itself. Fibers from one side of the batt or web are looped across to the other side. The resultant fabric is not as strong as Malimo or Maliwatt fabrics, but it is suitable for use in

Figure 17.10. Maliwatt stitch-bonding machine which forms fabrics from loose fiber webs. Courtesy of Chima, Inc.

garment linings or industrial cloths in which strength is not a major requirement. In the Voltex process, fibers are intermeshed with a backing fabric to form a voluminous pile fabric. Major applications are in blankets, imitation furs, plush fabrics, and lining materials.

Polymer Films

Fabrics coated with polymer films (Figure 17.11) are used for a variety of products ranging from apparel to table cloths. (See Chapter 21 for a fuller discussion of coated fabrics.)

Coated fabrics and poromerics, products with microscopic, open-celled structures, are used to produce imitations of leather. Vinyl-coated fabrics may have an imitation leatherlike grain embossed on the surface. These are the least satisfactory leather imitations both in terms of aesthetics and performance. Fabrics are cold and hard to the touch and do not allow the transmission of moisture vapor.

Expanded vinyl is manufactured so as to have internal air bubbles that improve flexibility and cause the material to feel warmer and softer. Urethane-coated fabrics are even more leatherlike in their qualities.

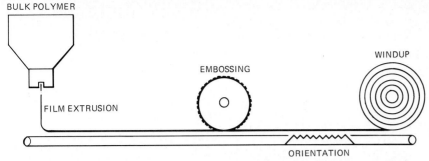

BULK POLYMER

WINDUP

EMBOSSING

FILM EXTRUSION

ORIENTATION

FIGURE 17.11.   *Extrusion process. Courtesy of INDA.*

Process: *Film extruded nonwovens are formed in a continuous process from a polymer melt of polypropylene, polypropylene copolymers or polyethylene. The web is formed by extruding the melt through a slotted film die. Any one of several patterns may then be cut into the web by an embossing roll. When the web is biaxially oriented, it opens up into a network structure or nonwoven fabric.*

Fabric characteristics: *Film extruded nonwovens exhibit excellent uniformity in very light weights. The embossing pattern, type of polymer, film thickness and degree of orientation are all key factors in determining the characteristics of film extruded nonwovens. Fabric weights usually range from 0.2 to 1.6 ounces per square yard. Thicknesses may range from 2 to 20 mils.*

Typical end uses: *Medical/surgical bandage facings, underpad facings, paper and fabric reinforcements, carpet and upholstery fabric backings, drybonding material for canvas and other fabrics, press cloths, scrims and industrial carriers.*

Apparel items made from film-coated fabrics vary in their care requirements. Consumers should follow care label instructions carefully as some products must be laundered; others can withstand dry cleaning.

Poromeric structures more closely match the moisture vapor permeability and other qualities of real leather.

Ultrasuede®, the tradename of a fabric created to look and feel like suede leather, is a nonwoven poromeric structure. Manufactured in Japan, the fabric is distributed in this country by the Skinner Division of Springs Mills, Inc. Little information is available concerning the process by which Ultrasuede® is manufactured; however, it appears to be composed of polyester and polyurethane. The polyester makes up about 40 per cent of the fabric, the polyurethane, 60 per cent.

Ultrasuede® is formed from a nonwoven structure made up of matrix fibers of a type called "islands in the sea." (See Figure 13.3 for depiction of a matrix fiber.) The sea phase is dissolved, leaving a highly entangled nonwoven web of very fine fibers that are then impregnated with polyurethane. Promotional materials from Skinner indicate that the fabric will not stretch out of shape, pill, fray, and crock (lose color through rubbing of the surface), or wrinkle. It is hand or machine washable and dry cleanable and colorfast and will not water spot or stiffen.

Ultrasuede® is used for apparel of all kinds, for furniture and wall

Other Methods of Fabric Construction   **317**

coverings, and for luggage. Special care must be used by home sewers using this fabric. In the fabric all face fibers run in the same direction, so all garment pieces must be cut in the same direction. Needle and pin holes will remain, so care must be taken to avoid ripping and pinning in areas where holes would be evident.

Economic Importance of Nonwoven Fabrics

With an annual growth rate of 11 per cent projected for the nonwoven industry through 1990, it is certain that consumers will select and use increasing numbers of products made from such fabrics.

At the present time, major marketing areas for nonwovens include durables such as interfacings, interlinings, carpet backings, furniture and bedding, automotive and furniture padding, indoor/outdoor carpet, blankets, and the construction industry. Disposable nonwovens are used in diapers, medical and surgical products, wipes, packaging, and filters.

Fibers used for durables include synthetics such as polyester, polypropylene, polyethylene, nylon, and modacrylic. Rayon is also used in large quantities for disposables. Smaller quantities of polyester, cotton, acetate, vinyon, and modacrylic are also utilized in disposables.

Future Directions for Nonwovens

Relatively new processes allow the manufacturer to create fabrics directly from synthetic solutions, avoiding even the steps of fiber spinning and drawing. These processes have obvious economic advantages in that, when steps are eliminated in manufacturing, costs are decreased.

Hercules manufactures a plastic netting material from high-density polyester or polypropylene. A film is extruded, embossed, and then stretched. During stretching, the fabric breaks into an open-work pattern of interconnected, thin bars. A variation of the embossing pattern is used to create a wide variety of patterns. Delnet® is the trademark for these fabrics.

In another of these processes, known as *melt blowing*, a molten polymer is extruded through a row of spinneret holes. Hot airstreams are directed in such a way that they cause the polymer to form into filaments and, at the same time, deposit them in a random web that can be bonded together at once, or later, as the manufacturer chooses.

Another process uses polyamide film that is programmed to break into continuous filaments or into an interconnecting filament network after drawing and heat treating the film.

Forecasts indicate that the quantities of nonwovens produced from dry staple fibers are likely to decrease, while those made by spun-bonding, spun-laced, and melt-blown processes are expected to increase.[3] At the present time, the manufacture of nonwovens utilizes existing man-made fibers. The future development of this industry is likely to lead to

[3]"Non-wovens: A Major Role, No Longer a Bit Player," *Textile Industries*, 148, No. 12 (December 1984), p. 38.

the synthesis of fibers that are engineered specifically for nonwovens. This will improve the quality of nonwoven goods. Although no one anticipates that nonwovens will ever totally replace woven goods, consumers will find an increasing quantity and variety of nonwoven goods from which to select in both disposable and durable items.

Nets

Nets are created by looping and knotting a continuous strand of yarn into an open mesh. In use since prehistoric times for trapping fish, birds, and other small animals, nets also have a long history as a decorative fabric. Egyptian burial chambers, for example, contained fabric made from open-work net with embroideries of pearls and precious stones.

Most netted fabrics are made with either a square or diamond-shaped mesh. The hand process is a fairly simple one of looping and knotting to form an open-work fabric. The decorativeness of the net can be increased by embroidering designs on the open mesh. The terms *filet* work or *lacis* are applied to decorated nets, and they are often classified as a type of lace. (See Figure 17.12.)

Machine-made nets are manufactured on a bobbinet lace machine. Raschel or compound needle tricot knitting machines also produce fabrics similar in appearance but with different structures. Net fabrics range from lightweight tulles to heavy fishing nets.

Macramé

Macramé might be considered as a variation of the principle used in making nets. Like netting, macramé uses the techniques of looping and knotting yarns. Unlike netting, however the decorative qualities of macramé are determined by the selection and use of a variety of ornamental knots. In netting, it is the open area that is important. In macramé the closed or knotted areas are emphasized.

The word *macramé* seems to be Arabic in origin, and the process itself probably was brought to Europe from the Arab world. Like filet or lacis, macramé may be classified as a lace. Its first use was in finishing off the unwoven yarns at the end of a fabric. In time, macramé was constructed separately and attached to linens or garments in the same way that other trimmings were sewn into place.

The first major surge of interest in macramé came during the seventeenth century during a period of emphasis on lace making in general. Since that time macramé has experienced periods of great favor and periods of relative obscurity. During the nineteenth century, it was an important decoration for clothes and household items, and fashion magazines of the 1800s are filled with instructions for macramé work. Macramé was not used widely during the early 1900s, but since the late 1960s there has been a resurgence of interest in the technique.

Nets, Macramé, and Lace

FIGURE 17.12. Examples of lacis or embroidered net fabric from the sixteenth century. Courtesy of the Metropolitan Museum of Art. Gift of Mrs. Magdalena Nuttall.

Since macramé does not require specialized tools, it can be made with a minimum of equipment. During the eighteenth and nineteenth centuries sailors on whaling ships often occupied their spare time in making macramé items that they bartered when they reached port.

The yarns or cords that are to be used in macramé are fastened to a holding cord, which in turn is clamped or pinned securely so that the cords will not slip. For complex work, the yarns are wound onto bobbins so that they do not become entangled. The work is done by creating a variety of knots that join the cords at different intervals. Placement of the knots and judicious selection of the type of knots make possible the creation of a variety of textures and decorative effects. Macramé is essentially a handcraft technique. (See Figure 17.13.)

FIGURE 17.13.   Macramé fabric, knotted from ivory cotton in the late nineteenth century. Courtesy of the Philadelphia Museum of Art. Given by Mrs. Edward F. Bailey, 1955.

Lace

Because of its delicate beauty, lace has been one of the most sought after of fabrics. The precise origins of lace making are unknown, but its development was related not only to knotting and netting but also to embroidery. Among the earliest lacelike fabrics were those that were called *drawn work*. In drawn work, individual yarns were unraveled from a woven fabric, and embroidery stitches were used to fasten groups of these yarns together into a decorative pattern. *Cut work* was also a forerunner of lace. In cut work, areas of fabric are cut out to form a pattern, and the raw edges around the open areas are embroidered both to prevent them from fraying and to add decoration. Ornamentation can be increased by throwing threads across the open area to form geometric patterns by weaving in and out or by embroidering over the threads that bridged the gap.

Although fabrics decorated by each of these techniques bear certain similarities to lace, true lace making dispensed with the base fabric and created the design from the threads alone. Laces are generally divided into two categories, according to their construction. One is called *needlepoint lace*, the other *bobbin lace.*

Needlepoint lace, which is slightly older than bobbin lace, probably originated in Venice sometime prior to the sixteenth century.[4] In making needlepoint laces, the design for the lace was first drawn on parchment or heavy paper. A piece of heavy linen was sewn to the back of the parchment to hold it straight. Threads were then laid along the lines of the pattern and basted lightly onto the parchment and linen. None of these threads was attached to any other. The lace was created by embroidering over the base threads with decorative stitches. These embroideries connected the base threads. The areas between the threads could also be filled in with fancy needlework, according to the requirements of the pattern. When the embroidery was complete, the basting threads that held the lace to the paper were clipped and the finished lace was released.

Bobbin lace or, as it is also termed, *pillow lace* uses twisted and plaited threads. It is more closely related to netting and to knotting, whereas needlepoint lace stems more from embroidery. Again the design is drawn on stiff paper. Holes are pricked into the paper in the area of the pattern. This pattern is then stretched over a pillow and small pins are placed at close intervals through the holes in the paper. The pins go through the paper and into the pillow. The thread is wound onto bobbins, and the threads are worked around the pins to form meshes, openings, and closed areas. Bobbin lace seems to have originated in Flanders or Belgium. (See Figure 17.14.)

The techniques for making both bobbin lace and needlepoint lace quickly spread throughout Europe. Each town developed its own style

---

[4]S. L. Goldenberg, *Lace, Its Origin and History* (New York: Brentano's, 1904), p. 2.

of lace, which had its traditional patterns and construction features. It is this localization of design that has given us the names for most laces. Chantilly lace, for example, was first made in the French city of Chantilly, Venice point lace originated in Venice, and Val lace was first made in Valenciennes, France.

In describing the construction of laces, certain basic terms are employed. It may be helpful to define several of the most important words from this vocabulary. Definitions are adapted from *Encyclopedia of Textiles, American Fabrics* (Englewood Cliffs, N.J.: Prentice-Hall, Inc., 1980), p. 558.

Allovers—Relating to the design that covers the body of net, as distinguished from motifs or borders.

Baby—A term for narrow or light laces.

Bars or *Brides*—Connecting threads ornamenting open spaces in lace.

Bead edge—A series of looped threads edging a lace.

Cordonnet—The cord outline applied to a pattern.

Fillings—Fancy stitches employed to fill in open spaces.

Ground—The net serving as a foundation for patterns or designs on lace.

Guipure—The term applied to heavy work. The word itself derives from *guipe*, a cord around which the silk is rolled.

Insertion—A strip of lace inserted as a band between other materials.

Picot—Tiny loops or knots worked on the edges of a design.

Among the best known and most widely used types of lace are the following:

Alençon, a needlepoint lace that originated in France. The lace has a sheer net background with a solid design outlined in cord.

Binche, bobbin lace from Belgium. The ground has a six-pointed star-shaped ground net that is sprinkled with snowflake like figures.

Carrickmacross, an Irish lace, the ground of which is knotted hexagonals with appliquéd lawn pieces. The edges of the appliqué are covered by buttonhole embroidery stitches.

Chantilly, French lace with a fine ground in which designs are outlined in heavy thread. At one time the lace was made of silk, but now it is made in rayon, nylon, and mercerized cotton as well.

Cluny, medium- to heavyweight bobbin lace that originated in France. The designs are often of a wheel, wheat ear, bat wing, or poinsettia design.

Milanese, bobbin lace originating in Italy with a strong pattern that is made with tapes joined into patterns by fine mesh and with picot edging.

Rose point, A Venetian-type needlepoint lace with strong relief cordonnet.

Venetian point, needlepoint lace not connected by mesh. The edge of the lace has an irregularly placed picot finish.

Valenciennes, flat bobbin lace that originated in France. Popular for edgings, the lace has a mesh ground often with a scroll or floral design.

The production of lace by machine began soon after 1800. Although an earlier machine had had good success in producing manufactured nets, machine-made laces were not perfected until John Leavers invented a machine that could make as much lace in one day as a skilled handworker would produce in six months.[5] Only an expert can tell the difference between machine- and hand-made lace. Most modern laces are produced by machine, on the Leavers machine. Knitted laces may be made on the Raschel machine, and some lacelike embroidered fab-

[5]F. R. Schwab, *The Story of Lace and Embroidery* (New York: Fairchild Publications, Inc., 1951), p. 10.

rics are produced by the Schiffli machine. Schiffli fabrics, however, are not true laces; rather, they are embroidered, woven fabrics.

Crochet

The origins of crochet are obscure. The technique of creating fabric by pulling one loop of yarn through another with a hook was brought to the United States by Irish immigrants of the nineteenth century. The craft was evidently practiced in Irish convents as an efficient means of copying lace fabrics. During the potato famine of the 1840s, the nuns taught many poor Irish women to crochet so that they could supplement the family income. When these families came to America, they brought Irish crochet with them, and soon women throughout the United States had learned to crochet.

Crocheting is closely related to knitting. Both join together a series of interlocked yarn loops into a variety of open and/or closed patterns. Crochet is made with a single needle or hook, whereas knitting uses several needles.

Recommended References

"Bark Fabrics," *CIBA Review* (May 1940).

Bogdanovic, B. "Medical/Hospital Nonwovens: An Indispensible Industry Becoming More Important," *Nonwovens Industry*, 16 (February 1985), p. 18.

Bouda, F. J. "An Overview: Nonwoven Sanitary Absorbent Products," *Nonwovens Industry*, 16 (January 1985), p. 9.

Conley, J. T. "Modern Air Forming," *Nonwovens Industry*, 15 (March 1984), p. 68.

Di Stefano, F. V. "Chemical Bonding of Air Laid Webs," *Nonwovens Industry*, 16 (June 1985), p. 16.

"Felt," *CIBA Review*, No. 129 (November 1958).

Floyd, K. L. "Nonwoven Fabrics," *Textiles*, 6 (February 1977), p. 21.

Frasier, A. F. "Applications of Nonwoven Materials in the Aerospace Industry," *Nonwovens Industry*, 13 (December 1982), p. 20.

Guide to Nonwoven Fabrics. New York: Association of the Nonwoven Fabrics Industry, 1978.

Harvey, V. *Macramé*. New York: Van Nostrand Reinhold Co., 1967.

Heydt, D. L., and W. E. Cowan. "New Trends in Stitch-bonding Technology," *America's Textiles*, 12 (October 1983), p. 43.

Holliday, T. M. "Needlepunched Nonwovens," *Nonwovens Industry*, 15 (March 1984), p. 54.

Holliday, T. M. "Stitchbonding—Alive and Well," *Nonwovens Industry*, 15 (February 1984), p. 16.

"Interlinings to Rooftops: Non-wovens Are There," *Textile World*, 134 (February 1984), p. 45.

"Lace," *CIBA Review*, No. 73 (April 1949), pp. 2670 ff.

Melen, L. *Knotting and Netting*. New York: Van Nostrand Reinhold Co., 1971.

"Needlepunched Nonwovens" (entire issue), *Nonwovens Industry*, 16 (March 1985).

"Nonwovens in Geotextiles" (entire issue), *Nonwovens Industry*, 16 (August 1985).

"Non-wovens: A Major Role, No Longer a Bit Player," *Textile Industries*, 148 (December 1984), p. 35.

SCHWAB, F. R. *The Story of Lace and Embroidery*. New York: Fairchild Publications, Inc., 1951.

SHIELDS, M. "Textiles for Road Vehicles," *Textiles*, 13 (Summer 1984), p. 50.

SIMON, R. "Out of Whole Cloth," *Forbes*, 133 (August 9, 1984), p. 144.

"Special Supplement on Non-woven Technology," *Daily News Record* (July 1, 1985).

"Technology Intensifies in Non-wovens Industries," *Textile Industries*, 148 (July 1984), p. 47.

WARD, D. "Spunbondeds," *Modern Textiles*, 57 (April 1976), p. 29.

Adding Color to Textiles

Most objects made by human beings are decorated in some way. Textiles are no exception. The decoration of textiles may be achieved through varying the construction of the fabric, by adding color through dyeing, or by applying color in patterns by printing.

Even the earliest fabrics excavated by archeologists show evidence of ornamentation, through the use of natural fibers of contrasting colors or by embroidery or dyes. Cave paintings made by prehistoric peoples of at least twenty-five thousand years ago clearly demonstrate that these people knew how to make pigment colors from natural materials. Pottery from many cultures was painted with designs. Probably the first addition of color to fabrics was made by painting designs on the cloth.

Dyeing

Natural Dyestuffs

The paints used on pottery or stone were not always serviceable on fabrics, but certain substances did have a particular affinity for cloth. These dyestuffs came from a wide variety of animal, vegetable, and mineral matter. The difficulty with most of the natural dyestuffs was that they lacked colorfastness. As a result, those dyes that proved to have excellent colorfastness became important items of international trade.

Few of these early dyes could be relied upon to produce strong colors on all fibers. The coloring of fibers results from the chemical reaction of the functional groups within the fibers and those within the dyestuff. The varying chemical composition or structure of the natural fibers caused each to react differently with the chemicals in each of the dyestuffs. The treatment of the fabrics with certain natural acids or oxides did, however, improve their colorfastness. These substances, called *mordants*, react both with the dyestuff and with the fiber to form an insoluble compound, thereby "fixing" the color within and on the fiber. The effect of mordants probably was discovered accidentally when it was realized that washing undyed fabrics in the water of some streams (those high in certain metallic compounds) resulted in their taking and holding colors better.

Some mordants were more effective on animal fibers such as silk and wool; others were preferable for cotton and linen. Those who worked in the dyer's trades developed skill in utilizing mordants to make fabrics of fairly good colorfastness, although it was not possible to obtain consistently excellent colorfastness until after the invention of synthetic dyes in the nineteenth century.

There were many sources of natural dyes. Vegetable dyes could be made from flowers, leaves, berries, barks, roots, grasses, weeds, vines, and lichens. The most famous of the traditional dyes made from plants included woad, indigo, madder, fustic, logwood, cutch, and safflower. The woad plant was cultivated in European villages for its blue color made from the bark of the plant. Its production continued from Roman times until the end of the Middle Ages, when woad was supplanted by indigo, a blue dye imported from India. The compound in the woad plant that creates the blue color is present in much greater concentrations in indigo. Madder was a source of reds, but it also had the peculiar quality of producing several different colors or color intensities when it was employed in combination with different mordants. The chemical reaction of the metallic salts in the various mordants with the chemical compound in madder resulted in colors that ranged from yellow to rose to red. Fustic for yellow, logwood and cutch for browns, and safflower for red were other widely known dyes. By combining the primary colors of red, blue, and yellow, it was possible to create additional colors in the green, purple, and orange ranges. A good, fast, dark black was exceedingly difficult to achieve.

Some iron oxides were employed, but in general mineral colors were less often used than were plant or animal substances. Animal sources provided some of the most effective dyestuffs. Kermes, a brilliant scarlet dyestuff, was obtained in ancient times from the bodies of small insects that lived in oak trees. This dye was replaced by cochineal, small insects that are native to South America and that had been used by the Indians as a dyestuff for many centuries. This cochineal bug, which became a major item of trade between the New and Old Worlds, produced a vivid red of excellent fastness.

The color purple has been associated with royalty for centuries. The origins of this association are based on the production of Tyrian purple, a color made from the juice secreted by a small shellfish. The technique for making the dye was known as early as 1000 B.C. and required a lengthy and complex series of steps. First, the dye was "milked" from the shellfish. This white liquid, as it oxidized, turned from milky white to green, to red, to deep purple. Careful control of the color range could be used to produce a wide range of red-purple colors, the most desirable being a deep, rich red-purple. Because the process was time consuming and difficult and the supply of the dye limited, fabrics dyed with Tyrian purple were very costly and therefore available only to the rich and, in particular, to the nobility. Royalty eventually gained a monopoly on the color, and so it has come to be known as "royal purple."[1]

Synthetic Dyes

William Perkin, an English chemist, discovered that a coal tar derivative, *aniline*, colored white silk. After further experimentation, Perkin was able to make a dyestuff that had potential commercial application. It was a reddish-purple in color, called mauve.

Perkin's discovery in 1856 stimulated additional research with other coal tar derivatives and related compounds, and the synthesis of a wide range of man-made dyestuffs resulted. Gradually an enormous range of synthetic dyes made from many chemical substances was developed. These have almost completely replaced natural dyes for commercial production.

The selection of dyestuffs for coloring fabrics is a decision requiring the attention not only of the highly trained dye technician but also of designers, stylists, and business managers who are knowledgeable about current fashion trends. Although some types of dyed fabrics can be bleached and redyed another color, or designs printed over plain-colored fabrics, dyeing a fabric to an unpopular color may spell financial disaster for a manufacturer of piece goods.

In addition, the choice of hue is only the first of many decisions about adding color to fabrics. It must be decided at what point the color will be added and the type of dyestuff that will be used.

Each fiber reacts differently to dyestuffs; therefore, the use of an appropriate dye is crucial to colorfastness. Since loss of color in use is a major source of consumer dissatisfaction, reputable manufacturers must choose dyes carefully.

Color is one of those areas in which the chemistry of textiles is most important. Although this text does not explore the complex chemical reactions that take place in dyeing, it is important to think of both the fiber and the dyestuff as chemical substances. The combination of fiber with dyestuff is a chemical as well as a physical reaction.

Types of Dyeing

Color may be added to fabric at any one of four steps in its processing. Color can be added to man-made fibers before the fiber is extruded, or dyes can be applied to fibers, to yarns, or to constructed fabrics or finished products.

---

[1]P. Gerhard, "Emperor's Dyes of the Mixtecs," *Natural History*, 73 (January 1964), pp. 26ff.

Addition of Color Before Extrusion

When color is added to man-made fibers before they are extruded, the fibers are known as *solution-dyed* or *dope-dyed* fibers. Pigment is dispersed throughout the liquid fiber solution. When the fiber is extruded, it carries the coloring material as an integral part of the fiber.

This "locked-in" color is extremely fast to laundering (i.e., it will not diminish); however, such colors can be sensitive to light and bleaching or may fade. The range of colors in which solution dyeing is done is rather limited for economic reasons. The fiber manufacturer must produce substantial quantities of fiber to justify the expense of adding an extra step during the manufacturing process. Furthermore, fiber production takes place well in advance of the time when fabrics reach the market. Fashion color trends may change fairly rapidly, so that, by the time a solution-dyed fabric reaches the market, the color may be out of fashion and not salable. For this reason, solution-dyed fabrics are generally produced in basic colors.

Solution dyeing is used on acetate to prevent gas fading. Gas fumes in the air may turn some blue or green dyes used for acetate to pink or brown.

The following is a list of some of the registered trademarks of some fibers that are solution dyed and the companies that manufacture them.

Camalon®—nylon	Sunshine Cordage Corporation
Chromespun®—acetate	Eastman Kodak Company
Coloray®—rayon	Courtaulds North America, Inc.
Kolorbon®—rayon (staple)	American Enka Company
Marvess CG®—olefin	Phillips Fibers Corp.

Addition of Color to Fibers

Fibers may be colored in the fiber state. When color is added at this point, this process is known as *fiber dyeing* or *stock dyeing*.

Loose (usually staple) fibers are immersed in a dyebath, dyeing takes place, and the fibers are dried. This is a relatively expensive type of dyeing because it takes longer to dye the fibers than it would to dye a comparable quantity of yarn or fabric, and because the cost of reopening fibers after dyeing is higher. It does achieve a high level of dye penetration into the fiber, and fibers tend to take up the dye evenly.

Stock-dyed fibers are most often used in tweed or heather effect materials in which delicate shadings of color are produced by combining fibers of varying colors. (See Figure 18.1.) Fiber-dyed fabrics can be identified by untwisting the yarns to see whether the yarn is made up of a variety of different colored fibers. In solid-colored yarns, untwisted stock-dyed fibers will be uniform in color, with no darker or lighter areas.

FIGURE 18.1. Multicolored spots of fiber-dyed fibers are used in this tweed fabric.

Fibers for worsted fabrics are sometimes made into a sliver before they are dyed. This variation of fiber dyeing is known as *top dyeing*. By dyeing the fibers after they have been combed, the manufacturer avoids the wasteful step of coloring the short fibers that would be removed in the combing process.

Yarn Dyeing

If color has not been added either to the solution or the fiber, it can be applied to the yarns before they are made into fabrics. Usually yarns are dyed to one solid color, but in a variant of the technique called *space dying*, yarns may be dyed in such a way that color-and-white or multicolored effects are formed along the length of the yarn.

Many types of fabrics utilize yarn of differing colors to achieve a particular design. Stripes in which contrasting sections of color alternate in the length or crosswise direction, chambrays in which one color is-used in one direction and another color is used in the other direction, complex dobby or Jacquard weaves, and plaids may all require yarns to which color has already been added.

Yarns may be dyed in skeins, in packages, or on beams. (Figure 18.2.) Special dyeing equipment is required for each of these processes. In skein dyeing, large, loosely wound skeins of yarn are placed in a vat for dyeing. Package dyeing utilizes a number of perforated tubes or springs into which the yarn is wound. The dye is circulated around and

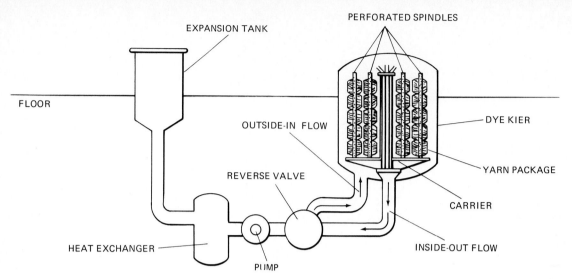

EXPANSION TANK

PERFORATED SPINDLES

FLOOR

OUTSIDE-IN FLOW

REVERSE VALVE

HEAT EXCHANGER

PUMP

DYE KIER

YARN PACKAGE

CARRIER

INSIDE-OUT FLOW

FIGURE 18.2 *Package dyeing of yarns.*
Courtesy of Badische Company.

through the tubes to assure that the yarns have maximum contact with the dyestuff. Beam dyeing is a variation of package dyeing, which uses a larger cylinder onto which a set of warp yarns is wound.

Yarn-dyed fabrics may be identified by unraveling several warp and several filling yarns from the pattern area to see whether they differ in color. Not only will each yarn be a different color, but the yarns will have no darker or lighter areas where they have crossed other yarns. (See Figure 18.3.)

FIGURE 18.3 *Gingham fabric in which the design is achieved by alternating rows of yarn-dyed yarns in the warp and filling directions.*

Piece Dyeing

Fabrics that are to be a solid color are usually piece dyed. In piece dyeing, the finished fabric is passed through a dye bath in which the fabric absorbs the dyestuff. A number of different methods are used for piece dyeing, each of which has some slight differences in the way in which the fabric is handled.

Fabrics may be dyed either continuously or in batches. In continuous dyeing, the cloth continually passes through the dyestuff. Where possible this method is used for dyeing large yardages. Batch dyeing is used for shorter fabric lengths, for yarn dyeing, and for dyeing individual items such as hosiery. Some fabrics are dyed in open, flat widths. Knitted fabrics and those woven materials that are not subject to creasing are handled in "rope" form, that is, bunched together and handled as a narrower strand. Some of these methods are especially suitable to certain types of fabrics and unsuitable for others. Many different kinds of machines can be used for piece dyeing.

Beck, box, or *winch dyeing* is frequently used in batch dyeing wool fabrics and knits, as it places relatively little tension on the fabric during dyeing. (See Figure 18.4.) Fabric is formed into an endless, circular chain and is rotated through the dye. Up to twelve ropes of fabric can be dyed side-by-side at the same time. Devices in the machine keep the ropes separate.

Jet dyeing is a relatively new method of dyeing that utilizes jet propulsion to improve dye penetration. Dyeing takes place in a closed system that carries a fast-moving stream of pressurized dye liquor.

A fluid jet of dye penetrates and dyes the fabric. After it passes through this jet, the fabric is floated through an enclosed tube in which the fluid moves faster than the fabric. This prevents the fabric from touching the walls, keeping it constantly immersed in the dyebath. Turbulence is created by locating elbows in the tube. The turbulence aids in diffusing dyes and other chemicals. Since no pressure is put on the fabric, even very delicate fabrics can be dyed by this process. Jet dying has the advantage of being economical in operation and at the same time allowing a high degree of quality control. (See Figure 18.5.)

Jig dyeing is a process that places greater tension on the fabric than either of the aforementioned processes. Fabrics are stretched across two rollers that are placed above a stationary dyebath. At regular intervals, the fabric is passed through the dyebath. The tension created by placing the fabric on the rollers means that this process must be reserved for fabrics with a fairly close weave that will not lose their shape under tension.

Beam dyeing, which is used for lightweight, fairly open-weave fabrics, utilizes the same principle as beam dyeing of yarns. The fabric is wrapped around a beam and immersed in the dyebath. Tightly woven fabrics would not allow sufficient dye penetration; hence, the need to apply this method to loosely woven cloth. It has the added advantage

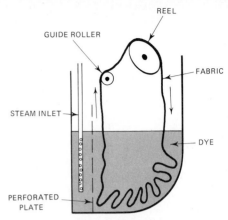

FIGURE 18.4   Sideview diagram of a typical dye beck showing movement of fabric through the dyebath. Courtesy of Badische Company.

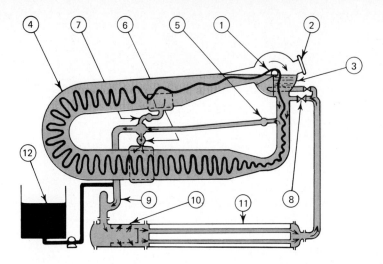

1. Fabric guide roll
2. Loading and unloading port
3. Header tank
4. "U" tube
5. Suction control
6. Suction control
7. Suction control
8. Delivery control
9. Main Pump
10. Filter
11. Heat exchanger
12. Service tank

FIGURE 18.5   Hiska jet-dyeing machine. Reprinted by permission of National Knitwear and Sportswear Association.

of not putting tension or pressure on the goods as they are processed. (See Figure 18.6.)

Pad dyeing is a continuous process used in producing large quantities of piece-dyed goods that can withstand tension and pressure. Fabrics pass through a dyebath, then through pads or rollers that squeeze out the excess dye, and then into a steam or heated chamber in which the dye is fixed or set.

Vacuum impregnation is a dye system introduced to improve the dyeing of heavyweight fabrics. Because of their thickness, it has been difficult to get good dye penetration of fabrics such as corduroy, sateens, and heavyweight ducks. Trapped air, caught in these denser fabrics, makes dyeing them difficult. In this vacuum system, the fabric comes into contact with a perforated stainless steel cylinder into which a vacuum pump draws air, while, at the same time, the dye liquor is applied to the fabric. This means that dye and fabric come into contact in a pressurized chamber, with the result that the dye penetrates the fabric more thoroughly. The vacuum system has been particularly useful in dyeing corduroy fabrics and other pile fabrics as it allows equal dye penetration of both the pile and the ground fabric.

Foam dyeing is a continuous process for applying color to the surface of fabrics. Currently used on a limited basis in the carpet industry, foam dyeing has been compared to "spreading colored shaving cream over the face of the carpet." The foam bubbles break down and deposit dye liquor over the surface of the fabric. The advantage of foam dyeing is

FIGURE 18.6 Beam dyeing of fabric. Courtesy of Allied Corporation Fibers Division.

that even though the material being dyed must be wet before foam application, the wet pickup is much reduced, and less time and energy are required to dry the dyed carpet. Foam can be applied in different colors and in selected areas to create designs. Only those dyestuffs that use a wet fixation technique can be applied through the foam process; therefore, neither vat nor sulfur dyes can be applied.

Cross-dyeing

The increased use of blended fabrics, that is, fabrics composed of two or more different fibers, has created problems for the dyer and yet has presented new techniques to use. Dyeing of piece goods is less expensive than is fiber or yarn dyeing. Cross-dyeing utilizes piece-dyeing techniques to produce a multicolored fabric, thereby decreasing the higher costs of production that are entailed in yarn or fiber dyeing.

Each fiber responds to dyeing in a different way. Because of the differences in the chemical composition of fibers and different dyestuffs, there are dyes that are specific to certain fibers or fiber groups. For example, there are dyes that will be effective on nylons, but not on acrylics, or dyes that will color silk, but not polyester. By mixing several dyes in one dyebath, each of which is specific to one fiber, the manufacturer can pass a blended fabric through a single dyebath, and each fiber will pick up only its specific dye. For example, if a black/red/gray tweed effect using a blend of rayon, acrylic, and nylon fibers, is desired, the fabric could be passed through a dyebath in which there was a black dye specific to rayon, a red specific to acrylics, and a gray specific to nylon. The resulting fabric would be made up of back rayon, red acrylic, and gray nylon fibers. Plaids or stripes can be created by alternating yarns of different fibers, so that, for instance, nylon yarns are dyed red and polyester yarns are dyed blue to make a blue and red stripe.

Union Dyeing

Conversely, the dyer has difficulty in piece dyeing solid-colored, blended fabrics because each fiber takes up the dye differently. It is sometimes necessary for the dyer to select several different types of dyes of the same color, mixing them together in the same dyebath, to achieve a uniform color in a fabric that is made of several different fibers. This type of piece dyeing is called union dyeing.

Tone-on-Tone Dyeing

A more subtle method of creating pattern with color is utilized in tone-on-tone fabrics. Here two different types of the same generic fiber might be used. Both types respond to the same type of dye, but one may be less reactive so that, for example, a lighter and darker shade of the same color results.

Dyestuffs and Colorfastness

The science of dyeing is highly complex, and the mechanisms of dyeing are not completely understood. This discussion is necessarily superficial, and does not provide an in-depth exploration of the subject. For additional background, readers may consult the references at the end of the chapter.

To be usable in coloring fabrics, dyes and pigments must have these properties: they must be highly colored and they must yield goods with resistance to color change or loss in use and care. This latter quality is known as *colorfastness*. Furthermore, dyes must be soluble or be capable of being made soluble in the medium in which they are to be applied or they must themselves be molecularly dispersible into the fibers. The medium most often used for dyes that require a solvent is water.

The rate of dyeing depends upon three factors. The first, the rate of migration of dye onto the fiber surface, is assisted by the agitation of the dyebath. The second, the rate of penetration of dye into the fiber, is generally fairly rapid in most cases; and the third, the rate of diffusion within the fiber itself, varies a good deal from one type of fiber to another.

Exhaustion is the rate of transfer of dye from the bath into the fiber. It is possible for all the dye to be removed from the bath and for the dyebath to be clear at the end of the process. *Leveling* is the depth of shade throughout the textile. Uneven leveling will result in a streaked appearance of the cloth.

A number of chemical reagents or auxiliaries are used in the dyeing process. These chemical auxiliaries act in a variety of ways, ranging from softening water or assisting with dye leveling to increasing dye solubility or the rate of penetration into the fiber. Substances that increase the acceptance of the dyestuff are called *mordants*. The temperature of the dyebath may also have an effect on the receptivity of the fiber to the dyestuff, although the optimum temperature will differ not only with the type of dye but also with the kind of fiber being dyed.

Once the dye has entered the fiber, it must be retained within the fiber not only during the dyeing but also when fabrics are laundered or dry-cleaned during use. Several mechanisms make for dye retention. In general, the number of chemically reactive sites in the fiber is the most crucial element in dyeability. Dyes may be physically bound to fibers by chemical forces such as hydrogen bonding, Van der Waals forces, or ionic forces. Ionic forces are created by the attraction between positively and negatively charged ions, one on the dye, the other on the fiber. The chemical structure of dyestuff and fiber may be such as to allow the formation of covalent chemical bonds between fiber and dye. Dyes may be carried in a temporary solvent that, when removed, leaves the dye stranded within the fiber.

Colorfastness

A fabric that retains its color during care and use is said to be *colorfast*. Fastness of dyestuffs is related to the chemical and physical forces holding the dye within the fiber, the stability of the combination of dye and fiber to environmental factors, and the location of the dye within the fiber. Small aggregates of dyestuff distributed evenly throughout the fiber makes for a more satisfactory result than does surface application of color.

Fabrics may be more or less colorfast to a variety of different substances or conditions. The importance of colorfastness depends on the use of the fabric. Colorfastness to laundering is, of course, important in those garments and household textiles that must undergo frequent laundering. Some colors are not fast to laundering but are fast to dry cleaning, or vice versa.

Perspiration may cause some color change and/or color transfer, and many colors are not fast to light. Ascertaining the colorfastness to sunlight of curtains, draperies, carpets, or other items that have prolonged exposure to sunlight may be important in evaluating the usefulness of fabrics for these items. Some colors may be lost or diminished by heat.

Some dyes tend to "crock" or rub off on fabrics or other materials with which they come in contact. Others will "bleed" into water during laundering and may be picked up by lighter-colored fabrics. Chlorine bleaches will remove color from most dyed fabrics, but some types of dyestuff are more sensitive than others to the action of chlorine bleaches.

Even dyes that belong to the same class of dyestuffs can have differing degrees of colorfastness to the same condition, so that the consumer has no real guarantee of permanence of color unless a label specifies that a particular fabric is colorfast. Dye performance labeling is not required by any form of legislation or regulation. Some manufacturers do, however, include colorfastness information on labels. Such labels will generally describe the conditions under which the fabric is colorfast, such as "colorfast to laundering, but not to chlorine bleaching" or "colorfast to sunlight." A few terms may be found on labels that carry an assurance of colorfastness, such as trademarks that have been applied to solution-dyed synthetic fibers. The colorfastness of one class of dyes, the *vat dyes*, is so consistently good for laundering that the term "vat dyed" on labels has come to be accepted as an assurance of good colorfastness.

A variety of tests has been developed to determine the colorfastness of fabrics. Fabrics can be tested to determine their colorfastness to laundering, dry cleaning, light, perspiration, and crocking. These tests are discussed in more detail in Chapter 24, Textile Testing and Standards.

Dye Classes

Dyestuffs are divided into a number of classifications. Within each of these classifications there exists a range of colors, and each of these colors may vary somewhat in its fastness to different conditions. The names given to the dye classes generally relate to the method of application and, to a lesser extent, the chemical composition of the dye class.

The ability of the fibers to accept each of these dye classes depends upon several factors. One is the availability of appropriate chemically reactive groups in both the fiber and the dyestuff, and the other is the chemical composition of the dye liquor. Dyes that must be applied in an alkaline medium, for example, are difficult to use on protein fibers because the alkalinity of the dyebath may harm the fiber. Likewise, dyebaths that are strongly acid may be harmful to cellulose fibers.

In the following discussion of specific dye classes, these classes are grouped according to the fiber types for which they are most widely (though not exclusively) used.

Dyes Most Often Used on Cellulosic Fibers

Azoic Dyes. Azoic dyes (also called naphthol dyes) are used primarily on cotton fibers, but they can also be applied to acetates, olefins, polyesters, and nylons. The reaction that produces dyeing takes place when two components, a diazonium salt and a naphthol compound, join together to form a highly colored, insoluble compound on the fabric.

These dyes are also known as "ice dyes" because the reaction takes place at lowered temperatures. Their colorfastness is good to laundering, bleaching, alkalis, and light. They do tend to crock somewhat, however. The color range is broad, although somewhat deficient in blues and greens.

Direct Dyes. Direct dyes are water-soluble dyes that are used primarily for cotton and rayon, although some polyamide and protein fibers are also dyed with these compounds. These dyes have the advantage of being applied directly in a hot aqueous dye solution in the presence of common salts required to stabilize the rate of dyeing, making the process relatively inexpensive. They also possess the disadvantage of poor fastness to laundering. An aftertreatment with copper salts is sometimes used to form a more stable dye compound. This improves colorfastness by forming a chemical compound of the dye molecule, the cellulose, and the copper salts. Other special finishes have also been developed to make the dye color more stable.

Vat Dyes. Vat dyes are insoluble in water. By chemical reduction they are converted to a soluble form. The dye is applied to the fibers, then the dye, now within the fiber, is reoxidized to the insoluble form. This creates a color that is fast to both light and washing.

Because vat dyes must be applied in an alkaline solution, they are not suitable for use with protein fibers. Primarily used with cottons and rayons, vat dyes are also used on acrylics, modacrylics, and nylon. These dyes provide a wide range of colors except for reds and oranges. Indigo is a vat dye.

Sulfur Dyes. Sulfur dyes produce mostly dark colors, such as black, brown, or navy. Applied in an alkaline solution to cottons and rayons, fabrics dyed with sulfur dyes must have carefully controlled processing or a buildup of excess chemicals on the fibers will eventually cause the fibers to be weakened. Colorfastness of sulfur dyes is good to washing and fair to light. Black and yellow sulfur dyes may accelerate light degradation of cellulosic fibers.

Reactive Dyes. In this class of dyes the dyestuff bonds chemically with the fiber. Reactive dyes are applied most commonly to the cellulosic fibers, cotton, viscose, and linen. Some colors are appropriate for use on wool. Wools that have been chlorinated, bleached, or shrink-proofed may present difficulties in colorfastness as they tend to have poor wetfastness. Reactive dyes can produce good wetfast colors on wool and on silk. Nylons and acrylics can be dyed to some shades with reactive dyes, although the dyes are difficult to apply evenly on synthetics. Colorfastness of these dyes is generally good to all types of use.

Dyes Used Primarily for Protein Fibers

Acid Dyes. Applied in an acid solution, acid dyes react chemically with the basic groups in the fiber structure. Because wool has both acid and basic groups in its structure, acid dyes can be used quite successfully on wools. These dyes are also utilized for dyeing nylon and to a lesser extent for acrylics, some modified polyesters, polypropylene, and spandex. Acid dyes cannot be used on cellulosic fibers because these fibers are susceptible to damage from acids. Colorfastness of acid dyes varies a good deal, depending on the color and the fiber to which the dye has been applied.

Chrome or Mordant Dyes. Used on the same general group of fibers as acid dyes, chrome or mordant dyes use a metallic salt that, when added to the dye molecule, reacts to form a relatively insoluble dyestuff with improved wet- and lightfastness. As the name of the dye indicates, chrome salts are most often used for the process, but salts of cobalt, aluminum, nickel, and copper can also be utilized. Especially effective for dyeing wool and silk, these dyes have excellent colorfastness to dry cleaning.

Dyes Used Primarily for Man-made Fibers

Basic Dyes. Basic dyes are alkaline in reaction because they contain amino groups. Since the reactive group is basic, they combine well with acid groups within fibers. The colored part of the dye molecule is positively charged (cationic). It was found that the positive ion in the dyestuff was strongly attracted to negatively charged ions in acrylic fibers, and as a result basic dyes are used in dyeing acrylic fibers. Modified nylon and polyester fibers can also be dyed with basic dyes. They had been used for coloring silk and cellulose acetate, but poor colorfastness has decreased their use.

The colors that these dyes produce are exceptionally bright. Unfortunately in natural fibers basic dyes have rather poor colorfastness to light, laundering, or perspiration. Recent developments of basic dyes for synthetics produce excellent colorfastness.

Disperse Dyes. Developed for coloring acetates, disperse dyes are now used to color many other man-made fibers. The dye is insoluble in water. Particles of dye disperse in the water without dissolving but, rather, dissolve in the fibers. Colors produced with these dyes cover a wide range and generally have good fastness. Blues, however, tend to be discolored by nitrous oxide gases in the atmosphere and may gradually fade to a pinkish color. Greens may fade to brown. This is known as "fume" fading. (See Chapter 5.)

Disperse dyes can be applied to a wide variety of fibers, including acetate, acrylic, aramid, modacrylic, nylon, olefin, polyester, saran, and triacetate. One author points out that disperse dyes are really the only practical means of coloring acetate, polyester, and triacetate fibers; most of the disperse dyes consumed today are used to dye these three fibers.[2] On acrylic fibers they are mostly used for pastel shades.

Disperse dyes can be applied in an aqueous solution, through a special process developed by DuPont called the Thermosol® process, and by heat transfer. (See Chapter 19 for discussion of heat transfer printing.) In the Thermosol® process no dyebath is used. Instead, the fabrics are padded with dye and are then passed through an oven. A partial vacuum is created inside the oven, which forces the dyestuff to migrate into the fibers.

Pigment Colors. Pigment colors are not soluble, cannot penetrate fiber surfaces, and therefore must be attached to the surface of the fabric by a binder. A polymeric resin serves as the binder. When the resin is "cured" or permanently fixed to the fabric, the dye is also fixed on the fabric surface. The colorfastness of pigment colors is dependent on the durability of the binder, not the pigment.

Fugitive Tints

Colors that are not permanent are sometimes called *fugitive tints*. In most dyeing processes, the manufacturer wishes to produce a color that is permanent and one that will not disappear in use or in processing. An exception is found in the use of fugitive tints such as Versatint®, a range of colors produced by Milliken Chemical Company.

These dyes are utilized to identify fibers or yarns during the manufacture of fabrics. By dyeing fibers or yarns of a particular generic type to a specific tint, the manufacturer has a readily identifiable color code. When the processing of the materials is complete, the manufacturer can remove the color by a simple wash, often in cold water.

ASPLAND, J. R. "What Are Dyes, What Is Dyeing?" *Textile Chemist and Colorist*, 12 (July, 1980), p. 24.

"Color and Textiles," *American Fabrics & Fashions*, No. 96 (Winter 1972), p. 43.

FAIRLIE, S. "Dyestuffs in the 18th Century," *Economic History Review*, 55 (April 1965), pp. 488 ff.

HUGHEY, C. S. "Indigo Dyeing: An Ancient Art," *Textile Chemist and Colorist*, 15 (June 1983), p. 13.

GRAFFIN, D. "Indigo," *American Fabrics & Fashions*, No. 112 (Spring 1977), p. 41.

Recommended References

[2]M. J. Schuler, "Dyeing with Disperse Dyes," *Textile Chemist and Colorist*, vol. 12 (August 1980), p. 33.

KAMRISCH, B. "Color in Clothing—Past and Present," *American Dyestuff Reporter*, 74 (March 1985), p. 15.

KRAMER, J. *Natural Dyes, Plants and Processes.* New York: Charles Scribner's Sons, 1972.

"The Magic of Fiber-mix Dyeing," *American Fabrics*, No. 79 (Summer 1968), p. 83.

McCONNELL, B. L. "A Survey of Yarn Dyeing Equipment," *Textile Chemist and Colorist*," 16 (June 1984), p. 13.

"Multi-Solid-Color Foam Dyeing Spreads Success," *Textile World*, 133 (February 1983), p. 59.

RABINOWITZ, B. "Dyeing with Acid Dyestuffs," *American Dyestuff Reporter*, 73 (February 1984), p. 26.

REAGEN, B. M. "Dyeing and Printing Basics," *Proceedings of the Association of College Professors of Textiles and Clothing*, 1982, p. 30.

SOMM, F., and R. BUSER. "Present and Future of Thermosol Dyeing," *American Dyestuff Reporter*, 73 (December 1984), p. 30.

STEVENS, C. B. "Recent Developments in Colourants and Colouration Methods," *Textile Month* (March 1976), p. 35.

Textile Chemist and Colorist (series of articles)
   "Dyeing with Acid Dyes," 12 (February 1980), p. 25.
   "Dyeing with Basic Dyes," 12 (March 1980), p. 42.
   "Dyeing with Direct Dyes," 12 (April 1980), p. 38.
   "Dyeing with Vat Dyes," 12 (May 1980), p. 38.
   "Dyeing with Sulfur Dyes," 12 (June 1980), p. 43.
   "Dyeing with Azoic Dyes," 12 (July 1980), p. 30.
   "Dyeing with Disperse Dyes," 12 (August 1980), p. 33.
   "Dyeing with Reactive Dyes," 12 (September 1980), p. 74.

TURNER, G. R. "New Developments in Carpet Dyeing," *Textile Chemist and Colorist*, 14 (October 1982), p. 13.

TURNER, G. R. "Textile Printing: The Changing Scene," *Textile Chemist and Colorist*, 17 (March 1985), p. 33.

Textile Printing and Design

Important decisions in the creation of a textile product must be made when its design and/or its color are chosen. Although many thousands of yards of fabrics are processed in solid colors, thousands more yards of fabric have designs applied through printing.

The application of a pattern to fabric by the use of dyes, pigments, or other colored substances may be effected by a variety of hand or machine processes. Free-hand painting of designs on fabrics is probably the oldest technique for applying ornament, but hand painting is a time-consuming procedure. Furthermore, it does not always result in a uniform repeat of a motif that is to be used more than once. If a design is transferred to a flat surface that can be coated with a dye and then stamped onto the fabric, the same design can be repeated many times over simply by pressing the decorated surface against the fabric. This process is known as *printing*. Over many centuries, a variety of techniques for printing designs have evolved. Printing can be applied to warp yarns, to fabrics, or to apparel pieces—for example, slogans or pictures on T-shirts.

Early Forms of Printing

Block Printing

Block printing appears to be the most ancient of these techniques. Some experts assign a date of 2000 B.C. to printed fabrics from the Caucasus in Russia. Blocks that were used in printing textiles have been recovered from Egyptian graves of the fourth century A.D.[1] This is the simplest of the printing techniques and requires only a limited technology. A block of material (usually wood) has a design drawn on one flat

---

[1]R. Haller, "The Technique of Early Cloth Printing," *CIBA Review*, No. 26 (October 1939), p. 933.

side. The design is carved by cutting away the spaces between the areas that form the pattern, thus placing the design in a raised position. (See Figure 19.1) Color is applied to the surface of the block, and the block is pressed onto the cloth. Anyone who has ever made a potato or linoleum print should recognize the technique. Sometimes during printing, the block was tapped with a mallet to assure complete contact of the block with the fabric.

To make the best possible print, the dye had to be in a viscous or pastelike form; otherwise, the incised areas would have been filled in by the water dye substance and the block would not have carried sufficient dye to make a clear image.

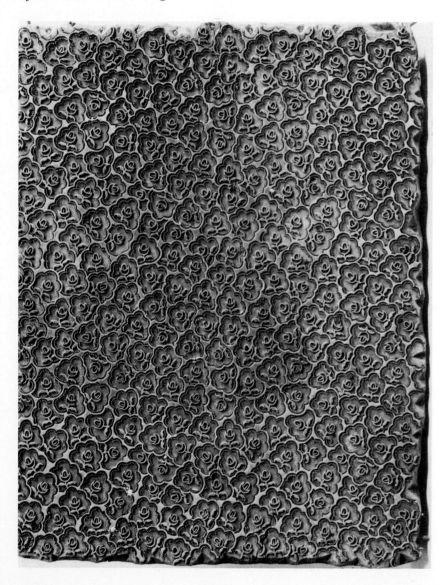

FIGURE 19.1 Woodblock used for printing textiles. This block was made in the eighteenth century. Courtesy of the Metropolitan Museum of Art. Gift of C. P. and J. Baker, 1927.

Mordant Printing

Inventive printers found another means of combining printing and dyeing to add color patterns to fabrics. Colorfastness without mordanting was very poor. The printer learned to print the mordant onto the surface of the fabric and then to pass the entire cloth into the dyebath. The mordanted areas absorbed the dye permanently; the rest of the cloth picked up dye only on the surface. When the fabric was rinsed after the dyebath, the dye washed out of the unprinted areas and left a colorful design on the section that had been impregnated with the mordant.

By using different mordant materials, different colors could be produced from the same dyestuff. Madder was especially useful in this respect. When the dyer printed the surface with several different mordants, immersed the fabric in the dyebath, and rinsed away the excess dye, a fabric printed with two or three different colors resulted. This process was evidently used in Egypt during Roman times. The Roman writer Pliny describes a mysterious process in which an "invisible ink" (the mordant) was painted onto fabric and the fabric passed through another solution (the dye). After rinsing, a multi-colored fabric "magically" appeared.[2]

Resist Printing

In resist printing, a substance coats the fabric in preselected areas, thus preventing the fabric from absorbing dye in the areas. Resist materials have included starch, clay, and wax. The technique has been used to produce designs in textiles in many different cultures, including those of Persia, India, South America, Egypt, and the Far East. Although the pattern of the resist material can be said to be "printed" onto the fabric, the application of color takes place by dyeing, just as in mordant printing.

Batik

Today the best known wax-resist process is that used for the making of *batik*. The name batik originates in the Indonesian Archipelago where resist printing has become an important art form. An analysis of the batik method will show clearly how resist printing is done. Wax is applied to the areas that the printer does not want to dye. In Indonesia, a small, spouted cup with a handle is used to apply the wax. As the wax is heated, it melts and the liquid wax is poured from the cup or *tjanting* onto the cloth. When it hardens, the wax coats the fabric so that the dye cannot reach the fibers. (See Figure 19.2.)

If several colors are to be used, the process becomes somewhat more

---

[2]E. Lewis, *Romance of Textiles* (New York: Macmillan Publishing Company, 1937), p. 66.

FIGURE 19.2 *Indonesian woman uses tjanting for applying wax to a batik fabric. Courtesy of Exxon corporation.*

complex. For example, if a fabric is to be colored white, red, and blue, the artisan begins with a creamy-white cotton cloth. Those areas that are to remain white are coated with wax and the areas to be red are also covered. Only the area to be colored blue remains exposed. The fabric is now subjected to a blue dyebath, and the exposed areas take on the blue tint.

Next, the wax is boiled off and reapplied to the blue and white areas. The fabric is placed in red dyebath. Since both the blue and white areas are covered with wax, the red color penetrates only the uncovered areas of the design. After dyeing is complete, the fabric is treated with a fixative (a mordant) to make the colors fast, and a final rinse in hot water removes all traces of wax.

For faster production, a technique was devised whereby the wax could be printed onto the surface of the fabric with a device called a *tjap*. As in block printing, the design is carved on a tjap block. The block is dipped in wax, the block is pressed onto the fabric, and the molten wax is thus imprinted on the cloth. Well-to-do Indonesians look upon the tjap-printed fabrics as inferior in quality, although to the untrained eye they look much the same as those made with the *tjanting*.

Tie and Dye

Resist designs can be produced by the tie-and-dye method in which parts of the fabric are tightly wound with other yarns, or the fabric may be tied into knots in selected areas. When the fabric is placed in a dye bath, the covered or knotted areas are protected from the dye. Careful attention to the shape of the wrapping and the placement of the tied areas can produce intricate and attractive patterns. In Indian textiles, the tie-and-dye method is known as *bandanna*. (See Figure 19.3.)

FIGURE 19.3 A tie-dyed fabric. Courtesy of the Metropolitan Museum of Art. Gift of Fay Halpern, 1972.

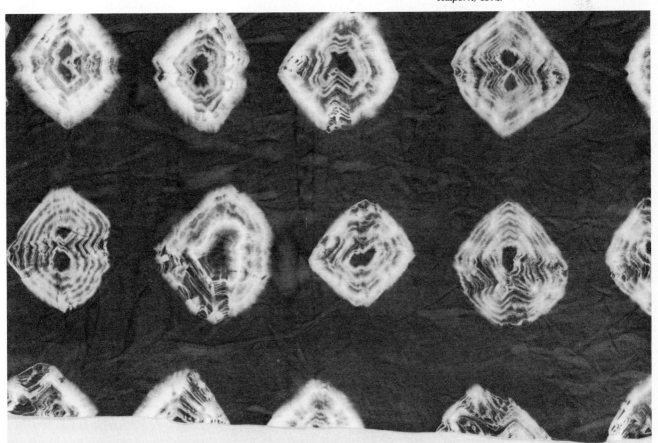

FIGURE 19.4 Ikat *fabric from the Dutch East Indies. The central portion of the fabric had the design applied to the warp yarns before the filling was inserted. Courtesy of the Metropolitan Museum of Art. Gift of Mrs. Delia Tyrwhitt, 1965.*

Ikat and Warp Printing

A complex and unusual variation of resist printing has been practiced in many places. The process, called *ikat*, required the weaver to prepare the warp yarns on the loom. Selected sections of the yarns were then covered with a resist material—wax, clay, or other yarns as in tie and dye. The warps were dyed, and the covered area did not absorb the dye. If a more complicated pattern were required, the warp yarns might be treated several times, as in the batik procedure. When dyeing was completed, the resist material was removed, and the filling was woven into place. This produced a fabric design of blurred, indistinct patterns. *Ikat* fabrics (Figure 19.4) often have a shimmering, soft quality that is very beautiful. The technique called *warp printing* grows out of the ancient *ikat* process. In warp printing, a design is printed onto the warp yarns by a roller printing device prior to the interlacing of the fillings. Warp prints have the same soft, shimmering patterns that are characteristic of *ikat* (See Figure 19.5.)

Block printing, batik, stenciling, and tie-dyeing are methods of color application used largely by either natives from Africa, South America, and the Orient or by persons using these techniques as hobbies or art forms. Such fabrics are sometimes produced commercially in small quantities, usually at very high prices.

FIGURE 19.5   Warp-printed silk fabric.

Screen Printing

Silk screen or screen printing is a method of applying colored design that is done either by hand or by an automated process. The fabric to be printed is spread out on a long table. A screen is prepared for each color of the design. At the time this procedure was developed, fine screens of silk were used; hence the name "silk screen printing." Today screens of synthetic fibers or metal mesh are more likely to be used.

A lacquer coating closes off all areas of the screen except the area in which one of the colors of the design is to be printed. For example, if a red rose with green leaves is to be printed, one screen is made that closes off all but the red rose area, and another is made that closes off all but the green leaves.

The design is transferred to the screen, often by a photochemical process that utilizes the following steps.

1. The design for each color is photographed separately to make a photographic plate for that part of the design.
2. A screen for each color is coated with a photosensitive material. This material will serve to opaque or close out the sections of the screen that will not be penetrated by the dye.
3. The photographic plate for each section is held in contact with a coated screen.
4. A high-intensity light is directed through the photographic plate to the screen. Those areas exposed to the light are changed chemically by action of the light on the plate, making it possible to wash out these sections. The unexposed areas remain opaque.
5. A layer of lacquer is placed over the opaque areas for additional reinforcement.

The printer takes the screen for one color, which is mounted on a frame, and places it in the correct position above and against the fabric. Dye paste is coated on the top of the screen, the fabric is underneath. A squeegee is run across the screen and presses the dye through the open area of the screen, onto the fabric. To color the next section of the fabric, the screen is moved farther along the fabric. After one color has been applied, a second color is added as are additional colors if they are required.

Hand screen printing is a slow process. Automation has been achieved in the manufacture of flatbed screen prints by making the frames stationary and moving the fabric along on a belt from screen to screen. The squeegee action, too, is done automatically. Flatbed screen printing machines can print from 10 to 15 meters per minute.[3] This is a limited production when compared with rotary screen printing and roller printing. (See Figure 19.6.)

[3]K. V. Datye and A. A. Vaida, *Chemical Processing of Synthetic Fibers and Blends* (New York: John Wiley & Sons, Inc., 1984), p. 353.

Industrial Printing Processes

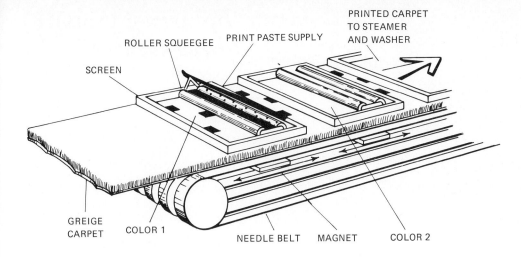

Flat-bed Zimmer carpet printing machine lays down each color separately from printing paste applied by means of two magnetic roller squeegees. Pressure is controlled by the selection of heavy or light squeegees and by varying the current going to the electromagnet. Endless belts fitted with needles assure a positive drive for good register.

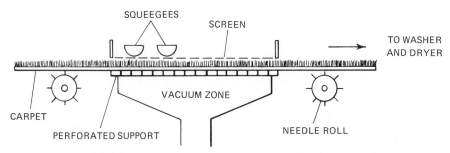

The BDA Screen printer uses a series of screens, one for each color; the basic unit is sketched above.

FIGURE 19.6 *Silk screen printing of carpets.*   *Courtesy of* Modern Textiles *magazine.*

Rotary Screen Printing

In addition to flatbed screen printing, a rotary screen printing technique has been developed that makes possible an output of quantities of 25 to 100 meters per minute. Instead of using a flat screen, screens are shaped into rollers. (See Figure 19.7.) As in the hand process, a screen is prepared for each color. The dye feeds through the unscreened area, pushed out from inside the roller by a squeegee. Fabrics move continuously under the rollers, and up to twelve colors may be printed on one fabric. The maximum length of the design repeat is limited to the circumference of the roller. The production of screens for rotary screen printing is less costly than the engraving of the heavy copper rollers used for roller printing, and the use of rotary screen printing techniques is increasing.

Roller Printing

Like rotary screen printing, roller printing utilizes a series of rollers, each imprinting a different color on the fabric. (See Figure 19.8.) Up to sixteen different colors can be used on one fabric. The length of the repeat (the interval at which the design is repeated) is determined by the diameter of the roller. Printing speeds of 100 to 150 meters per minute are possible.[4]

The rollers are made of copper, plated with chromium for durability. The design of each color is transferred accurately to the roller by one of several processes. In photoengraving, a photographic image of the

[4]Ibid.

FIGURE 19.7 Rotary screen printing machine. Each cylinder on the machine adds a different color and a different part of the total pattern. Courtesy of the American Textile Manufacturers Institute.

design is etched onto the roller, or a pantograph may be used to transfer the design from a flat surface to the roller. This device allows markings to be made on the roller simultaneously with the tracing of the design from a master design.

Once the rollers have been prepared, they are installed in exact position on the printing machine. The fabric to be printed moves over a rotating drum. Behind it is placed a layer of fabric that will absorb excess dye and keep it from being deposited on the drum. The design roller also rotates, moving against a rotary brush that rotates in a tray of print paste. This brush furnishes color to the roller. A *doctor blade* scrapes off excess dye from the roller, and the roller then rotates against the cloth and the design is imprinted. The fabric moves on to the second roller where a second color is imprinted, and so on, in a continuous printing operation.

Rollers must be aligned perfectly to keep the print in registration. If rollers are not positioned correctly, the resulting print will have one or more colors that do not fall in quite the correct position, causing the print to be distorted. The printed cloth is dried immediately and then passes to a chamber in which steam or heat sets the dye.

Roller printing is superior to other types of printing for fine or precise designs. However, roller printing requires skilled labor and much heavy manual work in the changing of the color troughs and rollers. The initial investment of time and money in the preparation of rollers for roller

FIGURE 19.8   Diagrammatic view of a roller printing system. Courtesy of Allied Chemical Corporation-Fibers Division.

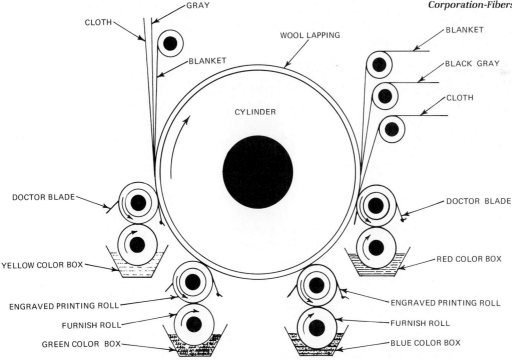

printing and in setting up the machine is such that production of small quantities of printed cloth is not economical. Roller printing is used more advantageously for lengthy runs of the same pattern.

Use of roller printing is declining in the United States. Rotary screen printing, by contrast, has overtaken roller printing and is continuing to increase.

Variations of Roller Printing

Duplex Printing. Duplex printing is done on a special machine that imprints designs on both sides of the fabric at the same time. Most often, the same design is printed on opposite sides, although different designs can be printed on each side. The resulting fabric looks like fabric with a woven design. This process is seldom used now, as it is almost as expensive to create duplex prints as it is to weave designs.

Blotch Prints. In blotch prints both a colored background and design motifs are printed onto the fabric. These prints should be differentiated from overprinting or printing of a design on a fabric that has already been piece dyed. Blotch prints can generally be distinguished from overprinting by a close examination of the fabric. Background colors of blotch-printed fabrics usually have a lighter color on the wrong side than on the right side of the fabric. Sometimes, too, minute, uncolored areas appear between the sections of background color and the design. Blotch prints can be made on either a rotary screen printing machine or on a roller printing machine. Blotch-printed fabrics made by screen printing may have better color penetration in background color areas than those made by roller printing.

Discharge Printing. Piece-dyed fabrics may be printed with a substance known as a *discharge paste* that removes color from specific areas of the fabric. Discharge printing is used only for small, light-colored or white designs on dark background. If fabrics are not processed carefully to remove all the discharge paste, these chemicals may eventually weaken the fabric in the areas from which color has been discharged. Discharge prints are recognizable because the color of the background design of the fabric is the same on both the front and back sides.

Flock Printing. By imprinting an adhesive material on the surface of a fabric in the desired pattern, and then sprinkling short fibers over the adhesive, a flocked print may be created. (See Figure 19.9.) Flocking as a type of finish is discussed at length in Chapter 20.

Resist Printing. Resist printing is a combination printing and dyeing method. A substance that resists dyes is printed onto the fabric in selected areas. Later, when the fabric is passed through the dyebath, the resist material prevents the fabric from absorbing the dye, thereby cre-

Figure 19.9   Flocked design printed on a sheer nylon fabric.

ating a design. This machine process follows the principle utilized in handmade batik fabrics.

Warp Printing. Warp yarns can be printed before they are woven into the fabric. The resulting fabrics have a delicate, shimmery quality that is achieved by the indistinct patterns created in warp printing. Warp printing is applied to higher-priced fabrics. (See Figure 19.5.)

Heat Transfer

Heat transfer or sublimation[5] printing is a system of printing in which dyes are printed onto a paper base and then transferred from the paper to a fabric. The transfer of colors takes place as the color sublimes through vaporization. This is achieved by rolling the paper and the fabric together under pressure and at high temperatures (424°F or 200°C). (See Figure 19.10.)

The system as generally applied, utilizes disperse dyes. Disperse dyes are effective only for some man-made fibers; therefore, heat transfer printing is most effective on nylons and polyesters. It can also be used on acrylics and triacetates and on polyester and cotton blends in which the proportion of polyester is relatively high. In spite of research into ways of using heat transfer printing on other fabrics, no commercially feasible processes have been developed.

[5]Sublistatic printing, a term often used in conjunction with heat transfer printing, is the trademark of the Sublistatic Corporation, a major producer of heat transfer printing paper.

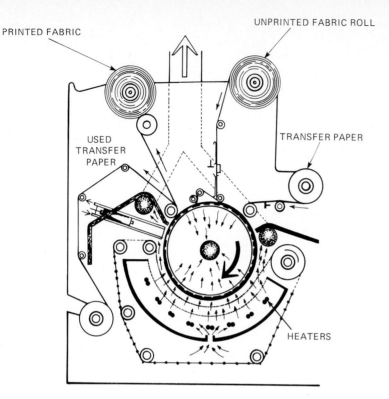

PRINTED FABRIC

UNPRINTED FABRIC ROLL

USED TRANSFER PAPER

TRANSFER PAPER

HEATERS

Figure 19.10   Heat transfer printing. This schematic diagram shows transfer-printing process. Unprinted fabric roll is at top to the right of the heat outlet. Gray fabric moves down to the drum where it is almost immediately joined by transfer paper from the right. The two pass through a bank of infrared heaters. Used transfer paper exits left and to the bottom, while printed fabric goes to roll at top left of the heat outlet. Schematic courtesy Textile World magazine. Copyright 1972 by McGraw-Hill, Inc.

Sublimation printing achieves a sharpness and clarity that other types of printing cannot match. All colors are printed at the same time, thereby simplifying the operation and requiring lower processing costs, with fewer personnel required. Production can change rapidly from one design to another simply by changing the design paper, whereas in roller or screen printing, each separate roller or screen must be removed from the machine and the machine set up for a new design with different rollers or screens. Short runs are feasible, fast deliveries are possible, given shorter time for processing, and companies need not keep costly inventories of fabric in stock.

Heat transfer printing has proved especially successful in printing knitted fabrics. Knitted goods are less dimensionally stable than are woven fabrics. Manufacturers using conventional screen and roller printing techniques on knit fabrics experienced difficulties in making multicolor prints in which the segments of the print must fit together accurately. In sublimation printing, all parts of the design are applied at once, eliminating the problem of stretching of fabrics as they move from one roller to another.

On the other hand, heat transfer printing is slower than is either roller or screen printing. Ten to 15 yards of printed fabric are produced per minute in sublimation printing operations, whereas roller printing can produce 35 yards of fabric per minute and rotary screen printing can produce 40 to 42 yards of fabric per minute.[6]

Heat transfer printing losses of fabric through faulty printing are substantially lower than are losses in conventional roller printing. Energy requirements are also lower. Garments and garment pieces can be printed, and precise placement of decorative motifs on a completed garment is possible.

Disadvantages of heat transfer printing that have been cited include off-grain printing. Some dyes used on nylons and acrylics have displayed variations in shade depth and, in some cases, problems with fastness to laundering. A yard of paper is required for each yard of fabric to be printed, so the disposal of paper can become a problem. On the other hand, conventional dyeing and printing systems produce problems of water pollution, whereas paper can be recycled.

Growth of heat transfer printing has not been as dramatic in recent years as it was when the technique was first introduced. This is probably due to the limited types of fabrics that can be produced.

Other Special Printing Techniques

Photographic printing is done in a manner similar to the photochemical preparation of screens for screen printing. A photosensitive dye is coated on the fabric, a negative is placed over the fabric, light is applied, and a photographic type of printing takes place.

Electrostatic printing is an experimental process in which a plate with an electrostatic charge is placed behind the fabric. A stencil in the form of the pattern is placed over the fabric. Special powdered inks that can be attracted by the electrostatic charge are passed over the surface fabric, and the inks are attracted into and color the fabric in the open areas of the stencil.

Ombre printing is the printing of a rainbow or varying tone effects. The tone may change from light to dark shades of one color, or vice versa, or the effect may be of a shading from one color into another. Ombre effects can also be obtained by weaving fabrics from yarns that have been yarn dyed into shaded colors.

Polychromatic printing or dyeing is actually a dyeing method that achieves a printed effect. Several different streams of dye liquor of different colors are utilized. The dye liquor is run over the surface of the fabric. By controlling the direction and flow of the dye, a variety of different effects can be achieved. Polychromatic® is a trademark of the ICI Company.

Foam printing, a variant of the foam dyeing process (see Chapter 18), can be used to apply dye to selected areas of fabric to create a multicolored effect. Foam printing offers the same energy-saving advantages as does foam dyeing.

[6]*American Fabrics*, No. 10 (Summer 1974), p. 45.

Printing Techniques for Carpets

Recent style trends have led to the production of substantial quantities of patterned carpet. Rotary screen and flatbed screen techniques can be used for printing carpets, though they require some special adaptations. Heat transfer printing is also applied to small area rugs and to floor carpet tiles. Foam and polychromatic coloring techniques can be used on carpeting, also.

A number of new and specialized processes used chiefly for carpets have gained acceptance recently. One such process, the Kustur TAK® process, is based on the use of a device that sprinkles droplets of dye solution onto a predyed or prepadded carpet. The simplest of these machines can produce two colors, plus the base shade. The MultiTAK® machine allows the application of dye liquor to specific areas of the carpet to produce a random pattern. Other variants of the process can create a multilayered color effect by applying a gum that resists the dye to the surface of the carpet, while allowing the TAK® droplets to penetrate below the surface.

Traditional roller printing on pile carpets would flatten or crush the pile; therefore, raised pattern areas are now being produced by mounting hard and soft rubber materials on a wood roller. These materials take up the dye from a dye trough and apply them to the carpet without flattening the pile.

Jet spray techniques for printing carpets have been developed by a number of textile machinery companies. The basic principle of this technique is that it utilizes small jets of dye that are controlled by computer. Production speeds can be very fast (up to 15 to 20 meters per minute). Rollers, screens, and other equipment requirements are simplified. One of the most versatile of these machines is the *Millitron*®, a machine developed by the Milliken Company that uses thousands of tiny jets to apply color. Since neither rollers nor screens are used, the pile is not distorted, and exceptional pattern clarity is possible. The machine can switch from one pattern to another in less than 1 second, allowing the production of relatively short runs quite economically. (See Figure 19.11.)

Textile fabrics utilize the same type of designs and design motifs that are used in a wide variety of other decorated items. These designs are often classified as being realistic, stylized, geometric, or abstract. Furthermore, certain traditional patterns in some of these categories have become classic designs used for either home furnishings or wearing apparel, or both.

Types of Textile Designs

Realistic Designs

Realistic or naturalistic designs depict real objects in a natural manner. Human, animal, plant forms, or any other object may be selected for representation.

FIGURE 19.11 *Carpet printed by the Millitron® printing machine is inspected. Courtesy of Milliken and Company.*

Certain traditional patterns in textile fabrics fall into this classification. *Toile de jouy*, for example, is a fine line representation of a pastoral or historic scene printed in one color on a white or off-white fabric. (See Figure 19.12.) Most often the fabric is cotton, a cotton blend, or linen. Many floral patterns realistically depict flower and plant forms.

Stylized Designs

Stylized designs distort real objects. The original source of inspiration for a stylized design is generally recognizable, but the object is exaggerated or simplified in such a way as to give it an unnatural form. Paisley prints are an example of a traditional design that is a stylized leaf form from India. In addition to distorting the real form of an object, stylized designs frequently use colors and proportions that are not natural.

Geometric Designs

Geometric patterns utilize geometric forms such as circles, squares, ovals, rectangles, triangles, ellipses, and so on. Polka dots are geometric patterns, as are plaids and stripes.

Abstract Designs

Abstract patterns have little or no reference to real objects. Although often somewhat geometric in form, they are less rigid than geometric designs. It is sometimes difficult to place certain designs clearly into one specific design category. The distinctions among stylized, geometric, and abstract patterns may sometimes become blurred.

Summary

These patterns may be created in small or large scale. The effect of the pattern may be altered by variations in scale, closeness of the design, or the colors in which it is printed. Except for hand-painted textiles, patterns must be repeated to cover the full length of a piece of fabric that may range from a few feet to many thousands of yards in length. The single pattern unit that is to be reproduced is called the *repeat*. The length of the repeat may range from a fraction of an inch to several feet.

A realistic pattern created in very small scale and repeated often may, from a distance, give the effect of a geometric or abstract pattern. Placing a large-scale realistic pattern against a sharply contrasting background color may emphasize its realism, whereas placing the same pattern against a low-contrast background may make it seem abstract. An enormous variety of design possibilities are open to the textile designer through manipulation of scale and proportion, placement of design, and selection of color.

Cross-cultural or Historic Influences on Design

Each historic period of Western civilization and each of the non-Western cultures has developed a wide variety of traditional patterns in textile fabrics. Modern designers frequently utilize these as sources of inspiration or may copy them directly.

Reproduction of, or designs inspired by, historic textiles are more often used in fabrics for interior design than in apparel fabrics. Particular historic designs may be chosen because they are associated with certain furniture styles. Historic textiles that are most often used as a source of design include oriental textiles, especially those of China, Japan, and India; Middle Eastern textiles, especially those of Persia and the Byzantine Empire; and Renaissance, baroque, and early American fabrics.

Oriental Textile Designs

The early invention in China of complex looms for weaving silk led to the development of elaborately woven patterned brocades and damasks. Embroidery was another important form of textile decoration, as were handblocked prints. Chinese designs lay heavy emphasis on religious symbols. Among the more widely used motifs are dragons, peacocks, chrysanthemums, peonies, and other flowers and stylized wave and cloud motifs. (See Figure 19.13.)

Japanese patterned fabrics are often reproduced. These fabrics are likely to emphasize human figures, blossoms, or Japanese scenes.

The influence of India in textile design is dramatically illustrated by the wide variety of fabric names that derive from Indian place names: madras, calico (from Calicut), and bengaline (from Bengali) are examples. In the seventeenth and eighteenth centuries vast quantities of Indian printed cotton were imported by European countries and Colonial Americans. Paisley prints, madras, and calicos with small, often stylized, design motifs are among the important Indian patterns. (See Figure 19.14.)

Middle Eastern Textiles

Persia, like China, developed elaborate looms for weaving textiles. Brocades, damasks, and similar fabrics were especially important Persian contributions to the history of textiles. Pattern motifs were many and varied and included floral forms, especially poppies, roses, and flower-

FIGURE 19.13   Embroidered Chinese fabric of the eighteenth century. Courtesy of the
Metropolitan Museum of Art, bequest of William Christian Paul, 1930.

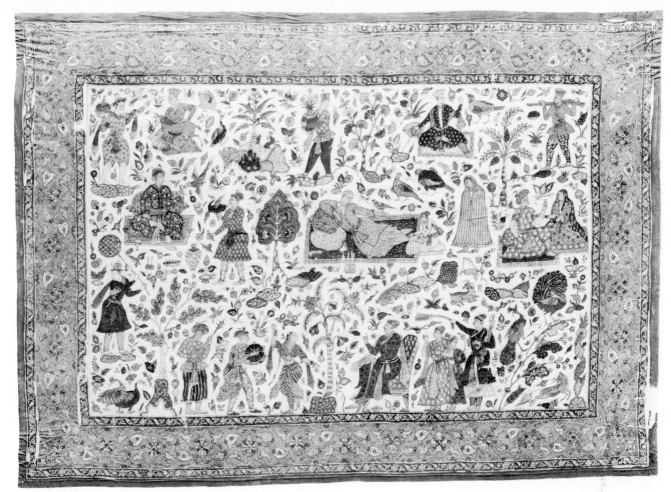

FIGURE 19.14 *Printed and painted cotton cushion cover made in India between 1615 and 1640. Courtesy of the Metropolitan Museum of Art, Rogers Fund, 1928.*

ing trees, cypresses, and the pomegranate, as well as animal forms, landscapes, hunting scenes, and birds. (See Figure 19.15.)

The textiles woven during the Byzantine Empire were rich and colorful. Brocades, damasks, and velvets predominated. Many ecclesiastical fabrics survive, and these place heavy emphasis on Christian symbolism. Secular fabrics utilize formal motifs, including fantastic birds and animals placed inside geometric forms. Byzantine textile design formed a bridge between East and West and melded oriental and Roman designs.

Renaissance Textiles

The earliest designs woven in Western Europe were made in Italy. Silk cultivation spread to Italy from Byzantium, and eleventh- to thirteenth-century Italian textiles showed strong Byzantine influence. After the fifteenth century, Italian and French Renaissance styles emphasized the use of velvets, brocades, and heavy satins in a variety of rich colors.

FIGURE 19.15 *Persian carpet of the seventeenth century. Courtesy of the Metropolitan Museum of Art, Rogers Fund, 1931.*

Design motifs took stylized shapes, especially flower and plant forms, the artichoke being a particular favorite. S-shaped scrolls, acanthus leaves, and geometric patterns in small- to medium-sized repeats were seen. (See Figure 19.16.)

Baroque Styles

The styles of the seventeenth century, known as *baroque* styles, were large in scale, with full, flowing, curved lines. Leafy plants, foliage, flowers, and fruit motifs predominated. Often somewhat stylized in form, they were generally made in clear, dark colors.

FIGURE 19.16 *Sixteenth-century Italian velvet with cut and uncut pile areas. Courtesy of the Metropolitan Museum of Art. Gift of Mrs. Valentine A. Blacque, 1933, in memory of Valentine A. Blacque.*

Rococo Designs

The rococo designs of the eighteenth century by contrast are more delicate in scale and more realistic in representation. Oriental design motifs may be incorporated, and it is not unusual to see representations of pastoral scenes. Colors are more pastel, and there is a greater use of printed cottons and fabrics with woven stripes. (See Figure 19.17.)

FIGURE 19.17 French brocade of the Louis XVI period with rococo floral pattern. Courtesy of the Metropolitan Museum of Art, Rogers Fund, 1920.

Early American Textiles

Many of the fabrics used in Colonial America were imported from Britain, the European continent, or India. Furthermore, American furniture styles were also copies of, or modifications of, other Western European furniture styles. For these reasons, many of the fabrics that are traditionally associated with Early American textiles are similar to English and French styles of the same time period, with special emphasis on the use of printed cottons and linens. American textiles in rural areas tended to be homespun. Often hand embroidery in crewel yarns was applied.

Many museums and historic sites have extensive collections of early American fabrics. Sometimes textile companies will reproduce one of these fabrics. When a modern reproduction of an authentic historic printed textile is made, the fabric is called a *documentary print*.

Textile Designs from Other Cultures

Textile designs from many non-Western cultures have become important influences in American textile fashions. African textiles have inspired many contemporary prints. Tie-dyed fabrics, block-printed fabrics, and resist prints by African artisans served as the basis for many copies and adaptations. Javanese batik fabrics have long been known and imitated. Both prehistoric textile designs and modern fabrics made by the Indians of South and North America also served to inspire contemporary designers.

Recommended References

AATCC Glossary of Printing Terms. Research Triangle Park, N.C.: American Association of Textile Chemists and Colorists, 1973.

"Batik: Design & Colors," *American Fabrics & Fashions*, No. 95 (Fall 1972), p. 34.

BUNT, C. *Byzantine Fabrics*. Atlantic Highlands, N.J.: Humanities, 1967.

CARAWAY, C. *Peruvian Textile Designs*. Owings Mills, Md.: Stemmer House, 1983.

CARAWAY, C. *Southeast Asian Textile Designs*. Owings Mills, Md.: Stemmer House, 1983.

"Developments in the Textile Printing Industry," *Textile Industries*, 147 (November 1983), p. 22.

FORD, P. R. *The Oriental Carpet: A History and Guide to Traditional Motifs, Patterns, and Symbols*. New York: Abrams, 1981.

FULMER, T. D. "The Changing Scene for Textile Printing," *America's Textiles* 14 (March 1985), p. 50.

GERSBACH, M. *Coptic Textile Design*. Magnolia, Mass.: Peter Smith, n.d.

HACKER, K. F., and K. JENSEN TURNBULL. *Courtyard, Bazaar, Temple: Traditions of Textile Design in India*. Seattle: University of Washington Press, 1982.

HALLER, R. "Techniques of Early Cloth Printing," *CIBA Review*, No. 26 (October 1939), p. 933.

HIGGENBOTTOM, R. S. "Heat Transfer Printing," *Textiles*, 4 (January 1975), p. 13.

"How Discharge Prints Are Made," *American Fabrics and Fashions*, No. 124 (Spring 1979), p. 27.

"Ikat," *American Fabrics and Fashions*, No. 105 (Fall 1975), p. 59; and No. 104 (Summer 1975), p. 39.

KELLER, I. *Batik, The Art and Craft.* Rutland, Vt.: Charles Tuttle Co., 1966.

MOCK, G. N. and E. JACUMIN, JR. "A Survey of Printing Machinery and Equipment," *Textile Chemist and Colorist*, 14 (March 1982), p. 17.

"Ornamentation: An AFF Portfolio of Ornamental Baroque Designs," *American Fabrics and Fashions*, No. 126 (Fall 1979), insert.

REAGAN, B. M. "Dyeing and Printing Basics," *ACPTC Combined Proceedings* (1982), p. 30.

"Recent Advances in Foam Printing of Carpet Tiles," *American Dyestuff Reporter*, 74 (June 1985), p. 16.

ROSSBACH, E. *The Art of Paisley.* New York: Van Nostrand Reinhold Co., 1980.

SCHAEFER, G. "The Earliest Specimens of Cloth Printing," *CIBA Review*, No. 26 (October 1939), pp. 914 ff.

"Special Report: Textile Printing," *Textile Chemist and Colorist*, 11 (May 1979), special issue.

SUCHECKI, S. M. "Technology: A Portfolio," *Textile Industries*, 147 (March 1983), p. 64.

Textile Printing. An Ancient Art and Yet So New. Research Triangle Park, N.C.: American Association of Textile Chemists and Colorists, 1975.

"Transfer Printing," *Textile Month* (January 1976), p. 46.

"Trends in the Manufacture of Carpets and Rugs," *American Dyestuff Reporter*, 74 (June 1985), p. 15.

TURNER, G. R. "Textile Printing: The Changing Scene," *Textile Chemist and Colorist*, 17, (March 1985), p. 33.

Routine and Mechanical Finishes

The finishing of woven, knitted, and nonwoven textiles consists of the application of a wide variety of treatments and special processes that give to the fabric some quality that is needed to enhance its aesthetic or performance properties. Some finishes modify appearance, some modify behavior, and some modify both appearance and behavior.

Classification of Finishes

Finishes may be classified on several bases. Certain finishes are routinely given to fabrics prior to dyeing or final processing. These are sometimes referred to as steps in fabric preparation rather than as finishes. Other finishes involve the mechanical manipulation of the fabric. Still others utilize chemical treatments to produce some change in fabric properties. Chemical treatments may be topical and applied to the surface of the fabric, or they may form chemical bonds with the fabric. In some instances, a finishing process may be both mechanical *and* chemical.

Finishes are also separated into those that are permanent, those that are durable, and those that are temporary. Permanent finishes will last for the lifetime of the product, durable finishes can be expected to function reasonably well for most of the lifetime of the fabric, and temporary finishes are removed after one or more launderings or dry cleanings. Renewable finishes can be added to fabrics when through use or care processes the original finish has been diminished or destroyed.

Some finishes are made permanent by utilizing the thermoplastic characteristics of synthetic fabrics. When heat-sensitive fibers are subjected to finishes involving heat treatment, the fabric may be permanently "set" in such a way that new characteristics are established. For example, in many finishes patterns are heat-set into thermoplastic fabrics by the use of heated, patterned rollers.

Chemical resins are frequently used in the treatment of fabrics. Many of the chemical resin treatments are intended to develop cross-links within the fibers. The mechanism of cross-linking is especially important in finishing fabrics made from cellulosic fibers or their blends.

In the process of cross-linking, chemical bonds are formed between molecules. (See Chapter 3 for a fuller discussion.) Fabrics treated to form cross-links are said to have a "memory" and will return to the state in which they were held during the cross-linking process. Fabrics held flat and smooth are expected to remain flat and smooth, and those that were held in a creased state (as in, for example, the formation of creases at the front of trousers) will return to that state after laundering. Since cross-linking interferes with the ability of the fiber to retain moisture, this process is generally applied after the fabric has been colored.

A single fabric can be given several finishes that are each intended to accomplish different purposes. For example, a fabric may be bleached to enhance whiteness and then given a durable press finish to make it resist wrinkling. Few fabrics are manufactured that do not undergo some type of finishing. The discussion in this chapter concentrates on routine and mechanical finishes. Chemical finishes are discussed in Chapter 21.

Application of Finishes

The application of finishes from a solution is generally accomplished through the steps of padding, drying, and curing. Figure 20.1 depicts the traditional process. In the padding stage, the fabric is wet by the finishing solution. Considerable amounts of energy are required to dry the fabric following padding. Because energy use contributes significantly to the cost of textile manufacture, a good deal of effort has been devoted to the development of processes that are less energy intensive. The basic principle underlying the development of these finishes is to decrease drying time. This is done by removing substantial quantities of liquid from the fabric before drying, wetting the fabric less during finishing, or combining several finishes into one so that instead of drying fabrics several times, they need be dried only once. Figure 20.2

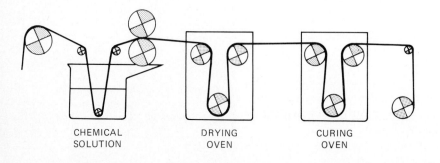

CHEMICAL SOLUTION   DRYING OVEN   CURING OVEN

FIGURE 20.1 Pad-dry-cure textile finishing. Diagram from Grayson, Encyclopedia of Textiles, Fibers, and Nonwoven Fabrics, *p. 468 reproduced courtesy of John Wiley and Sons, Inc.*

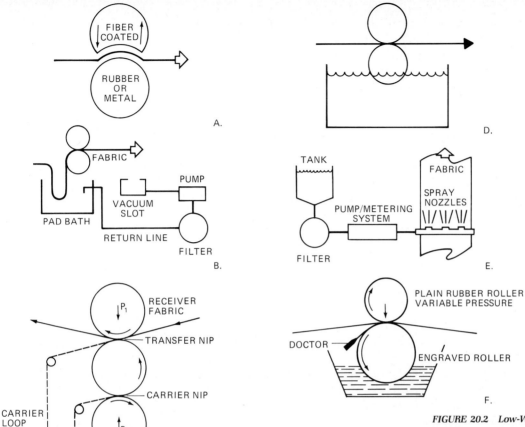

FIGURE 20.2 Low-Wet-Pickup Techniques in Finishing. A. Fiber-coated, high extraction roll. Highly porous, rubber-coated fiber rolls produce a suction effect that helps to remove more water. B. Pad/vacuum extraction. After padding, fabric is carried over a vacuum slot where a portion of the pad liquor is removed, filtered, and recirculated for re-use. C. Transfer padding. A continuous loop belt of material revolves through the finishing liquor, picks up the liquor, then is brought into contact with the fabric that is to be finished. The dry fabric picks up the finishing liquor from the wet belt. D. Kiss roll. Partially submerged roll picks up finishing solution as a film and carries it to the fabric. E. Spray. Finishing solution is sprayed onto the surface of the fabric. F. Engraved roll. An engraved metal roll passes through the pad mix, picks up finishing material in the engraved areas. A doctor blade removes excess finishing material before the fabric passes between the engraved roller and a rubber roller which facilitates transfer of the liquor evenly.

shows a number of variations of the "low-wet pickup" types of processes. Similar principles and techniques are utilized in some types of dyeing to save energy.

Removing Impurities from Fabrics

In the processing of natural fibers, impurities such as grease and vegetable matter in wool, gum in silk, or vegetable matter in cotton have been removed. Optimum conditions for spinning fibers into yarns, however, require some lubrication of fibers. Also in synthetic fibers some means must be found to decrease the static electricity that builds up during spinning. For these reasons natural lubricating substances in

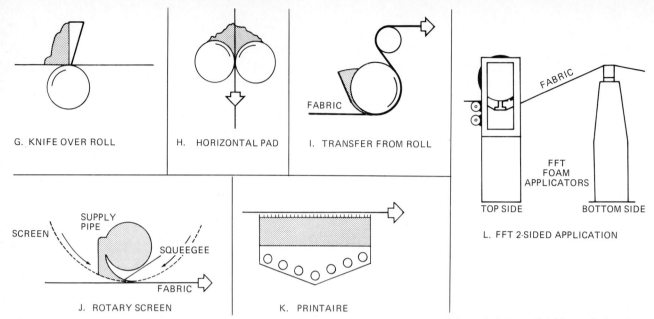

G. KNIFE OVER ROLL   H. HORIZONTAL PAD   I. TRANSFER FROM ROLL

J. ROTARY SCREEN   K. PRINTAIRE

FFT FOAM APPLICATORS

TOP SIDE   BOTTOM SIDE

L. FFT 2-SIDED APPLICATION

G through K. Foam finishing techniques. Finishing material is formed into foam by incorporation of air. Application of the foam can be made by any of the techniques of (G) knife over a roll, (H) horizontal pad, (I) transfer from a roll, (J) through a screen using a squeegee to force foam onto the fabric, (K) printed onto the fabric surface, or (L) using foam applicators that coat first one side, then the other. (In the diagrams, shaded areas represent the foam finishing material.) Reprinted from America's Textiles, May 1984. *T. D. Fulmer, author.*

cotton are not removed before spinning, and other fibers generally have had substances added that aid in spinning. Temporary starches (called sizings) may be utilized during weaving, or other special additives such as identifying dyes may have been used. Fabrics may become soiled during weaving. These substances and soils must be removed before further treatment is given to the fabrics.

Cotton

The general process of cleaning fabrics after weaving is called *scouring*. For cottons, or cotton blended with man-mades, this is generally done in a *kier vat*, a large iron vessel in which soap and boiling water wash the fabrics clean. Alternate procedures for scouring cottons include use of a *J box* in which a continuous scouring and bleaching of full-width fabrics takes place. Automatic machines pass fabric through the solution at the rate of 200 yards a minute.

Silk

In addition to removing the soil or additives used while weaving silk, degumming or scouring removes any gum or sericin that remains on the silk. Often a quantity of the natural gum has been allowed to remain on the silk fiber to give it additional body and to make it easier to handle in spinning and weaving. Although a few silk fabrics are manufactured in which the gum is retained purposely to provide body or produce a different texture, most silk fabrics are degummed as part of the finishing process. The resultant fabric has a much softer hand and a whiter appearance.

Wool

Wool fabrics that have some vegetable matter clinging to the woven or knitted yarns must be *carbonized*. Carbonizing is accomplished by the immersion of wool in sulfuric acid. Because strong acids readily attack the cellulose of the vegetable matter and do not immediately harm protein fibers like wool, the burrs, sticks, leaves, and the like that remain in the wool are destroyed. The treatment is carried out under carefully controlled conditions so that the wool is not damaged, and the fabric is given a careful scouring afterward to remove or neutralize all the acid that remains. The scouring of wool is done in solutions of less concentration and at lower temperatures than scouring of other fibers because most scouring solutions are alkaline and wool is damaged by alkali. (See Figure 20.3.)

FIGURE 20.3 *Fabric is scoured on a continuous basis as it passes through cleansing solution. Courtesy of West Point Pepperell.*

Bleaching

Problems can arise in dyeing if any small amount of impurity that is highly colored remains. Even man-made fabrics, especially those that have been heat set, may become yellowed as a result of processing. Therefore fabrics may require bleaching or whitening to prepare them for dyeing or printing or to produce a fabric that is of a clear white color. Bleaches are chemical substances, so that an appropriate bleach must be selected for each fiber. Most bleaches used by industry are either chlorine bleaches or peroxygen bleaches. The peroxygen bleaches, and particularly hydrogen peroxide bleaches, are used most frequently in commercial bleaching of greige (or untreated) goods, although for some fabrics other types of bleaches must be used. (Home bleaching is discussed in Chapter 22.)

Fluorescent Whiteners

In addition to bleaching, many white fabrics are treated with fluorescent whiteners (also known as optical brighteners) to enhance their whiteness. Fluorescent whiteners are not bleaches, but are dyelike compounds that emit a strong bluish fluorescence. This causes the white to appear whiter (a "bluish-white" instead of a "yellow-white") and brighter. Optical brighteners are most effective in daylight; they are not effective in artificial light, which does not contain ultraviolet light.

Optical brighteners are only moderately fast to laundering, and are not fast to chlorine bleaching. Since most detergents contain optical brighteners in their formulation, any loss of the original brightener is usually replaced in laundering. Wool fabrics treated with fluorescent brighteners may develop a brown discoloration as the brighteners fade as a result of exposure to sunlight.

Delustering

Many of the man-made fibers have a high natural luster or brightness. Some man-made fibers are treated to reduce this luster before the fiber is formed by adding titanium dioxide pigment, which causes the fiber to reflect less light and thereby decrease the brightness. Other methods of delustering fibers include etching or roughening of the fiber surface by chemical treatment to produce a more irregular surface that does not reflect but scatters light.

Fabrics may be delustered by applying a delustrant to the surface of the fabric and fixing it in place with a resin binder. Any process that roughens or brushes fibers onto the fabric surface (see brushing, napping, etc., later in this chapter) will also reduce luster.

Mercerization

In 1851, John Mercer discovered that the treatment of cotton with a strong solution of caustic soda (or sodium hydroxide) altered the strength, absorbency, and appearance of the fabric. Because fabric treated in this way shrunk as much as 25 per cent of its length, the finish was not applied commercially until an English chemist, H. A. Lowe, discovered that application of the finish under tension not only minimized shrinkage but also increased luster.

In *mercerization*, as this finish is called, the cotton fabric is immersed under tension in a strong solution of sodium hydroxide for a short, controlled period of time (usually 4 minutes or less), the alkali is washed off, and any excess alkali is neutralized.

Mercerized cotton fabrics have greatly increased luster. During mercerization the fiber swells, the natural convolutions of cotton are largely lost, and the fiber retains a fuller, rounder diameter. This smooth surface reflects more light than does the untreated, flatter fiber.

The strength of the fiber is increased as much as 20 per cent. The cotton becomes more absorbent and has a greater affinity for moisture and for dyestuffs. Vat-dyed cotton fabrics that have been mercerized have excellent colorfastness, and less dye is required to produce colors. Some decorative effects can be achieved by combining mercerized yarns and unmercerized yarns in one fabric because mercerized yarns dye to darker shades than do those that are untreated.

Mercerized fabrics are also more reactive. As a result, they are more easily damaged by acids and oxidizing agents. Probably for the same reason, mercerized fabrics are more receptive to resin finishes.

Mercerization can be applied to either yarns or fabrics. Most good-quality cotton sewing threads are mercerized to improve their strength. *Slack mercerization*, or mercerization of fabrics that are not held under tension, can be used to produce stretch fabrics. During slack mercerization, yarns shrink and develop a good degree of elasticity. The finished fabric can be stretched, and when the tension is removed, the goods will return to their original length. Yarns that have been slack mercerized do not have the high luster of yarns mercerized under tension; their strength is greater than is that of yarns that are mercerized under tension. This process is not widely used.

Mercerization is both inexpensive and permanent, and for these reasons it is widely used on cotton goods. Linen can also be mercerized, and since it has a natural luster and good strength, the major advantage of mercerizing linen is to improve the dyeability and receptivity of linen to other finishes.

Basic Finishes That Alter Hand or Texture

Fulling

Wool fabrics are *fulled* to give the fabric a more compact structure. In a type of preshrinking, fabrics are subjected to moisture, heat, soap, and pressure. This causes the yarns to shrink and to lie closer together and gives the fabric a denser structure. Wool cloth may be given more or less fulling, depending upon the desired characteristics of the resultant fabrics. Melton cloth, for example, is one of the most heavily fulled wool fabrics and has a dense, feltlike texture.

Singeing

To produce a smooth surface finish on fabrics made from staple fibers, fabrics are passed over a heated copper plate or above a gas flame. The fiber ends burn off. The fabric is moved very rapidly, and only the fiber ends are destroyed. Immediately after passing the flame, the fabric is passed through a water bath to put out any sparks that might remain. (See Figure 20.4.)

FIGURE 20.4   Fabric passes over gas flame that singes or burns off excess surface fiber. Courtesy of West Point Pepperell.

The burning characteristics of fibers must be taken into account when this process is applied, as heat-sensitive fibers melt, forming tiny balls on the surface of the fabric. These balls interfere with dye absorption, so that, as a general rule, heat-sensitive fibers would be singed after dyeing or printing. The tendency of some man-made fibers to pill may be decreased by singeing.

Filament yarns do not require singeing, as there are no short fiber ends to project onto the surface of the fabric. Fabrics that are to be napped are not singed.

Stiffening

Sizing. To add body to fabrics, some type of sizing is often applied. This may be in the form of starch, gelatin, or resin or a combination of these with softening substances such as oils or waxes.

Starches and gelatins are temporary sizings and are removed during laundering or dry cleaning. Inexpensive cotton or rayon fabrics are often heavily starched and after laundering may become quite limp. For fabrics sized with starch or gelatin, it is possible to determine how heavily sized a fabric is by rubbing hard at a section of the fabric. If small flakes of starch can be removed, the fabric has obviously been sized. If the same fabric is held up to the light, one can often see more light through the area in the section from which the sizing has been removed than in other areas.

Gelatins are used as sizing on rayons because they are clear in color and do not dim the luster of the fabric. The application of the sizing, plus a hard press, may create a deceptively full hand and surface luster that is lost after laundering.

Various resins can also be used to add body to fabrics. These resins produce a durable finish. The resin attaches to the surface of the fiber or actually impregnates the fiber. Sometimes resins are used in combination with starches to produce a reasonably durable finish in which the resin serves to "bind" the starch to the fiber.

Permanently Stiffened Cottons. By a special acid treatment known as *parchmentizing*, some cottons are given a permanently stiff character. The application of a carefully controlled acid solution causes the surface of the yarn to become softened and gelatinlike. An afterwash in cold water causes the gelatinous outer surface to harden, forming a permanently stiffened exterior. Permanently finished organdy, for example, is made by this process. Acid finishes are also used to create certain decorative effects, which are discussed later in this chapter.

Weighting of Silk. Raw silk contains from 25 to 30 per cent of its weight in sericin or gum. When the fiber is cleaned, this substance is removed. Silks may be weighted both to enable the producer to regain some of the loss in fiber weight and to add greater body to fabrics.

The silk fabric is first placed in an acid solution of stannic chloride (a chloride of tin). The fiber absorbs the substance, then is washed, placed into a solution of sodium phosphate, and then washed again. During this process, an insoluble compound (tin phosphate) is formed within the fiber, and the weight and body of the fiber is increased. A further treatment with sodium silicate solution forms another chemical compound and still greater weight.

These steps can be repeated a number of times, and with each repetition, greater weighting is achieved. The silk fiber can hold considerably more than its own weight of this added chemical weighting.

Heavily weighted silks may have very poor abrasion resistance and eventually will break from the weight of the silk. For this reason, legislation has been passed to restrict the quantity of weighting that may be added to silk without indicating on the label that the silk has been weighted. Any silk labeled Pure Dye Silk may not contain more than 10 per cent of weighting or 15 per cent for black fabrics. If heavily weighted silks are burned, the fabric is consumed, leaving a skeleton of the metallic compound in the shape of the woven fabric. In this way, silk samples may be tested for weighting.

Softening

Heat setting of man-made fabrics, durable press finishes, and some treatments given to acrylic fabrics may produce a harsh and unpleasant hand. Application of fabric softeners during finishing can overcome these negative qualities. The chemical compounds used penetrate intersections between yarns to allow a certain amount of yarn slippage, thereby creating a more supple, smoother, and more pleasant-feeling fabric.

Some of these products are available for use in home laundering. These are discussed in Chapter 22, Care of Textiles.

Surface Finishes

Many finishes are used because of the effect they have on the appearance of the fabric. Sometimes these finishes produce a related change in texture or hand, as well.

Calendering

Calendering is a broad, general term that refers to a mechanically produced finish achieved by passing fabrics between a series of two or more rollers. The object of calendering is to smooth the fabric and/or create interesting surface effects.

Simple Calendering. The simplest form of calendering is comparable to ironing a fabric. The calender rolls are heated and the dampened cloth is passed between the cylinders that smooth and flatten the fabric, producing a wrinkle-free, slightly glossy surface.

Glazing. A special calendar called a *friction calendar* is used to produce fabrics that have a highly glazed or polished surface, such as chintz or polished cotton. Prior to passing the fabric through the calender, the cloth is saturated with either starch or resin. The fabric is dried slightly and is then fed into the machine in which a rapidly moving, heated roller polishes the surface of the more slowly moving fabric. If starch is used to produce the glaze, the finish is temporary. If resins are used, the glaze is durable.

Ciréing. Ciré fabrics are characterized by a high surface polish. A fashion term, "the wet look," has sometimes been used to decribe ciré fabrics. Made by much the same process as friction calendering, ciré effects on natural fibers or rayon are produced by using waxes and thermoplastic resins. Heat-sensitive synthetics are given a permanent "wet look," by this procedure when the thermoplastic fibers fuse slightly under the heat of the rollers.

When hydrophobic fibers are given a ciré finish, some degree of water repellency is provided. This occurs as a result of the slight glazing or fusing that the fabrics undergo.

Embossing. Embossed designs are produced by pressing a pattern onto fabrics. Like other calendered finishes, they may be permanent when applied to thermoplastic fibers, durable when applied to fabrics that have been resin treated, and temporary on other fabrics.

Some embossed designs have a relatively flat design. The pattern is created by running an embossed roller with a raised pattern across the fabric. The opposite roller is made of paper and has a smooth surface. Because the paper roll can "give" with the pressure, the embossed roller "prints" the colorless design by flattening some sections of the cloth.

Three-dimensional embossed designs are made with embossed rollers also. In this method the embossed roller first presses the design onto the surface of the paper roller; then when the fabric is passed between the rollers, both the engraved roller and the shaped paper roll together to mold the shape of the pattern onto the cloth.

Embossed designs provide surface texture at a lower cost than do woven designs. If applied to nonthermoplastic fibers without special resin finishes, the embossing will be lost sooner or later. Embossed fabrics should not be ironed or pressed, as the design may be diminished by the pressure. (See Figure 20.5.)

Schreinering. The Schreiner calendar produces fabrics with a soft luster and a soft hand. One of the calenders is embossed with about 250 fine diagonal lines per inch. This roller passes over the fabric, flattening the yarns and producing a more opaque fabric with soft luster and hand. Unless the fabric is thermoplastic, the finish is a temporary one. Thermoplastic fibers are set permanently into position by the

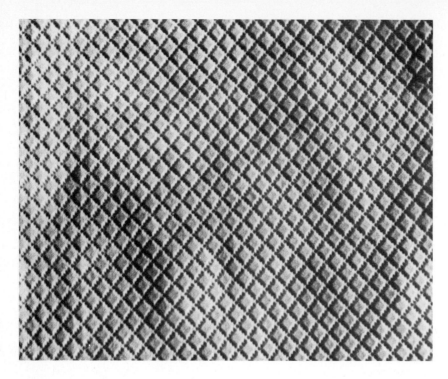

FIGURE 20.5 Embossed cotton fabric.

Schreiner calender's heat. If fabrics are given a resin finish before Schreinering, the finish will be fairly durable.

The Schreiner finish is designed to give fabrics a soft luster. Damask table linens and cotton sateens are among the fabrics given this finish routinely. Thermoplastic tricots use the finish to enhance surface luster.

Moiré. Moiré fabrics have a watered or clouded surface appearance on the fashion side of the fabric, which is sometimes called a wood grain pattern. (See Figure 20.6.) The original technique for producing moiré fabrics is an old one and luxurious silks of the eighteenth and nineteenth centuries are often made with a moiré finish.

To achieve an effective moiré pattern, ribbed fabrics such as taffeta, faille, or bengaline are usually selected. The pattern is temporary, durable, or permanent depending upon the fiber and/or chemicals used. In watermarked moiré, such as those used a hundred years ago, the pattern would be destroyed by laundering. Resin treatment makes the pattern reasonably durable to cleaning and laundering, and the use of heat-setting of thermoplastic fibers creates a permanent finish.

One of two methods is employed. The first, and more traditional method, places two lengths of a fabric from the same bolt face to face, with one layer slightly off-grain in relation to the other. Enormous pressure is put upon the fabrics by the smooth moiré rollers, and the ribs of one fabric press down on those of the other, flattening each other in some areas and causing the fabrics to reflect light differently across the

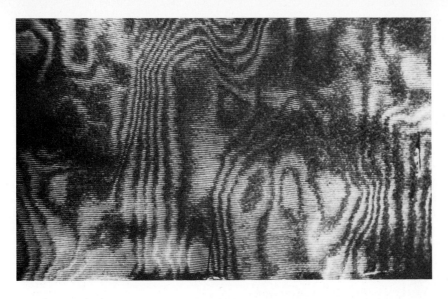

FIGURE 20.6   *Faille fabric with a moiré finish.*

surface of the fabric. The moiré produced in this manner has a random pattern with no discernible repeats.

The second method uses a roller with a moiré pattern etched into its surface. In this procedure, the roller flattens one area more than another, creating the same effect as in the first method. Here, however, the patterns are repeated at regular intervals.

Beetling

Linens and cottons that are intended to look like linens are beetled, by pounding the fabric (in a machine equipped with hammers that strike over the surface of the fabric) to flatten the yarns and make them smoother and more lustrous. Unless a resin treatment has been given to the fabric before beetling, this must be considered a temporary finish.

Napping and Sueding

Napped and sueded fabrics are fabrics in which fiber ends are brushed up onto the surface of the fabric. Napping and sueding are applied to woven or knitted goods, and, although the term "pile" is often used to refer to the fiber ends that appear on the surface of the cloth, these fabrics should not be confused with pile fabrics in which a separate set of yarns is used to create the pile through weaving.

Sueding develops a very low pile on the surface of the fabric, and the surface of the fabric can be finished to look and feel like suede leather, or the process may be used to develop a very low pile on the surface of the fabric. An abrasive material, a type of sandpaper, is used to achieve the finish. The fabric is rotated against the abrasive material, and the hand and appearance of the fabric are determined by the type of fiber used, the size of the yarn, and the intensity of the friction between the fabric and the abrasive material.

In periods when suedelike fabrics have been fashionable, woven and knitted fabrics finished on sueders have been widely available. Attempts to simulate suede leather have ranged from the development of nonwoven fabrics such as Ultrasuede, which approximates the hand and appearance of suede leather closely, to those in which finishing with a sueder provides the appearance of suede surface while maintaining the hand and drapability of woven or knitted cloth.

Napped fabrics, like suede fabrics, have a pile or nap on the surface of the fabric. Napping generally develops a deeper nap and utilizes machinery different from sueding.

Napped fabrics are used for clothing and household textiles in which warmth is desired. The loose fiber ends trap air that serves as insulation. Blankets, sleepwear, coating fabrics, sweaters, and the like are often made from napped fabrics.

The nap is created by rubbing the surface of the fabric with a rough device. Napped fabrics are generally made from yarns with a fairly loose twist, so that the surface fibers will brush up easily. Long ago this was done with teasels (thistle heads with many fine, hooklike, sharp projections). Today napping is more likely to be done with machines set with small, fine wires that approximate the teasel spine. These small hooklike projections catch fibers and pull them up to the surface of the fabric, creating a fuzzy, soft layer of fibers on the surface that are also caught into the yarn. Some very fine napped wools are still made by using natural teasels. The terms *gigging* and *raising* may also be used to describe the napping process. Excessive napping may tend to weaken fabrics by pulling up too many fibers, thereby weakening the basic structure of the fabric. Fabrics intended for apparel are generally napped on one side, whereas those for blankets are napped on both sides. (See Figure 20.7.)

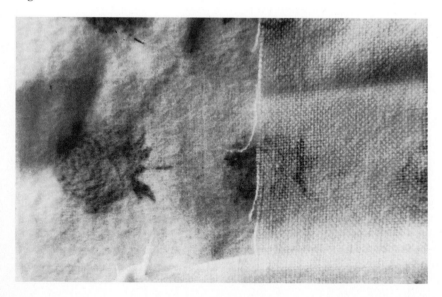

FIGURE 20.7 *Napped cotton flannel showing the unnapped wrong side contrasted with the napped right side.*

Brushing. Many napped and pile fabrics are brushed in such a way that the nap or pile runs in one direction. When this has been done, the fingers can be run across the surface of the fabric to feel that the fabric is smooth in one direction and rougher in the other direction. Items cut from such fabrics must be handled so that the direction of all pieces is the same. If this is not done, a fabric in which the grain runs down may reflect light differently from one in which the grain runs up. This difference in light reflection may cause pieces placed side by side to appear to be different in color.

Shearing

Napped or pile fabrics may be sheared to make the nap or the pile the same thickness in all parts of the fabric. The shearing is done in a machine in which sharp, rotating blades cut the pile or nap to the desired length. The machine has been compared by Potter and Corbman to a lawn mower.[1] If some sections of the pile or nap are flattened, and other areas sheared, brushing up the uncut sections can achieve a sculptured effect.

Flocking

A surface effect that is similar to a nap or pile may be created by flocking in which short fibers are "glued" onto the surface of fabrics by an adhesive material. If the adhesive coats the entire surface of the fabric, the flocking will cover the entire surface of the fabric, but if the adhesive is printed onto the fabric in a pattern of some sort, the flock will adhere only in the printed areas. (See Figure 19.9.) All-over flocked fabrics may have a suedelike appearance.

Short lengths of fiber flocking can be made from any generic fiber type. Rayon is most often used for flocking because of its relatively low cost. Nylon may be selected for situations in which good abrasion resistance is required.

Fibers for flocking are made from bundles of tow fiber (continuous filament fibers without twist). The tow is fed through a finish removal bath and then into a bank of cutters that cut flock of the desired length. The fibers may be dyed before they are attached to the fabric, or the completed fabric may be dyed.

The application of the flock to the fabric is done by either of two methods (See Figure 20.8.) The mechanical flocking process sifts loose flock onto the surface of the fabric to be coated. A series of beaters agitate the fabric causing most of the fabrics to be set in an upright position, with one end of the fiber "locked" into the adhesive.

The second method causes the fibers to be attached in an upright position by passing them through an electrostatic field. The fibers pick up the electric charge and align themselves vertically. One end pene-

[1]M. D. Potter and B. P. Corbman, *Textile, Fiber to Fabric* (New York: McGraw-Hill Book Company, 1967), p. 142.

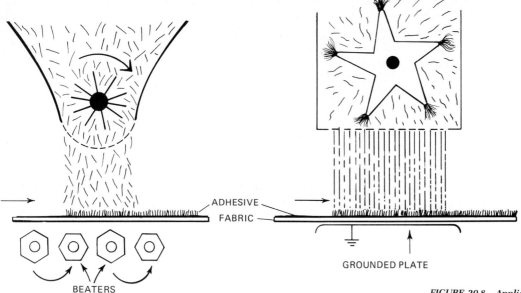

MECHANICAL FLOCKING PROCESS   ELECTROSTATIC FLOCKING PROCESS

ADHESIVE
FABRIC

BEATERS

GROUNDED PLATE

FIGURE 20.8   *Application of flock to fabrics.*

trates into the adhesive, and the flock is formed. Electrostatic flocking assures more complete vertical positioning, and the resultant fabrics are of better quality. It is a more costly process. There is no way for a consumer to tell which process was used when buying fabrics.

The durability of flocked fabrics depends largely on the adhesives that hold the flock firmly during either laundering or dry cleaning. In some cases, flock may be removed by dry-cleaning solvents. Permanent care labels should tell the consumer how flocked fabrics ought to be handled. A second factor in the durability of flocked fabrics has to do with the fiber from which the flock has been made. For example, rayon flocking tends to wear more readily than does nylon.

Burnt-out Designs

Chemicals that will dissolve some fibers can be used to produce alterations in fabric appearance. It is possible, for example, to create open areas in fabrics by imprinting a cellulosic fabric with a sulfuric acid paste that dissolves the printed area. Such fabrics are likely to fray around the edges of the dissolved area and are not especially durable.

In blended fabrics, this technique can be used to create a number of interesting effects. Two different fibers are used. When the dissolving material is imprinted on the fabric, one of the fibers is dissolved while the other is unharmed. Those areas that have not had chemical imprinted upon them remain intact and create the design. By contrasting texture, luster, or color of the fiber to be burnt out with that of the second fiber, a number of attractive decorative effects can be achieved. (See Figure 20.9.)

FIGURE 20.9 *Dark areas of this fabric have been dissolved out by chemicals to produce a "burnt-out" design.*

Plissé Designs

A puckered or plissé effect is achieved in some fabrics by imprinting them with chemicals that cause the fabric to shrink. When these chemicals are printed in a design, some areas of the fabric shrink while others do not. This causes untreated areas to pucker or puff up between the treated areas. (See Figure 20.10.) Cottons and rayons react in this way when treated with sodium hydroxide, an alkali, as do nylons that

FIGURE 20.10 *Cotton plissé puckered design created by printing with sodium hydroxide on the background to shrink the fabric, leaving puffed, untreated areas between.*

have been printed with phenol, an acid substance. Although this is a fairly durable finish, plissé fabrics should not be ironed because the pressing of the plissé flattens the surface.

Acid Design

In addition to stiffening the fabric, the acid treatment of cotton fabric causes it to become more transparent. The action can be utilized to create fabrics with a "frosted" design. Areas of the fabric are coated with acid-resistant materials. When the finish is applied, these areas remain opaque, while the acid-treated areas become quite transparent.

Drying

Every type of fabric is dried at least once and often more times during processing. Drying is costly both in terms of time and energy. As the application of heat to dry the cloth is the most costly part of this operation, mechanical devices such as mangles, which squeeze off water; suction dryers, which pull off water by vacuum extraction; or centrifuges, which spin off water, may be used to remove as much water as possible prior to thermal drying.

Thermal drying requires the application of heat to aid in the drying. Passing the cloth over heated cylinders is one such drying technique. This would be comparable, in principle, to ironing a wet garment to dry it. Another method uses hot air in a tentering or stentering machine. (See Figure 20.11) Tentering both dries and stretches the fabric smooth

FIGURE 20.11   Fabric entering tenter frame. Courtesy of West Point Pepperell.

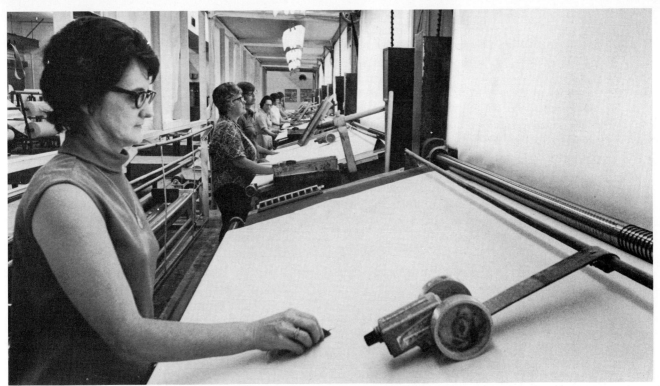

FIGURE 20.12 *Workers inspect and burl fabrics. Courtesy of West Point Pepperell.*

and free from wrinkles. Fabrics are stretched between two parallel chains of correct width. The fabric is held in place on the tenter frame by pins and clips. Examination of the selvage of fabrics will usually reveal either small pinholes or marks from the clips.

The tenter frame carries the fabric into a drying apparatus where the fabric is dried under tension and made wrinkle free. Fabrics that have not been set on the tenter frame straight will be off-grain. That is, the warp and filling yarns will not cross at right angles. Some fabrics that are off-grain can be straightened by pulling the yarns into the correct or straight position. However, fabrics that have had heat-setting or resin treatments cannot be straightened and will always be off-grain. The serviceability and aesthetic qualities of fabrics are, therefore, adversely affected by poor tentering.

Drying fabrics with hot air is more expensive than is drying with heated rollers. For this reason, some fabrics may be tentered after being passed over heated rollers for preliminary partial drying.

Before a fabric is ready to leave the factory, a visual or electronic inspection of the goods is made. (See Figure 20.12.) If done by a worker, the fabric is run over a roller. The process is called *perching*, and the machine used is known as a perch. The perch resembles the uprights on a football goal.

A Few Other Finishing Steps

Electronic scanning is done by laser that generates selvage markings of defective areas and a computer map showing where all the defects in a roll are located. This map can be used by apparel manufacturers using computer-controlled cutting systems that will cut automatically around defects in the cloth. The data generated by electronic inspection can help to pinpoint sources of defects so that these can be corrected.

For woolens and worsteds, both *burling* and *specking* may have to be done. Specking is the removal from woolens and worsteds of burrs, specks, or other small objects that might detract from the final appearance of the fabric. It is usually done with a tweezers or a burling iron.

Burling is the removal of loose threads and knots from woolens and worsteds by means of a burling iron, a type of tweezer. Many knots must be pulled or worked to the back of the fabric because pulling them out might leave a small hole in the fabric.

The finishes described in this chapter might be summed up as "the application of a pleasing or appealing effect to the fabric, comparable with the application of cosmetics to improve the facial effects of those who use them."[2]

Recommended References

Cowhig, W. T. "What Is Moiré?" 4, *Textiles* (June 1975), p. 46.

Evans, M. "Mechanical Finishing," *American Dyestuff Reporter*, 71 (May 1982), p. 36.

Hall, A. J. *Textile Finishing*. New York: American Elsevier Publishing Co., Inc., 1966.

Herard, R. A. "Yesterday's Finishing Techniques Applied to Today's Fabrics," *Textile Chemist and Colorist*, 11 (June 1979), p. 24.

Hodgson, A. "Desizing and Bleaching," *Textiles*, 11 (Spring 1982), p. 10.

Marsh, J. T. *Introduction to Textile Finishing*. Plainfield, N.J.: Textile Book Service, 1966.

Peeling, R. H. "Drying of Textiles," *Textiles*, 13 (Autumn 1984), p. 69.

Reisfeld, A. "Face Finishing: Techniques for Making Basic Fabrics into "Innovative" Looks," *Knitting Times*, 52 (October 3, 1983), p. 12.

[2]*A Dictionary of Textile Terms* (Danville, Va.: Dan River Mills, 1967), p. 41.

Chemical Finishes

Although Chapter 20 described preparatory treatments and mechanical finishes and this chapter concentrates on finishes that are achieved chiefly through the use of chemical applications, there are some finishes that defy strict classification. Mercerization, for example, uses chemical treatment as part of a preparatory process and could be classified as a chemical finish. Likewise, finishes for shrinkage control include both mechanical techniques or chemical finishes or a combination of both.

Shrinkage Control

A reduction in the length or width of a fiber, yarn, or fabric is known as *shrinkage.* If fabrics shrink after they have been made into garments or household items, they may decrease in size to such an extent that the item is no longer serviceable. For example, a garment with a 25-inch waist size will decrease by 1¼ inches if it shrinks 5 per cent.

Some fibers shrink naturally. Wool, animal hair fibers, and rayon are examples of such fibers. Most fibers, however, do not shrink because of inherent fiber qualities but because they have been stretched during the processing of yarns and fabrics. When tension is removed from these fabrics, the fabric relaxes and returns to its original unstretched size and shape.

The wetting of a fabric causes the tension that has been applied during the manufacture of the fabric to be relaxed, so that fabrics generally shrink after the first and up to the fifth laundering. This type of shrinkage is known as *relaxation shrinkage.* Procedures and solvents used in commercial dry cleaning, as a rule do not permit fabrics to relax, as washing does, so that items that are dry cleaned may not shrink as readily. Shrinkage in dry cleaning is generally the result of the high moisture content in the solvent or steaming during pressing.

The warp yarns of woven fabrics are subject to greater tension than are filling yarns, so that fabrics generally shrink more in the warp than in the filling direction. Knit goods tend to stretch more during manufacture than do woven goods, and therefore knit goods are likely to shrink and change shape even more than woven goods.

Tumble drying or cleaning in a coin-operated dry-cleaning machine may produce yet another type of shrinkage. Consolidation shrinkage results from the return of a distorted fiber to its natural shape. Often the fiber becomes shorter and wider. The bulk of the fabric may actually increase, whereas the length and/or width decrease. Consolidation shrinkage requires the presence of mechanical action. A number of finishes have been developed to improve the performance of fabrics in regard to shrinkage.

Compressive Shrinkage Control

For fabrics that are subject to relaxation shrinkage, such as cotton, linen, and rayons, it would seem logical to "wash" or wet the fabrics to allow them to return to their true dimensions. This is not, however, practical for the manufacturer, not only because the process would be time consuming but also because the required equipment would take up a great deal of space. Instead, a method has been devised in which the fabric is "mechanically" reduced to its correct dimensions.

A sample of fabric is measured, the measurements are recorded, and the fabric is laundered in such a way as to produce maximum shrinkage. The shrunken fabric is measured, and the percentages of warp and filling shrinkage are calculated. This tells the processor how much to compress the fabric.

Compression of the fabric requires that these steps be followed. The fabric is dampened and is then placed on a machine that is equipped either with a continuous woolen or felt blanket or a rubber pad. These pads are constructed so that they can be both stretched and compressed. The fabric is carried on top of the blanket (or pad). The fabric meets the carrier at a point where the carrier is stretched around a curve. As the carrier moves from the curve to a straight area, it squeezes or compresses into a smaller, flat area. When the carrier compresses, the fabric it carries is also compressed. The fabric is then set into this compressed position. The machines used are engineered to provide the degree of compression needed for each type of fabric. The various patented processes of the compressive shrinkage type guarantee residual (or remaining) shrinkage of less than 1 per cent unless the fabric is dryer dried.

The Sanforized Company has developed a number of different compressive shrinkage control processes for different types of fabrics. All provide for shrinkage of less than 1 per cent. The trademark *Sanforized*® is used on woven cotton and cotton blends. *Sanfor-set*® is used on "easy-care" 100 per cent cotton and cotton blends. This latter process consists of the treatment of cotton fabric with liquid ammonia, which causes the fiber to swell and relax. Then the fabric is subjected to mechanical, compressive shrinkage control treatment. When the treatment is complete, the ammonia is removed from the cotton and recycled. The resulting fabric is both shrinkage and wrinkle resistant. It can be laundered in the same way as any cotton fabric: washed and tumble dried, although prompt removal from the dryer is recommended.

Shrinkage Control for Knits

During knitting and finishing, knit fabrics are subject to tension and stretching, especially in the warp direction. The construction of knits allows for greater stretch. They often shrink far more than do comparable woven goods. Shrinkage may be particularly pronounced in the warp direction. Processes similar to that described in the preceding section on compressive shrinkage control have been developed recently for the treatment of knits made from natural fibers and rayon.

Although different methods are utilized to return fabrics to their relaxed position, the principle remains that of compression of the fabric. One such process feeds fabrics through a machine in which a series of rollers operating at different rates of speed cause the fabric to become compressed

In another, knitted fabrics are stretched in the crosswise direction. This shortens the lengthwise direction where most knit shrinkage occurs.

Sanfor-Knit®, another shrinkage control process of the Sanforized Company, addresses the problem of knit shrinkage in both length and width. In this process, test garments that have had compressive shrinkage control treatment are made up in the desired size, are washed, tumble dried, and checked by a testing instrument called the "Knitpicker." The test instrument determines whether the garments have held both the length dimension and the elasticity in girth that will provide comfortable wear. If the garment does not meet the established standard, the knitter is advised as to changes that should be made in construction, yarn characteristics, or production techniques, Sanfor-Knit® garments are available in men's T-shirts, athletic shirts, polo shirts, briefs, and sports knits.

Still another technique for controlling shrinkage in knits is known as Micrex® shrinkage control. Fabrics are moved between two conveyors, each 6 inches apart. The cloth is kept in constant motion, both vertically and horizontally, by hot air from a high-energy nozzle system. This action allows the relaxation of the tensions that were imposed in previous operations, thereby allowing the fabric to relax to its original dimensions.

Synthetic knits are stabilized by heat setting. If heat setting has not been done the fabrics will shrink. Low-priced double knits, for example, may display shrinkage as a result of inadequate heat-setting.

Shrinkage Control for Rayon Fabrics

Viscose rayon fabrics have a tendency to continue to shrink more with each successive laundering or cleaning (this is known as *progressive shrinkage*). High-wet-modulus rayon fabrics exhibit less shrinkage. Shrinkage control for rayons is most effective when compressive shrinkage control treatments are followed by a resin finish to stabilize the fabric.

Careful control is needed in the application of chemical resins, as excessive concentrations can lower the quality and durability of the fabric. However, if applied correctly, chemical resins penetrate the fibers to prevent further shrinkage.

Shrinkage Control for Wool

Wool and animal hair fibers are among those few fibers that show progressive shrinkage. Most textile experts believe that it is the scale structure of wool that causes this continuous shrinkage, and the scale structure is also thought to be related to the felting of wool in which fibers shrink and cling closely together. In felting, fibers become increasingly entangled. (See Chapter 6.)

In addition to felting shrinkage, wool fabrics display the same type of residual shrinkage from relaxation that other fibers show. Shrinkage treatments for wool are of two types: those that alleviate the problems of relaxation shrinkage and those that eliminate or ameliorate felting shrinkage.

Relaxation Shrinkage. Several methods can be utilized to eliminate relaxation shrinkage in wool. Because these processes do not protect against felting shrinkage, fabrics that have these finishes should be dry cleaned or handled carefully during laundering.

1. Damp Relaxing or Steam Relaxing. High-quality worsted fabrics are subjected to a step that permits them to relax before they are cut into garments. The fabric is dampened or steamed and then permitted to dry in a relaxed state. The tensions applied to the fabric during processing are thereby removed. The process is sometimes called "London shrinking," although this British term is not often used by American textile manufacturers.

2. Cylinder Method. In this method, wool fabric is passed across perforated cylinders. Jets of steam are released through the holes in the cylinders, causing the fabric to be dampened. The damp fabric, which relaxes in size, is dried without tension.

Washable Wools

Attempts to produce washable wool fabrics that will not show felting shrinkage have led to the development of processes that alter the basic fiber structure. The wool scale structure is the cause of shrinkage; thus, most of these techniques alter the scale structure in some way.

1. Chlorination. Chlorine gas or liquid chlorine compounds apparently partially dissolve the edges of the wool fiber scales, thereby decreasing their tendency to catch on each other. This chemical is, however, destructive, and unless the process is carefully controlled, it can weaken or seriously damage the cortex of the fiber. The texture of the fabric tends to become rough and harsh.

Fibers that have been subjected to chlorination are often blended with other wool or man-made fibers. When blended with other wool fibers, problems may be encountered in dyeing, as chlorinated fibers tend to accept dyes more readily than do untreated fibers, thereby causing an unevenness in color.

2. Resin Coatings. A second method for the creation of washable wools is the application of a thin layer of synthetic resin to the surface of the fabric. The resins coat the scales and/or "spot weld" the fibers together to decrease shrinkage.

Different processes utilize varying resins. Problems encountered in the use of resins include a tendency for the fabrics to become stiff or harsh to the touch when enough resin is used to make the fabrics completely shrinkproof. Also, some resins are lost after a number of launderings.

Superwash® is a finish that uses chlorination followed by a resin finish. It is used especially for sweaters and knitwear.

Shrinkage Control Through Heat Setting

Synthetic fabrics may be stabilized through heat setting. Synthetics can be permanently set into shape by subjecting them to heat that is close to, but not beyond, their melting temperatures. This process is used to establish permanent dimensions for these fabrics. Synthetic knits, for example, are relatively free from shrinkage problems if they are properly heat-set, because heat setting may be used to stabilize their dimensions.

Wrinkle Recovery

Resistance to the formation of persistent wrinkles can be imparted to fabrics by different means. First, the fiber itself may recover naturally from wrinkling because of its resiliency. This is true of many synthetics and of wool. Second, because of their construction, certain fabric types recover from or disguise wrinkling. Terry cloth, knits, seersucker, plissé, and some "busy" prints are such fabrics. Or special finishes may be applied to fabrics to improve their wrinkle resistance.

Since cellulosic fibers are most prone to wrinkling, most wrinkle-resistant finishes were applied to fabrics made from these fibers or their blends. Wrinkle-resistant finishes date back to 1929 when Tootal Broadhurst Lee Ltd.[1] patented a finish that could be used on cottons and rayons. The Tootal process utilized urea formaldehyde. According to the theory behind this process—accepted at the time the process was

Finishes That Minimize Fabric Care

[1]U.S. Patent No. 1,734,516, Cotton Textile Impregnation with Resin by Foulds, assignor to Tootal Broadhurst Lee Co., November 5, 1929.

developed—the resin penetrated into the fiber and combined chemically with itself to form a long-chain compound inside the fiber. Once inside, the resin was thought to "stuff" the fiber so that it was less flexible and therefore resisted wrinkling.

Recent textile finishing processes that have been designed to secure wrinkle resistance in cellulosic fibers also utilize synthetic resins. However, researchers today believe that wrinkle resistance and recovery are achieved by chemical reactions between the resins and the molecular structure of the fiber. The long-chain molecules of the fiber are "cross-linked" through the action of the chemicals, thereby providing greater stability in the position of the molecules and preventing them from being too greatly deformed, or upon deformation, pulling them back into alignment, thereby eliminating the wrinkles.

Moreover, although resin finishes improve wrinkle resistance, finishing reduces both the absorbency and abrasion resistance of treated fibers. The blending of cellulose with resilient synthetic fibers may have the effect of improving wrinkle resistance. Blended fabrics abrade less readily, but the use of synthetics does nothing to improve absorbency. Even though most of the resin finishes are classed as durable, some loss in effectiveness is generally observable over the lifetime of the item.

Wash and Wear

Wash-and-wear finishes were an outgrowth of crease-resistant finishes, and, historically, this name was given to the next group of "easy-care" finishes to be developed. In the 1950s, much effort was put into developing finishes that would eliminate the need for ironing after items were laundered. Many of these "wash-and-wear" finishes (as they were called) did require some touch-up pressing prior to use.

Permanent or Durable Press

In spite of problems of adequate performance, of yellowing and degradation of fabrics that were bleached with chlorine bleach, and of a harsher hand, consumer acceptance of "wash and wear" was enthusiastic. Continued research to improve these resin finishes led eventually to the development of finishes that came to be known as permanent or durable press. Unlike the "wash-and-wear" and "easy-care" processes that were applied to flat goods, durable press finishes can be applied to constructed garments and products. This provides durably set shaping and creases. When laundered correctly, durable press garments require no ironing.

The terms *permanent* and *durable* press are often used interchangeably by consumers, advertisers, and the textile industry. Durable press is a more accurate term, as some of these finishes are diminished over the lifetime of the garment. It is important to remember that, although synthetic fibers may be blended with cellulosics for durable press fabrics, the finishes themselves react only with the cellulose component. Like the crease-resistant and "wash-and-wear" finishes, durable press finishes utilize the properties of fibers, fabric construction and/or treatment with synthetic resins or other chemicals.

Utilizing Fiber Properties

Heat setting of synthetic fibers can provide durability for creases and pleats. Furthermore, synthetic fibers that are quite resilient may not require ironing after laundering. These fabrics are not given chemical finishes.

Resin Treatments

By far the largest quantity of durable press is achieved through resin treatment of cellulosic and cellulosic-blend fabrics. The manufacturer applies the resinous material and then follows the application of the resin with a "cure" period. The cure may be applied either before the goods are constructed into garments or other items or after construction. (See Figure 21.1)

Precure and Flat-Cure Durable Press. Fabrics given a "precure" treatment are finished prior to delivery to the manufacture of textile items. The resin is impregnated into the fabric. Next, the fabrics are subjected to heat in a curing oven, which "sets" the resin. This has the effect of setting the fabric in a flat position. "Durable press" yard goods used by home sewers are made by the precure process.

When precured goods are used in manufactured items, the items are pressed with a hot-head press. The heat and pressure of the press shape the item, chiefly by heat setting the thermoplastic fibers in the blend. Precured fabrics have been made into plain dresses or blouses, curtains, table and bed linens, and draperies, all of which require relatively little shaping.

Postcure Process. Manufacturers found that precured fabrics were difficult to handle in manufacture. Furthermore, these fabrics were difficult to press into permanent shape because they had been set as "flat." An alternative method of producing durable press items was, therefore, evolved.

In this new method, known as the *postcure* process, the fabric is impregnated with resin and dried. In this state, treated but not cured, the fabric is shipped to the manufacturer. Garments or other items are manufactured from the cloth, and then the finished item is cured in a special curing oven. Creases, pleats, hems, and the like are "permanently" set in this way. Care must be taken to be sure that the fabrics are free from wrinkles or puckers or these, too, will be permanently set.

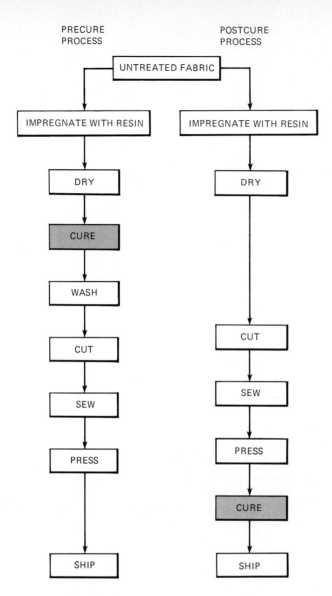

PRECURE PROCESS

POSTCURE PROCESS

UNTREATED FABRIC

IMPREGNATE WITH RESIN

IMPREGNATE WITH RESIN

DRY

DRY

CURE

WASH

CUT

CUT

SEW

SEW

PRESS

PRESS

CURE

SHIP

SHIP

FIGURE 21.1 Comparison of the sequence of processing of durable press treatments.

Problems of Durable Press

Manufacturing. The production of durable press items raises the cost of manufacture. The additional steps required and the cost of special equipment for finishing both contribute to this increase in price that is passed along to the consumer. Most consumers, however, appear to be willing to pay more for a product that requires less care.

In constructing items, the garment manufacturer must make changes in sewing techniques. Stitching of long seams may cause puckering unless special thread is used and unless changes in sewing machine tension, type of needle, and length of stitching are made.

It is also important for the garment manufacturer to select findings such as interfacings, linings, hem tape, and the like that will be compatible with durable press. They must not wrinkle or shrink differently from the fashion fabric.

Use and Care. Durable press fabrics, like their forerunners the crease-resistant and wash-and-wear fabrics, exhibit some loss in strength and particularly a decrease in abrasion resistance. One hundred per cent cotton fabrics have been known to undergo loss in strength as high as 50 per cent when given durable press finishes. In blends, areas such as collars and cuffs of men's shirts or the knees of children's pants often show the results of abrasion by fraying or "frosting." Frosting is a change in color that results from the breakage and loss of fibers because of abrasion. The soft, fuzzy ends of the fibers give abraded areas a lighter or darker shade of color, depending on the color of the synthetic fibers that have not been worn away. (See Figure 21.2.)

Blending of cellulosic fibers with synthetics, especially with polyesters that have increased abrasion resistance, can overcome the abrasion problem to a great extent. It is therefore relatively rare to find 100 per cent cellulose durable press items. Even with blends, however, the problem of different rates of abrasion for each fiber remains.

A variety of different blends of thermoplastic and cellulosic fibers are used for durable press. The most common of these are polyester (from 75 to 40 per cent) and cotton (from 25 to 60 per cent), polyester (from 65 to 50 per cent) and high-wet-modulus rayon (from 35 to 50 per cent),

FIGURE 21.2 Closeup view of durable press fabric in which frosting has taken place. Darker cotton fibers have worn away, leaving a line of lighter polyester fiber.

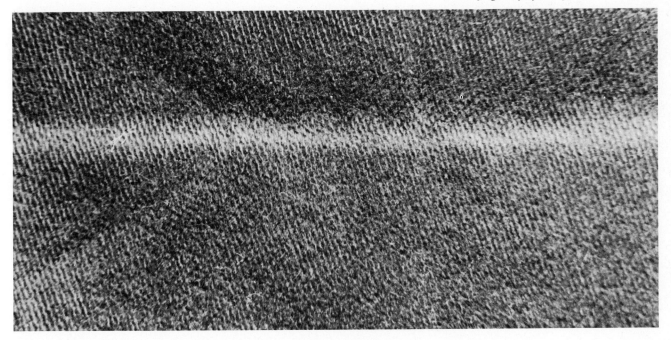

and varying other combinations such as rayon or cotton with nylon. Spandex is sometimes utilized for its stretch properties.

Once creases and pleats are permanently set in durable press garments, making alterations is difficult. It is easier to shorten skirts or trousers than it is to lengthen them, even though it may be difficult to get as crisp a press as the fabric had when it came from the manufacturer. The crease mark of the original hem will always show in a lengthened garment. For these reasons, durable press garments should be bought to fit and should not be given extensive alterations.

Some of the synthetic fibers used in durable press allow the penetration of oil but resist the penetration of water. This is also true of the synthetic resins used in creating durable press finishes. As a result, oil-borne soils may be absorbed by durable press fabrics. Since the fabrics resist wetting, laundering (even with detergents that would normally remove oil-based soils) does not clean them effectively. When this problem became a major source of consumer complaints, special "soil-releasing" finishes were developed to overcome these difficulties. (See the following section on Soil-Releasing Finishes.)

The quantities of resins needed to produce satisfactory durable press make some of these fabrics rather stiff. They may not drape as well as fabrics without the finish. For the same reason, these fabrics may not absorb moisture readily and may be less comfortable to wear in warm weather than untreated fabrics. Also, if fabrics are not given an adequate afterrinse, a "fishy" odor may cling to the new fabric. This odor is generally lost after one or more launderings.

Special care in home laundering is required to produce optimum durable press performance. Washing should be done at warm rather than hot temperatures. Best results are seen when a warm wash cycle is followed by a cool rinse. Durable press finishes are designed for use in automatic laundering equipment, especially tumble dryers. If items must be line dried, they should be removed from the washer before the "spin" cycle in which fabrics may become creased, unless the washer is equipped with a special durable press wash cycle.

Dry fabrics should be removed from the dryer immediately after the cycle ends to avoid having creases formed while the item lies wrinkled in the bottom of the dryer. (Dryers that have special "durable press" cycles have an initial warm drying phase, followed by a cool air phase.) If items do become wrinkled, wrinkles will be removed if they can be placed in a warm dryer for a few minutes with a damp item and then immediately removed from the dryer.

Safety. Formaldehyde is an important component of easy-care and durable press finishes. Questions have been raised about the possibility that health hazards result from exposure of textile industry workers to formaldehyde fumes. The levels of this chemical that are permitted to be present in the air during manufacture of any product in which formaldehyde is used are restricted; however, there is currently an unresolved debate about whether these levels should be lowered still more. (See Chapter 23 for a fuller discussion of this issue.)

Soil results when a textile comes into contact with soiled surfaces or with air- or water-borne soils. Soil is retained either by mechanical entrapment of soil within the yarn or fabric structure or by electrostatic forces that bond the soil to the fabric.

One way to approach the problem of soil is to prevent its deposition on the fabric. (See Figure 21.3.) Another is to seek ways to facilitate its removal. Special finishes have been developed that have taken both of these approaches.

Soil and Water Repellency

Stain Repellency

Scotchgard®, Zepel®, or other finishes that repel water and oil may be classified as stain-resistant finishes. They are applied to fabrics used in products such as upholstery fabrics and tablecloths to prevent soiling by staining. They may be applied to the fabric at the time of manufacture in a liquid form or sprayed onto the fabric after the fabric has been applied to a piece of furniture. Aerosol spray containers of some of these finishes can be purchased for home application. The finish tends to diminish with laundering, but it can be renewed by using the sprays.

Soil-Releasing Finishes

Soil-releasing finishes were developed largely as a result of the tendency of durable press and polyester fabrics to absorb and hold oil-borne stains. The soil-releasing finish should not be confused with soil-repellent finishes, although Zepel® and Scotchgard® are both stain resistant and soil releasing.

Soil-releasing finishes may be of two types. The first type prevents soil from entering the fabric by coating the surface of the fibers and yarns. Soil and stains are held on the surface of the fabric. When the fabric is laundered, the soil and stains are readily lifted away by the washing action.

Alternatively, soil-release finishes alter the characteristics that cause soil to bond to the fibers. Polyester presents particular soiling problems because of the chemical structure of the fiber. A relatively hydrophobic fiber, especially on the surface, those parts of the polyester fiber that are hydrophilic are deep within the fiber. Therefore, even during the washing process, soil may be deposited deep within the fiber and become very difficult to remove. A variety of soil-releasing finishes have been developed for polyester and polyester blends that make polyester and resin-treated cellulosics more water receptive.

One type of finish that forms hydrophilic grafts on the fiber results in improvements in soil release and soil redeposition. Most soil-release fin-

FIGURE 21.3 (A)   The drop of liquid on the left is oil, on the right is water. Note in Figure A how the fluorochemical stain resistant finish enables this nylon upholstery fabric to resist both oil and water based stains and soil.

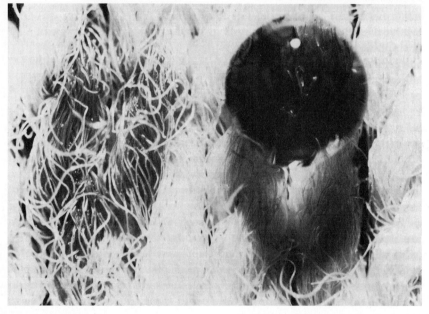

FIGURE 21.3 (B)   The silicone finish applied to this nylon upholstery fabric enables it to resist only water-based stains. Oil-based stains are absorbed by the silicone-treated fabric. (Note, however, that application of silicone finishes over fluorochemical finishes will cancel out oil repellency.) Courtesy of 3M Company

ishes for polyester are applied during the finishing of the fabric and are compatible with durable press finishes.

At the same time that soil-releasing finishes increase the receptivity of fibers to water, a second benefit is gained. Static electricity buildup is decreased as absorbency is increased. Increased absorbency also increases the comfort of the garment in warm weather. Fuzzing and pilling seem to be decreased by soil-releasing finishes as well, as the finish almost lubricates the fabric.

Effective soil-releasing finishes should result in fabrics from which common soil is removed during home laundering with normal detergents. Oily stains, often hard to remove from durable press fabrics, should be removable in home laundering. The disadvantage of most of these finishes is that they are gradually diminished through laundering.

Water Repellency

Waterproof Fabrics

A fabric that is waterproof allows no water to penetrate from the surface to the underside. Coated fabrics can be waterproof. Coatings made from rubber or synthetic plastic materials can create fabrics that are completely waterproof; however, these fabrics tend to be warm and uncomfortable because they create a barrier that traps air and perspiration close to the body.

Recent advances in fabric coating materials have led to the development of textiles that are said to be waterproof and yet allow the passage of moisture vapor from perspiration. GORE-TEX® is one of the best known of these products, and it is used extensively in outdoor clothing for active sports. Garments made of GORE-TEX® are made by placing a membrane of PTFE fluorocarbon underneath a layer of outer fabric. A lining fabric layer is also added. The manufacturer claims that this membrane has 9 billion microscopic pores per square inch that are 20,000 times smaller than a drop of water but 700 times larger than a molecule of water vapor. Therefore water from rain or snow is kept on the outside, but moisture vapor from perspiration can escape. (See Figure 21.4.)

Performance of these garments is closely related to their construction. Seamlines must be sealed, so that water does not pass through the fabric by way of the holes left by the sewing needle. Tears, rips, or worn spots are also areas in which leaks can occur. The manufacturer recommends that GORE-TEX® garments not be laundered in liquid detergents, as these tend to leave surfactants on the surface that may allow the wetting of the fabric. Instead, use cold-water temperatures and powdered detergent.

Other manufacturers have also produced treatments for fabrics that are said to make them "waterproof and breathable." Bion II® is made by Biotex Industries, and Dicrylan® is a product of Ciba-Geigy.

Water-Repellent Fabrics

The term *water repellent* should not be confused with the term *waterproof*. Water-repellent fabrics resist penetration by water but are not

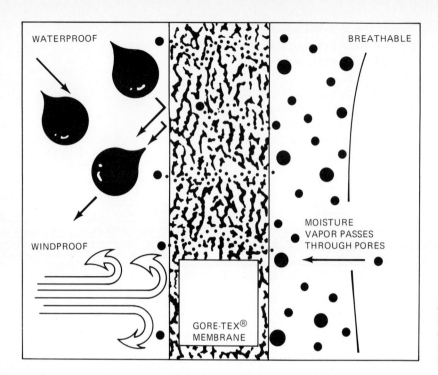

FIGURE 21.4 Manufacturer's diagram shows how GORE-TEX® membrane repels water but allows moisture vapor to pass through pores that are too small to permit passage of water. Courtesy W. L. Gore and Associates.

completely waterproof. Such fabrics represent a practical alternative to fabrics that keep out water and air, since they resist wetting and also allow the passage of air. The passage of air is imperative if one is to have a garment that is comfortable to wear.

Water repellency is conferred through a combination of the principles of fabric construction, the application of one of the finishes that are classified as either renewable finishes or durable finishes, and appropriate selection of fiber content.

Renewable Finishes. Renewable water-repellent finishes are removed during laundering and dry cleaning. These are relatively inexpensive and easily applied, so that they can be renewed after each laundering or dry cleaning.

Either wax emulsions or metallic soaps are used to secure renewable water repellency. Both these materials are naturally water repellent, and when they are applied in such a way that they coat the yarns of the fabric, they permit the passage of air between the yarns, but prevent the passage of water. If the fabric on which they are coated has a close, compact weave, water repellency is improved. Of course, in conditions in which the fabric is subjected to long periods of exposure and sufficient force, water will eventually penetrate any water-repellent fabric.

Durable Finishes. As in renewable finishes, the effectiveness of durable water-repellent finishes is improved if fabrics with high yarn counts and close weaves are selected. Although the first water-repellent finishes were of the renewable type, subsequent research has concentrated on effective durable finishes. A number of different materials have been developed that confer a more permanent finish.

1. *Water Repellency.* Many of these finishes begin with fatty or oily substances that possess natural water repellency; these substances are then treated with other chemicals to form compounds that can be absorbed by the fiber and are also insoluble in dry cleaning or soap solutions. Pyridinium compounds, methylol stearamides, and ammonium compounds are used.

Silicone compounds are also effective in producing durable water-repellent fabrics. Trade names for silicone finishes include Cravanette®, Hydro-Pruf®, and Syl-mer®.

2. *Water and Oil Repellency.* Most of the finishes under discussion repel water, but they do not repel oil. They are quite serviceable for products in which only water repellency is required. However, by using fluorochemical compounds, it is possible to produce finishes that repel both water and oil. Scotchgard®, and Zepel® are trade names of such finishes. (See Figure 21.3.)

Some of the durable finishes are durable only to laundering or only to dry cleaning. It is especially important, therefore, for the consumer to follow care instructions attached to these products.

Flame-Retardant Finishes

Flame Retardance

Finishes that make fabrics flame retardant have gained in importance since the passage of a series of laws known as the Flammable Fabrics Act. The act provides for the setting of certain standards in regard to flammability that must be achieved in wearing apparel, carpets, mattresses, and children's sleepwear.

The terminology employed in a discussion of flame retardancy can be confusing. For purposes of clarifying the following discussion, a series of definitions follows.[2]

1. *Flame-resistant* material (polymer, fiber, or fabric) is one that exhibits lower flammability than other well-known materials under identical, carefully specified conditions of testing.
2. *Self-extinguishing* material (fabric or garment) is one that, when ignited at the bottom edge in a vertical position, does not continue to burn after the source of ignition is removed.
3. *Flame-retardant* material is a material that decreases the flammability of a combustible polymer, fiber, or fabric to which it is added.

[2]Terms adapted from "Textile Flammability," by Joseph E. Clark and Giuliana Tesoro, paper presented to the State of the Art Symposium on Man-made Fibers, American Chemical Society, June 1974, Washington, D.C.

4. *Thermally stable* material (fiber or polymer) is one that has a high decomposition temperature and is thus inherently flame resistant because of chemical structure (rather than through the presence of added flame retardants.)

Thermally stable materials include fibers such as asbestos and glass fiber and certain synthetic fibers that have been developed for the aerospace industry, such as Kevlar® and Nomex® aramid. These could be called fireproof substances that will not burn. Glass fiber has had widespread commercial distribution, but it is limited to household textile products such as draperies, window shades, or lamp shades. Thermally stable synthetic fibers have not been developed for general use, but for specialized protective clothing for industrial and military uses. Not only are they expensive, but they lack the aesthetics that would make them useful in consumer products.

Some synthetic fibers are flame resistant. Modacrylics, for example, which offer adequate flame resistance at a moderate cost, are currently used in carpets, curtains, and children's sleepwear. Vinyon fibers and Cordelan®, a biconstituent matrix fiber, also exhibit flame-resistant qualities. These last two fibers are not especially useful in carpets, as their resilience is not adequate, but they can be made into children's sleepwear.

Man-made fibers can be modified to reduce flammability by the addition of flame-retardant materials to the solution prior to extrusion.

If inherently flame-resistant or -retardant fibers are not used, flame-retardant textiles can be produced by either of the following means: (1) incorporating a flame-retardant additive during or immediately after polymerization to produce modified fibers or (2) applying flame-retardant finishes to fiber, yarn, or fabric.

Polyester, acrylic, rayon, cellulose acetate, and triacetate are produced in flame-retardant fiber varieties. Polyester, polyester and cotton blends, cellulosics, and nylon are treated with finishes applied to fiber, yarn, or fabric. Wool is inherently moderately resistant to burning.

In addition to these so-called "durable fire-retardant finishes," a solution of 30 per cent boric acid and 70 per cent borax can be used as a rinse for products. This rinse will provide temporary flame retardancy, but it produces a decrease in the softness and drapability of the fabric to which it is applied.

Problems with Flame Retardance

Except for thermally stable materials, flame retardancy may be lost through normal use and care of products. Laundering of fabrics treated with flame-retardant finishes must be carefully controlled. Use of chlorine bleach, soaps, or low-phosphate detergents and some fabric softeners may result in a loss of the flame-retardant finish. Laundering in hard water will also diminish the effectiveness of the finish. Since some states have banned the sale of phosphate detergents, much of the treated children's sleepwear sold in these states will gradually become combustible.

Blends of synthetic and natural fibers also create problems in relation to flame retardancy. The finishes that are effective on cellulose fibers, for example, may not be effective when those fibers are blended with polyesters. Polyester retardants may also be rendered ineffective when the polyester is combined with cotton.

Yet other hazards result when layers of different fibers are combined. A cotton dress worn over a nylon slip will burn very differently from a cotton dress worn over a rayon slip. Often the effect of these combinations is not fully understood. These problems and others regarding flammability have yet to be overcome.

Flammable Fabrics Act

Flammability of textiles is an important contributor to serious injuries and loss of life and property in fires. After a number of injuries and deaths due to highly flammable garments, the Flammable Fabrics Act of 1953 was passed. In this legislation the use and sale of *highly* flammable materials for clothing were banned. This law was amended in 1967 to extend coverage to (excluding some types of hats, gloves, and footwear) carpets, draperies, bedding, and upholstery.

The Flammable Fabrics Act is a federal (national) law. Local and state laws and other regulations may impose restrictions on the use of flammable textile materials in public buildings, but there is no *national* regulation of such items as draperies or curtains for home or public places, other than that they may not be "highly flammable."

Since 1967, the regulations have been modified yet further. Originally only those materials that are *highly* flammable were prohibited, but now the manufacture of *all* flammable carpets, mattresses, and children's sleepwear (sizes 0 to 14) is banned.

In 1972, responsibility for administering and enforcing the law was given to the Federal Consumer Product Safety Commission. Products found to be in violation of the law may be confiscated and destroyed. Persons found guilty of "manufacturing for sale, offering for sale, or selling items that do not comply with the law are subject to a fine of not more than $5,000 and/or imprisonment of not more than a year." The secretaries of the Commerce and Health and Human Services departments are required to sponsor research concerning fire-related hazards. When, on the basis of these investigations, the secretary of Commerce determines that a new standard is needed, the Bureau of Standards is given the responsibility of conducting research analyses and developing test methods.

Standards that products must meet are established in a two-step procedure. Notice is given by the commission that there may be a need for a new standard, and a proposed standard is set forth. Individuals are invited to offer their opinions about the proposals. Finally, the standard and test method(s) are announced. Standards and test methods become effective one year after this final notification.

Highly Flammable Textiles

The standard for this part of the law requires that "a piece of fabric placed in holder at a 45 degree angle and exposed to a flame for 1.0 second must not spread flame up the length of the sample in less than 3.5 seconds for smooth fabrics or 4.0 seconds for napped fabrics."[3] Five specimens measuring 2 inches by 6 inches are required for each test. The time of flame spread is taken as an average of five specimens.

In 1983 the Consumer Product Safety Commission issued a rule that allows persons and firms performing testing of fabrics to use apparatus and procedures other than the ones specified in the standard, "provided that the apparatus or procedure is as stringent or more stringent than the apparatus and procedure prescribed by the Standard."

Carpets

Carpet standards (Standard no. FF2-70) require that manufacturers submit samples of carpet fabric for testing prior to marketing. Eight samples are tested by the "methenamine pill" test. This pill, which simulates a source of flame such as a lighted cigarette, is placed in the center of a bone-dry sample of carpet and is ignited. If the resulting flame does not extinguish itself before it spreads 3 inches in more than one of the samples, the carpet will not pass the test and must be withdrawn from manufacture.

The pill test determines only surface ignition. It does not assess the contribution of carpets to the spreading of fires, the behavior of carpets in an environment created by a general fire, or the toxicity of the fumes produced.

Other test methods are used to assess the performance of carpets during fires. These test methods are controversial and are not accepted by all authorities as valid. They are not required by the Flammable Fabrics Act. The most widely used test of this type is called the "tunnel test," which uses a horizontal furnace in which the test material is mounted on the ceiling. The sample is exposed from below, at one end of the tunnel, to a gas flame of 1400°F, which is fanned by an artificial draft. Measurements are made of the volume of smoke and of the time required to spread the flames over a given distance. These figures are compared with an established smoke index and flame spread scale. The governmental agencies that regulate programs have established a level of performance on the tunnel test that carpeting installed in hospitals and facilities participating in Medicare and Medicaid programs must meet.

[3]U.S. Consumer Product Safety Commission, *Fact Sheet* (Washington, D.C.: The Commission, June 1974), p. 1.

There are several exceptions to carpets covered under flammable fabrics legislation. One-of-a-kind carpets need not meet the standards. Handcraft items, oriental carpets, and the like are not covered by this law. Carpets that are 6 feet by 6 feet or smaller than 24 square feet that do not pass the pill test may be sold, provided that they are clearly labeled as being flammable.

Children's Sleepwear

Since 1972, children's sleepwear in sizes 0 to 6X (Standard no. FF 3-71) has been regulated under the Flammable Fabrics Act. For the first year that the law was in effect, sleepwear that did not meet the standards established had to be labeled as flammable. After July 1973, flammable children's sleepwear was banned from manufacture. Already existing stocks of flammable sleepwear, however, continued to be sold after that date. Coverage under the law was extended in May 1975 to sleepwear sizes 7 to 14 (Standard no. FF 5-71).

Standards for children's sleepwear sizes 0 to 6X and for sizes 7 to 14 differ slightly. The standard for the smaller sizes is more stringent, in that it is thought that older children are more likely to be able to protect themselves in the event of a fire.

In the established testing procedure for sleepwear, each of five samples of the fabric being tested is hung in a cabinet and exposed to a gas flame along its bottom edge for 3 seconds. The flame is then removed. Both size groups must conform to these standards: samples cannot have an average char length of more than 7 inches; no single sample may have a char length of 10 inches. For the sizes 0 to 6X, an additional criterion is imposed, limiting the length of time molten materials or fragments of the test specimens may continue to burn on the base of the test cabinet.

These standards must be met not only by new fabrics but also by those that have been laundered fifty times. All sleepwear must be labeled permanently with instructions as to the care required to maintain the flame-retardant finish. Both manufactured sleepwear items and fabrics intended for use in sleepwear must meet the standard. This includes fabrics and wearing apparel such as pajamas, nightgowns, robes, and sleepers, and underwear that is sold in children's sleepwear departments. (The Consumer Product Safety Commission has indicated that it will take legal action against manufacturing or retail firms that promote children's playwear that has not been made to be fire retardant as sleepwear.)

Mattresses

After December 1973, it became illegal for manufacturers to make mattresses that are combustible. The flammability of mattresses is tested using lighted cigarettes, which were selected as a source of ignition because statistics showed that the greatest number of mattress fires were caused by smoking in bed.

This testing procedure requires that nine cigarettes be placed at various points on the mattress and another nine cigarettes between two sheets on the mattress. To pass the standard (FF 4-72), the char length on the mattress surface may not be more than 2 inches in any direction from any cigarette. The legislation applies to mattress ticking filled with "any resilient material intended or promoted for sleeping upon" and includes mattress pads. Pillows, box springs, and upholstered furniture are excluded.

Other Standards

Consideration is also given to requirements of flame retardancy for other products. The Consumer Product Safety Commission has begun to solicit opinions as to the need for standards in upholstered furniture, blankets, and children's wearing apparel. Individual states have enacted their own flammability legislation. California, for example, has enacted legislation that forbids the sale of any combustible clothing for children, sizes 0 to 14.

Upholstered Furniture

In November 1978, the Consumer Product Safety Commission (CPSC) considered a draft of a mandatory standard for flammability of upholstered furniture. In response to this move by the CPSC, the Upholstered Furniture Action Council (UFAC), a trade organization for the furniture industry, proposed that a voluntary plan devised by the industry be utilized. The industry plan, as it evolved, included a fabric rating system, criteria for construction of furnishings, a labeling plan, and compliance procedures.

The CPSC gave the industry an opportunity to try the voluntary plan. The rating system grouped all upholstery fabrics into one of two classes, based on fiber content. Fabrics containing at least 50 per cent of thermoplastic fibers, which are less likely to ignite, are placed in Class I; all other fabrics are placed in Class II. Class II fabrics can be upgraded to Class I if they can pass a cigarette ignition test. Cigarettes are responsible for many of the fires that start in upholstered furniture.

Furthermore, various components of furniture such as welting, filling and padding, decking materials, and substances placed as a barrier between Class II fabrics and the cushion filling must be able to withstand cigarette ignition tests. Only furniture meeting the Class I standards could carry the UFAC approval label.

Compliance was to have been monitored through the UFAC by periodic inspections. UFAC expected that voluntary compliance would be extensive and predicted that, by 1984, 94 per cent of the dollar volume of sales in the field would comply with the standard.[4]

[4]"News from CPSC," November 1979, pp. 1 ff.

Compliance with the standard has not reached the predicted level; however, the commission considers that progress is being made. At present there are no plans to move ahead with mandatory flammability standards for furniture.

Consumer Reaction

Consumer and research interest in fabric flammability reached its peak in the ten-year period beginning in the late 1960s. In 1977, however, TRIS, one of the chemicals used in some finishes given to polyester, acetate, and triacetate fabrics, was banned by the Consumer Product Safety Commission after it was shown to have possibly mutagenic effects. TRIS-treated fabrics and garments were withdrawn from the market and other chemicals used in fire-retardant treatments were tested, and any that were not proved safe were also banned from use. Nevertheless, much of the public quickly became suspicious of fire-retardant treatments in general. As a result, interest in fire retardancy has waned. In spite of the obvious hazards from textile combustibility to certain high-risk groups such as the elderly, the handicapped, and cigarette smokers, there is little likelihood of increased regulation of textiles in regard to flammability at the present time.

Antistatic Finishes

Synthetic fibers, being poor conductors of electricity, tend to build up static electric charges. Electricity causes garments to cling or to build up charges that are dissipated through unpleasant, though mild, electric shocks when the wearer touches a conductor such as a metal door knob or another person's hand.

Some finishes have been developed that attempt to decrease static buildup. However, these finishes tend to have limited effectiveness, largely because they are gradually lost during laundering. The antistatic finishes work on either of two principles: either they coat the surface of the fiber with a more conductive substance, or they attract to the fiber small amounts of moisture that increase its conductivity.

More successful cutdown in static buildup of synthetics is achieved through the modification of the polymer prior to extrusion. These finishes, which are permanent, incorporate compounds in the fiber structure that increase the moisture absorbency that, in turn, increases conductivity.

Another approach is to use special, high-performance antistatic fibers. Metal, metallized, and bicomponent fibers containing metal or carbon are among those used. A small proportion of these fibers is blended with conventional synthetic fibers. Being more conductive, they serve to dissipate the static charges.

Antistatic sprays can be purchased for home use. Fabric softeners applied in the final rinse during laundering will also provide some reduction in static buildup.

A number of finishes have been developed to overcome problems of individual fibers or to meet a particular need. Such finishes are applied on a fairly limited basis to particular fibers, yarns, or fabrics, many of which are intended for rather specialized uses.

Special-Purpose Finishes

Abrasion Resistance

Fibers vary in their resistance to damage from abrasion (surface wear from rubbing or friction). Synthetics, generally, have better abrasion resistance than do natural fibers. Improved abrasion resistance can also be attained by the application of certain synthetic resins to fabrics. However, these finishes apparently create some difficulties by causing fabrics to soil more readily. Such finishes are not used widely.

Absorbency

Cellulosic fibers that are being used for diapers, towels, or other items in which absorbency is important may have ammonium compounds applied to them. These compounds increase the absorbency of the fabrics somewhat.

Some attempts have been made to increase the absorbency of synthetic fibers. Antistatic finishes for synthetics do make them more hydrophilic. Surface hydrolysis of polyester using sodium hydroxide does cause the fiber to be more absorbent, and a number of reports of this process have appeared in the literature. Nevertheless, this process is thought to have limited commercial use at present.[5]

Soil-releasing finishes on polyesters make them more absorbent.

Antislip Finishes

Smooth, filament yarns may have a tendency to slide against one another, creating flawed areas in a fabric or problems of seam slippage. This is known as yarn *slippage*. Resins coated on the surface of these fabrics will keep the yarns in place, as the resin holds yarns together at the points where the yarns interlace. Resin antislip finishes are durable.

Other antislip finishes can be created by coating silica compounds on fabrics. However, these are only temporary finishes.

Antimildew and Antirot Finishes

Mildew, a fungus or mold, is a whitish growth that affects certain textile fibers when they are stored in a damp condition in a warm place. This growth damages the fiber and causes serious staining. Cellulosic fibers

[5]S. Vail, "Finishing," in *Encyclopedia of Textiles, Fibers, and Nonwoven Fabrics* (New York: Wiley-Interscience, 1984), p. 488.

are most susceptible to mildew. Protein fibers are less likely to be attacked.

The best protection against mildew is to make certain that the fabrics are dry when stored and that they do not become damp during storage. Mildew is an especially serious problem in warm, humid climates. Mildew weakens fabrics, and home treatments to remove stains from mildew may be degrading to them as well.

Rotting is an acute problem with bast fibers, such as jute and hemp, when they are used for bags, ropes, and other materials that are exposed for long periods to water, damp soil, or wet floors. Rot- and mildew-resistant fabrics can be made by treating the fabrics with antiseptic substances. Since copper has bactericidal power, copper solutions may be used to confer rot resistance to fabrics. A variety of other chemical substances (among them phenol, formaldehyde, and pentachloral phenol) that are not harmful to the fabric and inhibit the growth of microorganisms are also used.

During experimentation with melamine resin finishes for crease resistance, it was learned that these finishes retarded mildew and rotting. Home processes can be used to guard against mildew. An afterrinse with boric acid will retard the formation of mildew.

Antibacterial Finishes

Chemical substances that inhibit the growth of bacteria are also used to finish goods that will be used in health care products, apparel, home furnishings, or fabrics used in the hotel/restaurant industry.

Although these finishes are classified as either renewable or durable, even so-called durable finishes are removed gradually during laundering. Renewable finishes can be replaced during laundering.

Certain specific organic ammonium compounds are known to combat diaper rash. Many diaper services routinely apply this finish to the diapers that they launder. Antimicrobial finishes are being applied to nonwoven fabrics used in surgical and medical products such as instrument packs, surgical packs, and surgical draping fabrics.

Heat-Reflectant Finishes

An increased level of insulation can be provided in garments and draperies by the addition of heat-reflectant finishes to textile products. Most of these products are treated with a spray coating of metal and resinous substances. The heat-reflectant material is sprayed onto the surface of a closely woven fabric. The finish is designed to keep heat either on one side or the other of the fabric. The finish is effective only with radiated heat.

Lining fabrics are usually constructed so that the finish is applied to the inside of the fabric. The finish reflects the body heat back toward the wearer, thus providing added warmth. In protective clothing to be worn under hot conditions, the finish is worn to the outside to deflect heat away *from* the body. Draperies may also be treated to provide greater insulation for homes. Treated draperies placed inside windows may serve to keep heat inside the home or to reflect heat outward, preventing it from warming the house.

Some of the processes designed to produce heat reflectance use aluminum in the finish, as it provides excellent reflectancy. The trade name for this process is Milium®.

A variant of this principle is utilized in fabrics in which a thin layer of aluminum, foams, resins, or synthetic rubber is coated or laminated to fabric.

Light-Reflectant Finishes

Light-reflectant finishes are created by the application of microscopic reflective beads to the surface of a fabric. The increased number of persons who jog or ride bicycles after dark is probably responsible for the application of this finish to a variety of garments for sports and to other items such as back packs. Three M produces a reflective finish called Scotchlite®. The manufacturer notes that the finish does not alter the color or appearance of the garment by day, but after dark the fabric "lights up" when directly in the path of the lights of an oncoming vehicle. (See Figure 21.5.)

Light Deterioration

Many textile fabrics are deteriorated by exposure to sunlight, so attempts have been made to protect fabrics from light damage. Of the rays in the spectrum of the sun, the ultraviolet are the most destructive of fibers. Although antilight finishes have yet to be perfected, those that are being tried either coat the fabric or impregnate the fibers with materials that absorb ultraviolet rays but are not themselves damaged by or removed by exposure to these rays. Such finishes are particularly important in olefin fabrics, which are degraded by sunlight unless ultraviolet stabilizers are added. Such additives to olefin fibers are permanent and are not lost during usage.

Synthetics that have been delustered with titanium dioxide are especially subject to damage from sunlight. This chemical apparently accelerates damage to the fiber and fading of dyes. The addition of certain chemical salts to the melt solution prior to spinning can ameliorate this problem.

Mothproofing Finishes

Wool and other animal hair fibers are attacked by the larva of the clothes moth. Silk is not attacked by moths as it lacks cystine, a sulfur-

FIGURE 21.5   Runner wears garments with Scotchlite light reflective finish. At night, light is reflected from headlight beams to alert motorists to the presence of the wearer. Courtesy of 3M Company.

containing amino acid moths seem to favor. The moth lays its eggs on the fabric, and when the larvae (or grubs) hatch, wool becomes their source of food. Although moth grubs will not attack all fibers, they will eat their way through most fabrics to reach wool. For this reason, other fabrics stored on top of wools that have not been mothproofed may be damaged by moth larvae trying to reach the wool.

To prevent moth damage, precautions must be taken in the care and storage of wool products. Since larvae more readily eat areas of the cloth that are soiled with food stains, clothing should be stored in a clean condition. A variety of moth-repellent substances are on the market to be applied to fabrics or placed in closed storage containers to keep the insects away.

Finishes to prevent moth damage operate according to one of two basic principles. Either the finish is a substance (an insecticide) that is poisonous to the moth larvae, or the finish alters the fiber in some way that makes the wool unpalatable to moth larvae, thereby "starving" the grubs.

The insecticide finishes may be applied during manufacture or during dry cleaning. Some of these finishes are durable, whereas others must be renewed with each cleaning.

The second type of finish effects a change in the chemical structure of the fiber. Through chemical treatment, the disulfide cross-linkages, which are attacked by the moth larvae, are changed and are replaced by larger linkages that the moths cannot digest. These finishes are permanent.

Summary

Whereas the finishes discussed in Chapter 20 were compared with "cosmetics," used to enhance the physical properties of fabrics, the finishes discussed in this chapter are designed to modify the actual behavioral properties of textiles. Although finishes may change the appearance, texture, and hand of a fabric, they do so for more than cosmetic reasons. Finishes that modify, or in some way improve, inherent fiber properties may result in an increase in price and/or a change in care requirements, but consumers have generally been receptive to the improvements and are willing to pay for them. But the costs of some finishes cannot be measured only by an increased price tag on the product. Durable press finishes do result in shorter wear life and may result in more frequent replacement of garments, and there are other kinds of trade-offs involved. For example, proper laundering of fire-retardant–finished products requires the use of phosphate-containing detergents. Phosphates have been cited as a cause of water pollution. The choice is between one kind of hazard and another. There are no easy answers and no simple solutions.

Recommended References

AVERELL, R. B. "Recent Trends in Finishing," *ACPTC Combined Proceedings* Monument Co: Association of College Professors of Textiles and Clothing, Inc., (1982), p. 26.

BOGLE, M. *Textile Dyes, Finishes, and Auxiliaries.* New York: Garland Publishing Co., 1977.

Book of Papers, 1978 Technical Conference. Research Triangle Park, N.C.: American Association of Textile Chemists and Colorists, 1978.

DATYE, K. V., and A. A. VAIDYA, *Chemical Processing of Synthetic Fibers and Blends*. New York: John Wiley & Sons, Inc., 1984.

"Establishing World Flammability Terms," *Textile World*, 125 (January 1975), p. 107.

FERGUSON, C. "Hydrophilic Finishes for Polyester: Durability and Processing Advantages," *American Dyestuff Reporter*, 71 (June 1982), p. 43.

"Finishing: An Overview," *Textile Industries*, 139 (May 1975), p. 99.

GAGARINE, D. M. "Hydrophilic Soil Release," *Textile Chemist and Colorist*, 10 (December 1978), p. 13.

HATCH, K. L., and R. R. KING. "Chemical Finish Information on Textile Labels: Will the Consumer Benefit?" *Textile Chemist and Colorist*, 12 (October 1980), p. 13.

HOLMES, F. H. "How Safe from Fire Need Textiles Be?" *Textiles*, 12 (Spring 1983), p. 2.

JOHN, C. A. "Developments in Carpet Finishing," *Canadian Textile Journal*, 101 (November 1984), p. 28.

KERSHAW, A., and J. LEWIS. "The Role of Polymer Treatments in Shrink-Proofing of Wool," *Textile Month* (April 1976), p. 40.

LOMAS, G. R. "Coated Fabrics. Part 1: Light Weight Breathable Fabrics," *Textiles*, 14 (Spring 1985), p. 2.

NAPHTA, R. "Internal Anti Stats," *American Dyestuff Reporter*, 64 (April 1975), p. 41.

NEEDLES, H. L. *Handbook of Textile Fibers, Dyes, and Finishes*. New York: Garland STPM Press, 1981.

RICHARDSON, G. A. "The Dyeing and Finishing of Cotton Knitgoods. The Balance Between Quality and Cost," *Canadian Textile Journal*, 102 (March 1985), p. 21.

RUSHFORTH, M. A. "Machine Washable Wool," *Textiles*, 10 (Autumn 1981), p. 58.

SHET, R. T., et al. "Modification of Polyester and Polyester/Cotton by Alkali Treatment," *Textile Chemist and Colorist*, 14 (November 1982), p. 21.

TATTERSALL, R. "Recent Progress in Textile Finishing," *Textile Month*, (March 1976), p. 42.

TAYLOR, M. A. "Fabrics and Garments for Rainwear," *Textiles*, 11 (Spring 1981), p. 25.

TOWNSEND, M. W. "Moths and Wool," *Textiles* 12 (Spring 1983).

TROTMAN, E. R. *Dyeing and Chemical Technology of Textile Fibres*. New York: John Wiley & Sons, Inc., 1984.

TURNER, J. D. "An Introduction to Foam Finishing," *Textile Chemist and Colorist*, 12 (March 1980), p. 19.

VIGO, T. "Antibacterial Fiber Treatments and Disinfection," *Textile Research Journal*, 51 (July 1981), p. 454.

The Care of Textile Products

Attention to the correct procedures for cleaning and maintaining textile products will extend the useful life of the product. Improper cleaning and storage can result in either severe damage to the fabric or an increased rate of wear over a period of time.

The accumulation of soil on fabrics is one of the factors that causes fabrics to deteriorate. Spilled food, for example, can make a fabric that is normally unappetizing to insects into an attractive meal for moths and carpet beetles. The "ground-in dirt" that television commercials decry can increase the abrasion of yarns as gritty soils rub against fibers, causing them to break. Soil removal is, therefore, one of the most important aspects of caring for fabrics if they are to be maintained in good condition.

Soil deposited on fabrics is made up of different materials. Some types of soil are soluble; other types are insoluble. Soluble dirt is made up of organic acids, mineral acids, alkaline substances, blood, starches, and sugars. All these substances dissolve in cool or warm water, and although they may sometimes require special stain-removal techniques, these soluble substances present no extraordinary problems in cleaning.

Water alone will remove soluble soil, but insoluble soils may be held onto the fabric by physical attraction or in films, greases, or oils. Such soil requires the use of some kind of cleaning aid.

Historical Development

Just when soap was developed is not clear. Soaplike materials dating from 2500 B.C. have been found in clay cylinders from the city of Babylon in the Near East, but whether this substance was used as a cleaning agent or as a dressing for the hair is not known. Other references from antiquity likewise provide no clear description of the uses of soap, although the Roman writer Pliny describes the process by which it was made. By the Middle Ages the craft of soapmaking was well enough developed that guilds or associations of soapmakers had been formed.

For many centuries, the making of soap from natural materials was a major household task. Animal fats and lye, made by soaking wood ashes in water, were boiled together to make a strong soap. Commercial soapmaking co-existed with the home process. Over time the commercial processes gradually improved and eventually replaced the homemade product as chemists found better ways of isolating and manufacturing the components used in the soapmaking process.

Soap is a good cleaning agent; however, soaps do not perform well in hard water, which is water with higher concentrations of minerals such as calcium and magnesium. The minerals in the water combine with soap to form an insoluble gray curd or scum. Once the soap has combined with these minerals, less soap is available for cleaning, and larger quantities of soap must be used. Also the hard-water scum may be deposited on clothing, leaving it gray or dull looking.

An alternative cleaning agent to soap was developed during World War I in Germany when fats and oils normally used for making soap were in short supply. This substance, a synthetic detergent, had another advantage: it did not combine with hard-water minerals.

The term *detergent* can create some confusion. Cleaning agents are known as detergents. Both soaps and synthetic detergents are, technically speaking, detergents, even though the term "detergent" is often used by the general public to refer only to synthetic detergents (sometimes abbreviated *syndets*). For purposes of this discussion the term "detergent" will be used to refer to synthetic detergents and to both soaps and detergents where those terms are interchangeable.

Although synthetic detergents were produced in the United States as early as the 1930s, it was only following World War II that their use increased dramatically. Today "syndets" dominate the home laundry market, and only a few brands of laundry soap remain.

Soil Removal

Soil can be removed from fabrics by laundering or by dry cleaning. These processes can be carried out in the home or by professional cleaners. The principles utilized are the same in both instances, but the equipment and laundry or dry-cleaning products that are used will vary.

Laundering

The process of laundering soiled fabrics consists of wetting the fabric and its soil, removing the soil from the fabric, and holding the soil in suspension so that it does not redeposit on the fabric during washing. Detergents increase the cleaning ability of water. The addition of detergent to water decreases the surface tension of water, thereby increasing its wetting power. When the wetting power of water is increased, textiles are penetrated more completely by water. A simple experiment will demonstrate this principle. Take a small piece of nylon fabric and float it on the surface of a small bowl of water. The surface tension of the water (molecular forces in the outer layer of water) enables the nylon to float for a time, until it becomes wet throughout. Drop a few drops of liquid detergent into the water. The fabric will become wet immediately and sink.

The wet fabric is agitated by the motion of the washing machine or by hand scrubbing. The soil is broken into smaller particles and is surrounded (emulsified) by the detergent and is then lifted off the fabric by the action of the detergent. The detergent surrounding the soil particles prevents their being redeposited on the fabric as the washing progresses. When fabrics are rinsed, the soil and detergent are rinsed away.

Soaps

Soap is made from fatty acids and alkali that react together to form the soap. Some degree of alkalinity is necessary for cleaning, and as the soap dissolves, the washing water becomes somewhat alkaline in reaction. Much soil is acid in chemical reaction and will tend to neutralize some of the alkalinity of the soap and decrease its effectiveness. Therefore, more heavily soiled items require more soap.

To assure that adequate alkalinity is present for thorough washing, extra alkali is added to increase the effectiveness of the soap. Soaps with added alkali are known as "built" or "heavy-duty" soaps and are designed for general laundering. Less alkaline soaps are also available for laundering more delicate fabrics. Because protein fibers are damaged by excessive alkali, only light-duty soaps should be used for washing wool, silk, and other delicate fabrics.

Synthetic Detergents

Synthetic detergents are synthetic products made from petroleum and natural fats and oils. Unlike soaps, synthetic detergents do not form hard-water scum but dissolve readily in both hard and soft water. Some detergents are made to maintain low suds levels, whereas others are made to produce more suds. Synthetic detergents are available in high-, medium-, and low-sudsing formulations. All suds levels clean equally well, but low-suds formulations are often necessary for optimum cleaning in front-loading washers, in which the laundry is carried up and around as the basket rotates. When the wet laundry reaches the top of the circle, it drops to the bottom, thereby providing the agitation necessary for releasing soil. High-suds detergents break the fall of the fabrics, thereby decreasing the washing action. Low-suds detergents provide the cleaning agent without interfering with the washing action.

Typically, synthetic detergents are formulated from the following materials: surfactants, builders, processing aids, agents to protect washer parts, antiredeposition agents, fluorescent whiteners, and perfumes.

1. *Surfactants.* Surfactants are organic chemicals, the active ingredient in synthetic detergents, that alter the properties of water and soil so that dirt can be removed. The surfactant molecule might be described as having a long "water-hating" or hydrophobic body with a "water-loving" or hydrophilic head. The action of the surfactant breaks up water droplets that surround soil particles, allowing water to penetrate. Groups of surfactant molecules (called *micelles*) surround the soil, with the hydrophobic section of the molecule attached to the soil and the water-loving head of the molecule oriented toward the water in which the particles become suspended. (See Figure 22.1.) The most commonly used surfactants are linear alkyl benzene sulfonate (LAS), alcohol sulfates (AS), nonionic surfactants, and soap. Both LAS and AS surfactants are anionic; that is, they generate negative electrostatic charges in water. Similar electric charges repel each other. Most fabrics also carry negative charges, so that the negative charge of the surfactant molecules surrounding the soil particles is effective in preventing the redeposition of soil on the fabrics being washed.

Nonionic surfactants do not carry electric charges as they dissolve. They are more effective in removing oily soil than are anionic surfactants. Soaps may also be used as a minor ingredient in detergent formulations because they help to break the foam produced by LAS-containing products. Soap is often used in controlled-suds products. Detergent manufacturers use one or more of these types of surfactants in their formulations. One of the popular detergent combinations is made up of LAS, soap, and nonionic surfactants.

SURFACTANT REMOVING AND SUSPENDING DIRT

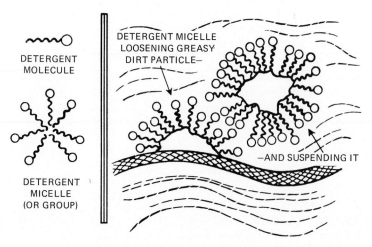

FIGURE 22.1 *Diagram showing the action of a surfactant removing and suspending dirt. Reprinted from Monograph #108, "The Technology of Home Laundering." Courtesy of the American Association for Textile Technology, Inc.*

2. *Builders.* Builders are substances that soften water and maintain alkalinity. Until recently, the majority of builders used in detergent formulations were phosphates, which are especially effective in counteracting water hardness. They also disperse and suspend dirt and maintain alkalinity, which is necessary to neutralize many soils that tend to be acid in chemical reaction.

   Fears that phosphates may be contributing to water pollution have led some states and communities to restrict the use of phosphate-containing detergents. As a result, detergent manufacturers have developed a variety of nonphosphate or low-phosphate detergents that utilize other builders. These nonphosphate builders include sodium silicate, sodium carbonate, sodium sulfate, and sodium citrate. Research has shown, however, that detergents containing these builders are not as effective in removing soil as are those with phosphates.[1]

   Some of these builders require high alkalinity to operate most efficiently and may irritate or harm the skin and/or mucous membranes. Such products must be labeled to warn consumers about using care in handling them.

3. *Processing aids.* Materials are added that maintain good powder properties in powdered detergents. Commonly used materials include sodium silicate (also cited previously as a builder), sodium sulfate, and small amounts of water.

4. *Agents to protect washing machine parts.* Silicates added to detergents help to prevent corrosion of the parts of the washer that are exposed to water and detergents.

5. *Antiredeposition agents.* Although anionic surfactants help to prevent the redeposition of soil, other agents are also added to the detergent to prevent redeposition. The most common chemical used for this purpose is sodium carboxymethyl cellulose.

6. *Fluorescent whiteners.* Fluorescent whiteners are additives that make white wash appear whiter and brighter. When light strikes a fabric on which these agents have been deposited, the agents absorb the ultraviolet wavelengths that are not visible to the human eye and reemit them in a visible wavelength. The formulation of the fluorescent whitening agent is such that the rays of light it emits cause fabrics to reflect a whiter light, rather than light that is more yellow. Fabric, therefore, appears whiter and brighter. Fluorescent whiteners do not remove soil.

7. *Perfumes.* Many detergents contain perfumes. These products give the laundered items a more pleasant odor.

8. *Other additives.* Enzymes, oxygen bleaches, blueing, and/or fabric softeners may be added to some detergents to create what the in-

---

[1]Carol E. Avery and Doris E. Harabin, *A Comparison of Phosphate and Non-Phosphate Detergents*, Bulletin No. 415 (Kingston, R.I.: Agricultural Experiment Station, University of Rhode Island, 1975), p. 72.

dustry calls "multifunctional products." Each of these additives can be purchased and used separately from the detergent by the consumer, as well.

The specific formulation of each synthetic detergent varies, of course, from one product to another. In some states or localities, environmental legislation has been enacted to restrict the use of some chemicals that had been used as builders in detergents, particularly phosphates, that have been used to soften water and provide alkalinity. Detergent manufacturers have revised formulations to conform with such restrictions. Also, concern about the slow decomposition of some detergents in sewage treatment and in surface water has led to the use of biodegradable surfactants, that is, surfactants that are readily decomposed after use.

Laundry detergents are produced in both liquid and powder form. Heavy-duty liquid detergents have shown remarkable growth in the last decade, increasing their market share from 2 per cent to 22 per cent between 1972 and 1982, and it is predicted that they will achieve a 25 to 30 per cent market share by the 1990s.[2] One reason for the increase in these products is that they can be formulated more readily without phosphates than can powdered detergents.

Water Softeners or Conditioners

Synthetic detergents do not produce hard-water scum as soaps do, but it is necessary to use larger quantities of detergent in hard water than in soft water. (Soft water is water free from these dissolved minerals.) Many families, therefore, find it helpful to decrease the hardness of water by some form of water conditioning. Hard water can be softened either by commercial softening systems installed in the home to soften all water used in the household or by the addition of powdered water softeners to the laundry. Powdered softeners are of two types: precipitating and nonprecipitating.

Precipitating water softeners combine with the minerals that cause water to become hard to form a compound that precipitates or settles out of solution into visible granules. These granules may be deposited on laundered items. Also, precipitating softeners must be added to wash water *before* the soap is added. They cannot dissolve soap scum once it has been formed. Washing soda and Climalene® are precipitating water softeners.

Nonprecipitating water softeners keep hard-water minerals tied up in chemical combination and in solution so that neither soap scum nor a precipitate is formed. Furthermore, nonprecipitating softeners can dissolve soap scum formed before the softener was added to the water and can strip scum left in clothes from previous washings in hard water.

[2]D. E. Haupt, "U.S. Detergent/Surfactant Trends—1980s," *Technical Bulletin SC:745-83* (Houston: Shell Chemical Company, 1983.)

Minerals, such as iron or manganese, in water may stain fabrics. The addition of bleach to such water may cause the formation of colored salts that, when deposited on fabrics, cause discoloration. Nonprecipitating water softeners will prevent such staining by tying up the minerals. Calgon® and Spring Rain® are nonprecipitating water softeners.

Bleaches

Bleaches are often used along with soaps and synthetic detergents in laundering. It is important to remember that bleaches do not *clean* clothing. Detergents do the cleaning; bleaches are used to whiten fabrics and remove stains.

Bleaches oxidize the coloring matter in fabric, and some stains are removed by the oxidation of the coloring matter in them. Two basic types of bleaches are used in the home: chlorine bleaches and perborate bleaches.

Chlorine bleaches are the stronger of the two. They utilize active chlorine to oxidize colored matter. But after the chlorine has oxidized all stains, color, and so on, it begins to oxidize susceptible fibers. For this reason, chlorine bleaches need to be used in correct concentrations, be dissolved thoroughly before application, and rinsed out thoroughly or they may damage the fibers. Some dyes are damaged by chlorine bleach; therefore, it is rarely recommended that colored fabrics be bleached with chlorine bleach.

The most frequent mistakes made in handling chlorine bleach are

1. Using too much bleach. Follow directions on the package. Do not assume that if a little bleach is good, twice as much is better.
2. Pouring bleach directly onto clothing. Bleach should be added to a full tub of water and agitated thoroughly before any laundry is added. Adding concentrated bleach to a washer full of clothing will result in concentrated bleach being poured over some garments, which may damage them. If bleach must be added to the wash at a later point, bleach should be diluted in one or more quarts of water before it is poured into the washer.
3. Bleaching items that should not be bleached. Read care labels carefully. Some resins or fibers such as spandex will yellow on contact with chlorine bleach. Chlorine bleach damages other fibers such as silk or wool or spandex.
4. Soaking heavily stained items in concentrated bleach solutions. Exposure to concentrated bleach solutions may damage certain fibers and should be avoided. Items should not be soaked in even low concentrations of chlorine bleach for longer than 15 minutes.

Chlorine bleaches are sold in both dry and liquid forms under a variety of trade names. Clorox® and Purex® are trademarks of chlorine bleaches.

Commercial laundries use bleaches routinely on white cottons and linens. To avoid damage from chlorine bleaches, these establishments control bleaching concentrations very carefully and follow the bleaching with a "sour" treatment in which a weak acid rinse is used. This neutralizes any excess bleach, which is alkaline. It is also important to rinse bleached fabrics carefully at home, or deterioration of the fibers can continue for as long as any bleach remains in the fiber.

Oxygen or perborate bleaches do not use chlorine for oxidation, but use other chemicals such as sodium perborate, hydrogen peroxide, and potassium monopersulfate. They also do not whiten as efficiently in a short period of time. These bleaches will work best if used in every laundering. Like chlorine bleaches, oxygen bleaches should be diluted before addition to the wash, as some colors may be sensitive to the bleaching action of these products. Some of the trade names of oxygen bleach include Clorox-2®, Miracle White®, Snowy®, Purex All Fabric/All Color®, and All-fabric Beads-O-Bleach®. Hydrogen peroxide is sold in drugstores.

Pretreatment Products

Certain types of stains are especially hard to remove. Among these are protein-based stains such as body soils, blood, eggs, baby formula, grass stains, and chocolate. Special enzyme presoak products contain selected types of enzymes that may break down these soils to simpler forms that are then more readily and completely removed by the laundry soap or detergent. Fabrics are soaked from 30 minutes to overnight, depending on the instructions and the age and amount of the stain. Enzymes may be incorporated into the formulation of some multipurpose detergents.

Aerosol prewash soil and stain removers that contain perchlorethylene or other petroleum-based solvents are sold for use on synthetics and durable press fabrics. They help to remove greasy stains such as those made by lipstick, bacon fat, coffee with cream, and ballpoint pen. Instructions on the label generally recommend that they be applied to fabrics 5 minutes or longer before washing.

Fluorescent Whiteners or Optical Brightners

Most detergent formulations contain fluorescent whiteners. It is also possible to purchase fluorescent whiteners or "optical brighteners" for use in the home. These agents do not attach themselves to different fibers to the same degree, so their effectiveness may vary from fiber to fiber. Also, chlorine bleach may destroy the active ingredients in fluorescent whiteners, so that the two products should never be added to the laundry at the same time.

Some optical brighteners for household use are called "blueing." In using blueing, which has a blue color, one must follow directions carefully. Too great a concentration of the brightener may give the white laundry a bluish tint, instead of reflecting the desired blue-white light.

Disinfectants

One of the purposes of laundering clothing and household items is to destroy bacteria. Ordinary laundering procedures using detergent and hot water will destroy many bacteria. Recent trends toward using cooler washing temperatures may have the effect of allowing higher levels of bacterial survival, however, so that when there is illness or infection in a home, special care may be required to sanitize items being washed.

To be suitable for sanitizing laundry, a disinfectant should kill bacteria without injuring or discoloring fabrics. Furthermore, disinfectants should not leave a residue that is harmful to the user and they must be compatible with detergents.

USDA researchers have found four types of disinfectant that satisfy these criteria that are readily available and reasonable in cost. These are

1. *Liquid chlorine bleaches.* (Labels should state that the bleach contains 5.25 per cent of sodium hypochlorite.)
2. *Quarternary disinfectants.* These disinfectants are colorless and odorless compounds that are effective in hot, warm, or cold water. Labels should carry the term *Benzalkonium, chloride.* Such substances are available in drugstores and from janitors', hospital, or dairy supply houses.
3. *Pine oil disinfectants.* These disinfectants are effective in hot or warm water. They have a characteristic pine oil odor that does not remain after laundering. The label should state that the product contains at least 70 per cent steam-distilled pine oil. Pine oil disinfectants are sold in supermarkets or grocery stores.
4. *Phenolic disinfectants.* Effective in warm or hot water, phenolic disinfectants are sold under such well-known trademarks as Pine-Sol®, Lysol®, and Texize 8304 Centex®. The label should contain the names "orthobenzyl-parachlorophenol" or "ortho-phenyl-chlorophenol."[3] Disinfectants should be used according to the directions on the package.

Fabric Softeners

Fabric softeners deposit a waxy, lubricative substance on fibers that causes fabrics to feel softer. All fabric softeners are based on quarternary ammonium compounds. Although different compounds are used, all have a long fatty chain that imparts the soft feel to the fabric. The softening effect is especially desirable for fabric with a napped or pile surface that may become stiffer and less soft after laundering, particularly if the fabrics are line dried rather than dryer dried. Towels, washable blankets, diapers, corduroy or other pile fabrics, and sweaters are often washed with fabric softeners.

[3]*Sanitation in Home Laundering,* Home and Garden Bulletin No. 97 (Washington, D.C.: U.S. Department of Agriculture, October 1971).

In addition to making fabrics feel softer, fabric softeners cut down static electricity, make ironing easier, and improve the performance of wash-and-wear finishes, often making touch-up ironing unnecessary. At the same time, the continual use of fabric softeners causes a buildup of the softener on the fibers, thereby decreasing absorbency. On items where absorbency is an important function, such as towels or diapers, it is recommended that fabric softeners not be used in every wash but in alternate washings or periodically.

Fabric softeners are designed for addition to the wash, the rinse, or the drying cycle. Add wash-added liquid fabric softeners to the wash water *before* the detergent and the clothes are placed in the water to prevent fabric staining. These products can generally be used in the final rinse cycle as well.

Rinse-added fabric softeners cannot be used in the wash cycle, nor should they be used along with other laundry additives such as blueing or water softeners. These products and detergents may interfere or react adversely with the softener. They should be diluted, unless machine dispenser instructions state that this is not necessary, and they should not be poured directly onto fabrics as they may cause staining.

Dryer-added fabric softeners are added to a load of clothes in the dryer and are supplied either in sheet or packet form. Sheet-type softeners are impregnated into a nonwoven fabric or polyurethane foam sheet. Packet-type softeners are attached to a fin of the dryer drum. In both cases, the heat of the dryer and the tumbling action of the clothes cause the softener to be transferred to the clothes and spread evenly on the fabric surfaces.

Specific instructions for the use of fabric softeners are provided on the package. Follow these instructions carefully to achieve best results.

Starches

Starches are sizings that are added during home laundering. They help to restore body to limp fabrics. Starches help to keep fabrics cleaner, as dirt tends to slide off the smooth finish produced by starching. Also, soil may become attached to the starching material rather than to the fiber, making the soil easier to remove.

Since vegetable starches were used originally for this purpose, the term *starch* was given to these products. Today, however, "starches" may be either vegetable or resinous compounds. Liquid or dry sizings are added in the rinse cycle of laundering. Aerosol sprays are added at the time of ironing. Vegetable starches must be renewed after each washing. Resins penetrate the fiber more thoroughly and will last through several washings.

Laundry Equipment

Washing Machines. Except for hand-laundered items, most laundry in the home is done in washing machines. Washing machines may be of three types: automatic, semiautomatic, and wringer style. Many households use automatic dryers.

Each of these appliances differs in its construction, features, and operation. It is beyond the scope of this book to discuss the variety of types of laundry equipment in relation to the care of fabrics.

Although some fully automatic washers have programmed cycles that require only the selection of a suitable term, such as *permanent press*, it is more likely that the user will have to select water temperature, time duration for washing, and type of agitation. Most washers offer a low, moderate, or high water temperature; washing time durations of from 2 to 14 minutes; and either gentle or normal agitation. Washing machine instruction manuals will give specific directions for settings that should be used for varying types and loads of laundry. Of course, the user will have to select the detergent and other laundry additives such as bleach, water softener, fabric softener, and so on that are to be used in the wash.

Table 22.1 offers typical time, speed of agitation, and water temperature for various fiber groups.

TABLE 22.1

Fiber	Time	Water Temperature	Agitation and Spin Speed
Wool	1–3 min	110–120°F	slow
Cotton and linen	10–12 min	120–140°F	normal
Man-made and			slow
durable press	5–7 min	110–120°F	

The expansion of the use of wash-and-wear and durable press finishes has led to the manufacture of washers and dryers that have "permanent press" cycles. These cycles are designed to produce optimum performance from durable press finishes by using varying water temperatures in washing and rinsing, decreased agitator speeds in extracting water, and by ending the drying cycle with a cool temperature to avoid heat-setting wrinkles into dried clothing. If durable press fabrics have been washed in a normal wash cycle rather than in a durable press cycle, the final rinse may have been made with hot water. During the extraction of the water in the spin cycle, clothes are compressed against the basket walls. If the fabric is warm, the cooling that takes place will cause the fabrics to wrinkle, whereas the cool water cycles of the special durable press cycle provide better wrinkle resistance. If the clothes are to be dried in an automatic dryer, these wrinkles will be tumbled out of the fabric. If clothes are to be line dried, however, durable press items should be removed from the washer before the final spin cycle.

Laundry Procedures

Although the washer and dryer do the physical work of laundering, the selection of appropriate laundry procedures is essential for efficient cleaning. Sorting, selecting washing time and water temperature, pretreating spots and stains, and carefully selecting laundry products for use all require that decisions be made by the person doing the washing.

Laundry should be sorted carefully according to color, fiber type, degree of soil, and delicacy of construction. Items should be grouped together that require the same laundry products, water temperature, length of washing, and speed of agitation.

White items should be washed together. White permanent press and nylon fabrics are most prone to discoloration if washed with items of color and should be washed only with other whites. Colorfast items may be laundered together, even if the colors are not the same, but it is advisable to separate light and dark colors at least until it has been ascertained that the dark colors will not bleed. Those items that are not colorfast should be washed separately; in some cases they may have to be washed by hand.

Fabrics that produce lint, such as bath towels, chenille fabrics, terry items, and the like, should be washed separately from those that attract lint; that is, corduroy, synthetic fabrics, and durable press. It is especially important to separate light-colored lint-producing fabrics from dark colored lint attractors, such as dark nylon underclothing or socks.

Loads should, as much as possible, be balanced with some small and some larger items. This will provide better washing action; however, lightweight man-made items should be dried separately from heavy cellulosic fabrics, such as towels, because the man-made items will dry first and then become overheated during the time required for the heavier, cotton fabrics to dry.

Heavy items such as blankets or bedspreads may have to be washed alone because of their size. When a heavy load is put into a washer, it should be arranged carefully so that the washer balance is maintained during spin cycles.

Heavily soiled items should not be washed with lightly soiled items, but alone. The lightly soiled items may pick up soil or discoloration from the wash water.

Before laundering, clothing should be checked carefully. Pockets should be emptied since coins or other items left in pockets can damage washers or dryers, and tissues left in pockets will produce lint that will be picked up by garments. Lint and dirt should be brushed out of pant cuffs. Zippers and hooks should be closed so that they do not catch onto other items and tear them. Pins, heavy ornaments, and buckles may also cause damage to fabrics and should be removed. Tears should be mended before laundering, as the agitation of washing and drying may cause them to be enlarged.

Some items may require pretreatment for optimum cleaning. Soil lines that are formed around collars and cuffs may be difficult to remove from synthetic and durable press fabrics. The area may be pretreated by dampening the area and then rubbing liquid detergent or a paste made of powdered detergent and water over the soiled area.

Stain Removal

Stain removal is easiest immediately after the fabrics have been subjected to staining. It is important to know the kind of material that caused the stain and the fiber of which the fabric is made. The selection of the method to use in removing the stain will be determined by the type of stain, and the type of stain remover to be used may be limited by the type of fabric.

Before any stain remover is used, the fabric should be tested to determine whether it is colorfast to the stain remover or whether it may have a finish that the stain remover will harm. Fabrics can be tested by sponging a small amount of stain remover onto a seam, hem, or other hidden part of the item. If a suitable stain remover cannot be found, the item should be taken to a professional dry cleaner for treatment.

Table 22.2 lists a wide variety of materials that may produce stains on fabrics and suggests an appropriate treatment for washable fabrics. Some stains cannot be removed. Extensive staining by hard-to-remove substances or stains on delicate and/or nonwashable fabrics are probably best removed by a professional dry cleaner who has a variety of spot- and stain-removing chemicals and an expert knowledge of stain removal. It is always helpful to the cleaner, however, if the customer points out the stain and identifies the staining substance.

TABLE 22.2   Stain Removal Chart

Stain	Treatment
Adhesive tape, chewing gum, rubber cement	Apply ice or cold water to harden surface; scrape with a dull knife. Saturate with cleaning fluid. Rinse; then launder.
Baby formula	Soak in a product containing enzymes for at least 30 minutes (several hours for aged stains). Launder.
Beverages (coffee, tea, soft drinks, wine, alcoholic beverages)	Sponge or soak stain in cool water. Then pretreat with prewash stain remover, liquid laundry detergent, liquid detergent booster, or paste of granular laundry product and water. Launder using chlorine bleach, if safe for fabric, or an oxygen bleach. Older stains may respond to soaking in a product containing enzymes, then laundering.
Blood	If stain is fresh, soak in cold water. For dried stains, soak in warm water with a product containing enzymes. Launder. If stain remains, rewash using a bleach safe for fabric.
Brown or yellow discoloration from iron, rust, manganese	Use a rust remover recommended for fabrics; launder. Do **not** use a chlorine bleach to remove rust stains because it may intensify discoloration. For a rusty water problem, use a nonprecipitating water softener in both wash and rinse water. For severe problems, install an iron filter in the system.

Stain	Treatment
Candle wax	Scrape off surface wax with a dull knife. Place stain between clean paper towels and press with a warm iron. Replace paper towels frequently to absorb more wax and to avoid transferring stains. Place stain face down on clean paper towels. Sponge remaining stain with cleaning fluid; blot with paper towels. Let dry. Launder. If any color remains, rewash using a chlorine bleach, if safe for fabric, or an oxygen bleach.
Chocolate	Prewash with a product containing enzymes in warm water or treat with a prewash stain remover. Launder. If stain remains, rewash using a bleach safe for fabric.
Collar, cuff soil	Pretreat with prewash stain remover, liquid laundry detergent, or paste of granular detergent and water. Launder.
Cosmetics	Pretreat with prewash stain remover, liquid laundry detergent, paste of granular detergent, or laundry additive and water or rub with bar soap. Launder.
Crayon	For a few spots, treat same as candle wax. For a whole load of clothes, wash with hot water using a laundry soap and 1 cup baking soda. If color remains, launder using chlorine bleach, if safe for fabric. Otherwise, soak in a product containing enzymes or an oxygen bleach using hottest water safe for fabric; then launder.
Dairy products (milk, cream, ice cream, yogurt, sour cream, cheese, cream soups)	Treat as for baby formula. Soak in a product containing enzymes. Launder.
Deodorants, antiperspirants	Pretreat with liquid laundry detergent. Launder. For heavy stains, pretreat with prewash stain remover. Allow to stand 5 to 10 minutes. Launder using an oxygen bleach.
Dye transfer	You can attempt restoration of white fabrics that have picked up color from other fabrics by using a packaged color remover, following label directions. Launder. If dye remains, launder again using a chlorine bleach, if safe for fabric. For colored fabrics and whites that cannot be chlorine bleached, soak in oxygen bleach. Launder. This type of stain can be prevented if proper sorting and laundering procedures are followed.
Egg	Treat as for baby formula. Soak in a product containing enzymes. Launder.
Fabric softener	Dampen the stain and rub with bar soap. Rinse out, then launder.
Fruit, juices	Wash with bleach safe for fabric.
Grass	Soak in a product containing enzymes. If stain persists, launder using chlorine bleach, if safe for fabric, or oxygen bleach.
Grease, oil (car grease, butter, animal fats, salad dressings, cooking oils, motor oils)	Pretreat with prewash stain remover, liquid laundry detergent, or liquid detergent booster. For heavy stains, place stain face down on clean paper towels. Apply cleaning fluid to back of stain. Replace paper towels under stain frequently. Let dry, rinse. Launder using hottest water safe for fabric.
Ink	Some inks in each of the following categories—ballpoint, felt tip and liquid—may be impossible to remove. Laundering may set some types of ink. Try a pretreatment method using a prewash stain remover, denatured alcohol or cleaning fluid. Use·one of the following methods with denatured alcohol or cleaning fluid. First, sponge the area around the stain with the stain remover before applying it directly on the stain. Place stain face down on clean paper towels. Apply denatured alcohol or cleaning fluid to back of stain. Replace paper towels under the stain frequently. Rinse thoroughly. Launder.

Stain	Treatment
Ink (continued)	Another method is to place the stain over the mouth of a jar or glass and hold the fabric in a taut position. Drip the stain remover through the spot so that the ink will drop into the container as it is being removed. Rinse thoroughly. Launder.
Mildew	Badly mildewed fabrics may be damaged beyond repair. Launder stained items using chlorine bleach, if safe for fabric. Or soak in oxygen bleach and hot water; then launder.
Mud	When dry, brush off as much as possible. Pretreat with a paste of granular detergent and water, liquid laundry detergent or a liquid detergent booster. Launder. For heavy stains, pretreat or presoak with a laundry detergent or a product containing enzymes. Launder.
Mustard	Pretreat with prewash stain remover. Launder using chlorine bleach, if safe for fabric.
Nail polish	May be impossible to remove. Try nail polish remover but do not use on acetate or triacetate fabrics. Place stain face down on clean paper towels. Apply nail polish remover to back of stain. Replace paper towels under stain frequently. Repeat until stain disappears, if it does. Rinse and launder.
Paint	**Water-based:** Rinse fabric in warm water while stains are still wet; then launder. Once paint is dry, it cannot be removed.
	Oil-based and varnish: Use the same solvent the label on the can advises for a thinner. If label is not available, use turpentine. Rinse. Pretreat with prewash stain remover, bar soap or laundry detergent. Rinse and launder.
Perfume	Pretreat with prewash stain remover or liquid laundry detergent. Launder.
Perspiration	Use a prewash stain remover or rub with bar soap. If perspiration has changed the color of the fabric, apply ammonia to fresh stains, white vinegar to old stains and rinse. Launder using hottest water safe for fabric. Stubborn stains may respond to washing in a product containing enzymes or oxygen bleach in hottest water safe for fabric.
Pine resin	Sponge cleaning fluid into the stain; let dry. Mix liquid laundry detergent and ammonia; soak stain in the solution. Launder using liquid laundry detergent.
Scorch	Treat as for mildew. Launder using chlorine bleach, if safe for fabric. Or soak in oxygen bleach and hot water, then launder.
Shoe polish	**Liquid:** Pretreat with a paste of granular detergent and water; launder.
	Paste: Scrape residue from fabric with a dull knife. Pretreat with a prewash stain remover or cleaning fluid. Rinse. Rub detergent into dampened area. Launder using a chlorine bleach, if safe for the fabric, or an oxygen bleach.
Tar	Scrape residue from fabric. Place stain face down on paper towels. Sponge with cleaning fluid. Replace paper towels frequently to absorb more tar and to avoid transferring stains. Launder in hottest water safe for fabric.
Tobacco	Dampen stain and rub with bar soap. Rinse. Soak in a product containing enzymes; then launder. If stain remains, launder again using chlorine bleach, if safe for fabric.
Typewriter correction fluid	Let stain dry thoroughly. Gently brush excess off with a clothes brush. Send to professional drycleaner and mention the type of stain.
Urine, vomit, mucous, feces or stool	Soak in a product containing enzymes. Launder using chlorine bleach, if safe for fabric, or use oxygen bleach.

SOURCE: Reprinted courtesy of the Soap and Detergent Association.

Drying

Automatic dryers generally provide both time and temperature settings. Temperatures for drying may range from no heat to moderate and high temperatures. The drying time is determined by the size of the load and the weight of the fabrics being dried. Some dryers have an automatic sensor that turns off the dryer when the wash is dry, whereas others will continue to tumble for the length of time set on the dial, even after the laundry is dry.

Fabrics that have been laundered may be either line dried or dried in an automatic dryer. Some fabrics should not be dried in dryers, because the heat and action of the dryer may cause some shrinkage in heat-sensitive fabrics. Elastics made with natural rubber may lose their elasticity over a period of time if dried in a very hot dryer. Permanent-care labels should be consulted to ascertain whether fabrics should be placed in a dryer.

Heat-sensitive fabrics should be dried at low-heat or no-heat settings. Durable press and synthetic fabrics should be removed from the dryer immediately after completion of the drying cycle to prevent the setting of wrinkles.

Dryers in coin-operated laundromats often operate at much higher temperatures than do home units. Synthetics that dry quickly and are thermoplastic sometimes melt when they come in contact with the sides of the hot dryer drum.

As in washing, fabrics of similar colors should be dried together. It is possible for colors to run from one fabric to another if damp, noncolor-fast fabrics are placed on top of other fabrics during drying.

Pressing

Although many synthetic and durable press fabrics will not require pressing, other items will need touch-up pressing before use. Linens and cottons require the highest temperature settings, synthetics the lowest. Even though irons have temperature settings for different fabric types, the iron temperature should be tested in an inconspicuous part of the item, as thermostats of irons vary in accuracy.

Fabrics are best pressed when they are slightly damp or with steam, as wrinkles are removed more easily. Dark-colored fabrics of all fibers, silks, acetates, and rayons should be ironed from the wrong side to prevent shine. When these fabrics require pressing on the right side, press over a press cloth, not directly on the fabric.

Wool fabrics should be pressed with steam or a dampened press cloth. Silk should be pressed with a dry press cloth. Fabrics with textured surface should be tested carefully to see if ironing will flatten the surface. Sometimes these fabrics can be pressed lightly on the wrong side over a folded terry towel or other soft surface. Corduroy can be pressed in this way, although it is better to use a special pressing board called a needle board. Velvets, velveteens, and plushes also require the use of a needle board. These fabrics may respond better to steaming (holding a steam iron or a "wrinkle remover" steamer several inches away), then hanging to dry to allow the wrinkles to hang out. The same effect may be achieved by hanging items in a bathroom that is warm and moist from a hot shower.

Commercial Laundering

Commercial laundering procedures are used by local dry-cleaning establishments to clean washable items such as men's shirts or household linens. Commercial laundering procedures are similar to those used in the home, except that the conditions under which laundry is done commercially are more controlled and wash loads are considerably larger than in the home laundry. These large wash loads are made up of items from a number of different customers, so that identification numbers or tags must be affixed to each item for identification purposes.

The first step in the commercial laundering process is to sort the fabrics. Items are separated according to color, fiber content, and degree of soil. As many as twelve different classifications can be used.

Different laundries utilize different detergent formulations and procedures, but, in general, bleachable items are subjected to several sudsings with soap or detergent and added alkali at temperatures of 125° to 160°F, a chlorine bleaching at 160°F for 3 to 5 minutes, three or four rinses at different temperatures, each one lower than the last, an acid sour, and blueing. In the rinse, starch is added for those items for which customers have requested it.

The purpose of the acid sour is to neutralize the alkalinity of the water, to remove iron stains, to kill bacteria, and to destroy excess or unused bleach. Some typical sours are acetic acid, sodium bisulfite, sodium acid fluoride, and oxalic acid.

Light-colored fabrics are washed at lower temperatures than are white fabrics, generally, 100° to 120°F, and no chlorine bleach is used. Dark-colored fabrics are laundered at still lower temperatures, 90° to 100°F, as they are more likely to lose color or bleed at higher temperatures. They, too, are not bleached.

After the final rinse, fabrics are spun in an extractor to remove excess water. The extraction may be done by the same machine that washes the items, or it may be done by a separate piece of equipment. This step is comparable to the spin-dry cycle on home washers.

After extraction, the fabrics are dryer dried and, if the customer wishes, pressed. Different types of pressing equipment are used for various items. Flat pieces are ironed on a machine called a *flatwork* ironer. A smooth, heated iron plate provides the heat and pressure, while the fabrics travel across a rotating, padded roll. Special equipment is made for ironing shirts, small pieces, and oversized items such as curtains.

Silk and wool fabrics may be laundered, but are handled in special machines and without the use of chlorine bleach. Neutral soaps and detergents are used without additional alkali, and the washing machine uses a gentle agitation. Three to five rinses are needed to remove all the soap and detergent, so that discoloration of the fabric does not take place. An acid sour is used. Extraction is done gently.

Dry Cleaning

The term *dry cleaning* derives from the use of special solvents for cleaning that dry quickly. Washing of cloth has been the chief method of cleaning washable fabrics since before the beginning of recorded history. Dry cleaning is a relatively recent development, supposedly discovered in 1825 by a Frenchman, Jean Batiste Jolly, who observed that a tablecloth over which the contents of a paraffin lamp were spilled lost its staining in the area of the spill. He recognized that he might be able to clean clothing using this solvent and established the first dry-cleaning business. Benzene replaced paraffin as the solvent fairly early, but the technique was still a far cry from present-day dry-cleaning processes. Originally, the entire garment was taken apart, each piece was cleaned separately by dipping it into pans of benzene, the piece was brushed on a scouring board, dipped again, then dried in a warm oven, and ultimately reassembled.

Modern dry-cleaning processes are a good deal simpler. Professional dry cleaning requires special equipment and techniques, some of which are similar to laundering. The steps in professional dry cleaning are sorting, cleaning, spotting, and finishing.

Sorting, as in laundering, is done according to fiber types, colors, degree of soil, and the like. Buttons or other trim that may be harmed by dry-cleaning solvents are removed. Cleaning takes place in a special washing cylinder comparable to the cylinder of a front-loading automatic washer. Dry-cleaning solvents are either petroleum solvents or synthetic solvents, specifically perchloroethylene or trichlorotrifluoroethane. Perchloroethylene is used by more dry-cleaning establishments than any of the other solvents.

Special soaps and detergents perform the same function in commercial dry cleaning as soaps and detergents do in home laundry. When added to solvents, these special preparations aid in soil removal.

Dry-cleaning solvents cannot be used and then discarded; instead, they are recycled and reused. Solvents are purified and accumulated soil is removed either by filtration or distillation. The continual use of dirty solvent will interfere with cleaning.

After cleaning, the garments are checked for spots or stains that have not been removed in the dry cleaning. Spotters are trained to handle different fabrics and stains as effectively as possible.

If dry cleaning and spotting have not been adequate to remove all soil, the garments may have to be wet cleaned. Wet cleaning is not laundering, but the treatment of fabrics with water to remove soil.

Final touches are given to the clean garment in the finishing department. Buttons or trimmings that have been removed are replaced, garments are steamed or, if necessary, pressed, and minor repairs are made.

To cut corners and costs, some dry-cleaning establishments may eliminate some of the steps that are usually part of the dry-cleaning process. Inferior-quality dry-cleaning establishments may

1. Sort inadequately.
2. Do no cleaning of pockets, cuffs, and so on.
3. Use dirty solvent.
4. Use inferior-quality solvents.
5. Fail to extract all of solvent from item, leaving an unpleasant odor.
6. Omit steps such as spotting, mending, and removal of buttons.
7. Do no wet cleaning.
8. Do no hand pressing.

Coin-Operated Dry Cleaning

Coin-operated dry cleaning is similar to the coin-operated "laundromat." The customer puts clothing to be cleaned into a machine that tumbles clothing in a nonflammable, dry-cleaning solvent (either perchloroethylene or fluorocarbon). The owner of the dry-cleaning establishment supplies only the machines and the cleaning fluid. The customer must sort items, put them into the machine, and take them out at the end of the cycle.

The cost of coin-operated dry cleaning is well below that of full-scale professional dry cleaning. The services that normally come with dry cleaning, that is, spotting, mending, pressing, and so on, are, of course, lacking. Sometimes the solvents used in coin-operated dry cleaning are not cleaned adequately.

Storage of Textile Products

Between uses, textile items may be put away for either short or long periods of time. Some attention to the way in which clothing is stored may help to prolong the life of textile products.

Textile products will wear longer if given a chance to "rest" between uses. Rotating items in use, either clothing or household textiles, will provide this rest period. Storage practices may encourage this rotation. For example, towels or bed linens that have been laundered may be placed at the bottom of the stack of items, and the next item to be used taken from the top of the stack.

When table linens, bed linens, or other items are pressed, care should be taken to fold these items at different places. Continuous folding of fabrics, especially where sharp creases are pressed into the material, in the same place will cause the yarns to break or wear first in those spots.

Fabrics that are to be put away for long-term storage should always be put away clean. Moths or other insects will more readily attack soiled fabrics. Furthermore, some spots or stains that are only slightly evident may be oxidized. Oxidized stains darken and are exceedingly difficult to remove. Fabrics should not be put away with pins left in them, as the pins may rust and cause stains to appear around the pinned area.

Fabrics that are subject to attack by insects and mildew should be stored carefully. Wool and animal hair fabrics can be mothproofed before storage or stored in tightly closed containers with moth repellants.

Fabrics that are susceptible to mildew should be stored dry, in a dry place. The fairly widespread use of central or room air conditioning has decreased humidity in many buildings. Closed closets can hold humidity, so that leaving doors slightly ajar or using ventilated doors will help to prevent humidity buildup in closed areas.

If fabrics that are normally starched are to be stored for a long period of time, it is best to store them without starching, as silverfish find the starch especially appetizing. If starch is required later, garments can be spray starched before use. If starched garments are stored, they should be put away in a closed container that insects cannot penetrate.

Permanent-Care Labeling Requirements

Since July 1972, wearing apparel and fabrics sold by the yard must carry a permanently affixed label giving instructions for the care of this item. Current provisions of the rules are as follows. All textile wearing apparel and piece goods sold for making home apparel are subject to the legislation except shoes, gloves, hats, and items not "used to cover and protect the body" such as belts, neckties, handkerchiefs, and suspenders. Nonwoven, one-time use garments are also excluded, as are manufacturers' fabric remnants up to 10 yards in length when the fiber content is not known and cannot easily be determined, and trim up to 5 inches wide. These provisions apply whether the items were manufactured in the United States or abroad.

Manufacturers are required to provide full care instructions about regular care, or provide warnings if a garment cannot be cleaned without harm. Care labels are attached to finished garments before they are sold. These labels must remain legible throughout the useful life of the garment. Piece goods information is to be provided on the end of each roll or bolt. Consumers, therefore, would need to make note of care procedures themselves when purchasing piece goods, as copies of instructions are not provided.

Labels must be placed so that they can be seen or easily found by consumers at the point of sale. If packaging obscures the label, additional information should appear on the outside of the package or on a hang tag fastened to the product.

Some types of products, however, need not include any care instructions. These are products sold to institutional buyers for commercial use, such as uniforms provided for hospital employees that are purchased by and cared for by the institution, garments custom made from fabric provided by the customer, and items completely washable and sold at retail for $3.00 or less.

Some other products need not have permanently affixed labels, but have to be provided with temporary labels. Totally reversible clothing without pockets and those granted exemptions because a label would harm their appearance or usefulness are cited in the rule, although special permission for items in the latter category must be obtained through petition. Products that may be washed, bleached, dried, ironed, or dry cleaned by the harshest procedures available are also exempt, provided that the instruction "wash or dry clean, any normal method" appears on a temporary label that is conspicuous at the point of sale.

The directions to manufacturers as to the contents of the care label make the following stipulations. The label must have either a washing or dry cleaning instruction. If a product can be both washed and dry cleaned, it can carry only one of these instructions. If it can be neither washed nor dry cleaned, the label must say "Do not wash—Do not dry clean."

The rule includes a glossary of terms. It is recommended, but not required, that the terms in this glossary be used when applicable. Symbols may be used in addition to words, but symbols alone are not permitted.

If a garment is labeled as washable, the label must say whether the product should be washed by hand or machine, and if regular use of hot water will harm the product, a water temperature must be stated. For example, a label that says "Machine wash, Cold" means that the consumer can machine wash the garment but only in cold water. A label that says "Machine wash" means that any temperature ranging from cold to hot could be used. The word "wash" cannot be used alone, but must stipulate whether the item should be machine or hand washed.

If all commercially available bleaches can be used on a regular basis, the label need not mention bleach. If chlorine bleach would harm the garment, but nonchlorine bleach would not, the label should say "only nonchlorine bleach when needed." If all commercially available bleaches would harm the product, the label should say "no bleach" or "do not bleach."

The appropriate drying method must be stipulated, and if regular use of high temperature would be harmful, the appropriate temperature setting must be given. "Machine wash, Tumble Dry" would indicate that there are no restrictions of washing or drying temperatures.

Ironing information is to be given if ironing will be needed on a regular basis. As in washing and drying instructions, temperature should be stipulated unless a hot iron can be used without harm.

The rule also requires that consumers be warned against processes that they might be expected to use that would harm the product. For example, if ironing would be harmful to a garment that consumers might "touch up" occasionally, the label should read "Do not iron." If an item is not colorfast, it must be labeled "Wash separately" or "Wash with like colors." It is not necessary to warn users about alternate procedures that may be harmful to the item. For example, if instructions say "Dry flat," it is not required that labels also say "Do not tumble dry."

For items labeled as dry cleanable, other provisions apply. If all commercially available types of solvents can be used, the label need not mention any type of solvent. If one or more solvents would harm the product, a solvent that is safe to use must be mentioned. If any part of the dry-cleaning process will harm the garment, the label must warn "Do not . . ." or "No . . ." or provide other wording that would clarify appropriate procedures. For example, "Professionally dry clean, No steam" would indicate that no steam should be used in pressing or finishing the garment. If the word "Dry clean" is used without the word "Professionally" in front of it, the item should be dry cleanable by any machine process with no restrictions on solvents, moisture content, heat, and steam. "Professionally dry clean" is used when the normal dry-cleaning process must be modified in some way. This term is not used alone, but must be followed by a description of the modifications that are needed. For example, "Professionally dry clean, Short cycle, No steam" would mean that any commercially available solvent could be used, the cleaning time should be reduced, and steam should not be used on pressing or finishing.[4]

Further Sources of Information

Many organizations publish booklets or pamphlets that offer information to the consumer about the care of textile products. Soap and detergent manufacturers and consumer magazines frequently publish materials that instruct the consumer in the appropriate care techniques for textiles of all kinds.

Consumers who wish to obtain further information about textile cleaning, storage, and maintenance can often find current information on these subjects from the Department of Agriculture and from State Home Economics Extension Offices. Lists of publications of the U.S. Department of Agriculture can be obtained from the U.S. Government Printing Office, Washington, D.C. 20402. Most of these materials are published as "Home and Garden Bulletins." Lists of state extension publications are generally available from the land-grant college in each state.

Manufacturers of detergents and other laundry products also write and distribute a variety of informational materials for consumers and professionals. The Soap and Detergent Association holds symposia for

---

[4]"Writing a Care Label." (Washington, D.C.: Bureau of Consumer Protection, Federal Trade Commission, March 1984).

its members and others at which new developments are examined. The *Proceedings* of these meetings are published and can be obtained by those who are unable to attend meetings. The International Fabricare Institute, an organization that does research and supplies current information to dry-cleaning establishments, publishes newsletters and fact sheets about dry-cleaning practices and problems. These materials can be obtained by purchasing a membership in the institute at a very reasonable fee.

Recommended References

AVERY, C., and D. HARRABIN. *A Comparison of Phosphate and Non-Phosphate Detergents*, Bulletin No. 415. Kingston: University of Rhode Island, November 1975.

BEVAN, G. "Mechanism of Soiling of Textiles," *Textiles*, 8 (October 1979), p. 69.

CLOUD, R. M., L. A. BONDURANT, and N. K. KEITH. "Efficacy of Four Cleaning Solutions in the Removing Smoke Damage from Apparel Fabrics," *Clothing and Textiles Research Journal*, 2 (Fall/Winter 1983–84), p. 55.

CORLESS, M. G. "How to Remove Stains," *Textiles*, 14 (Spring 1985), p. 13.

Detergents—In Depth. Proceedings of symposium sponsored by the Soap and Detergent Association, Chicago, April 1984.

"The Effect of Wash Water Temperature on Laundry Results," *Technical Bulletin No. 3.* Newton, Iowa: Maytag Company,

FORTRESS, F. "Problems of Cleaning Textiles," *Textile Industries*, 140 (March 1976), p. 65.

A Handbook of Industry Terms. New York: Soap and Detergent Association, 1981.

GAMPER, J. and C. L. RIGGS. "The Effect of Disinfectant Concentrations of Chlorine Bleach on Chlorine-Sensitive Fabrics," *Textile Chemist and Colorist*, 15 (April 1983), p. 29.

HAUPT, D. E. "U.S. Detergent/Surfactant Trends—1980s," *Technical Bulletin No. SC 745-83.* Houston: Shell Chemical Company, 1983.

HEBEISH, H., K. EL-ZOGHBY, and S. HALEEM. "Food Stain Removal from Cotton and PET/Cotton Fabrics," *American Dyestuff Reporter*, 73 (February 1984), p. 36.

KINCAID, C. J., and K. L. HATCH. "Do Consumers Understand Care Labels?" *Textile Chemist and Colorist*, 10 (February 1978), p. 13.

MOHAMED, S. S. "Comparison of Phosphate and Carbonate Built Detergents for Laundering Polyester/Cotton," *Textile Chemist and Colorist*, 14 (March 1982), p. 37.

MORRIS, M. A., and H. H. PRATO. "The Effect of Wash Temperature on Removal of Particulate and Oily Soil from Fabrics of Varying Fiber Content," *Textile Research Journal*, 52 (April 1982), p. 280.

POWDERLY, D. "Effect of Water Temperature on Dimensional Change," *Textile Chemist and Colorist*, 12 (October 1980), p. 36.

RAHEEL, M., and M. D. LIEN. "Effect of Detergents on Wear and Appearance Characteristics of Cotton Broadcloth," *Textile Chemist and Colorist*, 14 (June 1982), p. 27.

Removing Stains from Fabrics, Home and Garden Bulletin No. 63. Washington, D.C.: U.S. Department of Agriculture, 1973.

RHODE, R. O. "How Non-phosphate Detergents Affect Dyed Fabrics," *Textile Chemist and Colorist*, vol. 6 (October 1974), p. 33.

Sanitation in Home Laundering, Home and Garden Bulletin No. 97. Washington, D.C.: U.S. Department of Agriculture, October 1971.

SHEPLEY, M. A. "Drycleaning," *Textiles,* vol. 10 (Summer 1981), p. 47.

Soaps and Detergents, Home and Garden Bulletin No. 139. Washington, D.C.: U.S. Department of Agriculture, October 1973.

The Technology of Home Laundering, Textile Monograph #108. New York: American Association for Textile Technology, 1973.

"Tell Your Cleaner About Stains," *IFI Bulletin No. PCR-58.* International Fabricare Institute, 1985.

"What's New About Care Labels?" Washington, D.C.: *Federal Trade Commission,* April 1984.

Textiles and the Environment

As the general public has become more mindful of dangers to the natural environment from industrial production, the relationship of the production of modern textiles to ecological problems has become an issue of public concern. Environmental problems relating to the production and processing and use of both natural and man-made fibers occur in four areas. The first of these concerns the health of the workers in the textile industry and consumers of textiles. Second, textile manufacture can produce pollution of the air and the water, and used textile fibers may create waste disposal problems. Third, home care of textiles requires the use of detergents or soaps, which have been cited as pollutants of the water supply. And, finally, many synthetic fibers are made from petroleum and petroleum products. When shortages of these products occur, prices of the raw materials from which textiles are made rise, and textile products increase in cost.

Health Hazards to Textile Workers

Lung Disease

The deleterious effect of inhaling minute, invisible particles of grit or other hard inorganic matter has been recognized for many years. The constant exposure of the lungs to these irritants is harmful and may eventually produce lung disease in many of the persons exposed.

This has long been recognized as a hazard in the production of asbestos. Recently, two similar problem areas in textile processing have been given increased attention. Glass fibers are hard and fairly durable. Questions have been raised about whether the inhalation of fibers of glass may cause lung disease. To date, none of the research into this question has produced any solid evidence of a relationship between inhaling glass fiber and lung disease.

A third culprit has been identified, namely, cotton. Cotton workers may, after a period of exposure to cotton dust, develop byssinosis or "brown lung," as it is called by the workers.

Researchers had thought that the sand and other gritty particles present in bales of cotton might be responsible for the development of byssinosis. The most recent research, however, tends toward the conclusion that the cause of byssinosis is probably toxins from bacteria or fungi that are present in the leaf dust that is part of the raw cotton.

The Occupational Safety and Health Act (OSHA) has established maximum allowable levels of cotton dust that may be present in the air of factories where cotton is being processed. Maintaining these standards is costly. Either the amount of dust must be decreased to a safe level, or the worker must be given personal protective devices to filter out the dust.

The problem is still under study. Manufacturers are experimenting with air ventilation systems that remove a significant amount of dust and with personal safety devices, rather like gas masks, that can be worn by workers. Unfortunately, worker response to the discomfort of masks has been somewhat negative. It has also been found that the way in which workers carry out their tasks is related to the amount of dust inhaled. Researchers have recommended that workers be trained to change their work practices if they are detrimental.

Toxicity of Chemicals

Some of the chemical substances with which textile workers come into contact are highly toxic. For the most part, companies have been able to identify these substances and to protect workers from contact with them.

From time to time, however, research findings point out new materials that are harmful that have never been identified before as presenting any serious health problems. Vinyl chloride is such a chemical. An important ingredient in the production of polyvinyl chloride plastics, vinyl chloride, is used in the production of plastic backings and coatings for fabrics. Evidence indicates that continued exposure to vinyl chloride will produce cancer of the liver in some of the persons exposed. Unfortunately, this discovery has come too late to help those who have already been affected, but steps will now have to be taken to protect those workers who must handle this material in the future.

Some dyestuffs have been proven to be harmful to workers. When evidence is found linking dyes to health hazards, their use may be banned.

As of May 1986, OSHA employee health protection rules will require that information about hazardous chemical substances be communicated to employees by the employer. In summary, the requirements will be:

. . . Hazard information must be conveyed to employees through appropriate labels on the products that they use.
. . . Safety data sheets must provide hazard information.
. . . Affected industries must have a written hazards information communications program.
. . . Industries must establish and conduct employee chemical hazard training programs.

The specific means by which these requirements are met are not mandated, but both the producers of chemicals deemed hazardous and the industries using the chemicals must comply. The textile industry sectors that manufacture or process a wide variety of textile products will therefore be affected.[1]

Formaldehyde is another chemical that is widely used in the textile industry. Research has indicated that high levels of formaldehyde are associated with nasal cancer in rats. Whether it is a carcinogen in humans has not been proven. Long-term studies of workers exposed to formaldehyde have been inconclusive. The American Cancer Institute is conducting additional studies that may yield more reliable data.

The controversy about formaldehyde has centered on the workplace. The Consumer Product Safety Commission has concluded that consumers are not at risk because garments do not give off enough formaldehyde to affect wearers. Even so, investigations are continuing into the effect of the chemical on the skin.

About 1.4 million workers are estimated to be exposed to formaldehyde, of which about 744,000 work in the textile and apparel industries. In 1982 the Environmental Protection Agency (EPA) and OSHA decided not to reduce further allowable levels. Present allowable level is a day-long average of 3 parts per million (ppm), with a top limit of 5 ppm in any 30-minute period. However, a congressional investigation and lawsuits brought by environmental and trade union groups have led to a reconsideration of this decision. Spokespersons for the textile industry claim that any decrease in allowable formaldehyde levels in the workplace will work a severe economic hardship on the industry.

Although a final resolution has yet to be made about the formaldehyde issue, formaldehyde levels in textile mills and apparel factories have been reduced. Between 1975 and 1983, the levels of formaldehyde released by treated fabrics were cut by a third. The textile literature contains many reports of research into finishing techniques that reduce formaldehyde use or lower levels of its release.[2]

[1]G. S. Dominguez, "Industries Must Prepare Now for New OSHA Hazard Rule," *Textile Industries* (August 1984), p. 51.
[2]"Formaldehyde: Debating Rules and Risks," *Daily News Record*, June 19, 1985, p. 6.

Noise

Noise levels in textile manufacturing plants can be very high. The National Institute for Occupational Safety and Health has rated the textile industry as having the highest percentage of work force exposed to hazardous noise. Governmental standards regulating the noise levels have been imposed, and manufacturers must comply with these requirements. The standards limit noise on the basis of the level of noise in relation to the length of exposure of the employee to the noise.

These standards were imposed because of the relationship between high noise levels and hearing loss. It is the responsibility of the company to lower noise levels in those cases where the standards are not met. This presents a more difficult problem in factories using older equipment that operates at much higher sound levels than does newer textile equipment, which is engineered to satisfy these requirements. Shuttleless looms are an example of a newer type of textile machinery that has made a significant contribution to the reduction of noise levels.

Although investigations are underway as to how best to cope with the health and safety hazards of the textile industry, complete solutions to these problems do not yet exist. National Safety standards have been established by the Occupational Safety and Health Act of 1970, and companies must now adapt equipment and work situations to meet the requirements of the law.

Health Hazards to Consumers

The substances utilized in the manufacture of textiles may pose a hazard to the health of the consumers of these products as well as to workers in the textile industry. Probably the best known instance of public conern with textile chemicals is the TRIS case.

TRIS, which chemically is 2,3-dibromopropyl phosphate, also called TBPP and DBPP, is a chemical finish that had been used to make some polyester, acetate, and triacetate fabrics flame retardant. TRIS was found to be a possible carcinogen. All sleepwear for children sizes 0 to 14 is required to be made fire retardant, and much of the public failed to realize that not all sleepwear fabrics were being treated with this particular chemical. Many consumers rejected cotton sleepwear treated with safe substances. TRIS-treated garments were withdrawn from the market, and its use was discontinued.

Textiles as a Source of Air and Water Pollution

The Manufacturers

Textile production has always been a source of water pollution. Not only the man-made fibers but also natural fibers have created pollutants in the scouring of wool and in many of the dyeing and finishing operations. The recently awakened concern with the industrial pollution of air and water has focused attention on these unpleasant by-products of textile manufacture. Federally mandated standards for clean air and water have been imposed, and textile companies are required to comply with these regulations.

Problems in relation to air pollution seem to be generated during heat setting, in which the organic compounds used for finishing are vaporized and carried off in gaseous forms; in piece dyeing, where some dye materials are carried off in water vapor; and in a wide variety of processing steps that utilize chemical solvents.

Water pollution can take place at almost any step of textile production, from preparation of the fiber through to the finishing of fabrics, posing a threat to fish and the ecological balance of streams. Dyeing and finishing of fabrics utilize a great deal of water, and the disposal of the chemicals used in these processes presents serious problems for the manufacturer.

The legal requirements for meeting clean water standards imposed by local, state, or national governments have led the textile industry to look for means to dispose of wastes in ways that do not pollute streams. Recycling of water or other processing materials such as sizing, treating the water to render it safe or to remove pollutants, and using biodegradable substances are three measures that can be used by manufacturers to maintain clean water.

Disposal of solid wastes from textile firms and from chemical companies associated with the textile industry is another difficulty. Incineration and burial, which have been used to eliminate wastes, both present problems. Burial may lead to the contamination of ground water, to fires, or to the generation of noxious gases from the indiscriminate mixing of chemical substances. Incineration may produce air pollution or water pollution as a by-product of the incineration process. To be successful, both processes require careful monitoring and control.

The disposal of waste products of all kinds by textile manufacturers is an ongoing problem that the industry, like all other industries, is trying to solve. John Lomartine, in a paper presented to the American Chemical Society in June 1974, suggested the ways in which textile companies might respond to the requirement for a cleaner environment:

1. A heavy contaminator could be replaced by a light contaminator.
2. A new processing concept could be adopted whereby all water is cleaned before being returned to its source and/or water recycling processes could be used.
3. Operations could be improved so that they generate less waste and not only aid in the disposal problem but also generate more prime salable material.
4. Recycling of waste into the process will become more prevalent. An added advantage of this move will be more efficient conversion of raw materials.

5. Use of waste as fuel, feeding boilers to produce steam. At the very least, incineration of burnable waste will be done if for no other reason than to reduce the volume of material to be disposed. As energy sources become more expensive, the burning of waste becomes more attractive.[3]

The Consumer

In some respects, the problems of disposal of textile items after they have been used by the ultimate consumer are even more difficult than the disposal of waste products generated in the manufacture of textiles. Disposable nonwovens used for products such as diapers have increased the quantity of textile products that are discarded. Disposable items from medical institutions present particular problems. Patient-contact items must be separated and decontaminated before disposal.

Natural fibers are biodegradable and will eventually break down, but synthetics are quite resistant and are not so easily disposed of. Recycling has been recommended as a means of disposing of used textiles, but the recycling of textiles is complicated by a number of factors. (Purchases or gifts of secondhand clothing are one form of recycling clothing.) Only small quantities of textile wastes are recycled. The reasons that textile wastes are recycled so infrequently relate to the regulations that place limitations on the sale and use of products containing textile fibers. Companies that reclaim textile fibers may find it economically unproductive to handle all types of materials.

Textile waste from manufacturers of garments or other textile products is relatively easy to process, since the manufacturer can identify the textile fiber. In reclamation fibers must be sorted into different generic categories, and the identification of unknown man-made fibers or blends is difficult. Chemical analysis for identification purposes may be necessary. Recycling textiles used and discarded by consumers is extremely difficult. Not only is fiber content unidentified, but the quality of fibers may also be quite uneven as a result of wear.

Natural fibers and rayon present relatively few problems of identification and recycling. Wool is reprocessed or reused and is made into "new" fabrics. Cotton, linen, and rayon can be utilized in the production of fine rag paper or in battings and paddings.

The separation of blends into their component parts is more difficult. Often this is achieved by identifying the components of the blend and then dissolving out one of the fibers, leaving the other intact. Man-made fibers can be reused in making flock, as industrial fillers in the manufacture of plastic, or in the regeneration of synthetic fibers.

[3]John Lomartine, "Fibers and the Environment," paper presented to the American Chemical Society Symposium on Man-made Fibers, Washington, D.C., June 1974, pp. 2 ff.

Special finishes that are applied to fabrics may create additional problems for recycling. Many of these finishes are virtually impossible to recycle, and they contaminate the fibers, making their recycling impossible too.

As the raw materials from which many textiles are made become more scarce, the importance of recycling textile products becomes increasingly important. It is imperative that intensive research into the ways to turn discarded textile products into usable raw materials be given priority. See Figure 23.1 and 23.2 for summary of flow of products in textile waste utilization.

Pollution from Home Laundering

The fear of water pollution from household wastes that contain large quantities of phosphates has led some states and communities to restrict the sale of phosphate-containing detergents. These restrictions have generally been made as a result of local conditions that have generated public support for such measures.

Other local and state governments have passed regulations banning the sale of phosphate-containing detergents. Claims and counterclaims are made by the detergent manufacturers and the supporters of these laws. Environmentalists claim that phosphates stimulate the growth of algae (eutrophication), whereas detergent manufacturers respond by claiming that phosphates from detergents contribute negligibly to these levels and blame other sources of phosphates, such as chemical fertilizers. Furthermore, the manufacturers dispute the environmentalist's claim that increased phosphate levels do increase algae growth. More research is required to prove the case for or against phosphates in detergents.

For those areas where phosphates have been outlawed, detergent companies have produced phosphate-free detergents in which other alkaline salts, such as sodium carbonate and sodium silicate, are used as substitutes for the phosphates. One of the major disadvantages of substituting other nonphosphate detergents for phosphate-bearing detergents is that residues left by these substances have a detrimental effect on flame-retardant finishes.

The manufacturers of detergents are also working toward the production of a wide range of detergents that are more biodegradable, that is, substances that decompose more rapidly during sewage treatment.

Textiles and Energy

Increases in energy costs that accelerated after 1973–1974 created a ripple effect in the textile industry as they did in all areas of the national economy. Any changes in petroleum supply or increased prices adversely affect the textile industry since petroleum and petroleum by-products are the most important single raw material used in the manufacture of most synthetics. Since many of the chemicals used to manufacture synthetics are derived from oil, the cost of these chemicals will increase if oil prices rise. The supply of these chemicals will decrease if supplies of oil should decrease. Furthermore, there is the cost of energy to power the plants that produce fibers, yarns, fabrics and finishes.

A return to the use of larger quantities of natural fibers will not have a significant impact on energy consumption. There are not enough natural fibers to supply the demands of consumers from all over the world. Furthermore, natural fibers also require energy for their production and processing, so that these fibers are not "energy free." Many fertilizers are made from petrochemicals, and tractors and other farm machinery are run on petroleum fuels.

Already, techniques for processing textiles that save energy have achieved wide acceptance by the textile industry. Dyeing and finishing are aspects of the manufacture of textiles that are especially energy intensive. Among the energy-saving innovations already adopted for use in dyeing and finishing are the use of solar heating for water used in processing fabrics, reducing quantities of hot water required, recovering and reutilizing heat from processing, changing processes to permit use of lower temperatures, and adopting techniques that shorten time requirements.[4]

FIGURE 23.1 *Waste textile utilization flow. Reprinted from* Textile Industries, *December 1972, p. 43.*

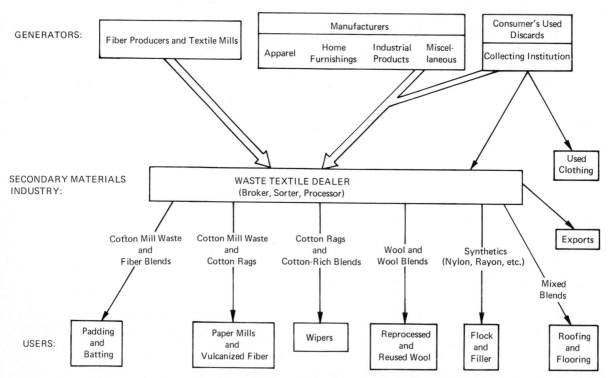

[4]E. S. Olson, "New Dyeing and Finishing Equipment and Processes Which Minimize Energy Requirements," *Textile Chemist and Colorist,* 9 (February 1977), p. 20.

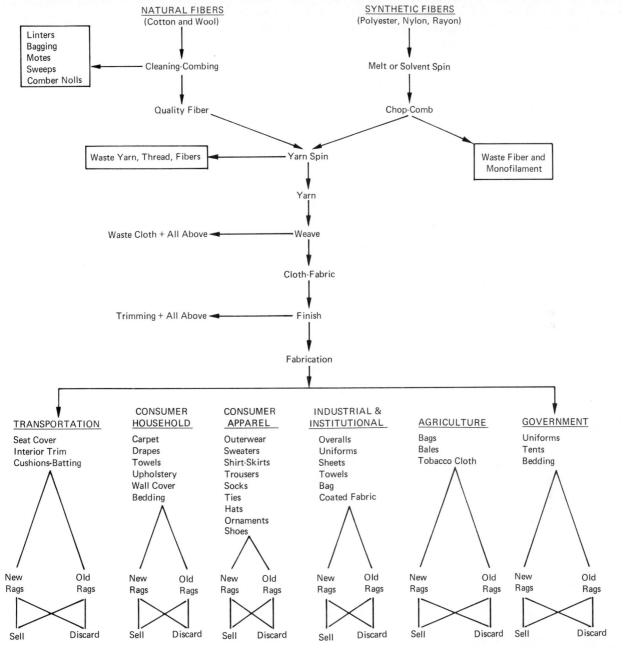

FIGURE 23.2 *Typical flow of textile fibers in process and the resulting generation of textile waste. Reprinted from* Textile Industries. *December 1972, p. 43.*

The consumer must also think in terms of energy use for the care of textile products. Washing, drying, and ironing all require the expenditure of energy. The selection of fabrics that require shorter drying time or can be line dried, as well as those that can be washed in cooler water or do not require ironing, will have the end result of costing the consumer less money because less energy will be used in their care.

One study reported that fiber production accounted for less than 15 per cent of the total energy required for production and manufacture of a garment, whereas care of the garment after purchase accounted for 55 to 80 per cent.[5]

An increased consumer emphasis on durability may also contribute to a reduction of energy needs. If textile items are used longer, they will have to be replaced less often, thereby reducing the amount of the raw materials needed. Longer use before disposal will also decrease the problem of disposal of used textiles. Fashion, however, is such an important aspect of the apparel industries that many items are discarded before they are outworn. Even a return of the energy crisis would not be likely to remove fashion as a factor in clothing choice. Consumers may find it useful to identify certain of their purchases as "fashion" items in which durability may not be so important as it is in "classic" or other items that do not go out of style quickly.

Summary

Both industry and the public have obligations for the protection of the environment. Whereas at first glance industry would seem to be more responsible for pollution, a deeper examination of the issues leads inexorably to the conclusion that this is a shared responsibility. In the long run, the public must be willing to pay for the improvements in pollution control that industries make. Environmentally safe manufacturing of textiles is expensive. The cost of cleaner factories and mills will be paid for by increasing prices of the items that are marketed. And at the same time consumers must recognize that imported fabrics and apparel are often produced in countries that have little or no regulation of the environment of the workplace. Such goods compete with domestically produced fabrics into which the costs of cleaner factories and mills must be calculated.

No one relishes increases in the cost of textiles, but the alternatives are unthinkable. The trade-off for lower prices would be to continue the deterioration of the environment that future generations will inherit.

Recommended References

BAJAJ, J. K. L. "Recycling Man-made Fibers," *Textile Industries*, 136 (December 1972), p. 42.

DAFOE, F. G. "Noise: The Industry's Greatest Health Threat," *Canadian Textile Journal*, 101 (April 1984), p. 11.

DOMINGUEZ, G. S. "Industries Must Prepare Now for New OSHA Hazard Rule," *Textile Industries*, 148 (August 1984), p. 51.

[5]T. L. Van Winkle et al., "Cotton versus Polyester," *American Scientist*, 66 (September–October 1978), pp. 280 ff.

"Flame Retardant Chemicals and Ecology," *Textile Industries*, 140 (February 1976), p. 74.

FRIEDMAN, H. L., and others. "Mutagenicity of Textile Dyes," *Environment, Science and Technology*, 14 (September 1980), p. 1145.

GOODSON, L. A. JR. "Formaldehyde and the Textile Industry," *Textile Chemist and Colorist*, 16 (January 1984), p. 15

GREENE, J. "Formaldehyde: Debating Rules and Risks," *Daily News Record*, June 19, 1985, p. 6.

GROSS, P., and D. C. BRAUN. *Toxic and Biomedical Effects of Fibers*. Park Ridge, N.J.: Noyes Publications, 1984.

HATCH, K. L. "Chemicals and Textiles. Part II: Dermatological Problems Related to Finishes," *Textile Research Journal*, 54 (November 1984), p. 721.

MUNSON, D. M., "Textiles' Role in an Energy Conscious Society," *Proceedings of the Association of College Professors of Textiles and Clothing*, 1981, p. 45.

NORTHRUP, H. L., and W. F. TURNER. "Air Pollution Control in Textile Finishing," *Textile Chemist and Colorist*, 7 (April 1975), p. 22.

POLYZOU, A. "Energy Consumption for Textiles and Apparel," *Family Economics Review* (Spring 1979), p. 3.

VAN WINKLE, T. L., et al. "Cotton versus Polyester," *American Scientist*, 66 (September–October 1978), p. 280.

WADE, R. H. "Vapor Phase Treatments of Cotton Dust to Deactivate Endotoxins," *Textile Research Journal*, 53 (October 1983), p. 615.

WALLENBERGER, F. T., et al. "The Effect of Fabric Composition on Energy Demand in Home Laundering," *Textile Chemist and Colorist*, 12 (July 1980), p. 20.

Textile Testing and Standards

Governmental agencies, product manufacturers, retailers, and consumer groups may all become involved in the establishment of standard performance specifications for textile products. A *standard specification* is a defined level of performance that a product much achieve to be considered as acceptable for use. The term "standards" is a sort of verbal shorthand used to refer to established standard specifications.

Except in the case of some flammability standard specifications, manufacturers are not required by law to conform to textile product standards. Some retailers, however, require that wholesale manufacturers from whom they buy must produce goods that meet specifications. The Department of Defense establishes minimum specifications for textiles used by the military, and some federal agencies and funding regulations for federally financed construction projects require that carpets, draperies, and the like conform to stated specifications. Standard specifications also provide a basis for the comparison of results of studies of textiles by different researchers. Although the general public does benefit from the use of standards by segments of the textile industry, most consumers are unaware of their existence.

Organizations That Establish Standards

The organization most actively involved in establishing textile standards is the American National Standards Institute (ANSI). ANSI is a nonprofit federation, whose membership is composed of trade, labor, technical, and consumer organizations and governmental agencies. ANSI does not originate standards but serves as a clearinghouse and coordinator for standards in many fields. The American Society for Testing Materials (ASTM) is an organization that establishes standard test methods and specifications through an organization of technical committees. One of these committees, Committee D-13, deals with textile materials. Textile fabric performance standards developed by ASTM Committee D-13 are accepted by ANSI.

Activities related to the setting of standards are not limited to the United States. International standardized systems of measurement and standard specifications have been developed by the International Organization for Standardization (ISO). A new system of measurement, the International System of Units (SI), is gradually being adopted. Its details are published and controlled by an international treaty organization called the International Bureau of Weights and Measures.

The federal government, through the Office of Engineering Standards Services, works with the textile industry to establish not only standards of performance but also standard sizes, grading, test methods, and the like. Although these standards are also voluntary, they are established cooperatively by government and industry, often at the request of industry, and are subsequently adopted rather widely.

The Consumer Product Safety Commission was established under the Consumer Product Safety Act of 1972. This commission has broad jurisdiction over product safety, one area of which is fabric flammability. The commission oversees the administration and revision of standards that items covered under flammability legislation must meet.

Specific federal agencies and the military establish standards that the products they buy must meet. Compliance with these standards is essential if companies wish to do business with such agencies.

Textile Testing and Textile Standards

To determine whether textile products meet established standards, such products must be tested. Textile standards and textile testing are, therefore, closely involved. The two groups that have developed the most widely used textile testing methods are the American Association of Textile Chemists and Colorists (AATCC) and the American Society for Testing and Materials (ASTM).

The American Association of Textile Chemists and Colorists is composed of persons from the textile wet processing industry, textile chemists, others working in varying segments of the textile industry, and educators. The association establishes testing methods, largely in the area of chemical testing, and maintains an active educational program implemented through national and regional meetings and a monthly journal, the *Textile Chemist and Colorist*. Specific test methodologies are described fully in an annual publication, *The Technical Manual*.

Tests established by the American Society for Testing and Materials are more specifically focused on physical testing and the testing of fabric construction. ASTM test methods are published annually in a book of *ASTM Standards*.

ASTM also issues *ASTM Standard Performance Specifications for Textile Fabrics.* Many are extensions and/or revisions of earlier guidelines known as L22, L24, or L14 standards of ANSI, which have been withdrawn from distribution by ANSI. This group of fabric performance standards is voluntary and serves as a guide to manufacturers and consumers. The publication can be purchased from ASTM.

Testing

Established testing methods have validity and are accepted by authorities in the field as reliable. Not only do industry and the government require testing of materials in ways that are accepted as reliable and standardized, but researchers also require a body of accepted tests for use in comparing data accumulated by different researchers working in different laboratories. Specific tests of the type established by AATCC and ASTM are too numerous to discuss here. These testing methodologies are given in detail in the technical publications of these organizations and can readily be obtained for use by interested persons.

Although most students in introductory textile courses do not become involved with extensive textile testing, it may be helpful for students to have some familiarity with testing equipment and the types of testing that can be done. There are, also, some simple forms of testing of textile products that can be carried out in the classroom or at home without specialized equipment that will provide a general evaluation of fabrics.

To assure accuracy and replicability, textile testing should be carried out under carefully controlled conditions. Atmospheric conditions, particularly the amount of moisture present that might be picked up by fibers, yarns, or fabrics, affect the performance of textiles. For this reason, testing is done with temperature and humidity being maintained at standard levels: 70°F (21°C) and 65 per cent relative humidity. Testing equipment must conform to specifications established in the testing methodology, and fabric specimens must be of uniform size. Test measurements are repeated a number of times because of variability in results from one specimen to another. Results are averaged, and these overall measurements more accurately characterize the materials being tested than does the measurement of a single example that might possess some atypical quality.

Classroom or home test methods cannot meet the same rigorous criteria for controlled conditions, but they should maintain as much control as possible over conditions under which testing is done, size of specimens, number of tests run, and so on.

Laboratory testing has limitations in that these tests do not simulate exactly the conditions under which textiles will be used. Consumers will differ from each other in terms of the stresses to which they subject textiles. A farmer will place different demands on a pair of jeans than will a suburban high school student. The research literature that deals with the evaluation of textile products contains numerous studies of actual wear tests or of correlations between consumer evaluations of products and standard testing procedures. Studies such as these add another dimension to the testing of textiles. The technical and research publications in the field regularly report new developments in testing as well as the results of tests performed in studies of various aspects of textile performance.

Dimensions, Weight, and Thickness

Certain data must often be collected about textiles prior to testing. Information about dimensions and construction is obtained in the following ways.

The length and width of the fabric or fabric sample are determined by measuring the fabric. Samples are placed flat, free from winkling, and unstretched. Length is measured parallel to the selvage, and width is measured perpendicular to the selvage. Measurements may have to be taken at several points and averaged, as distortions of the fabric may have taken place during handling.

Fabric weight may be expressed as ounces per square yard, ounces per linear yard, linear yards per pound, or grams per square meter. For the measurement of ounces per linear yard, 1 linear yard of fabric is weighed. The width of the yard must also be noted. In measuring linear yards per pound, 1 pound of fabric is weighed out, and then the fabric length is measured. Again, the width of the fabric must be noted. The same measurements may also be made in grams rather than ounces. Ounces per square yard are calculated as follows: 1 square yard is equal to 1,296 square inches. Ounces or grams per square yard equal 1,296 times the weight of the sample (in grams or ounces) divided by the area of the sample (expressed in square inches). The formula might be written as follows:

$$\text{ounces or grams per square yard} = \frac{1{,}296 \times \text{weight of sample}}{\text{area of sample}}$$

Or, using completely metric measurements to determine the number of grams per square meter, the formula would be

$$\text{grams per square yard} = \frac{10{,}000 \text{ cm}^2 \times \text{weight of sample in grams}}{\text{area of sample in square centimeters}}$$

Fabric thickness can be measured by using any of a number of thickness gauges, testers, or compressometers. This may be an important measurement for pile fabrics or may be used in conjunction with tests for shrinkage or abrasion.

FIGURE 24.1. Pick counter used to facilitate counting threads per inch or wales and courses of knitted goods. Courtesy of Alfred Suter Co. Inc.

Fabric Count

Fabric count is the number of yarns per inch in a woven fabric. This fabric is examined with a calibrated, square magnifying glass called either a *linen tester* or a *pick glass*. (See Figure 24.1.) The glass is marked off in fractions of an inch or in centimeters, and the number of warp and filling yarns beside these calibrations can be viewed in magnified form with the glass and counted. In knitted fabrics the number of wales or courses per inch is counted.

The glass is lined up along a lengthwise yarn or crosswise yarn, the yarns in that direction are counted, and the count is expressed as a whole number of warps by a whole number of fillings. A yarn count of 75 × 50, for example, would mean that the fabric has 75 yarns in the warp direction and 50 yarns in the filling.

If the number of warps and fillings are about the same, the fabric may be said to have a balanced count and could be written as a count of 75 square or 75 warps by 75 fillings. Sometimes the fabric count is written as warp plus the filling yarns per inch.

Strength

Fabric strength evaluations are made in terms of breaking strength, tearing strength, or bursting strength. A variety of machines (See Figure 24.2.) is used to measure strength, and fabric samples are prepared for testing according to ASTM test method procedures.

Breaking strength is the force required to break a woven fabric when it is pulled under tension. The measurement is made of the pounds or grams of force required to break the fabric. Half the specimens are pre-

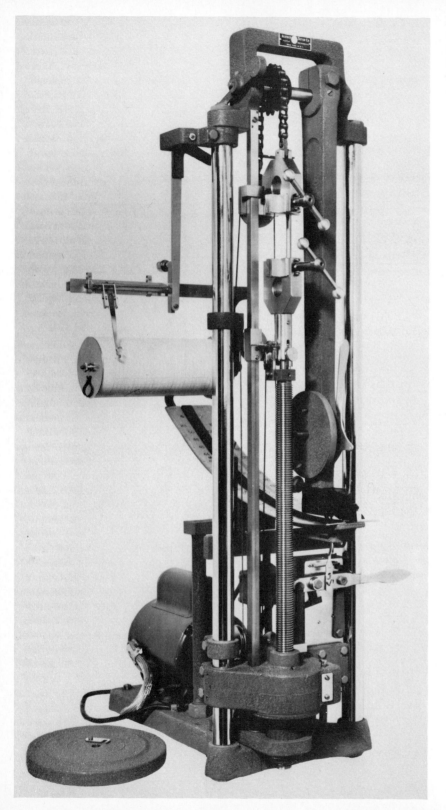

FIGURE 24.2. *Tensile tester used for testing tensile strength of fabrics and cords. Many tensile machines can be adapted to perform tearing and bursting strength tests. Courtesy of Alfred Suter Co., Inc.*

pared with warp yarns running in the direction of stress, and the other half with the stress in the filling direction. Breaking strength in each direction is calculated by averaging the measurements of the specimens for that direction.

The tearing strength of a fabric, expressed in pounds or grams, is the pressure required to continue a tear or rip already begun in a woven fabric. As in breaking strength, an average of values for warp yarns and average values for filling yarns are taken.

If yarns in one direction have low tear or breaking strength, performance will be affected. High levels of strength in one direction do not counterbalance low strength in the other.

Bursting strength is the pounds or grams of pressure required to rupture a knitted or woven fabric. Force is applied to the fabric from below or above the fabric as it is held flat.

Strength tests are often used as a measure of the effect of different treatments on fabrics. Researchers may use these tests to make comparisons between control or untreated fabrics and experimental fabrics. For example, breaking strength tests may be used to determine whether special finishes affect the strength of a fabric.

There are no hand tests for breaking strength that have the accuracy of testing performed on machines. Strength testing in the classroom or at home is limited to estimations of difference in strength. Yarns can be raveled from fabric samples and comparisons made of the strength required to break them by pulling. A tear can be started at the edge of a woven fabric, and some estimate is then made of the strength required to continue the tear.

Elongation and Recovery from Stretching

At the same time that breaking strength is being tested on a breaking strength testing machine, the degree of elongation that the fabric undergoes before breaking may be determined. The breaking strength machine is designed to record both the force required to break the sample and the inches of elongation before the sample broke. The percentage of stretch the sample underwent is calculated.

Fabrics may also be tested for recovery from elongation. Samples are stretched to a certain percentage of their original length (often 2 per cent) and then permitted to recover for a specific length of time. A remeasurement is made, and the percentage of elastic recovery is calculated by determining the length before stretching, length after stretching, and length after recovery. Since some fabrics recover gradually from stretching, measurements of recovery may be made after varying periods of time.

Although students in the classroom lack the sophisticated equipment required for very exact testing of elongation and recovery from stretching, fabric samples can be measured, subjected to stretching by pulling the fabric between two clamps or hanging weights from the bottom of the specimen for a period of time and then measured again to determine whether stretching has taken place. A second measurement taken after the fabric has been permitted to recover will allow some approximate determination of recovery from stretching.

Shrinkage

Fabric samples can be tested for shrinkage or stretching after laundering or dry cleaning, and the percentage of shrinkage can be calculated. Such tests can be done easily in the classroom or at home, although without temperature and humidity control, the results of these tests will always be approximate.

For best results, samples should be of an adequate size to make the calculations more exact. The smaller the sample, the greater the likelihood of error. Samples marked off at 10 or 20 inches also make numerical calculations easier. If the sample is large enough, an area 10 inches square is marked off in indelible ink following grain lines. The sample size should not be cut to 10 inches, but several inches on either side of the markings should be allowed; otherwise, the edges of the fabric may lose threads through raveling, and the results may not be accurate.

The sample should then be laundered by hand or by machine. The sample should be laundered by the same method that would be used for a garment made from the fabric. After laundering, the fabric is spread flat, dried, and then remeasured. The percentage of shrinkage is calculated by this formula.

$$\% \text{ shrinkage} = \frac{10 \text{ in. } - \text{ distance between marks after laundering}}{10 \text{ in. (marked length of original)}} \times 100$$

If only a small sample of fabric is available, it can be measured, then washed by hand, and remeasured with the shrinkage calculated as before, using the appropriate measurements:

$$\% \text{ shrinkage} = \frac{\text{length of original sample less length after laundering}}{\text{length of original sample}} \times 100$$

To prevent the fraying of small samples, it is best to overcast edges by hand, or some other method of preventing the sample from raveling should be used.

An evaluation of dimensional stability to dry cleaning can be made by immersing measured samples of fabric in dry-cleaning fluid, agitating the samples, then drying. The instructions on dry-cleaning fluids should be carefully followed since many are either flammable or toxic if inhaled in a closed area.

In those instances where samples stretch rather than shrink, calculations of the amount of stretch are made using this formula:

$$\% \text{ stretch} = \frac{\text{length of sample after laundering less original length}}{\text{original length}} \times 100$$

Abrasion Resistance and Pilling

Abrasion resistance is tested on different types of abrasion-testing machines. (See Figure 24.3.) The results of tests run on different machines cannot be compared, as each machine tests with a different motion and

FIGURE 24.3. *CSI Surface Abrader for testing surface abrasion. Other instruments will test for flex abrasion and edge abrasion. Courtesy of Custom Scientific Instruments, Inc.*

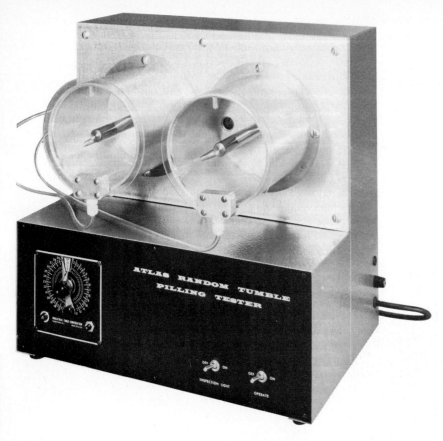

FIGURE 24.4.   *Random Tumble Pilling Tester for determining the pilling and fuzzing characteristics of all types of fabrics. Courtesy of Atlas Electric Devices Co.*

each holds the fabrics in different positions. (See discussion of abrasion in Chapter 2.)

No home test will provide a completely accurate measure of abrasion resistance; however, stroking a piece of sandpaper back and forth across the surface of a fabric may given a general indication of the tendency of the fabric to abrade. Machines such as the Brush Pilling Tester or Random Tumble Pilling Tester are used to evaluate the tendency of fabrics to pill. (See Figure 24.4.)

Abrasion is one of those factors most likely to be affected by each individual's unique use of textiles. For example, the linings of overcoats are subject to abrasion from garments worn beneath them. A person who favors soft, smooth-textured clothing would subject the lining of a coat to considerably less abrasion than one would who prefers coarse-textured, rough-surfaced textiles.

Colorfastness

The colorfastness of fabrics to a variety of substances and conditions can be measured by the use of a wide variety of specific testing methods and machinery. Atmospheric conditions may result in color loss of some fabrics. Fume fading—loss of color caused by an exposure to acidic atmospheric gases (specifically oxides of nitrogen) and ozone— can be measured in a device called a *gas fading chamber.* Fabrics in this enclosed chamber are exposed to these gases, and their color loss is determined.

Color change is ascertained by keeping a control or untreated sample of the fabric being tested. Tested samples can then be checked against the original. Comparison should always be made under the same kind of lighting, as different light sources can alter the appearance of colors. For laboratory testing, color scales have been established by AATCC that make it possible to determine more precisely the degree of color change that has taken place. The *gray scale* is made up of ten chips, each with two sections. One section of each chip is the same dark gray, the other section gradually lightens to provide a range of contrasts between the dark gray section of the chip and the changing section. A numerical value is assigned to each chip, with 5 (the highest rating) being given to the chip with no contrast and 1 (the lowest rating) being given to the chip with greatest contrast. Specimens being evaluated for color change are placed beside a control specimen that has undergone no treatment. The observer compares the color contrast between the test and control specimens to the color contrasts on the gray scale, determining at which step on the gray scale the contrast between sections of the chips most closely approximates the contrast in color between the two fabric specimens. A similar scale has been established for evaluating staining. The principle is the same; however, the gray scale for evaluating staining begins with a white chip, both sections being the same white, and carries the white chip throughout. (See Figure 24.5.)

FIGURE 24.5 *Using gray scale for evaluation of color change.*

Although visual evaluation can yield reasonably consistent results, computerized color evaluation instruments are more accurate than observers. It is likely that in the future these visual evaluation techniques will be superseded by electronic measuring devices. Samples of both treated fabrics and control fabrics are compared with the standard scales, and numerical ratings are assigned.

An exposure to sunlight may cause color loss in some fabrics. A simple home method for testing for fading from exposure to the sun is to tape a sample fabric in a sunny window. The sample is exposed to the sun for a period of time and is then compared to an unexposed sample. If part of the sample is covered, the color change can be compared more easily. This method does not provide a gauge of really long-term exposure, and the hours of exposure to sunlight are dependent upon the weather and time of year.

The Fade-o-meter®, a machine that duplicates the fading action of the sun, is used in laboratories to test for colorfastness to light. Samples may be exposed for varying periods of time and the loss of color is compared with a control sample. (See Figure 24.6.)

Some fabrics lose color through crocking, or rubbing against another fabric. Some fabrics crock when dry, some when wet, and some when both dry and wet. Testing for crocking is relatively easy.

1. *Dry crocking.* Place a sample of the fabric to be tested on a flat surface. Fold a piece of clean, dry, white cotton fabric over the forefinger. Rub back and forth across the test fabric. Examine the white fabric to determine whether any color has rubbed off.
2. *Wet crocking.* Wet the clean, white fabric and rub on the sample. Determine whether any color has rubbed off.

A laboratory device called a Crockmeter (Figure 24.7.), which can be used for testing for crocking, works on the same principle as the home test, by rubbing a white fabric sample across the fabric to be tested.

Laundering and dry cleaning may produce color loss in some fabrics. A machine known as the Launder-Ometer is used to perform laboratory washfastness tests. One 45-minute treatment in the Launder-Ometer is equivalent to five home launderings. The same device can be used to test for colorfastness to dry cleaning.

Home tests for washfastness are made as follows. A small sample of fabric is cut. A pint jar with a screw top is filled with water of the temperature appropriate for the fabric and a half-teaspoon of detergent or soap powder. The sample is placed in the water, and the top is placed on the jar and tightened. The jar is shaken briskly for a minute, is allowed to stand for 5 minutes, and is then shaken again for a minute. If a more severe laundry action is wanted, the water can be agitated with a spoon and the stirring repeated four times instead of two.

Pour the used wash water into a clear glass and look to see if the fabric has bled any color into the water. (It is possible for samples to

FIGURE 24.6. Fade-o-meter® for determining color fastness to sunlight. Courtesy of Atlas Electric Devices Company.

FIGURE 24.7. *AATCC Crockmeter that provides standard motion and pressure for determining colorfastness to crocking. The model on the left is operated manually, the model on the right is motorized. Courtesy of Atlas Electric Devices Co.*

lose some surface dye without undergoing noticeable color loss themselves.) Rinse the sample, dry, and then compare with the control sample.

It is possible to determine whether other fabrics are likely to pick up color lost by the test fabric during laundering. One or more samples of white fabric can be cut in half. Wash one half of the sample along with the test sample, rinse, dry, and then compare it with the unwashed white sample to determine whether any color has been picked up during washing. Special cloth containing a number of different fiber samples can be used for this testing to determine whether color pickup is general or limited to one fiber type.

Colorfastness to dry cleaning can be determined by immersing fabric in dry-cleaning fluid for 5 minutes. Fluid can be examined for color change, and when it is dry, the sample can be compared with the control.

AATCC has devised tests for colorfastness not only to laundering and dry cleaning but also to other conditions including perspiration (Figure 24.8.), chlorine bleach, chlorinated water (as in swimming pools), sea water, water spotting, and the like. Specific tests are described in the *Technical Manual.*

FIGURE 24.8. *AATCC Perspiration Tester for testing colorfastness to perspiration, and to chlorinated pool, sea, and distilled water. Up to twenty specimens can be tested simultaneously. Courtesy of Atlas Electric Devices Co.*

Tests to Determine Effectiveness of Special Finishes

Garments treated with wash and wear or durable press finishes are expected to look reasonably free of wrinkles after laundering. AATCC test methods have been developed for the evaluation of garments and other textiles treated with these finishes. The tests include a test for the appearance of durable press fabrics after repeated home laundering (Test Method 124), a test evaluating the appearance of seams in wash-and-wear items after home laundering (Test Method 88B), a test for the appearance of creases in wash-and-wear items after home laundering (Test Method 88C), and a test evaluating the appearance of apparel and other textile products after repeated home launderings (Test Method 143). The specifics of these test methods can be found in the AATCC publications.

In addition to testing that evaluates the appearance of garments, devices have been developed that will evaluate recovery of fabrics from wrinkling. The AATCC Wrinkle Tester allows an evaluation of wrinkle recovery by first subjecting a sample of fabric to wrinkling and then allowing a period of recovery. Finally, samples are evaluated by comparing them to specified visual standards (replicas of fabrics with varying degrees of wrinkling) and rating the samples.

A second method measures the angle of recovery of test samples. Samples of fabric are folded to make a crease, the creased sample is mounted on a Wrinkle Recovery Tester, and the angle of recovery after creasing is measured.

A quick test for crease recovery can be as simple as crushing a sample of fabric within a closed fist for 3 minutes and then removing the pressure, allowing the fabric to relax. Fabrics with good wrinkle recovery will appear less wrinkled than will those with poor recovery.

A sample of fabric can be folded and placed under a 1-pound box of sugar or other packaged material for a period of time. When the weight has been removed, the sample can be examined to see how sharp a crease has been formed. Allow the sample to relax for a while; then examine it again to determine whether the sharpness of the crease has diminished.

A number of tests have been devised to determine the effectiveness of other finishes. These tests cover such areas as durability of applied designs and finishes to dry cleaning, oil repellency, soil release, water resistance and repellency, and weather resistance. Specific instructions for testing in these and other areas are included in the *Technical Manual* of the American Association of Textile Chemists and Colorists and in the *Book of ASTM Standards* of the American Society for Testing materials.

Flammability Testing

Testing for flammability is required under the Flammable Fabrics Act. The requirements of that legislation and the performance standards that materials are required to meet under the law are discussed in Chapter 21. In addition to the tests required by law, a wide variety of additional tests for flammability can be conducted. Table 24.1 lists the various flammability tests that the United States Testing Company, an independent, commercial testing and inspection organization, will perform.

Researchers have devised a number of techniques to study flammability. Most of these devices require test samples of considerable size or even whole garments. They are intended to provide more extensive information about the effects of burning fabrics.

DuPont, Eastman Kodak and the University of Minnesota have developed "thermal" manikins with heat sensors located in various parts of the figure. Tests performed using these figures can determine not only the combustibility of the fabric being tested but also the location of "hot spots" and data about the transfer of heat.

Another device is called the "mushroom tester" or the MAFT. The device consists of a hollow cylindrical tube. A circular platform is mounted at the top of the tube. The sample to be tested is wrapped around the platform and hangs down (much as a skirt would hang from a person's waist). An air space is formed between the sample and the vertical tube. Temperature sensors are located in the tube and in the platform, and the device measures time of ignition and transfer of heat from the burning fabric.

Fiber Identification

In addition to the tests described that evaluate fabric characteristics and performance, a variety of procedures is used when it is necessary to identify the fiber composition of unknown fabrics.

The *Technical Manual* of AATCC Test Method 20-1973 "describes physical, chemical and microscopical techniques for identifying textile fibers used commercially in the United States."[1] Another useful publication is *Practical Fiber Identification* by David Hall.[2]

The identification of textile fibers generally follows these lines. A preliminary examination of the fibers or fabric is made. This may provide some clues as to the general category into which the fabric may fall. Experienced technologists may be able to exclude certain fibers or narrow the range of fibers into which the sample may fall simply by examining the fabric. For example, if a fabric exhibits no stretch, it cannot possibly contain spandex.

Burning a small sample of the fabric may help to distinguish its group still further. The odor and appearance of the fabric during and after burning, and the appearance of the residue may put it into a general category, such as cellulosic fiber, protein fiber, or synthetic. The results of this test help to determine the subsequent course of testing. Table 24.2 gives the results of burning tests for some fibers.

[1]"Fibers in Textiles: Identification," Test Method 20-1973, *Technical Manual* (Research Triangle Park, N.C.: AATCC, 1975) pp. 50 ff.
[2]David Hall, *Practical Fiber Identification* (Auburn, Ala.: Auburn University, 1976).

TABLE 24.1 Textile Flammability tests Conducted by the United States Testing Company, Inc.

Sponsoring Organization	Name of Test	Procedure Ident. No.	Sample	Specimen Size (In.)
1a CPSC	Flammability of Clothing Textiles	CS 191-53 16 CFR 1610.4	Fabrics	2 × 6
1b AATCC	Flammability of Clothing Textiles	AATCC-33-1962	Fabrics	2 × 6
1c ASTM	Flammability of Clothing Textiles	ASTM D-1230	Fabrics	2 × 6
1d NFPA	Flammability of Clothing Textiles	NFPA 702	Fabrics	2 × 6
2 CPSC	Wearing Apparel	MAFT	Clothing and fabrics	12½ × 24
3 CPSC	Children's Sleepwear	FF 3-71 16 CFR 1615.4	Sleepwear, sizes 0–6X	3½ × 10
4 CPSC	Children's Sleepwear	FF5-74 16 CFR 1615.4	Sleepwear, sizes 7–14	3½ × 10
5 Federal Test Method Standard	Flame Resistance of Cloth, Vertical	FTMS 191 Method 5903	Fabrics	2¾ × 12
6 Federal Test Method Standard	Burning Rate of Cloth, Horizontal	FTMS 191 Method 5906	Fabrics	4½ × 12½
7 Federal Test Method Standard	Burning Rate of Cloth, 45° Angle	FTMS 191 Method 5908	Fabrics	2 × 6
8 Federal Test Method Standard	Burning Rate of Cloth, 30° Angle	FTMS 191 Method 5910	Fabrics	1 × 6
9 CPSC	Mattresses	FF4-72 16 CFR 1632.4	Mattresses and mattress pads	Finished item
10a NFPA	Fire Tests for Flame-Resistant Textiles and Films	NFPA 701, Large Scale	Fabrics and films	Installed (1) in sheets—5 × 84 (2) in folds—25 × 84
10b NFPA	Fire Tests for Flame-Resistant Textiles and Films	NFPA 701, Small Scale	Fabrics and films	2¾ × 10
11a City of Boston	City Fire Code	11.2	Treated fabrics	Varies
11b City of Boston	City Fire Code	11.3	Inherent fire-resistant fabrics	Varies
12 City of New York	Board of Standards and Appeals	Calendar No. 294-40-SR	Fabrics	2 × 12.5
13a State of California	Fire Code Title 19	Par. 1273.3	Film, synthetic and coated fabrics	12 × 30
13b State of California	Fire Code Title 19	Par. 1237.1, Small Scale	Fabrics	2½ × 12½
13c State of California	Fire Code Title 19	Par. 1237.3, Large Scale	Fabrics	5 × 84
14a Federal Specifications	Surface Flammability of Carpets and Rugs	DDD-C-95	Carpets and rugs	9 × 9
14b CPSC	Surface Flammability of Carpets and Rugs	FF1-70 16 CFR 1630.4	Carpets and rugs	9 × 9
14c CPSC	Surface Flammability of Small Carpets and Rugs	FF 2-70 16 CFR 1631.4	Carpets and rugs	9 × 9
14d ASTM	Surface Flammability of Carpets and Rugs	ASTM D-2859	Carpets and rugs	9 × 9
15 State of California	Upholstery Materials	Bulletin 117	Fabrics and filing materials	
16 CPSC	Upholstery Materials	PFF 6-76	Fabrics and furniture	—
17a Federal Aviation Authority	FAA Regulations for Compartment Interiors	Par. 25.853	Compartment materials	4 × 14
17b Federal Aviation Authority	FAA Regulations for Compartment Interiors	Par. 26.863	Compartment materials	2¾ × 12½
18 Department of Transportation State of California	Flammability of Interior Materials—Cars, Trucks, Multipurpose Passenger Vehicles, Buses	FMVSS 302	Interior materials	4 × 14
19 Federal Test Method Standard	Mackey	FTMS 191 Method 5920	Cloth, related materials	2 × 12
20 Canvas Products Association International	Camping Tentage	CPAI-84	Tenting materials	Floors, 9 × 9; walls, 2¾ × 12
21 Canvas Products Association International	Sleeping Bags	CPAI-75	Sleeping bags	Entire bag

TABLE 24.1 Continued

Number of Specimens	Angle of Specimen	Ignition Source	Conditioning	Properties Measured
5 orig. 5 DC & W	45°	Butane burner	Oven-dry	Time of flame spread, ease of ignition, flame intensity
5 orig. 5 DC & W	45°	Butane burner	Oven-dry	Time of flame spread, ease of ignition, flame intensity
5 orig. 5 DC & W	45°	Butane burner	Oven-dry	Time of flame spread, ease of ignition, flame intensity
5 orig. 5 DC & W	45°	Butane burner	Oven-dry	Time of flame spread, ease of ignition, flame intensity
2 W, 2 L	Vertical	Micro burner	70° F, 50% RH	Ignition time, maximum heat transfer rate
5 Fabric 15 Seams	Vertical	Methane burner	Oven-dry	Residual flame time, char length
10 Fabric 15 Seams	Vertical	Methane burner	Oven-dry	Char length
5 W, 5 F	Vertical	Burner (mfg gas B)	70° F, 65% RH	Afterflame, afterglow, char length
5	Horizontal	Burner	Oven-dry	Time of flame spread
5	45°	Butane burner	4 hr at 140°F	Ease of ignition, rate of burning
3W, 3 F	30°	Match	4 hr at 140°F	Rate of burning
1	Horizontal	Cigarette	65–80°F 50% RH max.	Char length
5 W, 5 F, 2W, 2 F	Vertical	Burner	Oven-dry	Afterflame, afterglow, char length
5 W, 5 F	Vertical	Burner	Oven-dry	Afterflame, afterglow, char length
3	Vertical	Burner	Ambient	Afterflame, afterglow
3	Vertical	Burner	Ambient	Afterflame, afterglow
3	Vertical	Burner	Ambient	Afterflame, afterglow
3	Vertical	Burner	Ambient	Afterflame, afterglow
3 W, 3 F	Vertical	Burner	Oven-dry	Afterflame, char length
3 W, 3 F	Vertical	Burner	Oven-dry	Afterflame, char length
8	Horizontal	Methenamine burning tablet	Oven-dry	Area of flame spread (greatest diameter)
8	Horizontal	Methenamine burning tablet	Oven-dry	Area of flame spread (greatest diameter)
8	Horizontal	Methenamine burning tablet	Oven-dry	Area of flame spread (greatest diameter)
8	Horizontal	Methanamine burning tablet	Oven-dry	Area of flame spread (greatest diameter)
		Specimens and procedures vary with materials		
—	—	Cigarette	70°F, 50% RH	Char length, substrate ignition
3 min.	Horizontal	Burner	70°F, 50% RH	Time of flame spread
3 min.	Vertical	Burner	70°F, 50% RH	Afterflame, burn length
5 L, 5 W	Horizontal	Burner	70°F, 50% RH	Time of flame spread
2 min.	Not applicable	Not applicable	4 hrs. at 60°C	Tendency of material to undergo self-heating at moderate temp.
8 8 W, 8 F	Horizontal vertical	Pill burner	70°F, 65% RH Leached and Weathered	Area of flame spread, afterflame, char length
10	Horizontal	Bunsen burner	70°F, 50% RH	Burning rate

Table 24.2   Burning Tests—Results for Some Fibers

Nonthermoplastic

Burns leaving a hard black residue. Smell of burnt hair.	Wool, silk, and hair fibers
Burns readily leaving gray ash. Smell of burnt paper.	Cotton, linen, hemp, jute, sisal, viscose
Burns slowly, extinguishing on removal from flame. Carbonized residue. Pungent odor.	Flame-retardant viscose, cellulose fiber with flame-retardant finish
Burns readily leaving a dark skeletal residue. Strong fishy odor.	Cellulose with resin finish (e.g., cotton or viscose)

Thermoplastic

Burns rapidly. No soot. Not self-extinguishing	Acetate Triacetate
Burns with difficulty. Forms a hard bead. Smell of celery. Self-extinguishing.	Nylon 6 Nylon 66
Burns with sooty flame. Forms hard bead. Sweet smell. Self-extinguishing.	Polyester
Burns with sputtering sooty flame leaving an irregular crisp black mass. Self-extinguishing.	Acrylic

SOURCE: M. Greeves, "Fibre Identification," *Textiles*, 4 (1979) a periodical published by Shirley Institute, Manchester, England.

An examination with the microscope may also narrow the range of fibers with which the tester is working by providing a positive identification of those few fibers that have a distinctive appearance under the microscope. Wool or other animal hair are, for example, the only fibers with a scale structure. Generally, however, further analysis is required. Even if the identity of the fiber is reasonably certain, it may be desirable to verify the identification.

Different generic fiber types accept different types of dyes. Special fiber identification stains can be used to determine the fiber type, but this requires, of course, that the fiber being tested is a light shade or has been stripped of its color. These dye preparations come with a color shade chart showing the colors to which different generic fiber types will dye.

A further test of the solubility of the fiber in different chemicals can be made. Testing procedures specify the types of chemical solvents to be used, their concentrations, and the procedures to be used in handling the fibers and solvents. Many of these substances are hazardous and should be handled only in a laboratory under careful supervision. A comparison of the results of solubility testing with charts, such as those in the AATCC test method, should provide a final confirmation of fiber identity.

A determination of specific gravity, melting point, and/or moisture regain of the specimen may also help to verify the identity of fibers.

Identification of Finishes

The identification of special finishes for textiles is difficult. Except for mechanical finishes that can easily be identified by eye (such as moiréing and napping), the determination of chemical finishes may require extensive laboratory procedures. AATCC Test Method 94-1973 outlines a variety of tests for the identification of textile finishes.

Recommended References

American National Standards Institute Catalog. 1430 Broadway, New York, New York 10018.

ASTM Standard Performance Specifications for Textile Fabrics. Philadelphia: American Society for Testing Materials, 1983.

BARBIARZ, R. S., V. D. LYON, F. L. SIEVENPIPER. "Colorfastness to Washing," *Textile Chemist and Colorist*, 8 (February 1976), p. 34.

BURDETT, B. C. "Chemical Testing of Textiles," *Textiles*, 13 (Summer 1984), p. 44.

COHEN, A. C. *Beyond Basic Textiles.* New York: Fairchild Publications, Inc., 1982.

"Compilation of Laws Administered by the U.S. Consumer Product Safety Commission." Washington, D.C.: U.S. Consumer Product Safety Commission.

FELIX, E., and K. DOUGLAS, "Yarn Quality Specifications for Woven and Knitted Cloth," *Canadian Textile Journal*, 100 (November 1983), p. 21.

GOBEIL, N. B., and B. J. MUELLER. "Evaluating Colorfastness to Perspiration: Lab Tests vs. Wear Tests," *Textile Chemists & Colorist*, 6 (November 1974), p. 46.

HALL, D. *Practical Fiber Identification.* Auburn, Ala.: Auburn University, 1976.

HALL, D. *Chemical Testing of Textiles.* Auburn, Ala.: Auburn University, 1974.

HARNETT, P. R., and P. N. MEHTA. "A Survey and Comparison of Laboratory Test Methods for Measuring Wicking," *Textile Research Journal*, 54, No. 7 (July 1984), p. 471.

JOSEPH, M. *Introductory Textile Science.* New York: Holt, Rinehart and Winston, Inc., Chaps. 27, 31, and 34.

LYLE, D. C. *Performance of Textiles.* New York: John Wiley & Sons, Inc., 1977.

OLSEN, N. F., and E. R. BROOME. "Pupillometric and Subjective Assessment of Fabric Comfort," *Textile Chemist and Colorist* (June 1977), p. 30.

"The Physical Testing Laboratory in Weaving and Knitting," *International Textile Bulletin. World Edition: Weaving*, 1975, #1, p. 187; #3, p. 307.

RIDLEY, A., and D. WILLIAMS. *Simple Experiments in Textile Science.* London: Heinemann Educational Books, 1974.

TAYLOR, H. M. "Physical Testing of Textiles," *Textiles*, 14 (Spring 1985), p. 21.

Technical Manual. Research Triangle, N.C.: American Association of Textile Chemists and Colorists (published annually).

Textile Handbook. Washington, D.C.: American Home Economics Association, 1974.

"U.S. Testing: Busier than Ever at 96," *Modern Textiles*, 57 (May 1976), p. 38.

WARFIELD, C. L., and I. R. HARDIN, "Visual vs. Instrumental Evaluation of Fabric Whiteness," *Textile Research Journal*, 51 (November 1981), p. 725.

WEAVER, J. W., ed. *Analytical Methods for a Textile Laboratory.* Research Triangle Park, N.C.: American Association of Textile Chemists and Colorists, 1984.

Fabric Structure: The Sum of Its Parts

This chapter is a summary of the preceding chapters. In previous chapters the many aspects of textile fabrics have been discussed at length, but a fabric is, in the final analysis, not a set of individual components; it is the sum of its various parts.

Fabrics are three-dimensional structures; they have length, width, and thickness. A number of components must be assembled in different ways to create the structures. In the most complex fabric structures, the components are the fiber content, yarn construction, fabric construction, and applied finishes. In simpler structures, such as fiber webs, the elements are more limited. They are fiber content, the method of distribution of fibers, the bonding medium, and applied finishes. Each of these aspects of textiles has been discussed before, but it is also important to consider them in relation to each other. Stress in this discussion is placed on woven and knitted fabrics.

Because fiber, yarn, fabric structure, and finish each play a role in the way in which a given textile product will behave during its "use lifetime," this chapter is organized to lead the reader through a summary of considerations relating first to fibers, then to yarns, and finally to fabric structures and how, together, they relate to special aspects of textile behavior. When finished, the author hopes that the reader will be able to view textiles as the sum of their various parts and to have a more complete understanding of the meaning of that equation.

The Importance of the Fibers

"The properties of the single fiber are the basis on which fabric properties ultimately rest."[1] Fiber properties are discussed in Chapter 1 and in subsequent chapters dealing with individual fibers.

---

[1]N. J. Abbott, "The Relationship Between Fabric Structure and Ease of Care Performance of Cotton Fabrics," *Textile Research Journal*, 34 (December 1964), p. 1050.

To recapitulate, these properties are length, density, crimp, surface character, diameter, luster, toughness, strength, elongation, elasticity, resilience, moisture regain, conductivity, dimensional stability, and resistance to heat and fire, sun, weathering, microorganisms, insects, acids, alkalis, and other solvents. Taken together, these properties for any given fiber are the personal qualities that give the fiber its individual "personality." Although special finishes can be applied that alter some of these properties, the fiber properties are an essential part of the ultimate character of a textile fabric, and an understanding of textile fabrics requires knowledge of fiber characteristics.

The first question that must be asked, then, in coming to understand a particular textile product is, "What is the fiber?" What are the fiber characteristics?"

The Geometry of Yarns

In woven, in knitted, and in some other structures such as stitch-through, netting, or macramé, the fibers cannot be utilized unless they are made into yarns. The act of combining fibers into yarns creates a new structure that has properties of its own. Textile scientists speak of this as *yarn geometry*, that is, the three-dimensional structure of a yarn. The most significant aspects of yarn geometry are yarn diameter, the degree of fiber compactness within the yarn, yarn twist, yarn cross-sectional shape, yarn stiffness, and yarn crimp. Geometric characteristics of yarn are a product both of the type of fibers put into the yarn and of the yarn structure that is employed.

Yarn Diameter and Fiber Compactness

Yarn diameter is the width of the yarn. Fiber characteristics have an impact on yarn diameter. Yarn diameter can be increased by putting a larger number of fibers into a yarn or by using fibers of large diameter. Fibers with smooth, even surfaces will pack into a yarn more closely, giving the yarn a greater degree of fiber compactness. Fibers with rough or uneven surfaces will have the opposite effects. Yarn diameter is also affected by yarn twist.

Yarn Twist

The amount of twist given a yarn can be controlled. However, fiber characteristics must also be taken into account when considering the subject of yarn twist. Staple fibers require twist to form them into a yarn; filament fibers do not, although they frequently are twisted.

Twist is also related to the diameter of the yarn. If two yarns made from the same fiber have the same quantity of fiber in the yarn, the yarn that is given the higher degree of twist will have a smaller diameter.

Fibers have an impact on the diameter, the degree of twist, and other characteristics of yarns. Among the fiber characteristics having the greatest influence on the appearance and behavior of the twisted yarns are length, fineness, crimp, and cross-sectional shape.

The yarn, in turn, will cause the fabric into which it is woven or knitted to take on certain qualities. Tenacity of yarns is affected by twist. Up to a certain point, increasing twist increases strength in staple fibers. This is thought to be because increased twist decreases the ability of fibers to slip, thereby requiring more force to break the yarn. Some of the other physical properties of yarns that are affected by twist include bending behavior, resistance to creasing, resistance to abrasion, drapability, and elastic performance. Yarn twist may be utilized to create fabrics with special aesthetic qualities. For example, crepe yarns with high twist are used in weaving crepe fabrics with their pebbly surface texture. Low-twist staple yarns are selected for use in fabrics that are to be napped. Low-twist bright filament yarns are used in some satin fabrics to produce a high luster.

Yarn Cross-sectional Shape

Likewise, yarn cross-sectional shape will affect fabric characteristics. Twist, diameter, and yarn cross-sectional shape are related to fabric density and thickness. A yarn with a flat, ribbonlike cross section may be used to advantage in making a fabric with little depth. Round, thick yarns will increase fabric depth.

Yarn Stiffness

Yarn stiffness is related to fiber stiffness, and fabric stiffness is related to yarn stiffness. It is not possible to make a flexible yarn from an inflexible fiber or a flexible fabric from an inflexible yarn. Moreover, the way in which fibers are combined in the yarn will affect yarn flexibility. "To take advantage of the inherent flexibility, it is necessary to give the individual fiber the greatest freedom of movement possible . . . the fibers should be able to slip over one another."[2] From this description it is easy to see that more tightly twisted yarns, in which fibers have less freedom of movement, will be less flexible. The most flexible yarn of all should be one in which the filament fibers are combined with little or no twist. The least flexible yarns should be those in which the fibers are bonded together by an adhesive or fused by heat or chemical means. An excellent example of this principle can be seen after a heavily sized fabric with a water-soluble sizing has been laundered. The fabric after laundering will be much softer and more flexible when the sizing that has held the fibers together has been removed.

Added to the questions, "What is the fiber?" and "What are the fiber characteristics?" then are the questions, "What effect do these fiber

[2]P. R. Lord and M. H. Mohamed, *Weaving: Conversion of Yarn to Fabric* (Watford, England: Merrow Publishing Company Ltd., 1973), p. 129.

characteristics have on the structure of the yarn into which they are made?" and "What are the characteristics of the yarns, themselves? their diameter? degree of twist? shape? stiffness?"

Interrelationships between properties of yarns and fibers are important aspects of the complex relationships of the various building blocks of textile products. A similar interrelationship exists between yarns and fabric structures. One must consider the fiber and its characteristics, the yarn and its characteristics, and also fabric structure. Some of the aspects of fabric structure that must be taken into account are the method of construction (i.e., type of weave or knit), the number of yarns per inch, yarn crimp, and yarn cover power.

Yarn Crimp in Woven Fabrics

An important concept in understanding woven fabric behavior is the concept of the development of *crimp* in yarns during weaving. The term "crimp" has been used in relation to fiber properties. In that usage it was defined as the undulating or wavy form of the fiber. Crimp is also an important characteristic of woven structures.

When warp and filling yarns cross each other, they cannot continue to move in an absolutely straight line, but each set of yarns must bend over and under yarns in the other set. Each yarn, therefore, develops a wavy configuration. Some force is exerted at every point where warp and filling yarns cross, because each yarn has a tendency to want to return to a straight configuration. As a result, there is a sort of "ideal" balance between the forces of the yarns, and this "ideal balance" is the most stable state of the fabric. (See Figure 25.1.)

This balance can be altered by stretching the fabric in one direction. Pulling it in one direction causes it to contract in the other. To illustrate this principle, take a wide rubber band and stretch it in one, then in the other, direction and observe what happens. As the band stretches in one direction, it contracts in the other. "Crimp interchange" or "crimp transfer" can be used to create selected effects. For example, fabrics with some degree of stretch can be made by placing warp yarns under pronounced tension. When stress is exerted in the filling direction, crimp interchange takes place and the fabric "stretches" in the

Fabric Geometry

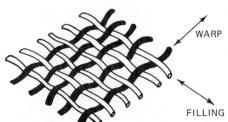

WARP

FILLING

FIGURE 25.1. *As warp and filling yarns pass over and under each other, they develop crimp. Smaller warp yarns (shown in black) develop greater crimp as they pass over larger filling yarns (shown in white).*

filling direction. When stress is released, the fabric returns to its "normal" state (i.e., as it has been set with tension in the warp), and the crimp transfers again to the filling direction.

Certain generalizations about the effect of yarns and of fabric weaves on crimp can be made.

1. The greater the number of yarn intersections, the more the crimp created in one or the other of the yarn directions. A logical outcome of this is that plain-weave fabrics have greater crimp than do satins, as yarns in plain-weave fabrics intersect more often.
2. Thick, bulky yarns will produce greater yarn crimp than will small-diameter yarns. Obviously thick yarns will have to move farther away from a straight path when they cross each other.
3. Double-cloth fabric constructions in which yarns travel from one side of the fabric to the other will develop exceptionally great crimp as the yarns move from front to back of the fabric.
4. If there are many warps per inch and few fillings, the crimp in the warp will be small and the crimp in the filling will be large. Weavers can compensate for this by adjusting the tension on yarns during weaving. When tension is applied to the yarns in one direction, the yarns tend to straighten. But as the yarns in one direction become straighter and less crimped, the yarns in the opposite direction must develop a greater amount of crimp through transfer or crimp interchange.
5. Stiffer yarns will develop less crimp than will more flexible yarns when both are used in the same fabric. If a smooth surface is desired, the crimp must be adjusted to bring the crests of the yarns into the same level. If a ribbed or corded fabric is desired, crimp will be purposely decreased in the direction of the cord or rib and increased in the yarns that cross the cord or rib yarns.

Special finishes can be given to fabrics to "set" a particular crimp configuration. For example if one wished to cause a fabric to return to a state in which warp yarns are under tension, those warp yarns must be set in some way, usually either through a resin finish or through a heat-setting process.

Knitted Structures

The methods of construction used to make woven fabrics as opposed to the methods of construction used to make knitted fabrics cause the fabrics to have different characteristics. Obviously the great variety of types of woven and knitted structures make it difficult to compare all woven with all knitted structures, but a few very general comments can be made. The structure of knitted fabrics is essentially that of a connected series of loops. Loops require little force to distort them; therefore, knitted fabrics, in theory, will extend readily in the length and width when subject to stress. After deformation, the yarns tend to return to their previous position. However, the differences in structure between warp and weft knits makes the preceding generalization true only to a limited extent. Warp knitting requires that yarns be carried from one wale to another, thereby giving warp knits increased stability. Furthermore, variations of weft knitting may incorporate long warp or weftwise floats or other structural variations that can also make fabrics more stable.

Given the enormous variety of knitted structures, any evaluation of fabrics that takes into account the method of construction must take careful note of the type of knit and its individual characteristics.

Covering Power

The terms "covering power" and "cover factor" refer to both the optical and the geometric properties of fabrics. Optical covering power is the ability of the fabric to hide that which is placed under it.

Fiber characteristics affect the optical covering power. If the fibers used are translucent or transparent, the fabric will be more translucent or transparent. The same fiber may have greater opacity if it has been delustered and will reflect more light, rather than allowing light to pass through the fiber. Fiber cross-sectional shape and degree of crimp also affect the optical covering power.

Yarn structure will be a factor. Smaller-diameter yarns or smoother yarns will cover less well. Fabric structure will influence optical covering power. An open-construction fabric will obviously cover less well than will a densely constructed fabric.

Fabric crimp is also related to covering power in woven fabrics. As yarns in one direction cross and exert pressure on the yarns in the opposite direction, these yarns may be flattened somewhat. Flatter yarns provide better cover.

Knitted fabrics tend to have lower cover than do woven fabrics, with weft knits having substantially more porous structures than warp knits, unless the fabric is deliberately made to have an open, lacy construction as in some Raschel knits. Use of thinner or thicker yarns can increase the cover of knitted fabrics.

Dyeing and finishing will also have an effect on cover. Darker colors tend to cover better than do lighter, for instance.

The geometric aspect of covering power is expressed as the cover factor, which is the ratio of fabric surface occupied by yarn to total fabric surface. A cover factor of 100 per cent means that all the fabric surface is covered completely by yarn. It would require that the yarns be packed densely, with no open spaces between the yarns. Few fabrics can actually achieve such complete cover, as there is generally some space, however small, between the yarns even in the most closely constructed fabrics.

Fabric Density and Thickness

Fabric density and thickness are achieved by the manipulation of yarn construction, fabric construction, and the application of some types of finishes. Fulling, used to produce a compact, denser fabric from wool fibers, is one such finish; napping of fabrics makes them thicker; and calendering makes them thinner.

Finishes

The appearance or behavior of fibers, yarns, and fabrics may also be altered by special finishes given to textiles. To cite only one example, durable press finishes given to fabrics composed of 50 per cent cotton and 50 per cent polyester do not have an appreciable effect on appearance of the fabric, but they do make a treated garment resist wrinkling more than one of the identical fiber composition, yarn structure, or weave that has not been treated. At the same time, the finish has the effect of decreasing abrasion resistance and making the fabric less moisture absorbent. The effects of any of the many finishes applied to fabrics must be taken into consideration when one tries to understand a particular fabric.

Fabric Behavior

The sum total of fabric behavior, then, is affected by fiber, yarn, fabric construction, and special finishes. Some of the aspects of fabric performance that are affected include appearance, durability, comfort, and care.

Appearance Factors

Wrinkle Resistance and Recovery

Different fibers have differing resiliency. When a manufacturer begins by making a yarn from a fiber that is resilient, the wrinkle resistance of the yarn into which it is made and the fabric into which that yarn is woven or knitted will be enhanced. When the fiber has poor wrinkle recovery, the opposite is true. A fabric of 100 per cent polyester should wrinkle less than one of 100 per cent cotton.

Yarn structure must also be considered. When a crease forms in a woven or knitted fabric, the yarns bend. The fibers in the outer side of the yarn are strained; those on the inner side are compressed. In more tightly twisted yarns the forces within the yarn will tend to keep yarns from being permanently deformed, and they will tend to return to their original shape.

Fabric structure affects the ability of yarns and fibers to move and must therefore be given specially close attention. In general, it is true that fabrics with few interlacings and knits wrinkle less than do other fabrics. Printed fabrics, especially those with "busy" designs, may mask or hide wrinkles. Researchers who have investigated the factors of fabric structure that are related to crease resistance and crease recovery suggest that the following principles operate.

1. "The most important factor in crease resistance is the freedom of the yarns and fibers to relax."[3] Loosely woven fabrics generally allow more fiber redistribution and motion and therefore have better crease recovery. However, because loosely woven fabrics allow more fiber redistribution and motion, when these fabrics do become creased or wrinkled, the wrinkles may be more permanent (assuming, of course, that all other factors, such as fiber resiliency, yarn twist, and so on are the same).
2. Stiffer fabrics will become creased to a lesser degree than will more flexible fabrics. Since greater pressure is required to form a crease in stiff fabrics, stiff fabrics will form fewer wrinkles during washing and drying. But once wrinkles have been formed, wrinkle recovery is less than it is for more flexible fabrics. Abbott recommends that, in engineering fabrics for increased crease resistance and wrinkle recovery, fabrics be made in which "stiffness is high enough to prevent easy formation of wrinkles, but not so high that ability to recover from wrinkling is impaired."[4]

Drape and Handle

Textile researchers speak about bending and shear properties. Shearing is the deformation of a structure in which a rectangle becomes lozenge shaped. In woven fabrics this results from movement of yarns from what one might call a normal position in which yarns run horizontally and vertically and interlace at right angles to other positions in which the interlacing is deformed to a less than 90 degree angle. (See Figure 25.2.)

Bending and shear formation have an effect on drape and handle of fabrics. Fabrics that shear easily will be softer and more drapable. To illustrate this principle, think about cutting a half-circle skirt from a fabric. Parts of the garment will lie along the straight grain (true warp or true filling directions), but other parts will lie along other directions, some at a diagonal called the *bias*. In the bias direction, fabric is particularly subject to shear deformation. If the fabric is unable to shear, it remains stiff and will not mold or drape softly.

These draping qualities are affected by the stiffness of the fiber and yarn, the size of the yarn, and particularly the fabric construction. In tight structures, especially where coarse yarns are packed tightly together, fabrics are likely to be stiff and less drapable. In loose structures where yarns can move easily over one another, fabrics are likely to be softer and drape more easily.

[3]Lord and Mohamed, *Weaving*, p. 167.
[4]Abbott, "The Relationship Between Fabric Structure and Ease of Care Performance," p. 1054.

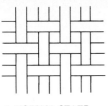
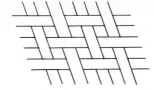

A. NORMAL STATE

B. SHEARED

C. LOW SHEARABILITY

D. HIGH SHEARABILITY

FIGURE 25.2. Shear deformation is the movement of yarns from a normal position (A) where yarns run horizontally and vertically to other position(s) (B) where interlacing is deformed to a less than ninety degree angle. Fabrics with low shearability (C) are not as soft and drapable as fabrics with high shearability (D).

Fabrics such as satin that have long floats in the weave can be more flexible, bending more easily and making possible softer, smoother handle and improved draping qualities. If at the same time these fabrics are made from filament yarns with little twist, the draping quality is enhanced still more.

In general, because of the ways in which yarns are combined, woven fabrics have higher shearability than do knitted fabrics, although knitted fabrics have good flexibility and are easily extended. Warp knits have lower shearability than do weft knits. These qualities must be taken into account by designers, although they may not be aware of the technical terminology used to describe these properties.

For example, a warp knit tricot fabric with low shearability would not be used to make a bias-cut garment in which the intention is to take advantage of high shearability. Instead, the designer would be likely to use a soft, gathered construction where the high flexibility of the fabric would work to good advantage, but where most of the draping would fall in the vertical direction of the fabric.

Finishes that make yarns more rigid or that restrict yarns from moving freely in relation to one another will reduce flexibility.

Durability Factors

Abrasion Resistance

The difficulty of assessing the complex interrelationships of fiber, yarn, and fabric structures is especially well illustrated in the question of abrasion resistance. H. M. Taylor, in an article about fabric abrasion, concluded that "The problems attached to the characterization of textiles in respect of abrasion are serious and by no means solved."[5]

---

[5]H. M. Taylor, "Abrasion in Fabrics," *Textiles*, 7 (June 1978), p. 40.

Some fibers have better abrasion resistance than do others. Yarn construction is also a factor. Loosely twisted yarns abrade more easily that do tightly twisted yarns, as in the loosely twisted yarns individual fibers are more likely to be subjected to being pulled up from the fabric surface.

In woven fabric construction, the aspect of crimp distribution seems to be particularly important. The crown—the part of the yarn that protrudes above the surface of the fabric—receives the pressure of surface or edge abrasion. The more crowns of the same height there are in a given area of cloth, the more evenly the wear will be distributed over the surface of the fabric. Interrelationships of construction and yarn structure may be observed in a fabric like shantung, in which uneven, loosely twisted slubbed yarns present higher crowns that are unevenly spaced; this is an example of a fabric that has poor abrasion resistance.

Weave also enters into abrasion resistance. In fabrics with floats, yarns and fibers are more free to move and are less consistently exposed to abradants. For this reason, twill and some sateen fabrics may show superior abrasion resistance.

Knitted fabrics sometimes seem to be less resistant than woven fabrics to abrasion when this resistance is measured on testing instruments. However, in actual wear, the pliability of knits may prevent the same area of fabric from being constantly subjected to the pressures that result in abrasive wear, so that "in the uses to which they are put, knitted fabrics compare well with the woven fabrics that would be chosen for the same purpose."[6] Pilling, as a result of abrasion, however, may be more of a problem in knitted than in woven fabrics because fibers are not held so closely into knitted structures as into woven structures and therefore can be pulled into pills on the surface of the fabric.

Some finishes may have a negative impact on resistance to abrasion. Durable press and other resin finishes have this effect, probably by making fabrics more rigid and therefore giving fibers less opportunity to move. To compensate for decreases in abrasion resistance resulting from the application of these finishes, fiber content is carefully selected. Instead of using 100 per cent of natural fibers such as cotton, which has lower abrasion resistance, cotton fibers are blended with synthetic fibers such as polyester, which has superior abrasion resistance.

Tensile Strength and Tear Strength

The major factors in tensile strength and tear strength are the strength of the yarn and the strength of the fabric structure. Fiber tenacity is relatively less important, because strong yarn or fabric structures can compensate for low individual fiber tenacities.

[6]H. M. Taylor, "Woven and Knitted Fabrics," *Textiles*, 8 (October 1979), p. 68.

Tear strength is more closely related to the serviceability of woven fabrics than is tensile strength. In testing tensile strength, all the yarns share equally in the stress applied, but in tear strength testing, a few yarns, at most, are subject to stress. Fabric constructions in which groups of yarns are woven together, such as basket or rib weaves, will have the greatest tear strength, since more yarns will group together to share the stress. Any construction that restricts the ability of yarns to function together will decrease tear strength. Finishes that coat fabrics or restrict yarn movement will tend to isolate yarns and decrease tear strength.

Strength of knitted fabrics is considered to be less important in durability than it is in woven goods. This is because knitted fabrics are easily stretched to accommodate changes of shape as a result of stress.

Elongation and Recovery

Fiber elongation may be a significant factor in the extensibility of fabrics when an elastomeric fiber such as spandex is used.

Crimp added to yarns, as in textured yarns, and the natural crimp created in all fabrics when yarns interlace are also related to extensibility and elongation. First, as a fabric is stretched, the crimp in the direction of the stretch is removed, permitting the fabric structure to reach its maximum extensibility. The second phase is one in which the crimp of the yarn (as opposed to fabric crimp) is removed. The greater the yarn crimp, the more extensible the fabric.

When woven and knitted fabrics are compared, it can be said that woven fabrics are firmer and have less extensibility and elongation than do knitted fabrics. But as was noted earlier, variations in knitting techniques can increase or decrease extensibility of knitted fabrics.

Dimensional Stability

A few fibers exhibit poor dimensional stability. Thermoplastic fibers that have not been heat stabilized may be plasticized by heat and shrink when agitated in hot water. Viscose shrinks and stretches unless specially treated. Assemblies of wool fiber felt and cause shrinkage in the fabrics into which they are made.

The fiber content is therefore a critical element in dimensional stability of yarns and fabrics. As noted before, however, special finishes can be given to fabrics to overcome these inherent properties.

In fabrics in which the fiber is dimensionally stable or has been stabilized through a finish, dimensional stability problems will be related to unreleased stresses introduced in the manufacturing processes, particularly where stress is applied to yarns or fabrics that causes them to be elongated beyond their natural dimensions. Finishes may be applied to compensate for any of these factors. Knitted fabrics, because of their greater extensibility, are more likely to lose their shape. Warp knits and double knits have better dimensional stability than do weft knits.

Comfort Factors

Thermal Conductivity

The thickness of the fabrics, and the ability of the fabric to entrap still air within the fabric are related to thermal conductivity. Still air provides excellent insulation. If the yarn structure and the fabric structure permit the entrapment of still air, a fabric may provide warmth by insulating the body. Napped wool and acrylic sweaters are an instance of the application of this principle. However, if the wind blows hard, the same garment may allow the passage of moving air through the fabric, and its insulating qualities may be lost or diminished. Thermal properties are, therefore, related to air permeability.

Air Permeability

Air permeability is the ability of air to pass through a fabric. Obviously, where openings between yarns or between fibers within yarns are large, a good deal of air will pass through the fabric. Conversely, where compact yarns are packed tightly into fabrics with little air space between them, the flow of air through the fabric is diminished.

Some finishes for fabrics—such as ciréing of thermoplastic fabrics—decrease air permeability by causing fibers and yarns to fuse slightly. Fabrics may be coated with another material that closes up interstices in the fabric. To make garments that are warm enough for sports such as skiing in which moving air may cool the athlete, a fabric with low air permeability (such as closely woven nylon) may be combined with materials of low thermal conductivity (such as polyester or acrylic fiberfill or with pile fabrics) that trap air close to the body.

Moisture Vapor Transmission and Water Repellency

Like air permeability, water vapor transmission is closely related to the density of fabric construction. Tight, close constructions allow little transmission of water vapor. Hydrophobic fibers may act as a shield to prevent passage of water vapor, whereas hydrophilic fibers allow some water vapor to pass through the fabric.

In some synthetic yarns, the empty spaces between the fibers may permit the wicking or spreading of water. These fibers are not, therefore, naturally water repellent, but must be given special treatments to render them water repellent. Dense cotton fabrics, by contrast, may provide better water repellency by virtue of the fact that they are hydrophilic. The fibers swell on exposure to water, jamming the construction and forming a barrier to keep out water.

Care Factors

Drying Rate and Drying Time

Although practical experience with home laundering leads to the conclusion that garments made from hydrophilic fibers such as cotton require longer to dry than do those from hydrophobic materials such as polyester, research indicates that drying time may be more closely related to yarn and fabric construction than to fiber content. "A thin, low weight, low moisture regain synthetic filament fabric dries faster than a thick, heavy, high moisture regain spun yarn fabric because more water must be evaporated from the latter, not because it is hydrophilic."[7] Studies have shown that identical fabrics made from acrylics and wool will dry in the same length of time.[8]

During drying, then, water must be evaporated from fabric, yarn, and fiber. A thick dense fabric will dry more slowly; a staple, fuzzy, or thick yarn will dry more slowly; and a hydrophilic fiber will contain more moisture that must be evaporated.

Soiling

The ability of soil to penetrate a fabric is related to the fabric structure. Smooth-surfaced fabrics will allow soil to slide off the surface. Fuzzy, unevenly textured fabrics may serve as traps for dirt and dust. Some fabric structures may mask soil better than others by hiding it and do not appear soiled as quickly. Fibers with uneven surfaces such as wool or multilobal fibers may have this quality.

If soil is deeply embedded in fiber, yarn, or fabric structures it may be difficult to remove. Soil held inside a fabric structure may serve as an abradant and tend to cut or break yarns. Some finishes may tend to attract soil; others are applied to decrease soiling.

Summary

The foregoing discussion shows clearly that no single characteristic of fibers, yarns, or fabrics can be judged by itself. All these characteristics are subject to modification either intentionally or unintentionally and are mutually dependent on each other in the final product.

It is essential to analyze the factors that are at work in any particular textile product and to relate the various factors one to the other. Most of the paradoxical elements of fabric behavior can be accounted for by this means, and predictions of fabric performance and evaluations of textiles for specific end uses will be more satisfactory. It is the recognition of the interrelatedness of fiber, yarn, fabric, construction, and finishes that makes an understanding of textiles possible.

Recommended References

ABBOT, N. J. "The Relationship Between Fabric Structure and Ease of Care Performance of Cotton Fabrics," *Textile Research Journal*, 34 (December 1964), p. 1049.

BACKER, S., and S. J. TANNENHOUS. "The Relationship Between the Structural Geometry of a Textile Fabric and Its Physical Properties. Part III: Textile Geom-

[7]E. R. Kaswell, *Handbook of Industrial Textiles* (New York: Wellington Sears Co., Inc., 1964), p. 467.
[8]Ibid.

etry and Abrasion Resistance," *Textile Research Journal*, 21 (September 1951), p. 635.

BERTOLI, P. "The Influence of Fibers and Yarn Properties on End-product Behavior," *Textile Month* (October 1975), 91.

CARNABY, G. "The Mechanics of Carpet Wear," *Textile Research Journal*, 51 (August 1981), p. 514.

EULER, R. D. "Creating "Comfort" Socks for the U.S. Consumer," *Knitting Times*, 54 (May 1985), p. 47.

GOLDBERG, J. B. "The Properties of Fabrics," in S. B. McFarlane, ed., *Technology of Synthetic Fibers*, New York: Fairchild Publications, Inc., 1953.

GOODINGS, A. C. "Air Flow Through Textile Fabrics," *Textile Research Journal*, 34 (August 1964), p. 713.

KASWELL, E. R. *Handbook of Industrial Textiles*. New York: Wellington Sears Co., Inc., 1963.

LORD, P. R., and M. H. MOHAMED. *Weaving: Conversion of Yarn to Fabric*. Watford, England: Merrow Publishing Company Ltd., 1973.

MORRIS, M. A., et al. "Relationship of Fiber Content and Fabric Properties to the Comfort of Socks," *Clothing and Textiles Research Journal*, 3 (Fall/Winter 1984–85), p. 14.

"Pilling and Chafing," *Bulletin No. FC-94*, International Fabricare Institute, Silver Springs, Md., 1985.

ROBINSON, A. T. C., and R. MARKS. *Woven Cloth Construction*. Manchester, England: The Textile Institute, 1973.

SCHERER, M. "How to Choose Outdoor Clothing," *Sierra*, 68 (March/April 1983), p. 71.

TAYLOR, H. M. "The Functional Design of Textiles," *Textiles*, 13 (Spring 1984), p. 23.

TAYLOR, H. M. "Thermal Comfort. Part I: Clothing," *Textiles*, 11 (Autumn 1982), p. 66; "Part II: Bedding, Carpets, and Curtains," 12 (Spring 1983).

Appendix: Bibliography

General References: Texts and Encyclopedias

ALEXANDER, P. R. *Textile Products: Selection, Use, and Care.* Boston: Houghton Mifflin Company, 1977.

BELCK, N., M. L. JOSEPH, and M. WAMHOFF, *Textiles: Decision Making for the Consumer.* East Lansing: Michigan State University Press, 1985.

BURNHAM, D. *Warp and Weft: A Dictionary of Textile Terms.* New York: Charles Scribner's Sons, 1982.

COHEN, A. C. *Beyond Basic Textiles.* New York: Fairchild Publications, Inc., 1982.

COLLIER, A. M. *A Handbook of Textiles,* 3rd ed. New York: Pergamon Press, 1980.

CORBMAN, B. *Textiles: Fiber to Fabric.* New York: McGraw-Hill Book Company, 1982.

DANTAYGI, S. *Fundamentals of Textiles and Their Care.* New York: Apt Books, Inc., 1983.

Dictionary of Textile Terms. New York: Dan River, 1980.

Encyclopedia of Textiles, American Fabrics, 3rd ed. Englewood Cliffs, N.J.: Prentice-Hall, Inc., 1980.

GIOELLO, D. *Understanding Fabrics: From Fiber to Finished Cloth.* New York: Fairchild Publications, Inc., 1982.

FARNFIELD, C. A., and P. J. ALVEY. *Textile Terms and Definitions.* New York: State Mutual Book and Periodical Service, 1975.

GRAYSON, M., ed. *Encyclopedia of Textiles, Fibers, and Nonwoven Fabrics.* New York: Wiley-Interscience, 1984.

HALL, A. J. *The Standard Handbook of Textiles.* New York: John Wiley & Sons, Inc., 1975.

HARDINGHAM, M. *Illustrated Dictionary of Fabrics.* London: Studio Vista, 1978.

HOLLEN, M., and J. SADDLER. *Textiles.* New York: Macmillan Publishing Company, 1979.

JOSEPH, M. L. *Essentials of Textiles;* 3rd ed. New York: Holt, Rinehart and Winston, Inc., 1984.

Joseph, M. *Introductory Textile Science;* 5th ed. New York: Holt, Rinehart and Winston, Inc., 1986.

Klapper, M. *Fabric Almanac.* New York: Fairchild Publications, Inc., 1971.

Kleeberg, I. C., ed. *Butterick Fabric Handbook.* New York: Butterick Publishing Company, 1975.

Labarthe, J. *Elements of Textiles.* New York: Macmillan Publishing Company, 1975.

Linton, G. E. *The Modern Textile and Apparel Dictionary,* 4th ed. Durham, England: Meadowfield Press, 1973.

Lyle, D. S. *Modern Textiles;* 2nd ed. New York: John Wiley & Sons, Inc., 1982.

————. *Performance of Textiles.* New York: John Wiley & Sons, Inc., 1977.

Miller, E. *Textiles: Properties and Behavior.* London, England: Batsford, 1984.

Pizzuto, J. *Fabric Science.* New York: Fairchild Publications, Inc., 1980.

Smith, B., and I. Block. *Textiles in Perspective.* New York: Englewood Cliffs, N.J.: Prentice-Hall, Inc., 1982.

Textile Handbook. Washington, D.C.: American Home Economics Association. Current edition.

Textile Terms and Definitions; 7th ed. Manchester, England: The Textile Institute, 1975.

Wingate, I. B. and J. Mohler. *Textile Fabrics and Their Selection;* 8th ed. Englewood Cliffs, N.J.: Prentice-Hall, Inc., 1984.

————. *Fairchild's Dictionary of Textiles.* New York: Fairchild Publications, Inc., 1979.

————, K. R. Gillespie, and B. G. Addison. *Know Your Merchandise.* New York: McGraw-Hill Book Company, 1975.

Woodhouse, J. M. *Science for Textile Designers.* London: Elek, 1976.

Historic Textiles

Broudy, E. *The Book of Looms—A History of the Handloom from Ancient Times to the Present.* New York: Van Nostrand Reinhold Co., 1979.

D'Harcourt, R. *Textiles of Ancient Peru and Their Techniques.* Seattle: University of Washington Press, 1974.

Emery, I., and P. Fiske, eds. *"Looms and Their Products,"* Proceedings of the Irene Emery Roundtable on Museum Textiles. Washington, D.C.: Textile Museum, 1977.

Gervers, V., ed. *Studies in Textile History.* Toronto: Royal Ontario Museum, 1977.

Leene, J. E. *Textile Conservation.* Washington, D.C.: Smithsonian Institution, 1972.

Mackie, L. W., and A. P. Rowe. *Masterpieces in the Textile Museum.* Washington, D.C.: The Museum, 1976.

Montgomery, E. *Textiles in America.* Wilmington, Del.: Winterthur, 1984.

Pianzola, M., and J. Coffinet. *Tapestry.* New York: Van Nostrand Reinhold Co., 1974.

Pollen, M. *Seven Centuries of Lace.* New York: Macmillan Publishing Company, 1908.

Powys, M. *Lace and Lace-making.* Boston: Charles T. Grandford Co., 1953.

Schwab, F. R. *The Story of Lace and Embroidery.* New York: Fairchild Publications, Inc., 1951.

Sieber, R. *African Textile and Decorative Arts.* New York: Museum of Modern Art, 1972.

Volbach, W. F. *Early Decorative Textiles.* New York: Paul Hamlyn, 1969.
Weibel, A. C. *Two Thousand Years of Textiles.* New York: Pantheon Books, 1952.
Wilson, K. *A History of Textiles.* Boulder, Colo.: Westview Press, 1979.

Textiles as an Art and Craft

Albers, A. *On Weaving.* Middletown, Conn.: Wesleyan University Press, 1965.
Birrell, V. L. *The Textile Arts.* New York: Harper & Row, Publishers, 1959.
Brown, R. *Weaving, Spinning and Dyeing Book.* New York: Alfred A. Knopf, Inc., 1979.
Clark, L. J. *The Craftsman in Textiles.* New York: Praeger Publishers, Inc., 1968.
Dendel, E. W. *African and Pacific Crafts.* New York: Taplinger Publishing Company, 1974.
Fannin, A. *Hand-spinning, Art and Technique.* New York: Van Nostrand Reinhold Co., 1970.
Gentille, T. A. *Printed Textiles: A Guide to Creative Design Fundamentals.* Englewood Cliffs, N.J.: Prentice-Hall, Inc., 1982.
Harvey, V. *Macramé.* New York: Van Nostrand Reinhold Co., 1967.
Held, S. B. *Weaving.* New York: Holt, Rinehart and Winston, Inc., 1972.
Keller, I. *Batik: The Art and Craft.* Rutland, Vt.: Charles Tuttle Co., 1966.
Kluger, M. *The Joy of Spinning.* New York: Simon & Schuster, Inc., 1971.
Kramer, J. *Natural Dyes, Plants, and Processes.* New York: Charles Scribner's Sons, 1972.
Melen, L. *Knitting and Netting.* New York: Van Nostrand Reinhold Co., 1971.
Proctor, R. M. *Surface Design for Fabric.* Seattle: University of Washington Press, 1984.
Proud, N. *Textile Dyeing and Printing Simplified.* New York: Arco Publishing Co., 1974.
Regenstein, E. *The Art of Weaving.* New York: Van Nostrand Reinhold Co., 1970.
Ward, M. *Art and Design in Textiles.* New York: Van Nostrand Reinhold Co., 1973.
Watson, W. *Watson's Advanced Textile Design: Compound Woven Structures.* London: Newnes-Butterworth, 1977.

Textile Care

"Detergents in Depth," *Proceedings.* New York: Soap and Detergents Association, 1984.
Finch, K. *Caring for Textiles.* New York: Watson-Guptill Publications, 1977.
Mailand, H. F. *Consideration for the Care of Textiles and Costumes: A Handbook for the Non-Specialist.* Indianapolis: The Indianapolis Museum, 1980.
Moss A. J. E. *Textiles and Fabrics: Their Care and Preservation.* New York: Chemical Publishing Company, 1961.
Preservation of Paper and Textiles of Historic and Artistic Value. Washington: D.C.: American Chemical Society, 1981.
"Soaps and Detergents for Home Laundering," Home and Garden Bulletin No. 139. Washington, D.C.: U.S. Department of Agriculture, 1973 (revised).
The Technology of Home Laundering. Textile Monograph 108. New York: American Association for Textile Technology, 1973.

BILLMEYER, F. W. *Textbook of Polymer Science*. New York: John Wiley & Sons, Inc., 1984.

CARTER, M. E. *Essential Fiber Chemistry*. New York: Marcel Dekker, Inc., 1971.

GOHL, E. P. G., and L. D. VILENSKY. *Investigations in Textile Science*. Glasgow: Blackie and Son, 1980.

HAPPEY, F., ed. *Applied Fibre Science*. New York: Academic Press, Inc., 1979.

HEARLE, J. W. S. *Polymers and Their Properties*. Vol. I: *Fundamentals of Structure and Mechanics*. Chichester, England: Ellis Horwood Ltd., 1982.

HIEMENZ, P. C. *Polymer Chemistry—The Basic Concepts*. Brookfield Center, Conn.: Society of Plastics Engineers, 1984.

KAUFMAN, H. S., and J. J. FALCETTA, eds. *Introduction to Polymer Science and Technology*. Brookfield Center, Conn.: Society of Plastics Engineers, 1977.

MILES, J. *Handbook of Chemistry Specialties. Textile Fiber Processing, Preparation, and Bleaching*. New York: Wiley-Interscience, 1983.

NEEDLES, H. L. *Handbook of Textile Fibers, Dyes, and Finishes*. New York: Garland STPM Press, 1981.

ROBINSON, J. S., ed. *Fiber-Forming Polymers*. Parkridge, N.J.: Noyes Data Company, 1980.

TROTMAN, E. R. *Dyeing and Chemical Technology of Textile Fibres*. New York: Wiley-Interscience, 1984.

Textile Chemistry

ALLEWELT, A. L; and J. BAUER, eds. *AATCC Handbook on Bonded and Laminated Fabrics*. Research Triangle Park, N.C.: American Association of Textile Chemists and Colorists, 1974.

Alternatives to Spun Yarns in Apparel Fabrics. A Book of Papers. Manchester, England: Shirley Institute, 1979.

BANCROFT, F., and C. A. LAWRENCE. *Progress in O. E. Spinning*. Manchester, England: Shirley Institute, 1975.

EMERY, I. *The Primary Structures of Fabrics*. Washington, D.C.: The Textile Museum, 1966.

FORD, J. E. *Fibrillated Yarns*. Watford, England: Merrow Publishing Company Ltd., 1975.

GIOELLO, D. *Profiling Fabrics: Properties, Performance, and Construction Techniques*. New York: Fairchild Publishers, Inc., 1981.

GOSWAMI, B. C., et al. *Textile Yarns, Technology, Structure and Applications*. New York: John Wiley & Sons, Inc., 1977.

GREENWOOD, K. *Weaving, Control of Fabric Structure*. Watford, England: Merrow Publishing Company Ltd., 1975.

Handbook of Bonded and Laminated Fabrics. Research Triangle Park, N.C.: American Association of Textile Chemists and Colorists, 1974.

HENSHAW, D. E. *Worsted Spinning*. Manchester; England: Textile Institute, 1981.

HENSHAW, D. E. *Self-twist Yarn*. Watford, England: Merrow Publishing Company Ltd., 1971.

HOSSACK, D. *Tape Yarns*. Watford, England; Merrow Publishing Company Ltd., 1971.

HUNTER, L. *The Production and Properties of Staple Fiber Yarns Made by Recently Developed Techniques*. New York: State Mutual Books, 1978.

HUTTON, H. *Textile Structures*. New York: Watson Gupthill Publishers, 1975.

LENNOX-KERR, P. *Flexible Textile Composites*. Manchester, England: Textile Trade Press, 1973.

Textile Construction (technical works)

Lord, P. R. *Spinning in the 70's.* Watford, England: Merrow Publishing Company Ltd., 1970.

———, and M. H. Mohamed. *Weaving: Conversion of Yarn to Fabric,* 2nd ed. Watford, England: Merrow Publishing Company Ltd., 1982.

Marks, R., and T. C. Robinson. *Principles of Weaving.* New York: State Mutual Book and Periodical Service, 1976.

McDonald, M. *Non-woven Fabric Technology.* Plainfield, N.J.: Textile Book Service, 1971.

Pierce, F. T., and J. R. Womersley. *Cloth Geometry.* Manchester, England: Textile Institute, 1978.

Piller, B. *Bulked Yarns: Production, Processing, and Applications.* Manchester, England: Textile Trade Press, 1973.

Reichman, C., ed. *Knitting Encyclopedia.* New York: National Knitted Outerwear Association, 1972.

———, et al. *Knitted Fabric Primer.* New York: National Knitted Outerwear Association, 1967.

Robinson, J. S., ed. *Manufacture of Yarns and Fabrics from Synthetic Fibers.* Park Ridge, N.J.: Noyes Data Corporation, 1980.

Robinson, A. T. C., and R. Marks. *Woven Cloth Construction.* London: Butterworth Co., 1973.

Rohlena, V. *Open-end Spinning.* New York: American Elsevier Publishing Co., Inc., 1975.

Schwartz, P., et al. *Fabric Forming Systems.* Park Ridge, N.J. Noyes Data Corporation, 1982.

Spencer, D. J. *Knitting Technology.* New York: Pergamon Press, 1984.

Talavsek, O. *Shuttleless Weaving Machines.* New York: American Elsevier Publishing Co., Inc., 1981.

Vincent, J. J. *Shuttleless Looms.* England: Durham, Meadowfield Press, 1979.

Wilson, D. K. *Production of Textured Yarns by the False Twist Technique.* New York: State Mutual Books, 1978.

———, *Production of Textured Yarns by Methods Other than the False Twist Method.* New York: State Mutual Books, 1978.

The Yarn Revolution. New Developments in the Production of Spun and Textured Yarns. Papers of the 60th Annual Conference of Textile Institute Manchester, England. Manchester: Textile Institute, 1976.

AATCC Glossary of Printing Terms. Research Triangle Park, N.C.: American Association of Textile Chemists and Colorists, 1973.

Backer, S., et al. *Textile Fabric Flammability.* Cambridge, Mass.: M.I.T. Press, 1976.

Bhatnagar, V. M., ed. *Advances in Fire Retardant Textiles.* New Holland, Pa.: Technomic Press, 1974.

Bird, C. L., and W. S. Boston. *The Theory of Coloration of Textiles.* New York: State Mutual Books, 1975.

Bogle, M. *Textile Dyes, Finishes, and Auxiliaries.* New York: Garland Publishers, 1977.

Book of Papers, Technical Conference. Research Triangle Park, N.C.: American Association of Textile Chemists and Colorists, published annually.

Cooper, C. G. *The Textile Industry: Environmental Control and Energy Conservation.* Park Ridge, N.J.: Noyes Data Corporation, 1978.

Textile Dyeing, Printing, and Finishing (technical works)

Datye, D. V., and A. A. Vaidya. *Chemical Processing of Synthetic Fibres and Blends*. New York: Wiley-Interscience, 1984.

Gutcho, M. H., ed. *Household and Industrial Fabric Conditioners*. Park Ridge, N.J.: Noyes Publishing Co., 1980.

Hearle, J. W. S., ed. *The Setting of Fibers and Fabrics*. Watford, England: Merrow Publishing Company Ltd., 1971.

Harrison, P. W. *Textile Finishing*. New York: State Mutual Books, 1978.

James, R. W. *Printing and Dyeing of Fabrics and Plastics*. Park Ridge, N.J.: Noyes Data Corporation, 1974.

Lee, R. W. *Printing on Textiles by Direct and Transfer Techniques*. Park Ridge, N.J.: Noyes Data Corporation, 1981.

Lewin, M., ed. *Flame-Retardant Polymeric Materials*, 2 vols. New York: Plenum Press, 1978.

Lewin, M., and S. B. Sello, eds. *Handbook of Fiber Science and Technology*. Vol. I: *Fundamentals and Preparation*. New York: Marcel Dekker, Inc., 1984.

Lewin, M., and S. B. Sello, eds. *Handbook of Fiber Science and Technology*. Vol. II: *Functional Finishes*. New York: Marcel Dekker, Inc., 1984.

Makinson. *Shrinkproofing of Wool*. New York: Marcel Dekker, Inc., 1979.

Miles, L. W. C. *Textile Printing*, 2nd ed. Watford, England: Merrow Publishing Company Ltd., 1982.

Nettles, J. E. *Handbook of Chemical Specialties: Textile Fiber Processing, Preparation, and Bleaching*. New York: John Wiley & Sons, Inc., 1983.

Olson, E. S. *Textile Wet Processes*. Vol. 1: *Preparation of Fibers and Fabrics*. Park Ridge, N.J.: Noyes Data Corporation, 1983.

Printing Symposium: Meeting the Challenge of the 80's. Research Triangle Park, N.C.: American Association of Textile Chemists and Colorists, 1978.

Proceedings of the Symposium on Transfer Printing. Princeton, N.J.: Textile Research Institute, 1976.

Ranney, M. W. *Textile Processing and Finishing Aids: Recent Advances*. Park Ridge, N.J.: Noyes Data Corporation, 1977.

Reichman, C., ed. *Transfer Printing Manual*. New York: National Knitted Outerwear Association, 1976.

Sodano, C. S. *Water and Soil Repellents for Fabrics*. Park Ridge, N.J.: Noyes Data Corporation, 1979.

Technology/Ecology Interface, proceedings of symposium. Research Triangle Park, N.C.: American Association of Textile Chemists and Colonists, 1977.

Textile Printing: An Ancient Art and Yet So New. Research Triangle Park, N.C.: American Association of Textile Chemists and Colorists.

Trotman, E. R. *Dyeing and Chemical Technology of Textile Fibres*. London: Griffin Publishers, 1975.

Williamson, R. *Fluorescent Brightening Agents*. New York: American Elsevier Publishing Co., Inc., 1980.

Yehaskel, A. *Fire and Flame Retardant Polyers: Recent Developments*. Park Ridge, N.J.: Noyes Data Corporation, 1980.

Aspin, C. *The Cotton Industry*. Aylesbury, England: Shire Publications, 1981.

Arthur, J. C. *Polymers for Fibers and Elastomers*. Washington, D.C.: American Chemical Society, 1984.

Textile Fibers (technical works)

BREARLY, A., and J. TREADLE. *The Woolen Industry.* New York: State Mutual Books, 1982.

———, and J. TREADLE. *The Worsted Industry.* New York: State Mutual Books, 1982.

CHAPMAN, C. B. *Fibres.* Plainfield, N.J.: Textile Book Service, 1974.

COOK, J. G. *Handbook of Textile Fibers,* vols. 1 and 2. Watford, England: Merrow, Technical Library, 1968.

———, *Handbook of Polyolefin Fibres.* Watford, England: Merrow Publishing Company Ltd., 1967.

GOHL, E. P. H., and L. D. VILENSKY. *Textile Science: An Explanation of Fibre Properties.* London: Longman Group Ltd., 1981.

HAMBY, D. S., ed *American Cotton Handbook,* 2 vols. New York: Wiley-Interscience, 1965–1966.

HAPPEY, F., ed. *Applied Fibre Science,* vols. 1 and 2. New York: Academic Press, Inc., 1978–1979.

HEARLE, J. W. S., and R. H. PETERS. *Fiber Structures.* London: Butterworth Co., 1963.

High Tech Fibers—Fiber Composites. Fort Lee, N.J.: Technical Insights, 1985.

HUGHES, A. J., et al. *The Production of Man-Made Fibres.* New York: State Mutual Books, 1976.

MONCRIEFF, R. W. *Man-Made Fibres,* 7th ed. New York: John Wiley & Sons, Inc., 1987.

MORTON, W. E., and J. W. S. HEARLE. *Physical Properties of Textile Fibers.* New York: John Wiley & Sons, Inc., 1975.

PAJGRT, O., et al., eds. *Processing of Polyester Fibres.* New York: American Elsevier Publishing Co., Inc., 1980.

PRESTON, J., and J. ECONOMY, eds. *High Temperature and Flame Resistant Fibers.* New York: John Wiley & Sons, Inc., 1973.

ROBINSON, J. S. *Spinning, Extruding, and Processing of Fibers: Recent Advances.* Park Ridge, N.J.: Noyes Data Corporation, 1980.

ROLLINS, M. L. *Cotton Fiber Structure.* Watford, England: Merrow Publishing Company Ltd., 1975.

RYDER, M. L. *The Production and Properties of Wool and Other Animal Hair Fibres.* New York: State Mutual Books, 1975.

SCHICK, M. J., ed. *Surface Characteristics of Fibers and Textiles,* 2 vols. New York: Marcel Dekker, Inc., 1975, 1977.

SITTIG, M. *Acrylic and Vinal Fibers.* Plainfield, N.J.: Textile Book Service, 1972.

———. *Polyamide Fiber Manufacture.* Plainfield, N.J.: Textile Book Service, 1972.

TURBAK, A. F., ed. *Solvent Spun Rayon, Modified Cellulose Fibers and Derivatives.* Washington, D.C.: American Chemical Society Symposium, 1977.

VON BERGEN, W., ed. *Wool Handbook,* vols. 1 and 2. New York: Wiley-Interscience, 1963, 1970.

WALCZAK, Z. *Formation of Synthetic Fibers.* New York: Gordon, 1977.

ZIABICKI, A. *Fundamentals of Fibre Formation.* New York: John Wiley & Sons, Inc., 1976.

BERKSTRESSER, G. A. *Textile Marketing Management*. Park Ridge, N.J.: Noyes Data Corporation, 1984.

Computers in the World of Textiles. Manchester, England: The Textile Institute, 1985.

ENRICH, N. L. *Management Control Manual for the Textile Industry*. New York: Krieger, 1980.

NORTHRUP, H. R., et al. *The Impact of OSHA*. Philadelphia: Wharton School, University of Pennsylvania, 1978.

OMEROD, A. *Management of Textile Production*. Boston: Newnes-Butterworth, 1979.

A Study of the Textile and Apparel Industries. Washington, D.C.: U.S. Government Printing Office, 1978.

TOYNE, B., et al. *The Global Textile Industry*. Boston: George Allen and Unwin, 1984.

———, et al. *The U.S. Textile Mill Products Industry*. Columbia: University of South Carolina, 1983.

WOODRUFF, J. L., and J. M. McDONALD, eds. *Handbook of Textile Marketing*. New York: Fairchild Publishers, Inc., 1982.

Textile Industry

Book of ASTM Standards. Philadelphia: American Society for Testing and Materials, published annually.

FARNFIELD, C. A., and D. R. PERRY. *Identification of Textile Materials*. New York: State Mutual Book and Periodical Service, 1975.

HALL, D. M. *Chemical Testing of Textiles: A Laboratory Manual*. Auburn, Ala: Auburn University, 1981.

Japan-Australia Joint Symposium on Objective Specifications of Fabric Quality, Mechanical Properties, and Performance, Kyoto, Japan, 1982.

Technical Manual. Research Triangle Park, N.C.: American Association of Textile Chemists and Colorists, published annually.

Textile Flammability, A Handbook of Regulations, Standards, and Test Methods. Research Triangle Park, N.C.: American Association of Textile Chemists and Colorists, n.d.

WEAVER, J. W. ed. *Analytical Methods for a Textile Laboratory*, 3rd ed. Research Triangle Park, N.C.: American Association of Textile Chemists and Colorists, 1984.

Textile Testing, Standards, and Legislation

BACKER, S. *Textile Fabric Flammability*. Cambridge, Mass.: M.I.T. Press, 1976.

CROWN, F. *The Fabric Guide for People Who Sew*. New York: Grosset & Dunlap, Inc., 1973.

FOURT, N., and N. R. HOLLIES. *Clothing/Comfort and Function*. New York: Marcel Dekker, Inc., 1970.

Technical bulletins of E. I. du Pont de Nemours & Company, Wilmington, Delaware 19898.

Miscellaneous

American Dyestuff Reporter, 630 Third Avenue, New York, N.Y. 10017.

American Fabrics and Fashions, Doric Publishing Company, 24 East 38th Street, New York, N.Y. 10016.

CIBA Review (until 1970).

America's Textiles, Box 88, Greenville, S.C. 29602.

Periodicals

Canadian Textile Journal, 4920 Maisonneuve Blvd., W., Montreal, Quebec, Canada.

Clothing and Textiles Research Journal, Association of College Professors of Textiles and Clothing, Inc., P.O. Box 1360, Monument, Colo. 80132.

Daily News Record, Fairchild Publications, Inc., 7 East 12th Street, New York, NY 10003.

Family Economics Review, Science and Education Administration—Agricultural Research, Northwestern Region, U.S. Department of Agriculture, Beltsville, Md. 20705.

Fibre and Fabric (until 1976).

Handweaver and Craftsman, Kutztown, Pa. 19530.

International Textile Bulletin: Dyeing, Printing and Finishing, International Textil-Service, GmbH Kesslerstrasse 9, P.O. Box CH-8952, Schlieren, Switzerland.

International Textile Bulletin: Knitting.

International Textile Bulletin: Spinning.

International Textile Bulletin: Weaving.

Journal of Coated Fabrics, Technomic Publishing Co., 851 New Holland Ave., Box 3535, Lancaster, Pa. 17604.

Journal of Industrial Fabrics, Industrial Fabrics Association, 345 Cedar, Suite 450, St. Paul, Minn. 55101.

Knitted Outerwear Times (to 1970).

Knitting Times, 51 Madison Avenue, New York, N.Y. 10010.

Modern Knitting Management, (to 1984).

Modern Textiles, (to 1984).

Nonwovens Industry, Box 555, 26 Lake Street, Ramsey, N.J. 07446.

Textile Bulletin (until 1971).

Textile Chemist and Colorist, P.O. Box 12215, Research Triangle Park, N.C. 27709.

Textile Forum, North Carolina State University School of Textiles, North Carolina State University, Raleigh, N.C. 27607.

Textile History, Butterworth Scientific Ltd., P.O. Box 63, Westbury House, Bury St., Guildford, Surrey, England.

Textile Industries, W. R. C. Smith Publishing Company, 1760 Peachtree Road, N. W., Atlanta, Ga. 30361.

Textile Month, 205 East 42nd Street, New York, N.Y. 10017.

Textile Museum Journal, The Textile Museum, 2320 "S" Street, N.W., Washington, D.C. 20008.

Textile Organon, Textile Economics Bureau, Inc., 489 Fifth Avenue, New York, N.Y. 10017.

Textile Research Journal, P.O. Box 625, Princeton, N.J. 08540.

Textile Technology Digest, Institute of Textile Technology, Charlottesville, Va. 22902.

Textile Topics, Textile Research Center, Texas Tech University, P.O. Box 5217, Lubbock, Tex. 79417.

Textile World, McGraw-Hill, Inc., 1175 Peachtree Drive, N.E., Atlanta, Ga. 30361.

Textiles, Shirley Institute, Manchester, England M 20 8 RX.

Appendix: Glossary

*Abrasion The wearing away of any part of a material by rubbing against another surface.

*Absorption A process in which one material (the absorbent) takes in or absorbs another (the absorbate): as the absorption of moisture by fibers

*Adsorption A process in which fluid molecules are concentrated on a surface by chemical or physical forces, or both.

Amorphous areas (in the fiber structure) Areas within fibers in which long-chain molecules are arranged in a random or unorganized manner.

Appliqué Attaching, usually by sewing, small pieces of cloth or other materials to the surface of a larger textile.

Bandanna Indian textiles decorated by the tie-and-dye method.

Bast fibers Fibers found in the woody stem of plants.

Batik Indonesian technique of resist printing in which areas of fabric that are to resist the dye are covered with wax.

*Bicomponent fiber A fiber or filament composed of two physically and chemically distinct polymeric components in continuous longitudinal contact within the fiber.

*Biconstituent fiber A fiber or filament consisting of a continuous matrix of one polymer in which a different fiber-forming polymer is dispersed as a second distinct discontinuous phase.

*Bleaching The procedure, other than by scouring only, of improving the whiteness of a textile material by oxidation or reduction of the coloring matter.

*Blended yarn A single yarn spun from a blend or mixture of different fiber species.

Block printing The application of printed designs by pressing dye-covered blocks onto a fabric.

Bobbin lace Lace made with a number of threads, each fastened to a spool. The pattern to be followed is anchored to a pillow, so that this lace is also called pillow lace.

Byssinosis A lung disease to which cotton mill workers are subject; thought to be caused by toxins in the cotton dust.

Calendering The process of passing fabric between rollers with the application of heat and pressure.

*Carbonized wool Scoured wool processed to destroy cellulosic impurities by treating with a mineral acid or an acid salt, drying and baking, crushing, and dusting out the embrittled cellulosic matter followed by neutralization of the acidified wool.

*Carding The process of untangling and partially straightening fibers by passing them between two closely spaced surfaces that are moving at different speeds, and at least one of which is covered with sharp points, thus converting a tangled mass of fibers to a filmy web.

Casement cloth A term used to refer to a wide variety of curtain fabrics.

Ciré A shiny, lustrous surface effect achieved by applying a wax finish or by heat treatment of thermoplastic fibers.

*Cohesiveness The resistance to separation of fibers in contact with one another.

Colorfastness The ability of a textile material to retain its color during use and care.

Combing A process that follows carding that pulls fibers into more parallel alignment.

*Courses In knitted fabrics, the series of successive loops lying crosswise of a knitted fabric, that is, lying at right angles to a line passing through the open throat to the closed end of the loops.

Cover factor The ratio of fabric surface occupied by the yarns to the total fabric surface.

Covering power (optical) The ability of a fabric to hide that which is placed under it.

*Crimp, fiber The waviness of a fiber expressed as waves or crimps per unit length.

Crochet A technique of creating fabric by pulling one loop of yarn through another with a hook.

*Crocking A transfer of color from the surface of a colored fabric to an adjacent area of the same fabric or to another surface principally by rubbing action.

*Cross-dye effect Variation in dye pickup between yarns or fibers resulting from their inherent dye affinities.

Cross-linking The attachment of one long-chain molecule to another by chemical linkages.

Crystallinity (in fiber structure) Orderly, parallel arrangements of molecules within a fiber.

Cut The number of needles per inch in the bed of a circular filling knit machine.

Cystine linkages Chemical cross-linkages in the wool fiber.

Delustered fiber A man-made fiber that has had its natural luster decreased by chemical or physical means.

Denier The weight of 9,000 meters of fiber or yarn expressed in grams.

*Density fiber, Mass per unit volume of the solid matter of which a fiber is composed, measured under specified conditions.

Dimensional stability The ability of a fiber or yarn to withstand shrinking or stretching.

Discharge printing The creation of design by applying a discharge material that removes color from treated areas of a dyed fabric.

Doupion or doupioni silk   A double strand of silk produced by two silkworms spinning a cocoon together.

Dry spinning   The formation of man-made textile fibers in which the polymer is dissolved in a solvent that is evaporated, leaving the filament to harden by drying in air.

Dull fiber   See *delustered fiber*.

Durable finishes   Those finishes that have good durability over a reasonably long period of use.

*Durable press   Having the ability to retain substantially the initial shape, flat seams, pressed-in creases, and unwrinkled appearance during use and after laundering or dry cleaning. The use of the term "permanent press" as a substitute for "durable press" is undesirable.

Dyes   Natural or synthetic substances that add color to materials.

*Elasticity   That property of a material by virtue of which it tends to recover its original size and shape immediately after removal of the force causing deformation.

*Elongation   Increase in length; extension; increase in length of a specimen during a tension test expressed in units of length, for example, centimeters and inches.

Embroidery   The use of yarns applied to fabrics with a needle in a variety of decorative stitches.

Ends   Warp yarns.

Fasciated yarns   Yarns made from a bundle of parallel fibers wrapped around by a surface wrapping of other fibers.

*Felt, wool,   A textile composed wholly of any one or combination of new, reprocessed, or reused wool fibers physically interlocked by the inherent felting properties of wool and produced by a suitable combination of mechanical work, chemical action, moisture and heat, but without weaving, knitting, stitching, thermal bonding, or adhesives.

Fiber dyeing   See *Stock dyeing*.

Fibrillation   The creation of fibers or yarns by drawing a polymer sheet in the lengthwise direction so as to cause the sheet to split into a network of fibers (that may be formed into yarns).

*Filament   A variety of fiber having an extreme length, not readily measured.

Filet   An embroidered net, also known as *lacis*.

Filature   A factory in which silk fibers are processed.

*Filling   Yarn running from selvage to selvage at right angles to the warp in a woven fabric.

*Fineness,   A relative measure of size, diameter, linear density, or mass per unit length expressed in a variety of units.

*Flexibility   That property of a material by virtue of which it may be flexed or bowed repeatedly without undergoing rupture.

*Flock   A material obtained by reducing textile fibers to fragments, as by cutting, tearing, or grinding, to give various degrees of comminution.

Fulling   In the processing of wool or animal hair fabrics, treatment with moisture, heat, soap, and pressure that causes yarns to shrink, lie closer together, and give the fabric a more dense structure.

Generic name   Names assigned by the Federal Trade Commission to the various types of man-made fibers according to the chemical composition of the fiber-forming substance.

Gigging   A synonym for napping or brushing up of loose fibers onto the surface of a fabric made from staple yarns.

*Glass transition   The reversible change in an amorphous polymer or in amorphous regions of a partially crystalline polymer from (or to) a viscous or rubbery condition to (or from) a hard and relatively brittle one.

*Graft polymers   A copolymer in which polymeric side chains have been attached to the main chain of a polymer of different structure.

*Greige goods,   Textile fabrics that have received no bleaching, dyeing, or finishing treatment after being produced by any textile process.

Hackling   A step in the processing of flax fibers that is comparable to combing.

Heat setting   The treatment of thermoplastic man-made fibers or fabrics with heat to set the fibers or fabrics into a specific shape or form.

Heat transfer printing   A system of textile printing in which dyes are applied to a paper base and are then transferred from the paper to a fabric under heat and pressure.

Heddle   A cord or wire eyelet through which warp yarns are passed on a loom.

Ikat   A form of resist printing in which sections of warp yarns are made to resist dyes. Dye is applied to the warp yarns, and filling yarns are inserted. The resultant patterns have an indistinct, shimmering pattern. (A type of warp print.)

High-wet-modulus   The quality in a fiber that gives that fiber very good stability when wet.

Kemp hairs   Coarse, straight hairs in a wool fleece that do not absorb dye readily.

Lacis   See *Filet.*

Latch needle   A needle used in knitting machines that has a latch that opens and closes to hold the yarn on the needle.

*Linters   The short fibrous material adhering to the cotton seed after the spinnable lint has been removed by ginning and that is subsequently recovered from the seed by a process called ''delinting.''

Loft   The ability of fibers to return to their original thickness after being flattened or compressed.

*Luster   That property of a textile material by virtue of which the latter exhibits differences in intensity of light reflected from within a given area of material when the angles of illumination or viewing are changed.

Macramé   A technique for creating fabric by knotting yarns together.

Malimo   See *Stitch-through.*

Man-made fibers   Fibers created through technology either from natural materials or from chemicals.

Matrix fiber   See *Biconstituent fiber.*

Melt spinning   The formation of man-made textile fibers in which the polymer is melted for extrusion and hardened by cooling.

*Mercerization   The process of subjecting a vegetable fiber to the action of a fairly concentrated aqueous solution of a strong base so as to produce great swelling with resultant changes in fine structure, dimensions, morphology, and mechanical properties.

Micron   A measurement that is 1/1000th of a millimeter or 0.000039 of an inch. See *Micrometer.*

*Micrometer (μm)   One millionth of a meter, 0.001 mm.

Mildew   A fungus that grows on some fibers under conditions of heat and dampness.

Moiré   A ribbed cloth that has a watermarked or wavy pattern on the surface.

*Moisture regain   The amount of moisture in a material determined under prescribed conditions and expressed as a percentage of the weight of the moisture-free specimen.

*Monofilament yarn   A single filament; also a single filament that can function as a yarn in commercial textile operations; that is, it must be strong and flexible enough to be knitted, woven, or braided.

*Monomer   A relatively simple compound that can react to form a polymer.

Mordant   Substance used in dyeing that reacts with both the dyestuff and the fiber to form an insoluble compound, thereby fixing the color within and on the fiber.

Multifilament yarn   Yarn made from two or more, usually more, filament fibers.

Nap   The "fuzzy" raised fibers that have been brushed up on the surface of a fabric.

Needlepoint lace   Lace made by embroidering over other threads held in a pattern across a sheet of parchment.

Needle punching   Fabric formation technique in which fabric is formed by the entangling that results when a series of needles are punched through a bat of fiber.

Netting   A technique of creating fabric by looping and knotting a continuous strand of thread into an open mesh.

Novelty yarns   Yarns made to create interesting decorative effects.

*Open-end spinning machine,   A textile machine for converting staple fiber into spun yarn by a continuous process in which the individual fibers or groups of fibers are caused to assemble at the open end of the forming yarn.

Orientation (of molecules within a fiber)   Arrangement of polymers in a position parallel to the length of the fiber.

OSHA   Occupational Safety and Health Act.

Permanent finish   A finish that will last for the lifetime of the fabric.

Picks   Filling yarns.

Piece dyeing   Dyeing of woven or knitted fabrics as opposed to dyeing of fibers or yarns.

*Pigment   An insoluble compounding material used to impart color.

*Pile (in pile fabric)   The raised loops or tufts (cut loops) that form all or part of the surface.

*Pills,   Bunches or balls of tangled fibers that are held to the surface of a fabric by one or more fibers.

Pillow lace   See *Bobbin lace.*

Pirns   Small metal pins around which yarns are wrapped. These pins are then inserted in a shuttle that carries the yarns across the fabric during weaving (also called quills).

Plissé   A puckered effect achieved on cotton fabrics by shrinking some areas of the fabric with sodium hydroxide.

*Ply yarns   Yarn formed by twisting together two or more single yarns in one operation.

*Polymer   A compound formed by the reaction of simple molecules having functional groups that permit their combination to proceed to high molecular weights under suitable conditions. Polymers may be formed by polymerization (addition polymer) or polycondensation (condensation polymer). When two or more monomers are involved, the product is called a copolymer.

Polymerization The formation of polymers.

Progressive shrinkage Shrinkage that continues after the first laundering and/or dry cleaning through successive cleanings.

Pure dye silk Silk with less than 10 per cent of weighting (or less than 15 per cent if it is black in color).

Quills See *Pirns.*

Regenerated fibers Fibers produced from natural materials that cannot be used for textiles in their original form but that can, through chemical treatment and processing, be made into textile fibers.

Relaxation shrinkage Shrinkage that takes place during initial laundering and/or dry cleaning as a result of the relaxation of tensions applied to yarns or fabrics during manufacture.

Residual shrinkage Shrinkage remaining in a fabric after it has been pre-shrunk. Residual shrinkage is generally expressed as a percentage.

*Resilience, That property of a material by virtue of which it is able to do work against restraining forces during return from a deformed state.

Resist printing The achieving of designs by causing sections of fabric to resist dye.

Retting The process of decomposing the woody stem and gums surrounding bast fibers to remove the fiber.

Ring spinning Method of spinning yarns from staple fibers in which the twist is imparted to the fibers by the concurrent movement of a spindle and a metal ring that moves around the spindle.

Roller printing The application of printed designs to fabrics by the use of engraved rollers over which the fabrics pass.

*Roving, A loose assemblage of fibers drawn or rubbed into a single strand, with very little twist. In spun yarn systems, the product of the stage, or stages, just prior to spinning.

Sanforization A trademarked compressive shrinkage control process.

Schreiner finish A finish that improves luster of fabrics that is produced by passing steel rollers engraved with fine lines over the cloth to flatten and smooth the surface.

Scrim An open-weave fabric that is often used as a backing material.

*Scouring A wet process of cleaning by chemical or mechanical means, or both.

Screen printing The application of printed design to fabrics by the use of screen coated with resist materials that permit dye to penetrate through the screen only in selected areas.

Seed hair fibers Those fibers that grow around the seeds of certain plants, such as cotton or kapok.

Sericin The gum that holds silk filaments together in a cocoon.

Sericulture The cultivation of the silkworm for the production of silk fiber.

Shed The passageway between the warp yarns through which the shuttle is thrown in weaving.

Shuttle The device that carries the yarn across the loom, through the shed, in weaving.

Shuttleless loom Loom in which the yarn is carried across the fabric by some means other than a shuttle. These looms may utilize jets of water, air, metal rapiers, metal grippers, or mechanical action.

*SI The International System of Units (abbreviation for "le Systemè International d'Unites) as defined by the General Conference on Weights and Measures (CGPM); based on seven base units, two supplementary units, and derived units, which together form a coherent system.

Simple yarn Yarn with uniform size and regular surface.

Singeing Treatment of woven fabrics with heat or flame to remove surface fibers from fabric to produce a smooth finish.

*Sizing A generic term for compounds which, when applied to yarn or fabric, form a more or less continuous solid film around the yarn and individual fibers.

*Sliver A continuous strand of loosely assembled fibers that is approximately uniform in cross-sectional area and without twist.

Solution dyeing Addition of color pigment to the liquid solution of man-made fibers before the fiber is formed.

*Specification A precise statement of a set of requirements to be satisfied by a material, product, system, or service, indicating, whenever appropriate, the procedure by means of which it may be determined whether the specified requirements have been met.

*Specific gravity The ratio of the mass of a unit volume of a material at a stated temperature to the mass of the same volume of distilled water at the same temperature.

Spindle A long, slender stick used in spinning to provide the necessary twist to fibers being formed into a yarn. Spindles may be hand devices or part of a spinning wheel.

Spring beard needle A needle used in knitting machines that holds yarns on the needle by means of a springlike action of the flexible hook.

Spun lace A fabric formation technique in which a fiber web is formed by air entanglement.

Spun bonding A fabric formation technique in which extruded fiber filaments are randomly arranged and bonded together by heat or chemical means.

*Standard A reference used as a basis for comparison or calibration; also a concept that has been established by authority, custom, or agreement to serve as a model or rule in the measurement of quantity or the establishment of a practice or a procedure.

Staple fibers Fibers of short, noncontinuous lengths.

Stitch-through A fabric formation technique in which fibers or yarns are held together by stitching through the materials.

Stock dyeing Dyeing of fibers before they are made into yarns or fabrics.

Striations Lengthwise markings on the surface of the man-made fibers when seen through a microscope.

Sublimation printing See *Heat transfer printing*.

Tapa Cloth made from bark.

Tapestry Woven designs, created on a tapestry loom.

Temporary finishes Those finishes that are removed through use and cleaning and must be renewed to be effective.

*Tenacity The tensile stress when expressed as force per unit linear density of the unstrained specimen; for example, grams per tex or grams-force per denier.

Tensile strength A measure of strength of textile fabrics.

Tentering Drying of wet fabrics after finishing or dyeing on a frame on which fabrics are stretched taut and flat.

*Tex A unit for expressing linear density, equal to the mass in grams of 1 km of yarn, filament, fiber, or other textile strand.

Textured fibers   Fibers that have had some alteration of their surface texture.

TFPIA   Textile Fiber Products Identification Act.

*Thermoplastic   A material that will repeatedly soften when heated and harden when cooled.

*Tow   (1) In bast fibers, the short fibers removed by hackling (2) in man-made fibers, a twistless multifilament strand suitable for conversion into staple fibers or sliver or for direct spinning into yarn.

Trademark name   A distinctive name placed on or attached to goods by a manufacturer to identify them as made or sold by that firm. Registration of a trademark is an aid in defending the legal right to exclusive use of the term.

Triaxial weave   A type of weaving in which three sets of yarns are utilized, with two sets of yarns moving in a diagonal direction to the third, rather than at right angles.

Tussah silk   Silk fiber from wild silkworms.

Union dyeing   The dyeing to the same color of two different fibers with different affinities for dye.

*Wale   In knitted fabrics, a column of loops in successive courses. The column is parallel with the loop axes; in woven fabrics, one of a series of raised portions or ribs lying warpwise in the fabric.

*Warp   The yarn running lengthwise in a woven fabric.

Warp knit   A hand- or machine-made knit in which the loops interlace vertically.

Warp print   A print in which the design is printed on the warp yarns before the filling yarns are interlaced. (See *Ikat*).

Weft   The crosswise direction of a woven fabric; the filling.

Weft knit   A knit in which the loops interlace horizontally rather than vertically.

Wet spinning   The formation of man-made textile fibers in which the fibers are hardened by extruding the fibers into a chemical bath.

*Wicking   Transmission of a gas or liquid along the fibers of the textile due to pressure differential or capillary action.

*Woolen yarns   Yarn spun from wool fibers that have been carded but not combed or gilled.

*Worsted yarns   Yarn spun from wool fibers which have been carded, and either gilled or combed, or both.

Yarn dyeing   The dyeing of yarns before they are woven or knitted into fabrics.

Appendix:
Summary of
Regulatory Legislation
Applied to Textiles

The following summarizes *briefly* the major pieces of legislation and/or regulations that apply to the textile products. Fuller details are provided about each of these acts or rulings in the body of the text. Only those items of legislation that have an impact on consumers are included. Those that regulate the industry, such as OSHA, are not included.

Textile Fiber Products
Identification Act

Passed 1960, Amended Subsequently

This legislation requires that each textile product carry a label listing the generic names of fibers from which it is made. These generic fiber categories are established by the Federal Trade Commission, which can add new generic categories as needed. At present there are twenty-one generic fiber categories for man-made fibers, as well as the names for the natural fibers.

The listing of fibers is made in order of percentage by weight of fiber present in the product, with the largest amount listed first, the next largest second, and so on. Fiber quantities of less than 5 per cent must be labeled as "other fiber" unless they serve a specific purpose in the product. Fibers that cannot be identified must be listed as "X per cent of undetermined fiber content."

The law prohibits the use of misleading names that imply the presence of fiber not in the product. Labels must carry either the name, trademark, or registered identification number of the manufacturer. All items covered under the law must be clearly and visibly labeled as to whether they are imported or produced in the United States. (For details, see Chapter 2, pages 22–26.)

Passed 1939

This legislation regulates the labeling of sheep's wool and other animal hair fibers. The Wool Products Labeling Act requires that all wool products be labeled and the fibers, except for ornamentation, be identified as either new or recycled wool. The rules and regulations of the Federal Trade Commission established in relation to the act require that the terms *wool*, *new wool*, or *virgin wool* be applied only to wool that has never been used before. Recycled wool is wool that has never been utilized in any way by the ultimate consumer, but has been spun into yarns or woven or knitted into cloth, (these formed but unused pieces of yarns or fabrics are pulled apart and the fibers are reprocessed into fabrics) or wool that has been used by consumers and is reclaimed by pulling the fabrics apart into fibers and spinning and weaving these fibers into other yarns and fabrics.

The law requires that the percentage of wool used in pile fabrics be identified as to the percentage of wool in the face and percentage of wool in the backing. The proportion of fiber used in face and backing must also be noted. Contents of paddings, linings, or stuffings are designated separately from the face fabric of products, but must be listed with the same items noted. Items of wool must be clearly and visibly labeled as to whether they are imported or produced in the United States. (See Chapter 6, pages 107–109.)

Passed 1951

This law requires that fur products carry the true English name of the fur-bearing animal from which it comes, and the name of the country of origin of the fur. (See Chapter 6, page 123.)

Original Provisions Enacted in 1953

The original provisions of the act stated that wearing apparel (excluding hats, gloves, and footwear) and fabrics that are highly flammable may not be sold. Standards were established for testing to determine whether items were highly flammable. (See Chapter 21, page 405 for discussion of the standard.)

Wool Products Labeling Act

Fur Products Labeling Act

Flammable Fabrics Act

Amendments to the Act, 1967, 1978

The scope of the act was broadened in 1967 to cover a wider range of clothing and interior furnishings. The act called for the establishment of standards for flammability for items covered by the act and banned from sale those carpets, mattresses, and items of children's sleepwear, sizes infant to 14, that do not meet the established standards. Some aspects of the standards were revised in 1978. (See Chapter 21, page 405, for discussion of the standards.) Labels giving care instructions for children's sleepwear that is flame retardant must be placed so that they can be read at the point of purchase. These instructions must be permanently affixed to the garment. Some small carpets and one-of-a-kind carpets are exempt from the provisions of the act, but must be labeled indicating that they do not meet the standard. The responsibility for administering and implementing the act was given to the Consumer Product Safety Commission. (See Chapter 21 for full discussion of the legislation.)

Permanent Care Labeling Ruling of the Federal Trade Commission

Established 1972

This ruling requires all wearing apparel and bolts of fabric sold by the yard to carry permanently affixed labels giving instructions for care. Exempt from the ruling are household textiles, retail items costing the consumer less than $3, footwear, head gear, and hand coverings, and all items that would be marred by affixing a label. The kind of information that must be provided is clearly specified. (See Chapter 23 for complete description of provisions.)

Federal Trade Commission Ruling on the Weighting of Silk

Established 1938

No silk products containing more than 10 per cent weighting except those colored black may carry a label saying that they are "silk" or "pure dye silk." Black silks can contain 15 per cent of weighting. Fabrics not meeting these standards must be labeled as "weighted silk." (See Chapter 6, page 127.)

Appendix D
Man-made Fibers and Trademarks

The following lists (alphabetically) the generic categories of man-made fibers, the FTC definition, and trademarks for fibers in each of these categories together with the name of the manufacturer and the types of yarns and fibers made under the trademark.[1]

acetate   A manufactured fiber in which the fiber-forming substance is cellulose acetate. Where not less than 92 per cent of the hydroxyl groups are acetylated, the term *triacetate* may be used as a generic description of the fiber.

	Trademark	Type of Yarn or Fiber	Manufacturer
acetate	Avetex acetate	filament	Avetex Fibers, Inc.
	Ariloft		Eastman Kodak Co.
	Avron		Avtex Fibers, Inc.
	Celanese acetate	staple, filament, cigarette filter tow, fiberfill	Celanese Corp.
	Chromespun	solution-dyed filament	Eastman Kodak Co.
	Estron	filament and cigarette filter tow	Eastman Kodak Co.
	Loftura	acetate yarn	Eastman Kodak Co.
triacetate	SLR	filament, dull yarn, resistant to weathering and sunlight	Eastman Kodak Co.
	Arnel	filament and staple	Celanese Corp.

acrylic   A manufactured fiber in which the fiber-forming substance is any long-chain synthetic polymer composed of at least 85 per cent by weight of acrylonitrile units ($-CH_2-CH-$).

$$\begin{array}{c} | \\ CN \end{array}$$

[1]Sources: "Man-made Fiber Desk Book," *Modern Textiles* (March 1980); *Man-made Fibers: A New Guide* (Washington, D.C.: Man-made Fiber Producers Association, 1984).

509

	Trademark	Type of Yarn or Fiber	Manufacturer
acrylic	Acrilan	staple and tow	Monsanto Co.
	Bi-loft	staple, bicomponent, tow	Monsanto Co.
	Creslan	staple and tow	American Cyanamid Co.
	Fi-Lana	ultrasoft fiber	Monsanto Fibers & Intermediates Co.
	Orlon	staple and tow	E. I. du Pont de Nemours & Co.
	Pa-Qel	bicomponent, high bulk	Monsanto Fibers & Intermediates Co.
	Remember		Monsanto Fibers & Intermediates Co.
	So-Lara	producer-colored fiber	Monsanto Fibers & Intermediates Co.
	Zefran	staple in both dyeable and producer-colored fiber	Badische Corp.

anidex   A manufactured fiber in which the fiber-forming substance is any long-chain synthetic polymer composed of at least 50 per cent by weight of one or more esters of a monohydric alcohol and acrylic acid (CH_2=Ch—COOH). No longer manufactured.

aramid   A manufactured fiber in which the fiber-forming substance is a long-chain synthetic polyamide in which at least 85 per cent of the amide

$$(-\overset{\parallel}{\underset{O}{C}}-NH-)$$ linkages are attached directly to two aromatic rings.

	Trademark	Type of Yarn or Fiber	Manufacturer
aramid	Kevlar	filament	E. I. du Pont de Nemours & Co.
	Nomex	filament and staple	E. I. du Pont de Nemours & Co.

azlon   A manufactured fiber in which the fiber-forming substance is composed of any regenerated naturally occurring proteins. Not manufactured in the United States.

carbon   No generic definition.

	Trademark	Type of Yarn or Fiber	Manufacturer
carbon	Celion	high-strength, high-modulus, and ultra-high-modulus	Celanese Corp.
	Panex	filament, staple	Stackpole Fibers Corp.

fluorocarbon, fluoropolymers   No generic definitions.

	Trademark	Type of Yarn or Fiber	Manufacturer
fluorocarbon	GORE-TEX	staple, filament, tow, and slit film	W. L. Gore
	Teflon	filament, monofilament	E. I. du Pont de Nemours & Co.

	Trademark	Type of Yarn or Fiber	Manufacturer
fluoropolymer	Halar	monofilament	Albany International Monofilament Plant
	Kynar	monofilament	Albany International Monofilament Plant
	Tefzel	monofilament	Albany International Monofilament Plant

glass   A manufactured fiber in which the fiber-forming substance is glass.

	Trademark	Type of Yarn or Fiber	Manufacturer
glass	Alumina Borosilicate	filament	PPG Industries, Inc.
	Beta	filament	Owens-Corning Fiberglas Co.
	Feneshield	filament	PPG Industries, Inc.
	Fiberglas	filament and staple	Owens-Corning Fiberglas Co.
	Fiber glass	filament	CertainTeed Corp.
	Fiber glass	filament	Johns-Manville Co.
	Fiber glass	plastic surfacing and reinforcing mats	Nicofibers, Inc.
	Lex	single-end textured yarn	PPG Industries, Inc.
	Modiglass	monofilament and filament	Reichhold Chemicals, Inc.
	Romhoglass	monofilament (metalized)	Lundy Electronics and Systems, Inc.
	RO 99	filament	CertainTeed Corp.
	SatinGlass	roving	PPG Industries, Inc.
	Stitchmat	filament	CertainTeed Corp.
	Texo	multistrand	PPG Industries, Inc.
	Trianti	filament	PPG Industries
	Unifilo	filament	CertainTeed Corp.

metallic   A manufactured fiber composed of metal, plastic-coated metal, metal-coated plastic, or a core completely covered by metal.

	Trademark	Type of Yarn or Fiber	Manufacturer
metallic	Alistran	flat, laminated yarn	Multi-Tex Corp.
	Brunsmet	stainless steel fiber in filament, staple, tow	Brunswick Co.
	Dura-Stran	flat, laminated filament	Multi-Tex Corp.
	Fairtex	flat, monofilament	Metlon Corp.
	Hudstat	monofilament	Hudson Wire Co.
	Lurex	yarn of slit film	Metal Film Co.
	Metlon F	flat monofilament, staple	Metlon Corp.

modacrylic   A manufactured fiber in which the fiber-forming substance is any long-chain synthetic polymer composed of less than 85 per cent but at least 35 per cent by weight of acrylonitrile units, ($-CH_2-CH-$), except fibers

$$\begin{array}{c} | \\ CN \end{array}$$

qualifying under subparagraph (2) of paragraph (j) of this section and fibers qualifying under paragraph (q) of this section.

	Trademark	Type of Yarn Fiber	Manufacturer
modacrylic	SEF	staple, flame retardant	Monsanto Co.

novoloid   A manufactured fiber containing at least 85 per cent by weight of a cross-linked novolac. Production discontinued.

nylon   A manufactured fiber in which the fiber-forming substance is a long-chain synthetic polyamide in which less than 85 per cent of the amide ($-C-NH-$) linkages are attached directly to two aromatic rings (as

$$\begin{array}{c} \| \\ O \end{array}$$

amended January 11, 1974).

	Trademark	Type of Yarn or Fiber	Manufacturer
nylon	A.C.E.	filament	Allied Co.
	Anso	nylon filament and staple soil-resistant carpet yarn modified cross section	Allied Corp.
	Anso-IV	filament, staple, modified cross section, static control, dull luster	Allied Chemical Corp.
	Antron	filament, staple, and tow	E. I. du Pont de Nemours & Co.
	Antron Plus	filament (semidull and bright), staple. Both control static, hide soil, and resist stain.	E. I. du Pont de Nemours & Co.
	Astro Turf	ribbon	Monsanto Co.
	Berkley nylon	flat and round monofilament	Berkley Co.
	Camalon	filament yarn, solution-dyed	Camac Corp.
	Cantrece	bicomponent filament or monofilament	E. I. du Pont de Nemours & Co.
	Caprolan	filament	Allied Corp.
	Caprolan Bright	filament, modified cross section, bright	Allied Corp.

Trademark	Type of Yarn or Fiber	Manufacturer
Caprolan Velour	filament, modified cross section	Allied Corp.
Cerex	spun bonded	Monsanto Co.
Cordura	bulked filament	E. I. du Pont de Nemours & Co.
Courtaulds nylon		Courtaulds North America, Inc.
Crepeset	patented continuous monofilament that develops a regular crimp	American Enka Co.
Crepeset Silver Label	monofilament	American Enka Co.
Crepeset Anti-cling	monofilament, inherent crepe effect, antistatic	American Enka Co.
DuPont nylon	filament, staple, tow, monofilament	E. I. du Pont de Nemours & Co.
Enkalon		American Enka Co.
Enkalure	filament, multilobal	American Enka Co.
Enkasheer	continuous monofilament torque yarn for ladies' stretch hosiery	American Enka Co.
Firestone nylon	monofilament, filament	Firestone Co.
Hanover nylon	monofilament, filament	Hanover Co.
Hyten		E. I. du Pont de Nemours & Co.
Lurelon		American Enka Co.
Multisheer	multifilament, producer-textured yarn for pantyhose	American Enka Co.
NM 1000, 1150, 1250, 1450, and 1500	monofilament (clear, melt-dyed)	Monofilaments, Inc.
Nylon by Ametek	round monofilament	Ametek Co.
nylon	monofilament	Albany International Monofilament Plant
PA 6, PA 66, PA 612	monofilament for industrial applications	Albany International Monofilaments
Shareen	monofilament textured yarn	Courtaulds North America, Inc.
Shareen Plus and Shareen SSS	filament	Courtaulds North America, Inc.
Shoeflex	monofilament, clear or melt-dyed	Shakespeare Co.
Softalon	filament	American Enka Co.
Sooflex	monofilament	Shakespeare Co.
Starbrite	staple	Star Fibers
Superflex	monofilament	Shakespeare Co.
T.E.N.		American Enka Co.
Ultron	filament, staple	Monsanto Co.
Vylor	monofilament	E.I. du Pont de Nemours & Co.
Wellon	staple	Wellman, Inc.
WN 1, 2, 4	monofilament	Shakespeare Corp.
Zeftron	filament, staple	Badische Corp.

nytril A manufactured fiber containing at least 85 per cent of a long-chain polymer of vinylidene dinitrile ($-CH_2-C(CN)_2-$) where the vinylidene dinitrile content is no less than every other unit in the polymer chain. Production discontinued in the United States.

olefin A manufactured fiber in which the fiber-forming substance is any long-chain synthetic polymer composed of at least 85 per cent by weight of ethylene, propylene, or other olefin units except amorphous (noncrystalline) polyolefins qualifying under category (1) of paragraph (j) of Rule 7.

	Trademark	Type of Yarn or Fiber	Manufacturer
olefin	Accord	spunbonded	Kimberly Clark Corp.
	Amco polyethylene	monofilament, slit film	American Mfg.
	Amco polypropylene	monofilament, slit film	American Mfg.
	American Polyethylene	monofilament, slit film	American Mfg.
	American Polypropylene	monofilament, slit film	American Mfg.
	Autotwine	slit film, high modulus	Blue Mountain Extrusions
	Avetex polypropylene	staple	Avetex Fibers Inc.
	Cala-line	monofilament	Sunshine Cordage Co.
	Camac	solution-dyed filament	Camac Corp.
	Celestra	spun bonded	Crown-Zellerbach Corp.
	Concorde polypropylene	textured, dyed filament	Concorde Fibers
	Cyclean	spunbonded, melt-blown, laminate	Kimberly Clark Corp.
	DUON	nonwoven fabrics and geotextiles	Phillips Fibers Corp.
	Evolution	spun bonded	Kimberly-Clark Corp.
	Evolution II	spunbonded and melt-blown	Kimberly Clark Corp.
	Fibretex	spun bonded	Crown-Zellerbach
	Fibri-Knit ⎫ Fibri-Cord ⎭	fibrillated filament for industrial use	Fibron, Inc.
	Fibrilawn ⎫ Fibrilon ⎭	fibrillated filament	Fibron, Inc.
	Geoseal	nonwoven	Phillips Fibers Corp.
	Herculon	continuous multifilament, bulked, continuous multifilament staple and tow	Hercules, Inc.
	Marquésa Lana	filament (bulked) yarn	Amoco Corp.
	Marvess	staple and tow, filament	Phillips Fibers Corp.
	Mirifi 100X, 500X, and 600X	woven polypropylene	Mirifi Inc.
	Oletex	monofilament	Sunshine Cordage
	Patlon	fibrillated	Amoco Corp.
	Patlon III	bulked filament, ultraviolet stabilized	Amoco Corp.
	Petromat ⎫ Petrotac ⎭	nonwoven	Phillips Fibers Corp.
	Polyethylene by Ametek	round monofilament	Ametek Co.
	Polyloom	fibrillated	Chevron Corp.
	Polytwine ⎫ Polywrap ⎭	slit-processed, high-modulus monofilament	Blue Mountain Extrusions
	Poncar	monofilament	Sunshine Cordage
	Propex	geotextile fabrics	Amoco Fabrics Co.
	Rufon		Phillips Fibers Corp.
	Ruftac		Phillips Fibers Corp.
	Sunshine	monofilament	Sunshine Cordage
	Supac	needle loomed	Phillips Fibers Corp.
	TY EZ ⎫ Tylon ⎬ Tytite ⎭	slit processed, high modulus	Indian Head Yarn and Thread Co.
	Typar	spun bonded	E. I. du Pont de Nemours & Co.
	Tyvek	spun bonded	E. I. du Pont de Nemours & Co.
	Welltite	Monofilament	Montair Division, Wellington Mills

polyester A manufactured fiber in which the fiber-forming substance is any long-chain synthetic polymer composed of at least 85 per cent by weight of an ester of a substituted aromatic carboxylic acid, including but not restricted to substituted therephthalate units $p(\text{—R—O—}\overset{\text{O}}{\overset{\|}{\text{C}}}\text{—C}_6\text{H}_4\text{—}\overset{\text{O}}{\overset{\|}{\text{C}}}\text{—O—})$ and parasubstituted hydroxybenzoate units, $p(\text{—R—O—C}_6\text{H}_4\text{—}\overset{\text{O}}{\overset{\|}{\text{C}}}\text{—O—})$ (as amended September 12, 1973).

	Trademark	Type of Yarn or Fiber	Manufacturer
polyester	A.C.E.	filament	Allied Chemical Corp.
	Avlin (Fiber 200)	filament	Avtex Fibers, Inc.
	Blue "C"	filament, staple	Monsanto Co.
	Comfort fiber	staple	Celanese Corp.
	Crepesoft	filament	American Enka Co.
	Dacron	filament yarn, staple, tow, and fiberfill	E. I. du Pont de Nemours & Co.
	Dacron Hollofil	staple	E. I. du Pont de Nemours & Co.
	Encron	continuous filament yarn	American Enka Co.
	ESP of Fortrel	filament yarn	American Enka Co.
	Firestone polyester	filament	Firestone Co.
	Fortrel	filament yarn, staple, tow, and fiberfill	Celanese Corp.
	Kodel	filament yarn, staple, tow, and fiberfill	Eastman Kodak Co.
	KodOfill and KodOsoft	staple, tubular	Eastman Kodak Co.
	Loftguard	staple for fiberfill	Celanese Corp.
	Matte Touch		American Enka Co.
	Plyloc		American Enka Co.
	Polar Guard	filament, tow	Celanese Corp.
	Polyester by Ametek	monofilament, round	Ametek Co.
	Polyester	monofilament	Albany International Monofilament Plant
	Polyextra		American Enka Co.
	Reemay	spun bonded	E. I. du Pont de Nemours & Co.
	Shakespeare Wonder Thread	monofilament	Shakespeare Co.
	Shanton		American Enka Co.
	Silky Touch		American Enka Co.
	Sontara	spun laced	E. I. du Pont de Nemours & Co.
	Spectran	staple	Monsanto Co.
	Trevira	filament, staple, high tenacity	Hoechst Fibers, Inc.
	Ultra Touch		American Enka Co.
	Varion	low pill, high bulk	American Hoechst Corp.
	Wellene	industrial applications	Wellman, Inc.
	Wellstrand	monofilament, staple	Wellman, Inc.

rayon A manufactured fiber composed of regenerated cellulose, as well as manufactured fibers composed of regenerated cellulose in which substituents have replaced not more than 15 per cent of the hydrogens of the hydroxyl groups.

	Trademark	Type of Yarn or Fiber	Manufacturer
rayon	Absorbit	staple, high-absorbency fiber	American Enka Co.
	Avetex Rayon	staple, filament	Avtex Fibers, Inc.
	Avril and Prima	high-wet-modulus staple	Avtex Fibers, Inc.
	Avril III	high-wet-modulus staple, multilobal	Avtex Fibers, Inc.
	Coloray	solution-dyed staple	Courtaulds North America, Inc.
	Courcel	hollow fiber	Courtaulds North America, Inc.
	Enkaire	staple (flat cross section)	American Enka Co.
	Enkrome	patented acid-dyeable staple and continuous filament yarn	American Enka Co.
	Fiber 700	high-wet-modulus staple	American Enka Co.
	Fibro	staple ⎫	Courtaulds North America, Inc.
	Fibro HT	high Tenacity ⎬	
	I.T.	improved-tenacity staple	American Enka Co.
	Kaycel	scrim	Kimberly Clark Corp.
	Kolorbon	solution-dyed staple	American Enka Co.
	Narco ⎫	industrial and regular yarn and tow	North American Rayon Co.
	Narcon ⎭		
	Regard	scrim	Kimberly Clark Corp.
	Skyloft	filament (bulked yarn)	American Enka Co.
	Super White	optically brightened rayon	American Enka Co.
	Suprenka Hi Mod	extrahigh-tenacity continuous filament industrial yarn	American Enka Co.
	Zantrel 700	high-wet-modulus, staple, resistant to caustics	American Enka Co.

rubber A manufactured fiber in which the fiber-forming substance is comprised of natural or synthetic rubber, including the following categories: (1) a manufactured fiber in which the fiber-forming substance is a hydrocarbon such as natural rubber, polyisoprene, polybutadiene, copolymers of dienes and hydrocarbons, or amorphous (noncrystalline) polyolefins; (2) a manufactured fiber in which the fiber-forming substance is a copolymer of acrylonitrile and a diene (such as butadiene) composed of not more than 50 per cent but at least 10 per cent by weight of acrylonitrile units:

$$(-CH_2-CH-)$$
$$|$$
$$CN$$

the term *lastrile* may be used as a generic description for fibers falling within this category; (3) a manufactured fiber in which the fiber-forming substance is a polychloroprene or a copolymer of chloroprene in which at least 35 per cent by weight of the fiber-forming substance is composed of chloroprene units:

$$(-CH_2 - C = CH - CH_2 -)$$
$$|$$
$$Cl$$

saran   A manufactured fiber in which the fiber-forming substance is any long-chain synthetic polymer composed of at least 80 per cent by weight of vinylidene chloride units.

$$(-CH_2 - CCl_2 -)$$

	Trademark	Type of Yarn or Fiber	Manufacturer
saran	Saran	round and flat monofilament	Ametek, Inc.

spandex   A manufactured fiber in which the fiber-forming substance is a long-chain synthetic polymer comprised of at least 85 per cent of a segmented polyurethane.

	Trademark	Type of Yarn or Fiber	Manufacturer
spandex	Cleerspan	filament	Globe Co.
	Glospan	filament	Globe Co.
	Lycra	filament	E. I. du Pont de Nemours & Co.

vinal   A manufactured fiber in which the fiber-forming substance is any long-chain synthetic polymer composed of at least 50 per cent by weight of vinyl alcohol units ($-CH_2-CHOH-$) and in which the total of the vinyl alcohol units and any one or more of the various acetal units is at least 85 per cent by weight of the fiber. Not manufactured in the United States.

vinyon   A manufactured fiber in which the fiber-forming substance is any long-chain synthetic polymer composed of at least 85 per cent by weight of vinyl chloride units.

$$(-CH_2 - CHCl -)$$

	Trademark	Type of Yarn or Fiber	Manufacturer
vinyon	Vinyon	modified staple	Avtex Fibers Inc.

Miscellaneous Fibers

	Trademark	Type of Yarn or Fiber	Manufacturer
Polybenzimidazole fiber*	PBI	staple	Celanese Corp.
polycarbonate (no generic definition)	Polycarbonate	monofilament	Monofilaments, Inc.
	Solvex	monofilament	Fibrex Co.
polyphenylene sulfide fiber*	Rhyton	staple	Phillips Fibers Corp.
silica	Q Fiber	bulk fiber	Johns Manville Corp.
	Temstran	bulk fiber	Johns Manville Corp.

*Currently no generic defintion. Company has petitioned FTC to establish a new definition for this fiber.

A

AATCC Technical Manual, 454
Abaca plant fiber, 83
Abrasion resistance, 35–36, 410, 461–462, 481–482
Absorbency, 36
  finishes to increase, 410
Acetate fibers, 93–100
  care, 98
  chemical properties, 97
  effect of environmental conditions, 97
  FTC definition, 93, 509
  manufacture, 93–95
  physical properties, 95–97
  thermal properties, 96–97
  uses, 98–99
Acid dyes, 340
Acid finishes, 386
Acids, effect on textiles, 55–56
  see also individual generic fiber listings
Acrilan acrylic fiber, 164–165
Acrylic fibers, 161–166
  care, 165–166
  chemical properties, 162
  effect of environmental conditions, 163
  FTC definition, 161, 509
  manufacture, 161, 163, 164
  physical properties, 162–163
  thermal properties, 162
  uses, 165
  varieties, 163–164
Agilon textured yarn, 217
Air jet spinning, 209–210
Air permeability, 484
Alginate fibers, 187
Alkalis, effect on textiles, 56–57
  see also individual generic fiber listings
Alpaca, 121
Aluminum silicate fibers, 137
American Association of Textile Chemists and Colorists, 454
American National Standards Institute, 453, 454
American Society for Testing Materials, 453, 454, 455, 497ff
Angora goat, 118–119

Angora rabbit, 122–123
Animal hair fibers, 103–123
Antibacterial finishes, 411
Antimildew finishes, 410–411
Antique satin, 257
Antirot finishes, 410–411
Antislip finishes, 410
Antistatic finshes, 409
Appliqué, 268–269
Arabeva machine, 315
Arachne machine, 315
Aralac milk protein, 131, 132
Araloop machine, 315
Aramid fiber, 148–149, 510
  FTC definition, 148, 510
  properties, 148–149
Ardil peanut fiber, 132
Arkwright, John, 196
Asbestos fiber, 133
ASTM Book of Standards, 454
Atmospheric fading, 97–98
Azlon fibers, 130–133, 510
Azoic dyes, 339

B

Bandanna, 347
Bark cloth, 307
Basic dyes, 340
Basket weave, 252
Bast fibers, 73–82
Batik, 345–346
Batiste, 251
Bedford cord, 253
Beetling, 381
Bengaline, 253
Beta glass fiber, 137
Bicomponent fibers, 188–190
Biconstituent fibers, 188–190
Bilateral agreements, 16
Bird's eye, 258
Bleaches, 422–424
  chlorine, 423–424
  hydrogen peroxide, 424
  oxygen, 424
  perborate, 424
Bleaching as a finish, 374
Blended yarns, 225–226
Blending of fibers, 197

Index

Bobtex Integrated Composite
    Spinning Machine, 215
Bonded fabrics, 273–274
Boron fibers, 137
Bottom-weight fabrics, 249
Bouclé yarns, 227
Braided fabrics, 231
Breaking strength, 457–458
Broadcloth, 253
Brocade, 258
Brocatelle, 258
Brown lung. *See* Byssinosis
Brushing, 383
Buckram, 251
Bulky yarns, 216–217
Burlap, 82
Burling, 388
Bursting strength, 457–458
Butcher linen, 252
Byssinosis, 68, 198, 442

C

Calendering, 378–379
Calico, 251
Camel's hair, 116–117
Carbon fibers, 138–139, 510
Carbonization, 107, 373
Carding, 107, 199
Care labeling, 434–438, 507
Care of textiles, 417–440, 484–485
    see also individual generic fiber
        listings; Home laundering;
        Drycleaning
Career opportunities, 19–20
Carothers, Wallace, 16
Carpets, 276–279
    Axminster, 276–277
    chenille, 277
    flammability testing, 406–407
    printing, 358
    tufted, 276
    velvet, 276
    Wilton, 276
Cartwright, Edmund, 234
Cashmere, 115–116
Cellulose acetate. *See* Acetate
Cellulose triacetate. *See* Triacetate
Cellulosic fibers, general
    characteristics, 61–63

man-made, 85–90
natural, 61–84
Ceramic fibers, 137
Cerex®, 313
Certification mark, 164
Challis, 251
Chambray, 252
Chardonnet, Count Hilaire de, 85
Cheesecloth, 251
Chemical reactivity of fibers, 38, 55–59
    see also individual generic fiber
        listings
Chemistry of textiles, 41–59
Chenille fabric, 265–266
Chenille yarns, 228
Chiffon, 251
Children's sleepwear, flammability
    testing of, 407
China grass. *See* Ramie
Chinon fiber, 131–132
Chlorination finish, 392–393
Chrome dyes, 340
Cidega knits, 300
Ciréing, 379
Civona® bicomponent fiber, 164
Cleerspan® spandex fiber, 181
Clip spot weave, 267
Cochineal, 7
Cohesiveness, 29
Coir, 73
Colorfastness, 59, 336–338, 462–465
    and crocking, 338
    and laundering, 337
    and perspiration, 338
    testing for, 462–465
Combing of fibers, 107, 199
Combustability of fibers, 37–38
    see also individual generic fiber
        listings
Commercial laundering, 423–434
Complex yarns, 227
Consumer Product Safety
    Commission, 454
Converters, 12, 13
Cord fabrics, 253
Cord yarns, 226, 227
Cordelan, 190
Corduroy, 264
Core-spun yarns, 228–229
Corkscrew yarns, 228
Coronizing, 135

Cotton Council, 9
Cotton fiber, 63–72
    botanical information, 65–66
    care, 71-72
    chemical reactivity, 71–72
    cultivation, 66
    economic importance, 64–65
    effect of environmental conditions
        on, 72
    history of, 63–64
    mercerization of, 374–375
    physical properties, 69–71
    production, 67–68
    structure, 69
    thermal properties, 70–71
    uses, 72
Cotton system of spinning, 199–202
Courses, in knits, 286–287
Covering power, 11, 478
Cow hair fiber, 123
Crash, 252
Crease resistance, 393–394
Crepe fabrics, 257
Crepe yarns, 222
Creslan® acrylic fiber, 165
Crimp, fiber, 29
    yarn, 216–219, 476–477
Crimp interchange, 476–477
Crinoline, 251
Crochet, 325
Crocking, 464–465
    testing for, 464–465
Crockmeter, 464, 465
Crompton, Samuel, 196
Cross dyeing, 335–336
Cross sectional shape of fibers, 27–29
Crosslinking of molecules, 48
Crystallinity, 46–47, 50
Cuperammonium rayon, 91
Cut of knit fabrics. See Gauge of knits

D

Damask, 258
Degumming, 372
Delustering of fiber, 27, 374
Denier, 30, 224
Denim, 254
Density of fibers, 32
    see also generic fiber listings

Design of textile products, 12, 14
Detergents, 418, 419–422
Dimensional stability of fabrics, 483
    of fibers, 34
    see also individual generic fiber
        listings
Dimity, 253
Direct dyes, 204–206
Direct spinning, 204–206
Dispersed dyes, 340–341
Dobby loom, 241
Dobby weave, 258–259
Documentary print, 367
Dotted swiss, 267
Double-cloth construction, 264, 271
Double-faced satin, 257
Double knits, 293
Doup weave. See Leno weave
Draw twisting, 153
Drawing of fibers, 54
Drill, 254
Dry cleaning, 434–435
    testing for colorfastness to, 465
Drying of textile fabrics, 386–387
Duchesse satin, 257
Durable press finishes, 394–399
    care of, 397–398
    problems of, 396–397, 398
Dye classes, 338–341
Dyeing, 6, 58–59, 327–342
    beam, 332–333
    beck, 333
    box, 333
    cross, 335–336
    fiber, 330–331
    history of, 327–329
    jet, 333
    jig, 333
    pad, 334
    piece, 333–335
    polychromatic. See Printing,
        polychromatic
    solution, 330
    stock. See Dyeing, fiber
    tone-on-tone, 336
    union, 336
    vacuum impregnation, 334
    winch, 333
    yarn, 331–341
Dyes, 338–341
    acid, 340

Dyes (*cont.*)
aniline, 329
azoic, 339
basic, 340
chrome, 340
direct, 339
dispersed, 340–341
naphthol. *See* Azoic dyes
pigment, 341
reactive, 339–340
sulfur, 339
vat, 339
Dyestuffs, 336–341
natural, 327–329
synthetic, 329
Dynel® modacrylic fiber, 169

E

Elastic recovery of fibers, 34
see also individual generic fiber
listings
Elastomeric fibers, 177–182
rubber, 177–178
spandex, 178–181
Elastomeric yarns, 220
Electrical conductivity of fibers, 37
see also individual generic fiber
listings
Elongation of fibers, 32, 34, 483
measurement of, 459–460
see also individual generic fiber
listings
Embossing, 379
Embroidery, hand, 268–269
machine, 270
Energy conservation, 370–371, 449–
450
Environment and textiles, 441–451
Environmental conditions, effects on
fibers, 38–39
see also individual generic fiber
listings
Extensibility. *See* Elongation of fibers

F

Fabric care, 417–440
bleaching, 422–424

dry cleaning, 434–435
laundering, 418–429
storage, 435–436
see also individual generic fiber
listings
Fabric construction, 4, 5
braiding, 231
felting, 231–232
fiber webs, 305–313
knitting, 231, 281–304
knotting, 231
looping, 231
needle punching, 311
stitch-through, 231, 313–316
tufting, 225
weaving, 231, 232–235
Fabric count, 248–249, 457
Fabric geometry, 476–479
Fabric softeners, 425–426
Fade-o-meter®, 461
Faille, 253
Fasciated yarns, 212
Fashion marks in knits, 297
Federal Trade Commission, 23–24, 26
Felt, 305–307
Fiber dyeing, 330–331
Fiber identification, testing for, 467,
470
Fiber webs, 305, 307–313
Fibers, acetate, 93–100
acrylics, 161–166
alginates, 187
aramid, 148–149
azlon, 130–133
bicomponent, 188–190
biconstituent, 188–190
chemical properties of, 38, 55–59
cotton, 63–72
cross-sectional shape of, 27–29
flax, 74–80
glass, 133–137
matrix, 188–190
modacrylic, 166–169
multilobal, 27–29
novoloid, 185
nylon, 141–147
olefin, 171–176
physical properties of, 21–39
polyester, 151–159
ramie, 80–82
rayon, 85–93

saran, 183–184
silk, 123–131
size, 30–31
surface contour, 29
thermal properties, 37–38
triacetate, 93–100
vinyon, 185
wool, 103–115
see also individual fiber listings
Fibrillation, 171, 220
Fibrolane azlon fiber, 132
Filament fibers, 29
Filament yarns, 216–220
Filet, 320, 322
Filling knits. *See* Weft knits
Filling yarns, 235–237
Film fibrillation. *See* Fibrillation
Film yarns, 220–221
Films, 231, 316–318
Finishes, 6, 369–415, 479
  abrasion resistant, 410
  absorbency, 410
  acid design, 386
  antibacterial, 411
  antimildew, antirot, 410
  antislip, 410
  antistatic, 409
  beetling, 381
  bleaching, 374
  brushing, 383
  calendering, 378–379
  carbonizing, 373
  chemical, 389–415
  ciréing, 379
  classification of, 369–370
  cleansing, 371–374
  durable, 369
  durable press, 394–399
  embossing, 379
  flame retardant, 403–405
  flocking, 383–384
  fulling, 375–376
  glazing, 379
  heat-reflectant, 411–412
  against light deterioration, 412
  light reflectant, 413
  mechanical, 369–388
  Mercerization, 374–375
  moiré, 380–381
  moth proofing, 412–414
  napping, 381–382

  permanent, 369
  Schreinerizing, 379–380
  scouring, 372
  shrinkage control, 389–393
  singeing, 376–377
  softening, 378
  soil-releasing, 400–401
  soil-repellent, 399–401
  stiffening, 372–378
  sueding, 381–382
  temporary, 369
  testing to identify, 471
  water repellency, 401–403
  waterproof, 401
  wrinkle resistant, 393–399
Flame retardant finishes, 403–405
Flammability testing, 466–467
Flammable Fabrics Act, 405–409, 506–507
Flannel, 254
Flax, 74–80
  chemical reactivity, 79
  cultivation, 75–76
  fiber preparation, 76–77
  physical properties, 77–79
  thermal properties, 78–79
  see also Linen
Foam finishing, 372
Fleece knits, 291
Flock yarns, 228
Flocking, 383–384
Fluorescent whiteners, 374, 424
Fluorocarbon fibers, 186, 511
Fluoropolymer fibers, 186, 511
Formaldehyde, concerns about toxicity, 398–399, 433
Fringed fibril theory, 49
Frisé, 264
Full-fashioned knits, 297
Fulling, 375–376
Fume fading, 97–98, 341
Fur fiber, 122–123
Fur Products Labeling Act, 123, 506

G

Gabardine, 254–255
Garment industry, 14–15
Gauge of knits, 287
Gauze, 251

General Agreement on Tariffs and
    Trade (GATT), 16
Generations, of fibers, 190–191
Generic fiber classification, 22
Geotextiles, 15
Gigging, 382
Gingham, 252
Ginning of cotton, 67–68
Glass fiber, 133–137, 511
    care of, 136
    chemical properties, 136
    coloring of, 135
    manufacture, 134
    physical properties, 134–136
    uses, 136–137
Glass transition temperature, 54–55
Glazing, 379
Glospan® spandex fiber, 181
GORE-TEX®, 186, 401
Graft-polymers, 45
Grain of fabrics, 247
Graphite fibers, 138–139
Gray scale, 463
Greige goods, 12, 249
Grenadine, 263
Grosgrain, 253
Guanaco, 121–122

H

Hackling, 77, 104
Hand, of fabrics, 29, 77, 204, 480–481
Hargreaves, James, 196
Hearle, J. W. S., 49
Heat-reflectant finishes, 411–412
Heat setting, 54–55
Heat-transfer printing, 355–357
Heddles, 233
Hemp, 82
Henequin, 83
Herringbone twill, 255
High pile knit fabrics, 288
High-wet-modulus rayon, 91
    properties, 92
    uses, 92–93
Hollow fibers, 28
Home laundering, 418–429
    equipment for, 426–429
    pollution from, 447
    procedures for, 428–429

Homespun, 252
Hooke, Robert, 85
Hopsacking, 252
Horizontal integration of textile firms,
    13
Horsehair fiber, 123
Huarzio, 121
Hydrogen bonding, 47–48

I

Ice dyes. *See* Azoic dyes
Ikat, 348–349
INDA, 308
Indigo dye, 7, 328
Industrial textiles, 15
Inorganic fibers, 133–138
Insects, resistance of fibers to attack
    by, 38
    see also individual generic fiber
        listings
Integrated composite spinning
        system, 215
Interlock knits, 294
International Linen Promotion
        Association, 9
International Organization for
        Standarization, 454
International Silk Association, 9
International System of Units (S. I.), 30
Interwoven fabrics, 271

J

Jacquard, Joseph, 239
Jacquard knits, 300–301
Jacquard loom, 239–241
Jacquard weave, 258
Jean, 254
Jersey knits, 288
Jobber, 13
Jute, 82

K

Kapok, 72–73
Kay, John, 234
Kevlar® aramid fiber, 149

Knit stitch sizes, 286–287
Knit-weave fabrics, 302–304
  warp insertion, 303
  weft insertion, 303
Knitted fabrics, 281–304, 477–478
  care of, 301–302
  creating pattern and design in,
    300–301
  dimensional stability of, 301–302
  high pile, 288
  mechanical damage of, 302
  performance of, 301–302
  plated fabrics, 291
  terry, 290
  velour, 290
Knitting, construction of fabrics by,
    281–304
  cidega, 300
  doubleknits, 293–294
  history of, 281–282
  Jacquard, 300–301
  jersey, 288
  loop formation, 284–286
  Milanese, 300
  plain, 288
  plated fabrics, 291
  purl, 294
  Raschel, 299–300
  rib, 292–293
  simplex, 300
  tricot, 298–299
  warp, 287, 297–300
  weft, 287, 287–297
Kustur TAK® printing, 358

L

Lace, 322–325
Lacis, 320, 322
Laminated fabrics, 273
Lanital fiber, 131, 132
Lappet weave, 268
Latch needle for knitting, 284–285
Laundering, colorfastness to, 464–465
  commercial, 433–434
  home, 418–429
  see also Home laundering;
    Commercial laundering
Laundr-ometer®, 464
Leaf fibers, 83

Lee, William, 282
Leno weave, 263
Linen, 74–80
  care, 79
  properties, 77–79
  uses, 79–80
  yarns, processing of, 204
  see also Flax
Liropol machine, 315
Llama, 121
Longcloth, 251
Looms
  air jet, shuttleless, 242, 245
  box, 252
  dobby, 241
  gripper, shuttleless, 242, 244
  hand, 232–234
  Jacquard, 239–241
  multiphase, 245
  rapier, shuttleless, 242, 244–245
  shuttle, 237–239
  shuttleless, 242–247
  water jet, shuttleless, 242, 245
Lurex®, Metallic yarn, 221
Luster, 27
Lycra® spandex fiber, 181

M

Macramé, 319
Madras, 258
Malimo, 313–316
Malipol machine, 315
Malivlies machine, 316
Maliwatt machine, 315
Man-made fiber formation, 50–54
  dry spinning, 52–53
  melt spinning, 51–52
  wet spinning, 53–54
Man-made Fiber Producers
    Association, 10
Marquisette, 263
Matelasse, 271
Matrix fibers, 189–190
Mauersberger, Heinrich, 313
Mercer, John, 374–375
Mercerization, 374–375
Merovina azlon fiber, 132
Metallic fibers, 137–138, 511–512
Microdenier fibers, 30–31

Microfibers. *See* Microdenier fibers
Milanese knits, 300
Millitron® printing machine, 358
Mineral fibers, 133
Misti, 121
Modacrylic fibers, 166–169, 512
  care, 169
  chemical properties, 168
  effect of environmental conditions
    on, 168
  FTC definition, 166, 512
  manufacture, 166
  physical properties, 166–168
  thermal properties, 168
  uses, 168–169
Modified cellulosic fibers, 93–99
  see also Acetate and Triacetate
Mohair, 118–119
Mohair Council, 9
Moiré, 380–381
Moisture regain of fibers, 36
  see also individual generic fiber
    listings
Molecular structure of textile fibers,
  44–50
Moncrieff, R. W., 47
Monk's cloth, 252
Monofilament yarns, 216, 227
Mordant dyes. *See* Chrome dyes
Mordant printing, 345
Mordants, 327–328
Mothproofing finishes, 412–414
Multicomponent fabrics, 270–279
Multifiber Agreement, 16
Multifilament yarns, 216, 227
Multilateral Agreements, 16
Musk ox, 119–120
Muslin, 252
Mylar, 221

N

Nainsook, 251
Naphthol dyes. *See* Azoic dyes
Napping, 381–382
Natural fibers, 9–10
Needlepunching, 311
Nets, 319
Network yarns, 220–222

Noise, standards for control of, 444
Nomex® aramid fiber, 149
Non-woven fabrics, 305–342
Novelty yarns, 227–229
Novoloid, 185, 512
Nylon, 141–147, 512–513
  care, 146–147
  chemical properties, 144
  effect of environmental conditions,
    144
  FTC definition, 141, 512
  manufacture of, 141–143, 145
  nylon 4, 147
  nylon 6, 145–146
  nylon 7, 147
  nylon 11, 147
  nylon 66, 141–145
  nylon 612, 147
  physical properties, 143–144
  thermal properties, 144
Nytril, 185, 513

O

Occupational Safety and Health Act of
  1970, 442
Offshore production of textile
  products, 17
Oil repellent finishes, 403
Olefin fibers, 171–176, 513–514
  FTC definition, 153, 171
  see also Polypropylene and
    Polyethylene
Open-end spinning, 207–211
Optical brighteners. *See* Fluorescent
  whiteners
Organdy, 251
Organza, 251
Oriental carpets, 278
Orlon acrylic fiber, 163
Orlon Sayelle bicomponent acrylic
  fiber, 164
OSHA, 68, 442
Osnaburg, 252
Ottoman, 253
Oxford cloth, 252
Oxidizing agents, effect on fibers, 57
  see also specific generic fiber
    listings

P

Pacific Converter, 204–205
Parchmentizing, 377
Partially-oriented yarn, 153
Paul, Lewis, 196
Pavena-Pavil bonded sliver spinning
    system, 212, 214–215
Peau de soie, 257
Percale, 251
Perching, 387
Perkin, William, 329
Perlock system, 205–206
Permanent Care Labeling Regulations,
    436–438, 507
Permanent press finishes. *See*
    Durable press finishes
Perspiration, colorfastness to, 465
PET, see polyethelylene tereph-
    thalate
Peters, R. H., 49
Piece dyeing, 333–335
Pigment dyes, 341
Pile fabric construction, 263–266
Pile fabrics,
    knitted, 288
    woven, 263–266
Pill test for flame retardancy, 406
Pilling, 35
    testing for, 461–462
Pina cloth, 83
Piqué, 258
Plain knit fabrics, 288
Plain weave fabrics, 250–252
Plated fabrics, 291
Plissé designs, 253, 385–386
Plush fabrics, 265
Ply yarns, 226, 227
Polyalkene fibers. *See* Olefins
Polyamide fibers. *See* Nylon
Polybenzimidazole fiber, 187, 518
Polycarbonate fibers, 518
Polyester, 151–159, 515
    care of, 156
    chemical properties, 154
    effects of environmental conditions,
        155
    FTC definition, 151, 515
    history, 151
    manufacture, 151–153
    physical properties, 153–155

thermal properties, 154
    uses for, 157
    varieties of, 155–156
Polyethylene, 176
Polyethylene terephthalate, 155
Polymerization, 44–46
    addition, 45–46
    condensation, 45
Polymers
    crystallinity, 46–47, 50
    orientation of, 46–47, 50
Polyphenylene sulfide fibers, 186–187,
    518
Polypropylene fibers, 171–176
    chemical properties, 172–173
    effect of environment on, 173
    manufacture, 171
    physical properties, 172–173
    thermal properties, 172
    uses, 173–174
Polyvinyl alcohol fiber, 187
Poplin, 253
Porometric structures, 317–318
POY. *See* partially-oriented yarn
Printing, 343–368
    block, 343–344
    blotch, 354
    discharge, 354
    duplex, 354
    electrostatic, 357
    flock, 354
    heat transfer, 355–357
    mordant, 345
    ombre, 357
    photographic, 357
    polychromatic, 357
    resist, 345–349, 354–355
    roller, 352–355
    rotary screen, 351
    screen printing, 350–351
    warp printing, 349, 355
Protein fibers, 101–102
    general properties, 101–102
Purl knits, 294

Q

Qiana® nylon, 147
Qivut, 119

Quality control, 18, 19
Quilted fabrics, 271, 273

R

Ramie, 80–82
Raschel knits, 299–300
Ratiné yarns, 228
Rayon, 8, 85–93, 516
  FTC definition, 86, 516
  history, 85
  see also Cuperammonium rayon;
    High-wet-modulus rayon; Viscose
    rayon
Reactive dyes, 339–340
Recycled wool, 108
Recycling of textiles, 446–447
Reemay, 312
Regenerated cellulose fibers, 85–93
Regenerated fibers, 21
Regenerated protein fibers, 130–133
Rep, 253
Repco spinning, 211–212
Resiliency, 34–35
Resin finishes, for durable press, 394–
    399
  for shrinkage control of wool, 393
Retailing of textile products, 14, 15
Retting, 76, 81
Rhyton® fiber, 186–187
Rib knits, 292–293
Ribbed fabrics, 253
Ring spinning, 206
Rilsan nylon, 147
Roller printing, 352–355
Rotor spinning. *See* Open-end
  spinning
Rubber fibers, 177–178, 516–517
Rya rugs, 278

S

S-twist of yarns, 223
Sacaton fiber, 83
Sanforized® finish, 390–391
Sanfor-Knit® finish, 391
Sanfor-Set® finish, 390
Saran, 183–184, 517

manufacture, 183
  properties, 183–184
  uses, 184
Sateen weave, 256
Satin weave, 256–257
Saturation regain, 36
Schiffli embroidery, 270
Schreinerizing, 379–380
Schusspol machine, 315
Scotchgard® finish, 403
Scotchlite® finish, 413
Scouring, 372
Seed hair fibers, 63–73
Seersucker, 253
SEF® modacrylic fiber, 169
Self-twist spinning, 211–212
Selvages, 247
Semi-worsted spinning system, 204
Serge, 254
Sericulture, 124–127
Shantung, 253
Shearing of napped fabrics, 383
Shrinkage, consolidation, 390
  control through finishing, 389–393
  of knits, 391
  progressive, 34, 391–392
  of rayon, 391–392
  relaxation, 34
  residual, 389
  testing for, 389
  of wool, 392–393
Shuttle, 237–238
Shuttle looms, 237–239
Shuttleless weaving machines, 242–
    247
S. I. *See* International System of Units
Silica fibers, 137, 518
Silicon carbide fibers, 137
Silk, 123–131
  care, 130
  chemical properties, 128
  effect of environmental conditions,
    129
  gum removal, 127
  history, 123–124
  physical properties, 128–129
  production, 124–127
  reeling, 126
  thermal properties, 129
  uses, 130

yarns, 127
Silk screen printing, 350–351
Silk weighting, 127
  FTC regulation of, 127
Silkworm, 124–126
Simplex knits, 300
Singeing, 376–377
Single knits, 288
Sisal fiber, 83
Sizing as a finish, 377
  during weaving, 235–236
  for home laundry, 426
Slack mercerization, 375
Slashing. *See* Sizing
Slipper satin, 257
Slit films, 220
Sliver, 200
Slub yarns, 228
Soaps, 418, 419
Softening of fabrics, 378
Soil-releasing finishes, 400–401
Soil-repellent finishes, 399–401
Soluble fibers, 187
Solution dyeing, 330
Sonic sewing, 273
Spandex, 178–181, 517
  care of, 181
  chemical properties, 179
  effect of environmental conditions,
    179–180
  FTC definition, 178
  manufacture, 178
  physical properties, 178–179
  thermal properties, 179
  uses, 180–181
Spanish moss, 83
Specialty hair fibers, 115–123
Specific gravity, 32
Specking, 388
Spinning, 193–230
  bonded sliver system, 214–215
  cotton system, 199–202
  direct, 204–206
  dry, 52–53
  hand, 194–195
  history of, 194–197
  integrated composite system, 215
  linen, 204
  man-made fibers, 204–206
  mechanization of, 196–197

  melt, 51
  open-end, 207–211
  preparation of fiber for, 198–199
  ring, 197, 206
  self-twist, 211–212
  wet, 53–54, 87
  woolen system, 202–203
  worsted system, 203–204
  zero-twist, 212–215
Spinning jenny, 196, 197
Spinning mule, 196, 197
Spinning wheel, 195–196
Split films, 220
Spot removal. *See* Stain removal
Spring beard needle, 283–285
Spun-bonding, 312–313
Spunlace, 311
Stain removal, 429–431
Standard specifications, 453–455
  carpets, flammability of, 406–407
  children's sleepwear, flammability
    of, 407
  mattresses, flammability of, 407–408
  upholstered furniture, flammability
    of, 408
Staple fibers, 29
Staple yarn formation, 197–215
Starches. *See* Sizing
Stiffening, 377–378
Stitch-bonding. *See* Stitch-through
  fabrics
Stitch-through fabrics, 313–316
Strength of textile fibers, 457–458
  see also individual generic fiber
    listings
Stretch-breaking, 205–206
Stretch yarns, 220
Stretching. *See* Elongation;
  Dimensional stability of fabrics
Striations, 29
Sublistatic printing. *See* Heat transfer
  printing
Suedelike fabrics, 317–318, 381–382
Sulfur dyes, 339
Superwash® finish, 393
Surah, 254
Surface effects, 267–268
Surfactants, 420
Swivel weave, 267–268
Syndets. *See* Detergents

Synthetic fibers. *See* individual generic fiber listings

T

Taffeta, 253
Tapa, 307
Tapestry weaving, 259–263
Tearing strength, 457–458, 482–483
Teflon fibers, 186
Tenacity of textile fibers, 31–32
  see also individual generic fiber listings
Tensile strength, 31–32, 482–483
Tentering, 386–387
Terry cloth, 265
Terry knits, 290
Terry weave, 265
Tex system, 30, 224
Textile Chemist and Colorist, 454
Textile chemistry, 41–59
Textile designs
  abstract, 350
  African, 367
  baroque, 365
  burnt-out, 384
  Byzantine, 363
  Chinese, 361
  early American, 367
  geometric, 359
  Indian, 361
  Japanese, 361
  Javanese, 367
  Middle Eastern, 361
  Oriental, 361
  Persian, 361
  realistic, 358–359
  Renaissance, 363
  rococo, 366
  South America, 367
  stylized, 359
Textile Fiber Products Identification Act, 19, 22–26, 505–506
Textile finishing, 369–415
  see also Finishes
Textile history, 6–9
Textile industry, 9–15
Textile testing, 453–471
  see also specific property categories

such as Abrasion; Colorfastness; Shrinkage; etc.
Textiles, care of, 417–440
  recycling, 446–447
  storage, 435–436
Textured yarns, 216–220
  air jet process, 219
  edge crimp process, 217
  false twist process, 217
  gear crimp process, 217, 219
  knit-deknit process, 217, 218
  stuffer box process, 217, 219
TFE fluorocarbon fiber, 186
Thermal conductivity, 484
Thermoplastic fibers, 37
Thermosol® process, 341
Thorpe, John, 197
Thread, 229
Thread count, *See* Fabric count
Throwsters, 12
Tie-and-dye, 347
Toile de jouy, 359
Tone-on-tone dyeing, 336
Top dyeing, 330–331
Top-weight fabrics, 249
Tow fiber, 77
Tow-to-top fiber processing, 204–206
Townshend, Matthew, 284
Trademarks, 10, 22
Triacetate, 93–100, 509
  care, 98
  chemical properties, 97
  effect of environmental conditions, 97
  manufacture, 93–94
  physical properties, 95–97
  thermal properties, 96–97
  uses, 98–99
Triaxial weave fabrics, 278–279
Tricot knits, 297–298
TRIS, 409
Tufted fabrics, construction, 275–276
Tunnel test for flame retardancy, 407
Turbo-stapler, 205–206
Twill angles in twill fabrics, 256
Twill weave, 253–255
Twist, effects of, 222–223, 474–475
Twistless spinning, 212, 214–215
Typar spun bonded fabric, 312
Tyvek spun bonded fabric, 313

U

Ultrasuede, 317–318
Unifil system, 237–238
Union dyeing, 336

V

Van der Waals forces, 47–48
Vat dyes, 337
VEEV knitting system, 303
Velour knits, 290
Velvet fabric, 264, 265
Velvet weave, 276
Velveteen, 264
Vicara, 132
Vicuña, 121
Vinal fibers, 186, 517
Vinyon fibers, 185, 517
Virgin wool, 108
Viscose rayon, 86–91
　care, 90
　chemical reactivity, 90
　effect of environmental conditions,
　　90
　manufacture, 86–87
　physical properties, 88–90
　thermal properties, 90
　uses, 91
Voile, 251
Voltex machine, 316

W

Wales, in knits, 286–287
　in twill weave, 255
Warp beam, 236–237
Warp knits, 297–300
Warp printing, 349, 355
Warp yarns, 235
Wash-and-wear finishes, 394
Water pollution, from home
　　laundering, 447
　from textile manufacture, 444–446
Water repellency, 484
　finishes for, 401–403
Waterproof finishes, 401
Weaves, 250–266

basket, 252
dobby, 258–259
Jacquard, 258
leno, 263
pile, 263–266
plain, 250–252
sateen, 256
satin, 257
surface, 266–270
tapestry, 259–263
terry, 265
triaxial, 278–279
twill, 253–255
Weaving, 232–235
　automation of, 234–235
　hand, 232–234
　history of, 232–235
Weft knits, 287–297
Weft yarn. *See* Filling yarns
Weighting, of silk, 377–378, 507
White-on-white, 259
Wicking, 36
Wintuk bicomponent fiber, 164
Woad, 7
Wool, 103–115
　care, 114–115
　chemical properties, 113
　definition, 108
　effects of environmental conditions,
　　114
　fleece removal, 82
　grading, 106–107
　history, 103–104
　labeling, 107–109
　molecular structure, 109–110
　mothproofing, 412–414
　physical properties, 111–113
　physical structure, 109–110
　processing, 105–107
　scouring, 107
　shrinkage, 392–393
　spinning, 107
　thermal properties, 113
　use, 115
Wool Bureau, 9
Wool Products Labeling Act, 107–109,
　506
Woolen spinning system, 202–203
Woolen yarns, 107
Worsted spinning system, 203–204

Worsted yarns, 203
Woven fabrics, 231–280
Wrinkle recovery, 393–394, 479–480
Wrinkle resistance finishes, 393–399
Wyatt, John, 196

Y

Yarn, 4, 193–230
    construction, 199–222
    count, 224
    crimp, 476–477
    cross-sectional shape, 475
    diameter, 474
    dyeing, 331–332
    geometry, 474–476
    preparation, 235–237
    slippage, 410
    twist, effect of, 222–223
Yarns
    bouclé, 227–228
    bulked, 216–217
    complex, 227–229
    cord, 226–227
    core-spun, 180, 181
    crepe, 222
    cross-belt textured, 218
    direction of twist, 223
    double-covered, 180, 181
    effect of twist, 222–223
    filament, 216–220

filling, 235–237
flake, 228
knop, 228
knot, 228
loopy, 217
monofilament, 216, 227
multifilament, 216, 227
network, 221–222
novelty, 227, 228–229
nub, 228
ply, 226–227
POY yarn, 153
S-twist, 223
simple, 227
single, 226
size of, 223–225
slit film, 220–221
snarl, 228
spiral, 228
split film, 220
spot, 228
stretch, 220
textured, 216–220
thick-and-thin, 228
warp, 235
Z-twist, 223

Z

Z-twist, 223
Zefran® acrylic fiber, 165
Zero-twist spinning, 212–215